ROTHMAN
RUGBY LE
YEARBOOK 1999

C000186134

Raymond Fletcher

ROTHMANS

HEADLINE

First published in 1999
by HEADLINE BOOK PUBLISHING

10 9 8 7 6 5 4 3 2 1

COVER PHOTOGRAPHS

Front cover; left to right: Kris Radlinski (Wigan Warriors), Brian McDermott (Bradford Bulls), Anthony Farrell (Leeds Rhinos)

Back cover; Top: David Hulme (Salford Reds). *Bottom:* Mark Johnson (Hull Sharks)

PHOTOGRAPHS

The bulk of the photographs in this *Rothmans Rugby League Yearbook* have been supplied by *League Express* and *Rugby Leaguer*. Thanks go to both weekly journals and their team of top class photographers, plus freelance photographer Andrew Varley, who has also made his vast file of photographs available, including the cover pictures.

ISBN 0 7472 7572 6

Copy-editing by Andrew Kinsman, First Rank Publishing, Brighton

Typeset by Wearset, Boldon, Tyne and Wear

Printed and bound in Great Britain by
Mackays of Chatham PLC,
Chatham, Kent

HEADLINE BOOK PUBLISHING
A division of Hodder Headline PLC
338 Euston Road
London NW1 3BH

ROTHMANS RUGBY LEAGUE YEARBOOK 1999

CONTENTS

EDITORIAL PREFACE

The last few years should have been the most progressive in Rugby League history. But the opportunity to take full advantage of the millions poured into the game by News Corporation was wasted because of internal squabbling. Just when there was never a greater need for everyone to work together for the good of the game, top officials fell out and splinter groups formed. Long-lasting progress will only be made when everyone is pulling in the same direction under the banner of the Rugby Football League.

One of the main reasons for the success of the *Rothmans Rugby League Yearbook* – now in a record-extending 19th edition – has been the great working relationship between the publishers and its authors. We have always pulled together with David Howes and myself nearly always in complete harmony. Any differences were soon overcome to the yearbook's benefit.

Now the partnership is broken as David devotes attention to his job as the Leeds Rugby Club managing director. He had been easing himself out as author in recent years, but the long hours put in during the early ground-breaking days prepared the foundations for the book's success. That I am now able to virtually go it alone is due greatly to David's valued partnership.

There are, of course, still several people to whom I am indebted for their assistance. High on the list is Mike Latham, who has checked almost every digit and whose thoroughness enhances the book's reputation for being as accurate as possible. Paul English provided an immense amount of statistics for cross-checking purposes and Mike Rylance was helpful in all matters French, while Terry Liberopoulos of the I. & T. Rugby League Statistics Service was responsible for much of the Overseas chapter. The trade journals *League Express* and *Rugby Leaguer* were again used regularly to cross-check facts.

I don't know where to begin to thank all those at the Rugby Football League who have put up with my pestering and supplied a mass of official information. Super League (Europe) has also always been willing to help whenever requested. You see, we *can* all work together.

This edition marks the 10th in which the prestigious *Coaches Select XIII* has appeared, and I would like to thank all who have supplied their nominations over the years.

Celia Kent and Ian Marshall at Headline leave me to carry on without interference, while continuing to give advice when requested. Copy-editor Andrew Kinsman has been equally laissez faire, and John Anderson's team at Wearset seem much closer to home now that Gateshead Thunder have entered Super League.

Another wise enough to have left me alone for many hours as the work piled up has been my wife, Muriel. But she has always been there to provide an encouraging pat.

An innovation this year is the introduction of a guest writer to give his *Viewpoint* and I cannot think of anyone better to be the first than John Kear.

Finally, one of Neil Tunnicliffe's first moves after taking over as the game's chief executive in 1998 was to restore the Rugby Football League's official approval to the yearbook. It is greatly appreciated.

● **Facts and figures in this *Rothmans Rugby League Yearbook* are as at 1 January 1999. The Christmas period challenge matches and other pre-season matches outside the major competitions do not count towards clubs' or players' records. It should also be noted that, except where stated, a player's statistics refer only to his record as a British-based player.**

RAYMOND FLETCHER

VIEWPOINT

By John Kear, Sheffield Eagles Coach

It is a tremendous honour and privilege to be asked to contribute to the 19th edition of the *Rothmans Rugby League Yearbook*. The book is established as the 'Bible' for all Rugby League journalists, statisticians, officials and coaches, as a veritable mine of relevant and in my job sometimes crucial, information. Consequently it is a source of great pride for me to have an input and I should like to think this reflects the standing of both my club and myself within the game as we approach the millennium.

A dream was fulfilled for Sheffield Eagles and myself last a year when the players and coaching staff predicted, worked for and, ultimately, realised success in the Challenge Cup. It was a memorable final, when the biggest underdogs in the history of the game overcame the hottest favourites. It saw the rebirth of the greatest traditional competition in the game; the day that ended a decade of Wigan/St. Helens domination and the air of predictability that accompanied it. I believe that the Eagles victory saw the rebirth of the Challenge Cup in the eyes of the nation, the BBC, the sponsors, the clubs but most importantly the regular Rugby League spectator. It was a massive result for all concerned.

A vision realised for myself. But what of the game generally? There are many positives attached to Rugby League and some would say many negatives. To discuss these would simply go over old ground. I should prefer to look forward, to perhaps five years down the line at what would be my dream or vision for Rugby League by 2004. It is essential that there is continued progress with the rules and stability with sensible evolution, so that the game continues to provide outstanding entertainment within a structure that incorporates the tradition of the game with the need to be innovative.

It is not necessary to make massive changes, but simply to tinker with the product that we have, allowing players and coaches to become more adept at playing within the Rugby League structure and not having to ape or adopt foreign structures. So 2004 should see the game very much as it is now with no amalgamation with Rugby Union to produce a bastardised version of both codes. Each can and should stand on their own.

A further essential is the continued rise in playing standards that the switch to summer, the advent of full-time professionalism and the improved standard in coaching has ushered in. There is no doubt that today's athlete is well conditioned, highly skilled and well educated in all aspects of Rugby League, but we can, will and need to progress if we are to match the consistent performances of our Antipodean cousins.

This will only happen if the RFL and BARLA continue to work together and address problems relating to player development, junior coaching standards and player participation at all levels. At the elite level, players and coaches need to continue to learn from every conceivable source while being bold, daring, and innovative themselves. Improvement at this level also comes from 'pressure cooker' competition where every game is a two-horse race and there are no foregone conclusions.

This level of competition can be attained through the enforcement of a salary cap, a draft system of recruitment and a ban on transferring players during a season. A club should declare its squad and then have to work with the chosen personnel or nurture their youngsters. This would force clubs to improve what they have and stop 'quick fix' transfers. For an intense Super League it is also essential that administration readopt the 'quality not quantity' philosophy of one game per week to allow our improved athletes time to recover and prepare for each fixture. This is vital for any improvements of playing standards.

The final piece in the playing standards issue is that of international Rugby League. The present third ranking on the international list galls myself and any other proud Englishman, but improvement can be made quickly and without too many tears. It is vital that there is a structured, rational programme of competition for all levels of international play from under-16 to full level. A planned programme dovetailing with the domestic league will allow the players to be adequately developed and prepared at these levels.

To cater for the expansion of international Rugby League, split the home nations but apply the same rule to all. The parentage rule should apply to England as well as the other home nations. So, if Australia's Laurie Daley has an English grandparent he should be actively pursued exactly as the Irish pursued Gary Connolly. This would immediately improve England at an administrator's stroke of the pen.

What else would I like to see by 2004? In an ideal world, rather than having only five British head coaches in Super League with the rest being Australian, I would really enjoy a situation where all head coaches and support staff were true Brits. That, however, is in the hands of the respective boards of directors at Super League clubs. Perhaps all the British coaches need is a chance. I believe that after 1998 Halifax and Sheffield may well agree with that. One way for our administrators to push our clubs in that direction could be to make sure that overseas coaches and support staff go on the clubs' overseas quota. Then chairmen and boards may prefer overseas players rather than coaching staff or, if indeed they prefer a coach to take up a quota place, it is a reasoned decision not simply 'let's follow the trend'.

Also in this brave new world, the game would be truly national in our major cities and there would be a meaningful French presence in the Super League. Gates would be significantly increased, TV viewers would be in the millions on BBC and the satellite channels, while the rest of the media would show coverage that I feel the game deserves. Then there would be true Rugby League sporting personalities regularly featured on Question of Sport, in advertising campaigns, etc.

So the year 2004 incorporates tradition, typified by the Challenge Cup final on a sunny May afternoon in front of a sell-out crowd shown on BBC television with the national anthem and gold medals an integral part of it. And along with this, innovation typified by the Grand Final in October, true theatre under lights with a capacity audience portrayed on Sky by the Americanised paraphernalia and gold ring that added so much to the inaugural Final's success. To cap it all: Great Britain regain the Ashes. Sounds good, doesn't it?

COACHES SELECT XIII

Jason Robinson and Gary Connolly of Wigan Warriors retained their places in the exclusive and prestigious *Rothmans Rugby League Yearbook* Coaches' Select XIII for an impressive fourth successive season. The feat has been achieved by only three other players during the ten seasons that the team has been selected with Martin Offiah making a record seven successive appearances while at Widnes and Wigan from 1988-89. Another Wigan pair, Denis Betts and Andy Gregory, also gained four successive selections in the early 1990s.

Winger Robinson and centre Connolly were chosen by nine of the 12 Super League coaches, who were invited to select their form team of the season without including players from their own club. The coaches were asked to base selections on individual form shown in Super League III before the play-offs and their choice would not necessarily be their best balanced team.

There were two positions which produced a tie and for the first time a casting vote was called for, with Great Britain coach Andy Goodway invited to be the adjudicator. He opted for Francis Cummins on the left wing ahead of Anthony Sullivan and Tevita Vaikona, while Paul Sculthorpe was preferred to Chris Joynt, Peter Gill and Gary Mercer for one of the second row berths. In each case the nominations had all received two votes. Adrian Morley had a clear majority for the other second row spot.

There was another tie at full back as Iestyn Harris and Kris Radlinski shared the 12 nominations equally. But with Harris also nominated at stand off and having a majority in that position, the 1998 Man of Steel and Super League player of the year was awarded the half back role with Radlinski at full back.

Harris's total of 10 selections made him the most nominated player along with Leeds Rhinos colleague Morley, who gained 10 second row votes. Morley has been selected in all three seasons since he was first chosen as a 19-year-old in 1996.

Five players were selected for the first time: Cummins, Dale Laughton and Neil Cowie plus the two overseas selections Brad Godden and Gavin Clinch of Australia. Clinch became the first Halifax Blue Sox player to be selected since the Coaches' Select XIII was introduced 10 years ago.

Grand Final winners Wigan Warriors provided the most players in the team with five, followed by four from beaten finalists Leeds.

A total of 45 players were nominated with the following gaining votes for two positions: Harris (6 full back, 4 stand off), Sean Long (3 scrum half, 1 stand off), Andrew Farrell (8 loose forward, 1 second row), Steele Retchless (1 prop, 1 second row).

Castleford Tigers, Huddersfield Giants and Salford Reds were the only clubs not to have at least one player nominated. In contrast, Wigan headed the list with 10 players nominated.

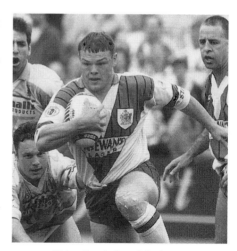

Keiron Cunningham: Select hooker.

The full list of nominations for the 1998 Coaches Select XIII was:

Full back

Kris Radlinski (Wigan Warriors) 6

Iestyn Harris (Leeds Rhinos) 6

Wing

Jason Robinson (Wigan Warriors) 9

Francis Cummins (Leeds Rhinos) 5*

Anthony Sullivan (St. Helens)........................4

Tevita Vaikona (Bradford Bulls) 4

Fili Seru (Hull Sharks) 1

Fereti Tuilagi (Halifax Blue Sox) 1

Chris Smith (St. Helens) 1

Centre

Gary Connolly (Wigan Warriors) 9

Brad Godden (Leeds Rhinos) 6

Paul Newlove (St. Helens)..............................4

Keith Senior (Sheffield Eagles) 3

Richard Blackmore (Leeds Rhinos) 2

Stand off

Iestyn Harris (Leeds Rhinos) 4

Henry Paul (Wigan Warriors) 3

Chris Chester (Halifax Blue Sox) 2

Tommy Martyn (St. Helens) 2

Sean Long (St. Helens) 1

Scrum half

Gavin Clinch (Halifax Blue Sox)....................6

Sean Long (St. Helens) 3

Tony Smith (Wigan Warriors) 2

Mark Aston (Sheffield Eagles) 1

Prop

Dale Laughton (Sheffield Eagles) 7

Neil Cowie (Wigan Warriors) 6

Karl Harrison (Halifax Blue Sox)...................4

Paul Broadbent (Sheffield Eagles).................2

Stephen Holgate (London Broncos)..............1

Darren Fleary (Leeds Rhinos).........................1

Apollo Perelini (St. Helens) 1

Steele Retchless (London Broncos) 1

Harvey Howard (Bradford Bulls) 1

Hooker

Keiron Cunningham (St. Helens) 6

Robbie McCormack (Wigan Warriors)...........5

Paul Rowley (Halifax Blue Sox) 1

Second row

Adrian Morley (Leeds Rhinos)....................10

Paul Sculthorpe (St. Helens) 3*

Gary Mercer (Halifax Blue Sox)....................2

Chris Joynt (St. Helens)..................................2

Peter Gill (London Broncos) 2

Steele Retchless (London Broncos) 1

Des Clark (Halifax Blue Sox) 1

Lee Gilmour (Wigan Warriors) 1

Denis Betts (Wigan Warriors) 1

Paul Carr (Sheffield Eagles)............................1

Andrew Farrell (Wigan Warriors)...................1

Loose forward

Andrew Farrell (Wigan Warriors)...................8

Martin Moana (Halifax Blue Sox)..................3

Mike Wainwright (Warrington Wolves)..........1

* Including casting vote by Great Britain coach Andy Goodway

COACHES SELECT XIII 1998

1. **Kris Radlinski** (Wigan Warriors)
2. **Jason Robinson** (Wigan Warriors)
3. **Gary Connolly** (Wigan Warriors)
4. **Brad Godden** (Leeds Rhinos)
5. **Francis Cummins** (Leeds Rhinos)
6. **Iestyn Harris** (Leeds Rhinos)
7. **Gavin Clinch** (Halifax Blue Sox)
8. **Dale Laughton** (Sheffield Eagles)
9. **Keiron Cunningham** (St. Helens)
10. **Neil Cowie** (Wigan Warriors)
11. **Adrian Morley** (Leeds Rhinos)
12. **Paul Sculthorpe** (St. Helens)
13. **Andrew Farrell** (Wigan Warriors)

TEN YEARS OF COACHES SELECT XIII

This is the tenth year of the *Rothmans* Coaches Select XIII, which has become a major feature of the yearbook with players taking pride in being selected for a team chosen by the game's top coaches. A compilation of every player who has been selected for the Select XIII reflects a decade of outstanding performers and reveals that only four have been chosen five or more times.

Top of the list is Martin Offiah, who made the final line-up on seven occasions to confirm his ranking as the outstanding winger of modern times. He was virtually an automatic choice in the first seven years when he was with Widnes and Wigan.

Shaun Edwards is next in line with six selections, three in each half back position, all while he was still at Wigan. Two other Wigan players were selected for the team five times: Denis Betts in the second row and Gary Connolly in the centre, including once as a St. Helens player.

COACHES SELECT XIII
TEAM OF THE DECADE
The following is a Coaches Select XIII of the past 10 years with each player having gained most selections in that position :

1. **Alan Tait** (Leeds)
2. **Jason Robinson** (Wigan)
3. **Dean Bell** (Wigan)
4. **Gary Connolly** (St. Helens, Wigan)
5. **Martin Offiah** (Widnes, Wigan)
6. **Shaun Edwards** (Wigan)
7. **Andy Gregory** (Wigan)
8. **Kevin Ward** (Castleford, St. Helens)
9. { **Phil McKenzie** (Widnes)
     Martin Dermott (Wigan)
10. { **Kelvin Skerrett** (Bradford N., Wigan)
      Andy Platt (Wigan)
11. **Denis Betts** (Wigan)
12. **Adrian Morley** (Leeds)
13. **Ellery Hanley** (Wigan, Leeds)

Martin Offiah: A record seven appearances in Coaches Select XIII.

COACHES SELECT XIII
1988-89 - 1997

1988-89
1. Alan Tait (Widnes)
2. Des Drummond (Warrington)
3. Andy Currier (Widnes)
4. Joe Lydon (Wigan)
5. Martin Offiah (Widnes)
6. Shaun Edwards (Wigan)
7. Andy Gregory (Wigan)
8. Kevin Ward (Castleford)
9. Phil McKenzie (Widnes)
10. Adrian Shelford (Wigan)
11. Mike Gregory (Warrington)
12. {Andy Platt (Wigan)
     {Ron Gibbs (Castleford)
13. Ellery Hanley (Wigan)

1991-92
1. Graham Steadman (Castleford)
2. John Devereux (Widnes)
3. Dean Bell (Wigan)
4. Gene Miles (Wigan)
5. Martin Offiah (Wigan)
6. Shaun Edwards (Wigan)
7. Andy Gregory (Wigan)
8. Kevin Ward (St. Helens)
9. Martin Dermott (Wigan)
10. Andy Platt (Wigan)
11. Denis Betts (Wigan)
12. Gary Mercer (Warrington)
13. Phil Clarke (Wigan)

1994-95
1. Henry Paul (Wigan)
2. Jason Robinson (Wigan)
3. Va'aiga Tuigamala (Wigan)
4. Gary Connolly (Wigan)
5. Martin Offiah (Wigan)
6. Tony Kemp (Castleford)
7. Bobbie Goulding (St. Helens)
8. Kelvin Skerrett (Wigan)
9. Lee Jackson (Sheffield E.)
10. Dean Sampson (Castleford)
11. Denis Betts (Wigan)
12. Chris Joynt (St. Helens)
13. Phil Clarke (Wigan)

1989-90
1. Alan Tait (Widnes)
2. Des Drummond (Warrington)
3. Kevin Iro (Wigan)
4. Paul Loughlin (St. Helens)
5. Martin Offiah (Widnes)
6. Shaun Edwards (Wigan)
7. Andy Gregory (Wigan)
8. {Kelvin Skerrett (Bradford N.)
    {Paul Groves (St. Helens)
9. {Phil McKenzie (Widnes)
    {Lee Jackson (Hull)
10. George Mann (St. Helens)
11. Denis Betts (Wigan)
12. Karl Fairbank (Bradford N.)
13. Ellery Hanley (Wigan)

1992-93
1. Alan Tait (Leeds)
2. Alan Hunte (St. Helens)
3. Dean Bell (Wigan)
4. Gary Connolly (St. Helens)
5. Martin Offiah (Wigan)
6. Tea Ropati (St. Helens)
7. Shaun Edwards (Wigan)
8. Kevin Ward (St. Helens)
9. Martin Dermott (Wigan)
10. Andy Platt (Wigan)
11. Denis Betts (Wigan)
12. Phil Clarke (Wigan)
13. Tawera Nikau (Castleford)

1996
1. Kris Radlinski (Wigan)
2. Jason Robinson (Wigan)
3. Gary Connolly (Wigan)
4. Paul Newlove (St. Helens)
5. Anthony Sullivan (St. Helens)
6. Henry Paul (Wigan)
7. Robbie Paul (Bradford B.)
8. Apollo Perelini (St. Helens)
9. Keiron Cunningham (St. Helens)
10. Tony Mestrov (London B.)
11. Adrian Morley (Leeds)
12. Paul Sculthorpe (Warrington)
13. Andrew Farrell (Wigan)

1990-91
1. Steve Hampson (Wigan)
2. Frano Botica (Wigan)
3. Kevin Iro (Wigan)
4. {Dean Bell (Wigan)
    {Daryl Powell (Sheffield E.)
5. Martin Offiah (Widnes)
6. Garry Schofield (Leeds)
7. Andy Gregory (Wigan)
8. Karl Harrison (Hull)
9. Phil McKenzie (Widnes)
10. Andy Platt (Wigan)
11. Denis Betts (Wigan)
12. Emosi Koloto (Widnes)
13. Ellery Hanley (Wigan)

1993-94
1. Dave Watson (Bradford N.)
2. St. John Ellis (Castleford)
3. Jonathan Davies (Warrington)
4. Paul Newlove (Bradford N.)
5. Martin Offiah (Wigan)
6. Frano Botica (Wigan)
7. Shaun Edwards (Wigan)
8. Kelvin Skerrett (Wigan)
9. Martin Dermott (Wigan) .
10. Lee Crooks (Castleford)
11. Andrew Farrell (Wigan)
12. Karl Fairbank (Bradford N.)
13. Ellery Hanley (Leeds)

1997
1. Stuart Spruce (Bradford B.)
2. Jason Robinson (Wigan W.)
3. Gary Connolly (Wigan W.)
4. Danny Peacock (Bradford B.)
5. Anthony Sullivan (St. Helens)
6. Iestyn Harris (Leeds R.)
7. Shaun Edwards (London B.)
8. Tony Mestrov (London B.)
9. James Lowes (Bradford B.)
10. {Paul Broadbent (Sheffield E.)
     {Brian McDermott (Bradford B.)
11. Peter Gill (London B.)
12. {Simon Haughton (Wigan W.)
     {Adrian Morley (Leeds R.)
13. Andrew Farrell (Wigan W.)

No team was selected for 1995-96, which was a shortened season bridging the gap between winter and summer rugby

COACHES SELECT XIII
1988-89 - 1998

The following is a list of all the players who have been chosen for the Coaches Select XIII since it was introduced in 1988-89:

Bell, Dean (Wigan)	3
Betts, Denis (Wigan)	5
Botica, Frano (Wigan)	2
Broadbent, Paul (Sheffield E.)	1
Clarke, Phil (Wigan)	3
Clinch, Gavin (Halifax B.S.)	1
Connolly, Gary (St. Helens, Wigan W.)	5
Cowie, Neil (Wigan W.)	1
Crooks, Lee (Castleford)	1
Cummins, Francis (Leeds R.)	1
Cunningham, Keiron (St. Helens)	2
Currier, Andy (Widnes)	1
Davies, Jonathan (Warrington)	1
Dermott, Martin (Wigan)	3
Devereux, John (Widnes)	1
Drummond, Des (Warrington)	2
Edwards, Shaun (Wigan, London B.)	6
Ellis, St. John (Castleford)	1
Fairbank, Karl (Bradford N.)	2
Farrell, Andrew (Wigan W.)	4
Gibbs, Ron (Castleford)	1
Gill, Peter (London B.)	1
Godden, Brad (Leeds R.)	1
Goulding, Bobbie (St. Helens)	1
Gregory, Andy (Wigan)	4
Gregory, Mike (Warrington)	1
Groves, Paul (St. Helens)	1
Hampson, Steve (Wigan)	1
Hanley, Ellery (Wigan, Leeds)	4
Harris, Iestyn (Leeds R.)	2
Harrison, Karl (Hull)	1
Haughton, Simon (Wigan W.)	1
Hunte, Alan (St. Helens)	1
Iro, Kevin (Wigan)	2

Jackson, Lee (Hull, Sheffield E.)	2
Joynt, Chris (St. Helens)	1
Kemp, Tony (Castleford)	1
Koloto, Emosi (Widnes)	1
Laughton, Dale (Sheffield E.)	1
Loughlin, Paul (St. Helens)	1
Lowes, James (Bradford B.)	1
Lydon, Joe (Wigan)	1
Mann, George (St. Helens)	1
McDermott, Brian (Bradford B.)	1
McKenzie, Phil (Widnes)	3
Mercer, Gary (Warrington)	1
Mestrov, Tony (London B.)	2
Miles, Gene (Wigan)	1
Morley, Adrian (Leeds R.)	3
Newlove, Paul (Bradford N., St. Helens)	2
Nikau, Tawera (Castleford)	1
Offiah, Martin (Widnes, Wigan)	7
Paul, Henry (Wigan)	2
Paul, Robbie (Bradford B.)	1
Peacock, Danny (Bradford B.)	1
Perelini, Apollo (St. Helens)	1
Platt, Andy (Wigan)	4
Powell, Daryl (Sheffield E.)	1
Radlinski, Kris (Wigan)	2
Robinson, Jason (Wigan W.)	4
Ropati, Tea (St. Helens)	1
Sampson, Dean (Castleford)	1
Schofield, Garry (Leeds)	1
Sculthorpe, Paul (Warrington, St. Helens)	2
Shelford, Adrian (Wigan)	1
Skerrett, Kelvin (Bradford N., Wigan)	3
Spruce, Stuart (Bradford B.)	1
Steadman, Graham (Castleford)	1
Sullivan, Anthony (St. Helens)	2
Tait, Alan (Widnes, Leeds)	3
Tuigamala, Va'aiga (Wigan)	1
Ward, Kevin (Castleford, St. Helens)	3
Watson, Dave (Bradford N.)	1

Lindsay bounces back – again

Eagles reach new heights at Wembley

Harris is a triple prize winner

Pauls apart no longer

GATESHEAD THUNDER IN

Kiwis claw Lions

MEMORIES

1998 HEADLINES

Behind the scoring feats and records there were a number of other stories which made the headlines in 1998.

Key: RFL – Rugby Football League; SLE – Super League (Europe); FASDA – First and Second Division Association; BARLA – British Amateur Rugby League Association

CHANGES AT THE TOP

Maurice Lindsay's controversial career took a sudden and sensational turn on 8 January when he departed as the Rugby Football League chief executive to become managing director of Super League (Europe). There was some dispute about Lindsay's actual transfer, but it is generally accepted that he was asked to leave by Sir Rodney Walker, chairman of the RFL board of directors, and he immediately accepted an invitation from SLE chairman Chris Caisley to join them. Lindsay had been the RFL chief executive since 1992 when he replaced the retiring David Oxley.

As part of the deal involving Lindsay's transfer, the RFL agreed to pay his £115,000 a year salary at SLE until the end of his contract in September 1999.

Neil Tunnicliffe, a former RFL projects manager who had been Lindsay's deputy for a few months, replaced him almost immediately. Initially, it was for a three-month trial period before his appointment was confirmed on 2 April.

The year ended with speculation that Lindsay would quit Rugby League in 1999 after he extended his interest as a bookmaker at horse racecourses. He had continued an on-rail bookmaking business throughout his time at the RFL and SLE despite increasing criticism.

Lindsay's appointment at SLE was followed by the announcement on 22 January that Australian Ian Robson was to become the organisation's public relations and marketing executive in time for the move to their Kings House, King Street headquarters in Leeds. A chartered accountant, Robson is a former Auckland Warriors chief executive and had headed the Australian Super League marketing department.

On 6 March, Colin Myler resigned as the SLE's chief executive, saying he had become disillusioned and professionally unfulfilled halfway through a three-year contract. Myler's departure left SLE without a base in London.

RFL media manager Peter Rowe left on 23 October to become director of communications for the Football League and was replaced by journalist John Huxley.

SIR RODNEY HANGS ON

RFL chairman Sir Rodney Walker just managed to retain his position as the British representative on the International Board in January after the failure of a controversial move to unseat him. The RFL's Annual General Meeting at Headingley was followed by a Council meeting at which Leeds Rhinos chief executive Gary Hetherington, seconded by Bradford Bulls and SLE chairman Chris Caisley, proposed that Sir Rodney should be replaced by an SLE member. Two clubs had already left the meeting, but all 12 Super League members voted in favour along with Bramley, Hunslet Hawks and Swinton Lions to give a 15-14 majority in favour of the proposal. The motion failed, however, because it needed 16 votes to carry it through.

In August, Sir Rodney beat Maurice Lindsay, chairman of the old International Board, by five votes to four in a straight fight for the post of vice-chairman of the newly-formed RL International Federation. Australian RL chairman John McDonald was elected unopposed as the Federation's first chairman.

There was another close call for Sir Rodney in April when FASDA chairman Bob Scott threatened a vote of no confidence in the RFL chairman and chief executive Neil Tunnicliffe after accusing them of 'selling out' by making concessions to Super League clubs at the expense of others. But they survived after the new TV contract with News Corporation received general approval.

Sir Rodney caused some controversy himself in July when he gave a strong indication that he would quit as the RFL chairman at the end of the season. But a week later he said he would stay on after receiving support from within the game.

GATESHEAD THUNDER IN

Gateshead were admitted to Super League after their franchise bid was finally accepted on 17 August. Chief executive Shane Richardson, an Australian and former top official at Eastern Suburbs and Cronulla, led the bid with Kath Hetherington, who had helped her husband Gary to found Sheffield Eagles in 1984. They soon appointed Shaun McRae, who was being released by St. Helens at the end of the season, as coach and the Australian recruited almost an entire playing squad of fellow countrymen.

The club became Gateshead Thunder early in November with the additional name having been the winning entry from five Boldon Comprehensive pupils in a schools' competition run by the *Newcastle Evening Chronicle*.

Gateshead, who were not admitted to the 1999 Silk Cut Challenge Cup at their own request, will be entitled to an estimated £500,000 from the News Corporation TV contract, which is £250,000 less than the other clubs receive. All their home matches will be played at Gateshead International Stadium.

There had been five applications for a Super League franchise in June before Northampton and Glasgow dropped out to leave Gateshead, Cardiff and Swansea on the short list. The RFL appointed accountants Deloitte & Touche to assess the strengths of their bids based on financial strategies, management structure, playing potential and population centres. After studying their report, the RFL and SLE boards of directors put forward their recommendations to the 12 Super League clubs, who rejected Cardiff and Swansea. In fact, the two Welsh applicants had already decided to defer their bids until 2000 after failing to meet the required standards. Gateshead were given another five days to satisfy the clubs that they could fulfil the required criteria and were then admitted.

TV DEAL UNITES CLUBS

Fears of a split between Super League and FASDA clubs were averted when they agreed a new £56.8m Sky TV contract with News Corporation at a special meeting of the RL Council on 15 July. The deal gave Super League £45m over five years from 1999 with £10.8m to be shared among First and Second Division clubs over two years. The RFL also received £1m. In an unconnected move, the FASDA clubs combined into one division at the end of the year and decided that the 13 clubs who would have been in the First Division should receive £325,000 and the five Second Division clubs £165,000.

The lower division clubs will receive no more money from News Corporation after 2000, but they are allowed to negotiate their own terrestrial television deals immediately. The original News Corporation contract for exclusive television rights was £87m for five years from 1996.

FASDA also won the right for the First Division champions to be considered for entry into Super League on the same basis as any new application for a franchise. This would require them to meet stringent financial and organisation criteria. The new requirement replaced the controversial condition that First Division champions would have to raise £500,000 for team strengthening.

The new deal ended several weeks of protests from FASDA, who had accused the RFL of a 'sell out' by allegedly making sweeping concessions to SLE, which gave them greater autonomy and a bigger share of the Sky TV money. At one stage, RFL chief executive Neil Tunnicliffe and chairman Sir Rodney Walker were threatened with a vote of no confidence by FASDA clubs.

BACK TO TWO DIVISIONS

There will be a return to two divisions in 1999 after FASDA decided to combine their First and Second Divisions as an 18-club structure outside Super League. The new First Division will involve each club playing 28 matches, but they will play six of their opponents only once instead of home and away. There will be a top five play-off at the end of the season to decide the championship.

The new set-up was accepted at a meeting on 27 November after FASDA scrapped plans for a First Division of 14 clubs and a five-club Second Division with a complicated cross-division fixture formula. They had to rethink when First Division champions Wakefield Trinity were granted promotion to Super League.

Super League will be increased to 14 clubs in 1999 following Wakefield's promotion and the admittance of new club Gateshead Thunder. The 14 clubs will play each other home and away with the first four rounds repeated to give a total of 30 matches for each club. This means that each club will play four others three times. For example, in addition to their 26 home and away matches, Wigan Warriors will play Hull Sharks and St. Helens at home again plus Leeds Rhinos and Wakefield away.

The Super League season has its earliest start – 5 March – to bring forward the Grand Final to 9 October and allow Great Britain to visit Australia and New Zealand for the Tri-Nations series. This will mean each club having to play up to three midweek matches.

The increase from 22/23 matches to 30 for each club and the reintroduction of midweek matches brought strong all-round criticism that it would set back the game to the pre-Super League era when quality was sacrificed for quantity, leaving Great Britain's players at a disadvantage in Test matches against Australia and New Zealand. But club officials argued the extra fixtures were necessary to bring in more income, especially after the new Sky TV contract meant less money from News Corporation.

ON THE ROAD

Super League officials made a bold move to give Rugby League a greater nationwide appeal when they staged six 'On the Road' matches in areas outside the game's Northern stronghold. In the original fixture list for 1998, no Super League matches were scheduled during most of July as it was hoped to stage an international tournament in the Southern Hemisphere during that period. It was also suggested that the three-week Super League break would avoid a clash with the media dominated Soccer World Cup in France, although that ended on 12 July. But when the international plan was abandoned, the three-week gap was filled by the innovative 'On the Road' fixtures.

The matches were fully competitive as they formed an additional Super League round – No. 14. Although a total attendance of 31,837 was nothing to get excited about, the venture was regarded as a success because the matches enhanced the game's profile with generally favourable media coverage in places where it would not normally be publicised.

The major drawback was that supporters did not see their team at home for over a month. In fact, Leeds Rhinos and Wigan Warriors went six weeks without a home match at a peak period of the season when both were battling for the League leadership.

Each Super League club played one match based on positions in the final 1997 table with 1st v. 2nd, 3rd v. 4th and so on. The matches were:

Gateshead, Friday 10 July: Leeds R. 34 v. Salford R. 16 (4,122); **Northampton, Friday 17 July:** Halifax B.S. 32 v. Sheffield E. 10 (3,087); **Edinburgh, Saturday 18 July:** Bradford B. 8 v. London B. 22 (6,863); **Gateshead, 24 July:** Huddersfield G. 10 v. Hull S. 21 (4,306); **Cardiff, Saturday 25 July:** Castleford T. 23 v. Warrington W. 16 (4,437); **Swansea, Sunday 26 July:** St. Helens 2 v. Wigan W. 36 (8,572).

BIG TRANSFER DEALS CURBED

The end of big transfer deals was virtually assured following a meeting of the RL Council on 24 June. They agreed that from 1999 there will be no transfer fees between clubs for players over 24 years of age. Young players will be asked to sign a contract which will bind them to their club until they are 24. Then they will become free agents, able to negotiate a new contract with the club of their choice. The age limit is believed necessary to give clubs who produce and develop their own young players some degree of protection and the chance of compensation if they are lured away before they reach 24.

The change was virtually forced on the RFL to bring it in line with European Law following the Bosman case in soccer two years earlier. Belgian player Jean-Marc Bosman won a court case which dramatically changed soccer's transfer system and granted players freedom of movement.

RULE CHANGES

The RL International Federation, at its meeting in Sydney, Australia, on 1-2 December, approved several changes to the International Rules of the Game to be effective from 1 January 1999. They included:

Kick-off to restart play after points have been scored: The non-scoring side will restart play with a place kick.

Ball finding touch after a restart: If the ball bounces into touch from a kick-off restart of play after points have been scored, 20-metre drop kick or goal-line drop out, the kicking side will receive the loose head and feed at the resultant scrum. If the ball bounces dead in-goal, play will recommence with a goal-line drop out.

40-20 rule: If a ball is kicked by a player in general play from within his own 40-metre area and bounces into touch in his opponent's 20-metre area, the kicking side will receive loose head and feed at the resultant scrum.

Substitutes: The International Rule is unlimited interchanges from four named substitutes. Provision is allowed for individual countries to vary the rule for domestic competitions.

Drop/field goals: A drop or field goal is awarded even if the ball is touched in flight by an opponent before going over the bar.

Zero tackle: The zero tackle will only operate from an error in general play, i.e. knock-on/forward pass. It will no longer apply to kicks in general play.

RACE CHARGE DISMISSAL

Anthony Gibbons of Bramley became the first player to be sent off for alleged verbal racial abuse when he was dismissed in the Second Division home match against Doncaster Dragons at Headingley on Easter Monday, 13 April. Although the RFL disciplinary committee accepted that Gibbons was not a racist they banned him for four matches for misconduct.

A second-half substitute, Gibbons was sent off in the 52nd minute by referee Nick Oddy for allegedly making racist remarks to black Doncaster winger Alex Goulbourne. But after the verdict an RFL statement said: 'The disciplinary committee were satisfied that the player was not a racist and, while he admitted using abusive language towards his opponent, it was accepted that this was done in the heat of the moment.' Bramley won the game 18-14.

Later in the season, the RFL decided that Leeds Rhinos forward Jamie Mathiou had no case to answer over allegations that he had made racist remarks to St. Helens' Western Samoan forward Apollo Perelini during the game on 4 September. The allegation had been made at a post-match Press conference by St. Helens coach Shaun McRae, who claimed that Saints hooker Keiron Cunningham had been sent to the sin bin by referee John Connolly after pushing Mathiou in response to the alleged remark. Mathiou admitted swearing at Perelini after the Saints forward had made a high tackle, but the RFL accepted that there was no racist intent.

RECORD FINE

Andy Kelly, Wakefield Trinity's coach, was fined a record £7,500 and banned from the touchline for bringing the game into disrepute following an incident immediately after the end of a First Division match at Featherstone Rovers on 5 July. Two-thirds of the fine was suspended until 31 December 1999. The touchline ban, which extended to all areas between the dressing rooms and the pitch, was for the remainder of the 1998 season and included Wakefield's matches at all levels. Kelly's previous good character and his high standing within Rugby League was taken into consideration before the former forward received the severest punishment ever handed out to an individual by the RFL.

Kelly was alleged to have assaulted a Featherstone official when they became involved in a scuffle after a home steward had stopped Trinity's coach from jumping over a perimeter wall to get to the dressing room when the final hooter sounded.

David Mycoe: Signed by Wakefield Trinity from Sheffield Eagles in January.

JANUARY

Bradford Bulls release 20 players after disbanding reserve team .... Featherstone Rovers sign Australian back Steve Collins from Parramatta .... Oldham win fight to be included in Silk Cut Challenge Cup draw .... Leigh Centurions sign Australian forward Steve Driscoll .... Wakefield Trinity forward Gary Divorty retires .... London Broncos sign Australian forward Mark Carroll from Manly .... Brisbane Broncos winger Wendell Sailor agrees two-year deal with Wigan Warriors .... Richard Evans replaces Steve Wagner as Featherstone Rovers chairman .... Maurice Lindsay leaves RFL to become managing director of SLE .... Leeds Rhinos deny some of their players are being pressured into joining Bramley .... Neil Tunnicliffe appointed chief executive of RFL board of directors for foreseeable future .... Wakefield Trinity sign David Mycoe on free transfer from Sheffield Eagles and Australian Garen Casey .... Dewsbury Rams sign Australians David O'Donnell and Paul Evans from Paris St. Germain .... Batley Bulldogs sign five players from Featherstone Rovers, including Roy Powell and Paul Gleadhill plus Australian forward Chad Fallins from Doncaster Dragons .... Salford Reds sign Phil Bergman from Paris St. Germain and release Fata Sini .... John Stabler and Russell Greenfield withdraw Hull Kingston Rovers takeover bid after Morrisons supermarket chain drop interest in buying Craven Park land for new store .... Swinton Lions sign Ian Blease from Salford Reds .... Tom Ellard replaces Eric Ashton as St. Helens chairman .... Phil Clarke joins Wigan Warriors board .... Hull Sharks sign Australian back David Baildon .... Super League clubs back Maurice Lindsay as SLE managing director .... Iestyn Harris denies he is switching codes in bid to play for Wales RU .... Swinton Lions re-sign Paul

Barrow from Warrington Wolves .... RFL decide not to make rule changes that have been accepted in Australia .... World Nines cancelled .... Tony Collins appointed RFL's official archivist .... Paul Rowley signs new three-year contract with Halifax Blue Sox .... Hull Sharks sign Glen Tomlinson from Bradford Bulls .... Sheffield Eagles sign Michael Jackson from Halifax Blue Sox .... Wigan Warriors appoint Andy Goodway as assistant coach .... Swinton Lions sign Ian Watson from Salford Reds .... Reborn Oldham beat Heworth in Silk Cut Challenge Cup play-off match .... Call for restriction on 'twinning' between Super League and First-Second Division clubs .... Graeme Bradley replaces Robbie Paul as Bradford Bulls captain .... High Court rejects Trevor Hobson's petition to wind up Batley Bulldogs .... SLE appoint Ian Robson as public relations and marketing executive .... Leeds Rhinos sign Australian utility back Brad Godden from Hunter Mariners .... York sign David Brook and Craig Booth from Hunslet Hawks .... Batley Bulldogs sign Deryck Fox on free transfer from Featherstone Rovers .... SLE and RFL in dispute over future News Corporation TV contract .... SLE withdraw Colin Myler from RFL operations board .... Tribunal orders Sheffield Eagles to pay Halifax Blue Sox £28,000 for Michael Jackson and St. Helens to pay Castleford Tigers £60,000 plus potential further payments totalling £20,000 for Chris Smith .... Sheffield Eagles sign Dave Watson, formerly of South Queensland Crushers .... Warrington Wolves sign former Oldham Bears centre Vince Fawcett .... Chris Caisley hints of SLE breakaway .... Clubs protest over agreement between RFL and Department of Employment over agreement that restricts signing of former Paris St. Germain players .... Rochdale Hornets sign Willie Swann

(Warrington Wolves), Adam Maher (Hunter Mariners) and Scott Opetaia (Gold Coast) .... Hunslet Hawks sign Ian Smales from Castleford Tigers .... Leigh Centurions sign Australian Steve Garces from South Perth .... Gary Hetherington becomes chief executive of both Leeds Rhinos and Leeds RU .... Castleford Tigers sign Danny Ellison and Gael Tallec from Wigan Warriors .... London Broncos complete signing of Australian Test forward Mark Carroll .... Oldham sign Mick Martindale from Wakefield Trinity .... Keighley Cougars out of administration .... Dewsbury Rams sign Alan Boothroyd from Bradford Bulls .... Dewsbury Rams coach Neil Kelly blames Maurice Lindsay for Paris St. Germain work permit breakdown .... Super League to go 'on the road' to fill summer break at neutral venues in new areas .... MPs vow to block any Super League plan to breakaway .... Dewsbury Rams sign Damian Ball from York .... Bramley sign David and Anthony Gibbons from Leeds Rhinos .... First and Second Division clubs announce Anglo-French tournament sponsored by EMAP .... RFL annual general meeting followed by RL Council meeting at which Super League clubs fail in bid to oust Sir Rodney Walker from the International Board .... Tom Smith elected RFL president .... Charity Commission to investigate RL Foundation's financial affairs .... Super League clubs deny breakaway threat after protests from David Hinchliffe MP and Lord Lofthouse .... Dewsbury Rams scrap twinning arrangement with Bradford Bulls in protest at Super League manoeuvres.

FEBRUARY
Dave Whelan of JJB Sports agrees two-year Super League sponsorship of about £1.5m .... First Division champions to receive £50,000

.... Sheffield Eagles chairman Tim Adams calls for transfer system to be scrapped .... St. Helens sign Australian centre Damien Smith from St. George .... Keighley Cougars sign Welsh RU winger Kirk Johnson .... Widnes Vikings' new ground to be renamed the Auto Quest Stadium .... RFL Players' consultative committee formed following official recognition of the RL Players' Association .... Players' agents to be licensed .... St. Helens report record £290,000 profit for 1997 .... Doncaster Dragons release Lee Trigg in disciplinary measure .... Workington Town sign former Widnes Vikings forward Anthony Samuel .... Sheffield Eagles sign Steve Molloy from Featherstone Rovers .... Pontypridd RU winger Jason Lee returns to Rugby League with Keighley Cougars .... Hunslet Hawks sign Grant Anderson from Castleford Tigers .... Keighley Cougars sign Western Samoan prop Fred Sapatu and take Australian second row Duncan Smith on trial .... Australia's decision not to discard four clubs puts Britain's Super League expansion plans in doubt because top class surplus Australian players would not now be available .... RFL rule former Carlisle Border Raiders captain Gary Charlton is not a free agent.

MARCH
RFL take no action after Halifax Blue Sox protest over referee Steve Presley's handling of Silk Cut Challenge Cup-tie at London Broncos, but Peter Gill and Terry Matterson are warned about their future conduct .... Colin Myler quits as chief executive of SLE .... Gary Connolly wanted by England RU .... Wigan Warriors shareholders back takeover by Dave Whelan .... Bob Scott quits Huddersfield Giants board to concentrate on FASDA duties .... Former Warrington Wolves forward Paul Hulme joins Swinton

Lions .... Geoff Berry retained as referees' coaching director .... Oldham sign Michael Edwards from Swinton Lions .... Lee Crooks replaces John Kain as Keighley Cougars coach .... Leeds Rhinos deny transfer of five players to Bramley .... Clubs from outside traditional RL areas may be invited to join an expanded Second Division .... Venues announced for Great Britain-New Zealand Test series included Bolton and Watford .... RFL announce financial penalties for salary cap infringements .... Nude poster campaign to launch Super League 1998 .... Halifax Blue Sox meet Leeds Rhinos in friendly farewell to Thrum Hall .... Hull K.R. query gate receipts from Cup-tie at London Broncos .... Wigan Warriors announce record £3.25m sponsorship deal with Tesco .... Hull Sharks' future in doubt after owner David Lloyd walks out of annual meeting .... JJB Super League launch announces record £275,000 for the champions .... David Lloyd agrees new deal to save Hull Sharks .... Wigan Warriors terminate injury-hit Nigel Wright's contract on medical grounds .... RFL agrees to pay Australian RL about £150,000 in an out-of-court settlement after conceding they withheld profits from 1995 World Cup .... Referee Stuart Cummings attacked by spectator at end of Sheffield Eagles' Silk Cut Challenge Cup semi-final defeat of Salford Reds at Headingley; Wigan Warriors beat London Broncos in the other semi-final, first time semis have been staged on successive weekend days .... Barrow Border Raiders sign Ayr RU and former Carlisle centre Stewart Magorian .... First and Second Divisions to be restructured in 1999 with potential for nine new clubs.

APRIL
Super League clubs win temporary relaxation of salary cap limits .... Neil Tunnicliffe con-

firmed as permanent RFL chief executive .... High Court awards Peter Regan £17,000 compensation for his sacking as Batley Bulldogs coach .... St. Helens cut players' winning bonus from £350 to £160 to keep within salary cap .... Tulsen Tollett returns to London Broncos on loan from Harlequins RU .... Keighley Cougars sign Davide Longo from Swinton Lions .... Paris unlikely to return to Super League in 1999 .... Maurice Lindsay admits mistakes in transferring RL Foundation money to RFL .... Great Britain coach Andy Goodway's contract extended to December 2000 .... SLE claim agreement with RFL over independent TV deal .... FASDA delay no confidence vote against Neil Tunnicliffe and Sir Rodney Walker over SLE's TV deal claim .... Shane Tupaea quits as Rochdale Hornets coach .... New international programme announced with a revived Wales meeting England, while France, Ireland and Scotland play in triangular tournament .... Super League's 'on the road' dates and venues announced .... Keighley Cougars sign Lee Hansen from Wigan Warriors .... Leeds Rhinos reject Wales RU move for Iestyn Harris .... Tribunal orders Halifax Blue Sox to pay money owed to Paul Moriarty .... Rochdale Hornets sign Australian back Ken Kerr .... Ray Unsworth appointed RFL Director of Coach Education .... Keighley Cougars sign former Warrington Wolves forward George Mann .... Robert Roberts transferred from Keighley Cougars to Hunslet Hawks after being banned for 10 matches .... Bramley's Anthony Gibbons banned four matches for misconduct after being sent off for alleged verbal racist abuse .... Castleford Tigers sign Martin Hall on loan from Wigan Warriors .... Bramley sign Castleford Tigers and Leeds RU winger Simon Middleton on loan .... RFL launch anti-racism drive with equal opportunities policy .... Protests after Leeds Rhinos prop Barrie McDermott joins Bramley on month's loan while serving five-match suspension .... Waisale Sovatabua of Sheffield Eagle cleared to play at Wembley after receiving a 'sending off sufficient' verdict .... Halifax Blue Sox sign Jamie Bloem from Widnes Vikings .... Oldham sign Joe Nadiole from Featherstone Rovers .... York sign former Salford Reds winger Fata Sini .... Silk Cut announce two-year extension to sponsorship of the Challenge Cup worth £1.8m.

MAY

Sheffield Eagles beat Wigan Warriors 17-8 in Silk Cut Challenge Cup final shock at Wembley .... Steve Ferres appointed Wakefield Trinity chief executive .... SLE fail in bid to block new Silk Cut Challenge Cup sponsorship deal .... Hull Sharks move to stamp out bad crowd behaviour .... Deryck Fox appointed player-coach of Rochdale Hornets .... RFL adopts Sports Aiding Medical Research for Kids as its official charity .... London Broncos sign Rob Smyth from Wigan Warriors .... Dewsbury Rams Australian hooker Dave O'Donnell granted work permit .... Castleford Tigers centre Barrie-Jon Mather to join Sale RU .... SLE calls for disciplinary meetings to be brought forward .... Professional Players' Association seek share of TV money .... FASDA give general manager Bob Scott vote of confidence .... Maurice Lindsay doubts Wakefield Trinity's chances of reaching Super League status .... Hunslet Hawks sign Richard Goddard from Castleford Tigers .... SLE and FASDA peace moves .... John Pendlebury quits and then stays as Halifax Blue Sox coach .... Swinton Lions sign George Mann while on loan to Keighley Cougars .... St. Helens list Karle Hammond at £150,000 .... St. Helens forward Dean Busby returns to Hull Sharks on loan .... St. Helens reject Bradford Bulls move for Paul Newlove .... St. Helens prop Brett Goldspink drops claim he was bitten by Hull Sharks player .... Eric Hughes returns to St. Helens as football operations manager .... Dewsbury Rams hooker Wayne Collins retires because of knee injury .... Andrew Whitelam appointed SLE broadcast and media manager .... Joint Policy Board for Rugby League awarded interim grant of £250,000 from Sports Council .... FASDA accept new Sky TV offer .... Keighley Cougars sign Adam Fogerty on loan .... Salford Reds coach Andy Gregory fined and banned from touchline until 31 October for verbal abuse of referees .... Hull K.R. coach Dave Harrison reprimanded for criticism of referee .... Keith Latham quits as Leigh Centurions coach and is succeeded by Norman Turley .... Controller of referees Geoff Berry defends referees against increasing criticism .... Wendell Sailor not to join Wigan Warriors .... Leroy Rivett transferred from Leeds Rhinos to Bramley after mix-up over loan move.

JUNE

Hull Sharks sign Craig Murdock on loan from Wigan Warriors .... Bradford Bulls announce £261,219 profit .... Former Cronulla Sharks official Shane Richardson and Kath Hetherington launch Gateshead's Super League bid .... Wakefield Trinity sign Australian centre Josh Bostock .... Music producer and songwriter Pete Waterman joins Salford Reds board .... Shell launch Super League discount promotion .... St. Helens reject Sheffield Eagles loan bid for Bobbie Goulding .... London Broncos sign Kris Chesney on loan from Harlequins RU .... Ian Riddoch to replace Rob Clayton as SLE marketing executive .... Hull Kingston Rovers

Garry Schofield: Released as coach by Huddersfield Giants in July.

forward Wayne Jackson retires because of head injury .... St. Helens takeover bid fails .... Chris Wood appointed RFL marketing manager .... FASDA start merit team and player of the week selections .... David Howes resigns as St. Helens chief executive .... Dewsbury Rams rename Crown Flatt ground Rams Stadium .... Hull Kingston Rovers sign Australian centre Keith Beauchamp .... Gateshead, Cardiff and Swansea make formal presentation of bid to enter Super League .... Bradford Bulls half back Shaun Edwards rejoins London Broncos .... RFL Council meeting votes to scrap fees for players over 24; delay decision on renegotiating News Corporation TV deal; change timing of disciplinary committee meetings .... salary cap limit amended for clubs who run Alliance teams .... David Howes appointed managing director of Leeds Rugby Club .... Ralph Rimmer becomes Sheffield Eagles' chief executive .... Director of referees Geoff Berry drops Steve Ganson after vital errors in match .... Wigan Warriors sign Australian international Greg Florimo from North Sydney .... Paul Rowley rescues girl from river, then stars for Halifax Blue Sox .... Silk Cut Challenge Cup final put on Government's list of great sporting events that cannot be sold to satellite TV .... Thomson Electronic Settlements Group to sponsor Emerging England and their match against Wales.

JULY

Former American player Chuck Wileman in Leicester franchise bid .... New Zealand call off matches against England and Wales .... Referees' Performance Advisory Panel formed .... Hull Sharks extend loan of Craig Murdock from Wigan Warriors .... Plans for new club at Goole called the East Riding Redskins .... Sir Rodney Walker to resign as RFL chairman .... 'On the road' series of matches starts with disappointing 4122 crowd at rain-soaked Gateshead who see Leeds Rhinos beat Salford Reds 34-16 .... Bradford Bulls deny signing Australian forward Wayne Richards, who is banned for taking steroids .... Peter Norbury succeeds Mike Nolan as Wigan Warriors chairman .... RFL chief executive Neil Tunnicliffe and SLE chairman Chris Caisley hold clear the air meeting .... RL Council special meeting: SLE and FASDA unite to agree new £54.8m Sky TV deal with News Corporation; First Division champions given hope of promotion to Super League; plans to reduce Super League overseas quota scrapped; New Alliance and Academy competitions planned .... Glasgow withdraws franchise bid .... Wigan Warriors sign St. Helens forward Brett Goldspink for next season .... London Broncos release Butch Fatnowna, Roger Best, Darren Higgins and Damien Chapman .... RFL reject Maurice Lindsay's call for referee appointments to be responsibility of SLE .... London Broncos sign Australian forward Shane Millward from South Sydney .... Huddersfield Giants release Garry Schofield as coach and he quits as a player .... Stan Martin quits as coach of Whitehaven Warriors and is replaced by Colin Armstrong as caretaker coach .... Salford Reds sign Garen Casey from Wakefield Trinity for next season .... St. Helens invite South African winger Gielle de Swardt to train with them .... Salford Reds sign Australian forward Shane Kenward from St. George .... York players call off threatened strike over club's failure to pay wages .... Tony Eagleton quits as RFL finance director .... Australian Test winger Wendell Sailor to play a few games for Leeds Rhinos during 16-week spell with Leeds Tykes RU .... BARLA's sacking of chief executive Maurice Oldroyd recalls long dispute with RFL

.... St. Helens not to renew coach Shaun McRae's contract .... Bobbie Goulding suspended by St. Helens for misconduct .... Wakefield Trinity coach Andy Kelly fined £7,500 (£5,000 suspended) and banned from touchline after assaulting Featherstone Rovers steward .... FASDA to consider return to winter season .... Bradford Bulls sign Nathan McAvoy from Salford Reds and Neil Harmon from Huddersfield Giants.

AUGUST

St. Helens sign Australian forward Phil Adamson from Penrith .... Blackpool Gladiators sue RFL for loss of League status .... St. John Ellis loses chance of coaching appointment at York .... Warrington Wolves sign Mike Pechey .... Super League International Board exclude Maurice Lindsay from top meeting .... York forward Stuart Flowers suspended three months after drugs test reveals traces of ephedrine .... John Kear rejects St. Helens and extends contract as Sheffield Eagles coach .... Widnes Vikings sack Graeme West as coach .... New Zealand threat to call off Tests against Great Britain if British-based players are not freed to face Australia .... London Broncos forward Steve Rosolen retires because of injury .... Bradford Bulls sign Australian centre Nick Zisti from Cronulla .... Hunslet Hawks sign Western Samoan hooker Willie Poching from St. George .... Cardiff and Swansea franchise bids rejected, but Gateshead's accepted a few days later .... First meeting of Referees' Performance Advisory Panel; ball stealing and sin bin to be reviewed .... Castleford Tigers sign Australians Aaron Raper from Parramatta and Paul Bell from Melbourne .... RL International Federation formed with John McDonald as chairman and Sir Rodney Walker beating Maurice Lindsay for the vice-chairmanship .... New Zealand agrees not to select British-based players for October Test series against Australia .... New referees' communication system introduced for all Super League matches .... World Cup planned for Britain in 2000 .... Ellery Hanley to be next St. Helens coach .... Bob McDermott condemns Sir Rodney Walker's decision to stay on as RFL chairman .... Oldham sack Paddy Kirwan as coach and put Mick Coates in charge .... Malcolm Reilly to be next Huddersfield Giants coach .... Shaun McRae to be Gateshead coach .... Australians Kerrod Walters and Danny Lee sign for Gateshead .... Harvey Howard joins Bradford Bulls on loan from Western Suburbs, Australia .... FASDA decide to award Wakefield Trinity a trophy for finishing as First Division leaders .... Simon Knox leaves Bradford Bulls for Salford Reds on loan .... Gateshead sign Luke Felsch from St. George, Australia .... London Broncos to release Mark Carroll.

SEPTEMBER

Leeds Rhinos sign Lee Jackson from Newcastle Knights, Australia .... Fereti Tuilagi to leave Halifax Blue Sox for St. Helens .... Gateshead sign Willie Peters from South Sydney, Australia .... SLE agree to start 1999 season early to facilitate Great Britain tour of Australia ... SLE and RFL in peace moves .... Leeds Rhinos forward Jamie Mathiou cleared of racist slur against Apollo Perelini of St. Helens .... Henry Paul to leave Wigan Warriors for Bradford Bulls next season .... Salford Reds coach Andy Gregory cleared of making abusive remarks to referee Karl Kirkpatrick .... Hull Sharks owner David Lloyd secures 75 per cent controlling interest in the club .... Former top administrator and Great Britain tour manager Tom Mitchell dies at 84 .... Hemel Hempstead's application to join Second

Division rejected .... Super League clubs call for up to 30 matches from next season .... RL Professional Players' Association breaks links with GMB trade union .... Leeds Rhinos owner Phil Carrick confirms interest in buying Hull K.R.'s Craven Park Stadium .... Scott Naylor to leave Salford Reds for Bradford Bulls ... Ian Millward appointed Leigh Centurions coach .... Maurice Lindsay defends criticism of extended Super League season in 1999 .... Salford Reds sign Craig Makin from Widnes Vikings .... Barrow Border Raiders sack Stuart Wilkinson as coach .... Whitehaven Warriors shareholders agree to merger talks with Workington Town .... Leeds Rhinos value Iestyn Harris at £2m after approaches by Welsh Rugby Union .... Abi Ekoku appointed chairman of RL Players' Association .... RFL aim to have Rugby League in 2002 Commonwealth Games .... New Challenge Cup trophy planned for 2002 .... Colin Whitfield appointed coach of Widnes Vikings .... Paul Mansson moves from Hunslet Hawks to Widnes Vikings .... Lancashire Lynx release Kevin Tamati as chief executive .... Wakefield Council give Castleford Tigers go ahead for new ground at Whitwood .... Shaun McRae steps down as Great Britain technical coach .... Swinton Lions forward Ian Skeech dies of leukaemia .... Plans to stage World Club Championship in South Africa .... St. Helens utility back Karle Hammond signs for London Broncos .... St. Helens deny signing Kevin Iro from Auckland Warriors .... Gateshead sign Australian full back Ian Herron from Parramatta .... Leeds City Council approve Headingley redevelopment application .... Castleford Tigers sign James Pickering from Sydney City .... Steve Simms departs as Featherstone Rovers coach .... Swinton Lions chairman Malcolm White admits he registered Manchester as a club .... Warrington Wolves sign Scott Wilson from Canterbury Bulldogs, Australia .... Paul Charlton appointed coach of Barrow Border Raiders .... St. Helens sign Kevin Iro from Auckland Warriors, New Zealand .... Steve Hampson appointed full-time coach of Lancashire Lynx following departure of team manager Kevin Tamati.

OCTOBER

Lancashire Lynx are the only British winners in first round of Treize Tournoi .... Warrington Wolves transfer list Mike Wainwright (£75,000), Warren Stevens (£45,000) and John Duffy (£25,000) .... Lincoln Financial Group to sponsor Great Britain-New Zealand Test series in £125,000 deal .... Greg McCallum to return as controller of referees .... Iestyn Harris elected RL Writers' Association player of the year .... Castleford Tigers' Jason Critchley joins Newport RU .... Halifax Blue Sox sign Craig Randall from Salford Reds .... Wendell Sailor refused work permit to player for Leeds RU .... Sheffield Eagles transfer list Paul Broadbent at his own request .... Huddersfield Giants sign Jim Lennihan from St. George, Australia .... Halifax Blue Sox release Karl Harrison .... John Kear resigns as France national coach to become Great Britain assistant coach .... Mick Coates appointed Oldham coach .... Tony Currie departs as London Broncos coach .... Dewsbury Rams sign Paul Medley on loan from Bradford Bulls .... Former Leeds and Salford back Phil Hassan joins Worcester RU .... Gary Connolly released from Australian RL contract .... Iestyn Harris named Man of Steel and Super League player of the season .... Andy Platt appointed Workington Town player-coach following departure of Robert Tew .... Wigan Warriors beat Leeds Rhinos in inaugural Grand Final .... Super League players vote to reject midweek matches .... Keighley Cougars sign Andrew Schick from Castleford Tigers .... Huddersfield Giants sign Ian Pickavance from St. Helens .... John Bentley leaves Halifax Blue Sox for Huddersfield Giants .... Hull Sharks sign Karl Harrison from Halifax Blue Sox .... Sheffield Eagles re-sign Jeff Hardy from St. George, Australia .... RFL appoint Darryl Keys non-executive finance director .... Oldham formally accepted as full members of RFL .... Decision on Wakefield Trinity's Super League application delayed .... Extra time to replace Challenge Cup replays .... Castleford Tigers sign Dale Fritz from North Queensland Cowboys, Australia .... Rochdale Hornets forward Karl Marriott dies after returning home from training .... Salford Reds sign winger Paul Carige from Parramatta, Australia .... Widnes Vikings sign George Mann .... Former Great Britain captain Garry Schofield makes surprise debut for Aberavon RU .... New Zealand beat Great Britain 22-16 in First Lincoln Test .... Roger Millward first winner of Tom Mitchell Trophy as 'Lion of the Year' .... New complicated fixture format proposed with First and Second Division clubs playing cross-division matches.

NOVEMBER

Mike Ford replaces Paul Fletcher as Bramley coach .... Kevin Tamati appointed Whitehaven Warriors coach .... Wakefield Trinity's Super League application decision deferred for second time .... Huddersfield Giants sign New Zealand forward Andrew Tangata-Toa from St. George, Australia .... London Broncos appoint Dan Stains as coach .... New Zealand clinch Lincoln Test series with record 36-16 defeat of Great Britain .... RFL give Andy Goodway vote of confidence as Great Britain coach .... Hull Sharks to go back to traditional irregular black and white hoops jerseys .... Wakefield Trinity's Super

League application accepted .... Sheffield Eagles re-sign Jeff Hardy from St. George, Australia .... Great Britain snatch 23-23 draw in final Test against New Zealand .... David Kirkwood replaces David Lloyd as Hull Sharks chairman .... Leeds Rhinos sign Karl Pratt from Featherstone Rovers in £100,000 deal .... France win Tri-Nations championship .... Hull Sharks sign Matt Calland from Bradford Bulls .... Wigan Warriors dispense with Phil Clarke as chief executive .... Adam Hughes becomes first player to sign jointly for Leeds Rhinos and Leeds Tykes RU .... Hull Sharks re-sign Karl Harrison from Halifax Blue Sox .... Warrington Wolves sign Simon Gillies from Canterbury Bulldogs, Australia .... RFL and BARLA Joint Policy Board sign new five-year agreement .... Swinton Lions sign Cliff Eccles from Salford Reds .... Featherstone Rovers' Post Office ground renamed Lionheart Stadium .... Wigan Warriors sign England Schools captain Sean O'Loughlin .... FASDA scrap complicated two divisions plan for one division of 18 clubs .... FASDA adjusts News Corp. income shareout to clubs .... Sheffield Eagles release Lynton Stott and Martin Wood .... Leeds Rhinos owner Phil Carrick bids £600,000 for Hull K.R. .... Whitehaven Warriors winger Les Quirk retires .... York sign Peter Edwards from Salford Reds .... St. Helens plan for match in Dubai as part of Millennium celebrations.

DECEMBER

Dublin Blues' winger Brian Carney signs for Gateshead Thunder .... Leeds Rhinos revert to traditional strip .... York issued with winding-up order by the Inland Revenue .... RL International Federation meeting in Sydney: Outline plans for 1999 Tri-Nations Series involving Great Britain, Australia and New Zealand; Great Britain to be split up into

England, Ireland, Wales and Scotland for 2000 World Cup; South Africa to stage World Nines at Johannesburg's Ellis Park .... Rule changes for 1999: Team finding touch inside opponents' 20-metre area from within 40 metres of own goal-line will get head and ball at scrum; non-scoring team to restart play after a score; zero tackles from downfield kicks scrapped .... Dewsbury Rams re-sign Nathan Graham from Bradford Bulls .... Dublin and Gateshead schools to meet in Wembley curtain-raiser .... Hull Sharks sign Robert Roberts from Hunslet Hawks .... Hunslet Hawks sign Richard Pachniuk from Rochdale Hornets .... Halifax Blue Sox sign Graham Holroyd from Leeds Rhinos .... Hull Sharks sign Andrew Purcell from Illawarra, Australia .... Widnes Vikings sign Lee Hansen from Keighley Cougars .... Featherstone Rovers sign Brendon Tuuta from Warrington Wolves .... Halifax Blue Sox sign Paul Broadbent and Nick Pinkney from Sheffield Eagles in exchange for Simon Baldwin, Daio Powell and Martin Pearson .... Wakefield Trinity sign Glen Tomlinson from Hull Sharks plus ex-Hunslet Warriors forward Willie Poching, ex-Salford Reds half back Shane Kenward and loose forward Frank Watene from Auckland Warriors, New Zealand .... Hull Sharks sign Wigan Warriors forwards Stephen Holgate and Steve Barrow .... Featherstone Rovers sign Ryan Horsley from Wakefield Trinity .... Maurice Lindsay extends interest in horse-race betting .... Paul Caddick withdraws Hull K.R. takeover bid .... Bradford Bulls release Jon Scales .... Wakefield Trinity sign Adrian Brunker from St. George, Australia .... Former Leeds United chairman Bill Fotherby appointed Hunslet Hawks managing director .... Rugby Football Union to forward plan for cross-code challenge matches between best young players in North and South England .... Huddersfield Giants sign Nigel Wright from Wigan Warriors .... Bradford Bulls sign David Boyle from Gold Coast Chargers, Australia .... Andy Hodgson leaves Bradford Bulls for Wakefield Trinity .... Widnes Vikings sign French international half-back Fabien Devecchi from Villeneuve .... Oldham sign French players Emmanuel Peralta and Laurent Minut from Villeneuve .... BBC to televise Silk Cut Challenge Cup draws .... Westferry Ltd takeover Doncaster Dragons .... RFL reprimand Graeme Bradley over criticism of referee Stuart Cummings .... Halifax Blue Sox sign Darryl Cardiss from Wigan Warriors .... England RFU drop £2m plan to sign Gary Connolly, Kris Radlinski and Alan Hunte .... Increasing speculation that Maurice Lindsay is to quit Rugby League .... Doncaster Dragons seek Garry Schofield as captain and development officer .... Oldham to play home games at Rochdale Hornets' Spotland Stadium .... Oldham sign Mark Perrett from Halifax Blue Sox .... Hull City Council launch 'Save Hull K.R. appeal' .... Huddersfield Giants sign former Adelaide Rams, Australia, forward David Boughton .... Peter Deakin rejects Warrington Wolves offer to become chief executive .... World Nines to be televised on Sky .... Roy Powell dies of suspected heart attack during training with Rochdale Hornets .... Salford Reds sign Mark Johnson from Hull Sharks .... Alex Murphy awarded OBE in New Year Honours.

Nathan McAvoy: Transferred from Salford Reds to Bradford Bulls.

CLUBS

CLUBS

The following is a focus on last season's 31 professional Rugby League clubs, the section providing each club with a profile and an analysis of their 1998 campaign on a match-by-match basis with a summary for each first team player.

KEY
In the individual club profiles the following headings are featured:
First season refers to when the club gained senior league status. In some instances clubs have disbanded and re-formed, sometimes under different titles. For record purposes these changes are ignored except where there has been a break of more than one full season.
Honours. Until they were scrapped in 1970, the Yorkshire and Lancashire Leagues were among the honours in the professional game. Before 1903 they operated under the title of the Lancashire and Yorkshire Senior Competitions. Winners of these competitions are included under the Lancashire and Yorkshire League Champions. The pre-1903 Yorkshire Senior Competition should not be confused with the league operating for A-teams in Yorkshire which had the same title.
Regal Trophy was previously known as John Player/Player's No. 6 Trophy competition.
Coaches. The clubs' individual coaching register is from the start of the 1974-75 season.
Attendances. Crowds in brackets are at neutral venues.
Appearances. Players' totals are based on official teamsheets submitted to the League after each first team match. + indicates playing substitute appearance.
Debut season. When a player goes back to a former club his return debut season is given.
Great Britain Register. The figure in brackets after a player's name is the number of Great Britain appearances he made while serving the club under whose entry he is listed, and the number after the + sign indicates playing substitute. This is followed by the time-span between his first and last British cap while at that club.
1998 Signings. The signing dates refer to when the players were registered at Rugby League headquarters. Players who signed but were not fully registered at RL headquarters before 31 December are not included, except in a few notable cases, which are listed without a registration date.
* Indicates where clubs have agreed to a player being signed 'on loan', a temporary transfer, the Rugby Football League prohibiting a subsequent transfer within 28 days. Where a player on loan has not been retained, his return to his original club is also marked *. When a player has been signed after a loan spell, his original loan signing date is given.
Key: Aust. – Australia; PNG – Papua New Guinea; ARL – Amateur Rugby League; Fr – France; RU – Rugby Union
Date of Birth. The dates are supplied in good faith by the Rugby Football League from their registration of players. This also applies to dates of signing and previous club.

In the match-by-match review for each club the following abbreviations are used:

SL	—	Super League	H	—	Home
FD	—	First Division	A	—	Away
SD	—	Second Division	N	—	Neutral
CC	—	Silk Cut Challenge Cup	W	—	Won
PO	—	Play-off	L	—	Lost
RR	—	Red Rose Championship	D	—	Drawn
WR	—	White Rose Championship	dg	—	Drop goal
TPF	—	Trans-Pennine Cup final			
TT	—	Treize Tournoi			
PR	—	Preliminary round			

BARROW BORDER RAIDERS

Ground: Craven Park (01229-830470)
First Season: 1900-01. Added Braves to title in 1995-96. Became Barrow Border Raiders after 'merging' with Carlisle Borders at end of 1997 season.
Chairman: Alan Winward
Honours: **Division Two** Champions, 1975-76, 1983-84
Challenge Cup Winners, 1954-55
Beaten finalists, 1937-38, 1950-51, 1956-57, 1966-67
Regal Trophy Beaten finalists, 1980-81
Lancashire Cup Winners, 1954-55, 1983-84
Beaten finalists, 1937-38

RECORDS

Match
Goals: 17 by Darren Carter v. Nottingham C., 27 Nov 1994
Tries: 6 by Val Cumberbatch v. Batley, 21 Nov 1936
Jim Thornburrow v. Maryport, 19 Feb 1938
Frank Castle v. York, 29 Sep 1951
Steve Rowan at Nottingham C., 15 Nov 1992
Points: 42 by Darren Carter v. Nottingham C., 27 Nov 1994

Season
Goals: 135 by Joe Ball, 1956-57
Tries: 50 by Jim Lewthwaite, 1956-57
Points: 305 by Ian Ball, 1979-80

Career
Goals: 741 by Willie Horne, 1943-59
Tries: 352 by Jim Lewthwaite, 1943-57
Points: 1,818 by Willie Horne, 1943-59
Appearances: 500 by Jim Lewthwaite, 1943-57
Highest score: 138-0 v. Nottingham C., 27 Nov 1994
Highest against: 90-0 at Leeds, 11 Feb 1990
Attendance: 21,651 v. Salford (League), 15 Apr 1938

COACHING REGISTER
● **Since 1974-75**

Frank Foster	May 73 - Apr 83
Tommy Dawes	May 83 - Feb 85
Tommy Bishop	Feb 85 - Apr 85
Ivor Kelland	May 85 - Feb 87
Dennis Jackson	Feb 87 - Nov 87
Rod Reddy	Nov 87 - Nov 89
Dennis Jackson	Nov 89 - Apr 90
Steve Norton	May 90 - Feb 91
Paul Kavanagh	Feb 91 - July 92
Geoff Worrall	July 92 - Apr 93
Dennis Ramsdale	May 93 - Sep 94
Peter Roe	Sep 94 - Jan 96
Steve Hogan	Feb 96 - Apr 96
Garry Schubert	May 96 - Apr 97
Stuart Wilkinson	Apr 97 - Sep 98
Paul Charlton	Sep 98 -

GREAT BRITAIN REGISTER
(19 players)

Bill Burgess	(16)	1924-29
Bill Burgess	(13)	1962-68
David Cairns	(2)	1984
Chris Camilleri	(2)	1980
Charlie Carr	(7)	1924-26
Frank Castle	(4)	1952-54
Roy Francis	(1)	1947
Harry Gifford	(2)	1908
Dennis Goodwin	(5)	1957-58
Jack Grundy	(12)	1955-57
Phil Hogan	(4+1)	1977-78
Willie Horne	(8)	1946-52
Phil Jackson	(27)	1954-58
Joe Jones	(1)	1946
Bryn Knowelden	(1)	1946
Eddie Szymala	(1+1)	1981
Ted Toohey	(3)	1952
Alec Troup	(2)	1936
Jack Woods	(1)	1933

BARROW BORDER RAIDERS 1998 MATCH ANALYSIS

Date	Competition	H/A	Opponents	Rlt	Score	Tries	Goals	Attendance	Referee
1.2.98	CC(3)	H	Farnworth R.O.B.	W	52-8	Carter (3), Ruddy (2), Burns, McMillan, Holt, Shaw	Marwood (8)	927	Cornish
15.2.98	CC(4)	H	Widnes V.	L	22-36	McMillan (3), Kerr	Marwood (3)	1313	Lowe
10.4.98	SD	H	Workington T.	W	26-10	Kerr (4), Hutton	Marwood (2), Carter	1748	Lee
13.4.98	SD	A	Lancashire L.	D	20-20	Carter, Halsall, McMillan, Ruddy	Marwood (2)	–	–
19.4.98	SD	H	Batley B.	W	19-17	Ruddy (2), Holt, Hutton	Marwood (1, dg)	1266	Atkin
26.4.98	SD	A	York	L	6-38	Carter	Marwood	–	–
10.5.98	SD	H	Doncaster D.	W	42-8	Halsall (2), Holt (2), Burns, Carter, Rhodes, Ruddy	Carter (3), Marwood (2)	1312	Lowe
17.5.98	SD	A	Oldham	L	4-13	Marwood	–	–	–
24.5.98	SD	H	Bramley	W	16-12	Carter, Hutton, McKelleher	Marwood (2)	973	Laughton
31.5.98	SD/RR	A	Workington T.	L	23-16	Wallis, McDermott	Marwood (2, dg)	–	–
7.6.98	SD/RR	H	Lancashire L.	L	12-22	Ruddy (2)	Marwood (2)	812	Atkin
14.6.98	SD/RR	A	Oldham	L	8-32	McKelleher, Ruddy	–	–	–
21.6.98	SD/RR	H	Workington T.	W	34-12	Rhodes (2), Kettlewell, Holt, Quayle, Spenceley	Marwood (5)	821	Lee
28.6.98	SD/RR	H	Oldham	W	19-2	Atkinson (2), Kavanagh, McKelleher	Marwood, Holt (dg)	1333	McGregor
5.7.98	SD/RR	A	Lancashire L.	L	14-32	Luxon, Rhodes, Ruddy	Marwood	–	–
26.7.98	SD	A	Workington T.	D	8-8	Hutton	Atkinson, Marwood	–	–
2.8.98	SD	H	Lancashire L.	L	12-21	Carter, Wilson	Atkinson (2)	821	McGregor
9.8.98	SD	A	Batley B.	L	16-17	Atkinson, Manihera, Rhodes	Atkinson (2)	–	–
16.8.98	SD	H	York	L	10-43	Burns, Kettlewell	Atkinson	808	Laughton
23.8.98	SD	A	Doncaster D.	W	22-8	Atkinson, Carter, Holt, Manihera	Atkinson (3)	–	–
30.8.98	SD	H	Oldham	W	31-20	Manihera (2), Atkinson, Burns, Hutton, McKelleher	Atkinson (3, dg)	896	Shaw
5.9.98	SD	A	Bramley	L	22-26	Marwood, Manihera, Atkinson, Burns	Atkinson (3)	–	–

1998 SIGNINGS REGISTER

Signed	Player	Club From
14.5.98	Alberty, Michael	Furness RU
4.8.98	Ayres, Phillip	Sale RU
24.7.98	Devlin, Ian	Workington T.
11.1.98	Farrimond, Jonathan	Carlisle B.R.
14.1.98	Gardner, John-Paul	Warrington W.
15.1.98	Hetherington, Gary	Whitehaven W.
11.1.98	Holt, Darren	Carlisle B.R.
20.1.98	Jackson, Steven	Carlisle B.R.
7.4.98	Magorian, Stewart	Ayr RU
30.7.98	Manihera, Tane	Widnes V.
14.5.98	McClure, Andrew	Roose ARL
14.4.98	McKelleher, John	Gold Coast (Aust.)
2 1.98	Oldcorn, Michael	Askam ARL
14.5.98	Rawlinson, Ian	Barrow Island ARL
22.7.98	Rigby, Andrew	Askam ARL
11.1.98	Ruddy, Gary	Carlisle B.R.
31.3.98	Stevens, Jamie	Carlisle B.R.
11.1.98	Thurlow, Jason	Carlisle B.R.
11.2.98	Wallis, Shaun	Western Suburbs (Aust.)
13.1.98	Whalley, Andy	Workington T.
6.8.98	Whitter, Damien	Workington T

Paul Charlton: New coach.

BARROW BORDER RAIDERS 1998 PLAYERS' SUMMARY

	Date of birth	App	T	G	D	Pts	Previous club	Debut
Atkinson, Phil	25.9.74	14+1	6	5	1	55	Ulverston ARL	1993-94
Bent, Peers	28.12.70	2+4	0	0	0	0	Blackpool G.	1993-94
Burns, Paul	9.2.67	16+1	5	0	0	20	Workington T.	1996
Carter, Darren	8.1.72	17+2	9	5	0	46	Workington T.	1997
Caunt, Nick	6.9.76	0+1	0	0	0	0	Ulverston ARL	1997
Chelton, Gavin	21.2.71	3+2	0	0	0	0	Holker Pioneers ARL	1995-96
Devlin, Ian	20.4.73	2+3	0	0	0	0	Workington T.	1998
Halsall, Ian	25.1.73	6+1	3	0	0	12	Warrington W.	1997
Holt, Darren	21.9.76	21	6	0	1	25	Carlisle B.R.	1998
Hutton, Glenn	17.8.74	19	5	0	0	20	Lock Lane ARL	1996
Kavanagh, Mike	5.2.71	10+4	1	0	0	4	Askam ARL	1998
Kerr, Gareth	17.1.76	10+1	5	0	0	20	Walney Central ARL	1994-95
Kettlewell, Ronnie	10.10.72	5+2	2	0	0	8	Warrington	1996
Luxon, Geoff	2.6.71	22	1	0	0	4		1995-96
Magorian, Stewart	28.1.73	0+2	0	0	0	0	Ayr RU	1998
Manihera, Tane	6.8.74	5	5	0	0	20	Widnes V.	1998
Marwood, Dean	22.2.70	18+1	2	32	2	74	Workington T.	1997
McAllister, Ian	27.4.72	1	0	0	0	0	Barrow Island ARL	1997
McDermott, Brett	10.9.78	5+2	1	0	0	4	Roose ARL	1995-96
McKelleher, John	21.8.70	16+2	4	0	0	16	Gold Coast (Aust.)	1998
McMillan, Paul	26.7.74	5	5	0	0	20	Walney Central ARL	1996
Procter, Steve	28.4.67	0+1	0	0	0	0	Dalton ARL	1996
Quayle, Stewart	22.4.68	4+6	1	0	0	4	Walney ARL	1994-95
Rawlinson, Ian	22.2.76	3+7	0	0	0	0	Barrow Island ARL	1998
Rhodes, Stuart	16.1.72	13+6	5	0	0	20	Carlisle	1998
Ruddy, Gary	9.12.73	19	10	0	0	40	Carlisle B.R.	1998
Shaw, Neil	29.9.68	15+1	1	0	0	4	Barrow Island ARL	1987-88
Spencely, Gary	5.2.67	5+14	1	0	0	4	Barrow Island ARL	1994-95
Stevens, Jamie	14.6.76	0+1	0	0	0	0	Carlisle B.R.	1998
Thurlow, Jason	18.12.69	2	0	0	0	0	Carlisle B.R.	1998
Waddell, Hugh	1.9.59	0+2	0	0	0	0	Carlisle B.R.	1997
Wallis, Shaun	8.12.72	17+1	1	0	0	4	Western Suburbs (Aust.)	1998
Whalley, Andy	4.3.75	0+1	0	0	0	0	Workington T.	1998
Whitehead, Mike	25.8.78	4+4	0	0	0	0	Wigan W.	1998
Whitter, Damien	25.11.76	1+3	0	0	0	0	Workington T.	1998
Wilson, Darren	7.3.73	6+3	1	0	0	4	Walney Central ARL	1994-95
TOTALS								
36 players			80	52	4	428		

BATLEY BULLDOGS

Ground:	Mount Pleasant (01924-470062)
First Season:	1895-96. Added Bulldogs to title at start of 1996 League season.
Chairman:	Kevin Nicholas
Honours:	**Championship** Winners, 1923-24 **Challenge Cup** Winners, 1896-97, 1897-98, 1900-01 **Yorkshire Cup** Winners, 1912-13 Beaten finalists, 1909-10, 1922-23, 1924-25, 1952-53 **Yorkshire League** Winners, 1898-99, 1923-24 **Trans-Pennine Cup** Winners 1998 **White Rose Championship** Winners 1998

RECORDS

Match

Goals:	13 by	Simon Wilson v. Leigh, 26 March 1995
Tries:	5 by	Joe Oakland v. Bramley, 19 Dec 1908 Tommy Brannan v. Swinton, 17 Jan 1920 Jim Wale v. Bramley, 4 Dec 1926 Jim Wale v. Cottingham, 12 Feb 1927 Tommy Oldroyd at Highfield, 6 Mar 1994
Points:	30 by	Simon Wilson v. Leigh, 26 Mar 1995

Season

Goals:	127 by	Simon Wilson, 1994-95
Tries:	29 by	Jack Tindall, 1912-13
Points:	308 by	Richard Price, 1997

Career

Goals:	463 by	Wharton "Wattie" Davies, 1897-1912
Tries:	123 by	Wharton "Wattie" Davies, 1897-1912
Points:	1,297 by	Wharton "Wattie" Davies, 1897-1912
Appearances:	421 by	Wharton "Wattie" Davies, 1897-1912

Highest score: 78-22 v. Leigh, 26 Mar 1995
Highest against: 78-9 at Wakefield T., 26 Aug 1967
Attendance: 23,989 v. Leeds (RL Cup), 14 Mar 1925

COACHING REGISTER

● **Since 1974-75**

Don Fox	Nov 72 - Oct 74
Alan Hepworth	Nov 74 - Apr 75
Dave Cox	May 75 - June 75
Trevor Walker	June 75 - June 77
Albert Fearnley	June 77 - Oct 77
Dave Stockwell	Oct 77 - June 79
* Tommy Smales	June 79 - Oct 81
Trevor Lowe	Oct 81 - May 82
Terry Crook	June 82 - Nov 84
George Pieniazek	Nov 84 - Nov 85
Brian Lockwood	Nov 85 - May 87
Paul Daley	July 87 - Apr 90
Keith Rayne	May 90 - Apr 91
David Ward	May 91 - Oct 94
Jeff Grayshon	Oct 94 - July 96
Mike Kuiti	July 96 - Sep 96
Peter Regan	Nov 96 - Sep 97
David Ward	Sep 97 -

* Ex-forward

GREAT BRITAIN REGISTER

(4 players)

Norman Field	(1)	1963
Frank Gallagher	(8)	1924-26
Carl Gibson	(+1)	1985
Joe Oliver	(4)	1928

Albert Fearnley: Coach in 1977.

BATLEY BULLDOGS 1998 MATCH ANALYSIS

Date	Competition	H/A	Opponents	Rlt	Score	Tries	Goals	Attendance	Referee
31.1.98	CC(3)	H	Oulton R.	W	44-2	Bargate (2), Harrison (2), Morgan, Jackson, Simpson, Walton	Price (6)	849	Lockton
15.2.98	CC(4)	H	London B.	L	20-44	Gleadhill, Jackson, Price	Price (4)	956	Bates
13.4.98	SD	H	York	W	25-11	Gleadhill (2), Barnett, Simpson	Price (4), Cass (dg)	745	Gilmore
19.4.98	SD	A	Barrow B.R.	L	17-19	Bargate, Cass, Mirfin	Price (2), Barnett (dg)	–	–
26.4.98	SD	H	Workington T.	W	42-18	Gleadhill (2), Jackson (2), Craven, Walker, Walton	Price (6), Fox	550	Oddy
6.5.98	SD	A	Doncaster D.	L	20-33	Bargate, Gleadhill, Price, Wray	Price (2)	–	–
10.5.98	SD	A	Oldham	L	20-28	Barnett, Cass, Price	Price (4)	–	–
17.5.98	SD	A	Bramley	L	14-24	Bargate, Morgan, Price	Price	–	–
24.5.98	SD	H	Lancashire L.	L	16-17	Barnett, Miers, Price	Price (2)	501	Lee
31.5.98	SD/WR	H	Doncaster D.	W	33-20	Barnett (2), Gleadhill, Walker, Harrison	Price (4), Dyson (2) Barnett (dg)	595	Lowe
7.6.98	SD/WR	A	York	W	13-4	Barnett, Wray	Price, Barnett (3dg)	–	–
14.6.98	SD/WR	H	Bramley	W	34-18	Hughes (3), Gleadhill, Wray, Simpson	Price (5)	627	McGregor
21.6.98	SD/WR	A	Doncaster D.	W	28-22	Gleadhill, Harrison, Price, McWilliam, Simpson	Price (4)	–	–
28.6.98	SD/WR	A	Bramley	L	16-24	Bargate, Mirfin, Walton	Price (2)	–	–
5.7.98	SD/WR	H	York	W	8-3	Simpson	Price (2)	617	Taberner
19.7.98	TPF	H	Oldham	W	28-12	Barnett (2), Simpson, Price	Price (6)	2696	Nicholson
26.7.98	SD	H	Doncaster D.	L	10-24	Hughes, Price	Price	568	I. Smith
2.8.98	SD	A	York	W	18-15	Bargate, Gleadhill, McWilliam	Price (3)	–	–
9.8.98	SD	H	Barrow B.R.	W	17-16	Cass, Walker	Price (4), Cass (dg)	400	Laughton
16.8.98	SD	A	Workington T.	W	28-12	Cass, Mirfin, Miers, Price	Price (6)	–	–
23.8.98	SD	H	Oldham	W	17-2	Harrison, Walker	Price (4), Barnett (dg)	1004	McGregor
30.8.98	SD	H	Bramley	W	30-22	Barnett, Gleadhill, Harrison, Mirfin, Walker	Price (5)	615	Presley
6.9.98	SD	A	Lancashire L.	W	31-22	Dyson (2), Simpson (2), Gleadhill	Price (5), Cass (dg)	–	–

1998 SIGNINGS REGISTER

Signed	Player	Club From
28.5.98	Ballentyne, Darren	Hunslet H.
1.1.98	Bargate, Lee	Featherstone R.
21.8.98	Braddon, John	BRK ARL
1.1.98	Brook, Richard	—
1.1.98	Cartledge, William	Batley Academy
1.1.98	Cowling, Stephen	BRK ARL
21.1.98	Fox, Deryck	Featherstone R.
7.5.98	Garside, Lee	Walton/Crofton ARL
1.1.98	Gleadhill, Paul	Featherstone R.
1.1.98	Haigh, Paul	Batley Academy
1.1.98	Harrison, Paul	York
22.5.98	Hughes, Darren	Featherstone R.
5.2.98	Lingard, Craig	Sharlston R. ARL
10.4.98	Miers, Grant	Oulton R. ARL
1.1.98	Morgan, Jonathan	Featherstone R.
—	Patterson, Brett	Dewsbury R.
19.6.98	Pennington, Matt	Leeds University ARL
1.1.98	Powell, Roy	Featherstone R.
1 1.98	Riley, Carl	Featherstone R.
4.4.98	Rumford, Tim	York
1 1.98	Sheridan, Brendon	Dewsbury Moor ARL
12.5.98	Simpson, Nick	Bradford B.
1.1.98	Smith, Simon	BRK ARL
24.2.98	Trigg, Lee	Doncaster D.
20.3.98	Wray, Andrew	Featherstone R.

BATLEY BULLDOGS 1998 PLAYERS' SUMMARY

	Date of birth	App	T	G	D	Pts	Previous club	Debut
Bargate, Lee	12.9.71	23	7	0	0	28	Featherstone R.	1998
Barnett, Gary	25.3.71	20+2	9	0	6	42	Bramley	1995-96
Bradbrook, Neil	6.1.72	1+11	0	0	0	0	Hunslet H.	1997
Brook, Richard	18.2.70	1	0	0	0	0		1998
Cass, Mark	17.11.71	18+2	4	0	0	19	Hull	1991-92
Craven, Nigel	24.11.70	0+6	1	0	0	4	Batley Boys ARL	1990-91
Dyson, Jeremy	15.2.72	12+2	2	2	0	12	Thornhill ARL	1998
Fox, Deryck	17.9.64	3	0	1	0	2	Featherstone R.	1998
Gibson, Carl	23.4.63	3	0	0	0	0	Featherstone R.	1996
Gleadhill, Paul	2.2.76	22+1	12	0	0	48	Featherstone R.	1998
Harrison, Paul	24.9.70	23	6	0	0	24	York	1998
Hewitt, Richard	7.10.74	2+2	0	0	0	0	Doncaster D.	1997
Hughes, Darren	19.6.74	7+1	4	0	0	16	Featherstone R.	1998
Jackson, Simon	4.2.77	10+4	4	0	0	16	St. John Fisher ARL	1996
Lingard, Craig	11.12.77	0+4	0	0	0	0	Sharlston R. ARL	1998
McWilliam, Chris	1.6.69	20	2	0	0	8	Ovenden ARL	1994-95
Middleton, Graham	2.10.70	9+6	0	0	0	0	Leeds	1993-94
Miers, Grant	22.4.75	14+3	2	0	0	8	Oulton R. ARL	1998
Mirfin, Phil	20.11.68	6+14	4	0	0	16	Castleford	1994-95
Morgan, Jonathan	21.11.74	1+6	2	0	0	8	Featherstone R.	1998
Powell, Roy	30.4.65	14	0	0	0	0	Featherstone R.	1998
Price, Richard	26.6.70	23	9	83	0	202	Sheffield E.	1996
Scott, Mark	30.1.65	0+2	0	0	0	0	Batley Boys ARL	1984-85
Simpson, Nick	13.11.74	1	0	0	0	0	Bradford B.	1998
Simpson, Roger	27.8.67	18	8	0	0	32	Bradford B.	1996
Turpin, David	21.1.73	1	0	0	0	0	Bradford B.	1996
Walker, Steve	8.11.69	15+6	5	0	0	20	Dudley Hill ARL	1992-93
Walton, Tony	20.12.63	18+2	3	0	0	12	Doncaster	1992-93
Wray, Andrew	21.10.77	14+7	3	0	0	12	Featherstone R.	1998
TOTALS								
29 players			87	86	9	529		

Deryck Fox: Former Featherstone Rovers scrum half had a brief spell with Batley Bulldogs in 1998.

BRADFORD BULLS

Ground: Odsal Stadium (01274-733899)
First Season: 1895-96 as 'Bradford'. Disbanded and became Bradford Northern in 1907-08. Disbanded during 1963-64 and re-formed for start of 1964-65. Retitled Bradford Bulls from the start of 1995-96.
Chairman: Chris Caisley
Honours: **Championship** Beaten finalists, 1947-48, 1951-52
War Emergency League Championship winners, 1939-40, 1940-41, 1944-45
Beaten finalists, 1941-42
Division One Champions, 1903-04, 1979-80, 1980-81
Super League Champions, 1997
Division Two Champions, 1973-74
Challenge Cup Winners, 1905-06, 1943-44, 1946-47, 1948-49
Beaten finalists, 1897-98, 1944-45, 1947-48, 1972-73, 1996, 1997
Regal Trophy Winners, 1974-75, 1979-80
Beaten finalists, 1990-91, 1992-93
Premiership Winners, 1977-78
Beaten finalists, 1978-79, 1979-80, 1989-90
Yorkshire Cup Winners, 1906-07, 1940-41, 1941-42, 1943-44, 1945-46, 1948-49, 1949-50, 1953-54, 1965-66, 1978-79, 1987-88, 1989-90
Beaten finalists, 1913-14, 1981-82, 1982-83, 1991-92
Yorkshire League Winners, 1899-1900, 1900-01, 1939-40, 1940-41, 1947-48

RECORDS

Match
Goals: 14 by Joe Phillips v. Batley, 6 Sep 1952
Tries: 7 by Jim Dechan v. Bramley, 13 Oct 1906
Points: 36 by John Woods v. Swinton, 13 Oct 1985

Season
Goals: 173 by Eddie Tees, 1971-72
Tries: 63 by Jack McLean, 1951-52
Points: 364 by Eddie Tees, 1971-72

Career
Goals: 779 by Keith Mumby, 1973-90 & 1992-93
Tries: 261 by Jack McLean, 1950-56
Points: 1,828 by Keith Mumby, 1973-90 & 1992-93
Appearances: 580+8 by Keith Mumby, 1973-90 & 1992-93
Highest score: 76-0 v. Leigh East, 17 Nov 1991
Highest against: 75-18 at Leeds, 14 Sep 1931
Attendance: 102,569 Warrington v. Halifax (RL Cup final replay), 5 May 1954
Home match: 69,429 v. Huddersfield (RL Cup), 14 Mar 1953

COACHING REGISTER
● **Since 1974-75**

Ian Brooke	Jan 73 - Sep 75
Roy Francis	Oct 75 - Apr 77
Peter Fox	Apr 77 - May 85
Barry Seabourne	May 85 - Sep 89
Ron Willey	Oct 89 - Mar 90
David Hobbs	Mar 90 - Oct 91
Peter Fox	Oct 91 - June 95
Brian Smith	June 95 - Aug 96
Matthew Elliott	Sep 96 -

GREAT BRITAIN REGISTER
(40 players)

David Barends	(2)	1979
Eric Batten	(4)	1946-47
Ian Brooke	(5)	1966
Len Casey	(5)	1979
Gerald Cordle	(1)	1990
Willie Davies	(3)	1946-47
Bernard Dwyer	(0+1)	1996
Karl Fairbank	(10+6)	1987-94
Tony Fisher	(8)	1970-78
Phil Ford	(7)	1987-88
Mike Forshaw	(0+3)	1997-98
Trevor Foster	(3)	1946-48
Deryck Fox	(1)	1992
Jeff Grayshon	(11)	1979-82
Ellery Hanley	(10+1)	1984-85
David Hobbs	(1+1)	1989
Harvey Howard	(0+1)	1998
Dick Jasiewicz	(1)	1984
Jack Kitching	(1)	1946

James Lowes	(3)	1997
Brian McDermott	(4)	1996-97
Steve McNamara	(0+2)	1997
Arthur Mann	(2)	1908
Keith Mumby	(11)	1982-84
Paul Newlove	(5+1)	1993-94
Brian Noble	(11)	1982-84
Terry Price	(1)	1970
Johnny Rae	(1)	1965
Bill Ramsey	(+1)	1974
Alan Rathbone	(4+1)	1982-85
Alan Redfearn	(1)	1979
David Redfearn	(6+1)	1972-74
Kelvin Skerrett	(8)	1989-90
Tommy Smales	(3)	1965
Bert Smith	(2)	1926
Stuart Spruce	(5)	1996
Jimmy Thompson	(1)	1978
Ken Traill	(8)	1950-54
Ernest Ward	(20)	1946-52
Frank Whitcombe	(2)	1946

Ernest Ward: 20 Test matches.

1998 SIGNINGS REGISTER

Signed	Player	Club From
26.1.98	Banks, Michael	Stanningley ARL
26.1.98	Bibb, Sam	Smawthorne P. ARL
25.4.98	Birchall, Christopher	—
—	Boyle, David	Gold Coast (Aust.)
26 1.98	Brown, Craig	Stanningley ARL
25.4.98	Hamilton, Lance	—
26.1.98	Handford, Gareth	Redhill ARL
28.7.98	Harmon, Neil	Huddersfield G.
29.8.98	*Howard, Harvey	Leeds R.
26.1.98	Langley, Christopher	Smawthorne ARL
22.5.98	Mason, Keith	—
29.7.98	McAvoy, Nathan	Salford R.
—	Naylor, Scott	Salford R.
—	Paul, Henry	Wigan W.
8.2.98	Pickles, Stephen	Leeds R.
11.9.98	Pryce, Leon	Queensbury ARL
—	Radford, Lee	Hull S.
26.1.98	Redfearn, Christopher	Magnet ARL
8.2.98	Smith, Richard	Halifax B.S.
19.2.98	Stanley, Gareth	Smawthorne P. ARL
19.2.98	Sykes, Paul	Thornhill ARL
—	Withers, Michael	Balmain (Aust.)
—	Zisti, Nick	Cronulla (Aust.)

Ken Traill: Eight Test matches.

BRADFORD BULLS 1998 MATCH ANALYSIS

Date	Com-petition	H/A	Opponents	Rlt	Score	Tries	Goals	Atten-dance	Referee
15.2.98	CC(4)	A	Rochdale H.	W	48-10	Forshaw (2), Calland, Edwards, Jowitt, Lowes, Paul, Spruce, Vaikona	McNamara (3), Lowes (3)	–	–
28.2.98	CC(5)	A	Castleford T.	L	21-26	Calland, Lowes, Spruce, Peacock	McNamara (1, dg), Lowes	–	–
3.4.98	SL	A	Huddersfield G.	W	38-6	Vaikona (2), Spruce, Peacock, Forshaw, Edwards, Bradley	McNamara (5)	–	–
12.4.98	SL	H	Leeds R.	L	6-26	Calland	McNamara	19,188	Cummings
17.4.98	SL	A	Sheffield E.	W	11-4	Edwards, Spruce	McNamara, Graham (dg)	–	–
26.4.98	SL	A	Hull S.	W	26-24	Calland (2), Peacock (2), Vaikona	McNamara (3)	–	–
10.5.98	SL	H	St. Helens	W	18-4	Lowes, Vaikona, McDermott	McNamara (3)	14,091	R. Smith
17.5.98	SL	H	Halifax B.S.	L	16-21	Paul (2), Vaikona	McNamara (2)	16,337	Cummings
22.5.98	SL	A	Castleford T.	W	52-10	Paul (3), Edwards (2), McDermott (2), Donougher, Peacock, Vaikona,	McNamara (6)	–	–
29.5.95	SL	H	London B.	W	17-14	Bradley, Lowes, McDermott	McNamara (2, dg)	11,893	Presley
7.6.98	SL	A	Warrington W.	L	10-28	Calland, Vaikona	McNamara	–	–
12.6.98	SL	H	Wigan W.	L	12-28	Vaikona, McDermott	McNamara (2)	14,103	Cummings
21.6.98	SL	A	Salford R.	L	10-11	Medley	McNamara (3)	–	–
28.6.98	SL	H	Huddersfield G.	W	36-10	Bradley (2), Deacon, Forshaw, Lowes, Spruce	McNamara (5), Deacon	12,024	Presley
3.7.98	SL	A	Leeds R.	W	33-22	Forshaw (2), Paul, Calland, Scales	McNamara (6, dg)	–	–
18.7.98	SL	N1	London B.	L	8-22	Bradley, Scales	–	(6863)	Presley
2.8.98	SL	H	Sheffield E.	L	18-38	Bradley (2), Lowes	McNamara (3)	11,493	Kirkpatrick
9.8.98	SL	H	Hull S.	W	38-18	Vaikona (2), Forshaw, Paul, McAvoy, Scales	McNamara (7)	11,294	Ganson
16.8.98	SL	A	St. Helens	L	25-33	Vaikona (2), Bradley, Spruce	McNamara (4, dg)	–	–
23.8.98	SL	A	Halifax B.S.	L	12-25	Deacon, McDermott	McNamara (2)	–	–
31.8.98	SL	H	Castleford T.	W	24-8	Lowes, Scales, Spruce	McNamara (6)	10,946	Cummings
6.9.98	SL	A	London B.	L	8-34	Bradley	McNamara (2)	-	-
13.9.98	SL	H	Warrington W.	W	36-8	Lowes (2), Bradley, Ekoku, Paul, Spruce	McNamara (4), Deacon (2)	10,815	Ganson
20.9.98	SL	A	Wigan W.	L	4-38	Ekoku	–	–	–
27.9.98	SL	H	Salford R.	W	40-18	Deacon (2), Bradley, Harmon, Howard, McNamara, Paul	McNamara (5), Deacon	11,102	J. Connolly
2.10.98	PO	A	St. Helens	L	24-46	Donougher (2), Graham, Crouthers	McNamara (4)	–	–

N1 at Hearts FC, Edinburgh

BRADFORD BULLS 1998 PLAYERS' SUMMARY

	Date of birth	App	T	G	D	Pts	Previous club	Debut
Anderson, Paul	25.10.71	1+1	0	0	0	0	Halifax B.S.	1997
Banks, Michael	5.7.80	0+1	0	0	0	0	Stanningley ARL	1998
Bradley, Graeme	20.3.64	24	11	0	0	44	St. George (Aust.)	1995-96
Calland, Matt	20.8.71	14+1	7	0	0	28	Featherstone R.	1995-96
Crouthers, Kevin	3.1.76	3+8	1	0	0	4	Dewsbury R.	1997
Deacon, Paul	13.2.79	12+1	4	4	0	24	Oldham B.	1998
Donougher, Jeremy	28.11.69	16+8	3	0	0	12	South Sydney (Aust.)	1995-96
Dwyer, Bernard	20.4.67	17	0	0	0	0	St. Helens	1995-96
Edwards, Shaun	17.10.66	10+2	5	0	0	20	London B.	1998
Ekoku, Abi	13.4.66	12+4	2	0	0	8	Halifax B.S.	1997
Fielden, Stuart	14.9.79	2+12	0	0	0	0	Illingworth ARL	1998
Forshaw, Mike	5.1.70	24+1	7	0	0	28	Saracens RU	1997
Graham, Nathan	23.11.71	10+11	1	0	1	5	Dewsbury	1995-96
Harmon, Neil	9.1.69	9+1	1	0	0	4	Huddersfield G.	1998
Hodgson, Andy	9.2.76	3+2	0	0	0	0	Wharfedale RU	1997
Howard, Harvey	29.8.68	4+2	1	0	0	4	Western Suburbs (Aust.)	1998
Jowitt, Warren	9.9.74	2+6	1	0	0	4	Hunslet H.	1995-96
Knox, Simon	14.10.72	2+3	0	0	0	0	Carlisle	1995-96
Lowes, James	11.10.69	20	9	4	0	44	Leeds	1996
McAvoy, Nathan	31.12.76	6+1	1	0	0	4	Salford R.	1998
McDermott, Brian	16.3.70	14+3	6	0	0	24	Eastmoor ARL	1993-94
McNamara, Steve	18.9.71	26	1	81	4	170	Hull	1996
Medley, Paul	21.9.66	2+10	1	0	0	4	Halifax	1989-90
Nickle, Sonny	4.5.69	5+6	0	0	0	0	St. Helens	1995-96
Paul, Robbie	3.2.76	23+2	10	0	0	40	Waitakere (NZ)	1994-95
Peacock, Danny	4.3.68	9	5	0	0	20	S. Queensland (Aust.)	1997
Pryce, Leon	9.10.81	1	0	0	0	0	Queensbury ARL	1998
Reihana, Tahi	15.3.72	9+12	0	0	0	0	Perth Reds (Aust.)	1997
Scales, Jonathan	28.7.74	14+4	4	0	0	16	Leeds	1995-96
Spruce, Stuart	3.1.71	23	8	0	0	32	Widnes	1996
Vaikona, Tevita	18.8.74	21	13	0	0	52	Hull S.	1998
TOTALS								
31 players			102	89	5	591		

Representative appearances 1998
Forshaw - Britain (0+1); Graham - Scotland (2); Harmon - Ireland (2); Howard - Britain (0+1); Paul - New Zealand (6, 3t)
Knox played for Scotland (1+1) while on loan to Salford Reds

BRAMLEY

Ground: Headingley (0113-224 2604)
First Season: 1896-97
Chairman: Jeff Wine
Honours: **BBC2 Floodlit Trophy** Winners,
              1973-74

RECORDS
Match
Goals: 11 by Bernard Ward v. Doncaster,
            1 Sep 1974
            Dean Creasser v. Chorley,
            17 Sep 1995
Tries: 7 by Joe Sedgewick v. Normanton,
            16 Apr 1906
Points: 28 by Bernard Ward v. Doncaster,
            1 Sep 1974

Season
Goals: 138 by Steve Carroll, 1991-92
Tries: 34 by Peter Lister, 1985-86
Points: 288 by Steve Carroll, 1991-92

Career
Goals: 926 by John Wilson, 1953-64
Tries: 140 by Peter Lister, 1982-91
Points: 1,903 by John Wilson, 1953-64
Appearances: 406+4 by John Wolford, 1962-76
Highest score: 74-0 v. Chorley, 17 Sep 1995
Highest against: 92-7 v. Australia, 9 Nov 1921
Attendance: 12,600 v. Leeds (League),
              7 May 1947 — at Barley Mow
              1,806 v. Widnes V. (Silk Cut Plate)
              2 March 1997 — at Headingley

COACHING REGISTER
● **Since 1974-75**

Arthur Keegan	May 73 - Sep 76
Peter Fox	Sep 76 - Apr 77
* Tommy Smales	May 77 - Dec 77
Les Pearce	Jan 78 - Oct 78
Don Robinson	Oct 78 - May 79
Dave Stockwell	June 79 - June 80
Keith Hepworth	June 80 - May 82
Maurice Bamford	May 82 - Oct 83
Peter Jarvis	Oct 83 - Apr 85
Ken Loxton	Apr 85 - Dec 85
Allan Agar	Dec 85 - Apr 87
Chris Forster	June 87 - Nov 87
Tony Fisher	Nov 87 - Feb 89
Barry Johnson	Mar 89 - Dec 90
John Kear	Dec 90 - Jan 91
Roy Dickinson	Jan 91 - Apr 92
Maurice Bamford	Apr 92 - Sep 93
Ray Ashton	Sep 93 - Dec 96
Paul Fletcher	Jan 97 - Nov 98
Mike Ford	Nov 98 -

* *Ex-forward*

1998 SIGNINGS REGISTER

Signed	Player	Club From
23.3.98	Brown, Gavin	Leeds R.
7.4.98	Cantillon, Phil	Leeds R.
1.5.98	Denham, Lee	Army
5.5.98	Eldershaw, Justin	York
—	Ford, Mike	Castleford T.
15.4.97	Gibbons, Anthony	Leeds R.
15.4.97	Gibbons, David	Leeds R.
23.3.98	Golden, Marvin	Leeds R.
16.3.98	Horner, Michael	Leeds R.
10.1.98	Kite, Neil	Leeds R.
16.7.98	*Lawford, Dean	Leeds R.
19.12.97	McDonald, Ryan	Leeds R.
—	McAllister, Danny	Gold Coast (Aust.)
9.4.98	*McDermott, Barrie	Leeds R.
23.4.98	Middleton, Simon	Castleford T.
15.6.98	*Newton, Terence	Leeds R.
12.4.98	Pickles, Stephen	Bradford B.
19.12.97	Potter, Daniel	Leeds R.
19.12.97	Poynter, Andrew	Leeds R.
28.5.98	Rivett, Leroy	Leeds R.
18.6.98	Smith, Kris	Leeds R.
6.6.97	Tiffany, Richard	Halifax B.S.
11.6.98	Webster, Mark	Wakefield T.

Roy Dickinson: Coach 1991-92.

BRAMLEY 1998 MATCH ANALYSIS

Date	Competition	H/A	Opponents	Rlt	Score	Tries	Goals	Attendance	Referee
1.2.98	CC(3)	H	Ellenborough R.	L	10-16	W. Freeman, D. Gibbons	Smith	1100	Johnson
10.4.98	SD	A	York	W	13-6	Brown, MacDonald	Smith (2), Gibbons (dg)	–	–
13.4.98	SD	H	Doncaster D.	W	18-14	Kite, Pickles, Stead	Brown (2), Smith	470	Oddy
22.4.98	SD	H	Oldham	W	12-10	Potter, Golden	Brown (2)	1089	Lee
29.4.98	SD	H	Lancashire L.	L	14-19	W. Freeman, Pickles, Potteer	Pitts	453	Gilmore
4.5.98	SD	A	Oldham	W	50-32	D. Gibbons (3), Middleton (2), Kite (2), Golden, Pickles	Smith (7)	–	–
9.5.98	SD	A	Workington T.	L	14-21	Potter, Render	Smith (3)	–	–
17.5.98	SD	H	Batley B.	W	24-14	Eldershaw (2), Poynter, Middleton	Smith (4)	450	McGregor
24.5.98	SD	A	Barrow B.R.	L	12-16	Potter, Poynter	Smith (2)	–	–
29.5.98	SD/WR	H	York	W	36-14	W. Freeman, McDermott, Kite, Pickles, Potter, Rivett	Smith (3), Brown (3)	771	McGregor
7.6.98	SD/WR	A	Doncaster D.	W	40-16	Middleton (2), Rivett (2), Eldershaw, Golden, Potter	Smith (4), Brown (2)	–	–
14.6.98	SD/WR	A	Batley B.	L	18-34	Potter (2), Denham	Brown (2) Smith	–	–
21.6.98	SD/WR	A	York	L	10-27	Potter	Brown (2), Smith	–	–
28.6.98	SD/WR	H	Batley B.	W	24-16	Eldershaw, A. Gibbons, Rivett, Smith, W. Freeman	Smith (2)	620	Atkin
5.7.98	SD/WR	H	Doncaster D.	W	57-12	A. Gibbons (2), Eldershaw, W. Freeman, Pickles, Potter, Poynter, Rivett, Tiffany	Smith (10), Gibbons (dg)	650	Silverwood
26.7.98	SD	H	York	L	20-21	Brown, W. Freeman, Lawford	Smith (4)	400	Lee
2.8.98	SD	A	Doncaster D.	D	24-24	D. Gibbons, Pickles, Potter, Poynter, Stead	Smith (2)	–	–
16.8.98	SD	A	Lancashire L.	W	23-22	Lawford, Poynter, Stead, Tiffany	Smith (2), Lawford (1, dg)	–	–
23.8.98	SD	H	Workington T.	W	30-16	Brown, W. Freeman, D. Gibbons, A. Gibbons Lawford	Lawford (3), Smith (2)	350	Dawber
30.8.98	SD	A	Batley B.	L	22-30	D. Gibbons (2), Poynter, Smith	Lawford (2, dg), Brown (dg)	–	–
5.9.98	SD	H	Barrow B.R.	W	26-22	A. Gibbons, Poynter, Lawford, W. Freeman	Lawford (3), Smith (2)	236	Lee

BRAMLEY 1998 PLAYERS' SUMMARY

	Date of birth	App	T	G	D	Pts	Previous club	Debut
Barnett, Steve	8.10.68	4+3	0	0	0	0	Huddersfield G.	1997
Blankley, Dean	28.10.68	0+1	0	0	0	0	Castleford	1990-91
Brown, Gavin	18.9.77	19	3	13	1	39	Leeds R.	1998
Cantillon, Phil	2.6.76	3	0	0	0	0	Leeds R.	1998
Currie, Eugene	25.2.65	5+3	0	0	0	0	Hunslet H.	1995-96
Denham, Lee	5.3.74	0+6	1	0	0	4	Army	1998
Eldershaw, Justin	9.12.75	15+2	5	0	0	20	York	1998
Freeman, Glen	9.4.72	14+6	0	0	0	0	Pudsey ARL	1992-93
Freeman, Wayne	30.4.74	16+3	8	0	0	32	Pudsey ARL	1992-93
Gibbons, Anthony	18.1.76	8+1	5	0	1	21	Leeds R.	1997
Gibbons, David	18.1.76	19	8	0	1	33	Leeds R.	1997
Gibson, Marc	16.11.75	5+3	0	0	0	0	Milford ARL	1997
Golden, Marvin	21.12.76	9	3	0	0	12	Leeds R.	1998
Horner, Michael	8.2.78	6+10	0	0	0	0	Leeds R.	1998
Julian, Alan	23.2.70	7	0	0	0	0	Keighley C.	1998
Kite, Neil	9.9.78	18+3	4	0	0	16	Leeds R.	1998
Lawford, Dean	9.5.77	6	4	9	2	36	Leeds R.	1998
McDermott, Barrie	22.7.72	4	1	0	0	4	Leeds R.	1998
McDonald, Ryan	24.2.78	19+1	1	0	0	4	Leeds R.	1998
Middleton, Simon	2.2.66	5+1	5	0	0	20	Castleford T.	1998
Newton, Terry	7.11.78	1+1	0	0	0	0	Leeds R.	1998
Pickles, Steve	2.11.73	7+9	6	0	0	24	Bradford B.	1998
Pitts, Dave	19.10.71	2+3	0	1	0	2	Stanningley ARL	1995-96
Potter, Dan	8.11.78	20	11	0	0	44	Leeds R.	1998
Poynter, Andy	24.10.78	21	7	0	0	28	Leeds R.	1998
Render, Nick	4.10.72	4+4	1	0	0	4	Bradley Arms ARL	1997
Rivett, Leroy	17.12.76	7	5	0	0	20	Leeds R.	1998
Smith, Kris	20.8.78	14+6	2	53	0	114	Leeds R.	1998
Stead, Richard	22.3.70	9+2	3	0	0	12	Normanton ARL	1992-93
Terry, Taniora	7.11.74	0+1	0	0	0	0	Milford ARL	1996
Tiffany, Richard	25.5.73	6+11	2	0	0	8	Halifax B.S.	1997
Webster, Mark	23.6.70	0+2	0	0	0	0	Wakefield T.	1998
TOTALS								
32 players			85	76	5	497		

CASTLEFORD TIGERS

Ground: Wheldon Road (01977-552674)
First Season: 1926-27. Added Tigers to title at the start of 1996 League season. There was also a Castleford team from 1896-97 to 1905-06 inclusive.
Chairman: Phil Hindle
Honours: **Championship** Beaten finalists, 1938-39, 1968-69
Challenge Cup Winners, 1934-35, 1968-69, 1969-70, 1985-86 Beaten finalists, 1991-92
Regal Trophy Winners, 1976-77, 1993-94
Premiership Beaten finalists, 1983-84, 1993-94
Yorkshire Cup Winners, 1977-78, 1981-82, 1986-87, 1990-91, 1991-92 Beaten finalists, 1948-49, 1950-51, 1968-69, 1971-72, 1983-84, 1985-86, 1987-88, 1988-89
Yorkshire League Winners, 1932-33, 1938-39, 1964-65
Eastern Division Championship Beaten finalists, 1963-64
Charity Shield Beaten finalists, 1986-87
BBC2 Floodlit Trophy Winners, 1965-66, 1966-67, 1967-68, 1976-77

RECORDS
Match
Goals: 17 by Geoff "Sammy" Lloyd v. Millom, 16 Sep 1973
Tries: 5 by Derek Foster v. Hunslet, 10 Nov 1972
John Joyner v. Millom, 16 Sep 1973
Steve Fenton v. Dewsbury, 27 Jan 1978
Ian French v. Hunslet, 9 Feb 1986
St. John Ellis at Whitehaven, 10 Dec 1989
Points: 43 by Geoff "Sammy" Lloyd v. Millom, 16 Sep 1973

Season
Goals: 158 by Geoff "Sammy" Lloyd, 1976-77
Tries: 40 by St. John Ellis, 1993-94
Points: 334 by Bob Beardmore, 1983-84
Career
Goals: 875 by Albert Lunn, 1951-63
Tries: 206 by Alan Hardisty, 1958-71
Points: 1,870 by Albert Lunn, 1951-63
Appearances: 585+28 by John Joyner, 1973-92
Highest score: 94-12 v. Huddersfield, 18 Sep 1988
Highest against: 62-12 at St. Helens, 16 Apr 1986
62-24 at St. Helens, 27 May 1996
Attendance: 25,449 v. Hunslet (RL Cup), 9 Mar 1935

COACHING REGISTER
● **Since 1974-75**

Dave Cox		Apr 74 - Nov 74
* Malcolm Reilly		Dec 74 - May 87
Dave Sampson		May 87 - Apr 88
Darryl Van de Velde		July 88 - May 93
John Joyner		May 93 - Apr 97
Stuart Raper		Apr 97 -

* *Shortly after his appointment Reilly returned to Australia to fulfil his contract before resuming at Castleford early the next season.*

GREAT BRITAIN REGISTER
(30 players)

Arthur Atkinson	(11)	1929-36
Kevin Beardmore	(13+1)	1984-90
Bill Bryant	(4+1)	1964-67
Lee Crooks	(5)	1992-94
Jim Croston	(1)	1937
Bernard Cunniffe	(1)	1937
Billy Davies	(1)	1933
Derek Edwards	(3+2)	1968-71
St. John Ellis	(+3)	1991-94
Keith England	(6+5)	1987-91
Mike Ford	(+2)	1993
Alan Hardisty	(12)	1964-70
Dennis Hartley	(9)	1968-70
Keith Hepworth	(11)	1967-70
Shaun Irwin	(+4)	1990
John Joyner	(14+2)	1978-84
Brian Lockwood	(7)	1972-74
Tony Marchant	(3)	1986
Roger Millward	(1)	1966
Steve Norton	(2+1)	1974
David Plange	(1)	1988
Malcolm Reilly	(9)	1970

(Contd)

CASTLEFORD TIGERS 1998 MATCH ANALYSIS

Date	Com-petition	H/A	Opponents	Rlt	Score	Tries	Goals	Atten-dance	Referee
14.2.98	CC(4)	A	Leeds R.	W	15-12	Mather, Schick	Davis (2), Maloney, Ford (dg)	–	–
28.2.98	CC(5)	H	Bradford B.	W	26-21	Davis, Tallec, Ellison, Flowers	Davis (5)	10,283	Cummings
14.3.98	CC(6)	H	Sheffield E.	L	22-32	Davis (2), Mather (2), Vowles	Maloney	7467	R. Connolly
5.4.98	SL	A	Wigan W.	L	4-18	Mather	–	–	–
10.4.98	SL	H	Sheffield E.	W	19-6	Critchley, Flowers, Orr	Davis (2, dg), Maloney	5248	Morris
17.4.98	SL	A	Leeds R.	L	10-20	M. Smith, Vowles	Davis	–	–
26.4.98	SL	A	Halifax B.S.	L	16-29	Gay, Sykes	Davis (4)	–	–
10.5.98	SL	H	Hull S.	W	31-18	Gay (2), Critchley, Ellison, Flowers, McKell	Davis (3), Ford (dg)	7722	Ganson
17.5.98	SL	A	Warrington W.	L	18-33	Ford (2), Mather	Maloney (3)	–	–
22.5.98	SL	H	Bradford B.	L	10-52	Maloney, Mather	Davis	8043	J. Connolly
31.5.98	SL	A	Salford R.	W	18-8	Ford, Mather, Wells	Benn (3)	–	–
7.6.98	SL	H	St. Helens	L	12-34	Flowers	Davis (2), Maloney, Benn	7192	R. Connolly
14.6.98	SL	H	Huddersfield G.	L	10-16	Orr	Davis (3)	5306	Ganson
21.6.98	SL	A	London B.	W	36-16	Davis, Ford, Gay, Sampson, M. Smith, Tonks, Vowles	Davis (4)	–	–
28.6.98	SL	H	Wigan W.	L	4-34	P. Smith	–	6734	Cummings
3.7.98	SL	A	Sheffield E.	L	16-22	Orr, Wells, Davis	Maloney, Davis	–	–
25.7.98	SL	N1	Warrington W.	W	23-16	Sampson, Ford, Critchley, M. Smith	Maloney (3), Davis (dg)	(4437)	Ganson
2.8.98	SL	H	Leeds R.	W	22-16	M. Smith, Orr, Wells, Flowers	Maloney (3)	8406	Cummings
9.8.98	SL	H	Halifax B.S.	L	16-36	Flowers, Gay, McKell	Orr (2)	6820	J. Connolly
16.8.98	SL	A	Hull S.	L	6-18	Orr	Orr	–	–
22.8.98	SL	H	Warrington W.	W	50-24	Wells (2), Ellison, Vowles, Davis, Schick, Sampson, Maloney, M. Smith	Orr (7)	4130	R. Connolly
31.8.98	SL	A	Bradford B.	L	8-24	Orr	Orr (2)	–	–
6.9.98	SL	H	Salford R.	W	30-12	Orr (2), Davis (2), M. Smith	Orr (3), Davis (2)	4865	R. Connolly
13.9.98	SL	A	St. Helens	D	32-32	Sampson (3), Maloney, Tallec, Vowles	Davis (2), Orr (2)	–	–
20.9.98	SL	A	Huddersfield G.	W	32-20	Maloney (2), Orr (2), Wells, Vowles	Davis (3), Orr	–	–
27.9.98	SL	H	London B.	W	23-18	Flowers (2), Harland, Veivers	Orr (3), Ford (fg)	5880	Kirkpatrick

N1 at Cardiff RU

GREAT BRITAIN REGISTER (Contd)

Dean Sampson	(0+1)	1997
Peter Small	(1)	1962
Tony Smith	(0+2)	1996
Graham Steadman	(9+1)	1990-94
Gary Stephens	(5)	1979
Doug Walton	(1)	1965
Johnny Ward	(3)	1963-64
Kevin Ward	(14)	1984-89

1998 SIGNINGS REGISTER

Signed	Player	Club From
—	Eagar, Michael	Warrington W.
—	Bell, Paul	Melbourne (Aust.)
3.5.98	Ellis, Dean	St. John Fisher ARL
26.1.98	Ellison, Daniel	Wigan W.
—	Fritz, Dale	N. Queensland (Aust.)
24.4.98	Hall, Martin	Wigan W.
—	Hill, Andy	York
—	Pickering, James	Sydney City (Aust.)
—	Raper, Aaron	Parramatta (Aust.)
—	Rogers, Darren	Salford R.
26.1.98	Tallec, Gael	Wigan W.
1.5.98	Waite, Daniel	Smawthorpe P. ARL
24.8.98	Wells, Paul	Oulton R. ARL
2.4.98	Williams, Martin	Smawthorpe P. ARL

45

CASTLEFORD TIGERS 1998 PLAYERS' SUMMARY

	Date of birth	App	T	G	D	Pts	Previous club	Debut
Benn, Jamie	4.5.77	0+3	0	4	0	8		1998
Chapman, David	19.2.73	4+3	0	0	0	0	Hunter M. (Aust.)	1996
Critchley, Jason	7.12.70	20+3	3	0	0	12	Keighley C.	1997
Davis, Brad	13.3.68	24	8	35	2	104	Wakefield T.	1997
Dobson, Gareth	31.12.78	0+2	0	0	0	0	Sharlston R. ARL	1998
Ellison, Danny	16.12.72	5+6	3	0	0	12	Wigan W.	1998
Flowers, Jason	30.1.75	19+4	8	0	0	32	Redhill ARL	1993-94
Ford, Mike	18.11.65	14+11	5	0	3	23	Wakefield T.	1997
Gay, Richard	9.3.69	21	5	0	0	20	Hull	1996
Hall, Martin	5.12.68	4	0	0	0	0	Wigan W.	1998
Harland, Lee	4.9.73	20+5	1	0	0	4	Halifax	1994-95
Maloney, Francis	26.5.73	19+7	5	14	0	48	Oldham B.	1998
Mather, Barrie-Jon	15.1.73	18	7	0	0	28	Perth Reds (Aust.)	1998
McKell, Richard	20.12.70	18+6	2	0	0	8	Wakefield T.	1997
Orr, Danny	17.5.78	17+5	10	21	0	82	Kippax ARL	1997
Russell, Richard	24.11.67	10+1	0	0	0	0	Oldham	1993-94
Sampson, Dean	27.6.67	22	6	0	0	24	Stanley R. ARL	1987-88
Schick, Andrew	27.5.70	17+5	2	0	0	8	Redcliffe (Aust.)	1995-96
Smith, Michael	10.5.76	14+9	6	0	0	24	Canterbury B. (Aust.)	1998
Smith, Paul	4.3.79	1+10	1	0	0	4	Dewsbury Moor ARL	1997
Sykes, Nathan	8.9.74	15+10	1	0	0	4	Moldgreen ARL	1991-92
Tallec, Gael	15.8.76	8+8	2	0	0	8	Wigan W.	1998
Tonks, Ian	13.2.76	2+4	1	0	0	4	Redhill ARL	1994-95
Vowles, Adrian	30.5.71	26	7	0	0	28	N. Queensland (Aust.)	1997
Wells, Jon	23.9.78	20+1	6	0	0	24	Sharlston R. ARL	1996
TOTALS								
25 players			89	74	5	509		

Representative appearances 1998

Critchley - Wales (1); Flowers - Scotland (1+1, 1t); Orr - Emerging England (0+1); Tallec - France (1)

DEWSBURY RAMS

Attendance: 26,584 v. Halifax (Yorks Cup),
30 Oct 1920 — at Old Crown Flatt
3,995 v. Batley (League), 26 Dec 1994
— at New Crown Flatt/Rams Stadium

Ground:	Rams Stadium (01924-465489)
First Season:	1901–02. Added Rams to title for the start of 1997 season.
Chairman:	Bob McDermott
Honours:	**Championship** Winners, 1972-73

Beaten finalists, 1946-47
War Emergency League Winners, 1941-42 (1942-43 won final but championship declared null and void because Dewsbury played an ineligible player.)
Beaten finalists, 1943-44
Division Two Champions, 1904-05
Challenge Cup Winners, 1911-12, 1942-43
Beaten finalists, 1928-29
Yorkshire Cup Winners, 1925-26, 1927-28, 1942-43
Beaten finalists, 1918-19, 1921-22, 1940-41, 1972-73
Yorkshire League Winners, 1946-47
BBC2 Floodlit Trophy Beaten finalists, 1975-76

RECORDS

Match

Goals:	13 by Greg Pearce at Blackpool G., 4 Apr 1993
Tries:	8 by Dai Thomas v. Liverpool C., 13 Apr 1907
Points:	32 by Les Holliday v. Barrow, 11 Sep 1994

Season

Goals:	145 by Nigel Stephenson, 1972-73
Tries:	40 by Dai Thomas, 1906-07
Points:	368 by Nigel Stephenson, 1972-73

Career

Goals:	863 by Nigel Stephenson, 1968-78 & 1984-86
Tries:	144 by Joe Lyman, 1913-31
Points:	2,082 by Nigel Stephenson, 1968-78 & 1984-86

Appearances: 454 by Joe Lyman, 1913-31
Highest score: 90-5 at Blackpool G., 4 Apr 1993
Highest against: 82-0 at Widnes, 30 Nov 1986

COACHING REGISTER

● **Since 1974-75**

Maurice Bamford	June 74 - Oct 74
Alan Hardisty	Oct 74 - June 75
Dave Cox	June 75 - July 77
Ron Hill	July 77 - Dec 77
Lewis Jones	Dec 77 - Apr 78
Jeff Grayshon	May 78 - Oct 78
Alan Lockwood	Oct 78 - Oct 80
Bernard Watson	Oct 80 - Oct 82
Ray Abbey	Nov 82 - Apr 83
* Tommy Smales	May 83 - Feb 84
Jack Addy	Feb 84 - Jan 87
Dave Busfield	Jan 87 - Apr 87
Terry Crook	Apr 87 - Dec 88
Maurice Bamford	Dec 88 - Dec 90
Jack Addy	Dec 90 - Aug 93
Norman Smith	Aug 93 - Apr 95
Tony Fisher	Apr 95 - Feb 96
Neil Kelly	Feb 96 -

* *Ex-forward*

GREAT BRITAIN REGISTER

(6 players)

Alan Bates	(2+2)	1974
Frank Gallagher	(4)	1920-21
Jim Ledgard	(2)	1947
Roy Pollard	(1)	1950
Mick Stephenson	(5+1)	1971-72
Harry Street	(4)	1950

Harry Street: Four Test matches.

DEWSBURY RAMS 1998 PLAYERS' SUMMARY

	Date of birth	App	T	G	D	Pts	Previous club	Debut
Agar, Richard	20.1.72	23+5	3	10	2	34	Rochdale H.	1998
Arrowsmith, Richard	1.12.78	16	7	0	0	28	Dewsbury M. ARL	1998
Bailey, Dennis	15.2.66	21+1	8	0	0	32	Queenswood ARL	1985-86
Ball, Damian	14.7.75	26+7	9	0	0	36	York	1998
Boothroyd, Alan	19.6.66	31+1	3	0	0	12	Bradford B.	1998
Bramald, Matthew	6.2.73	27+7	24	2	3	103	Westgate Redoubt	1995-96
Brent, Andrew	1.5.76	4+4	0	0	0	0	Wigan	1996
Collins, Wayne	24.6.67	8	0	0	0	0	Leeds R.	1998
Delaney, Paul	18.10.68	23+2	5	0	0	20	Leeds	1991-92
Eaton, Barry	30.9.73	34	7	132	0	292	Wakefield T.	1995-96
Evans, Paul	21.1.72	18+4	7	0	0	28	Paris S.G.	1998
Firth, Jason	16.6.77	4+10	0	0	0	0	Thornhill ARL	1995-96
Flynn, Adrian	9.9.74	31	9	0	0	36	Leeds R.	1997
Haigh, Mark	24.1.70	12+3	2	0	0	8	Hanging Heaton	1990-91
Halloran, Ryan	24.7.79	0+1	0	0	0	0	Thornhill ARL	1997
Jowitt, Robin	10.6.77	1+7	0	0	0	0	Stanley R. ARL	1996
Kelly, Neil	10.5.62	1+2	0	0	1	1	Wakefield T	1988-89
Kershaw, Billy	22.11.78	1+3	0	0	0	0	Oulton R. ARL	1997
Long, Matt	24.5.74	7+24	6	0	0	24	Hull S.	1998
McKelvie, Danny	10.10.69	1+21	2	0	0	8	Ryedale-York	1994-95
Milner, Lee	26.2.77	1+11	0	0	0	0	Huddersfield G.	1998
Moore, Craig	24.10.74	2+1	0	0	0	0	Bradford B.	1995-96
O'Donnell, David	6.4.68	17+2	2	0	0	8	Paris S.G.	1998
Patterson, Brett	13.12.69	8+3	3	0	0	12	Dubbo Westside (Aust.)	1997
Roche, Simon	31.12.71	3	0	0	0	0	BRK ARL	1997
Rose, Gary	25.7.65	34	2	0	0	8	Hull	1996
Spink, Andrew	12.1.79	23+7	2	0	0	8	Thornhill ARL	1997
Wilcock, Gilbert		0+1	0	0	0	0		1998
Williams, Brendan	15.1.75	30+3	13	0	0	52	Australia	1997
Williams, Shayne	20.10.71	28+3	11	0	0	44	Dewsbury C. ARL	1992-93
Williamson, Leon	22.8.74	19+1	7	0	0	28	Hunslet	1996
Wood, Danny	8.10.77	14+6	3	0	0	12	Hunslet Boys ARL	1995-96
TOTALS								
32 players			135	144	6	834		

1998 SIGNINGS REGISTER

Signed	Player	Club From
20.3.98	Agar, Richard	Rochdale H.
26.1.98	Ball, Damian	York
31.3.98	Beard, Stephen	Dewsbury M. ARL
23.1.98	Boothroyd, Alan	Bradford B.
19.3.98	Copley, Robert	Thornhill ARL
14.1.98	Evans, Paul	Paris S.G. (Fr.)
11.8.97	Flynn, Adrian	Leeds R.
—	Graham, Nathan	Bradford B.
—	Hicks, Simon	Wakefield T.
2.9.98	*Long, Matthew	Hull S.
6.2.98	Maskill, Steve	Bradford B.
—	*Medley, Paul	Bradford B.
12.5.98	Milner, Lee	Huddersfield G.
31.3.98	Morley, Daniel	Dewsbury Academy
5.5.98	O'Donnell, David	Paris S.G. (Fr.)
16.6.98	Patterson, Brett	Dubbo Westside (Aust.)
25.2.98	Roberts, Matthew	Thornhill ARL
21.1.98	*Simpson, Joseph	Bradford B.
24.9.98	Spivey, Joe	Dewsbury M. ARL
24.2.98	Thickbroom, Steven	Lock Lane ARL

DEWSBURY RAMS 1998 MATCH ANALYSIS

Date	Com- petition	H/A	Opponents	Rlt	Score	Tries	Goals	Atten- dance	Referee
1.2.98	CC(3)	H	Thornhill	W	40-2	S. Williams (2), Ball, Bramald, Eaton, Long, McKelvie	Eaton (6)	2355	Laughton
15.2.98	CC(4)	A	Lancashire L.	D	28-28	Boothroyd, Bramald, Flynn, Haigh	Eaton (6)	–	–
18.2.98 Replay	CC(4)	H	Lancashire L.	W	31-14	S. Williams, Bramald, Long, Flynn	Eaton (7), Kelly (dg)	900	Taberner
22.2.98	FD	H	Swinton L.	W	34-24	B. Williams (2), Bailey, Ball, Flynn, S. Williams	Eaton (5)	912	R. Connolly
1.3.98	CC(5)	H	Wigan W.	L	0-56	–	–	3100	Ganson
4.3.98	FD	A	Featherstone R.	L	20-36	Ball (2), Bailey	Eaton (4)	–	–
8.3.98	FD	H	Keighley C.	W	50-12	Bramald (3), Eaton (2), Bailey, Boothroyd, Haigh, Williamson	Eaton (7)	1416	R. Smith
15.3.98	FD	A	Rochdale H.	W	12-8	Flynn, Williamson	Eaton (2)	–	–
22.3.98	FD	H	Leigh C.	W	50-0	Bramald (3), B. Williams (2), Bailey, Flynn, S. Williams	Eaton (9)	1011	Bates
29.3.98	FD	A	Whitehaven W.	L	22-32	Eaton (2), Agar	Eaton (5)	–	–
5.4.98	FD	A	Widnes W.	W	15-12	Bramald, Delaney	Eaton (3), Agar (dg)	–	–
10.4.98	FD	H	Hunslet H.	D	14-14	Boothroyd, Williamson	Eaton (3)	1057	Taberner
13.4.98	FD	A	Hull K.R.	W	17-4	Bailey, Bramald, Williamson	Eaton (2), Agar (dg)	–	–
19.4.98	FD	A	Wakefield T.	D	26-26	Bramald, Delaney, Wood, B. Williams, Williamson,	Eaton (2)	–	–
10.5.98	FD	H	Featherstone R.	L	13-25	Evans, Flynn	Eaton (2), Bramald (dg)	1002	Gilmour
13.5.98	FD	H	Swinton L.	L	10-13	Bramald, McKelvie	Eaton	824	Oddy/Addy
17.5.98	FD	A	Keighley C.	L	20-22	Flynn, B. Williams, S. Williams	Eaton (4)	–	–
24.5.98	FD	H	Rochdale H.	W	40-4	Delaney, Eaton, O'Donnell, Long, Spink, Williamson	Eaton (8)	813	Nicholson
31.5.98	FD	A	Leigh C.	W	54-18	Bramald (4), Long (2), Flynn, Delaney, B. Williams	Eaton (9)	–	–
3.6.95	FD	H	Whitehaven W.	W	26-12	Evans (2), Arrowsmith, O'Donnell, S. Williams	Eaton (3)	809	Taberner
7.6.98	FD	H	Widnes V.	W	18-16	Evans (2), S. Williams	Eaton (3)	1117	Oddy
14.6.98	FD	A	Hunslet H.	W	24-2	Agar, Arrowsmith, Wood, B. Williams	Eaton (4)	–	–
21.6.98	FD	H	Hull K.R.	W	27-14	Arrowsmith, Flynn, Rose, S. Williams	Agar (5), Bramald (dg)	1547	Gilmour
24.6.98	FD	H	Wakefield T.	L	18-25	Delaney, Wood, Arrowsmith	Agar (3)	2436	McGregor
28.6.98	FD	A	Swinton L.	L	16-31	B. Williams, Arrowsmith, Bramald	Agar (2)	–	–
5.7.98	FD	A	Widnes V.	W	24-12	Bramald, Eaton, Patterson, Rose, S. Williams	Eaton (2)	–	–
10.7.98	FD	H	Featherstone R.	W	25-14	Bailey, Ball, Bramald	Eaton (6), Bramald (dg)	1102	J. Connolly
15.7.98	FD	A	Hull K.R.	L	12-18	Arrowsmith, Bailey	Eaton (2)	–	–
19.7.98	FD	H	Hunslet H.	W	24-21	B. Williams (2), Arrowsmith, Bramald	Eaton (4)	1073	Taberner
26.7.98	FD	A	Keighley C.	L	10-26	Ball, Williamson	Eaton	–	–
2.8.98	FD	H	Leigh C.	W	26-18	B. Williams (2), Agar, Ball	Eaton (5)	826	Bates
9.8.98	FD	A	Rochdale H.	W	40-12	Bramald (2), Bailey, Ball, S. Williams, Patterson	Eaton (8)	–	–
16.8.98	FD	H	Whitehaven W.	W	20-8	Ball, Evans, Patterson	Eaton (4)	1119	Shaw
30.8.98	FD	A	Wakefield T.	W	16-12	Evans, Long, Spink	Bramald (2)	–	–
6.9.98	PO	A	Hull K.R.	L	2-18	–	Eaton	–	–
13.9.98	PO	H	Featherstone R.	L	10-20	Bramald	Eaton (3)	2020	McGregor

DONCASTER DRAGONS

Ground: Belle Vue (01302-539441)
First Season: 1951-52. Added Dragons to title after re-forming for 1995-96 season.
Chairman: Peter Smith

RECORDS

Match

Goals: 12 by Tony Zelei v. Nottingham C., 1 Sep 1991
Robert Turner v. Highfield, 20 Mar 1994
Tries: 5 by Carl Hall v. Mysons, 31 Oct 1993
Points: 32 by Tony Zelei v. Nottingham C., 1 Sep 1991

Season

Goals: 123 by Robert Turner, 1993-94
Tries: 21 by Mark Roache, 1989-90
Points: 272 by Robert Turner, 1993-94

Career

Goals: 850 by David Noble, 1976-77, 1980-89 & 1992
Tries: 112 by Mark Roache, 1985-97
Points: 1,751 by David Noble, 1976-77, 1980-89 & 1992
Appearances: 306 + 21 by Audley Pennant, 1980-83 & 1985-97
308 + 8 by David Noble, 1976-77, 1980-89 & 1992
Highest score: 96-0 v. Highfield, 20 Mar 1994
Highest against: 75-3 v. Leigh, 28 Mar 1976
Attendance: 10,000 v. Bradford N. (RL Cup), 16 Feb 1952 — at York Road Stadium; 1,683 v. Hull K.R. (League), 20 Aug 1995-

COACHING REGISTER

● **Since 1974-75**

Ted Strawbridge	Feb 73 - Apr 75
Derek Edwards	July 75 - Nov 76
Don Robson	Nov 76 - Sep 77
Trevor Lowe	Sep 77 - Apr 79
* Tommy Smales	Feb 78 - Apr 79
Billy Yates	Apr 79 - May 79
Don Vines	Sep 79 - Jan 80
Bill Kenny	June 80 - May 81
Alan Rhodes	Aug 81 - Mar 83
Clive Sullivan	Mar 83 - May 84
John Sheridan	June 84 - Nov 87
Graham Heptinstall	Nov 87 - Jan 88
John Sheridan	Jan 88 - Apr 89
Dave Sampson	May 89 - Jan 92
Geoff Morris	Jan 92 - Nov 92
Tony Fisher	Nov 92 - Dec 94
Ian Brooke	Dec 94 - Apr 95
Peter Astbury } Andy Gascoigne }	July 95 - Sep 95
Peter Regan	Sep 95 - Oct 96
Tony Fisher	Dec 96 - May 97
Colin Maskill	May 97 -

* *Ex-forward, who shared the coaching post with Trevor Lowe for just over a year.*

1998 SIGNINGS REGISTER

Signed	Player	Club From
18.6.98	Conway, Mark	Dewsbury R.
13.3.98	Creasser, Dean	Bramley
14.1.98	Day, Michael	Moorends ARL
24.4.98	Edwards, John	Keighley C.
30.4.98	Fleming, Andrew	Oldham
23.4.98	*Goulbourne, Alfred	Hull K.R.
10.4.98	Green, Alex	Keighley C.
14.4.98	Higgins, Darren	Toll Bar ARL
14.4.98	*Kear, Mark	Castleford T.
31.3.98	Kini, Troy	Mt Wellington (NZ)
22.5.98	*Limb, Scott	York
24.7.98	*Maher, Lee	Featherstone R.
20.1.98	*Miller, Tony	Featherstone R.
25.2.98	Okul, John	Hull K.R.
14.1.98	Oldfield, David	Castleford T.
24.3.98	Saul, Carl	Dewsbury R.
26.1.98	Sims, Jason	Featherstone R.
28.5.97	Wilson, Warren	Featherstone R.

DONCASTER DRAGONS 1998 MATCH ANALYSIS

Date	Com-petition	H/A	Opponents	Rlt	Score	Tries	Goals	Atten-dance	Referee
1.2.98	CC(3)	H1	Featherstone Lions	L	18-23	Rothwell, Kear, Alex Goulbourne	L. Senior (3)	1012	McGregor
13.4.98	SD	A	Bramley	L	14-18	Creasser, Rowse	Creasser (3)	–	–
19.4.98	SD	A	Lancashire L.	L	6-40	Birdsall	Creasser	–	–
26.4.98	SD	H	Oldham	L	8-28	–	Creasser (4)	1020	Atkins
6.5.98	SD	H	Batley B.	W	33-20	Alex Goulbourne (2), Maskill, Miller, Rowse	Creasser (2), Fleming, L. Senior (1, dg). Edwards (4dg)	530	Lowe
10.5.98	SD	A	Barrow B.R.	L	8-42	I. Watson (2)	–	–	–
17.5.98	SD	H	York	L	8-29	Alex Goulbourne, Morgan	–	585	Cornish
24.5.98	SD	H	Workington T.	D	18-18	Limb, Morgan, Pell	Creasser (2) Edwards (2dg)	468	Atkin
31.5.98	SD/WR	A	Batley B.	L	20-33	Hepworth, Miller, Morgan, Penney	Green (2)	–	–
7.6.98	SD/WR	H	Bramley	L	16-40	Alfie Goulbourne, Creasser, Penney	Edwards (2)	442	Bates
14.6.98	SD/WR	A	York	L	12-44	Kear, Morgan	Edwards (2)	–	–
21.6.98	SD/WR	H	Batley B.	L	22-28	Miller (2), Okul (2)	Edwards (3)	432	Cornish
28.6.98	SD/WR	H	York	L	20-26	Alfie Goulbourne, Morgan, I. Watson	Edwards (4)	397	Shaw
5.7.98	SD/WR	A	Bramley	L	12-57	Morgan, Wilson	Edwards, Maskill	–	–
26.7.98	SD	A	Batley B.	W	24-10	Conway, Alfie Goulbourne, Green, Okul, I. Watson	Maskill (2)	–	–
2.8.98	SD	H	Bramley	D	24-24	Green, Morgan, Okul, Rowse	Maskill (4)	397	Laughton
9.8.98	SD	H	Lancashire L.	L	2-48	–	Maskill	440	Gilmour
16.8.98	SD	A	Oldham	L	16-26	Miller, Rowse, C. Watson	Edwards (2)	–	–
23.8.98	SD	H	Barrow B.R.	L	8-22	Alex Goulbourne	Edwards (2)	345	I. Smith
30.8.98	SD	A	York	L	6-46	Alfie Goulbourne	Edwards	–	–
6.9.98	SD	A	Workington T.	L	12-20	Alex Goulbourne, Alfie Goulbourne	Conway (2)	–	–

H1 at Wakefield T.

Colin Maskill: Former Wakefield, Leeds, Featherstone and Castleford hooker, still going strong as Doncaster's player-coach in 1998.

DONCASTER DRAGONS 1998 PLAYERS' SUMMARY

	Date of birth	App	T	G	D	Pts	Previous club	Debut
Bell, Glenn	26.3.65	6	0	0	0	0	Dewsbury R.	1998
Birdsall, David		1+4	1	0	0	4		1998
Brannan, Shaun	2.12.74	1	0	0	0	0	Hunslet H.	1997
Busby, Lance	1.2.73	6+4	0	0	0	0	Ship Inn	1995-96
Conway, Mark	31.1.64	6+4	1	2	0	8	Dewsbury R.	1998
Creasser, Dean	31.12.68	9+1	2	12	0	32	Bramley	1998
Day, Michael	21.2.78	0+1	0	0	0	0	Moorends ARL	1998
Dickinson, Alan	30.6.71	2+1	0	0	0	0	Lock Lane ARL	1997
Edwards, John	7.8.67	12+5	0	17	6	40	Keighley C.	1998
Fleming, Andy	16.8.67	2	0	1	0	2	Oldham	1998
Goulbourne, Alex	20.7.74	13+1	6	0	0	24	Featherstone R.	1995-96
Goulbourne, Alfie	23.6.75	15	5	0	0	20	Hull K.R.	1998
Green, Alex	9.2.71	12+8	2	2	0	12	York	1998
Hepworth, Scott		1+1	1	0	0	4	Lock Lane ARL	1998
Kear, Mark	31.3.78	17+1	2	0	0	8	Castleford T.	1998
Kini, Troy	15.10.66	1+2	0	0	0	0	Mt. Wellington (NZ)	1998
Limb, Scott	15.6.73	5	1	0	0	4	York	1998
Maher, Lee	29.10.75	2	0	0	0	0	Featherstone R.	1998
Maskill, Colin	15.3.64	11+2	1	8	0	20	Featherstone R.	1994-95
Miller, Tony	30.3.68	21	5	0	0	20	Featherstone R.	1998
Moore, Jon	8.7.74	0+1	0	0	0	0	Batley B.	1998
Morgan, Gavin	1.6.76	13+3	7	0	0	28	Sheffield E.	1995-96
Okul, John	24.11.72	11	4	0	0	16	Hull K.R.	1998
Pell, Richard	17.10.66	6+13	1	0	0	4	Hunslet H.	1990-91
Penney, Steve		5	2	0	0	8	Lock Lane ARL	1998
Pratt, Gareth	23.8.69	16+5	0	0	0	0	Dewsbury	1997
Rothwell, Andy	5.9.67	2	1	0	0	4	Featherstone R.	1992-93
Rowse, Martin	8.3.69	19	3	0	0	12	Hunslet H.	1997
Saul, Carl	13.6.69	2+3	0	0	0	0	Dewsbury R.	1998
Senior, Calum		0+4	0	0	0	0		1998
Senior, Lee	27.8.74	12+2	0	4	1	9	Featherstone R.	1997
Sims, Jason	15.7.70	8	0	0	0	0	Featherstone R.	1998
Trigg, Lee	24.11.68	0+1	0	0	0	0	Featherstone ARL	1996
Watson, Chris	9.9.67	15+2	2	0	0	8	Hunslet H.	1997
Watson, Ian	2.6.67	12+2	4	0	0	16	Lock Lane ARL	1997
Wilson, Warren	3.5.63	4	1	0	0	4	Featherstone R.	1997
Wolford, David	29.11.74	5+9	0	0	0	0	Lock Lane ARL	1997
TOTALS								
37 players			52	46	7	307		

FEATHERSTONE ROVERS

Points: 2,654 by Steve Quinn, 1976-88
Appearances: 440 by Jim Denton, 1921-34
Highest score: 86-18 v. Keighley, 17 Sep 1989
Highest against: 70-2 at Halifax, 14 Apr 1941
Attendance: 17,531 v. St. Helens (RL Cup),
21 Mar 1959

Ground: Post Office Road became Lionheart Stadium at end of 1998 season (01977-602723)
First Season: 1921-22
Chairman: Richard Evans
Honours: **Championship** Beaten finalists, 1927-28
Division One Champions, 1976-77
Division Two Champions, 1979-80, 1992-93
First Division Grand Final Beaten finalists, 1998
Challenge Cup Winners, 1966-67, 1972-73, 1982-83
Beaten finalists, 1951-52, 1973-74
Second Division/Divisional Premiership Winners, 1992-93
Beaten finalists, 1987-88
Yorkshire Cup Winners, 1939-40, 1959-60
Beaten finalists, 1928-29, 1963-64, 1966-67, 1969-70, 1970-71, 1976-77, 1977-78, 1989-90
Captain Morgan Trophy Beaten finalists, 1973-74

RECORDS

Match
Goals: 13 by Mark Knapper v. Keighley, 17 Sep 1989
Tries: 6 by Mike Smith v. Doncaster, 13 Apr 1968
Chris Bibb v. Keighley, 17 Sep 1989
Points: 40 by Martin Pearson v. Whitehaven, 26 Nov 1995

Season
Goals: 163 by Steve Quinn, 1979-80
Tries: 48 by Paul Newlove, 1992-93
Points: 391 by Martin Pearson, 1992-93

Career
Goals: 1,210 by Steve Quinn, 1976-88
Tries: 162 by Don Fox, 1953-65

COACHING REGISTER
● **Since 1974-75**

* Tommy Smales	July 74 - Sep 74
Keith Goulding	Sep 74 - Jan 76
† Tommy Smales	Feb 76 - May 76
Keith Cotton	June 76 - Dec 77
Keith Goulding	Dec 77 - May 78
Terry Clawson	July 78 - Nov 78
† Tommy Smales	Nov 78 - Apr 79
Paul Daley	May 79 - Jan 81
Vince Farrar	Feb 81 - Nov 82
Allan Agar	Dec 82 - Oct 85
George Pieniazek	Nov 85 - Nov 86
Paul Daley	Nov 86 - Apr 87
Peter Fox	May 87 - Oct 91
Allan Agar	Oct 91 - Aug 92
Steve Martin	Sep 92 - Oct 94
David Ward	Oct 94 - Apr 97
Steve Simms	Apr 97 - Oct 98
Kevin Hobbs	Oct 98 -

* *Ex-forward*
† *Ex-scrum half*

GREAT BRITAIN REGISTER
(16 players)

Tommy Askin	(6)	1928
Chris Bibb	(1)	1990
John "Keith" Bridges	(3)	1974
Terry Clawson	(2)	1962
Malcolm Dixon	(2)	1962-64
Steve Evans	(5+3)	1979-80
Deryck Fox	(9+4)	1985-92
Don Fox	(1)	1963
David Hobbs	(7+1)	1984
Gary Jordan	(2)	1964-67
Steve Molloy	(1+2)	1994-96
Arnold Morgan	(4)	1968
Steve Nash	(16)	1971-74
Paul Newlove	(7+3)	1989-93
Peter Smith	(1+5)	1977-84
Jimmy Thompson	(19+1)	1970-77

53

1998 SIGNINGS REGISTER

Signed	Player	Club From
26.2.98	*Allen, Christopher	Castleford T.
8.1.98	Amone, Asa	Halifax B.S.
2.4.98	Child, Lee	Hunslet H.
5.5.98	Clarkson, Michael	Wakefield T.
19.1.98	Collins, Steve	Parramatta (Aust.)
8.5.98	Coventry, James	Huddersfield G.
19.2.98	Hall, Carl	Moseley RU
30.3.98	Highton, Paul	Halifax B.S.
21.1.98	*Horne, Craig	Bradford B.
—	Horsley, Ryan	Wakefield T.
—	Isherwood, Matthew	Leeds R.
19.2.98	*Jackson, Anthony	Hull S.
—	Law, Martin	Wakefield T.
1.5.98	*Norton, Richard	Castleford P. ARL
17.7.98	*Peacock, James	Bradford B.
1.6.98	Smallman, Sam	Featherstone Jnrs ARL
27.3.98	Spurr, Christopher	Featherstone Jnrs ARL
25.2.98	Turner, Matthew	—
—	Tuuta, Brendon	Warrington W.
21.1.98	*Walker, Matthew	Bradford B.

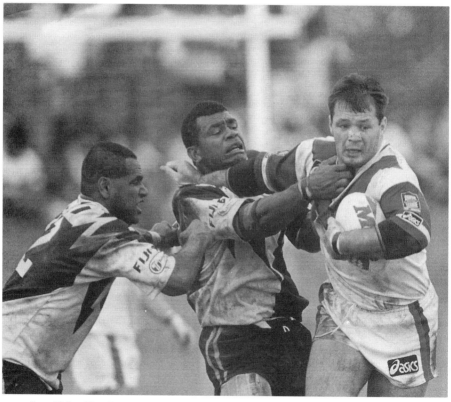

Steve Molloy: Three Test appearances for Great Britain as a Featherstone Rovers player before moving to Sheffield Eagles in 1998.

FEATHERSTONE ROVERS 1998 MATCH ANALYSIS

Date	Competition	H/A	Opponents	Rlt	Score	Tries	Goals	Attendance	Referee
1.2.98	CC(3)	H	Woolston R.	W	56-0	Baker (3), Handley (2), Pratt (2), Irwin, Jackson, Newlove, Slater	Fallins (6)	1126	Burke
8.2.98	FD	A	Whitehaven W.	L	14-32	Chapman, Padgett	Fallins (3)	–	–
15.2.98	CC(4)	H	St. Helens	L	24-56	Pratt (2), Fallins, Newlove	Fallins (4)	2759	R. Smith
22.2.98	FD	H	Hull K.R.	L	7-20	Evans	Fallins, Pratt (dg)	2221	Bates
4.3.98	FD	H	Dewsbury R.	W	36-20	Swinson (2), Baker, Handley, Irwin, Price	Fallins (6)	1587	J. Connolly
8.3.98	FD	A	Rochdale H.	W	34-24	Collins (2), Baker, Handley, Horne, Swinon	Fallins (5)	–	–
15.3.98	FD	H	Widnes V.	W	31-26	Hall, Horne, Irwin, Slater, Swinson, Walker	Chapman (2), Fallins (1, dg)	2035	Kirkpatrick
22.3.98	FD	A	Hunslet H.	L	12-34	Chapman, Horne	Fallins (2)	–	–
5.4.98	FD	H	Leigh C.	W	48-12	Child (2), Evans (2), Irwin, Chapman, Highton, Kimmell, A. Jackson	Chapman (6)	1746	Morris
10.4.98	FD	A	Wakefield T.	L	8-26	Collins	Chapman (2)	–	–
13.4.98	FD	H	Keighley C.	W	44-2	Collins (4), Hall, Handley, Irwin	Chapman (8)	1976	Laughton
19.4.98	FD	A	Swinton L.	L	30-31	Chapman, Child, Collins, Highton, Irwin	Chapman (5)	–	–
26.4.98	FD	H	Whitehaven W.	L	14-26	Collins	Fallins (4), Chapman	1530	Taberner
5.5.98	FD	A	Hull K.R.	L	6-18	Clarkson	Fallins	–	–
10.5.98	FD	A	Dewsbury R.	W	25-13	Collins (2), Clarkson, Price	Dickens (2), Fallins (2, dg)	–	–
17.5.98	FD	H	Rochdale H.	L	18-46	Fallins, Hall, Horne	Fallins (3)	1486	Bates
24.5.98	FD	A	Widnes V.	D	32-32	Kimmell (2), Chapman, Hall, Collins, Fallins	Fallins (4)	–	–
31.5.98	FD	H	Hunslet H.	W	18-10	Coventry, Fallins	Fallins (4, 2dg)	1726	Gilmour
7.6.98	FD	A	Leigh C.	W	48-16	Chapman (2), Dickens (2), Kimmell (2), Fallins, Pratt	Fallins (8)	–	–
14.6.98	FD	H	Wakefield T.	W	21-0	Chapman, Irwin, Maher, Pratt	Fallins (2, dg)	2440	Oddy
19.6.98	FD	A	Keighley C.	W	18-?	Baker, Coventry	Fallins	–	–
24.6.98	FD	H	Swinton L.	W	29-23	Dickens, Price, Hall, Coventry	Fallins (6, dg)	1342	Atkin
28.6.98	FD	A	Rochdale H.	W	50-27	Pratt (3), Collins (2), Evans, Hall, Irwin, Kimmell	Fallins (7)	–	–
5.7.98	FD	H	Whitehaven W.	W	37-0	Pratt (2), Chapman, Fallins, Irwin, Kimmell, Lowe	Chapman (4), Fallins (dg)	1478	Lowe
10.7.98	FD	A	Dewsbury R.	L	14-25	Clarkson, Irwin	Chapman (3)	–	–
15.7.98	FD	H	Wakefield T.	W	29-18	Collins (2), Pratt, Kimmell	Chapman (4, dg)	2607	Cummings
19.7.98	FD	A	Swinton L.	L	6-14	Collins	Chapman	–	–
26.7.98	FD	H	Widnes V.	W	28-26	Chapman, Collins, Handley, Irwin	Chapman (6)	1657	Shaw
9.8.98	FD	A	Hull K.R.	L	20-24	Chapman, Evans, Handley, A. Jackson,	Fallins (2)	–	–
14.8.98	FD	H	Hunslet H.	W	32-31	Pratt (2), Fallins, Baker,	Chapman (7), Kimmell (dg), Fallins (dg)	1826	McGregor
21.8.98	FD	A	Keighley C.	W	20-18	Baker, Chapman, Dickens, Pratt	Chapman (2)	–	–
30.8.98	FD	H	Leigh C.	W	58-4	Baker (3), Chapman (2), Pratt (2), Collins, Dooler, Lowe	Chapman (9)	2047	Oddy
6.9.98	PO	H	Swinton L.	W	22-12	Lowe (3), Pratt	Fallins (2, 2dg)	1770	Gilmour
13.9.98	PO	A	Dewsbury R.	W	20-10	Pratt (2), Hall, Handley	Fallins (2)	–	–
20.9.98	PO	A	Hull K.R.	W	54-6	Chapman (2), Collins (2), Pratt (2), Hall, Baker, Slater	Chapman (8), Fallins (2 dg)	–	–
26.9.98	POF	N1	Wakefield T.	L	22-24	Baker, Collins, Hall, A. Jackson	Chapman (3)	(8224)	Oddy
3.10.98	TT	A	Limoux	L	10-19	Lowe, Baker	Chapman	–	–
11.10.98	TT	H	St. Esteve	L	4-42	Hall	–	1130	Alibert (Fr)
17.10.98	TT	A	St. Esteve	L	24-48	Chapman, Handley, Riley, Peacock	Chapman (2), Rooney (2)	–	–
25.10.98	TT	H	Limoux	W	54-10	Pratt (2), Dickens (2), Spurr (2), Chapman, Swinson, Stokes	Chapman (9)	804	Frileux (Fr)

N1 at Huddersfield

FEATHERSTONE ROVERS 1998 PLAYERS' SUMMARY

	Date of birth	App	T	G	D	Pts	Previous club	Debut
Allen, Chris	15.10.78	2	0	0	0	0	Castleford T.	1998
Amone, Asa	8.1.66	24+6	0	0	0	0	Halifax B.S.	1998
Baker, Danny	9.12.75	20+15	14	0	0	56	Parramatta (Aust.)	1997
Chapman, Richard	5.9.75	32+5	18	83	1	239	Sheffield E.	1997
Child, Lee	28.9.74	9	3	0	0	12	Hunslet H.	1998
Clarkson, Mick	13.9.74	1+20	3	0	0	12	Wakefield T.	1998
Collins, Steve	9.4.74	31+1	22	0	0	88	Canberra R. (Aust.)	1998
Coventry, Jamie	9.2.77	16+6	3	0	0	12	Huddersfield G.	1998
Dean, Craig	20.10.76	2	0	0	0	0	Halifax B.S.	1998
Dickens, Stuart	23.3.80	24+3	6	2	0	28	Westgate Redoubt ARL	1998
Dooler, Steve	31.12.77	4+5	1	0	0	4		1998
Evans, Danny	15.10.74	8+15	5	0	0	20	Travellers ARL	1995-96
Fallins, Tyron	1.8.75	31+7	7	76	12	192	Australia	1996
Hall, Carl	10.8.69	27	10	0	0	40	Moseley RU	1998
Handley, Patrick "Paddy"	18.9.75	25+13	9	0	0	36	Leeds	1997
Highton, Paul	10.11.76	4	2	0	0	8	Halifax B.S.	1998
Horne, Craig	20.5.78	21	4	0	0	16	Bradford B.	1998
Irwin, Shaun	8.12.68	31	11	0	0	44	Oldham B.	1997
Jackson, Anthony "Chico"	20.11.69	28	3	0	0	12	Hull S.	1998
Jackson, Davy	25.10.73	1+1	1	0	0	4	Isberg Celtic ARL	1995-96
Kimmel, Davy	6.9.70	20+3	8	0	1	33	Australia	1997
Lowe, Neil	20.12.78	23+16	6	0	0	24	Hunslet Parkside ARL	1997
Maher, Lee	29.10.75	12	1	0	0	4	Leeds R.	1997
Newlove, Richard	18.7.78	4+1	2	0	0	8		1995-96
Padgett, Robert	23.6.80	4+3	1	0	0	4	Dewsbury Moor ARL	1998
Peacock, Jamie	14.12.77	2+2	1	0	0	4	Bradford B.	1998
Pratt, Karl	13.7.80	28+5	25	0	1	101	Hunslet Parkside ARL	1997
Price, Gary H.	28.10.69	35	3	0	0	12	Wakefield T.	1993-94
Riley, David	26.8.80	1+2	1	0	0	4	East Leeds ARL	1998
Rooney, Jamie	17.3.80	2+2	0	2	0	4	Featherstone Jnrs. ARL	1998
Slater, Richard	29.8.70	26+4	3	0	0	12	Wakefield T.	1995-96
Smallman, Ben	23.12.78	0+1	0	0	0	0	Featherstone Jnrs. ARL	1998
Spurr, Chris	7.7.80	1+2	2	0	0	8	Featherstone Jnrs. ARL	1998
Stokes, Jamie	13.8.79	4	1	0	0	4		1996
Swinson, Gavin	21.3.78	11+2	5	0	0	20	Kippax Welfare ARL	1997
Thompson, Ian	6.2.78	4	0	0	0	0	Wigan W.	1998
Walker, Matt	23.11.78	0+5	1	0	0	4	Bradford B.	1998
Wileman, Simon	23.4.76	1+7	0	0	0	0		1997
Williamson, Lee	21.9.80	1+3	0	0	0	0	Hunslet Parkside ARL	1998
TOTALS								
39 players			182	163	15	1069		

Representative appearances 1998
Child - Ireland (1+1)

GATESHEAD THUNDER

Ground: Gateshead International Stadium
(0191–4779158)
First Season: 1999
Coach: Shaun McRae

PLAYERS' REGISTER

	Club from
Allwood, Richard	Brisbane (Aust.)
Allwood, Sean	Brisbane (Aust.)
Bird, Deon	Adelaide (Aust.)
Carney, Brian	Dublin Blues ARL
Collins, Steve	Featherstone R.
Daylight, Matt	Adelaide (Aust.)
Felsch, Luke	St. George (Aust.)
Grimaldi, Tony	Canterbury B. (Aust.)
Green, Brett	Brisbane (Aust.)
Grogan, Brett	Newcastle (Aust.)
Herron, Ian	Parramatta (Aust.)
Hick, Andrew	Adelaide (Aust.)
Hugill, Russell	Gateshead Mets ARL
Lee, Danny	Cronulla (Aust.)
Maher, Adam	Rochdale H.
Maiden, David	Cairns (Aust.)
Peters, Willie	Sth Sydney (Aust.)
Robinson, Will	Illawarra (Aust.)
Sammut, Ben	Cronulla (Aust.)
Simon, Craig	Illawarra (Aust.)
Singleton, Stuart	Welsh Students ARL
Walters, Kerrod	Adelaide (Aust.)
Wilson, Craig	Illawarra (Aust.)

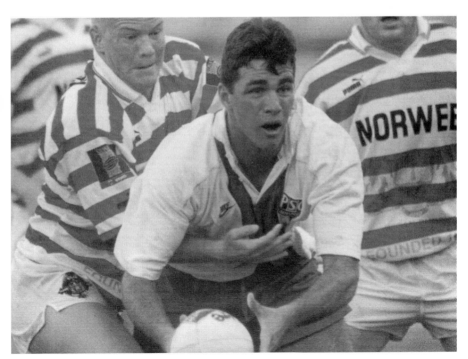

Deon Bird: Former Paris St. Germain and Adelaide Rams player signed by Gateshead Thunder.

HALIFAX BLUE SOX

Ground: The Shay (01422-250600)
First Season: 1895-96. Added Blue Sox to title at the start of 1996 League season.
Chairman: Chris Whiteley
Honours: **Championship** Winners, 1906-07, 1964-65
Beaten finalists, 1952-53, 1953-54, 1955-56, 1965-66
War Emergency League Beaten finalists, 1942-43, 1944-45
Division One Champions, 1902-03, 1985-86
Challenge Cup Winners, 1902-03, 1903-04, 1930-31, 1938-39, 1986-87
Beaten finalists, 1920-21, 1940-41, 1941-42, 1948-49, 1953-54, 1955-56, 1987-88
Regal Trophy Winners, 1971-72
Beaten finalists, 1989-90
Premiership Trophy Beaten finalists, 1985-86
Second Division Premiership Beaten finalists, 1990-91
Yorkshire Cup Winners, 1908-09, 1944-45, 1954-55, 1955-56, 1963-64
Beaten finalists, 1905-06, 1907-08, 1941-42, 1979-80
Yorkshire League Winners, 1908-09, 1920-21, 1952-53, 1953-54, 1955-56, 1957-58
Eastern Division Championship Winners, 1963-64
Charity Shield Winners, 1986-87
Beaten finalists, 1987-88

RECORDS

Match
Goals: 14 by Bruce Burton at Hunslet, 27 Aug 1972
Tries: 8 by Keith Williams v. Dewsbury, 9 Nov 1957
Points: 32 by John Schuster at Doncaster, 9 Oct 1994

Season
Goals: 147 by Tysul Griffiths, 1955-56
Tries: 48 by Johnny Freeman, 1956-57
Points: 362 by John Schuster, 1994-95

Career
Goals: 1,028 by Ron James, 1961-71
Tries: 290 by Johnny Freeman, 1954-67
Points: 2,191 by Ron James, 1961-71
Appearances: 482 by Stan Kielty, 1946-58
Highest score: 82-8 v. Runcorn H., 14 Oct 1990
Highest against: 76-0 at Brisbane B, 22 June 1997
By British club: 64-0 at Wigan, 7 Mar 1923; 64-18 at Featherstone R., 24 Nov 1991
Attendance: 29,153 v. Wigan (RL Cup), 21 Mar 1959 — at Thrum Hall
7,566 v. Bradford B. (League), 23 Aug 1998 — at The Shay

COACHING REGISTER
● **Since 1974-75**

Derek Hallas	Aug 74 - Oct 74
Les Pearce	Oct 74 - Apr 76
Alan Kellett	May 76 - Apr 77
Jim Crellin	June 77 - Oct 77
Harry Fox	Oct 77 - Feb 78
Maurice Bamford	Feb 78 - May 80
Mick Blacker	June 80 - June 82
Ken Roberts	June 82 - Sep 82
Colin Dixon	Sep 82 - Nov 84
Chris Anderson	Nov 84 - May 88
Graham Eadie	May 88 - Aug 88
Ross Strudwick	Aug 88 - Feb 89
Alan Hardisty	Feb 89 - Apr 89
John Dorahy	June 89 - Aug 90
Peter Roe	Aug 90 - May 91
Roger Millward	May 91 - Dec 92
Malcolm Reilly	Jan 93 - Sep 94
Steve Simms	Sep 94 - Feb 97
John Pendlebury	Mar 97 -

GREAT BRITAIN REGISTER
(32 players)

Alvin Ackerley	(2)	1952-58
Arthur Bassett	(2)	1946
Jack Beames	(2)	1921
Nat Bentham	(2)	1929
John Bentley	(1)	1994
Harry Beverley	(2)	1937
Oliver Burgham	(1)	1911

Arthur Daniels	(3)	1952-55
Will Davies	(1)	1911
Colin Dixon	(1)	1968
Paul Dixon	(3+3)	1987-88
Percy Eccles	(1)	1907
Terry Fogerty	(+1)	1966
Tony Halmshaw	(1)	1971
Karl Harrison	(8+3)	1991-94
Michael Jackson	(+2)	1993
Neil James	(1)	1986
Robbie Lloyd	(1)	1920
Alf Milnes	(2)	1920
Stuart Prosser	(1)	1914
Dai Rees	(1)	1926
Charlie Renilson	(7+1)	1965-68
Joe Riley	(1)	1910
Ken Roberts	(10)	1963-66
Asa Robinson	(3)	1907-08
Derrick Schofield	(1)	1955
John Shaw	(5)	1960-62
Cyril Stacey	(1)	1920
John Thorley	(4)	1954
Jack Wilkinson	(6)	1954-55
Frank Williams	(2)	1914
David Willicombe	(1)	1974

1998 SIGNINGS REGISTER

Signed	Player	Club From
14.4.98	Ashton, Paul	—
3.5.98	Bloem, Jamie	Widnes V.
—	Broadbent, Paul	Sheffield E.
—	Cardiss, Darryl	Wigan W.
26.1.98	Clark, Des	Gold Coast (Aust.)
26.1.98	Clarkson, Michael	Wakefield T.
26.1.98	Clinch, Gavin	St. George (Aust.)
—	Craig, Andy	Swinton L.
26.1.98	Dusher, Thomas	Hull Old Boys
15.1.98	Gibson, Damian	Leeds R.
24.6.98	Hall, Martin	Castleford T.
26.1.98	Halliwell, Christopher	Leigh East ARL
—	Holroyd, Graham	Leeds R.
16.2.98	Mercer, Gary	Leeds R.
13.7.97	O'Loughlin, Kevin	St. Helens
—	Pinkney, Nick	Sheffield E.
—	Randall, Craig	Salford R.

Paul Dixon: Six Test appearances for Great Britain as a Halifax player.

HALIFAX BLUE SOX 1998 MATCH ANALYSIS

Date	Competition	H/A	Opponents	Rlt	Score	Tries	Goals	Attendance	Referee
15.2.98	CC(4)	H1	Huddersfield G.	W	28-8	Tuilagi (2), Bouveng, Clark	Pearson (6)	5962	Ganson
1.3.98	CC(5)	A	London B.	L	18-21	Mercer, Moana, Rowley	Pearson (3)	–	–
5.4.98	SL	A	London B.	W	32-6	Clinch (2), Mercer, Gibson, Moana	Pearson (6)	–	–
10.4.98	SL	H	Huddersfield G.	W	30-6	Moana (2), Clinch, Pearson, Tuilagi	Pearson (5)	6392	Kirkpatrick
19.4.98	SL	A	Wigan W.	L	6-40	Gibson	Chester	–	–
26.4.98	SL	H	Castleford T.	W	29-16	Chester (2), Clark, Powell, Skerrett	Chester (3, dg), Pearson	5172	Kirkpatrick
10.5.98	SL	A	Warrington W.	L	20-31	Clinch (2), Clark	Chester (4)	–	–
17.5.98	SL	A	Bradford B.	W	21-16	Bouveng (2), Powell	Chester (4), Baldwin (dg)	–	–
24.5.98	SL	H	St. Helens	W	16-10	Moana, Tuilagi	Pearson (3), Chester	6760	R. Connolly
30.5.98	SL	A	Sheffield E.	W	28-22	Tuilagi (2), Bouveng, Rowley, Pearson	Pearson (3), Bloem	–	–
5.6.98	SL	H	Hull S.	W	30-16	Gibson (2), Bloem, Chester, Mercer	Pearson (5)	5198	Ganson
14.6.98	SL	H	Salford R.	W	34-6	Bentley, Bouveng, Clark, Powell, Rowley, Bloem	Pearson (5)	5218	R. Smith
19.6.98	SL	A	Leeds R.	L	18-35	Baldwin, Moana, Skerrett	Bloem (2), Pearson	–	–
27.6.98	SL	H	London B.	W	34-14	Bentley, Harrison, Marshall, Moana, Powell, Rowley	Clinch (5)	4443	R. Connolly
5.7.98	SL	A	Huddersfield G.	W	48-6	Powell (2), Tuilagi (2), Baldwin, Bentley, Gibson, Gillespie, Mercer	Clinch (5), Chester	–	–
17.7.98	SL	N1	Sheffield E.	W	32-10	Chester, Clark, Clinch, Mercer, Moana, Powell	Clinch (2), Bloem (2)	(3087)	R. Smith
31.7.98	SL	H	Wigan W.	L	14-20	Moana, Chester	Pearson (3)	6521	Ganson
9.8.98	SL	A	Castleford T.	W	36-16	Bouveng, Chester, Clark, Clinch, Marshall, Moana, Tuilagi	Clinch (3), Pearson	–	–
16.8.98	SL	H	Warrington W.	W	46-16	Bloem, Clinch, Marns, Mercer, Moana, Pearson, Powell, Tuilagi	Pearson (7)	4984	Presley
23.8.98	SL	H	Bradford B.	W	25-12	Chester, Gibson, Moana, Tuilagi	Pearson (4), Clinch (dg)	7566	J. Connolly
30.8.98	SL	A	St. Helens	L	6-36	–	Pearson (3)	–	–
6.9.98	SL	H	Sheffield E.	W	33-16	Bloem (3), Bouveng (2), Powell, Harrison,	Pearson (2), Clinch (dg)	4628	Cummings
11.9.98	SL	A	Hull S.	W	44-24	Powell (2), Rowley (2), Bloem, Clinch, Marns	Pearson (8)	–	–
20.9.98	SL	A	Salford R.	W	34-16	Bloem, Bouveng, Clinch, Gillespie, Pearson, Tuilagi	Pearson (5)	–	–
27.9.98	SL	H	Leeds R.	W	42-0	Clinch (3), Mercer (2), Bouveng, Moana	Clinch (5), Pearson (2)	5486	Presley
4.10.98	PO	A	Leeds R.	L	6-13	Tuilagi	Clinch	–	–
9.10.98	PO	H	St. Helens	L	30-37	Powell, Bloem, Clinch, Mercer, Moana	Pearson (5)	5451	Presley

H1 at Thrum Hall; N1 at Northampton T. FC

HALIFAX BLUE SOX 1998 PLAYERS' SUMMARY

	Date of birth	App	T	G	D	Pts	Previous club	Debut
Baldwin, Simon	31.3.75	6+16	2	0	1	9	Leigh	1994-95
Bentley, John	5.9.66	4+2	3	0	0	12	Leeds	1992-93
Bloem, Jamie	26.5.71	13+8	9	5	0	46	Widnes V.	1998
Bouveng, David	6.2.73	27	10	0	0	40	N. Queensland (Aust.)	1997
Chester, Chris	8.10.78	27	7	14	1	57	New Sharlston ARL	1995-96
Clark, Des	4.3.72	18+9	6	0	0	24	Gold Coast (Aust.)	1998
Clinch, Gavin	13.9.73	25	14	21	2	100	St. George (Aust.)	1998
Dean, Craig	20.10.76	0+1	0	0	0	0	Leigh East ARL	1994-95
Gibson, Damian	14.5.75	24+1	6	0	0	24	Leeds R.	1998
Gillespie, Carl	25.7.70	11+11	2	0	0	8	Old Crossleyans RU	1994-95
Hall, Martin	5.12.68	2+10	0	0	0	0	Castleford T.	1998
Harrison, Karl	20.2.64	26+1	2	0	0	8	Hull	1991-92
Hobson, Andy	26.12.78	0+6	0	0	0	0	New Sharlston ARL	1998
Marns, Oliver	10.10.78	0+5	2	0	0	8	Halifax Academy	1996
Marshall, Richard	9.10.75	10+16	2	0	0	8	St. Helens Academy	1994-95
Mercer, Gary	22.6.66	26+1	9	0	0	36	Leeds R.	1998
Moana, Martin	13.8.73	20+3	14	0	0	56	Auckland W. (NZ)	1995-96
O'Loughlin, Kevin	26.3.77	0+3	0	0	0	0	St. Helens	1997
Pearson, Martin	24.10.71	18+5	4	78	0	172	Featherstone R.	1997
Powell, Daio	9.3.73	26	12	0	0	48	Wakefield T.	1997
Rowley, Paul	12.3.75	25+2	6	0	0	24	Leigh	1994-95
Skerrett, Kelvin	22.5.66	20+3	2	0	0	8	Wigan	1997
Tuilagi, Fereti	9.6.71	23	13	0	0	52	Western Samoa RU	1995-96
TOTALS								
23 players			125	118	4	740		

Representative appearances 1998
Gibson - Wales (1); Hall - Wales (0+1); Pearson - Wales (0+1); Powell - Wales (1, 1t); Rowley - Emerging England (1); Skerrett - Wales (1)

Gary Mercer: Former Leeds Rhinos forward who made a big impact after moving to Halifax Blue Sox in 1998.

HUDDERSFIELD GIANTS

Ground: Alfred McAlpine Stadium
(01484-530710)
First Season: 1895-96; added Barracudas to title
from 1984-85 to 1987-88 inclusive.
Added Giants to title at the start of
1996 League season.
Chairman: Ken Davy
Honours: **Championship** Winners, 1911-12,
1912-13, 1914-15, 1928-29, 1929-30,
1948-49, 1961-62
Beaten finalists, 1913-14, 1919-20,
1922-23, 1931-32, 1945-46, 1949-50
Division Two Champions, 1974-75
Division Three Champions, 1991-92
Challenge Cup Winners, 1912-13,
1914-15, 1919-20, 1932-33, 1944-45,
1952-53
Beaten finalists, 1934-35, 1961-62
Premiership Divisional winners,
1997, Beaten finalists, 1994-95
Yorkshire Cup Winners, 1909-10,
1911-12, 1913-14, 1914-15, 1918-19,
1919-20, 1926-27, 1931-32, 1938-39,
1950-51, 1952-53, 1957-58
Beaten finalists, 1910-11, 1923-24,
1925-26, 1930-31, 1937-38, 1942-43,
1949-50, 1960-61
Yorkshire League Winners,
1911-12, 1912-13, 1913-14, 1914-15,
1919-20, 1921-22, 1928-29, 1929-30,
1948-49, 1949-50, 1951-52
Eastern Division Beaten finalists,
1962-63

RECORDS
Match
Goals: 18 by Major Holland v. Swinton Park,
28 Feb 1914
Tries: 10 by Lionel Cooper v. Keighley,
17 Nov 1951
Points: 39 by Major Holland v. Swinton Park,
28 Feb 1914

Season
Goals: 147 by Ben Gronow, 1919-20
Tries: 80 by Albert Rosenfeld, 1913-14
Points: 332 by Pat Devery, 1952-53

Career
Goals: 958 by Frank Dyson, 1949-63
Tries: 420 by Lionel Cooper, 1947-55
Points: 2,072 by Frank Dyson, 1949-63
Appearances: 485 by Doug Clark, 1909-29
Highest score: 142-4 v. Blackpool G., 26 Nov 1994
Highest against: 94-12 at Castleford, 18 Sep 1988
Attendance: 32,912 v. Wigan (League),
4 Mar 1950 — at Fartown,
12,417 v. Bradford B. (League), 3
April 1998 — at Alfred McAlpine
Stadium

COACHING REGISTER
● **Since 1974-75**

Brian Smith	Jan 73 - Mar 76
Keith Goulding	Mar 76 - Dec 76
Bob Tomlinson	Jan 77 - May 77
Neil Fox	June 77 - Feb 78
* Roy Francis	—
Keith Goulding	May 78 - July 79
Ian Brooke	July 79 - Mar 80
Maurice Bamford	May 80 - May 81
Les Sheard	June 81 - Nov 82
Dave Mortimer	Nov 82 - Aug 83
Mel Bedford	Aug 83 - Nov 83
Brian Lockwood	Nov 83 - Feb 85
Chris Forster	Feb 85 - Dec 86
Jack Addy	Jan 87 - Mar 88
Allen Jones ⎫ Neil Whittaker ⎭	Mar 88 - Nov 88
Nigel Stephenson	Nov 88 - Mar 90
Barry Seabourne	Mar 90 - Feb 91
Mick Blacker ⎫ Francis Jarvis ⎭	Feb 91 - Sep 91
Alex Murphy	Sep 91 - Apr 94
George Fairbairn	June 94 - Oct 95
Darryl Van de Velde	Dec 95 - Sept 96
Steve Ferres	Oct 1996 - Nov 97
Garry Schofield	Nov 97 - July 98
** Phil Veivers	July 98 - Oct 98
Malcolm Reilly	Nov 98 -

* *Although Roy Francis was appointed he was unable to
take over and Dave Heppleston stood in until the next
appointment.*
** *Caretaker coach*

HUDDERSFIELD GIANTS 1998 MATCH ANALYSIS

Date	Competition	H/A	Opponents	Rlt	Score	Tries	Goals	Attendance	Referee
15.2.98	CC(4)	A	Halifax B.S.	L	8-28	Barton	Cook (2)	–	–
3.4.98	SL	H	Bradford B.	L	6-38	Russell	Cook	12,417	R. Connolly
10.4.98	SL	A	Halifax B.S.	L	6-30	Sturm	Weston	–	–
19.4.98	SL	H	St. Helens	L	24-26	Arnold, Barton, Sturm, Weston	Weston (4)	4946	Presley
26.4.98	SL	H	Sheffield E.	L	18-48	Arnold (2), Veivers, Weston	Weston	3743	Ganson
10.5.98	SL	A	Salford R.	L	6-40	Arnold	Cook	–	–
17.5.98	SL	H	London B.	L	20-28	Arnold, Hanger, Loughlin, Russell	Cook (2)	4498	Nicholson
22.5.98	SL	A	Wigan W.	L	0-46	–	–	–	–
31.5.98	SL	H	Warrington W.	W	28-6	Booth, Cook, Hanger, Harmon, Weston	Loughlin (4)	4127	R. Connolly
5.6.98	SL	A	Leeds R.	L	4-54	Hanger	–	–	–
14.6.98	SL	A	Castleford T.	W	16-10	Booth, Russell, King	Booth (2)	–	–
21.6.98	SL	H	Hull S.	L	14-20	Arnold (2), Hanger	Booth	4250	R. Connolly
28.6.98	SL	A	Bradford B.	L	10-36	Arnold (2)	Cook	–	–
5.7.98	SL	H	Halifax B.S.	L	6-48	Wiitenberg	Cook	5091	Ganson
24.7.98	SL	N1	Hull S.	L	10-21	Arnold	Cook (3)	(4306)	Kirkpatrick
2.8.98	SL	A	St. Helens	L	18-68	Bunyan, Orr, Weston	Cook (3)	–	–
7.8.98	SL	A	Sheffield E.	L	10-56	Arnold, Berry	Weston	–	–
16.8.98	SL	H	Salford R.	L	12-16	Sturm, Weston	Goulding (2)	2932	J. Connolly
23.8.98	SL	A	London B.	L	8-20	Bunyan, King	–	5007	Kirkpatrick
30.8.98	SL	H	Wigan W.	L	14-38	Sturm (2)	Goulding (2, 2dg)	–	–
6.9.98	SL	A	Warrington W.	L	8-36	Cheetham	Goulding (2)	–	–
13.9.98	SL	H	Leeds R.	L	16-72	Cook, Russell, Sturm	Cook, Weston	5762	R. Connolly
20.9.98	SL	H	Castleford T.	L	20-32	Arnold, Hanger, Orr, Simpson	Goulding (2)	3791	Nicholson
27.9.98	SL	A	Hull S.	L	14-36	Arnold, Simpson	Goulding (3)	–	–

N1 at Gateshead

GREAT BRITAIN REGISTER

(24 players)

Jim Bowden	(3)	1954
Ken Bowman	(3)	1962-63
Brian Briggs	(1)	1954
Stan Brogden	(9)	1929-33
Jack Chilcott	(3)	1914
Doug Clark	(11)	1911-20
Don Close	(1)	1967
Dick Cracknell	(2)	1951
Jim Davies	(2)	1911
Frank Dyson	(1)	1959
Ben Gronow	(7)	1911-20
Fred Longstaff	(2)	1914
Ken Loxton	(1)	1971
Stan Moorhouse	(2)	1914
Bob Nicholson	(3)	1946-48
Johnny Rogers	(7)	1914-21
Ken Senior	(2)	1965-67
Tommy Smales	(5)	1962-64
Mick Sullivan	(16)	1954-57
Gwyn Thomas	(8)	1920-21
Dave Valentine	(15)	1948-54
Rob Valentine	(1)	1967
Harold Wagstaff	(12)	1911-21
Harold Young	(1)	1929

1998 SIGNINGS REGISTER

Signed	Player	Club From
18.2.98	Beevers, Chris	Elland Boxers ARL
—	Bentley, John	Halifax B.S.
1.4.98	Coventry, James	Castleford T.
24.4.98	*Field, Jamie	Leeds R.
13.5.98	Fielden, Jamie	Calder Valley ARL
10.5.98	Goodair, Mark	St. John Fisher ARL
19.8.98	Goulding, Bobbie	St. Helens
—	Lenihan, Jim	St. George (Aust.)
9.6.98	Marsden, Jamie	Huddersfield YMCA
—	Pickavance, Ian	St. Helens
17.8.98	Potter, Lee	Calder Valley ARL
20.4.98	Sellers, Luke	Dudley Hill ARL
8.4.98	Simpson, Darren	Lindley Swifts ARL
—	Tangata-Toa, Andrew	St. George (Aust.)
13.1.98	Wittenberg, Jeff	Bradford B.
—	Wright, Nigel	Wigan W.

HUDDERSFIELD GIANTS 1998 PLAYERS' SUMMARY

	Date of birth	App	T	G	D	Pts	Previous club	Debut
Adams, Guy	1.9.76	1+2	0	0	0	0		1996
Arnold, Danny	15.4.77	24	13	0	0	52	St. Helens	1998
Barton, Ben	4.12.74	2+6	2	0	0	8	Orrell St. James ARL	1993-94
Belle, Adrian	23.11.70	10+3	0	0	0	0	Oldham B.	1997
Berry, Joe	7.5.74	6+13	1	0	0	4	Keighley C.	1997
Booth, Steve	18.9.76	10+2	2	3	0	14	Oulton ARL	1995-96
Bowes, Tony	14.6.70	4+2	0	0	0	0	Doncaster D.	1997
Bunyan, James	2.11.77	7+3	2	0	0	8	Milford ARL	1995-96
Byrne, Shane	15.10.78	0+3	0	0	0	0	Moldgreen ARL	1998
Cheetham, Andy	25.1.75	12	1	0	0	4	Leigh C.	1997
Cook, Paul	23.7.76	11+6	2	15	0	38	Bradford B.	1997
Field, Jamie	12.12.76	15+5	0	0	0	0	Leeds R.	1998
Fielden, Jamie	9.5.78	2+3	0	0	0	0	Calder Valley ARL	1998
Fozzard, Nick	22.7.77	2+1	0	0	0	0	Leeds R.	1997
Goulding, Bobbie	4.2.72	5+1	0	11	2	24	St. Helens	1998
Hanger, Dean	24.2.70	20+1	5	0	0	20	Leigh	1994-95
Harmon, Neil	9.1.69	13	1	0	0	4	Leeds R.	1997
Hudson, Ryan	20.11.79	0+1	0	0	0	0	Stanley R. ARL	1998
Jackson, Paul	29.9.78	0+12	0	0	0	0	Stanningley ARL	1998
King, Dave	6.9.67	12+6	2	0	0	8	Warrington	1996
Loughlin, Paul	28.7.66	12+1	1	4	0	12	Bradford B.	1998
Milner, Lee	26.2.77	0+1	0	0	0	0	Huddersfield Acad.	1995-96
Moore, Adrian	27.9.77	0+4	0	0	0	0	Dewsbury M. ARL	1996
Moxon, Mark	22.8.80	3	0	0	0	0	Westgate Redoubt ARL	1998
Neill, Jonathan	19.12.68	8+1	0	0	0	0	St. Helens	1996
Orr, Chris	18.11.73	20+3	2	0	0	8	Gold Coast (Aust.)	1998
Richards, Basil	9.7.65	16+5	0	0	0	0	Warrington	1993-94
Russell, Danny	24.12.69	23	4	0	0	16	Carlisle	1997
Schofield, Garry	1.7.65	0+2	0	0	0	0	Leeds	1996
Simpson, Darren	13.11.77	5	2	0	0	8	Lindley Swifts ARL	1998
Sturm, Matt	13.12.72	24	6	0	0	24	Manukau Counties (NZ)	1997
Veivers, Phil	25.5.64	7+6	1	0	0	4	St. Helens	1996
Weston, Craig	20.12.73	19+1	5	8	0	36	Gold Coast (Aust.)	1997
Wittenberg, Jeff	19.3.73	19+1	1	0	0	4	Bradford B.	1998
TOTALS 34 players			53	41	2	296		

Representative appearances 1998

Arnold - Scotland (2, 1t); Berry - Scotland (2); Orr - Scotland (2); Russell - Scotland (2)

Ian Pickavance played for Ireland (1) after signing from St. Helens but before he had played for Huddersfield

HULL KINGSTON ROVERS

Ground: New Craven Park (01482-374648)
First Season: 1899-1900
Chairman: Barry Lilley
Honours: **Championship** Winners, 1922-23, 1924-25
Beaten finalists, 1920-21, 1967-68
Division One Champions, 1978-79, 1983-84, 1984-85
Division Two Champions, 1989-90
Division Two (3rd league) Champions, 1995-96, 1996
Challenge Cup Winners, 1979-80
Beaten finalists, 1904-05, 1924-25, 1963-64, 1980-81, 1985-86
Silk Cut Plate Winners, 1997
Regal Trophy Winners, 1984-85
Beaten finalists, 1981-82, 1985-86
Premiership Winners, 1980-81, 1983-84
Beaten finalists, 1984-85
Second Division Premiership Beaten finalists, 1989-90
Yorkshire Cup Winners, 1920-21, 1929-30, 1966-67, 1967-68, 1971-72, 1974-75, 1985-86
Beaten finalists, 1906-07, 1911-12, 1933-34, 1962-63, 1975-76, 1980-81, 1984-85
Yorkshire League Winners, 1924-25, 1925-26
Eastern Division Championship Winners, 1962-63
Charity Shield Beaten finalists, 1985-86
BBC2 Floodlit Trophy Winners, 1977-78
Beaten finalists, 1979-80

RECORDS

Match

Goals:	14 by Alf Carmichael v. Merthyr Tydfil, 8 Oct 1910
	Mike Fletcher v. Whitehaven, 18 Mar 1990
	Colin Armstrong v. Nottingham C. (at Doncaster), 19 Aug 1990
Tries:	11 by George West v. Brookland R., 4 Mar 1905
Points:	53 by George West v. Brookland R., 4 Mar 1905

Season

Goals:	199 by Mike Fletcher, 1989-90
Tries:	45 by Gary Prohm, 1984-85
Points:	450 by Mike Fletcher, 1989-90

Career

Goals: 1,268 by Mike Fletcher, 1985-98
Tries: 207 by Roger Millward, 1966-80
Points: 2,759 by Mike Fletcher, 1985-98
Appearances: 481+8 by Mike Smith, 1975-91
Highest score: 100-6 v. Nottingham C. (at Doncaster), 19 Aug 1990
Highest against: 76-8 at Halifax, 20 Oct 1991
Attendance: 27,670 v. Hull (League), 3 Apr 1953 — at Boothferry Park, Hull C. AFC
8,557 v. Hull (League), 1 Jan 1991 — at New Craven Park

COACHING REGISTER

● **Since 1974-75**

Arthur Bunting	Feb 72 - Nov 75
Harry Poole	Dec 75 - Mar 77
Roger Millward	Mar 77 - May 91
George Fairbairn	May 91 - May 94
Steve Crooks	May 94 - May 97
Dave Harrison	May 97 -

GREAT BRITAIN REGISTER

(26 players)

David Bishop	(+1)	1990
Chris Burton	(8+1)	1982-87
Alan Burwell	(7+1)	1967-69
Len Casey	(7+2)	1977-83
Garry Clark	(3)	1984-85
Alec Dockar	(1)	1947
George Fairbairn	(3)	1981-82
Jack Feetham	(1)	1929
Peter Flanagan	(14)	1962-70

Frank Foster	(1)	1967
David Hall	(2)	1984
Paul Harkin	(+1)	1985
Steve Hartley	(3)	1980-81
Phil Hogan	(2+2)	1979
Roy Holdstock	(2)	1980
Bill Holliday	(8+1)	1964-67
David Laws	(1)	1986
Brian Lockwood	(1+1)	1978-79
Phil Lowe	(12)	1970-78
Roger Millward	(27+1)	1967-78
Harry Poole	(1)	1964
Paul Rose	(1+3)	1974-78
Mike Smith	(10+1)	1979-84
Brian Tyson	(3)	1963-67
David Watkinson	(12+1)	1979-86
Chris Young	(5)	1967-68

1998 SIGNINGS REGISTER

Signed	Player	Club From
12.6.98	Beauchamp, Keith	St. George (Aust.)
23.1.98	Brown, Daniel	Parramatta (Aust.)
12.1.98	Chambers, Anthony	Skirlaugh Bulls ARL
22.1.98	Danby, Rob	Hull S.
25.1.98	Dixon, Mike	Hull S.
18.2.98	Jackson, Wayne	Halifax B.S.
23.1.98	Kennedy, Jamie	St. George (Aust.)
18.5.97	Kitching, Chris	Hull S.
22.1.98	McCracken, John	Hull S.
26.3.98	Smith, Richard	Bradford B.
22.1.98	Smith, Andy	Hull S.
—	Taewa, Whetu	Sheffield E.
25.6.97	Thompson, Alex	Sheffield E.

Chris Burton: Nine Test appearances for Great Britain as a Hull K.R. player.

HULL KINGSTON ROVERS 1998 MATCH ANALYSIS

Date	Com-petition	H/A	Opponents	Rlt	Score	Tries	Goals	Atten-dance	Referee
1.2.98	CC(3)	H	Queens	W	34-16	Bibby, Charles, Gene, Parker, Rouse, A. Smith	M. Fletcher (4), Sibary	1584	Shaw
8.2.98	FD	H	Leigh C.	W	48-14	Bibby (3), Gene (2), Danby, Rouse, P. Fletcher	M. Fletcher (7), Sibary	2228	Presley
13.2.98	CC(4)	A	Featherstone L.	W	56-20	M. Fletcher (2), Danby (2), Bibby (2), Gene, Harrison, P. Fletcher, A. Smith	M. Fletcher (8)	–	–
22.2.98	FD	A	Featherstone R.	W	20-7	Rouse (2), Bibby, Danby	M. Fletcher (2)	–	–
1.3.98	CC(5)	H	Swinton L.	W	46-24	P. Fletcher (2), Gene (2), Hill, Parker, Rouse	M. Fletcher (9)	2551	Kirkpatrick
4.3.98	FD	H	Widnes V.	W	26-8	Dixon (2), Charles, Gene	M. Fletcher (5)	2162	Shaw
8.3.98	FD	A	Whitehaven W.	W	24-14	McCracken (2), Dixon, Gene, P. Fletcher	M. Fletcher (2)	–	–
15.3.98	CC(6)	A	London B.	L	18-46	Gene, Danby, Hill, Rouse	M. Fletcher	–	–
22.3.98	FD	H	Rochdale H.	W	28-15	Charles, Danby, Harrison, Kitching	M. Fletcher (6)	2235	Morris
29.3.98	FD	H	Wakefield T.	W	36-6	Danby (2), M. Fletcher, Gene, Kennedy, R. Smith	M. Fletcher (6)	3504	R. Connolly
5.4.98	FD	A	Swinton L.	L	4-21	Gene	–	–	–
10.4.98	FD	A	Keighley C.	W	20-12	Dixon, M. Fletcher, Kitching	M. Fletcher (4)	–	–
13.4.98	FD	H	Dewsbury R.	L	4-17	Kitching	–	2958	Bates
19.4.98	FD	A	Hunslet H.	L	30-31	Dixon, P. Fletcher, Gene, Rouse, R. Smith	M. Fletcher (5)	–	–
26.4.98	FD	A	Leigh C.	L	14-22	Atkins (2), Bibby	M. Fletcher	–	–
5.5.98	FD	H	Featherstone R.	W	18-6	Atkins (2)	M. Fletcher (5)	2063	Nicholson
10.5.98	FD	A	Widnes V.	L	12-22	Danby, Kennedy	M. Fletcher (2)	–	–
17.5.98	FD	H	Whitehaven W.	W	25-16	Atkins, Dixon, Kennedy	M. Fletcher (6), Parker (dg)	1933	Morris
31.5.98	FD	A	Rochdale H.	D	26-26	P. Fletcher (2), Gene, Parker, Rouse	M. Fletcher (3)	–	–
3.6.98	FD	A	Wakefield T.	W	24-17	Rouse, Gene, P. Fletcher, Brown	M. Fletcher (3), Sibary	–	–
7.6.98	FD	H	Swinton L.	W	16-10	Kennedy, R. Smith	Charles (3, dg), Sibary (dg)	2076	Presley
14.6.98	FD	H	Keighley C.	W	28-16	P. Fletcher (2), Parker (2), R. Smith	M. Fletcher (3), Charles	2204	Gilmour
21.6.98	FD	A	Dewsbury R.	L	14-27	Gene (2)	M. Fletcher (3)	–	–
24.6.98	FD	H	Hunslet H.	W	44-18	Kennedy, Charles, P. Fletcher, Danby, R. Smith, Hill, Gene	Charles (8)	1941	Oddy
28.6.98	FD	A	Leigh C.	W	48-20	Gene (3), Danby (2), Dixon, P. Fletcher, Hill	Charles (8)	–	–
5.7.98	FD	H	Rochdale H.	W	34-6	Gene (3), Atkins, Dixon, Thompson	Charles (5)	1973	Nicholson
12.7.98	FD	A	Whitehaven W.	L	12-21	Bibby, Gene	M. Fletcher (2)	–	–
15.7.98	FD	H	Dewsbury R.	W	18-12	Beauchamp (2), Gene	Charles (3)	2187	R. Smith
19.7.98	FD	A	Wakefield T.	W	38-12	Gene (2), Dixon (2), Charles, R. Smith	M. Fletcher (6), Parker (2dg)	–	–
26.7.98	FD	H	Swinton L.	W	26-24	Charles, Gene, Kennedy, R. Smith	M. Fletcher (5)	2465	Presley
2.8.98	FD	A	Widnes V.	W	63-4	Gene (4), Beauchamp (2), Brown, Danby, Dixon, P. Fletcher	M. Fletcher (11), Parker (dg)	–	–
9.8.98	FD	H	Featherstone R.	W	24-20	Brown (2), Dixon, Gene,	M. Fletcher (4)	2463	Bates
23.8.98	FD	A	Hunslet H.	L	18-19	Beauchamp, Dixon, R. Smith	Charles (3)	–	–
30.8.98	FD	H	Keighley C.	L	6-17	Kitching	Charles	2142	Gilmour
6.9.98	PO	H	Dewsbury R.	W	18-2	Danby, Hill	M. Fletcher (4), Charles (dg), Gene (dg)	2649	Oddy
13.9.98	PO	A	Wakefield T.	L	16-19	Danby, Gene, R. Smith	M. Fletcher (2)	–	–
20.9.98	PO	H	Featherstone R.	L	6-54	Thompson	M. Fletcher	3813	Bates

67

HULL KINGSTON ROVERS 1998 PLAYERS' SUMMARY

	Date of birth	App	T	G	D	Pts	Previous club	Debut
Atkins, Gary	12.10.66	15+5	6	0	0	24	Ryedale-York	1994-95
Beauchamp, Keith	20.12.67	10	5	0	0	20	St. George (Aust.)	1998
Bibby, Mike	23.10.70	13+3	9	0	0	36	East Park ARL	1991-92
Brown, Danny	9.11.76	15+14	4	0	0	16	Parramatta (Aust.)	1998
Charles, Chris	7.3.76	36	6	32	2	90	Hull Boys ARL	1993-94
Crane, Mike	11.2.71	1+4	0	0	0	0	Greatfield ARL	1991-92
Danby, Rob	30.8.74	37	15	0	0	60	Hull S.	1998
Dannatt, Andy	20.11.65	25	0	0	0	0	St. Helens	1995-96
Dixon, Mike	6.4.71	31+5	13	0	0	52	Hull S.	1998
Fletcher, Mike	14.4.67	31+5	4	120	0	256	Hull KR Colts	1984-85
Fletcher, Paul	17.3.70	34+2	14	0	0	56	Eureka ARL	1987-88
Gene, Stanley	11.5.74	36	34	0	1	137	Papua New Guinea	1996
Hardy, Craig	24.8.73	1+2	0	0	0	0	Hull K.R. Acad.	1992-93
Harrison, Derek "Des"	10.10.64	9+18	2	0	0	8	Hull K.R. Colts	1984-85
Hartley, Jeremy "Jez"	30.12.77	1+4	0	0	0	0		1997
Hill, Howard	16.1.75	22+12	5	0	0	20	Oldham B.	1998
Jackson, Wayne	19.9.67	4+8	0	0	0	0	Halifax B.S.	1998
Kennedy, Jamie	7.3.75	20+9	6	0	0	24	St. George (Aust.)	1998
Kitching, Chris	1.8.77	4+13	4	0	0	16	Hull S.	1997
McCracken, John	14.1.78	4+1	2	0	0	8	Hull S.	1998
Okul, John	24.11.72	4+2	0	0	0	0	Papua New Guinea	1996
Parker, Wayne	2.4.67	23+2	5	0	4	24	Halifax B.S.	1997
Rouse, Paul	20.9.70	19	9	0	0	36	Skirlaugh ARL	1996
Sagar, Paul		0+1	0	0	0	0		1998
Scott, Paul	7.10.74	0+6	0	0	0	0	Hull Academy	1994-95
Sibary, Lee	19.9.70	19+5	0	3	1	7	Hull Dockers ARL	1998
Smith, Andy	4.1.76	8+17	2	0	0	8	Hull S.	1998
Smith, Richard	18.6.73	24	9	0	0	36	Bradford B.	1998
Thompson, Alex	29.7.74	35+2	2	0	0	8	Sheffield E.	1997
TOTALS								
29 players			156	155	8	942		

Representative appearances 1998

Dixon - Scotland (0+1); R. Smith - Ireland (2, 2t)

HULL SHARKS

Ground: The Boulevard (01482-327200)
First Season: 1895-96. Added Sharks to title at the start of 1997 League season.
Chairman: David Kirkwood
Honours: **Championship** Winners, 1919-20, 1920-21, 1935-36, 1955-56, 1957-58
Beaten finalists, 1956-57
Division One Champions, 1982-83
Division One (2nd league) Champions 1997
Division Two Champions, 1976-77, 1978-79
Challenge Cup Winners, 1913-14, 1981-82
Beaten finalists, 1907-08, 1908-09, 1909-10, 1921-22, 1922-23, 1958-59, 1959-60, 1979-80, 1982-83, 1984-85
Regal Trophy Winners, 1981-82
Beaten finalists, 1975-76, 1984-85
Premiership Winners, 1990-91
Beaten finalists, 1980-81, 1981-82, 1982-83, 1988-89
Divisional Premiership Beaten finalists, 1997
Yorkshire Cup Winners, 1923-24, 1969-70, 1982-83, 1983-84, 1984-85
Beaten finalists, 1912-13, 1914-15, 1920-21, 1927-28, 1938-39, 1946-47, 1953-54, 1954-55, 1955-56, 1959-60, 1967-68, 1986-87
Yorkshire League Winners, 1918-19, 1922-23, 1926-27, 1935-36
Charity Shield Beaten finalists, 1991-92
BBC2 Floodlit Trophy Winners, 1979-80

RECORDS

Match
Goals: 14 by Jim Kennedy v. Rochdale H., 7 Apr 1921
Geoff "Sammy" Lloyd v. Oldham, 10 Sep 1978
Tries: 7 by Clive Sullivan at Doncaster, 15 Apr 1968
Points: 36 by Jim Kennedy v. Keighley, 29 Jan 1921

Season
Goals: 170 by Geoff "Sammy" Lloyd, 1978-79
Tries: 52 by Jack Harrison, 1914-15
Points: 369 by Geoff "Sammy" Lloyd, 1978-79

Career
Goals: 687 by Joe Oliver, 1928-37 & 1943-45
Tries: 250 by Clive Sullivan, 1961-74 & 1981-85
Points: 1,842 by Joe Oliver, 1928-37 & 1943-45
Appearances: 501 by Edward Rogers, 1906-25
Highest score: 86-0 v. Elland, 1 Apr 1899
Highest against: 66-16 at Wigan, 23 Apr 1995
Attendance: 28,798 v. Leeds (RL Cup), 7 Mar 1936

COACHING REGISTER

● **Since 1974-75**

David Doyle-Davidson	May 74 - Dec 77
Arthur Bunting	Jan 78 - Dec 85
Kenny Foulkes	Dec 85 - May 86
Len Casey	June 86 - Mar 88
Tony Dean ⎫	
Keith Hepworth ⎭	Mar 88 - Apr 88
* Brian Smith	July 88 - Jan 91
* Noel Cleal	Sep 90 - Apr 92
Royce Simmons	May 92 - Apr 94
Tony Gordon	May 94 - Dec 94
Russ Walker/Phil Windley	Dec 94 - May 95
Phil Windley	May 95 - Nov 95
Phil Sigsworth	Jan 96 - July 97
Peter Walsh	July 97 -

* *Joint coaches Sep 90 - Jan 91.*

Brian Smith: Coach 1988-91.

GREAT BRITAIN REGISTER
(35 players)

Billy Batten	(1)	1921
Harold Bowman	(8)	1924-29
Frank Boylen	(1)	1908
Bob Coverdale	(4)	1954
Mick Crane	(1)	1982
Lee Crooks	(11+2)	1982-87
Andy Dannatt	(3)	1985-91
Gary Divorty	(2)	1985
Bill Drake	(1)	1962
Jim Drake	(1)	1960
Paul Eastwood	(13)	1990-92
Steve Evans	(2)	1982
Vince Farrar	(1)	1978
Dick Gemmell	(2)	1968-69
Emlyn Gwynne	(3)	1928-29
Tommy Harris	(25)	1954-60
Karl Harrison	(3)	1990
Mick Harrison	(7)	1967-73
Billy Holder	(1)	1907
Lee Jackson	(11)	1990-92
Mark Jones	(+1)	1992
Arthur Keegan	(9)	1966-69
Steve McNamara	(+2)	1992-93
Edgar Morgan	(2)	1921
Steve Norton	(9)	1978-82
Wayne Proctor	(+1)	1984
Paul Rose	(1)	1982
Garry Schofield	(15)	1984-87
Trevor Skerrett	(6)	1980-82
Billy Stone	(8)	1920-21
Clive Sullivan	(17)	1967-73
Bob Taylor	(2)	1921-26
Harry Taylor	(3)	1907
David Topliss	(1)	1982
Johnny Whiteley	(15)	1957-62

1998 SIGNINGS REGISTER

Signed	Player	Club From
13.1.98	Baildon, David	Workington T.
14.9.98	Balouchie, Faz	West Hull ARL
27.5.98	Barrow, Steve	Wigan W.
27.7.98	*Busby, Dean	St. Helens
—	Calland, Matt	Bradford B.
16.9.98	David, Kuki "Maea"	Illawarra (Aust.)
—	Harrison, Karl	Halifax B.S.
—	Holgate, Stephen	Wigan W.
25.3.98	Last, Andrew	Eureka ARL
22.3.98	Lee, Andy	York Acorn ARL
1.4.98	Lester, Gary	St. George (Aust.)
5.6.98	*Murdock, Craig	Wigan W.
13.2.98	Okesene, Hitro	Auckland W. (NZ)
12.9.98	Poucher, Craig	Isberg C. ARL
—	Purcell, Andrew	Illawarra (Aust.)
—	Roberts, Robert	Hunslet H.
24.2.98	Seru, Fili	Illawarra (Aust.)
18.1.98	Tomlinson, Glen	Bradford B.
2.4.98	Traynor, Christopher	Skirlaugh Bulls ARL

HULL SHARKS 1998 MATCH ANALYSIS

Date	Competition	H/A	Opponents	Rlt	Score	Tries	Goals	Attendance	Referee
15.2.98	CC(4)	A	Whitehaven W.	W	26-12	Baildon, Craven, Hunte, Johnson, Seru	Hallas (3)	–	–
1.3.98	CC(5)	H	Ellenborough R.	W	78-0	Hunte (5), R. Nolan (3), Hallas (2), Baildon, Campbell, Donohue, Prescott	Hallas (11)	3013	Morris
15.3.98	CC(6)	A	Salford R.	L	10-41	Booth, Seru	Hallas	–	–
5.4.98	SL	A	Sheffield E.	W	34-24	Prescott (2), Hallas, Hunte, Stephenson, Tomlinson	Hallas (5)	–	–
10.4.98	SL	H	London B.	W	6-4	Johnson	Hallas	6386	Presley
19.4.98	SL	A	Salford R.	L	4-12	Prescott	–	–	–
26.4.98	SL	H	Bradford B.	L	24-26	Campbell, Hepi, Hunte, Seru, Smith	Hallas (2)	9477	Campbell
10.5.98	SL	A	Castleford T.	L	18-31	Radford (2), Leatham, Stephenson	Hallas	–	–
17.5.98	SL	A	St. Helens	L	18-28	Baildon, Campbell, Prescott	Hallas (3)	–	–
25.5.98	SL	H	Warrington W.	L	28-32	Seru (2), Campbell, Prescott, Lester	Hallas (4)	5197	Presley
31.5.98	SL	H	Wigan W.	L	16-38	Campbell, Seru, Smith	Smith (2)	6908	R. Smith
5.6.98	SL	A	Halifax B.S.	L	16-30	Seru, Baildon	Smith (4)	–	–
14.6.98	SL	H	Leeds R.	W	22-10	Hallas, Hepi, Seru	Hallas (4, dg), Murdock (dg)	7189	R. Connolly
21.6.98	SL	A	Huddersfield G.	W	20-14	Murdock, Hepi, Schultz, Stephenson	Hallas (2)	–	–
28.6.98	SL	H	Sheffield E.	L	20-35	Craven, Hunte, Murdock	Hallas (2), Smith (2)	5020	J. Connolly
5.7.98	SL	A	London B.	L	6-38	Craven	Smith	–	–
24.7.98	SL	N1	Huddersfield G.	W	21-10	Campbell, Johnson, Lester	Prescott (4), Murdock (dg)	(4306)	Kirkpatrick
2.8.98	SL	H	Salford R.	W	32-0	Seru (2), Campbell, Johnson, Lester, Murdock	Prescott (3), Hallas	4593	J. Connolly
9.8.98	SL	A	Bradford B.	L	18-38	Johnson, Seru, Temu	Prescott (3)	–	–
16.8.98	SL	H	Castleford T.	W	18-6	Lester, Nolan, Prescott	Prescott (3)	5142	Kirkpatrick
23.8.98	SL	H	St. Helens	L	6-20	Booth	Prescott	5616	R. Smith
30.8.98	SL	A	Warrington W.	L	10-24	Baildon, Murdock	Prescott	–	–
6.9.98	SL	A	Wigan W.	L	6-58	Seru	Prescott	–	–
11.9.98	SL	H	Halifax B.S.	L	24-44	Hunte, Murdock, Prescott, Seru	Prescott (4)	3578	R. Smith
18.9.98	SL	A	Leeds R.	L	18-38	Hunte (2), Lester	Smith (3)	–	–
27.9.98	SL	H	Huddersfield G.	W	36-14	Lester (2), Campbell, Hunte, Murdock, Schultz, Smith	Hallas (4)	4031	Shaw

N1 at Gateshead

Alan Hunte: Made 24 appearances for Hull Sharks after signing from St. Helens.

HULL SHARKS 1998 PLAYERS' SUMMARY

	Date of birth	App	T	G	D	Pts	Previous club	Debut
Aston, Jon	5.6.76	0+1	0	0	0	0	Hull K.R.	1994-95
Baildon, David	26.1.71	17+1	5	0	0	20	Workington T.	1998
Barrow, Steve	8.12.75	1+1	0	0	0	0	Wigan W.	1998
Booth, Simon	9.12.71	15+3	2	0	0	8	St. Helens	1998
Busby, Dean	1.2.73	8+6	0	0	0	0	St. Helens	1998
Campbell, Logan	23.5.71	26	8	0	0	32	Workington T.	1997
Craven, Steve	9.4.72	16+5	3	0	0	12	Ryedale-York	1994-95
David, Maea	27.2.72	1	0	0	0	0	Illawarra (Aust.)	1998
Donohue, Jason	18.4.72	2	1	0	0	4	Bradford B.	1997
Gray, Kevin	10.12.75	0+1	0	0	0	0	Minehead ARL	1993-94
Hallas, Graeme	27.2.71	16+7	4	44	1	105	Halifax B.S.	1997
Hepi, Brad	11.2.68	16+1	3	0	0	12	Workington T.	1997
Hunte, Alan	11.7.70	24	13	0	0	52	St. Helens	1998
Ireland, Andy	6.12.71	11+9	0	0	0	0	Bradford B.	1997
Johnson, Mark	28.2.69	13+1	5	0	0	20	Workington T.	1997
King, Paul	28.6.79	0+1	0	0	0	0		1998
Leatham, Jim	10.10.74	5+13	1	0	0	4	Leeds R.	1997
Lester, Gary	15.5.72	22	7	0	0	28	St. George (Aust.)	1997
Murdock, Craig	24.10.73	15	6	0	2	26	Wigan W.	1998
Nolan, Rob	2.10.68	6+8	4	0	0	16	Hull Colts	1988-89
Okesene, Hitro	22.9.71	21+1	0	0	0	0	Auckland W. (NZ)	1998
Prescott, Steve	26.12.73	21	8	20	0	72	St. Helens	1998
Radford, Lee	26.3.79	0+9	2	0	0	8	Mysons ARL	1996
Schultz, Matthew	9.8.75	12+6	2	0	0	8	Leeds R.	1997
Seru, Fili	11.3.70	25	13	0	0	52	Illawarra (Aust.)	1998
Smith, Jamie	2.10.68	9+6	3	12	0	36	Workington T.	1998
Stephenson, David	6.10.72	12+7	3	0	0	12	Oldham B.	1998
Temu, Jason	17.4.72	15+2	1	0	0	4	Oldham B.	1998
Tomlinson, Glen	18.3.70	8	1	0	0	4	Bradford B.	1998
Wilson, Richard	5.2.75	1+12	0	0	0	0	Isberg ARL	1994-95
TOTALS								
30 players			95	76	3	535		

Representative appearances 1998

Busby - Emerging England (1); Campbell - Scotland (2, 1t); Prescott - Ireland (2)

HUNSLET HAWKS

Highest score: 82-0 v. Highfield, 21 Jan 1996
Highest against: 76-8 v. Halifax, 27 Aug 1972
Attendance: 24,700 v. Wigan (RL Cup),
15 Mar 1924 — at Parkside;
2,428 v. Hull K. R. (League),
30 June 1996 at South Leeds Stadium

Ground:	South Leeds Stadium (0113-2711675)
First Season:	1895-96. Disbanded at end of 1972-73. Re-formed as New Hunslet in 1973-74. Retitled Hunslet from start of 1979-80. Added Hawks to title in 1995-96.
Chairman:	Graham Liles
Honours:	**Championship** Winners, 1907-08, 1937-38

Beaten finalists, 1958-59
Division Two Champions, 1962-63, 1986-87
Division Two (3rd league) Champions, 1997
Challenge Cup Winners, 1907-08, 1933-34
Beaten finalists, 1898-99, 1964-65
Silk Cut Plate Beaten finalists 1997
Second Division Premiership Beaten finalists, 1986-87
Yorkshire Cup Winners, 1905-06, 1907-08, 1962-63
Beaten finalists, 1908-09, 1929-30, 1931-32, 1944-45, 1956-57, 1965-66
Yorkshire League Winners, 1897-98, 1907-08, 1931-32

RECORDS

Match
Goals: 12 by Billy Langton v. Keighley, 18 Aug 1959
Tries: 7 by George Dennis v. Bradford N., 20 Jan 1934
Points: 30 by Simon Wilson v. Highfield, 21 Jan 1996

Season
Goals: 181 by Billy Langton, 1958-59
Tries: 34 by Alan Snowden, 1956-57
Points: 380 by Billy Langton, 1958-59

Career
Goals: 1,044 by Billy Langton, 1955-66
Tries: 154 by Fred Williamson, 1943-55
Points: 2,202 by Billy Langton, 1955-66
Appearances: 569+10 by Geoff Gunney, 1951-73
572 by Jack Walkington, 1927-48

COACHING REGISTER

● **Since 1974-75**

Paul Daley	Apr 74 - Aug 78
Bill Ramsey	Aug 78 - Dec 79
Drew Broatch	Dec 79 - Apr 81
Paul Daley	Apr 81 - Nov 85
★ Peter Jarvis	Nov 85 - Apr 88
★ David Ward	July 86 - Apr 88
Nigel Stephenson	June 88 - Oct 88
Jack Austin ⎫	Oct 88 - Jan 89
John Wolford ⎭	
David Ward	Jan 89 - May 89
Graeme Jennings	Sep 89 - Apr 90
Paul Daley	May 90 - Dec 93
Steve Ferres	Jan 94 - Oct 96
David Plange	Nov 96 -

★ *Joint coaches from July 1986.*

GREAT BRITAIN REGISTER

(23 players)

Billy Batten	(9)	1907-11
Harry Beverley	(4)	1936-37
Alf Burnell	(3)	1951-54
Hector Crowther	(1)	1929
Jack Evans	(4)	1951-52
Ken Eyre	(1)	1965
Brian Gabbitas	(1)	1959
Geoff Gunney	(11)	1954-65
Dennis Hartley	(2)	1964
John Higson	(2)	1908
Dai Jenkins	(1)	1929
Albert Jenkinson	(2)	1911
Bill Jukes	(6)	1908-10
Bernard Prior	(1)	1966
Bill Ramsey	(7)	1965-66
Brian Shaw	(5)	1956-60
Geoff Shelton	(7)	1964-66
Fred Smith	(9)	1910-14
Sam Smith	(4)	1954
Cecil Thompson	(2)	1951
Les White	(7)	1932-33
Dicky Williams	(3)	1954
Harry Wilson	(3)	1907

1998 SIGNINGS REGISTER

Signed	Player	Club From
1.4.98	*Allen, Kieran	Wakefield T.
19.1.98	Barrow, Scott	—
4.8.97	Brown, Gary	Hull K.R.
6.1.98	Clarke, John	Oldham B.
5.6.98	*Conway, Billy	Wakefield T.
1.1.98	D'Arcy, Robert	Hull K.R.
1.6.98	Dobson, Nicky	Hunslet Parkside ARL
28.8.98	Dobson, Daniel	Hunslet Parkside ARL
23.2.98	Egan, James	—
—	Fatnowna, Abraham	London B.
—	Fletcher, Mike	Hull K.R.
29.4.98	Gittins, James	Dewsbury R.
12.5.98	Goddard, Richard	Castleford T.
19.6.98	*Gray, Kevin	Hull S.
28.8.98	Griffiths, Chris	Hunslet Parkside ARL
19.8.98	Hall, Lee	Oulton R. ARL
1.6.98	Henderson, Kelvin	Churwell ARL
14.7.98	Higgins, Robert "Iain"	London B.
—	Irwin, Shaun	Featherstone R.
—	Pachniuk, Richard	Rochdale H.
29.5.98	St. Hilaire, Lee	Castleford T.
19.1.98	Jessey, David	Oulton R. ARL
19.1.98	McCardle, Russell	Hull S.
3.6.98	Moore, Adam	East Leeds ARL
1.1.98	North, Christopher	Dewsbury R.
29.5.98	O'Connor, Daniel	Hunslet Parkside ARL
5.3.98	Parnell, Stephen	East Leeds ARL
30.3.98	Parry, David	Keighley C.
12.5.98	Phillips, Abraham	Batley B.
12.8.98	Poching, Willie	St. George (Aust.)
22.4.98	Roberts, Robert	Keighley C.
22.8.98	Skerrett, Ben	Hunslet Parkside ARL
26.1.98	Smales, Ian	Castleford T.
28.5.98	Tomlinson, Maxwell	Sandal RU
10.3.98	Walker, James	Bradford B.
23.1.98	Wilson, Rob	Hull K.R.
2.6.98	*Windley, Johan	Hull S.
19.8.98	Wykman, Ben	Oulton R. ARL

Ian Smales: 26 appearances after signing from Castleford Tigers in 1998.

HUNSLET HAWKS 1998 MATCH ANALYSIS

Date	Competition	H/A	Opponents	Rlt	Score	Tries	Goals	Attendance	Referee
1.2.98	CC(3)	H	Skirlaugh	W	44-12	Brown (2), Mansson (2), Tawhai (2), Ballot, Plange	Ellis (6)	830	Lowe
8.2.98	FD	A	Rochdale H.	W	36-12	Ballot, D'Arcy, Ellis, Mansson, North, Richards, Smales	Ellis (4)	–	–
15.2.98	CC(4)	A	Ellenborough R.	L	12-14	Butt, Smales	Ellis (2)	–	–
1.3.98	FD	H	Leigh C.	W	36-12	Wilson (2), Ellis, Plange, Richards, Smales	Ellis (6)	1280	Nicholson
8.3.98	FD	A	Widnes V.	L	26-32	Campbell, Clarke, Mansson, Smales, Ellis	Ellis (2), Smales	–	–
15.3.98	FD	A	Swinton L.	W	18-16	Coyle, D'Arcy, Plange	Mansson (3)	–	–
22.3.98	FD	H	Featherstone R.	W	34-12	Baker (2), Ellis, Filipo, North, Plange, Smales	Ellis (2), Plange	2020	Taberner
29.3.98	FD	A	Keighley C.	W	31-22	Plange (3), Coyle, Ellis	Ellis (5), Tawhai (dg)	–	–
5.4.98	FD	H	Whitehaven W.	W	35-4	Plange (2), Baker, D'Arcy, Ellis, Mansson	Ellis (5, dg)	1452	Shaw
10.4.98	FD	A	Dewsbury R.	D	14-14	D'Arcy, Mansson, Plange	Ellis	–	–
13.4.98	FD	H	Wakefield T.	L	4-15	–	Ellis (2)	2454	J. Connolly
19.4.98	FD	H	Hull K.R.	W	31-30	Baker (2), Ellis, Filipo, North	Ellis (5, dg)	2309	Gilmour
26.4.98	FD	H	Rochdale H.	W	47-6	Coyle (2), Thackray (2), Hayes, Manson, Plange, Tawhai	Ellis (7), Green (dg)	1402	Laughton
10.5.98	FD	A	Leigh C.	L	23-26	D'Arcy, Green, Ellis, Wilson	Ellis (3), Mansson (dg)	–	–
15.5.98	FD	H	Widnes V.	W	28-8	Baker (2), Ellis (2)	Ellis (5), Mansson	1554	Atkin
24.5.98	FD	H	Swinton L.	L	16-20	North, Wilson, Pryce	Ellis (2)	1752	Morris
31.5.98	FD	A	Featherstone R.	L	10-18	Baker, Tawhai	Ellis	–	–
3.6.98	FD	H	Keighley C.	W	14-8	Ellis, Wilson	Ellis (3)	2033	Nicholson
7.6.98	FD	A	Whitehaven W.	W	26-16	D'Arcy (2), Coyle, Windley	Ross (4), Ellis	–	–
14.6.98	FD	H	Dewsbury R.	L	2-24	–	Ross	1736	Bates
21.6.98	FD	A	Wakefield T.	L	22-36	Baker, Gray, Mansson, Thackray	Ellis (3)	–	–
24.6.98	FD	A	Hull K.R.	L	18-44	Baker (2), Ballot	Ross (3)	–	–
28.6.98	FD	A	Keighley C.	L	18-25	Baker, Goddard, St. Hilaire	Ross (3)	–	–
5.7.98	FD	H	Leigh C.	W	18-6	Gray, Mansson, Plange, Ross	Ross	1503	Oddy
12.7.98	FD	A	Rochdale H.	W	24-18	Clarke, Gray, Mansson, Tawhai	Ross (3), Tawhai (dg), Windley (dg)	–	–
15.7.98	FD	H	Whitehaven W.	W	37-18	Goddard (2), Higgins (2), Mansson, Plange, Tawhai	Ellis (4), Coyle (dg)	1021	McGregor
19.7.98	FD	A	Dewsbury R.	L	21-24	Tawhai (2), Goddard,	Ellis (4), Mansson (dg)	–	–
26.7.98	FD	H	Wakefield T.	L	12-20	Ross, Windley	Ross (2)	2006	Gilmour
2.8.98	FD	A	Swinton L.	W	27-16	Baker (2), Campbell, Coyle, Filipo	Ross (3), Goddard (dg)	–	–
7.8.98	FD	H	Widnes V.	W	41-10	Tawhai (2), Baker, Coyle, Filipo, Gray, Ross	Ross (6), Tawhai (dg)	1265	R. Connolly
14.8.98	FD	A	Featherstone R.	L	31-32	Baker (2), Thackray, Smales, Gray	Ross (4), Gray (1, dg)	–	–
23.8.98	FD	H	Hull K.R.	W	19-18	Baker, Mansson, North	Gray (3), Goddard (dg)	2356	Ganson

HUNSLET HAWKS 1998 PLAYERS' SUMMARY

	Date of birth	App	T	G	D	Pts	Previous club	Debut
Baker, Richard	26.1.75	24+3	18	0	0	72	East Leeds ARL	1995-96
Ballot, Andrew	27.5.71	5+9	3	0	0	12	Batley B.	1998
Brown, Gary	5.9.74	2	2	0	0	8	Hull K.R.	1997
Butt, Ikram	25.10.68	9+1	1	0	0	4	Huddersfield G.	1998
Campbell, Aaron	20.10.78	6+5	2	0	0	8	Hunslet Boys ARL	1997
Clarke, John	3.3.74	4	2	0	0	8	Oldham	1998
Coult, Mick	14.10.69	9+5	0	0	0	0	Doncaster D.	1997
Coyle, Michael	5.3.71	15+17	7	0	1	29	Middleton ARL	1990-91
D'Arcy, Rob	13.10.70	17+2	7	0	0	28	Hull K.R.	1998
Egan, James	12.11.75	0+1	0	0	0	0		1998
Ellis, St. John	3.10.64	24+1	11	73	2	192	Keighley C.	1997
Filipo, Lafaele	24.10.65	12+10	4	0	0	16	Keighley C.	1997
Goddard, Richard	28.4.74	13+1	4	0	2	18	Castleford T.	1998
Gray, Kevin	10.12.75	12	5	4	1	29	Hull S.	1998
Green, Matthew	25.8.78	14	1	0	1	5	Dudley Hill ARL	1997
Hayes, Richard	21.2.70	25+3	1	0	0	4	York	1998
Higgins, Robert "Iain"	14.9.76	1	2	0	0	8	London B.	1998
Luxford, Martin	5.3.77	1	0	0	0	0	Wakefield T.	1998
Mansson, Paul	13.3.72	29+3	12	4	2	58	Salford R.	1997
North, Chris	6.1.76	11+1	5	0	0	20	Dewsbury R.	1998
Pechey, Mike	16.10.68	2	0	0	0	0	Bedford RU	1997
Plange, David	24.7.65	15+7	13	1	0	54	Hull K.R.	1996
Poching, Willie	30.8.73	1+1	0	0	0	0	St. George (Aust.)	1998
Pryce, Steve	12.5.69	20+8	1	0	0	4	Ryedale-York	1994-95
Richards, Craig	27.1.70	18+8	2	0	0	8	Oldham B.	1998
Roberts, Robert	21.6.78	4+4	0	0	0	0	Keighley C.	1998
Ross, Chris	23.8.78	12+4	3	30	0	72	Hunslet Boys ARL	1995-96
Smales, Ian	26.9.68	22+4	6	1	0	26	Castleford T.	1998
Southernwood, Graham	5.11.71	2	0	0	0	0	Featherstone R.	1996
St. Hilaire, Lee	15.2.67	10+1	1	0	0	4	Castleford T.	1998
Tawhai, Latham	23.8.71	30+1	10	0	3	43	Keighley C.	1997
Thackray, Jamie	30.9.79	16+9	4	0	0	16	Oulton ARL	1997
Walker, James	22.11.73	1+6	0	0	0	0	West Hull ARL	1995-96
Wilson, Rob	31.8.72	20+2	5	0	0	20	Hull K.R.	1998
Windley, Johan	20.8.75	10+3	2	0	1	9	Hull S.	1998
TOTALS								
35 players			134	113	13	775		

KEIGHLEY COUGARS

Ground: Cougar Park (01535-213111)
First Season: 1901-02. Added Cougars to title at start of 1991-92.
Chairman: Howard Carter
Honours: **Division Two** Champions, 1902-03, 1994-95
                 Division Three Champions, 1992-93
                 Challenge Cup Beaten finalists, 1936-37
                 Second Division Premiership Winners, 1994-95
                 Beaten finalists, 1996
                 Yorkshire Cup Beaten finalists, 1943-44, 1951-52

RECORDS

Match
Goals: 15 by John Wasyliw v. Nottingham C., 1 Nov 1992
Tries: 6 by Jason Critchley v. Widnes, 18 Aug 1996
Points: 36 by John Wasyliw v. Nottingham C., 31 Oct 1993

Season
Goals: 187 by John Wasyliw, 1992-93
Tries: 45 by Nick Pinkney, 1994-95
Points: 490 by John Wasyliw, 1992-93

Career
Goals: 967 by Brian Jefferson, 1965-77
Tries: 155 by Sam Stacey, 1904-20
Points: 2,116 by Brian Jefferson, 1965-77
Appearances: 372 by Hartley Tempest, 1902-15
                   David McGoun, 1925-38
Highest score: 104-4 v. Highfield (away game at Rochdale), 23 Apr 1995
Highest against: 92-2 at Leigh, 30 Apr 1986
Attendance: 14,500 v. Halifax (RL Cup), 3 Mar 1951

COACHING REGISTER

● **Since 1974-75**

Alan Kellett	Jan 73 - May 75
Roy Sabine	Aug 75 - Oct 77
Barry Seabourne	Nov 77 - Mar 79
Albert Fearnley (Mgr)	Apr 79 - Aug 79
Alan Kellett	Apr 79 - Apr 80
Albert Fearnley	May 80 - Feb 81
Bakary Diabira	Feb 81 - Sep 82
Lee Greenwood	Sep 82 - Oct 83
Geoff Peggs	Nov 83 - Sep 85
Peter Roe	Sep 85 - July 86
Colin Dixon	July 86 - June 89
Les Coulter	July 89 - Apr 90
Tony Fisher	June 90 - Sep 91
Peter Roe	Sep 91 - Apr 94
Phil Larder	May 94 - Sep 96
Daryl Powell	Sep 96 - July 97
John Kain	July 97 - Mar 98
Lee Crooks	Mar 98 -

GREAT BRITAIN REGISTER

(2 players)

Terry Hollindrake	(1)	1955
Daryl Powell	(4+1)	1996

1998 SIGNINGS REGISTER

Signed	Player	Club From
—	Agar, Richard	Dewsbury R.
16.4.98	Anderson, Grant	Castleford T.
21.7.98	Antonik, Nathan	St. George (Aust.)
19.5.98	Bailey, Robert	Cougar Cubs ARL
23.7.98	*Benn, Jamie	Castleford T.
27.5.98	Calvert, Stuart	Clayton ARL
12.2.98	Campbell, Mark	Leeds R.
8.5.98	*Crouthers, Kevin	Bradford B.
17.6.98	*Dononue, Jason	Hull S.
26.5.98	Fogerty, Adam	Warrington W.
26.1.98	Foster, Matthew	Leeds R.
14.1.98	Guest, Daniel	Oldham
26.5.98	Gwilliam, Jonathan	Silsden ARL
14.4.98	Hansen, Liuaki "Lee"	Wigan W.
26.1.98	Irving, Simon	Leeds R.
16.2.98	Jones, David	—
3.4.98	Laurence, Jason	Hull S.
19.2.98	Lee, Jason	Dudley Hill ARL
6.4.98	Longo, David	Swinton L.
15.4.98	Mann, George	Leeds R.
20.1.98	McDonald, Brock	Freemantle (Aust.)
26.1.98	Roberts, Robert	Leeds R.
—	Schick, Andrew	Castleford T.

KEIGHLEY COUGARS 1998 MATCH ANALYSIS

Date	Com-petition	H/A	Opponents	Rlt	Score	Tries	Goals	Atten-dance	Referee
1.2.98	CC(3)	H	Saddleworth R.	W	66-16	Ramshaw (3), McDonald (2), Foster, Guest, Larder, Owen, Stephenson, Johnson	Robinson (11)	3116	Taberner
8.2.98	FD	A	Swinton L.	L	16-41	Billy (2), Irving	Robinson (2)	–	–
15.2.98	CC(4)	H	Wigan W.	L	0-76	–	–	4700	Presley
22.2.98	FD	H	Wakefield T.	L	10-14	Owen, Billy	Robinson	2529	Nicholson
3.3.98	FD	A	Rochdale H.	L	16-20	Robinson, McDonald,	Robinson (3), Lee	–	–
8.3.98	FD	A	Dewsbury R.	L	12-50	Billy, Foster, Larder	–	–	–
15.3.98	FD	H	Leigh C.	W	32-16	Foster, Kirk, Lee, David Smith, Robinson, Ramshaw	Robinson (4)	2191	Ganson
22.3.98	FD	A	Whitehaven W.	L	16-46	Irving, Parker, Ramshaw	Irving (2)	–	–
29.3.98	FD	H	Hunslet H.	L	22-31	Lee, Roberts, Sapatu	Irving (5)	2071	Kirkpatrick
10.4.98	FD	H	Hull K.R.	L	12-20	Lee, Wray	Irving (2)	2298	Nicholson
13.4.98	FD	A	Featherstone R.	L	2-44	–	Roberts	–	–
19.4.98	FD	H	Widnes V.	W	25-22	Foster, Laurence, Robinson, Sapatu	Irving (4), Longo (dg)	2363	Taberner
26.4.98	FD	H	Swinton L.	W	20-18	Foster, Larder, Lee, Robinson	Robinson (2)	2083	Morris
6.5.98	FD	A	Wakefield T.	L	0-18	–	–	–	–
10.5.98	FD	H	Rochdale H.	W	50-4	Foster (2), Lee (2), Campbell, Laurence, McDonald, Wray, Ramshaw	Lee (7)	2013	R. Connolly
17.5.98	FD	H	Dewsbury R.	W	22-20	Laurence (2), Hansen, Ramshaw	Lee (3)	2285	Lee
24.5.98	FD	A	Leigh C.	W	30-18	Larder, McDonald, Ramshaw, Robinson, Summerill	Lee (5)	–	–
31.5.98	FD	H	Whitehaven W.	W	22-18	Wray (2), Lee, Longo, Robinson	Lee	2169	Laughton
3.6.98	FD	A	Hunslet H.	L	8-14	Larder	Lee (2)	–	–
14.6.98	FD	A	Hull K.R.	L	16-28	Anderson, Foster, McDonald	Lee (2)	–	–
19.6.98	FD	H	Featherstone R.	W	15-10	Laurence, K. Smith, Tyrer	Lee, Longo (dg)	2069	Cummins
24.6.98	FD	A	Widnes V.	L	22-37	Longo (2), Sapatu, McDonald	Tyrer (2), Lee	–	–
28.6.98	FD	H	Hunslet H.	W	25-18	Donohue (2), K. Smith (2), McDonald	Longo (2), Tyrer (dg)	2016	Bates
12.7.98	FD	A	Leigh C.	W	26-18	Donohue (2), Hansen, Larder, McDonald	Lee (3)	–	–
15.7.98	FD	H	Rochdale H.	L	18-20	Lee, Longo, Walsh, Wray	Lee	1756	Lowe
19.7.98	FD	A	Whitehaven W.	W	25-14	Laurence (2), McDonald, Sapatu	Benn (4, dg)	–	–
26.7.98	FD	H	Dewsbury R.	W	26-10	Benn, Larder, Lee	Benn (7)	2028	Nicholson
2.8.98	FD	A	Wakefield T.	L	16-56	Lee (2), Laurence	Benn (2)	–	–
7.8.98	FD	H	Swinton L.	D	18-18	Foster, Laurence, Longo	Benn (3)	1842	Shaw
16.8.98	FD	A	Widnes V.	W	30-6	Lee (3), Laurence, Ramshaw	Benn (5)	–	–
21.8.98	FD	H	Featherstone R.	L	18-20	Lee (2), Laurence, McDonald	Benn	2038	Lee
30.8.98	FD	A	Hull K.R.	W	17-6	Antonik (2), McDonald	Antonik (2), Ramshaw (dg)	–	–

SIGNINGS (Contd)

16.2.98	Sapatu, Fred	Western Reds (Aust.)
27.3.98	*Simpson, Joseph	Bradford B.
3.6.98	Smits, Alex	Tonneins XIII (Fr.)
16.1.98	Summerill, Darren	Sheffield E.
7.5.98	Tonks, Ian	Castleford T.
28.5.98	Tyrer, Christian	Bath RU
5.2.98	Walker, John	Hunslet H.
30.5.98	Wilson, Matthew	Stanningley ARL
—	Wood, Martin	Sheffield E.

KEIGHLEY COUGARS 1998 PLAYERS' SUMMARY

	Date of birth	App	T	G	D	Pts	Previous club	Debut
Anderson, Grant	21.2.69	2+3	1	0	0	4	Castleford T.	1998
Antonik, Nathan	29.9.75	3+1	2	2	0	12	St. George (Aust.)	1998
Benn, Jamie	4.5.77	6	1	22	1	49	Castleford T.	1998
Billy, Marlon	22.11.73	8+1	4	0	0	16		1996
Cain, Alex	2.9.73	8+5	0	0	0	0	Sheffield E.	1997
Calvert, Stuart	14.12.79	0+1	0	0	0	0	Clayton ARL	1998
Campbell, Mark	19.10.78	16+1	1	0	0	4	Leeds R.	1998
Campbell, Steve	22.2.80	9+12	0	0	0	0	East Leeds ARL	1997
Cochrane, Gareth	18.9.74	0+3	0	0	0	0	Hunslet H.	1998
Crouthers, Kevin	3.1.76	3+2	0	0	0	0	Bradford B.	1998
Donohue, Jason	18.4.72	8	4	0	0	16	Hull S.	1998
Edwards, John	7.8.67	2+2	0	0	0	0	Chequerfield R. ARL	1997
Fogerty, Adam	6.3.69	4+2	0	0	0	0	Warrington W.	1998
Foster, Matthew	10.6.76	22+5	9	0	0	36	Doncaster	1995-96
Guest, Danny	20.4.77	1	1	0	0	4	Oldham B.	1998
Gwilliam, Jon	18.10.77	1	0	0	0	0	Silsden ARL	1996
Hansen, Liuaki "Lee"	23.7.68	20	2	0	0	8	Wigan W.	1998
Irving, Simon	22.3.67	11	2	13	0	34	Leeds	1994-95
Johnson, Kirk		1	1	0	0	4		1998
Julian, Alan	23.2.70	5+2	0	0	0	0	Leeds R.	1997
Kirk, Kristofer	16.9.78	2+1	1	0	0	4	East Leeds ARL	1998
Larder, David	5.6.76	24	7	0	0	28	Sheffield E.	1994-95
Laurence, Jason	23.1.70	23	11	0	0	44	Hull S.	1998
Lee, Jason	16.1.71	26+1	16	27	0	118	Dudley Hill ARL	1998
Longo, Davide	9.12.75	12+7	5	2	2	26	Swinton L.	1998
Mann, George	31.7.65	2+2	0	0	0	0	Warrington W.	1998
McDonald, Brock	14.8.76	27	12	0	0	48	Freemantle (Aust.)	1998
Owen, Paul	15.8.78	9+6	2	0	0	8	East Leeds ARL	1997
Parker, Chris		0+1	1	0	0	4		1998
Ramshaw, Jason	23.7.69	23+2	9	0	1	37	Halifax	1992-93
Rich, Pat	25.6.78	0+2	0	0	0	0	Gateshead ARL	1997
Roberts, Robert	21.6.78	5+2	1	1	0	6	East Leeds ARL	1995-96
Robinson, Chris	2.9.70	23+3	6	23	0	70	Halifax	1994-95
Sapatu, Fred	17.3.70	24+3	4	0	0	16	Perth Reds (Aust.)	1998
Senior, Andy	31.8.75	3+1	0	0	0	0	Keighley Academy	1994-95
Shackleton, Guy	9.9.77	2+2	0	0	0	0	East Leeds ARL	1998
Simpson, Joe	11.1.78	1+4	0	0	0	0	Bradford B.	1998
Smith, David		0+1	1	0	0	4		1998
Smith, Duncan		1	0	0	0	0	(Aust.)	1998
Smith, Karl	28.5.77	7+4	3	0	0	12		1997
Smits, Alex	5.8.74	1+6	0	0	0	0	Tonneins XIII (France)	1998
Stephenson, Phil	17.6.72	17+7	1	0	0	4	Clayton ARL	1990-91
Summerill, Darren	26.4.73	13+13	1	0	0	4	Sheffield E.	1998
Tonks, Ian	13.2.76	1+1	0	0	0	0	Castleford T.	1998
Tyrer, Christian	19.12.73	15+1	1	2	1	9	Bath RU	1998
Walsh, Peter	22.9.68	3+4	1	0	0	4	York	1998
Wray, Simon	19.5.70	22+2	5	0	0	20	Morley RU	1994-95
TOTALS								
47 players			116	92	5	653		

LANCASHIRE LYNX

Ground: Deepdale, Preston (01772-902020) Moved to Victory Park, Chorley, for 1999.

First Season: 1989-90 as Chorley. Became Chorley Borough in 1991-92. Not to be confused with the Chorley Borough who succeeded Springfield/Blackpool Borough in 1988-89. Demoted to the National Conference League for 1993-94 and regained senior status in 1995-96 when they became Chorley Chieftains. Dropped Chieftains from title at start of 1996 League season. Re-titled Lancashire Lynx for start of 1997 season after brief non-playing spell as Central Lancashire.

Chairman: Jeffrey Mallinson

Honours: **Division Two (3rd league)** Champions 1998
Treize Tournoi Beaten finalists 1998

RECORDS

Not including period in National Conference League

Match

Goals: 10 by Mike Smith v. Nottingham C., 1 Oct 1995
Phil Jones v. Workington T. 30 Aug 1998

Tries: 4 by Martin Holden v. Nottingham C., 1 Oct 1995
Neil Parsley v. Bramley, 9 Mar 1997
David "Doc" Murray at St. Esteve 3 Oct 1998

Points: 24 by Mike Smith v. Nottingham C., 1 Oct 1995
Phil Jones v. Workington T. 30 Aug 1998

Season

Goals: 101 by Phil Jones, 1998
Tries: 29 by Ray Waring, 1997
Points 254 by Phil Jones, 1998

Career

Goals: 288 by Mike Smith, 1989-96
Tries: 39 by Ray Waring, 1996-98
Points: 599 by Mike Smith, 1989-96
Appearances: 156+30 Carl Briscoe, 1989-98
Highest score: 92-0 v. Nottingham C., 1 Oct 1995
Highest against: 92-10 v. Hull K.R., 21 Apr 1996
Attendance: 1,079 v. Batley B. (League), 6 Sep 1998 — at Deepdale
5,026 v. Wigan (Lancs Cup), 15 Sep 1989 — at Leigh

COACHING REGISTER

Stan Gittins	June 89 - Apr 90
Bob Eccles	May 90 - Sep 91
John Taylor	Sep 91 - Jan 93
Carl Briscoe	Jan 93 - May 93
Bob Eccles	Aug 95 - Feb 96
Kevin Tamati	Feb 96 - Oct 97*
Steve Hampson	Oct 97 -*

Hampson appointed coach with Tamati remaining as manager until his departure in September 1998.

1998 SIGNINGS REGISTER

Signed	Player	Club From
15.1.98	Abram, Darren	Oldham B.
21.10.98	Bisping, Konrad	Army
26.6.98	Campbell, Craig	Blackpool Scorp. ARL
15.1.98	Cooksley, Jayson (Pekepo)	Hawkes Bay Unicorns (NZ)
—	Flanagan, Neil	Oldham
22.7.98	Jones, David	Rochdale H.
18.1.98	Mawdsley, Neil	Prescot P.
14.5.98	Murray, David "Doc"	Warrington W.
13.4.98	Prest, Lee	Wigan W.
2.4.98	Viller, Jason	Widnes V.
—	White, Kyle	Widnes V.

Darren Abram: 23 appearances after signing from Oldham in 1998.

LANCASHIRE LYNX 1998 MATCH ANALYSIS

Date	Competition	H/A	Opponents	Rlt	Score	Tries	Goals	Attendance	Referee
1.2.98	CC(3)	H	West Hull	W	46-0	P. Jones (2), Kelly (2), Gee, Abram, Byrne, Finney, C. Briscoe	Allday (5)	488	Bates
15.2.98	CC(4)	H	Dewsbury R.	D	28-28	Gee (2), Abram, Parsley, Taylor	Allday (3), Ruane	756	Taberner
18.2.98	CC(4) Replay	A	Dewsbury R.	L	14-31	Parsley, Pekepo, Ruane	Ruane	–	–
13.4.98	SD	H	Barrow B.R.	D	20-20	Parsley (2), Kelly	P. Jones (4)	721	Carter
19.4.98	SD	H	Doncaster D.	W	40-6	Kelly (2), Parsley (2), Donno, Ruane, Solomon, Taylor	P. Jones (4)	750	Bates
29.4.98	SD	A	Bramley	W	19-14	P. Jones, Pekepo, Solomon	P. Jones (3), Ruane (dg)	–	–
10.5.98	SD	H	York	L	12-25	P. Jones, Kelly	P. Jones (2)	853	McGregor
17.5.98	SD	A	Workington T.	W	40-6	Murray (2), Ashcroft, Kelly, Fairhurst, Pekepo, Solomon	P. Jones (6)	–	–
24.5.98	SD	A	Batley B.	W	17-16	Ashcroft, P. Jones	P. Jones (3), Ruane (3dg)	–	–
31.5.98	SD/RR	H1	Oldham	D	18-18	Ashcroft, P. Jones, Parsley	P. Jones (3)	1351	Cornish
7.6.98	SD/RR	A	Barrow B.R.	W	22-12	Abram (2), Parsley	P. Jones (4), Donno (dg), Kelly (dg)	–	–
14.6.98	SD/RR	A	Workington T.	W	26-25	Parsley (2), C. Briscoe, Donno, Solomon	P. Jones (3)	–	–
19.6.98	SD/RR	A	Oldham	L	20-25	Byrne (2), Parsley	P. Jones (4)	–	–
28.6.98	SD/RR	H	Workington T.	W	48-12	Byrne (2), Abram, Ashcroft, Donno, P. Jones, Parsley, Pekepo, Prest	P. Jones (6)	647	I. Smith
5.7.98	SD/RR	H1	Barrow B.R.	W	32-14	Abram, Kelly, Parsley, Ruane, Waring	P. Jones (6)	339	Laughton
26.7.98	SD	H1	Oldham	W	32-16	Gee, P. Jones, Kelly, Murray, David Jones, Solomon	P. Jones (4)	733	McGregor
2.8.98	SD	A	Barrow B.R.	W	21-12	P. Jones (2), Byrne	P. Jones (4), Ruane (dg)	–	–
9.9.98	SD	A	Doncaster D.	W	48-2	Gee (3), P. Jones (2), Murray (2), Kelly, Mawdsley	P. Jones (6)	–	–
16.8.98	SD	H	Bramley	L	22-23	Byrne, Gee, Murray	P. Jones (5)	431	Gilmour
23.8.98	SD	A	York	L	20-21	C. Briscoe, Donno, Ruane	P. Jones (4)	–	–
26.8.98	SD	A	Oldham	W	18-16	Murray, Donno, Ashcroft	P. Jones (3)	–	–
30.8.98	SD	H	Workington T.	W	64-25	Abram (2), Gee (2), David Jones (2), P. Jones, Kelly, Murray, Walsh, Ashcroft	P. Jones (10)	530	McGregor
6.9.98	SD	H	Batley B.	L	22-31	Abram (3), Donno	P. Jones (3)	1079	Bates
3.10.98	TT	A	St. Esteve	W	40-26	Murray (4), Walsh, Mawdsley, David Jones	P. Jones (6)	–	–
11.10.98	TT	H1	Villeneuve	W	28-24	Donno, Gee, Kelly, Parsley, Taylor	P. Jones (4)	370	Alba (Fr)
17.10.98	TT	A	Villeneueve	L	0-39	–	–	–	–
25.10.98	TT	H1	St. Esteve	W	26-18	Gee (2), Parsley, Campbell, Murray	P. Jones (3)	247	Alba (Fr)
1.11.98	TTF	N1	Villeneuve	L	10-16	Taylor, David Jones	P. Jones	(10,283)	G. Shaw

H1 at Preston Grasshoppers RU; N1 at Toulouse

LANCASHIRE LYNX 1998 PLAYERS' SUMMARY

	Date of birth	App	T	G	D	Pts	Previous club	Debut
Abram, Darren	27.9.67	23	11	0	0	44	Oldham B.	1998
Allday, Neil	27.9.75	3	0	8	0	16	Widnes	1996
Ashcroft, Steve	29.12.69	14+3	6	0	0	24	Barrow B.	1998
Briscoe, Carl	22.2.62	16+10	3	0	0	12	Chorley B.	1989-90
Briscoe, Neil	17.7.67	0+3	0	0	0	0	Ashton Eagles ARL	1995-96
Byrne, Steve	12.1.71	17+4	7	0	0	28	Huddersfield YMCA	1997
Campbell, Craig	4.1.77	5+2	1	0	0	4	Blackpool Scorp. ARL	1998
Charnley, Steve		0+2	0	0	0	0	Lancs. L. Acad.	1998
Donno, John	1.10.74	19+6	7	0	1	29	Widnes V.	1997
Fairhurst, Craig	9.12.70	6+2	1	0	0	4	Wigan St. Judes ARL	1996
Finney, Milton	26.10.67	8	1	0	0	4	Wigan St. Judes ARL	1996
Gee, Steve	15.4.72	17+3	13	0	0	52	Thatto Heath ARL	1996
Jones, Danny	23.10.77	0+2	0	0	0	0	Wigan St. Judes ARL	1997
Jones, David	7.12.68	13	5	0	0	20	Rochdale H.	1998
Jones, Phil	30.9.77	28	13	101	0	254	Hindley ARL	1997
Kelly, Chris	29.8.73	24+1	12	0	1	49	Widnes V.	1997
Mawdsley, Neil	28.7.72	7+15	2	0	0	8	Prescot P.	1998
McLoughlin, Robert	24.10.75	3+3	0	0	0	0	Hindley ARL	1996
Murray, David "Doc"	10.8.72	19+1	13	0	0	52	Wigan W.	1998
Norton, Paul	29.11.72	5+17	0	0	0	0	Wigan St. Judes ARL	1996
Parsley, Neil	18.4.74	23	15	0	0	60	Hoylake RU	1996
Pekepo, Jayson (Cooksley)	24.4.70	17+4	4	0	0	16	Hawkes Bay U. (NZ)	1998
Prest, Lee	14.7.76	15+9	1	0	0	4	Wigan W.	1998
Ruane, Andy	6.9.62	27	4	2	5	25	Barrow	1995-96
Smith, Simon	23.7.74	9+10	0	0	0	0	Wigan W.	1997
Solomon, Pehi James	17.8.76	24+3	5	0	0	20	Wellington Dukes (NZ)	1997
Taylor, Steve	30.4.74	14+2	4	0	0	16	Wigan	1996
Viller, Jason	29.10.72	0+1	0	0	0	0	Barrow B.R.	1998
Walsh, Joe	8.1.68	5+8	2	0	0	8	Salford	1992-93
Waring, Ray	6.1.74	3	1	0	0	4	Warrington	1996
TOTALS								
30 players			131	111	7	753		

Representative appearances 1998
Solomon - Scotland (2)

LEEDS RHINOS

Ground: Headingley (0113-278-6181)
First Season: 1895-96. Added Rhinos to title for start of 1997 season.
Chairman: Paul Caddick
Honours: **Championship** Winners, 1960-61, 1968-69, 1971-72
Beaten finalists, 1914-15, 1928-29, 1929-30, 1930-31, 1937-38, 1969-70, 1972-73
Super League Grand Final Beaten finalists 1998
League Leaders Trophy Winners, 1966-67, 1967-68, 1968-69, 1969-70, 1971-72
Challenge Cup Winners, 1909-10, 1922-23, 1931-32, 1935-36, 1940-41, 1941-42, 1956-57, 1967-68, 1976-77, 1977-78
Beaten finalists, 1942-43, 1946-47, 1970-71, 1971-72, 1993-94, 1994-95
Regal Trophy Winners, 1972-73, 1983-84
Beaten finalists, 1982-83, 1987-88, 1991-92
Premiership Winners, 1974-75, 1978-79
Beaten finalists, 1994-95
Yorkshire Cup Winners, 1921-22, 1928-29, 1930-31, 1932-33, 1934-35, 1935-36, 1937-38, 1958-59, 1968-69, 1970-71, 1972-73, 1973-74, 1975-76, 1976-77, 1979-80, 1980-81, 1988-89
Beaten finalists, 1919-20, 1947-48, 1961-62, 1964-65
Yorkshire League Winners, 1901-02, 1927-28, 1930-31, 1933-34, 1934-35, 1936-37, 1937-38, 1950-51, 1954-55, 1956-57, 1960-61, 1966-67, 1967-68, 1968-69, 1969-70
BBC2 Floodlit Trophy Winners, 1970-71
Charity Shield Beaten finalists, 1995-96

RECORDS

Match
Goals: 13 by Lewis Jones v. Blackpool B., 19 Aug 1957
Tries: 8 by Fred Webster v. Coventry, 12 Apr 1913
Eric Harris v. Bradford N., 14 Sep 1931
Points: 31 by Lewis Jones v. Bradford N., 22 Aug 1956

Season
Goals: 166 by Lewis Jones, 1956-57
Tries: 63 by Eric Harris, 1935-36
Points: 431 by Lewis Jones, 1956-57

Career
Goals: 1,244 by Lewis Jones, 1952-64
Tries: 391 by Eric Harris, 1930-39
Points: 2,920 by Lewis Jones, 1952-64
Appearances: 608+18 by John Holmes, 1968-89
Highest score: 102-0 v. Coventry, 12 Apr 1913
Highest against: 74-6 at Wigan, 10 May 1992
Attendance: 40,175 v. Bradford N. (League), 21 May 1947

COACHING REGISTER

● **Since 1974-75**

Roy Francis	June 74 - May 75
Syd Hynes	June 75 - Apr 81
Robin Dewhurst	June 81 - Oct 83
Maurice Bamford	Nov 83 - Feb 85
Malcolm Clift	Feb 85 - May 85
Peter Fox	May 85 - Dec 86
Maurice Bamford	Dec 86 - Apr 88
Malcolm Reilly	Aug 88 - Sep 89
David Ward	Sep 89 - May 91
Doug Laughton	May 91 - Sept 95
Dean Bell	Sep 95 - Oct 97
Graham Murray	Dec 97 -

GREAT BRITAIN REGISTER

(79 players)

Les Adams	(1)	1932
John Atkinson	(26)	1968-80
Jim Bacon	(11)	1920-26
Ray Batten	(3)	1969-73
John Bentley	(1)	1992
Jim Birch	(1)	1907
Stan Brogden	(7)	1936-37
Jim Brough	(5)	1928-36
Gordon Brown	(6)	1954-55

83

Mick Clark	(5)	1968
Terry Clawson	(3)	1972
David Creasser	(2+2)	1985-88
Lee Crooks	(1)	1989
Francis Cummins	(2)	1998
Willie Davies	(2)	1914
Kevin Dick	(2)	1980
Roy Dickinson	(2)	1985
Paul Dixon	(8+1)	1990-92
Les Dyl	(11)	1974-82
Richard Eyres	(+2)	1993
Tony Fisher	(3)	1970-71
Darren Fleary	(1+1)	1998
Phil Ford	(5)	1989
Dick Gemmell	(1)	1964
Carl Gibson	(10)	1990-91
Bobbie Goulding	(1)	1992
Jeff Grayshon	(2)	1985
Bob Haigh	(3+1)	1970-71
Derek Hallas	(2)	1961
Ellery Hanley	(2)	1992-93
Iestyn Harris	(1+1)	1998
Fred Harrison	(3)	1911
David Heron	(1+1)	1982
John Holmes	(14+6)	1971-82
Syd Hynes	(12+1)	1970-73
Billy Jarman	(2)	1914
David Jeanes	(3)	1972
Dai Jenkins	(1)	1947
Lewis Jones	(15)	1954-57
Ken Jubb	(2)	1937
John Lowe	(1)	1932
Paul Medley	(3+1)	1987-88
Steve Molloy	(1)	1993
Adrian Morley	(2+3)	1996-97
Terry Newton	(1)	1998
Ike Owens	(4)	1946
Steve Pitchford	(4)	1977
Harry Poole	(2)	1966
Roy Powell	(13+6)	1985-91
Dai Prosser	(1)	1937
Keith Rayne	(4)	1984
Kevin Rayne	(1)	1986
Bev Risman	(5)	1968
Don Robinson	(5)	1956-60
David Rose	(4)	1954
Garry Schofield	(29+2)	1988-94
Barry Seabourne	(1)	1970
Brian Shaw	(1)	1961
Mick Shoebottom	(10+2)	1968-71
Barry Simms	(1)	1962

Alan Smith	(10)	1970-73
Stanley Smith	(10)	1929-33
David Stephenson	(4+1)	1988
Jeff Stevenson	(15)	1955-58
Squire Stockwell	(3)	1920-21
Alan Tait	(1+4)	1992-93
Abe Terry	(1)	1962
Arthur "Ginger" Thomas	(4)	1926-29
Phil Thomas	(1)	1907
Joe Thompson	(12)	1924-32
Andrew Turnbull	(1)	1951
Hugh Waddell	(1)	1989
Billy Ward	(1)	1910
David Ward	(12)	1977-82
Fred Webster	(3)	1910
Dicky Williams	(9)	1948-51
Harry Woods	(1)	1937
Geoff Wriglesworth	(5)	1965-66
Frank Young	(1)	1908

Ray Batten: Three Test appearances.

1998 SIGNINGS REGISTER

Signed	Player	Club From
13.5.98	Cantillon, Philip	Bramley
23.10.98	Cook, Daniel	Milford ARL
19.1.98	Godden, Bradley	Hunter M. (Aust.)
8.6.98	Golden, Marvin	Bramley
21.9.98	Gornall, Arron	Castleford P. ARL
—	Jackson, Lee	Newcastle (Aust.)
—	Moore, Richard	Keighley C.
18.6.98	Orriss, Rhys	Oldham B.
—	Pratt, Karl	Featherstone R.
30.7.98	Rivett, Leroy	Bramley

LEIGH CENTURIONS 1998 MATCH ANALYSIS

Date	Competition	H/A	Opponents	Rlt	Score	Tries	Goals	Attendance	Referee
1.2.98	CC(3)	H	Hunslet W.	W	44-4	Liku (2), Burrows, Street, Hilton, Ingram, Jenkins, Pucill, Burgess	O'Loughlin (2), Wilkinson (2)	1259	R. Connolly
8.2.98	FD	A	Hull K.R.	L	14-48	Donlan, Nixon, Inrgam	Wilkinson	–	–
15.2.98	CC(4)	H	Sheffield E.	L	11-66	Fairclough, Ingram	Gunning (1, dg)	1391	Kirkpatrick
22.2.98	FD	H	Whitehaven W.	L	26-45	Costello (2), Fairclough (2), Ingram	O'Loughlin (2), Gunning	1370	R. Smith
1.3.98	FD	A	Hunslet H.	L	12-36	Fairclough, Garces, Ingram	–	–	–
8.3.98	FD	H	Wakefield T.	L	20-32	Bowker, Fairclough, Hudspith, Ingram	O'Loughlin (2)	1530	R. Connolly
15.3.98	FD	A	Keighley C.	L	16-32	Costello, Hudspith	O'Loughlin (3), Murray	–	–
22.3.98	FD	A	Dewsbury R.	L	0-50	–	–	–	–
29.3.98	FD	H	Widnes V.	W	19-14	Ingram, Murray	Wingfield (5), Wilkinson (dg)	1497	Nicholson
5.4.98	FD	A	Featherstone R.	L	12-48	Donohue (2)	O'Loughlin (2)	–	–
10.4.98	FD	A	Swinton L.	L	22-32	Hadcroft (2), Hill, Murray, Wingfield	Wingfield	–	–
13.4.98	FD	H	Rochdale H.	W	36-20	Murray (3), Costello, Street	Wingfield (8)	1310	Shaw
26.4.98	FD	H	Hull K.R.	W	22-14	Arkwright, Kendrick, O'Loughlin	Wingfield (5)	1800	Nicholson
6.5.98	FD	A	Whitehaven W.	L	12-34	Murray, Kendrick	Wingfield (2)	–	–
10.5.98	FD	H	Hunslet H.	W	26-23	Garces, Kendrick, Murray, Purtill	O'Loughlin (5)	1173	Bates
17.5.98	FD	A	Wakefield T.	L	14-60	Goulding, Murray	Wingfield (3)	–	–
24.5.98	FD	H	Keighley C.	L	18-30	Arkwright, Bowker, Murray, Purtill	Wingfield	1417	Gilmour
31.5.98	FD	H	Dewsbury R.	L	18-54	Gunning, Hadcroft, Hill	Wingfield (3)	1100	J.Connolly
3.6.98	FD	A	Widnes V.	L	16-36	Donlan, Hadcroft, Murray	Wingfield (2)	–	–
7.6.98	FD	H	Featherstone R.	L	16-48	Gunning, Street, Wingfield	Wingfield (2)	935	Lowe
14.6.98	FD	H	Swinton L.	L	28-34	Donhue (2), Bowker, Murray, Kendrick	Wingfield (4)	1100	Nicholson
21.6.98	FD	A	Rochdale H.	L	20-64	Grundy, Hill, Sarsfield	Wingfield (4)	–	–
28.6.98	FD	H	Hull K.R.	L	20-48	Arkwright, Purtill, Street	Wingfield (4)	774	Lowe
5.7.98	FD	A	Hunslet H.	L	6-18	Wingfield	Wingfield	–	–
12.7.98	FD	H	Keighley C.	L	18-26	Arkwright, Costello, Hadcroft, Street	Wingfield	970	Kirkpatrick
19.7.98	FD	A	Rochdale H.	L	10-28	Arkwright, Donlan	Wingfield	–	–
26.7.98	FD	H	Whitehaven W.	W	14-12	Fairclough, Jenkins	Wingfield (3)	698	Oddy
2.8.98	FD	A	Dewsbury R.	L	18-26	Donlan, Fairclough, Kendrick	Wingfield (3)	–	–
9.8.98	FD	H	Wakefield T.	L	12-28	Murray, Pucill	Kendrick, Gunning	1117	Taberner
16.8.98	FD	A	Swinton L.	L	4-32	–	Wingfield (2)	–	–
23.8.98	FD	H	Widnes V.	W	32-26	Dickinson (2), Fairclough, Liku, Wingfield	Wingfield (6)	1100	Morris
30.8.98	FD	A	Featherstone R.	L	4-58	Hill	–	–	–

LEIGH CENTURIONS 1998 PLAYERS' SUMMARY

	Date of birth	App	T	G	D	Pts	Previous club	Debut
Arkwright, James	8.5.76	14+1	5	0	0	20	St. Helens	1998
Bent, Peers	28.12.70	8+2	0	0	0	0	Barrow B.R.	1998
Bowker, Radney	5.2.79	7+2	3	0	0	12	Leigh East ARL	1998
Burgess, Barry	23.11.75	4	1	0	0	4	Wigan Academy	1995-96
Burrows, Mark	7.8.79	5+1	1	0	0	4	Leigh Miners ARL	1997
Conway, Dean	8.9.77	2+3	0	0	0	0	Rose Bridge ARL	1996
Costello, John	10.3.70	32	5	0	0	20	Leigh M. ARL	1991-92
Dickinson, Stuart	25.11.79	5	2	0	0	8	St. Helens	1998
Donlan, Stuart	29.8.78	28+2	4	0	0	16	Leigh East ARL	1997
Donohue, Jason	18.4.72	10+1	4	0	0	16	Hull S.	1998
Driscoll, Steve	1.6.77	0+6	0	0	0	0	S. Sydney (Aust.)	1998
Fairclough, Andy	18.9.71	12+2	8	0	0	32	Wigan St. Pats ARL	1997
Garces, Steve	31.3.75	12+15	2	0	0	8	South Perth (Aust.)	1998
Geritas, Sean	2.12.77	5+3	0	0	0	0	Warrington W.	1998
Goulding, Martin	23.3.78	0+2	1	0	0	4	Wigan St. Pats ARL	1996
Grundy, Andrew	19.1.77	16+4	1	0	0	4	Wigan W.	1998
Gunning, John	30.3.69	7+16	2	3	1	15	Swinton L.	1997
Hadcroft, Alan	31.3.77	19	5	0	0	20	Leigh East ARL	1995-96
Hartill, Dave	19.4.74	1+3	0	0	0	0	Swinton L.	1998
Hill, David	4.9.68	22+3	4	0	0	16	Blackbrook ARL	1988-89
Hilton, Scott	29.10.77	3+4	1	0	0	4	Leigh MW ARL	1997
Hudspith, Ian	27.7.74	2+6	2	0	0	8	Leigh East ARL	1997
Ingram, David	4.1.75	13	7	0	0	28	Leigh Academy	1994-95
Jenkins, Nick	24.2.74	12+8	2	0	0	8	Prescot P.	1997
Kay, Mark	26.11.77	4+1	0	0	0	0	Leigh East ARL	1996
Kendrick, Phil	31.10.77	12+3	5	1	0	22	Widnes V.	1998
Liku, Tau'alupe	21.2.71	13+8	3	0	0	12	Mau Saints (NZ)	1994-95
Murray, Anthony	25.5.77	26+2	12	1	0	50	Widnes V.	1998
Nixon, Matt	31.5.73	6	1	0	0	4	Australia	1997
Norman, Paul	25.3.74	3+1	0	0	0	0	Oldham B.	1998
O'Loughlin, Jason	29.11.70	12+4	1	16	0	36	St. Helens	1994-95
Patel, Safraz	20.10.76	2+2	0	0	0	0	Leigh East ARL	1996
Pucill, Andy	19.11.67	23+2	2	0	0	8	Huddersfield G.	1997
Purtill, Kieron	12.2.77	14+4	3	0	0	12	Wigan W.	1998
Sarsfield, Mark	22.3.71	0+1	1	0	0	4	Widnes	1993-94
Smith, Colin	29.9.72	2+1	0	0	0	0	Wigan St. Pats ARL	1997
Smith, Dave	23.11.74	0+2	0	0	0	0	Huddersfield G.	1997
Street, Tim	29.6.68	27	5	0	0	20	Hull	1996
Whittle, Dave	22.9.76	5	0	0	0	0	Wigan W.	1998
Wilkinson, Chris	2.3.65	5	0	3	1	7	Swinton	1994-95
Wingfield, Paul	16.8.78	23	4	61	0	138	Warrington W.	1998
TOTALS								
41 players			97	85	2	560		

LONDON BRONCOS

Highest score: 82-0 v. Highfield, 12 Nov 1995
Highest against: 72-6 v. Whitehaven, 14 Sep 1986
Attendance: 15,013 v. Wakefield T. (RL Cup),
15 Feb 1981 — at Craven Cottage
9,846 v. Brisbane B (World Club
Championship), 27 July, 1997 — The
Stoop

Ground: The Stoop (0181-410-5000)
First Season: 1980-81. Began as Fulham. Became
London Crusaders at start of 1991-92
and changed to London Broncos in
1994-95.
Chairman: Richard Branson
Honours: **Division Two** Champions, 1982-83
Second Division Premiership
Beaten Finalists, 1993-94

RECORDS
Match
Goals: 11 by Steve Guyett v. Huddersfield,
23 Oct 1988
Greg Pearce v. Runcorn H.,
26 Aug 1990
Terry Matterson v. Workington T.,
21 Apr 1996
Tries: 4 by Mark Riley v. Highfield,
17 Oct 1993
Mark Johnson at Highfield,
1 Apr 1994
Scott Roskell at Bramley,
19 Mar 1995
Evan Cochrane at Sheffield E.,
27 Sept 1995
Paul Hauff v. Workington T.
1 Oct 1995
Shane Vincent v. Highfield,
12 Nov 1995
Greg Barwick v. Castleford T.,
25 Aug 1996
Points: 28 by Greg Barwick v. Castleford T.,
25 Aug 1996

Season
Goals: 159 by John Gallagher, 1993-94
Tries: 43 by Mark Johnson, 1993-94
Points: 384 by John Gallagher, 1993-94

Career
Goals: 309 by Steve Diamond, 1981-84
Tries: 85 by Scott Roskell, 1992-97
Points: 691 by Steve Diamond, 1981-84
Appearances: 156+14 by Steve Rosolen 1991-98

COACHING REGISTER
● **Since formation in 1980**

Reg Bowden	July 80 - June 84
Roy Lester	June 84 - Apr 86
Bill Goodwin	Apr 86 - May 88
* Bev Risman	May 88 - Feb 89
Phil Sullivan	Feb 89 - Mar 89
Bill Goodwin	Mar 89 - Apr 89
Ross Strudwick	June 89 - Feb 93
Tony Gordon	Feb 93 - May 94
Gary Grienke	May 94 - Jan 96
Tony Currie	Jan 96 - Oct 98
Dan Stains	Nov 98 -

* *Team manager*

GREAT BRITAIN REGISTER
(1 player)
John Dalgreen   (1)   1982

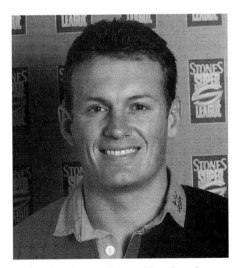

*Greg Barwick: Club record four tries and
28 points in a match.*

LONDON BRONCOS 1998 MATCH ANALYSIS

Date	Com-petition	H/A	Opponents	Rlt	Score	Tries	Goals	Atten-dance	Referee
15.2.98	CC(4)	A	Batley B.	W	44-20	Offiah (3), Timu (2), Toshack (2), D. Higgins, Ryan	Ryan (4)	–	–
1.3.98	CC(5)	H	Halifax B.	W	21-18	Chapman, Matterson, Offiah	Chapman (4, dg)	3092	Presley
15.3.98	CC(6)	H	Hull K.R.	W	46-18	Beazley (2), Ryan (2), Offiah, Dunford, Fatnowna, Timu, Toshack	Chapman (5)	4111	J. Connolly
29.3.98	CC(SF)	N1	Wigan W.	L	8-38	Mardon, Fatnowna	–	(11,058)	R. Smith
5.4.98	SL	H	Halifax B.S.	L	6-32	Ryan	Matterson	2442	R. Smith
10.4.98	SL	A	Hull S.	L	4-6	Chapman	–	–	–
19.4.98	SL	H	Warrington W.	W	14-4	Beazley, Retchless	Matterson (2, 2dg)	2167	Briers
26.4.98	SL	A	Wigan W.	L	10-24	Offiah, Toshack	Matterson	–	–
8.5.98	SL	H	Leeds R.	L	13-14	Offiah, Ryan	Matterson (2, dg)	2742	J. Connolly
17.5.98	SL	A	Huddersfield G.	W	28-20	Ryan (2), Air, Matterson, Smyth	Matterson (4)	–	–
24.5.98	SL	H	Salford R.	W	21-12	Beazley, Chapman, D. Higgins	Matterson (4), Chapman (dg)	2448	Ganson
29.5.98	SL	A	Bradford B.	L	14-17	Mardon (2), I. Higgins	Matterson	–	–
7.6.98	SL	H	Sheffield E.	W	26-22	Gill (2), Beazley, Cotton, D. Higgins	Chapman (3)	2581	Kirkpatrick
14.6.98	SL	A	St. Helens	L	6-58	Chapman	Chapman	–	–
21.6.98	SL	H	Castleford T.	L	16-36	Beazley, Goodwin, Matterson	Matterson (2)	2300	Morris
27.6.98	SL	A	Halifax B.S..	L	14-34	Cotton, Ryan, Smyth	Matterson	–	–
5.7.98	SL	H	Hull S.	W	38-6	Smyth (2), Matterson, Ryan, Spencer, Timu	Matterson (6), Ryan	3014	Morris
18.7.98	SL	N2	Bradford B.	W	22-8	Young, Edwards, Tollett, Timu	Matterson (3)	(6863)	Presley
2.8.98	SL	A	Warrington W.	W	23-14	Air (2), Edwards	Matterson (5, dg)	–	–
7.8.98	SL	H	Wigan W.	L	15-18	Air, Beazley, Cotton	Tollett (1, dg)	5762	Cummings
14.8.98	SL	A	Leeds R.	L	12-34	Ryan, Edwards	Tollett (2)	–	–
23.8.98	SL	H	Huddersfield G.	W	20-8	Goodwin (2), Millard, Tollett	Edwards, Tollett	2014	Presley
30.8.98	SL	A	Salford R.	L	20-23	Edwards, Smyth, Timu	Tollett (3), Goodwin	–	–
6.9.98	SL	H	Bradford B.	W	34-8	Air (3), Gill, Ryan, Timu	Tollett (5)	2954	R. Smith
11.9.98	SL	A	Sheffield E.	W	19-18	Dunford, Ryan, Timu	Ryan (3), Goodwin (dg)	–	–
18.9.98	SL	H	St. Helens	L	22-37	Air, Carroll, Williams, Young	Ryan (3)	3239	Cummings
27.9.98	SL	A	Castleford T.	L	18-23	Air, Gill, Timu	Ryan (3)	–	–

N1 at Huddersfield; N2 at Hearts FC, Edinburgh

1998 SIGNINGS REGISTER

Signed	Player	Club From
13.1.98	Air, Glen	Illawarra (Aust.)
—	Bradstreet, Darren	Illawarra (Aust.)
—	Calloway, Dean	Illawarra (Aust.)
14.1.98	Carroll, Mark	Manly (Aust.)
21.1.98	Chapman, Damien	Perth Reds (Aust.)
3.7.98	Edwards, Shaun	Bradford B.
—	Fleming, Greg	Canterbury B. (Aust.)
27.5.98	Goodwin, Luke	Oldham B.
—	Hammond, Karle	St. Helens
14.1.98	Higgins, Darren	Perth Reds (Aust.)
19.1.98	Jennings, Edward	—
—	McKenzie, Marty	Adelaide (Aust.)
29.7.98	Millard, Shane	Sth. Sydney (Aust.)
20.2.98	Oliver, Daniel	Staines RU
14.1.98	Retchless, Steele	S. Queensland (Aust.)
14.1.98	Ryan, Chris	Perth Reds (Aust.)
—	Simpson, Robbie	St. George (Aust.)
8.5.98	Smyth, Rob	Wigan W.
14.1.98	Timu, John	Canterbury B. (Aust.)
14.1.98	Toshack, Matt	S. Queensland (Aust.)
—	Warton, Brett	West. Suburbs (Aust.)
18.6.98	Williams, Bart	Sth. Sydney (Aust.)
19.1.98	Woad, Warren	Ruislip RU
14.1.98	Young, Grant	Auckland W. (NZ)

LONDON BRONCOS 1998 PLAYERS' SUMMARY

	Date of birth	App	T	G	D	Pts	Previous club	Debut
Air, Glen	17.11.73	17+2	9	0	0	36	Illawarra (Aust.)	1998
Beazley, Rob	18.3.74	17+5	7	0	0	28	Illawarra (Aust.)	1997
Best, Roger	18.3.74	1+5	0	0	0	0	Manly (Aust.)	1997
Carroll, Mark	26.2.67	19+3	1	0	0	4	Manly (Aust.)	1998
Chapman, Damien	6.3.74	9+2	4	13	2	44	Perth Reds (Aust.)	1998
Chesney, Kris		1+2	0	0	0	0	Harlequins RU	1998
Cotton, Wesley	9.6.77	11	3	0	0	12	Wigan W.	1997
Dunford, Matt	4.3.68	8+17	2	0	0	8	Manly (Aust.)	1997
Edwards, Shaun	17.10.66	8+1	4	1	0	18	Bradford B.	1998
Fatnowna, Abraham "Butch"	19.4.74	5+2	2	0	0	8	Workington T.	1997
Gill, Peter	14.12.64	27	4	0	0	16	Gold Coast (Aust.)	1995-96
Goodwin, Luke	18.1.73	9+2	3	1	1	15	Oldham B.	1998
Higgins, Darren	1.9.65	8+7	3	0	0	12	Perth Reds (Aust.)	1998
Higgins, Robert "Iain"	14.9.76	1+4	1	0	0	4	Cambridge Univ. ARL	1997
Jennings, Edward	11.3.79	0+1	0	0	0	0	London B. Academy	1998
Mardon, Nick	24.9.71	6	3	0	0	12	Boroughmuir RU	1997
Matterson, Terry	4.3.67	18	4	32	4	84	Brisbane B. (Aust.)	1995-96
Millard, Shane	30.7.75	5+4	1	0	0	4	South Sydney (Aust.)	1998
Offiah, Martin	29.12.65	11	7	0	0	28	Wigan	1996
Peters, Dominic	11.12.78	1+3	0	0	0	0	London B. Academy	1998
Retchless, Steve	16.6.71	25+2	1	0	0	4	Sth. Queensland (Aust.)	1998
Rosolen, Steve	16.11.68	2+1	0	0	0	0	North Sydney (Aust.)	1991-92
Ryan, Chris	3.1.73	25	12	14	0	76	Perth Reds (Aust.)	1998
Salter, Matt	2.12.76	4+14	0	0	0	0	Blackheath RU	1997
Smyth, Rob	22.2.77	16	5	0	0	20	Wigan W.	1998
Spencer, Adrian	3.3.73	3+14	1	0	0	4	Cambridge Univ. ARL	1992-93
Thomas, Giles	23.11.76	0+1	0	0	0	0	London B. Academy	1997
Timu, John	8.5.69	21+1	9	0	0	36	Canterbury B. (Aust.)	1998
Tollett, Tulsen	6.5.73	21	2	12	1	33	Parramatta (Aust.)	1996
Toshack, Matt	18.2.73	23+1	4	0	0	16	Sth. Queensland (Aust.)	1998
Williams, Bart	12.1.76	5+3	1	0	0	4	South Sydney (Aust.)	1998
Young, Grant	30.7.70	24+2	2	0	0	8	Auckland W. (NZ)	1998
TOTALS								
32 players			95	73	8	534		

Representative appearances 1998
Edwards - Ireland (1, 2t)

OLDHAM

Ground:	Boundary Park. (0161-628-3677) Moved to Spotland, Rochdale, in 1999.
First Season:	1895-96. Added Bears to title in 1995-96. Went into liquidation at the end of 1997 and re-formed as a new Oldham club.
Chairman:	Christopher Hamilton
Honours:	**Championship** Winners, 1909-10, 1910-11, 1956-57 Beaten finalists, 1906-07, 1907-08, 1908-09, 1921-22, 1954-55 **Division One** Champions, 1904-05 **Division Two** Champions, 1963-64, 1981-82, 1987-88 **Challenge Cup** Winners, 1898-99, 1924-25, 1926-27 Beaten finalists, 1906-07, 1911-12, 1923-24, 1925-26 **Second Division/Divisional Premiership** Winners, 1987-88, 1989-90 Beaten finalists, 1991-92 **Lancashire Cup** Winners, 1907-08, 1910-11, 1913-14, 1919-20, 1924-25, 1933-34, 1956-57, 1957-58, 1958-59 Beaten finalists, 1908-09, 1911-12, 1918-19, 1921-22, 1954-55, 1966-67, 1968-69, 1986-87, 1989-90 **Lancashire League** Winners, 1897-98, 1900-01, 1907-08, 1909-10, 1921-22, 1956-57, 1957-58 **Red Rose Championship** Winners 1998 **Trans–Pennine Cup** Beaten finalists 1998

RECORDS

Match

Goals:	14 by Bernard Ganley v. Liverpool C., 4 Apr 1959
Tries:	7 by James Miller v. Barry, 31 Oct 1908
Points:	30 by Abe Johnson v. Widnes, 9 Apr 1928

Season

Goals:	200 by Bernard Ganley, 1957-58
Tries:	49 by Reg Farrar, 1921-22
Points:	412 by Bernard Ganley, 1957-58

Career

Goals:	1,365 by Bernard Ganley, 1951-61
Tries:	173 by Alan Davies, 1950-61
Points:	2,775 by Bernard Ganley, 1951-61
Appearances:	626 by Joe Ferguson, 1899-1923

Highest score: 70-10 v. Bramley, 12 Feb 1995
Highest against: 67-11 at Hull K.R., 24 Sep 1978
Attendance: 28,000 v. Huddersfield (League), 24 Feb 1912 — at Watersheddings
11,284 v. Bradford B. (RL Cup), 9 Mar 1997 — at Boundary Park

COACHING REGISTER

● **Since 1974-75**

Jim Challinor	Aug 74 - Dec 76
Terry Ramshaw	Jan 77 - Feb 77
Dave Cox	July 77 - Dec 78
Graham Starkey (Mgr)	Jan 79 - May 81
Bill Francis	June 79 - Dec 80
Frank Myler	May 81 - Apr 83
Peter Smethurst	Apr 83 - Feb 84
Frank Barrow	Feb 84 - Feb 84
Brian Gartland	Mar 84 - June 84
Frank Myler	June 84 - Apr 87
★ Eric Fitzsimons	June 87 - Nov 88
★ Mal Graham	June 87 - Apr 88
Tony Barrow	Nov 88 - Jan 91
John Fieldhouse	Jan 91 - Apr 91
Peter Tunks	Apr 91 - Feb 94
Bob Lindner	Feb 94 - Apr 94
Andy Goodway	May 94 - Apr 97
Bob Lindner	Apr 97 - Sept 97
Paddy Kirwan	Nov 97 - Aug 98
Mick Coates	Aug 98 -

★ *Joint coaches June 87 - Apr 88*

GREAT BRITAIN REGISTER

(40 players)

Albert Avery	(4)	1910-11
Charlie Bott	(1)	1966
Albert Brough	(2)	1924
Terry Clawson	(9)	1973-74
Alan Davies	(20)	1955-60
Evan Davies	(3)	1920
Terry Flanagan	(4)	1983-84
Des Foy	(3)	1984-85
Bernard Ganley	(3)	1957-58
Andy Goodway	(11)	1983-85
Billy Hall	(4)	1914
Herman Hilton	(7)	1920-21

(Contd)

94

OLDHAM 1998 MATCH ANALYSIS

Date	Competition	H/A	Opponents	Rlt	Score	Tries	Goals	Attendance	Referee
18.1.98	CC(PO)	H	Heworth	W	36-14	Cooper (2), Diggle (2), Hough, Mead, Wilde	Quinlan (4)	2943	Crabtree
1.2.98	CC(3)	A	Widnes V.	L	8-48	Hough	Quinlan (2)	–	–
13.4.98	SD	A	Workington T.	W	22-18	Darkes, Edwards, Flanagan, Leuila, Round	Cooper	–	–
22.4.98	SD	A	Bramley	L	10-12	Eckersley, Robinson	Darkes	–	–
26.4.98	SD	A	Doncaster D.	W	28-8	Cooper, Eckersley, Flanagan, Martindale, Barker	Darkes (4)	–	–
4.5.98	SD	H	Bramley	L	32-50	Barker, Darkes, Hough, Leuila, Martindale, Prescott, Round	Darkes (2)	2921	McGregor
10.5.98	SD	H	Batley B.	H	28-20	Eckersley (2), Edwards, Leuila, Naidole, Round	Darkes, Wilkinson	1929	Atkin
17.5.98	SD	H	Barrow B.R.	W	13-4	Darkes, Eckersley	Wilkinson (2, dg)	1967	Laughton
24.5.98	SD	A	York	L	6-27	Mead	Wilkinson	–	–
31.5.98	SD/RR	A	Lancashire L.	D	18-18	Flanagan, Robinson, Wilde	Wilkinson (3)	–	–
7.6.98	SD/RR	A	Workington T.	W	27-10	Shaw (2), Darkes, Eckersley, Martindale	Wilkinson (3, dg)	–	–
14.6.98	SD/RR	H1	Barrow B.R.	W	32-8	Eckersley (2), Leuila (2), Hough, Wilde	Wilkinson (4)	1686	Cornish
19.6.98	SD/RR	H1	Lancashire L.	W	25-20	Wilde (2), Martindale, Mead	Wilkinson (4, dg)	1856	Shaw
28.6.98	SD/RR	A	Barrow B.R.	L	2-19	–	Wilkinson	–	–
5.7.98	SD/RR	H1	Workington T.	W	56-8	Edwards (3), Leuila (3), Eckersley (2), Cooper, Hough, Mead	Wilkinson (6)	1620	Cornish
19.7.98	TPF	A	Batley B.	L	12-28	Martindale, Sinfield	Wilkinson (2)	–	–
26.7.98	SD	A	Lancashire L.	L	16-32	Eckersley, Edwards, Hough	Wilkinson (2)	–	–
2.8.98	SD	H	Workington T.	W	12-9	Crook, Eckersley	Wilkinson (2)	1551	Silverwood
16.8.98	SD	H	Doncaster D.	W	26-16	Eckersley (3), Darkes, Quinlan	Wilkinson (3)	1605	Lowe
23.8.98	SD	A	Batley B.	L	2-17	–	Quinlan	–	–
26.8.98	SD	H	Lancashire L.	L	16-18	Mead, Wilde, Proctor	Quinland (2)	1710	Oddy
30.8.98	SD	A	Barrow B.R.	L	20-31	Hough, Jackman	Quinlan (6)	–	–
6.9.98	SD	H	York	L	8-38	Jackman	Quinlan (2)	1440	Nicholson

H1 at Rochdale H.

GREAT BRITAIN REGISTER (Contd)

David Hobbs	(2)	1987
Dave Holland	(4)	1914
Bob Irving	(8+3)	1967-72
Ken Jackson	(2)	1957
Ernest Knapman	(1)	1924
Syd Little	(10)	1956-58
Tom Llewellyn	(2)	1907
Jim Lomas	(2)	1911
Bill Longworth	(3)	1908
Les McIntyre	(1)	1963
Terry O'Grady	(5)	1954
Jack Oster	(1)	1929
Dave Parker	(2)	1964
Doug Phillips	(3)	1946
Frank Pitchford	(2)	1958-62
Tom Rees	(1)	1929
Sid Rix	(9)	1924-26
Bob Sloman	(5)	1928
Arthur Smith	(6)	1907-08
Ike Southward	(7)	1959-62
Les Thomas	(1)	1947
Derek Turner	(11)	1956-58
George Tyson	(4)	1907-08
Hugh Waddell	(4)	1988
Tommy White	(1)	1907
Charlie Winslade	(1)	1959
Alf Wood	(4)	1911-14
Mick Worrall	(3)	1984

OLDHAM 1998 PLAYERS' SUMMARY

	Date of birth	App	T	G	D	Pts	Previous club	Debut
Barker, Craig	3.11.76	12+1	2	0	0	8	Waterhead ARL	1998
Clegg, Jason	24.3.71	1+14	0	0	0	0	Bradford B.	1998
Cooper, Sean	29.12.70	15	4	1	0	18	Bradford B.	1998
Crook, Paul	12.2.74	6+4	1	0	0	4	Hull S.	1998
Darkes, Richard	5.10.69	18+2	5	8	0	36	Huddersf'd YMCA RU	1998
Diggle, Craig	2.4.75	2+1	2	0	0	8	Rochdale H.	1998
Eckersley, Chris	16.10.74	19+2	15	0	0	60	Warrington W.	1998
Edwards, Mike	14.4.75	16+4	6	0	0	24	Swinton L.	1998
Flanagan, Neil	11.6.70	20	3	0	0	12	Rochdale H.	1998
Fleming, Andrew	16.8.67	0+2	0	0	0	0	Lancashire L.	1998
Hough, John	14.4.76	21	7	0	0	28	Warrington W.	1998
Jackman, Emmerson	29.4.73	2+3	2	0	0	8	Oldham St. Annes ARL	1998
Leuila, Peaufai "Afi"	24.10.69	20	8	0	0	32	St. Helens	1995-96
Maders, Martin	29.6.73	12+1	0	0	0	0	Huddersfield G.	1998
Martindale, Michael	13.9.74	15+1	5	0	0	20	Wakefield T.	1998
McNicholas, Joe	26.12.78	3+1	0	0	0	0	Spotland R. ARL	1997
Mead, Adrian	6.4.78	13+6	5	0	0	20	Oldham B. Academy	1998
Naidole, Joe	23.12.68	14+1	1	0	0	4	Featherstone R.	1998
Prescott, Mike	26.3.76	1+5	1	0	0	4	Oldham B. Academy	1998
Proctor, Andrew	9.3.69	11	1	0	0	4	Wakefield T.	1998
Quinlan, Brian	9.4.70	7+1	1	17	0	38	Bramley	1998
Robinson, Darren	28.5.79	1+6	2	0	0	8		1998
Round, Paul	24.9.63	13+7	3	0	0	12	Castleford T.	1998
Shaw, Graeme	13.6.75	14+4	2	0	0	8	Bradford B.	1998
Sinfield, Ian	7.4.77	10+6	1	0	0	4	Salford R.	1998
Varley, Nathan	22.2.76	3+18	0	0	0	0	Bradford B.	1998
Wilde, Steven	1.4.74	17	6	0	0	24	Saddleworth ARL	1998
Wilkinson, Chris	2.3.66	13	0	34	3	71	Leigh C.	1998
TOTALS								
28 players			83	60	3	455		

Representative appearances 1998
Shaw - Scotland (0+2)

1998 SIGNINGS REGISTER

Signed	Player	Club From
—	Appleby, Darren	Rochdale H.
—	Casey, Leo	Rochdale H.
15.1.98	Clegg, Jason	Bradford B.
1.1.98	Cooper, Sean	Bradford B.
9.6.98	Crook, Paul	Hull S.
25.3.98	Darkes, Richard	Huddersfield YMCA
1.1.98	Diggle, Craig	Rochdale H.
1.1.98	Eckersley, Chris	Warrington W.
5.3.98	Edwards, Michael	Swinton L.
—	Farrell, Mick	Rochdale H.
15.1.98	Fleming, Andrew	Lancashire L.
1.1.98	Hough, John	Warrington W.
20.7.98	Jackson, Emmerson	Oldham St. Annes ARL
13.1.98	Maders, Martin	Huddersfield G.
23.1.98	Martindale, Michael	Wakefield T.
—	Minut, Laurent	Villeneuve (Fr.)
29.4.98	Naidole, Joseph	Featherstone R.
—	Peralta, Emmanuel	Villeneuve (Fr.)
—	Perrett, Mark	Halifax B.S.
29.5.98	Proctor, Andrew	Wakefield T.
1.1.98	Quinlan, Brian	Bramley
1.1.98	Round, Paul	Castleford T.
14.1.98	Shaw, Graeme	Bradford B.
1.1.98	Sinfield, Ian	Salford R.
28.1.98	Varley, Nathan	Bradford B.
7.5.98	Wilkinson, Chris	Leigh C.

ROCHDALE HORNETS

Ground: Spotland (017066-48004)
First Season: 1895-96
Chairman: Ray Taylor
Honours: **Challenge Cup** Winners, 1921-22
Regal Trophy Beaten finalists, 1973-74
Lancashire Cup Winners, 1911-12, 1914-15, 1918-19
Beaten finalists, 1912-13, 1919-20, 1965-66, 1991-92
Lancashire League Winners, 1918-19
BBC2 Floodlit Trophy Beaten finalists, 1971-72

RECORDS

Match

Goals: 14 by Steve Turner v. Runcorn H., 5 Nov 1989
Tries: 5 by Jack Corsi v. Barrow, 31 Dec 1921
Jack Corsi v. Broughton Moor, 25 Feb 1922
Jack Williams v. St. Helens, 4 Apr 1933
Norman Brelsford v. Whitehaven, 3 Sep 1972
Points: 32 by Steve Turner v. Runcorn H., 5 Nov 1989
Steve Turner v. Blackpool G., 31 Oct 1993

Season

Goals: 150 by Martin Strett, 1994-95
Tries: 30 by Jack Williams, 1934-35
Points: 346 by Martin Strett, 1994-95

Career

Goals: 741 by Walter Gowers, 1922-46
Tries: 103 by Jack Williams, 1931-37
Points: 1,497 by Walter Gowers, 1922-46
Appearances: 456 by Walter Gowers, 1922-46
Highest score: 92-0 v. Runcorn H., 5 Nov 1989
Highest against: 79-2 at Hull, 7 Apr 1921
Attendance: 8,150 v. Oldham (Div. 2), 26 Dec 1989 — at Spotland
26,664 v. Oldham (RL Cup), 25 Mar 1922 — at Athletic Ground

COACHING REGISTER

Frank Myler	May 71 - Oct 74
Graham Starkey	Oct 74 - Nov 75
Henry Delooze	Nov 75 - Nov 76
Kel Coslett	Nov 76 - Aug 79
Paul Longstaff	Sep 79 - May 81
Terry Fogerty	May 81 - Jan 82
Dick Bonser	Jan 82 - May 82
Bill Kirkbride	June 82 - Sep 84
Charlie Birdsall	Sep 84 - Apr 86
Eric Fitzsimons	June 86 - June 87
Eric Hughes	June 87 - June 88
Jim Crellin	June 88 - June 89
Allan Agar	July 89 - Jan 91
Neil Holding	Jan 91 - Apr 91
Stan Gittins	Apr 91 - Jan 93
Peter Regan	Jan 93 - Oct 93
Steve Gibson	Oct 93 - May 96
Shane Tupaea	May 96 - Apr 98
Deryck Fox	May 98 -

GREAT BRITAIN REGISTER (8 players)

Johnnie Baxter	(1)	1907
Jack Bennett	(6)	1924
Joe Bowers	(1)	1920
Terry Fogerty	(1)	1974
Ernest Jones	(4)	1920
Malcolm Price	(2)	1967
Jack Robinson	(2)	1914
Tommy Woods	(2)	1911

1998 SIGNINGS REGISTER

Signed	Player	Club From
30.6.97	Appleby, Darren	Batley B.
5.4.98	Aston, Jon	Hull S.
8.2.98	Best, Jason	Saddleworth R. ARL
31.5.98	Best, David	Saddleworth R. ARL
22.1.98	Bradwell, Michael	Rochdale RU
—	Burgess, Andy	Salford R.
—	Cooper, Shaun	Oldham
—	Coussons, Phil	Salford R.
15.7.98	Coult, Mick	Hunslet H.
13.2.98	Eyres, Richard	Warrington W.
14.5.98	Fox, Deryck	Batley B.
5.4.98	Gray, Kevin	Hull S.
23.1.98	Jones, David	Oldham
3.4.98	Jukes, Neil	Leigh C.
8.3.98	Kearsley, Gavin	Langworthy Jnrs. ARL

(Contd)

ROCHDALE HORNETS 1998 MATCH ANALYSIS

Date	Competition	H/A	Opponents	Rlt	Score	Tries	Goals	Attendance	Referee
1.2.98	CC(3)	H	Leigh M.R.	W	44-4	Fitzgerald (2), Bunce, Casey, Dixon, S. Hall, Maher	Fitzgerald (8)	737	Silverwood
8.2.98	FD	H	Hunslet H.	L	25-36	Fitzgerald (2), S. Hall, Pachniuk	Fitzgerald (4, dg)	850	Kirkpatrick
15.2.98	CC(4)	H	Bradford B.	L	10-48	Pachniuk, Scarisbrick	Fitzgerald	5466	Nicholson
22.2.98	FD	A	Widnes V.	L	20-22	S. Hall, Jones, Stevens	Fitzgerald (3), Pachniuk	–	–
3.3.98	FD	H	Keighley C.	W	20-16	Bunce (2), Pachniuk, Stevens	Dixon (2)	830	A. Bates
8.3.98	FD	H	Featherstone R.	L	24-34	Maher (2), Lowe, Pachniuk	Dixon (4)	916	Presley
15.3.98	FD	H	Dewsbury R.	L	8-12	Lowe, McKinney	–	818	Nicholson
22.3.98	FD	A	Hull K.R.	L	15-28	Bunce, Pachniuk, Stevens	Dixon, Swann (dg)	–	–
29.3.98	FD	H	Swinton L.	L	6-38	Appleby	Dixon	743	J. Connolly
5.4.98	FD	A	Wakefield T.	L	0-38	–	–	–	–
13.4.98	FD	A	Leigh C.	L	20-36	Dixon, Pachniuk, Stevens	Topping (3), Dixon	–	–
19.4.98	FD	H	Whitehaven W.	L	16-38	McKinney, Pachniuk	Gray (4)	721	Lowe
26.4.98	FD	A	Hunslet H.	L	6-47	A. Eyres	Gray	–	–
4.5.98	FD	H	Widnes V.	L	20-26	Aston, Gray, A. Eyres, Pachniuk	Gray (2)	930	Gilmour
10.5.98	FD	A	Keighley C.	L	4-50	Maher	–	–	–
17.5.98	FD	A	Featherstone R.	W	46-18	Pachniuk (2), Stevens (2), Appleby, Cameron, A. Eyres, McKinney	Fox (7)	–	–
24.5.98	FD	A	Dewsbury R.	L	4-40	Bunce	–	–	–
31.5.98	FD	H	Hull K.R.	D	26-26	A. Eyres (3), Gray, Stevens	Fox (3)	914	Bates
3.6.98	FD	A	Swinton L.	L	12-36	Aston, Stevens	Fox (2)	–	–
7.6.98	FD	H	Wakefield T.	L	28-46	Kerr (2), Aston, Farrell, Swann	Gray (4)	1014	Nicholson
21.6.98	FD	H	Leigh C.	W	64-20	Swann (4), Kerr (2), Shaw (2), Cameron, A. Eyres, Maher	Fox (10)	932	Lowe
24.6.98	FD	A	Whitehaven W.	L	6-24	Eyres	Fox	–	–
28.6.98	FD	H	Featherstone R.	L	27-50	Stevens (3), Aston, Swann	Farrell (3), Topping (dg)	896	Lee
5.7.98	FD	A	Hull K.R.	L	6-34	Swann	Topping	–	–
12.7.98	FD	H	Hunslet H.	L	18-24	Bunce (3), Stevens	Fox	838	Atkin
15.7.98	FD	A	Keighley C.	W	20-18	Farrell, Kerr, Shaw, Stevens	Farrell (2)	–	–
19.7.98	FD	H	Leigh C.	W	28-10	Bunce, Kerr, Shaw, Topping	Fox (6)	832	Laughton
2.8.98	FD	A	Whitehaven W.	L	22-30	A. Eyres, Kerr, McKinney, Shaw	Fox (3)	–	–
9.8.98	FD	H	Dewsbury R.	L	2-40	–	Farrell	980	Oddy
16.8.98	FD	A	Wakefield T.	L	21-28	Cameron, Kerr, Shaw	Farrell (4), Topping (dg)	–	–
23.8.98	FD	H	Swinton L.	W	41-16	R. Eyres (2), Swann (2), Shaw, Coult, A. Eyres	Fox (6), Topping (dg)	914	Gilmour
30.8.98	FD	A	Widnes V.	L	16-31	Shaw (2), Coult	Fox (2)	–	–

1998 SIGNINGS REGISTER (Contd)

Signed	Player	Club From
17.4.98	Kerr, Kenneth	Newcastle Sth (Aust.)
—	Knowles, Matthew	Swinton L.
14.3.98	Lord, Paul	Saddleworth R. ARL
21.1.98	Maher, Adam	Hunter M. (Aust.)
21.1.98	Powell, Mark	Oldham B.
—	Powell, Roy	Featherstone R.
15.7.98	*Robinson, Darren	Oldham
4.7.98	Sculthorpe, Les	Halifax B.S.
30.4.98	Sculthorpe, Daniel	Warrington W.
—	Stephenson, David	Hull S.
23.1.98	Swann, William	Warrington W.
26.2.98	Topping, Paul	Oldham B.
17.4.98	Webster, John	Oldham B.
—	Wilde, Steve	Oldham

ROCHDALE HORNETS 1998 PLAYERS' SUMMARY

	Date of birth	App	T	G	D	Pts	Previous club	Debut
Appleby, Darren	14.6.67	14+2	2	0	0	8	Batley B.	1997
Aston, Jon	5.6.76	17+4	4	0	0	16	Hull S.	1998
Bradbury, Gary	20.12.79	0+1	0	0	0	0	Wigan St. Patricks ARL	1997
Bunce, Martin	9.2.75	24+1	9	0	0	36	Waterhead ARL	1994-95
Cameron, Steve	14.3.78	12+11	3	0	0	12		1997
Casey, Leo	17.9.65	16+4	1	0	0	4	Swinton L.	1998
Coult, Mick	14.10.69	7	2	0	0	8	Hunslet H.	1998
Crowther, Steve	6.5.77	1	0	0	0	0	Waterhead ARL	1996
Dixon, Keith	16.9.66	8	2	9	0	26	Dewsbury R.	1998
Eyres, Andy	1.10.68	30	10	0	0	40	Keighley C.	1998
Eyres, Richard	7.12.64	18+1	2	0	0	8	Warrington W.	1998
Farrell, Mick	21.3.77	7+5	2	10	0	28	Waterhead ARL	1996
Fitzgerald, Peter	22.10.69	4	4	16	1	49	York	1998
Fox, Deryck	19.9.64	11	0	41	0	82	Batley B.	1998
Gray, Kevin	10.12.75	10+1	2	11	0	30	Hull S.	1998
Green, Jason	19.1.72	9+2	0	0	0	0	Widnes V.	1995-96
Hall, Rob	13.5.71	2+2	0	0	0	0	Oldham St. Annes ARL	1990-91
Hall, Steve	7.9.67	7	3	0	0	12	Keighley C.	1998
Hayes, Ian	23.9.77	1+1	0	0	0	0		1997
Holland, Chris	20.10.78	0+3	0	0	0	0	Hindley ARL	1997
Jones, David	7.12.68	13	1	0	0	4	Oldham B.	1998
Jukes, Neil	23.5.76	0+5	0	0	0	0	Leigh C.	1998
Kerr, Ken	18.10.69	21	8	0	0	32	Newcastle Souths (Aust.)	1998
Lowe, Robert	8.12.77	8+17	2	0	0	8	Wigan St. Judes ARL	1996
McKinney, Chris	12.11.76	25+1	4	0	0	16	Oldham B.	1998
Maher, Adam	22.8.72	22+1	5	0	0	20	Hunter M. (Aust.)	1998
Marriott, Karl	21.11.69	7+10	0	0	0	0	Mayfield ARL	1989-90
Meadows, Mark	9.5.65	0+2	0	0	0	0	Leigh	1994-95
Morrison, Tony	17.12.65	0+2	0	0	0	0	Swinton L.	1996
Opetaia, Scott		0+2	0	0	0	0	Gold Coast (Aust.)	1998
Pachniuk, Richard	24.3.71	17	10	1	0	42	Oldham	1992-93
Parr, Chris	31.5.71	8+5	0	0	0	0	Oldham B.	1996
Reid, Wayne	15.12.69	9+11	0	0	0	0	Salford	1994-95
Scarisbrick, Chris	10.10.77	5+15	1	0	0	4		1997
Sculthorpe, Danny	8.9.79	0+2	0	0	0	0	Warrington W.	1998
Shaw, Mick	16.7.75	12	9	0	0	36	Bramley	1998
Stevens, Paul	7.10.74	21+1	13	0	0	52	London B.	1997
Swann, Willie	25.2.74	26+1	9	0	1	37	Warrington W.	1998
Topping, Paul	18.9.65	19+1	1	4	3	15	Oldham B.	1998
Tupaea, Shane	24.12.63	2+3	0	0	0	0	Keighley C.	1996
Waters, Ryan		2+1	0	0	0	0	Wakefield T.	1998
Webster, John	2.12.71	1	0	0	0	0	Oldham B.	1998
Winrow, Jamie	19.8.77	0+3	0	0	0	0	Wigan St. Judes ARL	1997
TOTALS								
43 players			109	92	5	625		

Representative appearances 1998
R. Eyres - Wales (1)

ST. HELENS

Ground: Knowsley Road (01744-23697)
First Season: 1895-96
Chairman: Tom Ellard
Honours: **Championship** Winners, 1931-32, 1952-53, 1958-59, 1965-66, 1969-70, 1970-71
Beaten finalists, 1964-65, 1966-67, 1971-72
League Leaders Trophy Winners, 1964-65, 1965-66
Club Championship (Merit Table) Beaten finalists, 1973-74
Division One Champions, 1974-75
Super League Champions, 1996
Challenge Cup Winners, 1955-56, 1960-61, 1965-66, 1971-72, 1975-76, 1996, 1997
Beaten finalists, 1896-97, 1914-15, 1929-30, 1952-53, 1977-78, 1986-87, 1988-89, 1990-91
Regal Trophy Winners, 1987-88
Beaten finalists, 1995-96
Premiership Winners, 1975-76, 1976-77, 1984-85, 1992-93
Beaten finalists, 1974-75, 1987-88, 1991-92, 1996, 1997
Lancashire Cup Winners, 1926-27, 1953-54, 1960-61, 1961-62, 1962-63, 1963-64, 1964-65, 1967-68, 1968-69, 1984-85, 1991-92
Beaten finalists, 1932-33, 1952-53, 1956-57, 1958-59, 1959-60, 1970-71, 1982-83, 1992-93
Lancashire League Winners, 1929-30, 1931-32, 1952-53, 1959-60, 1964-65, 1965-66, 1966-67, 1968-69
Western Division Championship Winners, 1963-64
Charity Shield Winners, 1992-93
BBC2 Floodlit Trophy Winners, 1971-72, 1975-76
Beaten finalists, 1965-66, 1968-69, 1970-71, 1977-78, 1978-79

RECORDS

Match

Goals: 16 by Paul Loughlin v. Carlisle, 14 Sep 1986
Tries: 6 by Alf Ellaby v. Barrow, 5 Mar 1932
Steve Llewellyn v. Castleford, 3 Mar 1956
Steve Llewellyn v. Liverpool C., 20 Aug 1956
Tom Van Vollenhoven v. Wakefield T., 21 Dec 1957
Tom Van Vollenhoven v. Blackpool B., 23 Apr 1962
Frank Myler v. Maryport, 1 Sep 1969
Shane Cooper v. Hull, 17 Feb 1988
Points: 40 by Paul Loughlin v. Carlisle, 14 Sep 1986

Season

Goals: 214 by Kel Coslett, 1971-72
Tries: 62 by Tom Van Vollenhoven, 1958-59
Points: 452 by Kel Coslett, 1971-72

Career

Goals: 1,639 by Kel Coslett, 1962-76
Tries: 392 by Tom Van Vollenhoven, 1957-68
Points: 3,413 by Kel Coslett, 1962-76
Appearances: 519+12 by Kel Coslett, 1962-76
Highest score: 112-0 v. Carlisle, 14 Sep 1986
Highest against: 78-6 at Warrington, 12 Apr 1909
Attendance: 35,695 v. Wigan (League), 26 Dec 1949

Chris Arkwright: Two Test appearances.

GREAT BRITAIN REGISTER
(61 players)

Chris Arkwright	(+2)	1985
Len Aston	(3)	1947
Paul Atcheson	(2+1)	1997
Billy Benyon	(5+1)	1971-72
Tommy Bishop	(15)	1966-69
Frank Carlton	(1)	1958
Eric Chisnall	(4)	1974
Gary Connolly	(7+3)	1991-93
Eddie Cunningham	(1)	1978
Keiron Cunningham	(7)	1996-98
Bob Dagnall	(4)	1961-65
David Eckersley	(2+2)	1973-74
Alf Ellaby	(13)	1928-33
Les Fairclough	(6)	1926-29
John Fieldhouse	(1)	1986
Alec Fildes	(4)	1932
Alf Frodsham	(3)	1928-29
Peter Gorley	(2+1)	1980-81
Bobbie Goulding	(9+2)	1994-97
Doug Greenall	(6)	1951-54
Jonathan Griffiths	(1)	1992
Paul Groves	(1)	1987
Roy Haggerty	(2)	1987
Karle Hammond	(1+1)	1996
Joey Hayes	(1)	1996
Mervyn Hicks	(1)	1965
Neil Holding	(4)	1984
Dick Huddart	(12)	1959-63
Alan Hunte	(15)	1992-97
Les Jones	(1)	1971
Chris Joynt	(14+4)	1993-98
Tony Karalius	(4+1)	1971-72
Vince Karalius	(10)	1958-61
Ken Kelly	(2)	1972
Barry Ledger	(2)	1985-86
Sean Long	(1+1)	1997-98
Paul Loughlin	(14+1)	1988-92
Stan McCormick	(1)	1948
Tom McKinney	(1)	1957
John Mantle	(13)	1966-73
Roy Mathias	(1)	1979
Glyn Moses	(9)	1955-57
Alex Murphy	(26)	1958-66
Frank Myler	(9)	1970
Paul Newlove	(4)	1997-98
George Nicholls	(22)	1973-79
Sonny Nickle	(1+5)	1992-94
Harry Pinner	(5+1)	1980-86
Andy Platt	(4+3)	1985-88

Alan Prescott	(28)	1951-58
Austin Rhodes	(4)	1957-61
Paul Sculthorpe	(3)	1998
Jim Stott	(1)	1947
Anthony Sullivan	(6)	1991-97
Mick Sullivan	(10)	1961-62
John Tembey	(2)	1963-64
Abe Terry	(10)	1958-61
John Walsh	(4+1)	1972
Kevin Ward	(1+2)	1990-92
John Warlow	(3+1)	1964-68
Cliff Watson	(29+1)	1963-71

1998 SIGNINGS REGISTER

Signed	Player	Club From
—	Adamson, Phil	Penrith (Aust.)
10.2.98	Braddish, John	Crosfields ARL
5.3.98	Camman, Nicholas	Pilkington Recs ARL
19.8.98	Cunliffe, David	—
22.1.98	Hall, Steven	—
5.3.98	Hill, Stuart	St. Helens Academy
2.8.98	Howell, Ifan	Henby RU
9.3.98	Ireland, Neil	Ashton ARL
—	Iro, Kevin	Auckland W. (NZ)
19.2.98	Johnson, Jason	—
22.7.98	Jonkers, Timothy	Blackbrook ARL
20.4.98	McConnell, David	St. Helens Academy
5.3.98	Peachey, Ian	—
19.1.98	Peet, Kelvin	St. Helens Academy
1.1.98	Sculthorpe, Paul	Warrington W.
23.1.98	Smith, Chris	Castleford T.
10.2.98	Smith, Damien	St. George (Aust.)
—	Tuilagi, Fereti	Halifax B.S.
3.6.98	Wellens, Paul	Blackbrook ARL

COACHING REGISTER
● **Since 1974-75**

Eric Ashton	May 74 - May 80
Kel Coslett	June 80 - May 82
Billy Benyon	May 82 - Nov 85
Alex Murphy	Nov 85 - Jan 90
Mike McClennan	Feb 90 - Dec 93
Eric Hughes	Jan 94 - Jan 96
Shaun McRae	Jan 96 - Oct 98
Ellery Hanley	Oct 98 -

ST. HELENS 1998 MATCH ANALYSIS

Date	Competition	H/A	Opponents	Rlt	Score	Tries	Goals	Attendance	Referee
15.2.98	CC(4)	A	Featherstone R.	W	56-24	Hammond (2), Martyn (2), Sculthorpe (2), Cunningham, Goulding, Joynt, C. Smith	Goulding (8)	–	–
1.3.98	CC(5)	H	Warrington W.	W	35-22	Newlove (2), Cunningham, Martyn, Sullivan	Goulding (7, dg)	8499	R. Smith
15.3.98	CC(6)	A	Wigan	L	10-22	Sullivan, C. Smith	Goulding	–	–
5.4.98	SL	A	Salford R.	W	18-14	Haigh, Long, Newlove	Goulding (3)	–	–
10.4.98	SL	H	Wigan W.	L	18-38	Haigh, Martyn, Newlove	Goulding (3)	11,414	R. Smith
19.4.98	SL	A	Huddersfield G.	W	26-24	Long (2), Newlove, Sullivan	Goulding (5)	–	–
26.4.98	SL	H1	Warrington W.	W	36-14	Long (2), Anderson, C. Smith, D. Smith, Sullivan	Goulding (5), Long	10,058	R. Connolly
10.5.98	SL	A	Bradford B.	L	4-18	Long	–	–	–
17.5.98	SL	H	Hull S.	W	28-18	Atcheson, Hammond, D. Smith, C. Smith	Goulding (6)	7396	Kirkpatrick
24.5.98	SL	A	Halifax B.S.	L	10-16	Sculthorpe, Sullivan	Goulding	–	–
31.5.98	SL	H	Leeds R.	W	18-31	Hammond, Joynt, Sullivan	Long (3)	7825	Cummings
7.6.98	SL	A	Castleford T.	W	34-12	Newlove (2), Hammond, Long, Joynt, Perelini	Long (5)	–	–
14.6.98	SL	H	London B.	W	58-6	Sullivan (3), Hammond (2), D. Smith (2), Cunningham, Joynt, Newlove	Long (9)	5631	J. Connolly
20.6.98	SL	A	Sheffield E.	L	17-18	Newlove, Sullivan, C. Smith	Long (1, dg), Goulding	–	–
28.6.98	SL	H	Salford R.	W	48-12	Goulding (2), C. Smith (2), Goldspink, Long, Perelini, Sullivan	Goulding (8)	6130	Morris
5.7.98	SL	A	Wigan W.	L	14-38	Newlove, Sculthorpe	Long (3)	–	–
26.7.98	SL	N1	Wigan W.	L	2-36	–	Goulding	(8572)	Cummings
2.8.98	SL	H	Huddersfield G.	W	68-18	Atcheson (3), C. Smith (2), Davidson, Hammond, Joynt, Newlove, O'Neill, D. Smith, Sullivan	Long (10)	4227	R. Smith
9.8.98	SL	A	Warrington W.	W	48-18	Long (2), Atcheson, Joynt, Cunningham, Sculthorpe, Matautia, Sullivan	Long (8)	–	–
16.8.98	SL	H	Bradford B.	W	33-25	Cunningham (2), Atcheson, Long, Martyn	Long (6, dg)	6955	Cummings
23.8.98	SL	A	Hull S.	W	20-6	Davidson (2), Newlove, Sullivan	Long (2)	–	–
30.8.98	SL	H	Halifax B.S.	W	36-6	Anderson, Atcheson, Perelini, Cunningham, Davidson, Stewart	Long (5), Hamond (2dg)	7762	R. Connolly
5.9.98	SL	A	Leeds R.	L	18-37	Newlove, Sculthorpe, Matautia	Long (3)	–	–
13.9.98	SL	H	Castleford T.	D	32-32	Martyn (2), Goldspink, Newlove, Pickavance	Long (6)	5887	Kirkpatrick
18.9.98	SL	A	London B.	W	37-22	Sullivan (5), Sculthorpe, Martyn	Long (4, dg)	–	–
25.9.98	SL	H	Sheffield E.	W	50-0	Sullivan (3), Newlove (2), Joynt (2), Long, Davidson	Long (7)	4609	R. Connolly
2.10.98	PO	H	Bradford B.	W	46-24	Martyn (2), D. Smith (2), Long, Newlove, Sculthorpe, Sullivan	Long (7)	8793	Cummings
9.10.98	PO	A	Halifax B.S.	W	37-30	Sullivan (2), Martyn, Joynt, Newlove, Cunningham	Long (6), Martyn (dg)	–	–
18.10.98	PO	A	Leeds R.	L	16-44	Perelini, D. Smith, Sullivan, Newlove	–	–	–

H1 at Liverpool FC; N1 at Swansea C. FC

ST. HELENS 1998 PLAYERS' SUMMARY

	Date of birth	App	T	G	D	Pts	Previous club	Debut
Anderson, Paul	2.4.77	1+19	2	0	0	8	St. Helens Acad.	1995-96
Atcheson, Paul	17.5.73	29	7	0	0	28	Oldham B.	1998
Barrow, Scott	28.6.80	0+1	0	0	0	0	Blackbrook ARL	1997
Busby, Dean	1.2.73	0+1	0	0	0	0	Hull	1995-96
Cunningham, Keiron	28.10.76	23+1	8	0	0	32	Wigan St.Judes ARL	1994-95
Davidson, Paul	1.8.69	13+12	5	0	0	20	Oldham B.	1998
Goldspink, Brett	16.7.70	22+5	2	0	0	8	Oldham B.	1998
Goulding, Bobbie	4.2.72	12+2	3	49	1	111	Widnes	1994-95
Haigh, Andy	3.9.75	9+4	2	0	0	8	Crosfields ARL	1993-94
Hamilton, John	18.10.79	3	0	0	0	0	Blackbrook ARL	1998
Hammond, Karle	25.4.74	19+8	8	0	2	34	Widnes	1995-96
Hayes, Joey	4.1.76	1	0	0	0	0	Crosfields ARL	1995-96
Joynt, Chris	7.12.71	25	9	0	0	36	Oldham	1992-93
Leathem, Andy	30.3.77	2	0	0	0	0	Crosfields ARL	1994-95
Long, Sean	24.9.76	24+5	13	86	3	227	Widnes V.	1997
Martyn, Tommy	4.6.71	20+2	11	0	1	45	Oldham	1993-94
Matautia, Vila	31.8.69	3+8	2	0	0	8	Doncaster	1994-95
Newlove, Paul	10.8.71	28	19	0	0	76	Bradford B.	1995-96
O'Neill, Julian	24.7.73	24	1	0	0	4	Auckland W. (NZ)	1997
Perelini, Apollo	16.7.69	15+10	4	0	0	16	Western Samoa RU	1994-95
Pickavance, Ian	20.9.68	1+20	1	0	0	4	Swinton	1993-94
Sculthorpe, Paul	22.9.77	25+1	8	0	0	32	Warrington W.	1998
Smith, Chris	31.10.75	28	9	0	0	36	Castleford T.	1998
Smith, Damien	4.7.74	21+1	8	0	0	32	St. George (Aust.)	1998
Stewart, Anthony	5.3.79	0+5	1	0	0	4	St. Helens Academy	1997
Sullivan, Anthony	23.11.68	29	26	0	0	104	Hull K.R.	1991-92
Wellens, Paul	27.2.80	0+3	0	0	0	0	Blackbrook ARL	1998
TOTALS								
27 players			149	135	7	873		

Representative appearances 1998

Atcheson - Wales (1); Cunningham - Britain (2), Wales (1, 1t); Davidson - Emerging England (0+1, 1t); Hammond - Wales (1); Joynt - Britain (3); Long - Britain (1, 1t), Emerging England (1, 1dg); Martyn - Ireland (2, 1t, 5g); Newlove - Britain (1, 1t); Sculthorpe - Britain (3); Sullivan - Wales (1)
Busby played for Wales (1) while on loan to Hull Sharks

SALFORD REDS

Ground: The Willows (0161-736-6564)
First Season: 1896-97. Added Reds to title in 1995-96.
Chairman: John Wilkinson
Honours: **Championship** Winners, 1913-14, 1932-33, 1936-37, 1938-39
Beaten finalists, 1933-34
Division One Champions, 1973-74, 1975-76
Division Two Champions, 1990-91
Division One (2nd league) Champions, 1995-96, 1996
Challenge Cup Winners, 1937-38
Beaten finalists, 1899-1900, 1901-02, 1902-03, 1905-06, 1938-39, 1968-69
Regal Trophy Beaten finalists, 1972-73
Premiership Beaten finalists, 1975-76
Second Division/Divisional Premiership Winners, 1990-91; 1996
Lancashire Cup Winners, 1931-32, 1934-35, 1935-36, 1936-37, 1972-73
Beaten finalists, 1929-30, 1938-39, 1973-74, 1974-75, 1975-76, 1988-89, 1990-91
Lancashire League Winners, 1932-33, 1933-34, 1934-35, 1936-37, 1938-39
BBC2 Floodlit Trophy Winners, 1974-75

RECORDS
Match
Goals: 13 by Gus Risman v. Bramley, 5 Apr 1933
Gus Risman v. Broughton R., 18 May 1940
David Watkins v. Keighley, 7 Jan 1972
Steve Rule v. Doncaster, 4 Sep 1981
Tries: 6 by Frank Miles v. Lees, 5 Mar 1898
Ernest Bone v. Goole, 29 Mar 1902
Jack Hilton v. Leigh, 7 Oct 1939
Points: 39 by Jim Lomas v. Liverpool C., 2 Feb 1907

Season
Goals: 221 by David Watkins, 1972-73
Tries: 46 by Keith Fielding, 1973-74
Points: 493 by David Watkins, 1972-73

Career
Goals: 1,241 by David Watkins, 1967-79
Tries: 297 by Maurice Richards, 1969-83
Points: 2,907 by David Watkins, 1967-79
Appearances: 496+2 by Maurice Richards, 1969-83
Highest score: 78-0 v. Liverpool C., 2 Feb 1907
Highest against: 70-6 at Wigan, 14 Mar 1993
Attendance: 26,470 v. Warrington (RL Cup), 13 Feb 1937

GREAT BRITAIN REGISTER
(28 players)

Bill Burgess	(1)	1969
Paul Charlton	(17+1)	1970-74
Mike Coulman	(2+1)	1971
George Curran	(6)	1946-48
Ephraim Curzon	(1)	1910
Tom Danby	(3)	1950
Colin Dixon	(11+2)	1969-74
Alan Edwards	(7)	1936-37
Jack Feetham	(7)	1932-33
Keith Fielding	(3)	1974-77
Ken Gill	(5+2)	1974-77
Jack Gore	(1)	1926
Chris Hesketh	(21+2)	1970-74
Barney Hudson	(8)	1932-37
Emlyn Jenkins	(9)	1933-37
Jim Lomas	(5)	1908-10
Tom McKinney	(7)	1951-54
Alf Middleton	(1)	1929
Steve Nash	(8)	1977-82
Maurice Richards	(2)	1974
Gus Risman	(17)	1932-46
Jack Spencer	(1)	1907
Johnny Ward	(1)	1970
Silas Warwick	(2)	1907
Billy Watkins	(7)	1933-37
David Watkins	(2+4)	1971-74
Billy Williams	(2)	1929-32
Peter Williams	(1+1)	1989

SALFORD REDS 1998 MATCH ANALYSIS

Date	Competition	H/A	Opponents	Rlt	Score	Tries	Goals	Attendance	Referee
14.2.98	CC(4)	A	Ovenden	W	74-0	Rogers (3), White (3), McAvoy (2), Randall (2), Coussons, Crompton, Martin, Naylor	Blakeley (9)	–	–
1.3.98	CC(5)	A	Widnes V.	W	48-6	Martin (2), Randall (2), Blakeley, Bradbury, Naylor, Rogers, Savelio	Blakeley (6)	–	–
15.3.98	CC(6)	H	Hull S.	W	41-10	McAvoy (2), White (2), Broadbent, Forber, Naylor	Blakeley (4,dg,) White (2)	6210	R. Smith
28.3.98	CC(SF)	N1	Sheffield E.	L	18-22	Edwards, Rogers, White	Blakeley (2, dg), Crompton (dg)	(6961)	Cummings
5.4.98	SL	H	St. Helens	L	14-18	Crompton, Eccles, Hulme	White	7337	J. Connolly
10.4.98	SL	A	Warrington W.	W	37-4	Rogers (2), Bradbury, Broadbent, Forber, Hulme, Naylor	Crompton (4, dg)	–	–
19.4.98	SL	H	Hull S.	W	12-4	Blakeley, Rogers	Blakeley (2)	5227	Morris
24.4.98	SL	A	Leeds R.	L	12-31	Crompton, E. Faimalo	Blakeley (2)	–	–
10.5.98	SL	H	Huddersfield G.	W	40-6	Bradbury (2), McAvoy (2), Blakeley, Edwards, Hassan, Rogers,	Blakeley (4)	4195	Kirkpatrick
17.5.98	SL	H	Sheffield E.	L	8-28	McAvoy	Blakekley (2)	3752	Ganson
24.5.98	SL	A	London B.	L	12-21	Crompton, Martin	Crompton (2)	–	–
31.5.98	SL	H	Castleford T.	L	8-18	Martin, Rogers	–	4143	Morris
7.6.98	SL	A	Wigan W.	L	6-34	Alker	Russell	–	–
14.6.98	SL	A	Halifax B.S.	L	6-34	McAvoy	Southern	–	–
21.6.98	SL	H	Bradford B.	W	11-10	Bradbury, White	White, Lee (dg)	6319	Kirkpatrick
28.6.98	SL	A	St. Helens	L	12-48	Alker, Randall	White (2)	–	–
5.7.98	SL	H	Warrington W.	L	14-25	Alker (2), Randall	White	4538	Presley
10.7.98	SL	N2	Leeds R.	L	16-34	Martin, McAvoy, Alker	Svabic (2)	(4122)	R. Connolly
2.8.98	SL	A	Hull S.	L	0-32	–	–	–	–
9.8.98	SL	H	Leeds R.	L	6-40	Hassan	Svabic	4043	Kirkpatrick
16.8.98	SL	A	Huddersfield G.	W	16-12	Naylor (2), White	Svabic (2)	–	–
21.8.98	SL	A	Sheffield E.	D	18-18	Littler, Randall, Rogers	Svabic (2), Southern	–	–
30.8.98	SL	H	London B.	W	23-20	Highton, Naylor, Rogers	Blakeley (5) White (dg)	3681	R. Smith
6.9.98	SL	A	Castleford T.	L	12-30	Hulme, Waring	Blakeley (2)	–	–
13.9.98	SL	H	Wigan W.	L	2-34	–	Blakeley	4895	Presley
20.9.98	SL	A	Halifax B.S.	L	16-34	White (2), Southern	Svabic (2)	3487	Ganson
27.9.98	SL	A	Bradford B.	L	18-40	Bradbury, Broadbent, White	Svabic (3)	–	–

N1 at Leeds; N2 at Gateshead

COACHING REGISTER

● Since 1974-75

Les Bettinson	Dec 73 - Mar 77
Colin Dixon	Mar 77 - Jan 78
Stan McCormick	Feb 78 - Mar 78
Alex Murphy	May 78 - Nov 80
Kevin Ashcroft	Nov 80 - Mar 82
Alan McInnes	Mar 82 - May 82
Malcolm Aspey	May 82 - Oct 83
Mike Coulman	Oct 83 - May 84
Kevin Ashcroft	May 84 - Oct 89
Kevin Tamati	Oct 89 - July 93
Garry Jack	July 93 - Mar 95
Andy Gregory	Mar 95 -

1998 SIGNINGS REGISTER

Signed	Player	Club From
—	Briggs, Carl	Wakefield T.
—	Brown, Darren	Penrith (Aust.)
—	Carige, Paul	Parramatta (Aust.)
—	Casey, Garen	Wakefield T.
31.3.98	*Hassan, Phil	Leeds R.
23.4.98	Highton, Paul	Featherstone R.
—	Johnson, Mark	Hull S.
6.8.98	Kenward, Shane	St. George (Aust.)
28.8.98	*Knox, Simon	Bradford B.
5.6.98	Littler, Stuart	Salford Academy
—	Makin, Craig	Widnes V.
—	Smith, Hudson	Balmain (Aust.)
—	Thompson, Bobby	Penrith (Aust.)

SALFORD REDS 1998 PLAYERS' SUMMARY

	Date of birth	App	T	G	D	Pts	Previous club	Debut
Alexander, Neil	18.2.77	0+1	0	0	0	0	Salford Academy	1998
Alker, Malcolm	4.11.78	10+1	5	0	0	20	Wigan St. Patricks ARL	1997
Blakeley, Steve	17.10.72	13+1	3	39	2	92	Wigan	1992-93
Bradbury, David	16.3.72	13+1	6	0	0	24	Oldham B.	1997
Broadbent, Gary	31.10.76	27	3	0	0	12	Widnes V.	1997
Coussons, Phil	2.8.73	4	1	0	0	4	Salford U-18s	1992-93
Crompton, Martin	27.9.69	12+2	4	6	2	30	Oldham B.	1998
Eccles, Cliff	4.9.67	15+5	1	0	0	4	Rochdale H.	1994-95
Edwards, Peter	4.7.69	17+2	2	0	0	8	Auckland W. (NZ)	1995-96
Faimalo, Esene	11.10.66	8+18	1	0	0	4	Leeds R.	1997
Faimalo, Joe	28.7.70	14+7	0	0	0	0	Oldham B.	1998
Forber, Paul	29.4.64	7+9	2	0	0	8	St. Helens	1992-93
Hassan, Phil	18.8.74	15	2	0	0	8	Leeds R.	1998
Highton, Paul	10.11.76	10+3	1	0	0	4	Halifax B.S.	1998
Hulme, David	6.2.64	24	3	0	0	12	Leeds R.	1997
Kenward, Shane	7.3.72	1	0	0	0	0	St. George (Aust.)	1998
Knox, Simon	14.10.72	1+1	0	0	0	0	Bradford B.	1998
Lee, Mark	27.3.68	7+4	0	0	1	1	St. Helens	1989-90
Littler, Stuart	19.2.79	5	1	0	0	4	Salford Academy	1998
Marsh, Iain	6.10.80	1	0	0	0	0	Widnes Tigers ARL	1998
Martin, Scott	29.12.74	18+6	6	0	0	24	Leigh	1994-95
McAvoy, Nathan	31.12.76	18	9	0	0	36	Eccles ARL	1993-94
Naylor, Scott	2.2.72	15	7	0	0	28	Wigan	1993-94
Neal, Mike	4.9.73	0+1	0	0	0	0	Oldham B.	1998
Penni, Julian	20.11.79	3	0	0	0	0	Salford Academy	1998
Platt, Andy	9.10.63	10+2	0	0	0	0	Auckland W. (NZ)	1997
Randall, Craig	22.9.72	5+12	7	0	0	28	Leigh Miners ARL	1991-92
Rogers, Darren	6.5.74	25	12	0	0	48	Dewsbury	1995-96
Russell, Robert	12.3.79	2	0	1	0	2	Eccles ARL	1998
Savelio, Lokeni	24.11.69	9+15	1	0	0	4	Hutt Valley (NZ)	1995-96
Southern, Paul	18.3.76	12+5	1	2	0	8	Folly Lane ARL	1993-94
Svabic, Simon	18.1.80	7	0	12	0	24	Oldham B.	1998
Waring, Phil	5.3.75	1+4	1	0	0	4	Widnes V.	1997
White, Josh	9.8.71	22+3	11	7	1	59	London B.	1998
TOTALS								
34 players			90	67	6	500		

Representative appearances 1998

Broadbent - Emerging England (1); Burgess - Ireland (1+1); Crompton - Ireland (2, 1t, 1dg); Eccles - Ireland (0+2); Knox - Scotland (1+1); McAvoy - Emerging England (1);

SHEFFIELD EAGLES

Ground: Don Valley Stadium
(0114-261-0326)
First Season: 1984-85
Chairman: Tim Adams
Honours: **Challenge Cup** Winners 1998
Division Two Champions, 1991-92
Second Division/Divisional Premiership Winners, 1988-89, 1991-92
Yorkshire Cup Beaten finalists, 1992-93

RECORDS

Match

Goals: 12 by Roy Rafferty at Fulham, 21 Sep 1986
Mark Aston v. Keighley C., 25 Apr 1992
Mark Aston v. Egremont R. 1 Mar 1998

Tries: 5 by Daryl Powell at Mansfield M., 2 Jan 1989

Points: 32 by Roy Rafferty at Fulham, 21 Sep 1986

Season

Goals: 148 by Mark Aston, 1988-89
Tries: 30 by Iva Ropati, 1991-92
Points: 307 by Mark Aston, 1988-89

Career

Goals: 927 by Mark Aston, 1986-94 and 1995-
Tries: 114 by Daryl Powell, 1984-95
Points: 2,013 by Mark Aston, 1986-94 and 1995-
Appearances: 318+32 by Mark Gamson, 1984-96
Highest score: 84-6 v. Egremont R., 1 Mar 1998
Highest against: 80-2 v. Australia, 26 Oct 1994;
By British club: 68-2 at St. Helens, 18 Aug 1996
Attendance: 10,603 v. Bradford B. (Super League), 16 Aug 1997

COACHING REGISTER

● **Since formation in 1984**

Alan Rhodes	Apr 84 - May 86
Gary Hetherington	July 86 - Apr 93
Bill Gardner	May 93 - Dec 93
Gary Hetherington	Dec 93 - Oct 96
Phil Larder	Nov 96 - May 97
John Kear	May 97 -

GREAT BRITAIN REGISTER

(6 players)

Mark Aston	(+1)	1991
Paul Broadbent	(8)	1996-97
Lee Jackson	(6)	1993-94
Dale Laughton	(2+1)	1998
Daryl Powell	(19+9)	1990-94
Keith Senior	(3+2)	1996

1998 SIGNINGS REGISTER

Signed	Player	Club From
21.4.98	*Allen, Christopher	Castleford T.
—	Baldwin, Simon	Halifax B.S.
22.7.98	Bettinson, Lee	Doncaster Toll Bar ARL
1.4.98	Duckett, Gareth	Dodworth ARL
17.2.98	Greaves, Ben	Hillsborough H. ARL
6.8.98	Greenwood, Lee	Siddal ARL
—	Hardy, Jeff	St. George (Aust.)
23.1.98	Jackson, Michael	Halifax B.S.
—	Lovell, Karl	Parramatta (Aust.)
24.2.98	Martin, Kevin	Wakefield T.
16.2.98	Molloy, Steve	Featherstone R.
—	Pearson, Martin	Halifax B.S.
—	Powell, Daio	Halifax B.S.
1.4.98	Rice, Andrew	Walney Central ARL
5.8.98	Smith, Nicholas	Siddal ARL
23.1.98	Watson, David	S. Queensland (Aust.)
25.4.98	Wilkes, Oliver	Ulverston ARL
17.8.98	Windas, Christopher	Castleford T.

SHEFFIELD EAGLES 1998 MATCH ANALYSIS

Date	Competition	H/A	Opponents	Rlt	Score	Tries	Goals	Attendance	Referee
15.2.98	CC(4)	A	Leigh C.	W	66-11	Crowther (4), Carr (2), Senior (2), Laughton (2), Watson, Wood	Aston (9)	–	–
1.3.98	CC(5)	H	Egremont R.	W	84-6	Pinkney (4), Crowther (2), Aston, Broadbent, Carr, Doyle, Lawless, Senior, Sodje, Taewa, Wood	Aston (12)	1100	Taberner
14.3.98	CC(6)	A	Castleford T.	W	32-22	Senior (2), Crowther (2), Carr, Sovatabua	Aston (4)	–	–
28.3.98	CC(SF)	N1	Salford R.	W	22-18	Aston, Jackson, Laughton, Taewa	Aston (3)	(6961)	Cummings
5.4.98	SL	H	Hull S.	L	24-34	Crowther, Sovatabua, Turner	Aston (6)	4511	Kirkpatrick
10.4.98	SL	A	Castleford T.	L	6-19	Stott	Aston	–	–
17.4.98	SL	H	Bradford B.	L	4-11	–	Aston (2)	4678	R. Smith
26.4.98	SL	A	Huddersfield G.	W	48-18	Carr (2), Crowther (2), Turner, Jackson, Pinkney, Senior	Aston (5), Crowther	–	–
2.5.98	CC(F)	N2	Wigan W.	W	17-8	Pinkney, Crowther, Turner	Aston (2, dg)	(60,669)	Cummings
9.5.98	SL	H	Wigan W.	L	6-36	Senior	Aston	7365	Presley
17.5.98	SL	A	Salford R.	W	28-8	Crowther (2), Molloy, Senior	Crowther (6)	–	–
23.5.98	SL	H	Leeds R.	L	23-24	Carr, Pinkney, Senior, Sovatabua	Vassilakopoulos (3, dg)	6283	Cummings
30.5.98	SL	H	Halifax B.S.	L	22-28	Pinkney, Law, Senior, Turner	Vassilakopoulos (3)	3811	Ganson
7.6.98	SL	A	London B.	L	22-26	Senior (3), Sovatabua, Shaw	Vassilakopoulos	–	–
14.6.98	SL	A	Warrington W.	D	18-18	Senior, Vassilakopoulos, Carr	Vassilakopoulos (3)	–	–
20.6.98	SL	H	St. Helens	W	18-17	Stott (2), Sovatabua	Morganson (2), Wood	3675	Presley
28.6.98	SL	A	Hull S.	W	35-20	Sodje (3), Doyle, Senior, Turner	Wood (4), Morganson, Vassilakopoulos (dg)	–	–
3.7.98	SL	H	Castleford T.	W	22-16	Stephens, Taewa, Sodje	Wood (4, 2dg)	3151	Kirkpatrick
17.7.98	SL	N3	Halifax B.S.	L	10-32	Doyle, Morganson	Aston	(3087)	R. Smith
2.8.98	SL	A	Bradford B.	W	38-18	Sodje (2), Molloy, Senior, Sovatabua, Turner	Aston (6g, dg) Sovatabua (dg)	–	–
7.8.98	SL	H	Huddersfield G.	W	56-10	Sodje (3), Laughton (2), Senior, Sovatabua, Taewa, Turner	Aston (10)	2550	Presley
16.8.98	SL	A	Wigan W.	L	6-44	Turner	Aston	–	–
21.8.98	SL	H	Salford R.	D	18-18	Laughton, Sodje	Aston (5)	2571	Nicholson
28.8.98	SL	A	Leeds R.	L	22-36	Carr (2), Sodje, Senior	Aston (3)	–	–
6.9.98	SL	A	Halifax B.S.	L	16-33	Carr, Morganson, Senior	Aston, Wood	–	–
11.9.98	SL	H1	London B.	L	18-19	Carr (2), Sodje	Wood (3)	2420	Cummings
18.9.98	SL	H	Warrington W.	W	35-6	Cardoza, Carr, Taewa, Turner, Watson, Wood	Wood (5), Aston (dg)	3083	R. Connolly
25.9.98	SL	A	St. Helens	L	0-50	–	–	–	–

N1 at Leeds; N2 at Wembley; N3 at Northampton T. FC; H1 at Sheffield U. FC

SHEFFIELD EAGLES 1998 PLAYERS' SUMMARY

	Date of birth	App	T	G	D	Pts	Previous club	Debut
Aston, Mark	27.9.67	17+3	2	72	3	155	Featherstone R.	1995-96
Broadbent, Paul	24.5.68	25	1	0	0	4	Lock Lane ARL	1987-88
Cardoza, Dale	13.9.79	0+3	1	0	0	4	East Leeds ARL	1998
Carr, Paul	13.5.68	23+2	14	0	0	56	Hunslet	1992-93
Crowther, Matt	6.5.74	12	14	7	0	70	Kippax ARL	1992-93
Doyle, Rod	18.7.69	22+4	3	0	0	12	Sth. Queensland (Aust.)	1997
Jackson, Michael	11.10.69	4+9	2	0	0	8	Halifax B.S.	1998
Laughton, Dale	10.10.70	23+5	6	0	0	24	Dodworth ARL	1991-92
Law, Neil	23.10.74	1+1	1	0	0	4	Northampton RU	1998
Lawless, Johnny	3.11.74	15+4	1	0	0	4	Halifax	1995-96
Molloy, Steve	11.3.69	6+15	2	0	0	8	Featherstone R.	1998
Morganson, Willie	11.9.72	10+4	2	3	0	14	N. Queensland (Aust.)	1997
Pinkney, Nick	6.12.70	15+1	8	0	0	32	Keighley C.	1997
Senior, Keith	24.4.76	25	19	0	0	76	Sheffield E. Acad.	1994-95
Shaw, Darren	5.10.71	27+1	1	0	0	4	Canberra R. (Aust.)	1998
Sodje, Bright	21.4.67	18	13	0	0	52	Hull K.R.	1994-95
Sovatabua, Waisale	26.6.73	22+4	7	0	1	29	Carpenters Motors (Fiji)	1995-96
Stephens, Gareth	15.4.74	9+5	1	0	0	4	Hull S.	1997
Stott, Lynton	9.5.71	12+3	3	0	0	12	Halifax	1992-93
Taewa, Whetu	29.10.71	19+7	5	0	0	20	N. Queensland (Aust.)	1997
Turner, Darren	13.10.73	13+11	10	0	0	40	Leeds Academy	1992-93
Vassilakopoulos, Marcus	19.9.76	11+7	1	10	2	26	Leeds R.	1997
Watson, Dave	24.5.66	25+2	2	0	0	8	S. Queensland (Aust.)	1998
Wilkes, Oliver	2.5.80	0+1	0	0	0	0	Ulverston ARL	1998
Wood, Martin	24.6.70	10+14	3	18	2	50	Keighley C.	1997
TOTALS								
25 players			122	110	8	716		

Representative appearances 1998
Laughton - Britain (2+1); Lawless - Ireland (2); Molloy - Emerging England (1); Senior - Britain (3, 1t), Emerging England (1); Shaw - Scotland (2); Stephens - Wales (0+1)

SWINTON LIONS

Ground: Gigg Lane, Bury (0161-761-2328)
First Season: 1896-97. Added Lions to title at the start of 1996 League season.
Chairman: Malcolm White
Honours: **Championship** Winners, 1926-27, 1927-28, 1930-31, 1934-35
Beaten finalists, 1924-25, 1932-33
War Emergency League Beaten finalists, 1939-40
Division One Champions, 1962-63, 1963-64
Division Two Champions, 1984-85
Challenge Cup Winners, 1899-1900, 1925-26, 1927-28
Beaten finalists, 1926-27, 1931-32
Second Division Premiership Winners, 1986-87
Beaten finalists, 1988-89
Lancashire Cup Winners, 1925-26, 1927-28, 1939-40, 1969-70
Beaten finalists, 1910-11, 1923-24, 1931-32, 1960-61, 1961-62, 1962-63, 1964-65, 1972-73
Lancashire League Winners, 1924-25, 1927-28, 1928-29, 1930-31, 1960-61
Lancashire War League Winners, 1939-40
Western Division Championship Beaten finalists, 1963-64
BBC2 Floodlit Trophy Beaten finalists, 1966-67

RECORDS
Match
Goals: 12 by Ken Gowers v. Liverpool C., 3 Oct 1959
Tries: 6 by Mark Riley v. Prescot P., 11 Aug 1996
Points: 30 by Greg Pearce v. Prescot P., 11 Aug 1996

Season
Goals: 128 by Albert Blan, 1960-61
Tries: 42 by John Stopford, 1963-64
Points: 283 by Albert Blan, 1960-61

Career
Goals: 970 by Ken Gowers, 1954-73
Tries: 197 by Frank Evans, 1921-31
Points: 2,105 by Ken Gowers, 1954-73
Appearances: 593+8 by Ken Gowers, 1954-73
Highest score: 90-0 v. Prescot P., 11 Aug 1996
Highest against: 78-0 v. Wigan, 29 Sep 1992
Attendance: 26,891 v. Wigan (RL Cup), 12 Feb 1964 — at Station Road
3,501 v. Wigan (Lancs Cup), 29 Sep 1992 — at Gigg Lane

COACHING REGISTER
● **Since 1974-75**

Austin Rhodes	June 74 - Nov 75
Bob Fleet	Nov 75 - Nov 76
John Stopford	Nov 76 - Apr 77
Terry Gorman	June 77 - Nov 78
Ken Halliwell	Nov 78 - Dec 79
Frank Myler	Jan 80 - May 81
Tom Grainey	May 81 - Oct 83
Jim Crellin	Nov 83 - May 86
Bill Holliday } Mike Peers }	June 86 - Oct 87
Frank Barrow	Oct 87 - June 89
Jim Crellin	July 89 - July 91
Chris O'Sullivan	July 91 - Dec 91
Tony Barrow	Jan 92 - Jan 96
Peter Roe	Jan 96 - Mar 97
Les Holliday	Mar 97 -

GREAT BRITAIN REGISTER
(15 players)

Tom Armitt	(8)	1933-37
Alan Buckley	(7)	1963-66
Fred Butters	(2)	1929
Billy Davies	(1)	1968
Bryn Evans	(10)	1926-33
Frank Evans	(4)	1924
Jack Evans	(3)	1926
Ken Gowers	(14)	1962-66
Hector Halsall	(1)	1929
Martin Hodgson	(16)	1929-37
Ron Morgan	(2)	1963
Billo Rees	(11)	1926-29
Dave Robinson	(12)	1965-67
John Stopford	(12)	1961-66
Joe Wright	(1)	1932

SWINTON LIONS 1998 MATCH ANALYSIS

Date	Competition	H/A	Opponents	Rlt	Score	Tries	Goals	Attendance	Referee
1.2.98	CC(3)	H	Folly Lane	W	74-6	Ashcroft (2), Evans (2), Longo (2), T. Barrow, Coley, Casey, P. Barrow, Veikoso, Watson, Welsby, Cannon	Watson (8), Price-Jones	2425	Cummings
8.2.98	FD	H	Keighley C.	W	41-16	Adams, Gartland, Hodgkinson, Knowles, Price-Jones, Welsby	Gartland (7), Watson (3 dg)	2096	Ganson
15.2.98	CC(4)	H	York	W	39-21	Ashcroft (2), T. Barrow, Craig, Casey, Gartland	Gartland (7), Casey (dg)	780	Burke
22.2.98	FD	A	Dewsbury R.	L	24-34	Price-Jones, Craig, Gartland, Veikoso	Gartland (4)	–	–
1.3.98	CC(5)	A	Hull K.R.	L	24-46	Coley, Casey, Gartland, Price-Jones	Gartland (4)	–	–
4.3.98	FD	H	Whitehaven W.	W	27-6	Ashcroft (3), Price-Jones (2),	Gartland (3, dg)	708	Laughton
15.3.98	FD	H	Hunslet H.	L	16-18	Ashcroft, Coley, Watson	Gartland (2)	1134	Morris
22.3.98	FD	A	Wakefield T.	L	13-18	Cannon, Price-Jones	Gartland (2, dg)	–	–
29.3.98	FD	A	Rochdale H.	W	38-6	Craig (3), Price-Jones (2), Ashcroft, Watson	Gartland (5)	–	–
5.4.98	FD	H	Hull K.R.	W	21-4	Craig (2), Casey, Gartland	Gartland (2, dg)	1475	Taberner
10.4.98	FD	H	Leigh C.	W	32-22	P. Barrow (2), Gartland (2), Cannon, Casey	Gartland (4)	1246	Gilmour
13.4.98	FD	A	Widnes V.	L	18-34	Craig (2), Welsby	Gartland (3)	–	–
19.4.98	FD	H	Featherstone R.	W	31-30	Adams, Ashcroft, P. Barrow, Cannon, Knowles	Gartland (4), Casey, Price-Jones (dg)	1128	Kirkpatrick
26.4.98	FD	A	Keighley C.	L	18-20	Watson (2), Coley	Gartland (3)	–	–
10.5.98	FD	A	Whitehaven W.	L	10-12	Ashcroft, Craig	Gartland	–	–
13.5.98	FD	A	Dewsbury R.	W	13-10	P. Barrow, Watson	Gartland (2), Watson (dg)	–	–
24.5.98	FD	A	Hunslet H.	W	20-16	Adams, Cannon, Craig, Price-Jones	Watson (2)	–	–
31.5.98	FD	H	Wakefield T.	W	13-12	Veikoso	Gartland (4), Price-Jones (dg)	1406	Nicholson
3.6.98	FD	H	Rochdale H.	W	36-12	Casey (2), Adams, Coley, Gartland, Veikoso	Gartland (6)	1033	McGregor
7.6.98	FD	A	Hull K.R.	L	10-16	Gartland	Gartland (2, 2dg)	–	–
14.6.98	FD	A	Leigh C.	W	34-28	P. Barrow, Coley, Craig, Evans, Price-Jones, Watson	Gartland (5)	–	–
21.6.98	FD	H	Widnes V.	W	44-11	Mann (3), Cannon, Coley, Craig, Cushion, Watson	Gartland (6)	1349	Bates
24.6.98	FD	A	Featherstone R.	L	23-29	Veikoso (2), Price-Jones, Gartland, Coley	Gartland (1, dg)	–	–
28.6.98	FD	H	Dewsbury R.	W	31-16	Coley, Gartland, Welsby, Watson, Casey	Gartland (5), Price-Jones (dg)	1178	Oddy
5.7.98	FD	H	Wakefield T.	L	15-26	Blease (2)	Gartland (2), Watson (1, dg)	1520	Gilmour
15.7.98	FD	A	Widnes V.	W	34-12	Price-Jones (2), Cannon, Cleary, Craig, Watson, Casey	Gartland (3)	–	–
19.7.98	FD	H	Featherstone R.	W	14-6	Craig, Evans, Price-Jones	Gartland	1113	Ganson
26.7.98	FD	A	Hull K.R.	L	24-26	Casey (2), Gartland	Gartland (4)	–	–
2.8.98	FD	H	Hunslet H.	L	16-27	Ashcroft, Gartland, Mann	Gartland, Casey	1063	Taberner
7.8.98	FD	A	Keighley C.	D	18-18	Casey, Veikoso, Watson	Gartland (3)	–	–
16.8.98	FD	H	Leigh C.	W	32-4	Craig (2), Price-Jones, Adams, Veikoso	Gartland (6)	1182	R. Connolly
23.8.98	FD	A	Rochdale H.	L	16-41	Ashcroft, Casey, Watson	Gartland (2)	–	–
30.8.98	FD	H	Whitehaven W.	W	20-14	Cannon, Coley, Welsby	Gartland (4)	1007	J. Connolly
6.9.98	PO	A	Featherstone R.	L	12-22	Casey, Hulme	Gartland (2)	–	–

SWINTON LIONS 1998 PLAYERS' SUMMARY

	Date of birth	App	T	G	D	Pts	Previous club	Debut
Adams, Gareth	14.10.71	25+3	5	0	0	20	Counties-Manakau (NZ)	1997
Ashcroft, Simon	27.6.70	32+1	13	0	0	52	Highfield	1992-93
Barrow, Paul	20.10.74	29+3	6	0	0	24	Warrington W.	1998
Barrow, Tony	19.10.71	24+7	2	0	0	8	Oldham	1991-92
Blease, Ian	1.1.65	14+8	2	0	0	8	Salford R.	1998
Cannon, Peter	22.3.74	22+11	8	0	0	32	St. Helens	1995-96
Casey, Sean	9.12.71	33	15	2	1	65	Whitehaven W.	1997
Cleary, Damien	2.8.78	0+9	1	0	0	4	Rose Bridge ARL	1997
Coley, Andy	7.7.78	20+11	10	0	0	40	Laporte ARL	1997
Craig, Andrew	16.3.76	29+2	17	0	0	68	Wigan W.	1997
Cushion, Phil	15.6.78	2+1	1	0	0	4	Orrell St. James ARL	1998
Evans, Jim	14.6.72	16+14	4	0	0	16	Folly Lane ARL	1994-95
Gartland, Steve	3.10.70	33	13	110	6	278	Oldham B.	1998
Hodgkinson, Tommy	15.4.70	1+16	1	0	0	4	Bradford B.	1997
Hulme, Paul	19.4.66	19	1	0	0	4	Warrington W.	1998
Knowles, Matt	2.9.75	12+6	2	0	0	8	Wigan W.	1997
Longo, Davide	9.12.75	2+1	2	0	0	8	Bradford B.	1997
Mann, George	31.7.65	13+4	4	0	0	16	Keighley C.	1998
McComas, Dave	23.7.77	5+4	0	0	0	0		1997
Price-Jones, Gavin	19.12.70	34	15	1	3	65	Wagga M. (Aust.)	1994-95
Rogers, Wesley	3.11.77	1+15	0	0	0	0	Widnes V.	1997
Stazicker, Ryan	28.7.79	0+7	0	0	0	0		1997
Veikoso, Jimmy	31.5.71	25+1	8	0	0	32	Leigh C.	1997
Watson, Ian	27.10.76	34	12	11	5	75	Salford R.	1998
Welsby, Mark	7.7.70	17	5	0	0	20	Wigan	1992-93
TOTALS								
25 players			147	124	15	851		

1998 SIGNINGS REGISTER

Signed	Player	Club From
9.1.98	Barrow, Paul	Warrington W.
9.1.98	Blease, Ian	Salford R.
—	Eccles, Cliff	Salford R.
22.7.98	English, Wayne	Kirkholt WMC & A
6.6.98	Furey, Sean	Swinton Academy
—	Hill, Howard	Hull K.R.
6.3.98	Hulme, Paul	Warrington W.
12.5.98	Mann, George	Keighley C.
—	Stevens, Paul	Rochdale H.
12.1.98	*Watson, Ian	Salford R.

George Mann: 17 appearances.

WAKEFIELD TRINITY

Ground: Belle Vue (01924-211611)
First Season: 1895-96
Chairman: Ted Richardson
Honours: **Championship** Winners, 1966-67, 1967-68
Beaten finalists, 1959-60, 1961-62
Division Two Champions, 1903-04
First Division Grand Final Winners, 1998
First Division League leaders, 1998
Challenge Cup Winners, 1908-09, 1945-46, 1959-60, 1961-62, 1962-63
Beaten finalists, 1913-14, 1967-68, 1978-79
Regal Trophy Beaten finalists, 1971-72
Yorkshire Cup Winners, 1910-11, 1924-25, 1946-47, 1947-48, 1951-52, 1956-57, 1960-61, 1961-62, 1964-65, 1992-93
Beaten finalists, 1926-27, 1932-33, 1934-35, 1936-37, 1939-40, 1945-46, 1958-59, 1973-74, 1974-75, 1990-91
Yorkshire League Winners, 1909-10, 1910-11, 1945-46, 1958-59, 1959-60, 1961-62, 1965-66

RECORDS

Match

Goals: 13 by Mark Conway v. Highfield, 27 Oct 1992
Tries: 7 by Fred Smith v. Keighley, 25 Apr 1959
Keith Slater v. Hunslet, 6 Feb 1971
Points: 34 by Mark Conway v. Highfield, 27 Oct 1992

Season

Goals: 163 by Neil Fox, 1961-62
Tries: 38 by Fred Smith, 1959-60
David Smith, 1973-74
Points: 407 by Neil Fox, 1961-62

Career

Goals: 1,836 by Neil Fox, 1956-69 & 1970-74
Tries: 272 by Neil Fox, 1956-69 & 1970-74

Points: 4,488 by Neil Fox, 1956-69 & 1970-74
Appearances: 605 by Harry Wilkinson, 1930-49
Highest score: 90-12 v. Highfield, 27 Oct 1992
Highest against: 86-0 at Castleford, 17 Apr 1995
Attendance: 37,906 Leeds v. Huddersfield (RL Cup SF), 21 Mar 1936
Home Match: 30,676 v. Huddersfield (RL Cup), 26 Feb 1921

COACHING REGISTER

● **Since 1974-75**

Peter Fox	June 74 - May 76
Geoff Gunney	June 76 - Nov 76
Brian Lockwood	Nov 76 - Jan 78
Ian Brooke	Jan 78 - Jan 79
Bill Kirkbride	Jan 79 - Apr 80
Ray Batten	Apr 80 - May 81
Bill Ashurst	June 81 - Apr 82
Ray Batten	May 82 - July 83
Derek Turner	July 83 - Feb 84
Bob Haigh	Feb 84 - May 84
Geoff Wraith	May 84 - Oct 84
Dave Lamming	Oct 84 - Apr 85
Len Casey	Apr 85 - June 86
Tony Dean	June 86 - Dec 86
Trevor Bailey	Dec 86 - Apr 87
David Topliss	May 87 - Apr 94
David Hobbs	May 94 - Jan 95
Paul Harkin/ Andy Kelly	Jan 95 - Jan 96
Mitch Brennan	Jan 96 - June 97
Andy Kelly	June 97 -

Bob Haigh: Coach in 1984.

GREAT BRITAIN REGISTER
(24 players)

Ian Brooke	(8)	1967-68
Neil Fox	(29)	1959-69
Bob Haigh	(2)	1968
Bill Horton	(14)	1928-33
Michael Jackson	(2+2)	1991-92
David Jeanes	(5)	1971-72
Berwyn Jones	(3)	1964-66
Herbert Kershaw	(2)	1910
Frank Mortimer	(2)	1956
Harry Murphy	(1)	1950
Tommy Newbould	(1)	1910
Jonty Parkin	(17)	1920-29
Charlie Pollard	(1)	1924
Ernest Pollard	(2)	1932
Harold Poynton	(3)	1962
Gary H. Price	(0+1)	1991
Don Robinson	(5)	1954-55
Gerry Round	(8)	1959-62
Trevor Skerrett	(4)	1979
Stanley Smith	(1)	1929
David Topliss	(3)	1973-79
Derek Turner	(13)	1959-62
Don Vines	(3)	1959
Jack Wilkinson	(7)	1959-62

Jack Wilkinson: Seven Test appearances as a Wakefield Trinity player.

1998 SIGNINGS REGISTER

Signed	Player	Club From
2.6.98	Bostock, Joshua	Adelong Batlon (Aust.)
11.6.98	*Briggs, Carl	Halifax B.S.
—	Brunker, Adrian	St. George (Aust.)
15.1.98	Casey, Garen	Penrith (Aust.)
—	*Crouthers, Kevin	Bradford B.
9.4.98	*Fisher, Andrew	Hull S.
8.1.98	Fuller, Matthew	Perth West. Reds (Aust.)
4.9.98	*Gray, Kevin	Hull S.
—	Hodgson, Andy	Bradford B.
26.3.98	*Hughes, Adam	Leeds R.
—	Kenward, Shane	Salford R.
25.2.98	Lord, Gary	Oldham
6.1.98	Mycoe, David	Sheffield E.
—	Poching, Willie	Hunslet H.
—	Price, Gary H.	Featherstone R.
1.8.98	Richardson, Sean	Widnes V.
—	Stott, Lynton	Sheffield E.
—	Talbot, Ian	Wigan W.
—	Tomlinson, Glen	Hull S.
—	Watene, Frank	Auckland W. (NZ)
4.8.98	Westwood, Ben	Normanton Knights ARL

Berwyn Jones: Three Test appearances.

WAKEFIELD TRINITY 1998 MATCH ANALYSIS

Date	Competition	H/A	Opponents	Rlt	Score	Tries	Goals	Attendance	Referee
1.2.98	CC(3)	H	B.R.K.	W	44-6	McDonald (2), Whakarau (2), Wray (2), Judge, Southernwood, Waters	Mycoe (3), Rika	1369	I. Smith
8.2.98	FD	H	Widnes V.	W	24-22	Fuller, I. Hughes, P. March, Whakarau	Casey (4)	1980	R. Smith
15.2.98	CC(4)	H	Warrington W.	L	6-42	Casey	Casey	2844	Morris
22.2.98	FD	A	Keighley C.	W	14-10	Casey (2), Judge	Rika	–	–
8.3.98	FD	A	Leigh C.	W	32-20	Whakarau (2), Wray (2), I. Hughes, Rika	Casey (4)	–	–
15.3.98	FD	H	Whitehaven W.	W	38-22	Casey (3), McDonald (3), Holland, Rika	Casey (3)	1374	Presley
22.3.98	FD	H	Swinton L.	W	18-13	P. March, McDonald, Southernwood	Casey (3)	1406	J. Connolly
29.3.98	FD	A	Hull K.R.	L	6-36	McDonald	Casey	–	–
5.4.98	FD	H	Rochdale H.	W	38-0	Holland (3), Casey, S. Hicks, A. Hughes, Judge	Casey (5)	1110	Nicholson
10.4.98	FD	H	Featherstone R.	W	26-8	Casey (2), A. Hughes (2)	Casey (5)	1543	Bates
13.4.98	FD	A	Hunslet H.	W	15-4	A. Hughes (2), M. Law	Casey (1, dg)	–	–
19.4.98	FD	H	Dewsbury R.	D	26-26	Southernwood, (2) Fuller, A. Hughes	A. Hughes (5)	2285	Shaw
26.4.98	FD	A	Widnes V.	W	30-20	Horsley, A. Hughes, I. Hughes, McDonald	Casey (7)	–	–
6.5.98	FD	H	Keighley C.	W	18-0	Holland, A. Hughes, Southernwood	Casey (3)	1899	Shaw
17.5.98	FD	H	Leigh C.	W	60-14	P. March (2), Rika (2), Wray (2), Casey, Fisher, Horsley, Kenworthy, McDonald	Casey (8)	1400	Taberner
24.5.98	FD	A	Whitehaven W.	W	30-16	Kenworthy (2), S. Hicks, Horsley, A. Hughes, Wray	Casey (3)	–	–
31.5.98	FD	A	Swinton L.	L	12-13	Holland, Horsley, A. Hughes	–	–	–
3.6.98	FD	H	Hull K.R.	L	17-24	Holland, Kenworthy, Southernwood	Casey (2, dg)	2087	Gilmour
7.6.98	FD	A	Rochdale H.	W	46-28	Bostock (3), McDonald (2), Casey, I. Hughes, A. Hughes, Southernwood	Casey (5)	–	–
14.6.98	FD	A	Featherstone R.	L	0-21	–	–	–	–
21.6.98	FD	H	Hunslet H.	W	36-22	Briggs, Casey, I. Hughes, Wray, Southernwood, M. Law	Casey (6)	1580	Nicholson
24.6.98	FD	A	Dewsbury R.	W	25-18	Rika (2), Southernwood, Wray, Fisher	Casey (2), Briggs (dg)	–	–
5.7.98	FD	A	Swinton L.	W	26-15	Fisher, Kenworthy, McDonald, Stephenson	Casey (5)	–	–
12.7.98	FD	H	Widnes V.	W	64-8	Bostock (3), Southernwood (2), Fisher (2), Casey, S. Hicks, A. Hughes, Kenworthy, Rika	Casey (8)	2021	Bates
15.7.98	FD	A	Featherstone R.	L	18-29	Bostock, Casey, Kenworthy	Casey (3)	–	–
19.7.98	FD	H	Hull K.R.	L	12-38	Casey, Southernwood	Casey (2)	3106	Oddy
26.7.98	FD	A	Hunslet H.	W	20-12	Bostock, Fuller, A. Hughes	Casey (4)	–	–
2.8.98	FD	H	Keighley C.	W	56-16	Kenworthy (4), Mycoe (2), S. Hicks, A. Hughes, Wray	Casey (10)	2497	Nicholson
9.8.98	FD	A	Leigh C.	W	28-12	Fisher, Horsley, I. Hughes, M. Law, Whakarau	Casey (4)	–	–
16.8.98	FD	H	Rochdale H.	W	28-21	A. Hughes (3), Kenworthy	Casey (6)	1576	Morris
23.8.98	FD	A	Whitehaven W.	W	15-2	Casey, Kenworthy	Casey (3, dg)	–	–
30.8.98	FD	H	Dewsbury R.	L	12-16	A. Hughes, Wray	Casey (2)	3107	Bates
13.9.98	PO	H	Hull K.R.	W	19-16	Bostock, Holland	Casey (3, dg)	3290	Shaw
26.9.98	POF	N1	Featherstone R.	L	24-22	Bostock (2), Southernwood, Casey, Stephenson	Casey (2)	(8224)	Oddy
3.10.98	TT	A	Villeneuve	L	12-34	Stephenson, A. Hughes	A. Hughes (2)	–	–
11.10.98	TT	H	Limoux	W	38-36	Bostock (3), Gray (2), Mycoe, P. March	A. Hughes (5)	1506	Segura (Fr)
17.10.98	TT	A	Limoux	W	24-10	McDonald (2), Wray, Briggs, A. Hughes	Gray (2)	–	–
25.10.98	TT	H	Villeneuve	L	22-25	Fisher, Bostock, P. March, Mycoe	Hughes (3)	1270	Alibert (Fr)

N1 at Huddersfield

115

WAKEFIELD TRINITY 1998 PLAYERS' SUMMARY

	Date of birth	App	T	G	D	Pts	Previous club	Debut
Bostock, Josh	24.1.74	14+1	16	0	0	64	Adelong Batlon (Aust.)	1998
Briggs, Carl	27.9.74	11+5	2	0	1	9	Halifax B.S.	1998
Casey, Garen	25.6.74	32	17	115	4	302	Penrith (Aust.)	1998
Fisher, Andy	17.11.67	16+10	7	0	0	28	Hull S.	1998
Fuller, Matt	31.1.70	30	3	0	0	12	Perth Reds (Aust.)	1998
Gray, Kevin	10.12.75	6	2	2	0	12	Rochdale H.	1998
Griffin, Matt	16.9.78	1	0	0	0	0	Dewsbury Moor ARL	1998
Hicks, Paul	22.6.77	2+11	0	0	0	0	Normanton ARL	1994-95
Hicks, Simon	30.8.73	25+9	4	0	0	16	Stanley R. ARL	1993-94
Holland, Martyn	21.3.77	32	8	0	0	32	Crigglestone AB ARL	1996
Horsley, Ryan	21.8.78	16+3	5	0	0	20	Crigglestone AB ARL	1996
Hughes, Adam	1.10.77	30	20	15	0	110	Leeds R.	1998
Hughes, Ian	13.3.72	26+8	6	0	0	24	Sheffield E.	1997
Judge, Chris	7.11.72	6+11	3	0	0	12	York	1996
Kenworthy, Roger	14.1.71	20+7	13	0	0	52	Canberra R. (Aust.)	1997
Law, Graham	24.7.79	0+4	0	0	0	0	Westgate Redoubt ARL	1997
Law, Martyn	11.3.76	27+7	3	0	0	12	Leeds	1996
Lord, Gary	6.7.66	33	0	0	0	0	Oldham B.	1998
March, David	25.7.79	0+2	0	0	0	0	Thornhill ARL	1997
March, Paul	25.7.79	16+5	6	0	0	24	Thornhill ARL	1997
McDonald, Wayne	3.9.75	11+20	14	0	0	56	Middleton ARL	1993-94
Mycoe, David	1.5.72	15+6	4	3	0	22	Sheffield E.	1998
Proctor, Andy	9.3.69	1+4	0	0	0	0	Saddleworth R.	1996
Richardson, Sean	20.8.73	4+3	0	0	0	0	Widnes V.	1998
Rika, Craig	18.1.74	11+4	7	2	0	32	Halifax B.S.	1997
Sebine, Paul	2.1.75	6+2	0	0	0	0	Bisons ARL	1997
Southernwood, Roy	23.6.68	27+4	13	0	0	52	Halifax B.S.	1997
Stephenson, Francis	20.1.76	14+14	3	0	0	12	Dewsbury M. ARL	1993-94
Waters, Ryan		2	1	0	0	4		1998
Westwood, Ben	25.7.81	0+1	0	0	0	0	Normanton Knights ARL	1998
Whakarau, Sonny	13.1.66	30+6	6	0	0	24	Keighley C.	1997
Wray, Jon	19.5.70	30+1	12	0	0	48	Castleford	1995-96
TOTALS								
32 players			175	137	5	979		

Leading the way: Wakefield Trinity captain Matt Fuller leads by example in the First Division Grand Final defeat of Featherstone Rovers.

WARRINGTON WOLVES

Ground: Wilderspool (01925-635338)
First Season: 1895-96. Added Wolves to title for start of 1997 season.
Chairman: —
Honours: **Championship** Winners, 1947-48, 1953-54, 1954-55
Beaten finalists, 1925-26, 1934-35, 1936-37, 1948-49, 1950-51, 1960-61
League Leaders Trophy Winners, 1972-73
Club Championship (Merit Table) Winners, 1973-74
Challenge Cup Winners, 1904-05, 1906-07, 1949-50, 1953-54, 1973-74
Beaten finalists, 1900-01, 1903-04, 1912-13, 1927-28, 1932-33, 1935-36, 1974-75, 1989-90
Regal Trophy Winners, 1973-74, 1977-78, 1980-81, 1990-91
Beaten finalists, 1978-79, 1986-87, 1994-95
Premiership Trophy Winners, 1985-86
Beaten finalists, 1976-77, 1986-87
Lancashire Cup Winners, 1921-22, 1929-30, 1932-33, 1937-38, 1959-60, 1965-66, 1980-81, 1982-83, 1989-90
Beaten finalists, 1906-07, 1948-49, 1950-51, 1967-68, 1985-86, 1987-88
Lancashire League Winners, 1937-38, 1947-48, 1948-49, 1950-51, 1953-54, 1954-55, 1955-56, 1967-68
BBC2 Floodlit Trophy Beaten finalists, 1974-75
Captain Morgan Trophy Winners, 1973-74

RECORDS
Match
Goals: 14 by Harold Palin v. Liverpool C., 13 Sep 1950
Tries: 7 by Brian Bevan v. Leigh, 29 Mar 1948
Brian Bevan v. Bramley, 22 Apr 1953

Points: 33 by George Thomas v. St. Helens, 12 Apr 1909

Season
Goals: 170 by Steve Hesford, 1978-79
Tries: 66 by Brian Bevan, 1952-53
Points: 363 by Harry Bath, 1952-53

Career
Goals: 1,159 by Steve Hesford, 1975-85
Tries: 740 by Brian Bevan, 1945-62
Points: 2,416 by Steve Hesford, 1975-85
Appearances: 620 by Brian Bevan, 1945-62
Highest score: 78-6 v. St. Helens, 12 Apr 1909
Highest against: 80-0 at St. Helens, 4 Jan 1996
Attendance: 34,304 v. Wigan (League), 22 Jan 1949

COACHING REGISTER
● **Since 1974-75**

Alex Murphy	May 71 - May 78
Billy Benyon	June 78 - Mar 82
Kevin Ashcroft	Mar 82 - May 84
Reg Bowden	June 84 - Mar 86
Tony Barrow	Mar 86 - Nov 88
Brian Johnson	Nov 88 - Jan 96
John Dorahy	Jan 96 - Mar 97
Darryl Van de Velde	Mar 97 -

GREAT BRITAIN REGISTER
(48 players)

Jack Arkwright	(6)	1936-37
Kevin Ashcroft	(+1)	1974
Willie Aspinall	(1)	1966
Allan Bateman	(1+2)	1992-94
Billy Belshaw	(2)	1937
Nat Bentham	(2)	1929
John Bevan	(6)	1974-78
Tom Blinkhorn	(1)	1929
Ernie Brooks	(3)	1908
Jim Challinor	(3)	1958-60
Neil Courtney	(+1)	1982
Billy Cunliffe	(11)	1920-26
Jonathan Davies	(4)	1993-94
George Dickenson	(1)	1908
Billy Dingsdale	(3)	1929-33
Des Drummond	(2)	1987-88
Ronnie Duane	(3)	1983-84
Bob Eccles	(1)	1982
Kevin Ellis	(+1)	1991

(Contd)

WARRINGTON WOLVES 1998 MATCH ANALYSIS

Date	Com- petition	H/A	Opponents	Rlt	Score	Tries	Goals	Atten- dance	Referee
15.2.98	CC(4)	A	Wakefield T.	W	42-6	Roach (4), Doyle (2), Fawcett, Penny, Wainwright	Briers (3)	–	–
1.3.98	CC(5)	A	St. Helens	L	22-35	Roach, Penny, Forster	Briers (5)	–	–
5.4.98	SL	A	Leeds R.	L	8-30	Eagar	Briers (2)	–	–
10.4.98	SL	H	Salford R.	L	4-37	Kohe-Love	–	5567	R. Connolly
19.4.98	SL	A	London B.	L	4-14	Tuuta	–	–	–
26.4.98	SL	A	St. Helens	L	14-36	McCurrie, Penny, Doyle	Briers	–	–
10.5.98	SL	H	Halifax B.S.	W	31-20	Kohe-Love (2), Farrar, Forster, Roper	Briers (5, dg)	4790	Morris
17.5.98	SL	H	Castleford T.	W	33-18	McCurrie (2), Briers, Eagar, Wainwright	Briers (6, dg)	4918	J. Connolly
25.5.98	SL	A	Hull S.	W	32-28	Penny (2), Forster, Farrar, Rudd, Roper	Briers (4)	–	–
31.5.98	SL	A	Huddersfield G.	L	6-28	Rudd	Briers	–	–
7.6.98	SL	H	Bradford B.	W	28-10	Forster (2), Eagar, McCurrie, Wainwright	Roper (4)	6054	R. Smith
14.6.98	SL	H	Sheffield E.	D	18-18	Kohe-Love (2), Wainwright	Rudd (2), Roper	5220	Presely
21.6.98	SL	A	Wigan W.	L	8-56	Forster	Rudd (2)	–	–
28.6.98	SL	H	Leeds R.	L	14-27	Tuuta	Rudd (5)	5334	R. Smith
5.7.98	SL	A	Salford R..	W	25-14	Doyle (2), Briers, Forster, Rudd	Rudd (2), Briers (dg)	–	–
25.7.98	SL	N1	Castleford T.	L	16-23	Rudd, McCurrie, Briers	Rudd (2)	(4437)	Ganson
2.8.98	SL	H	London B.	L	14-23	Highton, Roach	Briers (3)	3476	R. Connolly
9.8.98	SL	H	St. Helens	L	18-48	Doyle, McCurrie, Pechey	Briers (3)	4538	R. Smith
16.8.98	SL	A	Halifax B.S.	L	16-46	Wainwright (2), Forster	Briers (2)	–	–
22.8.98	SL	A	Castleford T.	L	24-50	Roach (2), Farrar, Penny, Tuuta	Briers (2)	–	–
30.8.98	SL	H	Hull S.	W	24-10	Fawcett, Forster, Penny, Tuuta	Briers (3, 2dg)	3301	Nicholson
6.9.98	SL	H	Huddersfield G.	W	36-8	Eagar (2), Briers, Farrar, Forster, Pechey, McCurrie	Briers (4)	4908	Presley
13.9.98	SL	A	Bradford B.	L	8-36	Roach (2)	–	–	–
18.9.98	SL	A	Sheffield E.	L	6-35	McCurrie	Briers	–	–
27.9.98	SL	H	Wigan W.	L	24-30	Eagar, Forster, Knott, Penny	Briers (4)	5762	Cummings

N1 at Cardiff RU

GREAT BRITAIN REGISTER (Contd)

Jim Featherstone	(6)	1948-52
Mark Forster	(2)	1987
Eric Fraser	(16)	1958-61
Laurie Gilfedder	(5)	1962-63
Bobby Greenough	(1)	1960
Andy Gregory	(1)	1986
Mike Gregory	(19+1)	1987-90
Iestyn Harris	(4+1)	1996
Gerry Helme	(12)	1948-54
Keith Holden	(1)	1963
Albert Johnson	(6)	1946-47
Ken Kelly	(2)	1980-82
Tom McKinney	(3)	1955
Joe "Jack" Miller	(6)	1933-36
Alex Murphy	(1)	1971
Albert Naughton	(2)	1954
Terry O'Grady	(1)	1961
Harold Palin	(2)	1947
Ken Parr	(1)	1968
Albert Pimblett	(3)	1948

Ray Price	(9)	1954-57
Bob Ryan	(5)	1950-52
Ron Ryder	(1)	1952
Paul Sculthorpe	(7+1)	1996-97
Frank Shugars	(1)	1910
George "Jack" Skelhorne	(7)	1920-21
George Thomas	(1)	1907
Derek Whitehead	(3)	1971
John Woods	(+1)	1987

1998 SIGNINGS REGISTER

Signed	Player	Club From
12.1.98	Buckley, Daniel	Wigan St. Judes ARL
—	Busby, Dean	St. Helens
9.2.98	Dootson, Stephen	Wigan St. Judes ARL
19.1.98	Eagar, Michael	S. Queensland (Aust.)
16.2.98	Farrar, Daniel	Penrith (Aust.)
23.1.98	Fawcett, Vince	Oldham
16.1.98	Finney Phillip	Widnes Tigers ARL
—	Gillies, Simon	Canterbury B. (Aust.)
—	Hanger, Dean	Huddersfield G.

(Contd.)

WARRINGTON WOLVES 1998 PLAYERS' SUMMARY

	Date of birth	App	T	G	D	Pts	Previous club	Debut
Briers, Lee	14.6.78	22	4	49	5	119	St. Helens	1997
Causey, Chris	17.9.78	0+11	0	0	0	0	Orrell St. James	1997
Chambers, Gary	5.1.70	15+8	0	0	0	0	Kells ARL	1989-90
Cowell, Will	31.12.79	1+4	0	0	0	0	Kells ARL	1998
Doyle, Adam	26.4.78	11+3	6	0	0	24	West. Suburbs (Aust.)	1998
Duffy, John	2.7.80	4+2	0	0	0	0	Wigan St. Patricks ARL	1997
Eagar, Michael	15.8.73	23	6	0	0	24	S. Queensland (Aust.)	1998
Farrar, Danny	2.4.68	23	4	0	0	16	Penrith (Aust.)	1998
Fawcett, Vince	13.11.70	4+9	2	0	0	8	Oldham	1998
Finney, Phil	16.1.81	1	0	0	0	0	Widnes Tigers ARL	1998
Fogerty, Adam	6.3.69	4	0	0	0	0	St. Helens	1998
Forster, Mark	25.11.64	23	11	0	0	44	Woolston R. ARL	1982-83
Highton, David	31.1.80	6	1	0	0	4	Wigan St. Patricks ARL	1998
Hilton, Mark	31.3.75	7+6	0	0	0	0	Warrington Academy	1993-94
Knott, Ian	2.10.76	6+12	1	0	0	4	Wigan St. Judes ARL	1995-96
Kohe-Love, Toa	2.12.76	14	5	0	0	20	New Zealand	1996
McCurrie, Steve	2.7.73	22+3	8	0	0	32	Bedford RU	1998
Morley, Chris	22.9.73	2+10	0	0	0	0	St. Helens	1998
Nutley, Danny	4.1.74	25	0	0	0	0	S. Queensland (Aust.)	1998
Pechey, Mike	16.10.68	6+3	2	0	0	8	Bedford RU	1998
Penny, Lee	24.9.74	22	8	0	0	32	Orrell St. James ARL	1992-93
Roach, Jason	2.5.71	18	10	0	0	40	Castleford T.	1998
Roper, Jonathan	5.5.76	8	2	5	0	18	Hensingham ARL	1993-94
Rudd, Chris	17.12.69	13+2	4	13	0	42	Kells ARL	1988-89
Stevens, Warren	4.10.78	0+9	0	0	0	0	Orrell St. James ARL	1996
Tuuta, Brendon	29.4.65	20+2	4	0	0	16	Castleford T.	1998
Wainwright, Mike	25.2.75	25	6	0	0	24	Woolston R. ARL	1994-95
Whittle, Danny	18.7.70	0+2	0	0	0	0	Swinton L.	1998
Wilson, Scott	8.11.70	0+1	0	0	0	0	Canterbury B. (Aust.)	1998
TOTALS								
29 players			84	67	5	475		

Representative appearances 1998

Briers - Wales (1); Duffy - Scotland (2, 1t, 4g); Forster - Ireland (2, 1t); Hilton - Emerging England (0+1); Penny - Scotland (2); Roach - Scotland (2, 2t); Wainwright - Scotland (2)

1998 SIGNINGS REGISTER (Contd)

Signed	Player	Club From
10.1.98	Kirkbride, Stephen	Kells ARL
5.1.98	McCurrie, Steve	Bedford RU
1.1.98	Morley, Chris	St. Helens
2.4.98	Noone, Paul	Widnes Tigers ARL
5.1 98	Nutley, Daniel	S. Queensland (Aust.)
2.4.98	Parry, Ian	Wigan St. Judes ARL
31.7.98	Pechey, Michael	Bedford RU
5.1 98	Roach, Jason	Castleford T.
15.1.98	Tuuta, Brendon	Castleford T.
17.7.97	Whittle, Daniel	Swinton L.
24.9.98	Wilson, Scott	Canterbury B. (Aust.)

WHITEHAVEN WARRIORS

Ground: Recreation Ground (01946-692915)
First Season: 1948-49. Added Warriors to title for
            1997 season.
Chairman: Ralph Calvin

RECORDS

Match

Goals: 13 by Lee Anderson at Highfield,
            25 Jan 1995
Tries: 6 by Vince Gribbin v. Doncaster,
            18 Nov 1984
Points: 30 by Lee Anderson at Highfield,
            25 Jan 1995

Season

Goals: 141 by John McKeown, 1956-57
Tries: 34 by Mike Pechey, 1994-95
Points: 291 by John McKeown, 1956-57

Career

Goals: 1,050 by John McKeown, 1948-61
Tries: 148 by Bill Smith, 1950-62
Points: 2,133 by John McKeown, 1948-61
Appearances: 417 by John McKeown, 1948-61
Highest score: 86-6 at Highfield, 25 Jan 1995
Highest against: 92-10 at Hull K.R., 18 Mar 1990
Attendance: 18,500 v. Wakefield T. (RL Cup),
                19 Mar 1960

Eric Fitzsimons: Coach 1989-90.

COACHING REGISTER

● **Since 1974-75**

Jeff Bawden	May 72 - May 75
Ike Southward	Aug 75 - June 76
Bill Smith	Aug 76 - Oct 78
Ray Dutton	Oct 78 - Oct 79
Phil Kitchin	Oct 79 - Jan 82
Arnold Walker	Jan 82 - May 82
Tommy Dawes	June 82 - May 83
Frank Foster	June 83 - June 85
Phil Kitchin	June 85 - Oct 87
John McFarlane	Oct 87 - May 88
Barry Smith	July 88 - Sep 89
Eric Fitzsimons	Oct 89 - Mar 90
Norman Turley	June 90 - Apr 91
Jackie Davidson	May 91 - June 92
Gordon Cottier	June 92 - May 93
Kurt Sorensen	May 93 - Aug 95
Stan Martin	Oct 95 - July 98
Colin Armstrong	July 98 - Oct 98
Kevin Tamati	Oct 98 -

GREAT BRITAIN REGISTER

(5 players)

Vince Gribbin	(1)	1985
Bill Holliday	(1)	1964
Dick Huddart	(4)	1958
Phil Kitchin	(1)	1965
Arnold Walker	(1)	1980

1998 SIGNINGS REGISTER

Signed	Player	Club From
5.6.98	Armstrong, David	Biggar RU
9.5.98	Armstrong, Derek	Carlisle B.R.
16.2.98	Bretherton, Liam	Warrington W.
12.2.98	Brown, Leslie	Kells ARL
22.5.98	*Cantillon, Phillip	Leeds R.
11.3.98	Charlton, Gary	Carlisle B.R.
28.1.98	Frazer, Neil	Seaton R. ARL
24.6.98	Hetherington, Gary	Barrow B.R.
4.6.98	Hill, Simon	London B.
20.3.98	*Knox, Simon	Bradford B.
29.5.98	Stoddart, Stephen	Carlisle B.R.
7.3.98	Vaughan, Dean	Kells ARL
27.1.98	Wilson, Martin	Cockermouth ARL

WHITEHAVEN WARRIORS 1998 MATCH ANALYSIS

Date	Competition	H/A	Opponents	Rlt	Score	Tries	Goals	Attendance	Referee
1.2.98	CC(3)	H	Lock Lane	W	48-7	K. Hetherington (2), Williams (2), Joe (2), Kiddie, P. Smith, Wallace	K. Hetherington (6)	830	Roberts
8.2.98	FD	H	Featherstone R.	W	32-14	Lewthwaite (2), K. Hetherington, Kiddie, Quirk, Wilson	K. Hetherington (4)	1306	J. Connolly
15.2.98	CC(4)	H	Hull S.	L	12-26	Joe, Muliumu	K. Hetherington (2)	2030	R. Connolly
22.2.98	FD	A	Leigh C.	W	45-26	Bretherton (2), Kiddie (2), Allen, Joe, Lewthwaite, Morton	K. Hetherington (6) Kiddie (dg)	–	–
4.3.98	FD	A	Swinton L.	L	6-27	Morton	K. Hetherington	–	–
8.3.98	FD	H	Hull K.R.	L	14-24	Lewthwaite (2), Kiddie	K. Hetherington	1402	Cummings
15.3.98	FD	A	Wakefield T.	L	22-38	K. Hetherington, Lester, Walsh, Malietoa-Brown	K. Hetherington (3)	–	–
22.3.98	FD	H	Keighley C.	W	46-16	Morton (2), Muliumu (2), Kiddie, Lester, Wilson, Malietoa-Brown	K. Hetherington (7)	1364	Shaw
29.3.98	FD	H	Dewsbury R.	W	32-22	Seeds (2), K. Hetherington, Joe, Kiddie, Lester	K. Hetherington (4)	1113	Presley
5.4.98	FD	A	Hunslet H.	L	4-35	Seeds	–	–	–
10.4.98	FD	H	Widnes V.	W	44-12	Kiddie (3), Charlton, Joe, Knox, Muliumu, Seeds	Wilson (6)	1120	Ganson
19.4.98	FD	A	Rochdale H.	W	38-16	Lewthwaite (3), Wilson (2), Malietoa-Brown, (2), Allen, Joe	K. Hetherington	–	–
26.4.98	FD	A	Featherstone R.	W	26-14	Bretherton, Knox, Seeds, Malietoa-Brown, Wallace	K. Hetherington (2), Kitchin	–	–
6.5.98	FD	H	Leigh C.	W	34-12	Allen, Charlton, Fatialofa, Knox, Wallace	K. Hetherington (6), Bretherton	957	Oddy
10.5.98	FD	H	Swinton L.	W	12-10	Wallace (2)	K. Hetherington, Bretherton	1107	Lee
17.5.98	FD	A	Hull K.R.	L	16-25	Wallace (2), Lester	Armstrong, K. Hetherington	–	–
24.5.98	FD	H	Wakefield T.	L	16-30	Kiddie (2)	K. Hetherington (3), Bretherton	1324	Shaw
31.5.98	FD	A	Keighley C.	L	18-22	Lester, Wallace, Wilson	Armstrong (3)	–	–
3.6.98	FD	A	Dewsbury R.	L	12-26	Charlton, Quirk	Armstrong (2)	–	–
7.6.98	FD	H	Hunslet H.	L	16-26	Kiddie, Quirk, Walsh	Armstrong (2)	903	McGregor
14.6.98	FD	A	Widnes V.	L	12-40	Kiddie, Quirk	Armstrong (2)	–	–
24.6.98	FD	H	Rochdale H.	W	24-6	K. Hetherington, Wallace, Kiddie, Cox	Armstrong (4)	647	Taberner
28.6.98	FD	H	Widnes V.	W	48-14	Kiddie (2), Wilson (2), Quirk, K. Hetherington, Cantillon, Wallace, Williams	Armstrong (5), K. Hetherington	785	Kirkpatrick
5.7.98	FD	A	Featherstone R.	L	0-37	–	–	–	–
12.7.98	FD	H	Hull K.R.	W	21-12	Malietoa-Brown (2), Lewthwaite	K. Hetherington (4), Kiddie (dg)	949	Shaw
15.7.98	FD	A	Hunslet H.	L	18-37	Charlton, K. Hetherington, Muliumu, Lewthwaite	K. Hetherington	–	–
19.7.98	FD	H	Keighley C.	L	14-25	Charlton, Kiddie	K. Hetherington (3)	899	Morris
26.7.98	FD	A	Leigh C.	L	12-14	Walsh	K. Hetherington (4)	–	–
2.8.98	FD	H	Rochdale H.	W	30-22	Lewthwaite (3), Joe, Kitchin	K. Hetherington (5)	654	Morris
16.8.98	FD	A	Dewsbury R.	L	8-20	Kiddie	K. Hetherington, Kitchin	–	–
23.8.98	FD	H	Wakefield T.	L	2-15	–	K. Hetherington	1007	Oddy
30.3.98	FD	A	Swinton L.	L	14-20	Quirk (2)	Kitchin (2), K. Hetherington	–	–

WHITEHAVEN WARRIORS 1998 PLAYERS' SUMMARY

	Date of birth	App	T	G	D	Pts	Previous club	Debut
Abram, Dave	26.6.78	0+1	0	0	0	0	Aspatria RU	1998
Allen, John	16.6.72	12+10	3	0	0	12	Workington T.	1998
Armstrong, Colin	26.1.63	32	0	19	0	38	Swinton L.	1997
Bretherton, Liam	20.6.79	6+7	3	3	0	18	Warrington W.	1998
Brown, Les	31.5.73	0+5	0	0	0	0	Kells ARL	1998
Calvin, Graeme	19.3.77	0+1	0	0	0	0	Kells ARL	1997
Cantillon, Phil	2.6.76	6+1	1	0	0	4	Leeds R.	1998
Chambers, Craig	25.4.73	5+4	0	0	0	0	Kells ARL	1993-94
Charlton, Gary	5.3.67	27	5	0	0	20	Carlisle B.R.	1998
Cox, Mark	22.1.78	2+16	1	0	0	4	Wath Brown H. ARL	1997
Dymtowski, Tony	28.4.78	6+4	0	0	0	0		1997
Fatialofa, David	11.6.74	30	1	0	0	4	Palau (Fr.)	1996
Fieldhouse, John	28.6.62	0+7	0	0	0	0	Orrell RU	1997
Hetherington, Gary	5.7.65	0+1	0	0	0	0	Kells ARL	1985-86
Hetherington, Kevin	7.6.76	24+4	8	69	0	170	Aspatria RU	1996
Hill, Simon	25.2.75	0+1	0	0	0	0	London B.	1998
Joe, Leroy	31.12.74	19+3	8	0	0	32	Counties-Manakau (NZ)	1997
Kiddie, Lee	2.1.75	32	20	0	2	82	Kells ARL	1993-94
Kitchin, Wayne	26.11.70	11+11	1	4	0	12	Workington T.	1997
Knox, Simon	14.10.72	7+3	3	0	0	12	Bradford B.	1998
Lester, Aaron	16.5.73	23	5	0	0	20	Auckland W. (NZ)	1997
Lewthwaite, Graeme	5.7.72	19+2	13	0	0	52	Hensingham ARL	1993-94
Malietoa-Brown Gus	28.7.75	12+2	7	0	0	28	Counties-Manakau (NZ)	1997
Morton, Graeme	15.1.73	19+7	4	0	0	16	Kells ARL	1993-94
Muliumu, Siose	26.4.76	15+3	5	0	0	20	Western Samoa	1996
Parsley, Lee		0+1	0	0	0	0		1998
Quirk, Les	6.3.65	28	7	0	0	28	St. Helens	1994-95
Seeds, David	23.6.74	12+6	4	0	0	16	Kells ARL	1993-94
Smith, Leigh	1.9.75	2	0	0	0	0	Workington T.	1997
Smith, Peter	13.8.66	1+8	1	0	0	4	Kells ARL	1994-95
Stoddart, Stephen	22.10.76	0+1	0	0	0	0	Carlisle B.R.	1998
Vaughan, Dean	9.2.78	2+5	0	0	0	0	Kells ARL	1998
Wallace, Mark	21.2.78	22+2	10	0	0	40	Workington T.	1998
Walsh, Craig	19.9.78	5+6	3	0	0	12	Kells ARL	1997
Williams, Darren	27.4.74	9+1	3	0	0	12	Wigan	1995-96
Wilson, Wesley	30.5.77	28	7	6	0	40	Wath Brow H. ARL	1997
TOTALS								
37 players			123	101	2	696		

WIDNES VIKINGS

Ground: Auto Quest Stadium
(0151 - 495 2250)
First Season: 1895-96. Added Vikings to title for start of 1997 season.
Chairman: Tony Chambers
Honours: **Championship** Beaten finalists, 1935-36
Division One Champions, 1977-78, 1987-88, 1988-89
Challenge Cup Winners, 1929-30, 1936-37, 1963-64, 1974-75, 1978-79, 1980-81, 1983-84
Beaten finalists, 1933-34, 1949-50, 1975-76, 1976-77, 1981-82, 1992-93
Regal Trophy Winners, 1975-76, 1978-79, 1991-92
Beaten finalists, 1974-75, 1977-78, 1979-80, 1983-84, 1988-89
Premiership Winners, 1979-80, 1981-82, 1982-83, 1987-88, 1988-89, 1989-90
Beaten finalists, 1977-78, 1990-91
Lancashire Cup Winners, 1945-46, 1974-75, 1975-76, 1976-77, 1978-79, 1979-80, 1990-91
Beaten finalists, 1928-29, 1939-40, 1955-56, 1971-72, 1981-82, 1983-84
Lancashire League Winners, 1919-20
Western Division Championship Beaten finalists, 1962-63
Charity Shield Winners, 1988-89, 1989-90, 1990-91
World Club Challenge Winners, 1989-90
BBC2 Floodlit Trophy Winners, 1978-79
Beaten finalists, 1972-73, 1973-74

RECORDS
Match
Goals: 11 by Robin Whitfield v. Oldham, 28 Oct 1965

Tries: 5 by Eddie Cunningham v. Doncaster, 15 Feb 1981
John Basnett at Hunslet, 17 Oct 1981
John Basnett v. Hull K.R., 2 Nov 1986
David Hulme v. Dewsbury, 30 Nov 1986
Andy Currier v. Featherstone R., 25 Sep 1988
Martin Offiah v. Warrington, 15 Mar 1989
Points: 34 by Andy Currier v. Featherstone R., 25 Sep 1988
Jonathan Davies v. Whitehaven, 26 Aug 1990

Season
Goals: 140 by Mick Burke, 1978-79
Tries: 58 by Martin Offiah, 1988-89
Points: 342 by Jonathan Davies, 1990-91
Career
Goals: 1,083 by Ray Dutton, 1966-78
Tries: 234 by Mal Aspey, 1964-80
Points: 2,195 by Ray Dutton, 1966-78
Appearances: 587+4 by Keith Elwell, 1970-86
Highest score: 82-0 v. Dewsbury, 30 Nov 1986
Highest against: 64-12 at Keighley C., 18 Aug 1996; 64-8 at Wakefield T., 12 July 1998
Attendance: 24,205 v. St. Helens (RL Cup), 16 Feb 1961

COACHING REGISTER
● **Since 1974-75**

Vince Karalius	Jan 72 - May 75
Frank Myler	May 75 - May 78
Doug Laughton	May 78 - Mar 83
Harry Dawson ⎫ Colin Tyrer ⎭	Mar 83 - May 83
* Vince Karalius ⎫ Harry Dawson ⎭	May 83 - May 84
Eric Hughes	June 84 - Jan 86
Doug Laughton	Jan 86 - May 91
Frank Myler	June 91 - May 92
Phil Larder	May 92 - May 94
Tony Myler	May 94 - Aug 95
Doug Laughton	Aug 95 - May 97
Graeme West	May 97 - Aug 98
Colin Whitfield	Aug 98 -

* *Dawson quit as coach in March 1984 with Karalius continuing as team manager.*

GREAT BRITAIN REGISTER
(46 players)

Mick Adams	(11+2)	1979-84
John Basnett	(2)	1984-86
Keith Bentley	(1)	1980
Mick Burke	(14+1)	1980-86
Frank Collier	(1)	1964
Andy Currier	(2)	1989-93
Jonathan Davies	(8+1)	1990-93
John Devereux	(6+2)	1992-93
Ray Dutton	(6)	1970
Keith Elwell	(3)	1977-80
Richard Eyres	(3+4)	1989-93
John Fieldhouse	(6)	1985-86
Ray French	(4)	1968
Les Gorley	(4+1)	1980-82
Andy Gregory	(8+1)	1981-84
Ian Hare	(1)	1967
Fred Higgins	(6)	1950-51
Harold Higgins	(2)	1937
Les Holliday	(3)	1991-92
Eric Hughes	(8)	1978-82
David Hulme	(7+1)	1988-89
Paul Hulme	(3+5)	1988-92
Albert Johnson	(4)	1914-20
Vince Karalius	(2)	1963
George Kemel	(2)	1965
Doug Laughton	(4)	1973-79
Joe Lydon	(9+1)	1983-85
Tommy McCue	(6)	1936-46
Steve McCurrie	(1)	1993
Jim Measures	(2)	1963
Jim Mills	(6)	1974-79
Paul Moriarty	(1+1)	1991-94
Frank Myler	(14+1)	1960-67
Tony Myler	(14)	1983-86
George Nicholls	(7)	1971-72
Martin Offiah	(20)	1988-91
Dennis O'Neill	(2+1)	1971-72
Mike O'Neill	(3)	1982-83
Harry Pinner	(1)	1986
Glyn Shaw	(1)	1980
Nat Silcock	(12)	1932-37
Stuart Spruce	(1)	1993
Alan Tait	(9)	1989-92
John Warlow	(3)	1971
Darren Wright	(+1)	1988
Stuart Wright	(7)	1977-78

1998 SIGNINGS REGISTER

Signed	Player	Club From
27.2.98	Allday, Neil	Lancashire L.
4.6.98	Argent, Paul	Sims Cross ARL
—	Cantillon, Phil	Leeds R.
2.7.98	Charlton, Guy	St. Chads RU
5.1.98	Cragg, Paul	Woolston R. ARL
—	Devecchi, Fabien	Villeneuve (Fr.)
18.2.98	Earner, Adrian	Swinton L.
3.2.98	Fitpatrick, Karl	Wigan St. Patricks ARL
23.7.98	Flanagan, Mark	Widnes Academy
5.1.98	Garcia, Antonio	Wigan St. Patricks
27.2.98	Gildart, Ian	Oldham B.
17.6.98	Gray, David	Weaverham ARL
—	Hansen, Liuaki "Lee"	Keighley C.
5.4.98	Hewitt, Mark	Hull S.
4.6.98	Hobin, Michael	Portico P. ARL
15.1.98	Hussey, Stephen	Wigan St. Judes ARL
25.6.98	Jones, Daniel	Lancashire L.
5.1.98	Leatherbarrow, David	Widnes Academy
5.1.98	Litherland, Roy	Prescot P.
21.1.98	Manihera, Tane	Carlisle B.R.
—	Mann, George	Swinton L.
—	Mansson, Paul	Hunslet H.
5.1.98	McNulty, John	Widnes Academy
12.3.98	Moore, Martin	Sth. Sydney (Aust.)
3.5.98	Munro, Damien	Halifax B.S.
3.5.98	O'Loughlin, Kevin	Halifax B.S.
5.1.98	Salisbury, James	Liverpool St. Helens RU
5.1.98	Shea, Alan	Widnes Academy
5.1.98	Shields, Christopher	Widnes Academy
17.6.98	Smith, Paul	Eccles ARL
5.2.98	Viller, Jason	Fylde RU
11.1.98	Wilson, Shane	Sth. Sydney (Aust.)
5.1.98	Woods, Daniel	Widnes Academy

WIDNES VIKINGS 1998 MATCH ANALYSIS

Date	Competition	H/A	Opponents	Rlt	Score	Tries	Goals	Attendance	Referee
1.2.98	CC(3)	H	Oldham	W	48-8	Bloem (2), Salisbury (2), White (2), Ashton, Briers, Hunter	Howell (6)	4500	Nicholson
8.2.98	FD	A	Wakefield T.	L	22-24	P. Smith (2), Manihera, Salisbury	Howell (3)	–	–
15.2.98	CC(4)	A	Barrow B.R.	W	36-22	Bloem, Cross, George, Howell, Manihera, Salisbury	Howell (6)	–	–
22.2.98	FD	H	Rochdale H.	W	22-20	Bloem, Salisbury, White	Howell (4), Bloem	2974	Shaw
1.3.98	CC(5)	H	Salford R.	L	6-48	Hunter	Howell	5019	R. Connolly
4.3.98	FD	A	Hull K.R.	L	8-26	Bloem	Howell (2)	–	–
8.3.98	FD	H	Hunslet H.	W	32-26	Bloem, Cunningham, Wilson, P. Smith, Manihera	Howell (6)	2641	J. Connolly
15.3.98	FD	A	Featherstone R.	L	26-31	P. Smith (2), Howell, White, Manihera	Howell (3)	–	–
29.3.98	FD	A	Leigh C.	L	14-19	Fenlon, Howell	Howell (3)	–	–
5.4.98	FD	H	Dewsbury R.	L	12-15	Manihera, Moore	Hewitt (2)	2000	Laughton
10.4.98	FD	A	Whitehaven W.	L	12-44	Manihera	Hewitt (4)	–	–
13.4.98	FD	H	Swinton L.	W	34-18	Bloem (2), Ashton, Cunningham	Hewitt (9)	2502	
19.4.98	FD	A	Keighley C.	L	22-25	Salisbury (2), Moore	Hewitt (5)	–	–
26.4.98	FD	H	Wakefield T.	L	20-30	Richardson (2), Bloem,	Hewitt (4)	2555	Lee
4.5.98	FD	A	Rochdale H.	W	26-20	Wilson (2), Hewitt, Moore	Hewitt (5)	–	–
10.5.98	FD	H	Hull K.R.	W	22-12	Manihera, White	Hewitt (7)	2442	Laughton
15.5.98	FD	A	Hunslet H.	L	8-28	Litherland	Hewitt (2)	–	–
24.5.98	FD	H	Featherstone R.	D	32-32	Salisbury (2), Manihera, Percival, P. Smith, Wilson	Hewitt (4)	2272	Taberner
3.6.98	FD	H	Leigh C.	W	36-16	Salisbury (3), Wilson (2), Makin, Munro	Hewitt (4)	2274	Atkin
7.6.98	FD	A	Dewsbury R.	L	16-18	Manihera, Munro, P. Smith	Hewitt (2)	–	–
14.6.98	FD	H	Whitehaven W.	W	40-12	Makin (2), Munro (2), P. Smith, Gartland, Wilson	Hewitt (6)	2065	Morris
21.6.98	FD	A	Swinton L.	L	11-44	Gartland, Moore	Hewitt (1, dg)	–	–
24.6.98	FD	H	Keighley C.	W	37-22	Garcia (2), Manihera, Gartland, Percival	Hewitt (8, dg)	2102	Nicholson
28.6.98	FD	A	Whitehaven W.	L	14-48	Munro, Percival, Salisbury	Wood	–	–
5.7.98	FD	H	Dewsbury R.	L	12-24	Munro (2), Harris	–	2000	R. Connolly
12.7.98	FD	A	Wakefield T.	L	8-64	Makin	Wood (2)	–	–
15.7.98	FD	H	Swinton L.	L	12-34	Percival, Salisbury	Hewitt (2)	1701	Shaw
26.7.98	FD	A	Featherstone R.	L	26-28	George, Hewitt, Hunter, Long	Hewitt (4), Munro	–	–
2.8.98	FD	H	Hull K.R.	L	4-63	Long	–	1758	Oddy
7.8.98	FD	A	Hunslet H.	L	10-41	Munro, Percival	Hewitt	–	–
16.8.98	FD	H	Keighley C.	L	6-30	Moore	Hewitt	1668	Taberner
23.8.98	FD	A	Leigh C.	L	26-32	Cassidy, Moore, O'Loughlin, Percival	Hewitt (5)	–	–
30.8.98	FD	H	Rochdale H.	W	31-16	Garcia (2), Cross, Salisbury	Hewitt (7, dg)	1474	I. Smith

WIDNES VIKINGS 1998 PLAYERS' SUMMARY

	Date of birth	App	T	G	D	Pts	Previous club	Debut
Argent, Steve	7.5.78	1+2	0	0	0	0	Halton H. ARL	1998
Ashton, Lee	29.9.72	14+4	2	0	0	8		1994-95
Birdseye, Lee		1+1	0	0	0	0		1998
Bloem, Jamie	26.5.71	12	9	1	0	38	Doncaster	1997
Briers, James		3+8	1	0	0	4		1998
Cassidy, Jim	28.7.72	4	1	0	0	4	Leigh	1994-95
Connor, Ian	21.3.70	1+5	0	0	0	0	Swinton L.	1997
Cross, Dean	5.6.80	15+4	2	0	0	8	Widnes Academy	1997
Cunningham, Gareth	16.9.75	7+7	2	0	0	8	St. Helens	1996
Doherty, John-Paul	6.1.77	1+1	0	0	0	0	S. Wales	1997
Earner, Adrian	19.11.66	1+3	0	0	0	0	Swinton L.	1998
Emery, Paul	12.9.72	3+1	0	0	0	0	Lancashire L.	1997
Fenlon, Anthony	2.2.72	1+2	1	0	0	4	Whitehaven W.	1997
Fieldhouse, John	28.6.62	2+4	0	0	0	0	Whitehaven W.	1998
Garcia, Antonio	7.9.79	7+1	4	0	0	16	Wigan St. Patricks ARL	1998
Gartland, Paul	2.11.72	12+4	3	0	0	12	Swinton	1995-96
George, Paul	9.10.77	3+5	2	0	0	8	Wigan W.	1998
Gildart, Ian	14.10.69	18+3	0	0	0	0	Oldham B.	1998
Harris, Paul	18.4.74	16	1	0	0	4	St. Maries ARL	1993-94
Hewitt, Mark	17.3.74	22	2	83	3	177	Hull S.	1998
Hill, Mike	26.11.74	0+4	0	0	0	0		1998
Hobin, Mike	18.3.74	2+1	0	0	0	0	Portico Panthers ARL	1998
Howell, Paul	6.12.69	9	3	34	0	80	Wellington Dukes (NZ)	1997
Hunter, Jason	27.8.71	10+10	3	0	0	12	Blackbrook ARL	1993-94
Litherland, Roy	1.11.71	0+5	1	0	0	4	Prescot P.	1998
Long, Karl	18.11.80	1+6	2	0	0	8	Wigan St. Judes ARL	1998
Makin, Craig	13.4.73	31+1	4	0	0	16	Orrell St. James ARL	1993-94
Manihera, Tane	6.8.74	25	10	0	0	40	Carlisle B.R.	1998
Measures, Neil	11.1.71	7+2	0	0	0	0	Barrow B.R.	1998
Moore, Martin	5.11.69	21	6	0	0	24	South Sydney (Aust.)	1998
Munro, Damien	6.10.76	19	8	1	0	34	Halifax B.S.	1998
Murphy, Chris	25.11.78	1	0	0	0	0	Leigh East ARL	1998
Myler, Danny	7.8.79	3+1	0	0	0	0	St. Helens Crus. ARL	1997
Myler, Paul	11.11.72	6+1	0	0	0	0	Warrington	1994-95
O'Loughlin, Kevin	26.3.77	10+2	1	0	0	4	Halifax B.S.	1998
O'Neill, Andrew	4.1.76	11+8	0	0	0	0		1997
Percival, Chris	25.12.79	12+7	6	0	0	24	Laporte ARL	1996
Richardson, Sean	20.8.73	6+7	2	0	0	8	Castleford T.	1997
Salisbury, Jim	3.6.73	25	15	0	0	60	Liverpool-St. Helens RU	1998
Smith, David	21.12.78	2+2	0	0	0	0	Leigh M. ARL	1997
Smith, Peter	1.9.73	23+1	8	0	0	32	Widnes Tigers	1993-94
White, Kyle	12.1.71	29+1	5	0	0	20	St. Marys (Aust.)	1997
Wilson, Shane	27.4.72	27	7	0	0	28	Sth. Sydney (Aust.)	1998
Wood, Paul	13.1.78	5+9	0	3	0	6	Halton H. ARL	1998
TOTALS								
44 players			111	122	3	691		

WIGAN WARRIORS

Ground: Central Park (01942-231321)
First Season: 1895-96. Added Warriors to title for start of 1997 season.
Chairman: Peter Norbury
Honours: **Championship** Winners, 1908-09, 1921-22, 1925-26, 1933-34, 1945-46, 1946-47, 1949-50, 1951-52, 1959-60
Beaten finalists, 1909-10, 1910-11, 1911-12, 1912-13, 1923-24, 1970-71
Super League Grand Final Winners, 1998
War Emergency League Winners, 1943-44
Beaten finalists, 1940-41
League Leaders Trophy Winners, 1970-71
Division One Champions, 1986-87, 1989-90, 1990-91, 1991-92, 1992-93, 1993-94, 1994-95, 1995-96 (Centenary Champions)
Challenge Cup Winners, 1923-24, 1928-29, 1947-48, 1950-51, 1957-58, 1958-59, 1964-65, 1984-85, 1987-88, 1988-89, 1989-90, 1990-91, 1991-92, 1992-93, 1993-94, 1994-95
Beaten finalists, 1910-11, 1919-20, 1943-44, 1945-46, 1960-61, 1962-63, 1965-66, 1969-70, 1983-84, 1998
Regal Trophy Winners, 1982-83, 1985-86, 1986-87, 1988-89, 1989-90, 1992-93, 1994-95, 1995-96
Beaten finalists, 1993-94
Premiership Winners, 1986-87, 1991-92, 1993-94, 1994-95, 1996, 1997
Beaten finalists, 1992-93
Lancashire Cup Winners, 1905-06, 1908-09, 1909-10, 1912-13, 1922-23, 1928-29, 1938-39, 1946-47, 1947-48, 1948-49, 1949-50, 1950-51, 1951-52, 1966-67, 1971-72, 1973-74, 1985-86, 1986-87, 1987-88, 1988-89, 1992-93
Beaten finalists, 1913-14, 1914-15, 1925-26, 1927-28, 1930-31, 1934-35, 1935-36, 1936-37, 1945-46, 1953-54, 1957-58, 1977-78, 1980-81, 1984-85
Lancashire League Winners, 1901-02, 1908-09, 1910-11, 1911-12, 1912-13, 1913-14, 1914-15, 1920-21, 1922-23, 1923-24, 1925-26, 1945-46, 1946-47, 1949-50, 1951-52, 1958-59, 1961-62, 1969-70
Lancashire War League Winners, 1940-41
Charity Shield Winners, 1985-86, 1987-88, 1991-92, 1995-96
Beaten finalists, 1988-89, 1989-90, 1990-91, 1992-93
World Club Challenge Winners, 1987-88, 1991-92, 1993-94
Beaten finalists, 1992-93
BBC2 Floodlit Trophy Winners, 1968-69
Beaten finalists, 1969-70

RECORDS

Match

Goals: 22 by Jim Sullivan v. Flimby & Fothergill, 14 Feb 1925
Tries: 10 by Martin Offiah v. Leeds, 10 May 1992
Shaun Edwards at Swinton, 29 Sep 1992
Points: 44 by Jim Sullivan v. Flimby & Fothergill, 14 Feb 1925

Season

Goals: 186 by Frano Botica, 1994-95
Tries: 62 by Johnny Ring, 1925-26
Points: 423 by Frano Botica, 1992-93

Career

Goals: 2,317 by Jim Sullivan, 1921-46
Tries: 478 by Billy Boston, 1953-68
Points: 4,883 by Jim Sullivan, 1921-46
Appearances: 774 by Jim Sullivan, 1921-46
Highest score: 116-0 v. Flimby & Fothergill, 14 Feb 1925
Highest against: 58-3 at Leeds, 14 Oct 1972
Attendance: 47,747 v. St. Helens (League), 27 Mar 1959

GREAT BRITAIN REGISTER

(93 players)

Ray Ashby	(1)	1965
Ernest Ashcroft	(11)	1947-54
Eric Ashton	(26)	1957-63
Bill Ashurst	(3)	1971-72
Frank Barton	(1)	1951
John Barton	(2)	1960-61
Jack Bennett	(1)	1926
Denis Betts	(24+1)	1990-94
Dai Bevan	(1)	1952
Billy Blan	(3)	1951
Dave Bolton	(23)	1957-63
Billy Boston	(31)	1954-63
Tommy Bradshaw	(6)	1947-50
Frank Carlton	(1)	1962
Brian Case	(6+1)	1984-88
Mick Cassidy	(1+3)	1994-97
Norman Cherrington	(1)	1960
Colin Clarke	(7)	1965-73
Phil Clarke	(15+1)	1990-94
Percy Coldrick	(4)	1914
Frank Collier	(1)	1963
Gary Connolly	(10)	1993-98
Neil Cowie	(3)	1993-98
Jack Cunliffe	(4)	1950-54
Martin Dermott	(11)	1990-93
Shaun Edwards	(32+4)	1985-94
Joe Egan	(14)	1946-50
Roy Evans	(4)	1961-62
George Fairbairn	(14)	1977-80
Andrew Farrell	(16)	1993-98
Terry Fogerty	(1)	1967
Phil Ford	(1)	1985
Bill Francis	(4)	1967-77
Danny Gardiner	(1)	1965
Ken Gee	(17)	1946-51
Henderson Gill	(14+1)	1981-88
Lee Gilmour	(1+1)	1998
Andy Goodway	(12)	1985-90
Bobbie Goulding	(5)	1990
John Gray	(5+3)	1974
Andy Gregory	(16)	1987-92
Steve Hampson	(11+1)	1987-92
Ellery Hanley	(23)	1985-91
Simon Haughton	(0+5)	1997-98
Cliff Hill	(1)	1966
David Hill	(1)	1971
Jack Hilton	(4)	1950
Tommy Howley	(6)	1924
Bill Hudson	(1)	1948
Danny Hurcombe	(8)	1920-24
Bert Jenkins	(12)	1907-14
Keri Jones	(2)	1970
Roy Kinnear	(1)	1929
Nicky Kiss	(1)	1985
Doug Laughton	(11)	1970-71
Johnny Lawrenson	(3)	1948
Jim Leytham	(5)	1907-10
Ian Lucas	(1+1)	1991-92
Joe Lydon	(14+6)	1986-92
Barrie McDermott	(1+2)	1994
Billy McGinty	(4)	1992
Brian McTigue	(25)	1958-63
Barrie-Jon Mather	(0+1)	1994
Joe Miller	(1)	1911
Jack Morley	(2)	1936-37
Terry O'Connor	(5+2)	1996-98
Martin Offiah	(13)	1992-94
Andy Platt	(17+1)	1989-93
Ian Potter	(7+1)	1985-86
Jack Price	(4)	1924
Kris Radlinski	(11)	1996-98
Dick Ramsdale	(8)	1910-14
Gordon Ratcliffe	(3)	1947-50
Johnny Ring	(2)	1924-26
Dave Robinson	(1)	1970
Jason Robinson	(10)	1993-98
Martin Ryan	(4)	1947-50
Bill Sayer	(7)	1961-63
Jim Sharrock	(4)	1910-11
Dick Silcock	(1)	1908
Nat Silcock	(3)	1954
Kelvin Skerrett	(6+2)	1992-93
Tony Smith	(3)	1998
David Stephenson	(5)	1982-87
Jim Sullivan	(25)	1924-33
Mick Sullivan	(19)	1957-60
Gwyn Thomas	(1)	1914
Johnny Thomas	(8)	1907-11
Shaun Wane	(2)	1985-86
Ted Ward	(3)	1946-47
Les White	(2)	1947
David Willicombe	(2)	1974
Billy Winstanley	(3)	1911

COACHING REGISTER
● **Since 1974-75**

Ted Toohey	May 74 - Jan 75
Joe Coan	Jan 75 - Sep 76
Vince Karalius	Sep 76 - Sep 79
Kel Coslett	Oct 79 - Apr 80
George Fairbairn	Apr 80 - May 81
Maurice Bamford	May 81 - May 82
Alex Murphy	June 82 - Aug 84
Colin Clarke } Alan McInnes }	Aug 84 - May 86
Graham Lowe	Aug 86 - June 89
John Monie	Sep 89 - May 93
John Dorahy	June 93 - May 94
Graeme West	May 94 - Feb 97
Eric Hughes	Mar 97 - Nov 97
John Monie	Nov 97 -

1998 SIGNINGS REGISTER

Signed	Player	Club From
12.6.98	Bretherton, Liam	Warrington W.
28.9.98	Dean, Gareth	Cardiff Demons ARL
—	Florimo, Greg	Nth Sydney (Aust.)
—	Goldspink, Brett	St. Helens
4.9.98	Jackson, Robert	—
1.7.98	Lacey, Daryl	Blackbrook ARL
12.4.98	Lee, Craig	Woolston R. ARL
5.1.98	McCormack, Robbie	Hunter M. (Aust.)
14.1.98	Moore, Danny	Manly (Aust.)
20.5.98	Roden, Martin	Wigan Academy
18.8.98	Smith, Mark	Wigan Academy
5.9.98	Turner, Danny	Ince St. Williams ARL

Denis Betts: 20 appearances on his return to Wigan Warriors.

WIGAN WARRIORS 1998 MATCH ANALYSIS

Date	Competition	H/A	Opponents	Rlt	Score	Tries	Goals	Attendance	Referee
15.2.98	CC(4)	A	Keighley C.	W	76-0	Robinson (3), Murdock (2), Paul (2), Bell, Clarke, Gilmour, Haughton, Holgate, McCormack, Connolly	Farrell (10)	–	–
1.3.98	CC(5)	A	Dewsbury R.	W	56-0	Robinson (3), Murdock (2), Cardiss, Farrell, P. Johnson, Moore	Farrell (10)	–	–
15.3.98	CC(6)	H	St. Helens	W	22-10	Robinson, Moore, Betts, Haughton	Farrell (3)	17,179	Cummings
29.3.98	CC(SF)	N1	London B.	W	38-8	Radlinski (2), Moore (2), Robinson , Bell	Farrell (7)	(11,058)	R. Smith
5.4.98	SL	H	Castleford T.	W	18-4	Smith (2), Paul	Farrell (3)	10,920	Cummings
10.4.98	SL	A	St. Helens	W	38-18	Connolly, Gilmour, Robinson, P. Johnson, Radlinski, Smith	Farrell (7)	–	–
19.4.98	SL	H	Halifax B.S.	W	40-6	Connolly (3), Bell, Betts, Radlinski, Smith	Farrell (6)	12,841	Ganson
26.4.98	SL	H	London B.	W	24-10	Gilmour, P. Johnson, Moore, Smith	Farrell (4)	9233	Presley
2.5.98	CC(F)	N2	Sheffield E.	L	8-17	Bell	Farrell (2)	(60,669)	Cummings
9.5.98	SL	A	Sheffield E.	W	36-6	Moore (2), Bell, Radlinski, Smith, Robinson	Farrell (6)	–	–
15.5.98	SL	A	Leeds R.	L	8-16	Haughton	Farrell (2)	–	–
22.5.98	SL	H	Huddersfield G.	W	46-0	Cardiss, Cowie, Farrell, Paul, Gilmour, Radlinski, Smith, Robinson	Farrell (4), Connolly (2) Paul	8966	Kirkpatrick
31.5.98	SL	A	Hull S.	W	38-16	Moore (2), Connolly, Cowie, Haughton, Robinson	Farrell (7)	–	–
7.6.98	SL	H	Salford R.	W	34-6	Bell, Gilmour (2), Betts, Moore	Farrell (5)	10,075	Cummings
12.6.98	SL	A	Bradford B.	W	28-12	Connolly (2), Bell, Cowie, Paul	Farrell (4)	–	–
21.6.98	SL	H	Warrington W.	W	56-8	P. Johnson (2), Betts, Cassidy, Connolly, Gilmour, McCormack, Paul, Robinson	Farrell (10)	10,149	R. Smith
28.6.98	SL	A	Castleford T.	W	34-4	Paul (2), Connolly, Farrell, Moore, P. Johnson	Farrell (5)	–	–
5.7.98	SL	H	St. Helens	W	38-14	Haughton (2), Bell, Farrell, P. Johnson, O'Connor	Farrell (7)	12,461	R. Smith
26.7.98	SL	N3	St. Helens	W	36-2	Radlinski (2), Smith (2), Connolly, Farrell	Farrell (6)	(8572)	Cummings
31.7.98	SL	A	Halifax B.S.	W	20-14	Radlinski, Paul, McCormack	Farrell (4)	–	–
7.8.98	SL	A	London B.	W	18-15	Bell (2), Smith	Farrell (3)	–	–
16.8.98	SL	H	Sheffield E.	W	44-6	Paul (2), Farrell, Haughton, Holgate, Moore, Radlinski	Farrell (8)	10,175	Ganson
21.8.98	SL	H	Leeds R.	L	8-15	Haughton	Farrell (2)	12,786	Cummings
30.8.98	SL	A	Huddersfield G.	W	38-14	Connolly (2), P. Johnson (2), Radlinski, Robinson, Smith	Farrell (5)	–	–
6.9.98	SL	H	Hull S.	W	58-6	Gilmour (2), Robinson (2), Paul (2), Bell, Connolly, Farrell, P. Johnson, Radlinski, Smith	Farrell (5)	7930	Ganson
13.9.98	SL	A	Salford R.	W	34-2	Baynes, Bell, Davies, Holgate, Smith	Paul (5), Farrell (2)	–	–
20.9.98	SL	H	Bradford B.	W	38-4	Connolly (2), P. Johnson (2), Haughton, Mestrov	Farrell (7)	11,181	R. Smith
27.9.98	SL	A	Warrington W.	W	30-24	Smith (2), Bell, P. Johnson, Paul, Radlinski	Farrell (3)	–	–
11.10.98	PO	H	Leeds R.	W	17-4	Bell, Gilmour, Paul	Farrell (2, dg)	12,941	Cummings
24.10.98	POF	N4	Leeds R.	W	10-4	Robinson	Farrell (3)	(43,533)	(R. Smith)

N1 at Huddersfield; N2 at Wembley; N3 at Swansea C. FC; N4 at Manchester U. FC

131

WIGAN WARRIORS 1998 PLAYERS' SUMMARY

	Date of birth	App	T	G	D	Pts	Previous club	Debut
Ball, Rob	22.3.76	0+1	0	0	0	0	Leigh C.	1998
Baynes, Neil	14.9.77	0+5	1	0	0	4	Wigan St. Judes	1995-96
Bell, Mark	19.3.67	27	15	0	0	60	St. George (Aust.)	1998
Betts, Denis	14.9.69	18+2	4	0	0	16	Auckland W. (NZ)	1998
Cardiss, Darryl	13.7.78	4+3	2	0	0	8	Hunslet Boys	1995-96
Cassidy, Mick	3.7.73	11+13	1	0	0	4	Wigan St. Judes	1991-92
Clarke, Jonathan	4.4.79	1+8	1	0	0	4	Orrell St. James ARL	1997
Connolly, Gary	22.6.71	30	16	2	0	68	St. Helens	1993-94
Cowie, Neil	16.1.67	15+8	3	0	0	12	Rochdale H.	1991-92
Davies, Wes	20.1.78	0+1	1	0	0	4	Wigan St. Judes ARL	1998
Farrell, Andrew	30.5.75	30	7	152	1	333	Orrell St. James	1991-92
Gilmour, Lee	12.3.78	13+17	10	0	0	40	Dewsbury Moor ARL	1997
Hansen, Liuaki "Lee"	23.7.68	0+1	0	0	0	0	Widnes V.	1997
Haughton, Simon	10.11.75	18+9	9	0	0	36	Dudley Hill ARL	1993-94
Holgate, Stephen	15.12.71	11+11	3	0	0	12	Workington T.	1997
Isherwood, Andrew	23.11.79	0+3	0	0	0	0	Wigan St. Patricks ARL	1998
Johnson, Paul	25.11.78	5+19	13	0	0	52	Hindley ARL	1995-96
McCormack, Robbie	14.10.64	29	3	0	0	12	Hunter M. (Aust.)	1998
Mestrov, Tony	11.3.70	28+1	1	0	0	4	London B.	1998
Moore, Danny	2.11.71	25+2	12	0	0	48	Manly (Aust.)	1998
Murdock, Craig	24.10.73	2	4	0	0	16	Hensingham	1993-94
O'Connor, Terry	13.10.71	11+12	1	0	0	4	Salford	1994-95
Paul, Henry	10.2.74	28	15	6	0	72	Auckland W. (NZ)	1994-95
Radlinski, Kris	9.4.76	30	13	0	0	52	Wigan Academy	1993-94
Robinson, Jason	30.7.74	29+1	17	0	0	68	Hunslet Parkside	1992-93
Smith, Tony	16.7.70	25	15	0	0	60	Castleford T.	1997
Smyth, Rob	22.2.77	0+1	0	0	0	0	Rose Bridge ARL	1995-96
TOTALS								
27 players			167	160	1	989		

Representative appearances 1998

Cassidy - Ireland (2); Connolly - Britain (3), Ireland (1); Cowie - Britain (2), Wales (1); Farrell - Britain (3, 11g); Gilmour - Britain (1+1), Emerging England (1); Haughton - Britain (0+3), Emerging England (1); Johnson - Emerging England (0+1); O'Connor - Britain (1+2), Ireland (1); Paul - New Zealand (1+3, 2t); Radlinski - Britain (3); Robinson - Britain (3, 3t); Smith - Britain (3, 1t, 1dg)

WORKINGTON TOWN

Ground: Derwent Park (01900-603609)
First Season: 1945-46
Chairman: Geoff Tubman
Honours: **Championship** Winners, 1950-51
Beaten finalists, 1957-58
Division Two Champions, 1993-94
Challenge Cup Winners, 1951-52
Beaten finalists, 1954-55, 1957-58
**Second Division/Divisional
Premiership** Winners 1993-94,
Beaten finalists, 1992-93
Lancashire Cup Winners, 1977-78
Beaten finalists, 1976-77, 1978-79,
1979-80
Western Division Championship
Winners, 1962-63

RECORDS

Match

Goals: 13 by Dean Marwood v. Highfield,
1 Nov 1992
Dean Marwood v. Leigh, 26 Feb
1995
Wayne Kitchin v. Thatto Heath,
26 Jan 1997
Tries: 7 by Ike Southward v. Blackpool B.,
17 Sep 1955
Points: 42 by Dean Marwood v. Highfield,
1 Nov 1992
Dean Marwood v. Leigh,
26 Feb 1995

Season

Goals: 186 by Lyn Hopkins, 1981-82
Tries: 49 by Johnny Lawrenson, 1951-52
Points: 438 by Lyn Hopkins, 1981-82

Career

Goals: 809 by Iain MacCorquodale, 1972-80
Tries: 274 by Ike Southward, 1952-59 & 1960-68
Points: 1,800 by Iain MacCorquodale, 1972-80
Appearances: 415+4 Paul Charlton, 1961-69 &
1975-80
Highest score: 94-4 v. Leigh, 26 Feb 1995
Highest against: 78-4 at Wigan, 24 Aug 1996
Attendance: 17,741 v. Wigan (RL Cup), 3 Mar
1965 — at Derwent Park

20,403 v. St. Helens (RL Cup), 8 Mar
1952 — at Borough Park

COACHING REGISTER

● **Since 1974-75**

Ike Southward	Aug 73 - June 75
Paul Charlton	June 75 - June 76
Ike Southward	June 76 - Feb 78
Sol Roper	Feb 78 - Apr 80
Keith Irving	Aug 80 - Oct 80
Tommy Bishop	Nov 80 - June 82
Paul Charlton	July 82 - Dec 82
Dave Cox	Mar 83 - Mar 83
Harry Archer/Bill Smith	May 83 - June 84
Bill Smith	June 84 - Apr 85
Jackie Davidson	Apr 85 - Jan 86
Keith Davies	Feb 86 - Mar 87
Norman Turley	Mar 87 - Apr 88
Maurice Bamford	July 88 - Dec 88
Phil Kitchin	Dec 88 - May 90
Ray Ashton	June 90 - Dec 91
Dean Williams	Dec 91 - Apr 92
Peter Walsh	May 92 - July 95
Kurt Sorensen	Aug 95 - Mar 96
Ross O'Reilly	Mar 96 - Mar 97
Robert Tew	Apr 97 - Oct 98
Andy Platt	Oct 98 -

GREAT BRITAIN REGISTER

(10 players)

Eddie Bowman	(4)	1977
Paul Charlton	(1)	1965
Brian Edgar	(11)	1958-66
Norman Herbert	(6)	1961-62
Vince McKeating	(2)	1951
Billy Martin	(1)	1962
Albert Pepperell	(2)	1950-51
Rowland Phillips	(+1)	1996
Ike Southward	(4)	1958
George Wilson	(3)	1951

WORKINGTON TOWN 1998 MATCH ANALYSIS

Date	Competition	H/A	Opponents	Rlt	Score	Tries	Goals	Attendance	Referee
1.2.98	CC(3)	H	Haydock	W	12-8	Bibby, Williams	Fisher (2)	1139	Gillespie
13.2.98	CC(4)	A	Egremont R.	L	0-18	–	–	–	–
10.4.98	SD	A	Barrow B.R.	L	10-26	Highton, Williams	Fisher	–	–
13.4.98	SD	H	Oldham	L	18-22	Fisher, Mafi, Riley	Fisher (3)	1344	Lee
19.4.98	SD	A	York	L	14-18	Arnold, Henare	Fisher (3)	–	–
26.4.98	SD	A	Batley B.	L	18-42	Arnold, Henare, Samuels	Fisher (3)	–	–
9.5.98	SD	H	Bramley	W	21-14	Bethwaite, Crellin, Williams, Samuels	Maguire (1, dg), Fisher	759	Cornish
17.5.98	SD	H	Lancashire L.	L	6-40	Crellin	Maguire	869	Lowe
24.5.98	SD	A	Doncaster D.	D	18-18	Henare, Keenan, Mafi, Williams	Richardson	–	–
31.5.98	SD/RR	H	Barrow B.R.	W	16-13	Mafi, Sullivan, Woodcock	Cook, Sullivan	781	Shaw
7.6.98	SD/RR	H	Oldham	L	10-27	Roden	Fisher (3)	1057	Taberner
14.6.98	SD/RR	H	Lancashire L.	L	25-26	Henare (2), Close, Mafi	Fisher (4), Maguire (dg)	709	Griffiths
21.6.98	SD/RR	A	Barrow B.R.	L	12-34	Arnold, Henare	Fisher (2)	–	–
28.6.98	SD/RR	A	Lancashire L.	L	12-48	Close, Little	Richardson, Close (dg), Maguire (dg)		
5.7.98	SD/RR	A	Oldham	L	8-56	Little, Roden	–	–	–
26.7.98	SD	H	Barrow B.R.	D	8-8	Little	Branthwaite (2)	626	Lowe
2.8.98	SD	A	Oldham	L	9-12	Close	Branthwaite (2), Maguire (dg)	–	–
9.8.98	SD	H	York	L	15-20	Keenan, Richardson	Branthwaite (3), Close (dg)	577	I. Smith
16.8.98	SD	H	Batley B.	L	12-28	Close, Roden	Branthwaite (2)	561	Lee
23.8.98	SD	A	Bramley	L	16-30	Close, Richardson, Stalker	Branthwaite (2)	–	–
30.8.98	SD	A	Lancashire L.	L	25-64	Branthwaite, Keenan, Samuels, Stalker	Branthwaite (4), Maguire (dg)	–	–
6.9.98	SD	H	Doncaster D.	W	20-12	Close, Henare, Keenan, Stalker	Branthwaite (2)	726	Laughton

1998 SIGNINGS REGISTER

Signed	Player	Club From
5.9.98	Abram, Barry	—
—	Allen, John	Whitehaven W.
—	Armstrong, Colin	Whitehaven W.
16.1.98	Arnold, Stephen	Warrington W.
8.5.98	Birkett, Lee	Pack Horse ARL
21.1.98	Close, Graeme	Salford R.
26.5.98	Cusack, Sean	Carlisle B.R.
17.7.98	Hayter, Gregory	Dundee High School
8.5.98	*Hetherington, Gary	Barrow B.R.
16.2.98	McDonald, Lee	Maryport ARL
16.2.98	McDougall, Stuart	Ellenborough R. ARL
26.5.98	McKenzie, Paul "George"	Westfield ARL
27.8.98	Newell, John	Carlisle B.R.
5.9.98	Nicholson, Michael	Ellenborough R. ARL
5.9.98	Pearson, Simon	Flimby ARL
—	Platt, Andy	Salford R.
22.5.98	*Richardson, Willie	Carlisle B.R.
25.4.97	Roden, Carl	Warrington W.
27.5.98	Rudd, Warren	Carlisle B.R.
15.2.98	Samuel, Anthony	Widnes V.
2.4.98	Thompson, Chris	Seaton Packhorse ARL
30.7.98	Thurlow, Jason	Barrow B.R.
16.6.98	Walker, Eddie	Seaton Packhorse ARL
—	Wallace, Mark	Whitehaven W.
29.5.98	Warwick, David	Carlisle B.R.
—	White, Josh	Salford R.
11.6.98	*Wright, Ricky	Sheffield E.

WORKINGTON TOWN 1998 PLAYERS' SUMMARY

	Date of birth	App	T	G	D	Pts	Previous club	Debut
Anderson, Phil	26.9.66	2	0	0	0	0	Carlisle B.R.	1998
Armstrong, Craig	30.1.78	8+9	0	0	0	0	Westfield Hotel ARL	1997
Arnold, Steve	24.6.78	16+2	3	0	0	12	Warrington W.	1998
Barker, Craig	1.9.75	1+4	0	0	0	0		1996
Beaumont, Jamie		0+1	0	0	0	0	Workington T. Acad.	1998
Bethwaite, Mike	2.10.72	5+3	1	0	0	4	Glasson R. ARL	1995-96
Bibby, Dennis	7.11.74	4	1	0	0	4	Penrith ARL	1997
Branthwaite, Paul	15.10.73	7	1	17	0	72	Wigton ARL	1998
Close, Graeme	8.5.77	19	6	0	2	26	Salford R.	1998
Cook, Graeme	22.8.73	4+1	0	1	0	2	Workington RU	1998
Crellin, Nicky	20.5.77	4+12	2	0	0	4	Glasson R. ARL	1996
Fisher, Craig	16.9.77	9+4	1	22	0	48	Glasson R. ARL	1997
Heaton, Steve	2.7.76	9+4	0	0	0	0	Warrington W.	1997
Henare, Richard	12.10.68	18	7	0	0	28	Warrington W.	1998
Hetherington, Gary	5.7.65	0+1	0	0	0	0	Barrow B.R.	1998
Highton, Chris	11.1.78	2	1	0	0	4	Warrington W.	1998
Houston, Chris	6.7.76	2+4	0	0	0	0	West of Scotland RU	1998
Keenan, Mark	11.11.75	13+1	4	0	0	16	Workington Acad.	1995-96
Little, Andrew	12.1.68	14+1	3	0	0	12	Broughton Red Rose ARL	1998
Mafi, Mateaki	19.9.72	15+1	4	0	0	16	Warrington W.	1997
Maguire, Steve	12.8.63	16	0	2	5	9	Whitehaven W.	1998
Moore, Jason	27.12.70	2	0	0	0	0	Ellenborough ARL	1993-94
Penrice, Paul	27.2.66	1	0	0	0	0	Gt. Clifton ARL	1987-88
Petrie, Adrian	4.3.77	2	0	0	0	0	Seaton R. ARL	1996
Richardson, Willie	6.10.60	8+3	2	2	0	12	Carlisle B.R.	1998
Riley, Peter	1.3.68	16+4	1	0	0	4	Gt. Clifton ARL	1987-88
Roden, Carl	4.11.77	21	3	0	0	12	Warrington W.	1997
Samuel, Anthony	21.9.73	19	3	0	0	12	Widnes V.	1998
Scales, Ryan		0+1	0	0	0	0		1998
Smith, Garry	2.10.62	0+1	0	0	0	0	Egremont ARL	1984-85
Sowerby, Daniel	6.9.78	2+2	0	0	0	0	Ellenborough R. ARL	1997
Stalker, Craig	8.6.75	7+1	3	0	0	12	St. Nicholas Arms ARL	1998
Sullivan, Chris	12.4.72	3+5	1	1	0	6	Leigh C.	1998
Thurlow, Jason	18.12.69	0+1	0	0	0	0	Barrow B.R.	1998
Thursfield, John	22.10.69	5	0	0	0	0	Warrington W.	1997
Tubman, Mark	26.7.79	1	0	0	0	0	Ellenborough R. ARL	1997
Tunstall, Matthew		0+2	0	0	0	0		1998
Walker, Scott	7.9.74	4+1	0	0	0	0	Widnes V.	1997
Whitter, Damien	25.11.76	6	0	0	0	0	Warrington W.	1997
Williams, Barry	15.5.71	15+1	4	0	0	16	Carlisle B.R.	1997
Woodcock, Matthew		4	1	0	0	4		1998
Wright, Ricky	15.3.77	2	0	0	0	0	Sheffield E.	1998
TOTALS								
42 players			52	45	7	305		

YORK

Ground:	Ryedale Stadium (01904-634636)
First Season:	1901-02 as York. Became Ryedale-York at start of 1989-90. Reverted to York at the start of 1995-96.
Chairman:	Trevor Cox
Honours:	**Division Two** Champions, 1980-81 **Challenge Cup** Beaten finalists, 1930-31 **Yorkshire Cup** Winners, 1922-23, 1933-34, 1936-37 Beaten finalists, 1935-36, 1957-58, 1978-79

RECORDS

Match

Goals:	12 by Gary Pearce at Nottingham C., 4 Oct 1992
Tries:	7 by Brad Davis v. Highfield, 17 Sep 1995
Points:	28 by Gary Pearce at Nottingham C., 4 Oct 1992 Brad Davis v. Highfield, 17 Sept 1995

Season

Goals:	146 by Vic Yorke, 1957-58
Tries:	35 by John Crossley, 1980-81
Points:	318 by Graham Steadman, 1984-85

Career

Goals: 1,060 by Vic Yorke, 1954-67
Tries: 167 by Peter Foster, 1955-67
Points: 2,159 by Vic Yorke, 1954-67
Appearances: 449 by Willie Hargreaves, 1952-65
Highest score: 84-0 at Nottingham C., 4 Oct 1992
Highest against: 75-3 at Warrington, 23 Sep 1950
Attendance: 14,689 v. Swinton (RL Cup), 10 Feb 1934 — at Clarence Street 4,977 v. Halifax (Div. 2), 5 Jan 1990 — at Ryedale Stadium

COACHING REGISTER

● **Since 1974-75**

Keith Goulding	Nov 73 - Sep 74
Gary Cooper	Dec 74 - Sep 76
Mal Dixon	Sep 76 - Dec 78
Paul Daley	Jan 79 - May 79
David Doyle-Davidson	July 79 - July 80
Bill Kirkbride	Aug 80 - Apr 82
Alan Hardisty	May 82 - Jan 83
Phil Lowe	Mar 83 - Mar 87
Danny Sheehan	Mar 87 - Apr 88
Gary Stephens	Apr 88 - June 91
Derek Foster	July 91 - Nov 92
Steve Crooks	Nov 92 - May 94
Roger Millward	June 94 - Dec 94
Stewart Horton	Jan 95 - Dec 96
Dean Robinson	Dec 96 -

GREAT BRITAIN REGISTER
(7 players)

Edgar Dawson	(1)	1956
Harry Field	(3)	1936
Geoff Smith	(3)	1963-64
Jeff Stevenson	(4)	1959-60
Mick Sullivan	(1)	1963
Basil Watts	(5)	1954-55
Les White	(4)	1946

1998 SIGNINGS REGISTER

Signed	Player	Club From
19.3.98	*Aston, Jon	Hull S.
26.1.98	Austerfield, Shaun	Dewsbury R.
16.4.98	*Benn, James	Castleford T.
8.1.98	Booth, Craig	Hunslet H.
10.1.98	Brook, David	Hunslet H.
15.1.98	Darley, Paul	Hull S.
11.5.98	*Dobson, Gareth	Castleford T.
13.1.98	*Dunning, Robert	Hull S.
—	Edwards, Peter	Salford R.
24.2.98	Eldershaw, Justin	Ryde Eastwood (Aust.)
1.1.98	Flowers, Stuart	Hunslet H.
13.1.98	Godfrey, Alex	Hull S.
1.1.98	Hanlan, Lee	Hunslet H.
2.4.98	*Hargrave, Spencer	Castleford T.
19.3.98	*Hewitt, Mark	Hull S.
5.1.98	Hill, Andrew	Castleford T.
5.1.98	Hill, Stephen	Castleford T.
26.1.98	Lambert, Matthew	Featherstone R.
9.4.98	Moore, Craig	Dewsbury R.
15.1.98	*Ramsden, Michael	Wakefield T.
8.5.98	Sini, Iefata "Fata"	Salford R.
19.2.98	Strange, John	Featherstone R.
25.6.98	White, Paul	Hunslet H.
13.1.98	*Windas, Neil	Hull S.
8.1.98	Woodward, Geoff	—

YORK 1998 MATCH ANALYSIS

Date	Com-petition	H/A	Opponents	Rlt	Score	Tries	Goals	Atten-dance	Referee
1.2.98	CC(3)	H	Norland	W	37-5	Deakin (2), Pallister (2), Austerfield	Precious (8), Hanlan (dg)	900	Lee
15.2.98	CC(4)	A	Swinton L.	L	21-39	Godfrey, Lambert, Limb, Woodward	Precious (2), Hanlan (dg)	–	–
10.4.98	SD	H	Bramley	L	6-13	Deakin	Hopcutt	639	Atkin
13.4.98	SD	A	Batley B.	L	11-25	Moore (2),	Precious, Brook (dg)	–	–
19.4.98	SD	H	Workington T.	W	18-14	Booth, Deakin, Hanlan, Moore	Hopcutt	670	Laughton
26.4.98	SD	H	Barrow B.R.	W	38-6	Deakin, Austerfield, Cain, Dobson, Hanlan, Moore, Hopcutt	Hopcutt (5)	649	Shaw
10.5.98	SD	A	Lancashire L.	W	25-12	Deakin (3), Brook, Godfrey	Booth (2), Cain (dg)	–	–
17.5.98	SD	A	Doncaster D.	W	29-8	Austerfield, Deakin, Hanlan, Hopcutt, Sini	Hopcutt (4), Strange (dg)	–	–
24.5.98	SD	H	Oldham	W	27-6	Benn (2), Sini, Tichener	Benn (5), Strange (dg)	1482	Lowe
29.5.98	SD/WR	A	Bramley	L	14-36	Brook, Strange	Hopcutt (3)	–	–
7.6.98	SD/WR	H	Batley B.	L	4-13	Godfrey	-	718	Cornish
14.6.98	SD/WR	H	Doncaster D.	W	44-12	Cain (2), Sini (2), Austerfield, Darley, Strange	Booth (6), Cain (2)	554	Lee
21.6.98	SD/WR	H	Bramley	W	27-10	Deakin (2), Flowers, Cain, Moore	Cain (3), Precious (dg)	621	Laughton
28.6.98	SD/WR	A	Doncaster D.	W	26-20	Austerfield, Benn, Deakin, Godfrey, White	Benn (3)	–	–
5.7.98	SD/WR	A	Batley B.	L	3-8	–	Booth, Precious (dg)	–	–
26.7.98	SD	A	Bramley	W	21-20	Godfrey, Hopcutt, Pallister, Sini	Hopcutt (2), Strange (dg)	–	–
2.8.98	SD	H	Batley B.	L	15-18	Crane, Strange	Precious (3), Strange (dg)	677	Lowe
9.8.98	SD	A	Workington T.	W	20-15	Austerfield, Cain, Pallister	Hopcutt (2), Precious, Crane (dg), Austerfield (dg),	–	–
16.8.98	SD	A	Barrow B.R.	W	43-10	Austerfield, Booth, Cain, Godfrey, Pallister, Strange, Crane	Booth (6), Precious, Crane (dg)	–	–
23.8.98	SD	H	Lancashire L.	W	21-20	Booth, Deakin, S. Hill, A. Hill	Booth, Hopcutt, Cain (dg)	900	Bates
30.8.98	SD	H	Doncaster D.	W	46-6	Booth (2), Deakin (2), Strange (2), Austerfield, Godfrey, Preston	Booth (5)	1003	Taberner
6.9.98	SD	A	Oldham	W	38-8	Austerfield (2), Godfrey (2), Preston, Ramsden, Strange	Booth (4), Cain	–	–

YORK PLAYERS' 1998 SUMMARY

	Date of birth	App	T	G	D	Pts	Previous club	Debut
Austerfield, Shaun	11.9.75	19	10	0	1	41	Dewsbury R.	1998
Benn, Jamie	4.5.77	1+2	3	8	0	28	Castleford T.	1998
Booth, Craig	28.10.70	16+2	5	25	0	70	Hunslet H.	1998
Brook, David	4.2.71	10+1	2	0	1	9	Hunslet H.	1998
Cain, Mark	3.5.76	19+3	6	6	2	38	New Earswick ARL	1994-95
Crane, Mike	11.2.71	10	2	0	2	10	Hull K.R.	1997
Darley, Paul	26.1.74	14+3	1	0	0	4	Hull S.	1998
Deakin Leigh	27.12.72	15+1	15	0	0	60	Hull S.	1997
Dobson, Gareth	31.12.78	10+8	1	0	0	4	Castleford T.	1998
Flowers, Stuart	18.4.71	11+1	1	0	0	4	Hunslet H.	1998
Godfrey, Alex	2.12.78	12+7	9	0	0	36	Hull S.	1998
Hanlan, Lee	6.10.71	9	3	0	2	14	Hunslet H.	1998
Hargrave, Spencer	12.7.78	7+4	0	0	0	0	Castleford T.	1998
Hill, Andy	16.12.76	16+6	1	0	0	4	Castleford T.	1998
Hill, Steve	17.11.76	14+5	1	0	0	4	Castleford T.	1998
Hopcutt, Chris	6.12.69	11+2	3	19	0	50	Scarborough P.	1991-92
Lambert, Matthew	6.8.71	8+6	1	0	0	4	Featherstone R.	1998
Limb, Scott	15.6.73	2+2	1	0	0	4	Hunslet H.	1997
Moore, Craig	24.10.74	10+2	5	0	0	20	Dewsbury	1996
Pallister, Alan	4.12.70	14+2	5	0	0	20	York All Blacks	1991-92
Precious, Andrew	10.10.70	5+11	0	16	2	34	Hunslet	1993-94
Preston, Andy	19.5.78	4+3	2	0	0	8	Heworth ARL	1997
Ramsden, Mick	13.11.71	4+5	1	0	0	4	Wakefield T.	1991-92
Sini, Fata	24.12.66	15	5	0	0	20	Salford R.	1998
Strange, John	22.1.75	14+1	7	0	4	32	Featherstone R.	1998
Tichener, Lee	5.8.71	13+3	1	0	0	4	Bramley	1993-94
White, Paul	5.11.64	0+1	1	0	0	4	Hunslet H.	1998
Woodward, Geoff	28.7.71	3	1	0	0	4		1998
TOTALS								
28 players			93	74	14	534		

Stanley Gene of Hull K.R.: Top tryscorer in all matches in 1998 with 34.

RECORDS

LEADING SCORERS 1998

● All club and representative matches

TOP TEN TRIES

1. Stanley Gene (Hull Kingston Rovers).......................34
2. Anthony Sullivan (St. Helens)................................26
3. Karl Pratt (Featherstone Rovers)............................25
4. Matthew Bramald (Dewsbury Rams)......................24
5. Steve Collins (Featherstone Rovers)........................22
6. Francis Cummins (Leeds Rhinos)............................21
7. Adam Hughes (Wakefield Trinity)...........................20
   Jason Robinson (Wigan Warriors)..........................20
   Keith Senior (Sheffield Eagles)...............................20
   Paul Newlove (St. Helens).......................................20

TOP TEN GOALS

● Including drop goals
1. Andrew Farrell (Wigan Warriors)...........................164
2. Barry Eaton (Dewsbury Rams)...............................132
3. Mike Fletcher (Hull Kingston Rovers)....................120
4. Garen Casey (Wakefield Trinity)............................119
   Iestyn Harris (Leeds Rhinos)...................................119
6. Steve Gartland (Swinton Lions).............................116
7. Phil Jones (Lancashire Lynx).................................101
8. Sean Long (St. Helens)...90
9. Tyron Fallins (Featherstone Rovers) ... .88
10. Mark Hewitt (Widnes Vikings)...............................86

TOP TEN POINTS

		T	G	DG	Pts
1.	Andrew Farrell (Wigan W.)	7	163	1	355
2.	Garen Casey (Wakefield T.)	17	115	4	302
3.	Barry Eaton (Dewsbury R.)	7	132	0	292
4.	Iestyn Harris (Leeds R.)	14	116	3	291
5.	Steve Gartland (Swinton L.)	13	110	6	278
6.	Mike Fletcher (Hull K.R.)	4	120	0	256
7.	Phil Jones (Lancashire L.)	13	101	0	254
8.	Richard Chapman (F'stone R.)	18	83	1	239
9.	Sean Long (St. Helens)	14	86	4	232
10.	Richard Price (Batley B.)	9	83	0	202

TOP FIVE DROP GOALS

1. Tyron Fallins (Featherstone Rovers) 12
2. Gary Barnett (Batley Bulldogs)................................. 6
   John Edwards (Doncaster Dragons)......................... 6
   Steve Gartland (Swinton Lions)............................... 6
5. Steve Maguire (Workington Town)......................... 5
   Andy Ruane (Lancashire Lynx).............................. 5
   Ian Watson (Swinton Lions).................................... 5
   Lee Briers (Warrington Wolves).............................. 5

Key:
SL....................	Super League
FD....................	First Division
SD	Second Division
PO	Play-off
TT	Treize Tournoi
CC	Challenge Cup
N	Neutral venue
NA..................	Non-appearance
SF...................	Semi-final
Fr....................	France

*Graeme Hallas of Hull Sharks: Best match tally in 1998
with 30 points.*

140

OUTSTANDING SCORING FEATS 1998

INDIVIDUAL

Most tries in a match:

5   by Alan Hunte (Hull S.) v. Ellenborough R.   CC

    Anthony Sullivan (St. Helens) at London B. ......   SL

Most goals in a match:

12 by Mark Aston (Sheffield E.) v. Egremont R.   CC

11 by Chris Robinson (Keighley C.) v. Saddleworth R.   CC

    Graeme Hallas (Hull S.) v. Ellenborough R.   CC

    Mike Fletcher (Hull K.R.) v. Widnes................   FD

10 by Andrew Farrell (Wigan W.) at Keighley C.   CC

    Andrew Farrell (Wigan W.) at Dewsbury R.   CC

    Andrew Farrell (Wigan W.) v. Warrington W. ...   SL

    Iestyn Harris (Leeds R.) at Huddersfield G........   SL

    Sean Long (St. Helens) v. Huddersfield G. ....   SL

    Mark Aston (Sheffield E.) v. Huddersfield G. ....   SL

    Deryck Fox (Rochdale H.) v. Leigh C. ....   FD

    Garen Casey (Wakefield T.) v. Keighley C. ....   FD

    Phil Jones (Lancashire L.) v. Workington T.......   SD

    Kris Smith (Bramley) v. Doncaster D................   SD

Most points in a match:

30 by Graeme Hallas (Hull S.) v. Ellenborough R.   CC

26 by Richard Chapman (Featherstone R.) v. Leigh C.   FD

Deryck Fox: 10 goals in a match for Rochdale Hornets.

TEAM

Highest scores:

● There was a total of 38 Cup and League matches in which a team scored 50 points or more compared with 64 in 1997.

60-plus scores:

Home:

Sheffield E. 84 v. Egremont R. 6   CC

Hull S. 78 v. Ellenborough R. 0..................................   CC

Swinton L. 74 v. Folly Lane 6   CC

St. Helens 68 v. Huddersfield G.18 ....   SL

Keighley C. 66 v. Saddleworth R. 16   CC

Lancashire L. 64 v. Workington T. 25 ....   SD

Wakefield T. 64 v. Widnes V. 8 ....   FD

Rochdale H. 64 v. Leigh C. 20 ....   FD

Wakefield T. 60 v. Leigh C. 14 ....   FD

Away:

Keighley C. 0 v. Wigan W. 76   CC

Ovenden 0 v. Salford R. 74   CC

Huddersfield G. 16 v. Leeds R. 72 ....   SL

Leigh C. 11 v. Sheffield E. 66...................................   CC

Widnes V. 4 v. Hull K.R. 63 ....   FD

Highest score by a losing team:

Wakefield T. 38 v. Limoux (Fr.) 36...........................   TT

Oldham 32 v. Bramley 50 ....   SD

● There was a total of 90 Cup and League matches in which a team scored 20 points or more and lost.

High-scoring draws:

St. Helens 32 v. Castleford T. 32 ....   SL

Widnes V. 32 v. Featherstone R. 32...........................   FD

Wakefield T. 26 v. Dewsbury R. 26 ....   FD

Rochdale H. 26 v. Hull K.R. 26 ....   FD

Doncaster D. 24 v. Bramley 24 ....   SD

Lancashire L. 20 v. Barrow B.R. 20...........................   SD

● **Substitute appearances do not count towards players' full appearance records.**

● **Although abandoned League match points and appearances are included in players' overall totals, they do not count towards League records.**

● **The 1998 season ended with the completion of the international series involving Ireland, Scotland and France.**

RECORD-BREAKING FEATS IN 1998

AT A GLANCE

PHIL JONES of Lancashire Lynx set club records of 101 goals and 254 points in a season and equalled the match records of 10 goals and 24 points.

ANDREW FARRELL of Wigan Warriors scored in every one of his club's matches throughout the season. He is also the only player to have appeared in all 67 rounds of Super League since its launch in 1996, including a record scoring run of 37 matches.

RICHARD PRICE of Batley Bulldogs scored in every one of his club's matches throughout the season.

MIKE FLETCHER of Hull Kingston Rovers finished the season with a club record career total of 1,268 goals.

ANTHONY SULLIVAN of St. Helens equalled the Super League match record of five tries.

DAVID "DOC" MURRAY of Lancashire Lynx equalled the club record of four tries in a match.

MARK ASTON of Sheffield Eagles kicked a club record-equalling 12 goals in a match.

PAUL NEWLOVE of St. Helens took over as the scorer of most Super League career tries with 52.

SHEFFIELD EAGLES ran up their highest score with an 84-6 Silk Cut Challenge Cup home defeat of Egremont Rangers.

WIDNES VIKINGS conceded a club record-equalling points total with a 64-8 defeat at Wakefield Trinity.

LEEDS RHINOS scored a club and Super League record away victory with a 72-16 win at Huddersfield Giants.

ST. HELENS and CASTLEFORD TIGERS clashed in a Super League record high-scoring draw of 32-32.

WIGAN WARRIORS equalled the top division record of dropping only four points in a season.

HUDDERSFIELD GIANTS suffered a Super League record run of 13 successive defeats and the lowest points haul of four points from only two wins.

EGREMONT RANGERS beat Workington Town 18-0 to become first amateur club for over 90 years to nil professional opponents in the RL Challenge Cup.

NEW ZEALAND scored a record 36-16 win over Great Britain.

NEW RECORDS IN DETAIL

PHIL JONES of Lancashire Lynx broke or equalled four club records: 101 goals and 254 points in a season plus 10 goals and 24 points in a match. All four records had been held by full back Mike Smith.

Smith had set the two season records with 142 points from 73 goals, including four drop goals, in 30 matches during the club's inaugural 1989-90 campaign when they began as Chorley. Jones passed the points record with 16 in the 21-12 Second Division victory at Barrow Border Raiders on 2 August.

The 20-year-old stand off broke Smith's 73 goals record with three in Lancashire's 18-16 League win at Oldham on 26 August.

Four days later Jones equalled the match records with 10 goals and 24 points, including a try, in the 64-25 home League defeat of Workington Town. Smith had also scored 10 goals and 24 points in the 92-0 home Regal Trophy defeat of Nottingham City on 1 October 1995 when the club was Chorley Chieftains.

Jones played in all 28 of Lancashire's matches in 1998 as follows:

		T	G	Pts
West Hull	(H)	2	0	8
Dewsbury R. (CC)	(H)	0	0	0
Dewsbury R. (CC replay)	(A)	0	0	0
Barrow B.R.	(H)	0	4	8
Doncaster D.	(H)	0	4	8
Bramley	(A)	1	3	10
York	(H)	1	2	8
Workington T.	(A)	0	6	12
Batley B.	(A)	1	3	10
Oldham	(H)	1	3	10
Barrow B.R.	(A)	0	4	8
Workington T.	(A)	0	3	6
Oldham	(A)	0	4	8
Workington T.	(H)	0	6	16
Barrow B.R.	(H)	0	6	12
Oldham	(H)	1	4	12
Barrow B.R.	(A)	2	4	16
Doncaster D.	(A)	2	6	20
Bramley	(H)	0	5	10
York	(A)	0	4	8
Oldham	(A)	0	3	6
Workington T.	(H)	1	10	24
Batley B.	(H)	0	3	6
St. Esteve (TT)	(A)	0	6	12
Villeneuve (TT)	(H)	0	4	8
Villeneuve (TT)	(A)	0	0	0
St. Esteve (TT)	(H)	0	3	6
Villeneuve (TT)	(N)	0	1	2
Totals				
30 appearances		13	101	254

ANDREW FARRELL of Wigan Warriors joined the increasing number of players who have scored in every one of their club's matches throughout a season. The loose forward totalled 333 points for Wigan from seven tries and 153 goals, including a drop goal. In doing so, he became the first player to score in every Super League round during a season. He is also the only player to have appeared in all 67 Super League rounds since it was launched in 1996 and has the longest overall pointscoring run covering 37 matches.

Farrell's match-by-match record for Wigan in 1998:

	T	G	Pts
Keighley C. (CC) ....(A)	0	10	20
Dewsbury R. (CC) ....(A)	1	10	24
St. Helens (CC) ....(H)	0	3	6
London B. (CC) ....(N)	0	7	14
Castleford T. ....(H)	0	3	6
St. Helens ....(A)	0	7	14
Halifax B.S. ....(H)	0	6	12
London B. ....(H)	0	4	8
Sheffield E. (CC) ....(N)	0	2	4
Sheffield E............................(A)	0	6	12
Leeds R...............................(A)	0	2	4
Huddersfield G. ....(H)	1	4	12
Hull S. ....(A)	0	7	14
Salford R. ....(H)	0	5	10
Bradford B. ....(A)	0	4	8
Warrington W. ....(H)	0	10	20
Castleford T. ....(A)	1	5	14
St. Helens ....(H)	1	7	18
St. Helens ....(N)	1	6	16
Halifax B.S. ....(A)	0	4	8
London B..............................(A)	0	3	6
Sheffield E. ....(H)	1	8	20
Leeds R. ....(H)	0	2	4
Huddersfield G.....................(A)	0	5	10
Hull S..................................(H)	1	5	14
Salford R..............................(A)	0	2	4
Bradford B. ....(H)	0	7	14
Warrington W. ....(A)	0	3	6
Leeds R. (PO).......................(H)	0	3(1)	5
Leeds R. (POF) ....(N)	0	3	6
Totals			
30 appearances	**7**	**153(1)**	**333**

( ) Denotes drop goals included in total

Farrell also totalled 11 goals scoring in all three Test matches for Great Britain against New Zealand.

Richard Price: Scored in every match for Batley Bulldogs.

RICHARD PRICE of Batley Bulldogs scored in every one of his club's 23 matches. The stand off totalled 202 points from nine tries and 83 goals.

Price's match-by-match record for Batley in 1998:

	T	G	Pts
Oulton R. (CC)....................(H)	0	6	12
London B. (CC) ....(H)	1	4	12
York...................................(H)	0	4	8
Barrow B.R. ....(A)	0	2	4
Workington T. ....(H)	0	6	12
Doncaster D..........................(A)	1	2	8
Oldham ....(A)	1	4	12
Bramley................................(A)	1	1	6
Lancashire L. ....(H)	1	2	8
Doncaster D. ....(H)	0	4	8
York...................................(A)	0	1	2
Bramley ....(H)	0	5	10
Doncaster D..........................(A)	1	4	12
Bramley................................(A)	0	2	4
York ....(H)	0	2	4
Oldham (TPF)......................(H)	1	6	16
Doncaster D. ....(H)	1	1	6
York....................................(A)	0	3	6
Barrow B.R. ....(H)	0	4	8
Workington T........................(A)	1	6	16
Oldham ....(H)	0	4	8
Bramley ....(H)	0	5	10
Lancashire L. ....(A)	0	5	10
Totals			
23 appearances	**9**	**83**	**202**

MIKE FLETCHER of Hull Kingston Rovers finished the season with a club career record of 1,268 goals, including one one-point drop goal, in 360 appearances. The old record of 1,192 goals was set by Cyril Kellett in 382 matches from 1956 to 1967.

Fletcher equalled the record in his 333rd match with six goals in the 28-15 home League defeat of Rochdale Hornets on 22 March and beat it with another six at home to Wakefield Trinity a week later.

Fletcher passed Kellett's club career points record in 1997 and his total now stands at 2,759 points, including 56 tries.

The centre or full back also holds two club records for a season with 199 goals and 450 points, including 13 tries, in 1989-90. During that season he equalled a club match record with 14 goals against Whitehaven. He has twice kicked 12 goals in a match, 11 twice and 10 five times.

In 1989-90 he headed the goals charts with 199 and has finished in the top ten on four other occasions.

The former Rovers Colt made his first team debut at full back on 23 April 1985 when they lost 32-10 at home to Widnes in the old Division One. He has not played for any other senior club, but also kicked a goal for a Humberside XIII against Papua New Guinea, and four goals in two appearances for Great Britain Under-21s.

Goalscoring record for Hull K.R.:

	App.	Goals
1984-85	1	0
1985-86	3+7	4
1986-87	5+5	2
1987-88	28	90
1988-89	20+1	63
1989-90	35	199
1990-91	23+5	59
1991-92	30	71
1992-93	29	71
1993-94	32	90
1994-95	31+1	142
1995-96	22	117 (1)
1996	24	151
1997	18 +4	89
1998	31+5	120
Totals...............**332+28**		**1,268 (1)**

(1) Drop goal included in total

ANTHONY SULLIVAN of St. Helens scored a Super League record-equalling five tries in the 37-22 win at London Broncos on 18 September. The winger is the only player to achieve the feat away from home.

Others to score five tries in a Super League match are: Mike Umaga (Halifax Blue Sox stand off) v. Workington Town on 21 July 1996; Jason Robinson (Wigan winger) v. Leeds on 9 August 1996; Tony Smith (Wigan Warriors scrum half) v. Sheffield Eagles on 29 June 1997.

DAVID "DOC" MURRAY of Lancashire Lynx equalled a club match record with four tries from full back in the 40-26 win at St. Esteve in the Treize Tournoi on 3 October.

Others to score four tries for the club are: Martin Holden (winger) v. Nottingham City in a Regal Trophy first round tie on 1 October 1995 and Neil Parsley (centre) v. Bramley in a League match on 9 March 1997.

MARK ASTON of Sheffield Eagles kicked a club record-equalling 12 goals for a second time in the 84-6 Silk Cut Challenge Cup fifth round home defeat of Egremont Rangers amateur club on 1 March. The scrum half also kicked 12 goals in a 72-14 Divisional Premiership home defeat of Keighley Cougars on 25 April 1992.

The record was set by Roy Rafferty with 12 in a 68-14 League win at Fulham on 21 September 1986.

PAUL NEWLOVE of St. Helens took over as the top scorer of Super League tries with a total of 52 in 59 matches over the three seasons since it was launched. The centre scored a season's record 28 in 1996; 10 in 1997 and 14 in 1998.

Wigan Warriors winger Jason Robinson had led the way after two seasons with 39 and is now in second place with 47.

SHEFFIELD EAGLES ran up their highest score with an 84-6 Silk Cut Challenge Cup fifth round home defeat of amateur club Egremont Rangers on 1 March. The Eagles' 15 tries equalled the touchdown tally when they ran up their previous highest score with an 80-8 home defeat of Wigan St. Patricks amateurs in a John Player Special Trophy first round home tie on 13 November 1988.

WIDNES VIKINGS conceded a club record-equalling points total with a 64-8 First Division defeat at Wakefield Trinity on 12 July. They conceded the same points total when losing 64-12 at Keighley Cougars in a League match on 18 August 1996, the opposition scoring 12 tries on each occasion.

LEEDS RHINOS scored a club and Super League record away victory with a 13-try 72-16 win at Huddersfield Giants on 13 September. The previous Super League record away score was Wigan Warriors' 65-12 win at St. Helens on 26 May 1997 when they scored 11 tries.

Leeds' victory produced a club record away score and winning margin, beating the 54-5 League win at Acton and Willesden on 20 April 1936 when they scored 12 tries and the 13-try 51-0 League win at Doncaster on 25 February 1973.

ST. HELENS and CASTLEFORD TIGERS clashed in a Super League record high-scoring draw of 32-32 on 13 September with the latter scoring six tries to five. Castleford were also involved in the previous record, a 30-30 home draw against Leeds Rhinos on 26 May 1997 when both teams scored four tries.

WIGAN WARRIORS finished at the head of Super League with only two defeats, to equal the record of dropping only four points in a top division season. Their two defeats (both against Leeds Rhinos) matched the Super League records of St. Helens (1996) and Bradford Bulls (1997), while Wigan lost two matches in the old Division One seasons of 1986-87, 1994-95 and 1995-96.

HUDDERSFIELD GIANTS suffered a Super League record run of 13 successive defeats and the lowest points haul of four from only two wins. The previous lowest total of points gained in a Super League season was five by Workington Town from two wins and a draw in 1996. The old record of 11 successive defeats had been held by Castleford Tigers, who lost their last match of 1996 and the first 10 of 1997.

EGREMONT RANGERS became the first amateur club for over 90 years to nil professional opponents in the RL Challenge Cup when they beat Workington Town 18-0 in their fourth round home tie at Whitehaven. The previous time a non-League club nilled senior opponents at a main stage of the Challenge Cup was in 1906 when Victoria Rangers (Bradford) held Widnes to a scoreless first round draw before losing the replay 8-3. The following year Savile Green beat Bramley 10-0 in a preliminary round.

NEW ZEALAND ran up their highest ever score against Great Britain and equalled their widest winning margin with a 36-16 second Test win at Bolton. It beat the 32-16 win in the third Test at Auckland in 1984 and the 32-12 third Test win at Christchurch in 1996, while equalling the widest margin in the latter match. For other records in the 1998 Test series see GREAT BRITAIN chapter.

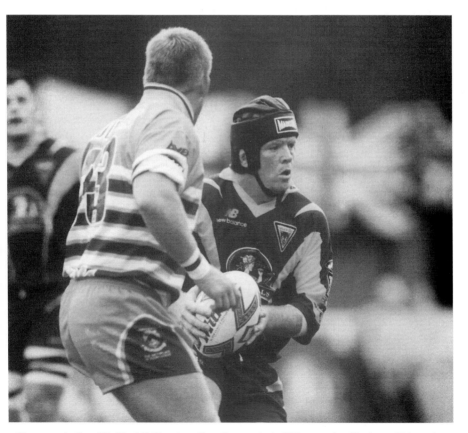

Giants struggle: One of Huddersfield Giants' two Super League wins in 1998 was against Warrington Wolves, whose captain Danny Farrar finds his way blocked by Bobbie Goulding in the return match.

MILESTONES ...

GARY CONNOLLY of Wigan Warriors passed two century milestones during the season. The centre scored his 100th try for Wigan in the 58-6 JJB Super League home defeat of Hull Sharks on 6 September and his 100th League touchdown with the second of two in the 38-4 home defeat of Bradford Bulls on 20 September.

His overall try total for Wigan at the end of the season was 102 in 191 matches. His total of 100 Super League and old Division One tries consisted of 77 for Wigan and 23 for St. Helens in 212 matches.

Connolly has totalled five hat-tricks for Wigan, including a Premiership final record-equalling three tries against Leeds in 1995. His three League hat-tricks were all for Wigan.

A former Blackbrook amateur, Connolly made his debut with St. Helens as a 17-year-old full back on 22 January 1989 in a 29-0 home League defeat of Hull Kingston Rovers. Connolly totalled 46 Cup and League tries for Saints before moving to Wigan in 1993 for £250,000 - still a joint record cash fee for a centre. He made his debut for Wigan with a try in a 32-2 home League defeat of Widnes on 24 September 1993.

Tryscoring record in League matches:

	App	Tries
St. Helens		
1988-89	6	1
1989-90	13+1	1
1990-91	15	2
1991-92	20	10
1992-93	23	9
Wigan		
1993-94	24	7
1994-95	28+2	19
1995-96	17	10
1996	21	13
1997	19	13
1998	23	15
Totals		
St. Helens	77+1	23
Wigan	132+2	77
GRAND TOTALS	**209+3**	**100**

Cup and League totals for Wigan

1993-94	41	10
1994-95	43+2	30
1995-96	22	16
1996	25	15
1997	28	15
1998	30	16
Totals	**189+2**	**102**

Gary Connolly: Two century milestones.

DENNIS BAILEY of Dewsbury Rams scored the 100th try of his career with one in the 50-0 First Division home defeat of Leigh Centurions on 22 March. The winger's total of 104 at then end of the season included his 100th try for Dewsbury in the 40-2 home League win at Rochdale Hornets on 9 August. He also scored four tries during a four-match loan spell with Bramley, giving him a total of 202 appearances.

Bailey returned to Dewsbury in 1998 after four seasons playing amateur rugby, apart from his brief period with Bramley in 1997. He played for Leeds amateur club Queens in the 1998 Silk Cut Challenge Cup before making a tryscoring return for Dewsbury in the 34-24 First Division home defeat of Swinton Lions on 22 February.

Bailey has scored four hat-tricks for Dewsbury, including two four-try feats. He also scored a hat-trick on his debut for Bramley. His most prolific season was 1991-92 when he scored 22 tries for Dewsbury.

Bailey signed for Dewsbury in December 1985 and made his debut in a 52-0 First Division home defeat against Warrington on 6 April 1986.

Tryscoring record:

	App	Tries
Dewsbury		
1985-86	5	0
1986-87	12+4	3
1987-88	6	1
1988-89	10	5
1989-90	33	19
1990-91	33	14
1991-92	30	22
1992-93	30	18
1993-94	14	10
1998	21+1	8
Bramley		
1994-95	4	4
Totals		
Dewsbury	194+4	100
Bramley	4	4
GRAND TOTALS	**198+4**	**104**

ROGER SIMPSON of Batley Bulldogs scored the 100th try of his career with one in the 28-12 Trans-Pennine Cup final home defeat of Oldham on 19 July. At the end of the season had totalled 27 tries for Batley, 72 Bradford Northern and three for Great Britain on the 1990 tour to New Zealand and Papua New Guinea. He has played in 340 matches. The utility back has scored one hat-trick each for Bradford and Batley.

A former Moldgreen (Huddersfield) amateur, Simpson signed for Bradford on his 17th birthday in August 1984 and gained Great Britain Colts honours. He made his debut on the wing in a 15-8 League defeat at Featherstone Rovers on 4 September 1985.

After 11 seasons he moved to Batley and made his debut at full back in a 20-13 home League defeat of Whitehaven on 31 March 1996.

Tryscoring record:

	App	Tries
Bradford N.		
1985-86......................	22	6
1986-87......................	19+4	8
1987-88......................	25+3	5
1988-89......................	29+1	9
1989-90......................	32+1	8
1990-91......................	34+2	9
1991-92......................	29+1	5
1992-93......................	34+3	6
1993-94......................	4+4	0
1994-95......................	21+1	11
1995-96......................	9+1	5
Batley B.		
1996...........................	10	3
1997...........................	26+1	16
1998...........................	18	8
Totals		
Bradford N.	258+21	72
Batley B........................	54+1	27
England......................	0+1	0
Tour 1990	5	3
GRAND TOTALS	**317+23**	**102**

MARK ASTON of Sheffield Eagles passed the 1,000 career goals mark with 10 in the 56-10 JJB Super League home defeat of Huddersfield Giants on 7 August and scored his 2,000th point for Sheffield in the 18-18 home League draw against Salford Reds 14 days later.

The scrum-half's goals total at the end of the season was 1,014, including 43 drop goals. He has kicked 927 for Sheffield and 87 for Featherstone Rovers in a total of 355 matches, including representative games and a loan spell with Bramley.

His total of 2,013 points for Sheffield comes from 50 tries and 927 goals, including 41 drop goals, in 313 matches. Aston's holds the following Sheffield records:

Most goals in a match: 12 v. Keighley C., 25 April 1992; v. Egremont R.,1 March 1998

Most goals in a season: 148 in 1988-89

Most goals in a career: 927
Most points in a season: 307 1988-89
Most points in a career: 2,013
In 1988-89 he scored in every match for Sheffield.
He also holds the following records:
Most goals in a Premiership match: 11 at London B., 14 September 1997
Most goals in a Divisional Premiership match: 12 v. Keighley C., 25 April 1992

A former amateur with Selby club Gaffers, he made his senior debut for Sheffield at scrum half in a 36-6 home League defeat of Huddersfield on 30 March 1986. He had a two-match loan spell with Bramley in 1987-88 before settling at Sheffield.

After nine seasons he joined Featherstone for a Tribunal-fixed fee of £100,000 in July 1994 and made his debut for Rovers in a 24-36 home League defeat against Wigan on 21 August 1994.

Aston went back to Sheffield in a £70,000 deal and made his return debut with three goals in a 10-42 home League defeat against London Broncos on 24 September 1995.

Scoring record:

	App	T	G	Pts
Sheffield E.				
1985-86......................	7	0	0	0
1986-87......................	22	7	26	80
Bramley				
1987-88......................	2	0	0	0
Sheffield E.				
1987-88......................	16+2	0	0	0
1988-89......................	36	6	148(13)	307
1989-90......................	29	1	99(5)	197
1990-91......................	22	6	60(2)	142
1991-92......................	31+1	2	104(6)	210
1992-93......................	30+1	4	62(3)	137
1993-94......................	35	14	123(5)	297
Featherstone R.				
1994-95......................	28+1	5	87(2)	192
1995-96......................	6	1	0	4
Sheffield E.				
1995-96......................	8	1	27(2)	56
1996...........................	21+1	2	88(1)	183
1997...........................	31	5	115(1)	249
1998...........................	17+3	2	75(3)	155
Totals				
Sheffield E.	305+8	50	927(41)	2013
Featherstone R.............	34+1	6	87(2)	196
Bramley......................	2	0	0	0
Great Britain..............	0+1	0	0	0
1992 Tour	1+3	0	0	0
GRAND TOTALS	**342+13**	**56**	**1014(43)**	**2,209**

ANDREW FARRELL of Wigan Warriors passed milestones for 500 goals and 1,000 points during the season.

The loose forward passed the 1,000 career points mark for the club with 10 goals in the 76-0 Silk Cut Challenge Cup fourth round win at Keighley Cougars on 15 February.

He reached 500 club and representative goals with six in the 36-6 JJB Super League win at Sheffield Eagles on 9 May and 500 for Wigan alone with the first of 10 in a 56-8 home League defeat of Warrington Wolves on 21 June.

Farrell also became the first player to total 500 Super League points.

At the end of the season his club and representative totals were 51 tries and 606 goals, including seven drop goals, for 1,409 points in 218 matches.

He has finished at the top of the overall goals and pointscoring charts for the last two seasons and in 1998 scored in all 30 of Wigan's matches. He also holds the record for most Super League career goals (327) and points (723).

He is a joint holder of most Super League goals in a match with 11 against St. Helens, including a drop goal, and Paris St. Germain in May 1997. Farrell also scored a try against Paris for a personal best match tally of 26 points. He has kicked 10 goals in a match on three other occasions but has yet to score a try hat-trick.

A former Orrell St. James amateur, Farrell made his senior debut for Wigan as a substitute in a 32-8 Regal Trophy second round home tie against Keighley Cougars on 24 November 1991. He made seven more substitute appearances before starting in the second row in a 27-14 League win at Warrington on 12 April 1993, scoring one try.

Scoring record:

	App.	T	G	Pts
Wigan W.				
1991-92	0+2	0	0	0
1992-93	5+7	2	6	20
1993-94	34+7	9	5(1)	45
	+1t,1g GB; 2t GB U-21			
1994-95	32+4	5	60(1)	139
				+2g GB
1995-96	14	6	85	194
				+1t,7g England
1996	25+1	7	113	254
1997	33	9	150(4)	332
				+1t,13g GB
1998	30	7	153(1)	333
				+11g GB
Totals				
Wigan W.	173+21	45	572(7)	1317
Great Britain	16	3	27	66
England	5	1	7	18
Great Britain U-21	1	2	0	8
Tour 1996	1	0	0	0
(Not inc. 1t in 5 Tests)				
GRAND TOTALS	196+21	51	606(7)	1,409

( ) Drop goals included in total

STEVE BLAKELEY of Salford Reds took his club and total career number of goals past the 500 mark with six in the 48-6 Silk Cut Challenge Cup fifth round win at Widnes Vikings on 1 March. The stand-off's tally at the end of the season was 530 with 527 for Salford, including seven drop goals, and three for Wigan in a total of 163 matches.

A former Leigh Rangers amateur, Blakeley made his senior professional debut for Wigan as a substitute in a 26-31 Premiership first round home defeat by Featherstone Rovers on 21 April 1991.

He made seven more substitute appearances before being transferred to Salford for £28,000 and making his debut against Wigan when he kicked three goals in an 18-26 home League defeat on 29 November 1992.

Blakeley was the First Division's top goal scorer in 1996 with 82 League goals, including a personal match best of 10 against Batley Bulldogs.

Goalscoring record:

	App.	Goals
Wigan		
1990-91	0+1	0
1991-92	0+6	3
1992-93	0+1	0
Salford		
1992-93	14	34
1993-94	27+5	71(1)
1994-95	24	81(2)
1995-96	17	93
1996	22+1	106(1)
1997	29	101(1)
1998	13+1	41(2)
Totals		
Wigan	0+8	3
Salford	146+7	527(7)
England	1+1	0
GRAND TOTALS	147+16	530(7)

( ) Drop goals included in total

DERYCK FOX of Rochdale Hornets scored the 2,000th point of his career with the second of three goals in the 26-26 First Division home draw against Hull Kingston Rovers on 31 May. It was only his third match after taking over as Rochdale's player-coach.

Fox's career total at the end of the season was 2,064 points with 82 for Rochdale, 1,145 Featherstone Rovers, 744 Bradford Northern, two for Batley Bulldogs and 91 in representative matches, including 20 for Britain. The scrum half has scored 109 tries and 854 goals, including 80 drop goals, in 517 matches.

A former St. John Fisher (Dewsbury) amateur, Fox turned professional with Featherstone after his return from BARLA's 1983 Great Britain youth tour of New Zealand. He made his debut as a substitute in Featherstone's 24-8 Yorkshire Cup first round defeat at Hull on 4 September 1983. His full debut came 14 days later in an 18-14 League win at Whitehaven.

Fox was transferred to Bradford ten years later for £140,000, then a record for Northern and the most paid by any club for a scrum half. He made a substitute debut for Bradford in a 34-22 Yorkshire Cup first round win at Bramley on 13 September 1993. His full debut was a week later when he kicked three goals in a 24-12 League win at Widnes.

He returned to Featherstone after two years and made his second debut in a 34-18 home League defeat of Hull on 19 November 1995. He moved to Batley two years later and made his debut in a 42-18 home League defeat of Workington Town on 25 April 1998.

Scoring record:

Featherstone R.

	App.	T	G	Pts
1983-84	30+2	6	26(7)	69
1984-85	34	6	6(4)	32 + GB 2t, 1g
1985-86	31	11	16(3)	73 + Yorks. 5g
1986-87	36	14	38(5)	127
1987-88	38	16	16(9)	87 + Yorks. 1g
1988-89	35	9	28(9)	83
1989-90	34	3	78(8)	160 + Yorks. 1t
1990-91	33	12	58(2)	162
1991-92	36	1	114(5)	227 + GB 1t, Yorks. 1t, 1dg

Bradford N.

	App.	T	G	Pts
1992-93	23+1	5	40(2)	98 + GB 3g
1993-94	39	8	148(11)	317
1994-95	34	3	126(3)	261 + England 1t, 5g
1995-96	10	1	32	68

Featherstone R.

	App.	T	G	Pts
1995-96	9	1	0	4
1996	21	3	10(6)	26
1997	13+1	2	46(5)	95

Batley B.

	App.	T	G	Pts
1998	3	0	1	2

Rochdale H.

	App.	T	G	Pts
1998	11	0	41	82

Totals

	App.	T	G	Pts
Featherstone R.	350+3	84	436(63)	1145
Bradford N.	106+1	17	346(16)	744
Batley B.	3	0	1	2
Rochdale H.	11	0	41	82
Great Britain	10+4	3	4	20
Tour 1990	7+1	2	0	8 Not inc. Tests
Tour 1992	5+4	0	14	28 Not inc. Tests
England	2	1	5	14
Great Britain U-21	1	0	0	0
Chairman's XIII	1	0	0	0
Yorkshire	8	2	7(1)	21
GRAND TOTALS	**504+13**	**109**	**854(80)**	**2,064**

( ) denotes drop goals included in total

IESTYN HARRIS of Leeds Rhinos passed the 1,000 points career milestone with a try and 10 goals in the 72-16 JJB Super League win at Huddersfield Giants on 13 September. His end of season total stood at 1,057 with 466 for Leeds, 516 for Warrington and 75 in representative matches. He has scored 65 tries and 403 goals, including nine drop goals in 164 matches.

Harris's best match tally is 24 points twice, once each for Warrington and Leeds. He has scored 20 or more on five other occasions. His three try hat-tricks include one for Wales against France in 1996 when he also kicked five goals. A former Oldham St. Annes amateur, Harris signed for Warrington in August 1993 and played for Great Britain Under-21s before he made his first team debut. He kicked four goals playing on the wing for the Under-21s in a 37-24 defeat against New Zealand at Workington on 26 October 1993.

His Warrington debut came three days later when he again played on the wing and kicked four goals in a 24-6 home League defeat of Leigh.

After four seasons at Warrington, Harris asked for a move and was listed at a world record £1,350,000 in July 1996. Leeds signed him in April 1997 for a reported £325,000 plus teenage reserve prop Danny Sculthorpe in part exchange. The deal was rated at £350,000, a record for both clubs and for the transfer of a stand off.

Harris made his debut for Leeds as a substitute on 4 April 1997, scoring a goal in a 16-17 Super League home defeat by Wigan Warriors. He was stand off in Leeds' next match seven days later when he kicked five goals, including a drop goal, in a 13-12 Super League home defeat of St. Helens.

Scoring record:

Warrington

	App.	T	G	Pts
1993-94	10	4	19	54 + 1t, 8g GB Under-21s
1994-95	39	18	38	148 + 1t Wales
1995-96	22+1	11	57(2)	156 + 2t, 1g, 1dg Wales
1996	18	4	69(2)	152 + 3t, 7g Wales
1997	1+1	0	3	6

Leeds R.

	App.	T	G	Pts
1997	23+2	7	78(1)	183
1998	27	13	117(3)	283 + 1t GB, 2g Wales

Totals

	App.	T	G	Pts
Warrington	90+2	37	186(4)	516
Leeds R.	50+2	20	195(4)	466
Britain	6+2	1	0	4
Tour 1996	1	0	3	6 Not inc. 4+1 Test app.
Wales	9*	6	11(1)*	45*
GB Under-21s	2	1	8	20
GRAND TOTALS	**158+6**	**65**	**403(9)**	**1,057**

( ) Drop goals included in total

* Including 2 goals in non-full international against Emerging England

STEVE McNAMARA of Bradford Bulls passed the 1,000 points career milestone with five goals and a try in the JJB Super League 40-18 home defeat of Salford Reds on 27 September. The loose forward's total of 1,014 at the end of the season consisted of 639 for Bradford, 369 for Hull and six in representative matches. He has totalled 37 tries and 439 goals, including 12 drop goals, in 258 matches.

His best match tally is 24 points for Hull, while he has twice scored 22 points for Bradford.

A former Skirlaugh (Hull) amateur, McNamara made his senior professional debut with Hull as a substitute when he scored their only try in a 30-12 League defeat at Bradford on 3 September 1989. McNamara made his full debut at loose forward in his next senior match, a 44-8 defeat against the New Zealand tourists on 1 November 1989.

Bradford signed McNamara for £100,000 seven years later and he made his debut for the Bulls in a 31-24 Super League home defeat of London Broncos on 8 April 1996.

Scoring record:

Hull

	App.	T	G	Pts
1989-90	6+1	2	0	8
1990-91	11+8	4	0	16
1991-92	29	0	2	4
1992-93	25	5	0	20
1993-94	21+4	2	6(4)	16
1994-95	32	2	12	32
1995-96	22	10	101(1)	241
1996	3	1	14	32
Bradford B				
1996	21	1	84(2)	170 + 1g England
1997	33	8	134(1)	299
1998	26	1	85(4)	170
Totals				
Hull	149+13	26	135(5)	369
Bradford B.	80	10	303(7)	639
Britain	0+4	0	0	0
Tour 1992	4	1	0	4
England	2+1	0	1	2
GB U-21s	5	0	0	0
GRAND TOTALS	**240+18**	**37**	**439(12)**	**1,014**

( ) Drop goals included in total

ST. JOHN ELLIS of Hunslet Hawks passed the 1,000 career points mark with a try and four goals in the 36-25 First Division victory at Rochdale Hornets on 8 February. The utility back's total at the end of the season was 1,172 points from 155 tries and 279 goals, including six drop goals, in 325 matches with six clubs and Great Britain.

Ellis scored a club record 40 tries for Castleford in 1993-94. He is also a joint holder of Castleford's match record of five tries, at Whitehaven on 10 December 1989, and has scored seven other hat-tricks for various clubs. His best match points tally is 26 from nine goals and two tries for Hunslet against York on 20 July 1997.

Ellis made his senior debut as a winger with York on 21 December 1986, scoring two goals in an 18-16 defeat at

Fulham. His debuts for other clubs are as follows:

Castleford v. New Zealand (H), 3 October 1989, wing, 4 goals, lost 20-22

Bradford Bulls v. London B. (H), 3 September 1995, full back, 1 try, won 26-16

Halifax v. Bradford B. (A), 1 January 1996, centre, won 22-18

Keighley C. v. Workington T. (A), 9 February 1997, full back, won 24-14, Cup-tie

Hunslet H. v. Barrow B.R. (H), 23 May 1997, full back, won 72-10, 1 goal

Season-by-season record:

	App.	T	G	Pts
York				
1986-87	14	9	15	66
1987-88	29	12	63	174
1988-89	29	10	38	116
1989-90	3	1	9	22
Castleford				
1989-90	26	23	9	110
1990-91	31+1	8	0	32
1991-92	39+1	15	4	68
1992-93	36	11	0	44
1993-94	41	40	4	168
Bradford B.				
1995-96	11+1	5	14	48
Halifax				
1995-96	5	0	0	0
1996	2	1	0	4
Keighley C.				
1997	11	3	0	12
Hunslet H.				
1997	18	6	48(4)	116
1998	24+1	11	75(2)	192
Totals				
York	75	32	125	378
Castleford	173+2	97	17	422
Bradford B.	11+1	5	14	48
Halifax	7	1	0	4
Keighley C.	11	3	0	12
Hunslet H.	42	17	123(6)	308
Great Britain	0+3	0	0	0
GRAND TOTALS	**319+6**	**155**	**279(6)**	**1,172**

( ) Drop goals included in total
Ellis missed the 1994-95 season while playing in Australia

LEADING SCORERS

	TRIES	GOALS	POINTS
1895-96	Hurst (Oldham) 28	Lorimer (Manningham).........35	Cooper (Bradford) 106
			Lorimer (Manningham).......106
1896-97	Hannah (Hunslet) 19	Goldthorpe (Hunslet)............26	Rigg (Halifax) 112
		Sharpe (Liversedge)...............26	
1897-98	Hoskins (Salford) 30	Goldthorpe (Hunslet)............66	Goldthorpe (Hunslet)..........135
1898-99	Williams (Oldham)................39	Goldthorpe (Hunslet)............67	Jacques (Hull) 169
1899-00	Williams (Oldham)................36	Cooper (Bradford) 39	Williams (Oldham)..............108
1900-01	Williams (Oldham)................47	Goldthorpe (Hunslet)............44	Williams (Oldham)..............141
1901-02	Wilson (Broughton R.) 38	James,W. (Broughton R.) 75	Lomas (Salford) 172
1902-03	Evans (Leeds) 27	Goldthorpe (Hunslet)............48	Davies (Batley)....................136
1903-04	Hogg (Broughton R.) 34	Lomas (Salford) 66	Lomas (Salford) 222
1904-05	Dechan (Bradford) 31	Ferguson (Oldham)...............50	Lomas (Salford) 146
1905-06	Leytham (Wigan) 40	Ferguson (Oldham) 49	Leytham (Wigan) 160
1906-07	Eccles (Halifax)....................41	Lomas (Salford) 86	Lomas (Salford) 280
1907-08	Leytham (Wigan) 44	Goldthorpe (Hunslet)..........101	Goldthorpe (Hunslet)..........217
1908-09	Miller (Wigan) 49	Lomas (Salford) 88	Lomas (Salford) 272
	Williams (Halifax) 49		
1909-10	Leytham (Wigan) 48	Carmichael (Hull K.R.) 78	Leytham (Wigan) 232
1910-11	Kitchen (Huddersfield)..........41	Carmichael (Hull K.R.) 129	Carmichael (Hull K.R.).......261
1911-12	Rosenfeld (Huddersfield).......78	Carmichael (Hull K.R.) 127	Carmichael (Hull K.R.).......254
1912-13	Rosenfeld (Huddersfield).......56	Carmichael (Hull K.R.) 93	Thomas (Wigan) 198
1913-14	Rosenfeld (Huddersfield).......80	Holland (Huddersfield) 131	Holland (Huddersfield) 268
1914-15	Rosenfeld (Huddersfield).......56	Gronow (Huddersfield) 136	Gronow (Huddersfield) 284

● Competitive matches suspended during war years

	TRIES	GOALS	POINTS
1918-19	Francis (Hull) 25	Kennedy (Hull).....................54	Kennedy (Hull)....................135
1919-20	Moorhouse (Huddersfield) 39	Gronow (Huddersfield) 148	Gronow (Huddersfield) 332
1920-21	Stone (Hull).........................41	Kennedy (Hull) 108	Kennedy (Hull)....................264
1921-22	Farrar (Oldham) 49	Sullivan (Wigan) 100	Farrar (Oldham) 213
1922-23	Ring (Wigan) 41	Sullivan (Wigan) 161	Sullivan (Wigan) 349
1923-24	Ring (Wigan) 49	Sullivan (Wigan) 158	Sullivan (Wigan) 319
1924-25	Ring (Wigan) 54	Sullivan (Wigan) 138	Sullivan (Wigan) 282
1925-26	Ring (Wigan) 63	Sullivan (Wigan) 131	Sullivan (Wigan) 274
1926-27	Ellaby (St. Helens) 55	Sullivan (Wigan) 149	Sullivan (Wigan) 322
1927-28	Ellaby (St. Helens) 37	Thompson (Leeds)..............106	Thompson (Leeds)...............233
1928-29	Brown (Wigan) 44	Sullivan (Wigan) 107	Sullivan (Wigan) 226
	Mills (Huddersfield) 44		
1929-30	Ellaby (St. Helens) 39	Thompson (Leeds)..............111	Thompson (Leeds)...............243
1930-31	Harris, E. (Leeds).................58	Sullivan (Wigan) 133	Sullivan (Wigan) 278
1931-32	Mills (Huddersfield) 50	Sullivan (Wigan) 117	Sullivan (Wigan) 249
1932-33	Harris, E. (Leeds).................57	Sullivan (Wigan) 146	Sullivan (Wigan) 307
1933-34	Brown (Salford) 45	Sullivan (Wigan) 194	Sullivan (Wigan) 406
1934-35	Morley (Wigan)....................49	Sullivan (Wigan) 165	Sullivan (Wigan) 348
1935-36	Harris, E. (Leeds).................63	Sullivan (Wigan) 117	Sullivan (Wigan) 246
1936-37	Harris, E. (Leeds).................40	Sullivan (Wigan) 120	Sullivan (Wigan) 258
1937-38	Harris, E. (Leeds).................45	Sullivan (Wigan) 135	Sullivan (Wigan) 285
1938-39	Markham (Huddersfield).......39	Sullivan (Wigan) 124	Risman (Salford)................267

● For the next six seasons emergency war-time competitions resulted in a reduction of matches and players were allowed to 'guest' for other clubs

1939-40	Batten (Hunslet) 38	Hodgson (Swinton) 98	Hodgson (Swinton) 208
1940-41	Walters (Bradford N.) 32	Lockwood (Halifax)..........70	Belshaw (Warrington) 174
1941-42	Francis (Barrow) 30	Lockwood (Halifax)..........91	Lockwood (Halifax) 185
1942-43	Batten (Hunslet) 24	Lockwood (Halifax)..........65	Lockwood (Halifax) 136
1943-44	Lawrenson (Wigan) 21	Horne (Barrow)................57	Horne (Barrow) 144
1944-45	Batten (Bradford N.) 41	Stott (Wakefield T.) 51	Stott (Wakefield T.) 129

● Normal peace-time rugby resumed

1945-46	Batten (Bradford N.) 35	Ledgard (Dewsbury) 89	Bawden (Huddersfield) 239
1946-47	Bevan (Warrington)...........48	Miller (Hull) 103	Bawden (Huddersfield) 243
1947-48	Bevan (Warrington)...........57	Ward (Wigan) 141	Ward (Wigan) 312
1948-49	Cooper (Huddersfield) 60	Ward (Wigan) 155	Ward (Wigan) 361
1949-50	Nordgren (Wigan)..............57	Gee (Wigan) 133	Palin (Warrington) 290
		Palin (Warrington) 133	
1950-51	Bevan (Warrington)...........68	Cook (Leeds) 155	Cook (Leeds) 332
1951-52	Cooper (Huddersfield) 71	Ledgard (Leigh) 142	Horne (Barrow) 313
1952-53	Bevan (Warrington)...........72	Bath (Warrington) 170	Bath (Warrington)..............379
1953-54	Bevan (Warrington)...........67	Metcalfe (St. Helens)..........153	Metcalfe (St. Helens) 369
		Bath (Warrington) 153	
1954-55	Cooper (Huddersfield) 66	Ledgard (Leigh) 178	Ledgard (Leigh) 374
1955-56	McLean (Bradford N.) 61	Ledgard (Leigh) 155	Bath (Warrington)..............344
1956-57	Boston (Wigan)..................60	Jones (Leeds) 194	Jones (Leeds) 496
1957-58	Sullivan (Wigan) 50	Ganley (Oldham) 219	Ganley (Oldham) 453
1958-59	Vollenhoven (St. Helens).......62	Ganley (Oldham) 190	Griffiths (Wigan)................394
1959-60	Vollenhoven (St. Helens).......54	Rhodes (St. Helens) 171	Fox (Wakefield T.)............453
		Fox (Wakefield T.) 171	
1960-61	Vollenhoven (St. Helens).......59	Rhodes (St. Helens) 145	Rhodes (St. Helens) 338
1961-62	Boston (Wigan)..................51	Fox (Wakefield T.) 183	Fox (Wakefield T.)..............456
1962-63	Glastonbury (Work'ton T.)....41	Coslett (St. Helens) 156	Coslett (St. Helens) 321
1963-64	Stopford (Swinton)..............45	Coslett (St. Helens) 138	Fox (Wakefield T.)..............313
1964-65	Lake (Wigan) 40	Kellett (Hull K.R.) 150	Killeen (St. Helens)..........360
1965-66	Killeen (St. Helens)..............32	Killeen (St. Helens) 120	Killeen (St. Helens)..........336
	Lake (Wigan) 32		
1966-67	Young (Hull K.R.) 34	Risman (Leeds) 163	Killeen (St. Helens)..........353
	Howe (Castleford)...............34		
1967-68	Millward (Hull K.R.)..............38	Risman (Leeds) 154	Risman (Leeds)..................332
1968-69	Francis (Wigan) 40	Risman (Leeds) 165	Risman (Leeds) 345
1969-70	Atkinson (Leeds)..................38	Tyrer (Wigan) 167	Tyrer (Wigan) 385
1970-71	Haigh (Leeds) 40	Coslett (St. Helens) 193	Coslett (St. Helens) 395
	Jones (St. Helens)................40		
1971-72	Atkinson (Leeds)..................36	Coslett (St. Helens) 214	Watkins (Salford) 473
	Lamb (Bradford N.) 36		
1972-73	Atkinson (Leeds)..................39	Watkins (Salford) 221	Watkins (Salford) 493
1973-74	Fielding (Salford) 49	Watkins (Salford) 183	Watkins (Salford) 438
1974-75	Dunn (Hull K.R.) 42	Fox (Hull K.R.) 146	Fox (Hull K.R.) 333
1975-76	Richards (Salford) 37	Watkins (Salford) 175	Watkins (Salford) 385
1976-77	Wright (Widnes) 31	Lloyd (Castleford) 163	Lloyd (Castleford)..............341
1977-78	Wright (Widnes) 33	Pimblett (St. Helens)..........178	Pimblett (St. Helens)..........381
1978-79	Hartley (Hull K.R.) 33	Lloyd (Hull)......................172	Lloyd (Hull) 373

LEADING SCORERS 1979-97

TRIES

1979-80

Keith Fielding (Salford)	30
Steve Hubbard (Hull K.R.)	30
Geoff Munro (Oldham)	29
Ian Ball (Barrow)	27
Keith Bentley (Widnes)	27
Peter Glynn (St. Helens)	27
Roy Mathias (St. Helens)	27
John Bevan (Warrington)	26
David Redfearn (Bradford N.)	26
David Smith (Leeds)	24

1980-81

John Crossley (York)	35
Terry Richardson (Castleford)	28
Steve Hubbard (Hull K.R.)	25
Steve Hartley (Hull K.R.)	23
Paul McDermott (York)	23
Ian Slater (Huddersfield)	23
Des Drummond (Leigh)	20
Ian Ball (Barrow)	19
John Bevan (Warrington)	19
Peter Cramp (Huddersfield)	19
Gary Hyde (Castleford)	19
Denis Ramsdale (Wigan)	19

1981-82

John Jones (Workington T.)	31
Des Drummond (Leigh)	26
John Basnett (Widnes)	26
Ray Ashton (Oldham)	26
Mick Morgan (Carlisle)	25
Steve Hartley (Hull K.R.)	23
Lyn Hopkins (Workington T.)	23
Terry Day (Hull)	23
Steve Evans (Hull)	22
David Hobbs (Featherstone R.)	21
David Moll (Keighley)	21

1982-83

Bob Eccles (Warrington)	37
Steve Evans (Hull)	28
John Crossley (Fulham)	27
Tommy David (Cardiff C.)	26
David Topliss (Hull)	24
Hussain M'Barki (Fulham)	23
Gary Hyde (Castleford)	22
Paul McDermott (York)	22

James Leuluai (Hull)	21
Phil Ford (Warrington)	20
Garry Clark (Hull K.R.)	20

1983-84

Garry Schofield (Hull)	38
Joe Lydon (Widnes)	28
Graham King (Hunslet)	28
John Woods (Leigh)	27
John Basnett (Widnes)	26
Carl Gibson (Batley)	26
Steve Herbert (Barrow)	25
Graham Steadman (York)	25
Gary Prohm (Hull K.R.)	25
Garry Clark (Hull K.R.)	24

1984-85

Ellery Hanley (Bradford N.)	55
Gary Prohm (Hull K.R.)	45
Henderson Gill (Wigan)	34
Barry Ledger (St. Helens)	30
Mal Meninga (St. Helens)	28
Vince Gribbin (Whitehaven)	27
Carl Gibson (Batley)	26
Gary Peacham (Carlisle)	25
Ged Byrne (Salford)	25
Steve Evans (Hull)	24
John Ferguson (Wigan)	24

1985-86

Steve Halliwell (Leigh)	49
Ellery Hanley (Wigan)	38
Peter Lister (Bramley)	34
John Henderson (Leigh)	31
Tommy Frodsham (Blackpool B.)	30
Phil Fox (Leigh)	29
Stewart Williams (Barrow)	27
Brian Garrity (Runcorn H.)	24
Carl Gibson (Leeds)	23
David Beck (Workington T.)	23

1986-87

Ellery Hanley (Wigan)	63
Garry Schofield (Hull)	37
Henderson Gill (Wigan)	32
Derek Bate (Swinton)	31
Phil Ford (Bradford N.)	30
John Henderson (Leigh)	27
Shaun Edwards (Wigan)	26
Brian Johnson (Warrington)	25
Joe Lydon (Wigan)	24
Brian Dunn (Rochdale H.)	23
Barry Ledger (St. Helens)	23
Kevin McCormack (St. Helens)	23

1987-88

Martin Offiah (Widnes)	44
Ellery Hanley (Wigan)	36
Garry Schofield (Leeds)	25
Carl Gibson (Leeds)	24
Andy Goodway (Wigan)	23
Kevin Pape (Carlisle)	23
Shaun Edwards (Wigan)	21
Des Foy (Oldham)	21
Peter Smith (Featherstone R.)	21
Chris Bibb (Featherstone R.)	20
Mark Conway (Wakefield T.)	20
Mark Elia (St. Helens)	20
Les Quirk (St. Helens)	20

1988-89

Martin Offiah (Widnes)	60
Barry Ledger (Leigh)	34
Derek Bate (Swinton)	32
Ellery Hanley (Wigan)	29
Peter Lister (Bramley)	28
Daryl Powell (Sheffield E.)	28
Peter Lewis (Bramley)	26
Les Quirk (St. Helens)	24
Grant Anderson (Castleford)	24
Paul Burns (Barrow)	24

1989-90

Martin Offiah (Widnes)	45
Greg Austin (Hull K.R.)	38
Anthony Sullivan (Hull K.R.)	35
Mark Preston (Wigan)	33
Gerald Cordle (Bradford N.)	32
Steve Larder (Castleford)	29
Paul Lord (Oldham)	29
Shaun Edwards (Wigan)	26
Andy Goodway (Wigan)	26
John Cogger (Oldham)	24
St. John Ellis (Castleford)	24
Wilf George (Halifax)	24
Mark Lord (Rochdale H.)	24
Owen Simpson (Keighley)	24

1990-91

Martin Offiah (Widnes)	49
Greg Austin (Halifax)	47
Martin Wood (Halifax)	31
Adrian Hadley (Salford)	31
Jonathan Davies (Widnes)	30
Ellery Hanley (Wigan)	29
Les Quirk (St. Helens)	26
Alan Hunte (St. Helens)	26
Garry Schofield (Leeds)	25
Graham Steadman (Castleford)	23
Andy Currier (Widnes)	23
John Devereux (Widnes)	23

1991-92

Shaun Edwards (Wigan)	40
John Devereux (Widnes)	35
Iva Ropati (Oldham)	33
Greg Austin (Halifax)	33
Vince Gribbin (Whitehaven)	31
Graham Steadman (Castleford)	31
Martin Offiah (Wigan)	30
David Myers (Wigan)	29
Paul Newlove (Featherstone R.)	28
Mark Preston (Halifax)	27

1992-93

Paul Newlove (Featherstone R.)	52
Shaun Edwards (Wigan)	46
Ellery Hanley (Leeds)	34
Owen Simpson (Featherstone R.)	34
Martin Offiah (Wigan)	32
Alan Hunte (St. Helens)	30
John Wasyliw (Keighley C.)	29
Martin Pearson (Featherstone R.)	29
Greg Austin (Halifax)	27
Martin Wood (Keighley C.)	27

1993-94

Mark Johnson (London C.)	43
St. John Ellis (Castleford)	40
Paul Newlove (Bradford N.)	37
Martin Offiah (Wigan)	37
Stuart Cocker (Workington T.)	35
Nick Pinkney (Keighley C.)	31
Mark Riley (London C.)	30
Carl Hall (Bradford N.)	27
Darren Moxon (Batley)	27
Jason Critchley (Salford)	25
John Bentley (Halifax)	25
Ellery Hanley (Leeds)	25

1994-95

Martin Offiah (Wigan)	53
Greg Austin (Huddersfield)	52
Nick Pinkney (Keighley C.)	46
Ellery Hanley (Leeds)	41
David Plange (Hull K.R.)	35
Mike Pechey (Whitehaven)	34
Gary Connolly (Wigan)	30
John Bentley (Halifax)	29
Alan Hunte (St. Helens)	29
Scott Limb (Hunslet)	29

1995-96
Martin Offiah (Wigan) 28
David Plange (Hull K.R.) 28
Anthony Sullivan (St. Helens)...................24
Va'aiga Tuigamala (Wigan)......................22
Jason Robinson (Wigan) 21
Simon Ashcroft (Swinton) 20
Joey Hayes (St. Helens) 18
Jason Viller (Hunslet H.) 18
Gary Atkins (Hull K.R.) 18
Jason Roach (Swinton) 17
Nathan McAvoy (Salford R.) 17

1996
Paul Newlove (St. Helens) 38
Gary Atkins (Hull K.R.) 27
Jason Robinson (Wigan) 27
Stanley Gene (Hull K.R.) 26
David Plange (Hunslet H.) 26
Jason Roach (Swinton L.) 26
Danny Arnold (St. Helens) 25
Jason Critchley (Keighley C.)....................25
Rob D'Arcy (Hull K.R.) 23
David Ingram (Leigh C.) 23
Robbie Paul (Bradford B.) 23
Mark Riley (Swinton L.) 23

1997
Tevita Vaikona (Hull S.)...........................40
Dean Hanger (Huddersfield G.)................31
Gary Ruddy (Carlisle B.R.) 30
Ray Waring (Lancashire L.) 29
Mick Coult (Hunslet H.) 27
Alan Hunte (St. Helens) 27
Anthony Sullivan (St. Helens)...................27
Richard Baker (Hunslet H.) 25
Paul Rouse (Hull K.R.) 24
Stanley Gene (Hull K.R.) 23
Jason Robinson (Wigan W.) 23

GOALS
● including drop goals
1979-80
Steve Quinn (Featherstone R.) 163
Steve Hubbard (Hull K.R.) 138
Steve Rule (Salford) 134
Steve Hesford (Warrington) 128
Mick Burke (Widnes) 127
Ian Ball (Barrow) 119
Steve Diamond (Wakefield T.) 116
Eric Fitzsimons (Oldham) 108
Mick Parrish (Hunslet) 98
Jimmy Birts (Halifax) 97

1980-81
Steve Hesford (Warrington) 147
Steve Quinn (Featherstone R.) 123
Steve Diamond (Wakefield T.) 112
Mick Burke (Widnes) 110
Steve Hubbard (Hull K.R.) 109
Ian Ball (Barrow) 104
Jimmy Birts (Halifax) 100
Graham Beale (Keighley) 97
Mick Parrish (Oldham) 95
George Fairbairn (Wigan) 94

1981-82
Lyn Hopkins (Workington T.) 190
George Fairbairn (Hull K.R.) 168
Mick Parrish (Oldham) 164
John Woods (Leigh) 158
Steve Rule (Salford) 130
Kevin Dick (Leeds) 125
Steve Quinn (Featherstone R.) 120
Malcolm Agar (Halifax) 119
Lee Crooks (Hull) 118
Steve Hesford (Warrington) 116

1982-83
Steve Diamond (Fulham) 136
Eric Fitzsimons (Hunslet) 121
Lee Crooks (Hull) 120
Bob Beardmore (Castleford) 117
Steve Hesford (Warrington) 113
Steve Fenwick (Cardiff C.) 111
Ken Jones (Swinton) 110
Colin Whitfield (Wigan) 104
Shaun Kilner (Bramley) 104
Steve Quinn (Featherstone R.) 98

1983-84
Steve Hesford (Warrington) 142
Bob Beardmore (Castleford) 142
Lyn Hallett (Cardiff C.) 140
Eric Fitzsimons (Hunslet) 131
John Woods (Leigh) 124
Colin Whitfield (Wigan) 122
Ian Ball (Barrow) 104
Mick Parrish (Oldham) 101
Malcolm Agar (Halifax) 94
Steve Tickle (Barrow) 91

1984-85
Sean Day (St. Helens) 157
George Fairbairn (Hull K.R.) 141
Peter Wood (Runcorn H.) 126
Graham Steadman (York) 122
Clive Griffiths (Salford) 118

Mick Parrish (Oldham) 117
Garry Schofield (Hull) 105
David Creasser (Leeds) 102
Malcolm Agar (Halifax) 87
Ken Jones (Swinton) 87

1985-86
Chris Johnson (Leigh) 173
David Stephenson (Wigan) 128
David Noble (Doncaster) 118
Kevin Harcombe (Rochdale H.) 115
Shaun Kilner (Bramley) 110
John Dorahy (Hull K.R.) 101
John Woods (Bradford N.) 98
David Creasser (Leeds) 84
Dean Carroll (Carlisle) 83
Gary Smith (Workington T.) 83

1986-87
Paul Loughlin (St. Helens) 190
Paul Bishop (Warrington) 117
David Noble (Doncaster) 114
Colin Whitfield (Halifax) 109
Alan Platt (Hunslet) 102
Paul Topping (Swinton) 100
Chris Johnson (Leigh) 86
Martin Ketteridge (Castleford) 80
David Wood (Rochdale H.) 80
Steve Quinn (Featherstone R.) 77

1987-88
John Woods (Warrington) 152
Steve Quinn (Featherstone R.) 128
Kevin Harcombe (Wakefield T.) 116
Paul Loughlin (St. Helens) 114
Gary Pearce (Hull) 111
Mike Smith (Springfield B.) 98
David Stephenson (Leeds) 95
Mike Fletcher (Hull K.R.) 94
David Hobbs (Bradford N.) 83
Ken Jones (Salford) 79

1988-89
Mark Aston (Sheffield E.) 148
Martin Ketteridge (Castleford) 129
David Hobbs (Bradford N.) 118
Chris Johnson (Leigh) 117
Dean Marwood (Barrow) 115
Paul Loughlin (St. Helens) 113
David Noble (Doncaster) 110
John Woods (Warrington) 107
Andy Currier (Widnes) 107
Steve Turner (Rochdale H.) 104

1989-90
Mike Fletcher (Hull K.R.) 199
Paul Loughlin (St. Helens) 145
Duncan Platt (Oldham) 126
Colin Maskill (Leeds) 114
Mark Conway (Wakefield T.) 107
David Hobbs (Bradford N.) 104
Paul Eastwood (Hull) 101
Mark Aston (Sheffield E.) 99
Jonathan Davies (Widnes) 98
Steve Turner (Rochdale H.) 98

1990-91
Steve Kerry (Salford) 177
Frano Botica (Wigan) 126
Paul Eastwood (Hull) 119
Jonathan Davies (Widnes) 112
Simon Irving (Leeds) 99
Graham Sullivan (Ryedale-York) 94
Paul Loughlin (St. Helens) 94
Alan Platt (Halifax) 91
Barry Vickers (Carlisle) 88
Tim Lumb (Hunslet) 85

1991-92
Frano Botica (Wigan) 161
Steve Carroll (Bramley) 138
Deryck Fox (Featherstone R.) 115
Lee Crooks (Castleford) 113
David Hobbs (Bradford N.) 110
Chris Vasey (Dewsbury) 109
Paul Eastwood (Hull) 108
Steve Parrish (Batley) 106
Mark Aston (Sheffield E.) 104
Jonathan Davies (Widnes) 99

1992-93
John Wasyliw (Keighley C.) 187
Frano Botica (Wigan) 184
Dean Marwood (Workington T.) 179
Martin Pearson (Featherstone R.) 145
Paul Bishop (Halifax) 118
Lee Crooks (Castleford) 116
Jonathan Davies (Widnes) 116
Steve Gartland (Rochdale H.) 105
Steve Maguire (Whitehaven) 95
Andy Precious (Hunslet) 90

1993-94
Frano Botica (Wigan) 188
John Gallagher (London C.) 159
Deryck Fox (Bradford N.) 148
Lee Crooks (Castleford) 137
Jonathan Davies (Warrington) 132

Mark Conway (Dewsbury) 130
Robert Turner (Doncaster) 123
Mark Aston (Sheffield E.) 123
Graham Holroyd (Leeds) 103
Dean Marwood (Workington T.) 100

1994-95
Frano Botica (Wigan) 186
Bobbie Goulding (St. Helens) 158
Simon Irving (Keighley C.) 152
Martin Strett (Rochdale H.) 150
John Schuster (Halifax) 144
Mike Fletcher (Hull K.R.) 142
Graham Holroyd (Leeds) 135
Deryck Fox (Bradford N.) 131
Simon Wilson (Batley) 127
Jonathan Davies (Warrington) 126

1995-96
Bobbie Goulding (St. Helens) 135
Mike Fletcher (Hull K.R.) 117
Steve McNamara (Hull) 101
Paul Cook (Bradford B.) 99
Willie Richardson (Carlisle) 96
Steve Blakeley (Salford R.) 93
Andrew Farrell (Wigan) 92
Martin Pearson (Featherstone R.) 86
Simon Irving (Keighley C.) 81
Chris Wilkinson (Leigh C.) 81

1996
Bobbie Goulding (St. Helens) 162
Mike Fletcher (Hull K.R.) 151
Andrew Farrell (Wigan) 113
John Schuster (Halifax B.S.) 113
Greg Pearce (Swinton L.) 110
Willie Richardson (Carlisle) 107
Steve Blakeley (Salford R.) 106
Simon Wilson (Hunslet H.) 102
Steve McNamara (Bradford B.) 99
Dean Purtill (Leigh C.) 90
Graham Holroyd (Leeds) 90

1997
Andrew Farrell (Wigan W.) 163
Mark Hewitt (Hull S.) 140
Steve McNamara (Bradford B.) 134
Mark Aston (Sheffield E.) 115
Richard Price (Batley B.) 110
Steve Gartland (Rochdale H.) 109
Kevin Hetherington (Whitehaven W.) 107
Dean Purtill (Leigh C.) 107
Willie Richardson (Carlisle B.R.) 106
Steve Blakeley (Salford R.) 101

DROP GOALS

1978-79	Norman Turley (Blackpool B.)	18
1979-80	Tony Dean (Hunslet)	18
1980-81	Arnold Walker (Whitehaven)	22
1981-82	Malcolm Agar (Halifax)	17
	Steve Donlan (Leigh)	17
1982-83	Harry Pinner (St. Helens)	13
1983-84	Lyn Hallett (Cardiff C.)	29
1984-85	Peter Wood (Runcorn H.)	28
1985-86	Paul Bishop (Warrington)	13
1986-87	Billy Platt (Mansfield M.)	18
1987-88	Wayne Parker (Hull K.R.)	15
1988-89	Gary Pearce (Hull)	16
1989-90	Paul Harkin (Bradford N.)	12
1990-91	Ray Ashton (Workington T.)	13
	Dean Carroll (Doncaster)	13
1991-92	Andy Ruane (Leigh)	17
1992-93	Paul Shuttleworth (Dewsbury)	11
1993-94	Jonathan Davies (Warrington)	14
1994-95	Jonathan Davies (Warrington)	14
1995-96	Carl Briggs (Halifax)	9
1996	Deryck Fox (Featherstone R.)	6
1997	Brad Davis (Castleford T.)	10

POINTS

1978-79	Geoff "Sammy" Lloyd (Hull)	373
1979-80	Steve Quinn (Featherstone R.)	375
1980-81	Steve Hesford (Warrington)	310
1981-82	Lyn Hopkins (Workington T.)	446
1982-83	Steve Diamond (Fulham)	308
1983-84	John Woods (Leigh)	355
1984-85	Sean Day (St. Helens)	362
1985-86	Chris Johnson (Leigh)	400
1986-87	Paul Loughlin (St. Helens)	424
1987-88	John Woods (Warrington)	351
1988-89	Mark Aston (Sheffield E.)	307
1989-90	Mike Fletcher (Hull K.R.)	450
1990-91	Steve Kerry (Salford)	427
1991-92	Frano Botica (Wigan)	364
1992-93	John Wasyliw (Keighley C.)	490
1993-94	Frano Botica (Wigan)	422
1994-95	Frano Botica (Wigan)	408
1995-96	Bobbie Goulding (St. Helens)	285
1996	Bobbie Goulding (St. Helens)	348
1997	Andrew Farrell (Wigan W.)	362

ALL-TIME RECORDS

Most goals in a match:
22 by JIM SULLIVAN (Wigan) v. Flimby & Fothergill (Challenge Cup), 14 February 1925

Most goals in a season:
DAVID WATKINS holds the record for most goals in a season with 221 — all for Salford — in 1972-73. Watkins played and scored a goal in every match that season as follows:

1972			
Aug. 19	Leeds	(H)	5
23	Featherstone R.	(A)	3
26	Whitehaven	(A)	4
28	Swinton	(H)	1
Sep. 1	Oldham	(LC) (H)	10
9	Leeds	(A)	2
15	Rochdale H.	(LC) (H)	11
17	Leigh	(A)	6
24	Barrow	(JP) (A)	4
29	Huyton	(H)	10
Oct. 3	Oldham	(FT) (A)	4
6	Wigan	(LC)(A)	4
8	Blackpool B.	(A)	5
13	Blackpool B.	(H)	8
21	Swinton	(Warrington, LC Final)	5
Nov. 5	Huyton	(A)	8
10	Rochdale H.	(H)	6
17	Warrington	(A)	4
19	New Zealand	(H)	10
24	Dewsbury	(JP) (H)	4
26	Workington T.	(H)	6
Dec. 1	Barrow	(H)	9
10	Bradford N.	(JP) (H)	9
13	Oldham	(A)	4
15	Leigh	(H)	3
24	Bradford N.	(A)	5
26	Workington T.	(A)	3
30	Hull K.R.	(JP) (A)	5

1973			
Jan. 3	Bradford N.	(H)	6
7	Rochdale H.	(A)	2
12	Featherstone R.	(H)	4
28	Featherstone R.	(RL Cup) (A)	4
Feb. 2	Whitehaven	(H)	4
11	Barrow	(A)	5
23	St. Helens	(H)	3
Mar. 7	Widnes	(A)	3
9	Dewsbury	(H)	3
16	St. Helens	(A)	2
24	Leeds	(Huddersfield, JP Final)	2
30	Warrington	(H)	1

Apr. 6	Widnes	(H)	4
13	Oldham	(H)	3
15	Dewsbury	(A)	2
17	Wigan	(A)	3
20	Swinton	(A)	7
23	Wigan	(H)	3
29	Rochdale H.	(top 16) (H)	2

	App	Goals
League	34	147
Lancs Cup	4	30
John Player	5	24
Tour match	1	10
RL Cup	1	4
Floodlit Cup	1	4
Top 16	1	2
Totals	47	221

Fastest goals century:
BOBBIE GOULDING of St. Helens holds the record of scoring the fastest 100 goals from the start of the season in terms of number of matches. Goulding reached his century in St. Helens' 17th Cup and league match of the 1996 season, having missed two of the matches because of injury.

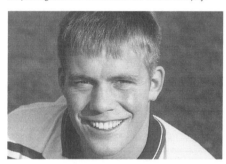

Bobbie Goulding: Fastest 100 goals.

Most goals in a career:
JIM SULLIVAN holds the record for most goals in a career with 2,867 between 1921-22 and 1945-46. He scored a century of goals in every season after leaving Welsh Rugby Union for Wigan until the war interrupted the 1939-40 campaign. The Test full back played all of his club rugby for Wigan apart from war-time appearances with Bradford Northern, Dewsbury and Keighley.

Sullivan's total includes 441 in representative matches, including three tours of Australasia. These figures are accepted by the Record Keepers' Club following research by James Carter and Malcolm Bentley.

Most one-point drop goals in a match:
5 by DANNY WILSON (Swinton) v. Hunslet (John
Player Special), 6 November 1983
PETER WOOD (Runcorn H.) v. Batley, 21 October
1984
PAUL BISHOP (Warrington) at Wigan (Premiership
semi-final), 11 May 1986

Most one-point drop goals in a season:
29 by LYN HALLETT (Cardiff C.) 1983-84

Most one-point drop goals in a career:
97 by NORMAN TURLEY (Warrington, Runcorn H.,
Swinton, Blackpool B., Rochdale H., Barrow,
Workington T., Trafford B.,
Whitehaven)..1974-91

Longest successful goal kick:
ARTHUR ATKINSON of Castleford is credited with the
longest successful goal kick, covering 75 yards (68.5 metres)
to the posts. The centre's wind-assisted penalty kick was
taken during Castleford's 20-10 League win at St. Helens on
26 October 1929.

Martin Hodgson of Swinton has often been credited with
the longest successful kick, but his goal at Rochdale Hornets
on 13 April 1940 was measured at 77¾ yards (71.06m) to
beyond the posts where the ball landed. Reports at the time
referred to a 58-yard (53m) goal.
● Details of the record kick were discovered following
research by Graham Morris.

Longest successful drop goal:
JOE LYDON of Wigan is credited with the longest successful drop goal of 61 yards (55¾ metres) in a Challenge Cup
semi-final against Warrington at Manchester City's Maine
Road ground on 25 March 1989. The distance was officially
measured after the match.

The centre took the kick from within the still visible soccer
centre circle and inside his own half. The ball cleared the
crossbar by about 10 feet and landed just beyond the dead
ball line. It came in the 73rd minute and edged Wigan 7-6
ahead towards a 13-6 victory.

Longest tryscoring run:
JOE BARDGETT of Carlisle is credited with the longest
solo tryscoring run of 139 yards (127 metres) in an old
Second Division home match at Brunton Park against
Halifax on 21 February 1982. The distance covered was
measured by a Carlisle official after the match.

Playing on the left wing, Bardgett fielded an opposition
kick a few inches from the touchline and ran back 10 yards
to his own in-goal area. Just before reaching the posts he
turned in-field and burst through a bunch of Halifax defenders to sprint down the middle for a try between the opposition's posts. The try came late in the game, which Carlisle
won 20-0.

Paul Bishop: Record five drop goals.

Most tries in a match:
11 by GEORGE WEST (Hull K.R.) v. Brookland Rovers
(Challenge Cup), 4 March 1905

Most tries in a career:
BRIAN BEVAN holds the record for most tries in a career
with 796 between 1946 and 1964. His season-by-season
record is:

1946-47	48
1947-48	57
1948-49	56
1949-50	33
1950-51	68
1951-52	51
1952-53	72
1953-54	67
1954-55	63
1955-56	57
1956-57	17
1957-58	46
1958-59	54
1959-60	40
1960-61	35
1961-62	15
1962-63	10
1963-64	7

Totals

Warrington	740
Blackpool Borough	17
Other Nationalities	26
Other representative matches	13
Grand Total	**796**

The Australian winger played his first game for
Warrington on 17 November 1945 and his last on 23 April
1962 before having two seasons at Blackpool Borough. His
last match for Borough was on 22 February 1964.

Most tries in a season:
ALBERT ROSENFELD holds the record for most tries in a
season with 80 – all for Huddersfield – in 1913-14.

Rosenfeld's match-by-match record:

1913
Sep.	6	York	(A)	4
	8	Warrington	(H)	2
	13	Leeds	(H)	5
	20	Halifax	(A)	1
	27	Batley	(A)	0
Oct.	4	Oldham	(H)	2
	11	Rochdale H.	(A)	0
	18	Bramley	(YC) (H)	2
	25	Dewsbury	(A)	4
Nov.	1	Halifax	(YC) (A)	2
	8	Wigan	(A)	1
	15	Dewsbury	(YC) (H)	3
	19	Bradford N.	(H)	3
	22	Leeds	(A)	3
	29	Bradford N.	(Halifax, YCF)	1
Dec.	3	Halifax	(H)	3
	6	Hunslet	(A)	2
	13	Rochdale H.	(H)	3
	20	Hull K.R.	(A)	2
	25	Hull	(A)	1
	26	Wakefield T.	(H)	3
	27	Hunslet	(H)	0

1914
Jan.	1	St. Helens	(A)	0
	3	Warrington	(A)	0
	10	York	(H)	3
	17	Keighley	(A)	2
	24	Dewsbury	(H)	1
	31	Batley	(H)	0
Feb.	7	Oldham	(A)	0
	14	Bramley	(H)	5
	21	Wigan	(H)	3
	28	Swinton Park R.	(RL Cup) (H)	7
Mar.	7	Wakefield T.	(A)	2
	14	Hull K.R.	(RL Cup) (H)	2
	18	Bramley	(A)	3
	21	Widnes	(RL Cup) (H)	0
	25	Keighley	(H)	3
	28	Hull K.R.	(H)	1
	30	Bradford N.	(A)	1
Apr.	4	Hull	(Leeds, RL Cup SF)	0
	11	Hull	(H) did not play	
	13	St. Helens	(H)	0
	20	Hull	(Play-off) (H) did not play	
	25	Salford	(Leeds, Championship Final)	0

	App	Tries
League	33	63
Yorks Cup	4	8
RL Cup	4	9
Play-off	1	0
Totals	**42**	**80**

Most points in a season:
LEWIS JONES holds the record for most points in a
season with 496 from 194 goals and 36 tries for Leeds and
representative teams in 1956-57.

Jones's match-by-match record:

For Leeds

1956
				G	T	Pts
Aug.	17	Halifax	(H)	3	0	6
	22	Bradford N.	(A)	11	3	31
	25	Wigan	(A)	4	0	8
	27	Featherstone R.	(H)	4	1	11
Sep.	1	Wakefield T.	(YC) (A)	3	1	9
	8	Dewsbury	(A)	6	0	12
	15	Warrington	(H)	7	0	14
	22	Huddersfield	(A)	3	0	6
	29	York	(H)	6	0	12
Oct.	6	Batley	(A)	4	2	14
	13	Australia	(H)	Did not play		
	20	Hull K.R.	(A)	Did not play		
	27	Wigan	(H)	2	0	4
Nov.	3	Hunslet	(A)	1	0	2
	10	Barrow	(H)	3	2	12
	17	Halifax	(A)	4	0	8
	24	Keighley	(H)	3	3	15
Dec.	1	Barrow	(A)	4	0	8
	8	Bramley	(A)	5	0	10
	15	Doncaster	(H)	1	2	8
	22	Bradford N.	..(abandoned) (H)	1	1	5
	25	Batley	(H)	8	1	19
	29	Keighley	(A)	3	0	6

1957
				G	T	Pts
Jan.	5	Hull	(H)	5	2	16
	12	Warrington	(A)	0	3	9
	19	St. Helens	(H)	5	1	13
	26	Doncaster	(A)	Did not play		
Feb.	2	Huddersfield	(H)	6	0	12
	9	Wigan	(RL Cup) (H)	2	1	7
	16	York	(A)	7	1	17
	23	Warrington	(RL Cup) (H)	5	1	13
	27	Castleford	(H)	4	1	11
Mar.	9	Halifax	(RL Cup) (A)	5	0	10
	16	Wakefield T.	(H)	5	1	13
	20	Bradford N.	(H)	5	1	13
	23	Hull	(A)	2	0	4
	30	Whitehaven ...(Odsal, RL Cup SF)		1	0	2
Apr.	3	Wakefield T.	(A)	3	0	6
	6	St. Helens	(A)	0	0	0
	12	Hull K.R.	(H)	Did not play		
	13	Dewsbury	(H)	6	2	18
	19	Hunslet	(H)	5	2	16
	20	Featherstone R.	(A)	2	0	4
	22	Castleford	(A)	2	0	4
	23	Bramley	(H)	7	1	17
May	4	Oldham	(Play-off) (A)	3	0	6
	11	Barrow ....(Wembley, RL Cup final)		0	0	0

Representative matches
For Great Britain:

Jan.	26	France ....(at Leeds)	9	1	21
Mar.	3	France ....(at Toulouse)	5	1	13
Apr.	10	France..............(at St. Helens)	7	1	17

For The Rest:

Oct.	3	Britain XIII ....(at Bradford)	4	0	8

For RL XIII:

Oct.	29	Australia ....(Leigh)	3	0	6

	App	G	T	Pts
League	36	147	30	384
RL Cup.......................................	5	13	2	32
Yorks Cup..................................	1	3	1	9
Play-off.....................................	1	3	0	6
Representative	5	28	3	65
Totals.......................................	**48**	**194**	**36**	**496**

Lewis Jones: Record 496 points in a season.

Most points in a match:
53 (11t,10g) by GEORGE WEST (Hull K.R.) v. Brookland Rovers (RL Cup), 4 March 1905

Most points in a career:
NEIL FOX holds the record for most points in a career with 6,220 between 1956 and 1979. This total does not include points scored during a spell of club rugby in New Zealand.

Fox was a month short of his 17th birthday when he made his debut for Wakefield Trinity on 10 April 1956. Apart from a brief time at Bradford Northern, Fox had 19 seasons at Wakefield before moving to a succession of clubs in later years.

After a long career as an international centre Fox moved into the forwards and played his last professional match for Bradford in their opening fixture of the 1979-80 season, on 19 August. That match enabled him to join the elite few who have played first team rugby at 40 years of age.

Fox's season-by-season tally is as follows:

	G	T	Pts
1955-56	6	0	12
1956-57	54	10	138
1957-58	124	32	344
1958-59	148	28	380
1959-60	171	37	453
1960-61	94	20	248
1961-62	183	30	456
1962 Tour			
Australasia	85	19	227
South Africa...............................	19	4	50
1962-63	125	14	292
1963-64	125	21	313
1964-65	121	13	281
1965-66	98	11	229
1966-67	144	16	336
1967-68	98	18	250
1968-69	95	9	217
1969-70	17	5	49
1970-71	110	12	256
1971-72	84	6	186
1972-73	138	8	300
1973-74	62	8	148
1974-75	146(1)	14	333
1975-76	102(1)	4	215
1976-77	79(1)	6	175
1977-78	95(1)	9	216
1978-79	50	4	112
1979-80	2	0	4

A breakdown of Fox's club and representative totals is as follows:

	App	G	T	Pts
Wakefield T.	574	1,836	272	4,488
Bradford N.	70	85(1)	12	205
Hull K.R.......................	59	212(2)	16	470
York	13	42	2	90
Bramley	23	73	6	164
Huddersfield	21	73(1)	5	160
Club Totals	**760**	**2,321(4)**	**313**	**5,577**
Yorkshire	17	60	9	147
Britain v. Australia..........	8	26	3	61
New Zealand..................	4	11	1	25
France	17	56	10	142
Other representative				
games including tour ...	22	101	22	268
Representative Totals...	**68**	**254**	**45**	**643**
Grand Totals.................	**828**	**2,575(4)**	**358**	**6,220**

( ) Figures in brackets are one-point drop goals included in total.

RECORDS

Score-a-match:
The following players have appeared and scored in all of their club's matches in one season:

Jim Hoey (Widnes)	1932-33
Billy Langton (Hunslet)	1958-59
Stuart Ferguson (Leigh)	1970-71
David Watkins (Salford)	1972-73
David Watkins (Salford)	1973-74
John Woods (Leigh)	1977-78
Steve Quinn (Featherstone R.)	1979-80
Mick Parrish (Hunslet)	1979-80
John Gorton (Swinton)	1980-81
Mick Parrish (Oldham)	1981-82
Peter Wood (Runcorn H.)	1984-85
David Noble (Doncaster)	1986-87
Mark Aston (Sheffield E.)	1988-89
Mike Fletcher (Hull K.R.)	1989-90
Steve Carroll (Bramley)	1991-92
Paul Bishop (Halifax)	1992-93
John Wasyliw (Keighley C.)	1992-93
John Schuster (Halifax)	1994-95
Mike Fletcher (Hull K.R.)	1995-96
Willie Richardson (Carlisle)	1996
Simon Wilson (Hunslet)	1996
Richard Price (Batley B.)	1998
Andrew Farrell (Wigan W.)	1998

Longest scoring run:
DAVID WATKINS holds the record for the longest scoring run, playing and scoring in 92 consecutive matches for Salford from 19 August 1972 to 25 April 1974. He totalled 403 goals, 41 tries and 929 points.

Longest run of appearances:
KEITH ELWELL holds the record for the longest run of appearances with one club with a total of 239 for Widnes. The consecutive run started at Wembley in the 1977 Challenge Cup final against Leeds on 7 May, and ended after he played in a Lancashire Cup tie at home to St. Helens on 5 September 1982. He was dropped for the match at Featherstone Rovers a week later. Although he went on as a substitute the record refers to full appearances only. Elwell played as a substitute in the next match and then made a full appearance before his run of all appearances ended at 242.

TEAM
Highest score:
Huddersfield 142 v. Blackpool Gladiators 4 (Regal Trophy) ..... 26 November 1994

Widest margin:
As above and
Barrow 138 v. Nottingham City 0 (Regal Trophy) ..... 27 November 1994

Highest score away:
Highfield 4 v. Keighley Cougars 104 (Division Two, played at Rochdale Hornets) .....23 April 1995

● The highest score on an opponent's ground is:
Chorley 10 v. Hull K.R. 92 (Division Two) ..... 21 April 1996

Widest margin:
Runcorn Highfield 2 v. Leigh 88 (Division Two) ..... 15 January 1989

Most points in all matches in a season:
1,735 by Wigan from 45 matches in 1994-95 as follows:

30 Division One matches	1,148
6 Challenge Cup	230
5 Regal Trophy	170
3 Premiership	167
1 Australia	20

Most League points in a season:
1,156 by Leigh from 34 Division Two matches in 1985-86.

Longest winning run:
29 by Wigan from February to October 1987, as follows:
20 Division One, 3 Premiership, 4 Lancashire Cup, 1 Charity Shield and 1 World Club Challenge.

Longest unbeaten run:
43 Cup and League matches, including two draws, by Huddersfield from 1914 to 1919 during a period interrupted by World War One.
They were unbeaten in the last 38 matches of 1914-15 and after the interruption of the First World War won their next five competitive matches — four Yorkshire Cup ties in 1918-19 and the first League match of 1919-20.

Longest winning run in the League:
31 matches by Wigan. Last 8 matches of 1969-70 and first 23 of 1970-71.
● In 1978-79 Hull won all of their 26 Division Two matches, the only time a club has won all its League matches in one season.

Longest losing run:
61 Cup and League matches by Runcorn Highfield from January 1989 to February 1991. Made up of 55 Division Two, 2 Challenge Cup, 2 Regal Trophy and 2 Lancs Cup.

Longest run without a win:
75 Cup and League matches (including two draws) by Runcorn Highfield from October 1988 to March 1991. Made up of 67 Division Two, 3 Challenge Cup, 3 Regal Trophy and 2 Lancs Cup.

Longest League losing run and run without a win:
Included in the above.
● Only three teams have lost all their matches in a season: Liverpool City (1906-07)*, Runcorn Highfield (1989-90) and Nottingham City (1991-92).
*Liverpool drew a League match against Bramley but this was expunged from the records as the return fixture was cancelled.

162

ALL-TIME RECORD SCORING AND APPEARANCE CHARTS
The following are extended charts of outstanding scoring and appearance records established by British-based players.

*Denotes amateur or non-league team

EIGHT OR MORE TRIES IN A MATCH

11	George West (Hull K.R.) v. Brookland R.*	4 Mar. 1905
10	Lionel Cooper (Huddersfield) v. Keighley	17 Nov. 1951
	Martin Offiah (Wigan) v. Leeds	10 May 1992
	Shaun Edwards (Wigan) at Swinton	29 Sep. 1992
9	Ray Markham (Huddersfield) v. Featherstone R.	21 Sep. 1935
	Greg Austin (Huddersfield) v. Blackpool G.*	26 Nov. 1994
8	Dai Thomas (Dewsbury) v. Liverpool C.	13 Apr. 1907
	Albert Rosenfeld (Huddersfield) v. Wakefield T.	26 Dec. 1911
	Fred Webster (Leeds) v. Coventry	12 Apr. 1913
	Eric Harris (Leeds) v. Bradford N.	14 Sep. 1931
	Lionel Cooper (Huddersfield) v. Yorkshire Amateurs*	11 Sep. 1948
	Keith Williams (Halifax) v. Dewsbury	9 Nov. 1957

14 OR MORE GOALS IN A MATCH

22	Jim Sullivan (Wigan) v. Flimby & Fothergill*	14 Feb. 1925
18	Major Holland (Huddersfield) v. Swinton Park*	28 Feb. 1914
17	Geoff "Sammy" Lloyd (Castleford) v. Millom*	16 Sep. 1973
	Darren Carter (Barrow) v. Nottingham C.*	27 Nov. 1994
16	Paul Loughlin (St. Helens) v. Carlisle	14 Sep. 1986
15	Mick Stacey (Leigh) v. Doncaster	28 Mar. 1976
	John Wasyliw (Keighley C.) v. Nottingham C.	1 Nov. 1992
14	Alf Carmichael (Hull K.R.) v. Merthyr Tydfil	8 Oct. 1910
	Jim Kennedy (Hull) v. Rochdale H.	7 Apr. 1921
	Harold Palin (Warrington) v. Liverpool S.	13 Sep. 1950
	Joe Phillips (Bradford N.) v. Batley	6 Sep. 1952
	Bernard Ganley (Oldham) v. Liverpool C.	4 Apr. 1959
	Bruce Burton (Halifax) v. Hunslet	27 Aug. 1972
	Geoff "Sammy" Lloyd (Hull) v. Oldham	10 Sep. 1978
	Chris Johnson (Leigh) v. Keighley	30 Apr. 1986
	Steve Turner (Rochdale H.) v. Runcorn H.	5 Nov. 1989
	Mike Fletcher (Hull K.R.) v. Whitehaven	18 Mar. 1990
	Colin Armstrong (Hull K.R.) at Nottingham C.	19 Aug. 1990

On tour with Great Britain:

17	Ernest Ward v. Mackay (Australia)	2 Jul. 1946
15	Alf Wood v. South Australia	23 May 1914
	Jim Ledgard v. Wide Bay (Australia)	28 Jun. 1950
	Lewis Jones v. Southern New South Wales (Australia)	21 Aug. 1954
	Eric Fraser v. North Queensland (Australia)	29 Jun. 1958

35 POINTS OR MORE IN A MATCH

53 George West (Hull K.R.) v. Brookland R.* .... 4 Mar. 1905
44 Jim Sullivan (Wigan) v. Flimby & Fothergill* .... 14 Feb. 1925
43 Geoff "Sammy" Lloyd (Castleford) v. Millom* .... 16 Sep. 1973
42 Dean Marwood (Workington T.) v. Highfield .... 1 Nov. 1992
    Darren Carter (Barrow) v. Nottingham C.* .... 27 Nov. 1994
    Dean Marwood (Workington T.) v. Leigh .... 26 Feb. 1995
40 Paul Loughlin (St. Helens) v. Carlisle .... 14 Sep. 1986
    Martin Offiah (Wigan) v. Leeds .... 10 May 1992
    Shaun Edwards (Wigan) at Swinton .... 29 Sep. 1992
    Martin Pearson (Featherstone R.) v. Whitehaven .... 26 Nov. 1995
39 James Lomas (Salford) v. Liverpool C. .... 2 Feb. 1907
    Major Holland (Huddersfield) v. Swinton Park* .... 28 Feb. 1914
38 John Woods (Leigh) v. Blackpool B. .... 11 Sep. 1977
    Bob Beardmore (Castleford) v. Barrow .... 22 Mar. 1987
    John Woods (Leigh) v. Ryedale-York .... 12 Jan. 1992
36 Jim Kennedy (Hull) v. Keighley .... 29 Jan. 1921
    Mick Stacey (Leigh) v. Doncaster .... 28 Mar. 1976
    John Woods (Bradford N.) v. Swinton .... 13 Oct. 1985
    Graham Steadman (Castleford) v. Salford .... 1 Apr. 1990
    John Wasyliw (Keighley C.) v. Nottingham C.* .... 31 Oct. 1993
    Greg Austin (Huddersfield) v. Blackpool G.* .... 26 Nov. 1994
35 Jeff Bawden (Huddersfield) v. Swinton .... 20 Apr. 1946

Paul Loughlin: 40 points in a match for St. Helens.

50 TRIES OR MORE IN A SEASON

80 Albert Rosenfeld (Huddersfield)............1913-14
78 Albert Rosenfeld (Huddersfield).............1911-12
72 Brian Bevan (Warrington)......................1952-53
71 Lionel Cooper (Huddersfield)................1951-52
68 Brian Bevan (Warrington)......................1950-51
67 Brian Bevan (Warrington).....................1953-54
66 Lionel Cooper (Huddersfield)................1954-55
63 Johnny Ring (Wigan)............................1925-26
   Eric Harris (Leeds)...............................1935-36
   Jack McLean (Bradford N.)...................1951-52
   Brian Bevan (Warrington)......................1954-55
   Ellery Hanley (Wigan)..........................1986-87
62 Tom Van Vollenhoven (St. Helens)........1958-59
61 Jack McLean (Bradford N.)...................1955-56
60 Lionel Cooper (Huddersfield)................1948-49
   Billy Boston (Wigan)............................1956-57
   Martin Offiah (Widnes)........................1988-89
59 Lionel Cooper (Huddersfield)................1950-51
   Jack McLean (Bradford N.)...................1952-53
   Tom Van Vollenhoven (St. Helens)........1960-61
58 Eric Harris (Leeds)..............................1930-31
57 Eric Harris (Leeds)..............................1932-33
   Brian Bevan (Warrington)......................1947-48
   Brian Nordgren (Wigan).......................1949-50
   Brian Bevan (Warrington)......................1955-56
56 Albert Rosenfeld (Huddersfield)............1912-13
   Albert Rosenfeld (Huddersfield)............1914-15
   Brian Bevan (Warrington)......................1948-49
55 Alf Ellaby (St. Helens)........................1926-27
   Ellery Hanley (Bradford N.)...................1984-85
54 Stan Moorhouse (Huddersfield)............1911-12
   Johnny Ring (Wigan)............................1924-25
   Brian Bevan (Warrington)......................1958-59
   Billy Boston (Wigan)............................1958-59
   Tom Van Vollenhoven (St. Helens)........1959-60
53 Ray Markham (Huddersfield)................1935-36
   Martin Offiah (Wigan)..........................1994-95
52 Jack Harrison (Hull)............................1914-15
   Frank Castle (Barrow)..........................1951-52
   Jack McLean (Bradford N.)...................1953-54
   Paul Newlove (Featherstone R.)............1992-93
   Greg Austin (Huddersfield)...................1994-95
51 Brian Bevan (Warrington)......................1951-52
   Jim Lewthwaite (Barrow)......................1956-57
   Billy Boston (Wigan)............................1961-62
50 Ernest Mills (Huddersfield)..................1931-32
   Lionel Cooper (Huddersfield)................1952-53
   Mick Sullivan (H'field and Wigan).........1957-58

170 GOALS OR MORE IN A SEASON

●   Including drop goals
221 David Watkins (Salford).....................1972-73
219 Bernard Ganley (Oldham)...................1957-58
214 Kel Coslett (St. Helens).....................1971-72
199 Mike Fletcher (Hull K.R.)...................1989-90
194 Jim Sullivan (Wigan)..........................1933-34
    Lewis Jones (Leeds)............................1956-57
193 Kel Coslett (St. Helens).....................1970-71
    David Watkins (Salford).....................1971-72
190 Bernard Ganley (Oldham)...................1958-59
    Lyn Hopkins (Workington T.)............1981-82
    Paul Loughlin (St. Helens)..................1986-87
189 Bernard Ganley (Oldham)...................1956-57
188 Frano Botica (Wigan).........................1993-94
187 John Wasyliw (Keighley C.)................1992-93
186 Frano Botica (Wigan).........................1994-95
184 Frano Botica (Wigan).........................1992-93
183 Fred Griffiths (Wigan)........................1961-62
    Neil Fox (Wakefield T.)......................1961-62
    David Watkins (Salford).....................1973-74
181 Billy Langton (Hunslet)......................1958-59
179 Dean Marwood (Workington T.)........1992-93
178 Jim Ledgard (Leigh)...........................1954-55
    Geoff Pimblett (St. Helens)................1977-78
177 Steve Kerry (Salford).........................1990-91
176 Fred Griffiths (Wigan)........................1958-59
175 David Watkins (Salford).....................1975-76
173 Eddie Tees (Bradford N.)...................1971-72
    Chris Johnson (Leigh).........................1985-86
172 Geoff "Sammy" Lloyd (Hull)............1978-79
171 Austin Rhodes (St. Helens)................1959-60
    Neil Fox (Wakefield T.)......................1959-60
170 Harry Bath (Warrington)...................1952-53
    Steve Hesford (Warrington)................1978-79

Kel Coslett of St. Helens: 214 goals in 1971-72.

165

370 OR MORE POINTS IN A SEASON

496	Lewis Jones (Leeds)............................1956-57	399	Austin Rhodes (St. Helens) 1959-60
493	David Watkins (Salford) 1972-73	395	Kel Coslett (St. Helens) 1970-71
490	John Wasyliw (Keighley C.) 1992-93	394	Fred Griffiths (Wigan) 1958-59
476	David Watkins (Salford) 1971-72	392	Simon Irving (Keighley C.) 1994-95
456	Neil Fox (Wakefield T.).....................1961-62	390	Fred Griffiths (Wigan) 1961-62
453	Bernard Ganley (Oldham)..................1957-58	385	Colin Tyrer (Wigan) 1969-70
	Neil Fox (Wakefield T.).....................1959-60		David Watkins (Salford) 1975-76
452	Kel Coslett (St. Helens) 1971-72	384	Bernard Ganley (Oldham)..................1956-57
450	Mike Fletcher (Hull K.R.)..................1989-90		John Gallagher (London C.) 1993-94
446	Lyn Hopkins (Workington T.) 1981-82	383	Bernard Ganley (Oldham)..................1958-59
438	David Watkins (Salford) 1973-74	381	Geoff Pimblett (St. Helens)................1977-78
427	Steve Kerry (Salford) 1990-91	380	Neil Fox (Wakefield T.).....................1958-59
424	Paul Loughlin (St. Helens).................1986-87		Billy Langton (Hunslet) 1958-59
423	Frano Botica (Wigan) 1992-93	379	Harry Bath (Warrington) 1952-53
422	Frano Botica (Wigan) 1993-94		Mick Parrish (Oldham) 1981-82
418	Dean Marwood (Workington T.) 1992-93	376	Nigel Stephenson (Dewsbury)............1972-73
408	Frano Botica (Wigan) 1994-95	375	Steve Quinn (Featherstone R.) 1979-80
406	Jim Sullivan (Wigan) 1933-34	374	Jim Ledgard (Leigh) 1954-55
405	Martin Pearson (Featherstone R.) 1992-93	373	Geoff "Sammy" Lloyd (Hull) 1978-79
400	Chris Johnson (Leigh)........................1985-86	372	John Woods (Leigh)...........................1981-82

300 TRIES OR MORE IN A CAREER

796	Brian Bevan (Warrington, Blackpool B.)..	1945-1964
571	Billy Boston (Wigan, Blackpool B.)	1953-1970
446	Alf Ellaby (St. Helens, Wigan)	1926-1939
445	Martin Offiah (Widnes, Wigan, London B.)	1987-
443	Eric Batten (Wakefield T., Hunslet, Bradford N., Featherstone R.)	1933-1954
441	Lionel Cooper (Huddersfield)..	1947-1955
428	Ellery Hanley (Bradford N., Wigan, Leeds)	1978-1995
415	Johnny Ring (Wigan, Rochdale H.)	1922-1933
406	Clive Sullivan (Hull, Hull K.R., Oldham, Doncaster)	1961-1985
401	John Atkinson (Leeds, Carlisle)...	1966-1983
399	Eric Harris (Leeds)..	1930-1939
395	Tom Van Vollenhoven (St. Helens)..	1957-1968
386	Albert Rosenfeld (Huddersfield, Wakefield T., Bradford N.)	1909-1924
383	Jim Lewthwaite (Barrow)	1943-1957
374	Ike Southward (Workington T., Oldham, Whitehaven)	1952-1969
372	Barney Hudson (Salford)..	1928-1946
358	Neil Fox (Wakefield T., Bradford N., Hull K.R., York, Bramley, Huddersfield)	1956-1979
342	Mick Sullivan (Huddersfield, Wigan, St. Helens, York, Dewsbury)	1952-1966
328	Garry Schofield (Hull, Leeds, Huddersfield G.)...	1983-
321	Johnny Lawrenson (Wigan, Workington T., Swinton)...	1939-1954
321	Shaun Edwards (Wigan, London B., Bradford B.)	1983-
319	Eric Ashton (Wigan)..	1955-1969
314	Jim Leytham (Lancaster, Wigan)..	1901-1912
312	Brian Nordgren (Wigan)	1946-1955
311	Alan Smith (Leeds)	1962-1983
310	Jim Lomas (Bramley, Salford, Oldham, York)	1902-1923
304	Alan Hardisty (Castleford, Leeds)..	1958-1974
302	Maurice Richards (Salford)..	1969-1983

1,000 OR MORE GOALS IN A CAREER

2,867	Jim Sullivan (Wigan)	1921-1946
2,575	Neil Fox (Wakefield T., Bradford N., Hull K.R., York, Bramley, Huddersfield)	1956-1979
1,768	Cyril Kellett (Hull K.R., Featherstone R.)	1956-1974
1,698	Kel Coslett (St. Helens, Rochdale H.)	1962-1979
1,677	Gus Risman (Salford, Workington T., Batley)	1929-1954
1,591	John Woods (Leigh, Bradford N., Warrington, Rochdale H.)	1976-1992
1,578	Steve Quinn (York, Featherstone R.)	1970-1988
1,560	Jim Ledgard (Leeds, Dewsbury, Leigh)	1944-1961
1,478	Lewis Jones (Leeds)	1952-1964
1,398	Bernard Ganley (Oldham)	1951-1961
1,376	Ray Dutton (Widnes, Whitehaven)	1966-1981
1,342	David Watkins (Salford, Swinton, Cardiff C.)	1967-1983
1,306	George Fairbairn (Wigan, Hull K.R.)	1974-1990
1,273	Mike Fletcher (Hull K.R.)	1985-
1,272	Colin Tyrer (Leigh, Wigan, Barrow, Hull K.R.)	1962-1978
1,189	Frank Dyson (Huddersfield, Oldham)	1949-1965
1,179	Terry Clawson (Featherstone R., Bradford N., Hull K.R., Leeds, Oldham, York, Wakefield T., Huddersfield, Hull)	1957-1980
1,169	Steve Hesford (Warrington, Huddersfield B.)	1975-1986
1,154	Derek Whitehead (Swinton, Oldham, Warrington)	1964-1979
1,127	Geoff "Sammy" Lloyd (Castleford, Hull)	1970-1983
1,092	John McKeown (Whitehaven)	1948-1961
1,081	Vic Yorke (York)	1954-1967
1,075	Ken Gowers (Swinton)	1954-1973
1,060	Lee Crooks (Hull, Leeds, Castleford T.)	1980-1997
1,044	Billy Langton (Hunslet)	1955-1966
1,030	Ron James (Halifax)	1961-1971
1,016	Iain MacCorquodale (Salford, Workington T., Fulham, Blackpool B., Rochdale H.)	1970-1982
1,014	Mark Aston (Sheffield E., Bramley, Featherstone R.)	1986-

2,500 OR MORE POINTS IN A CAREER

6,220	Neil Fox (Wakefield T., Bradford N., Hull K.R., York, Bramley, Huddersfield)	1956-1979
6,022	Jim Sullivan (Wigan)	1921-1946
4,050	Gus Risman (Salford, Workington T., Batley)	1929-1954
3,985	John Woods (Leigh, Bradford N., Warrington, Rochdale H.)	1976-1992
3,686	Cyril Kellett (Hull K.R., Featherstone R.)	1956-1974
3,545	Kel Coslett (St. Helens, Rochdale H.)	1962-1979
3,445	Lewis Jones (Leeds)	1952-1964
3,438	Steve Quinn (York, Featherstone R.)	1970-1988
3,279	Jim Ledgard (Leeds, Dewsbury, Leigh)	1944-1961
3,117	David Watkins (Salford, Swinton, Cardiff C.)	1967-1982
2,902	Colin Tyrer (Leigh, Wigan, Barrow, Hull K.R.)	1962-1978
2,894	George Fairbairn (Wigan, Hull K.R.)	1974-1990
2,844	Bernard Ganley (Oldham)	1951-1961
2,786	Ray Dutton (Widnes, Whitehaven)	1966-1981
2,769	Mike Fletcher (Hull K.R.)	1985-

2,574   Terry Clawson (Featherstone R., Bradford N., Hull K.R., Leeds,
        Oldham, York, Wakefield T., Huddersfield, Hull)... 1957-1980
2,561   Frank Dyson (Huddersfield, Oldham) 1949-1965

650 APPEARANCES OR MORE IN A CAREER

● Figures in brackets denote substitute appearances included in main total.

928	Jim Sullivan (Wigan)...	1921-1946
873	Gus Risman (Salford, Workington T., Batley)..	1929-1954
828 (28)	Neil Fox (Wakefield T., Bradford N., Hull K.R., York, Bramley, Huddersfield)	1956-1979
776 (57)	Jeff Grayshon (Dewsbury, Bradford N., Leeds, Featherstone R., Batley).................	1969-1995
740 (46)	Graham Idle (Bramley, Wakefield T., Bradford N., Hunslet, Rochdale H., Sheffield E., Doncaster, Nottingham C., Highfield).............................	1969-1993
738 (25)	Colin Dixon (Halifax, Salford, Hull K.R.)	1961-1981
727 (9)	Paul Charlton (Workington T., Salford, Blackpool B.)	1961-1981
695 (26)	Keith Mumby (Bradford N., Sheffield E., Keighley C., Ryedale-York, Wakefield T.)..	1973-1995
691 (1)	Ernie Ashcroft (Wigan, Huddersfield, Warrington)	1942-1962
688	Brian Bevan (Warrington, Blackpool B.)	1945-1964
683 (24)	John Wolford (Bramley, Bradford N., Dewsbury, Hunslet)........................	1962-1985
682	Joe Ferguson (Oldham)...	1899-1923
679	Joe Oliver (Huddersfield, Batley, Hull, Hull K.R.)	1923-1945
669 (33)	John Joyner (Castleford)...	1973-1992
665	George Carmichael (Hull K.R., Bradford N.)	1929-1950
663 (25)	John Holmes (Leeds)	1968-1989
662 (28)	Mal Aspey (Widnes, Fulham, Wigan, Salford)	1964-1983
651	Jack Miller (Warrington, Leigh)..	1926-1947

Champions: A triumphant Wigan Warriors captain
Andrew Farrell after leading his side to victory in the first
Super League Grand Final.

LEAGUE

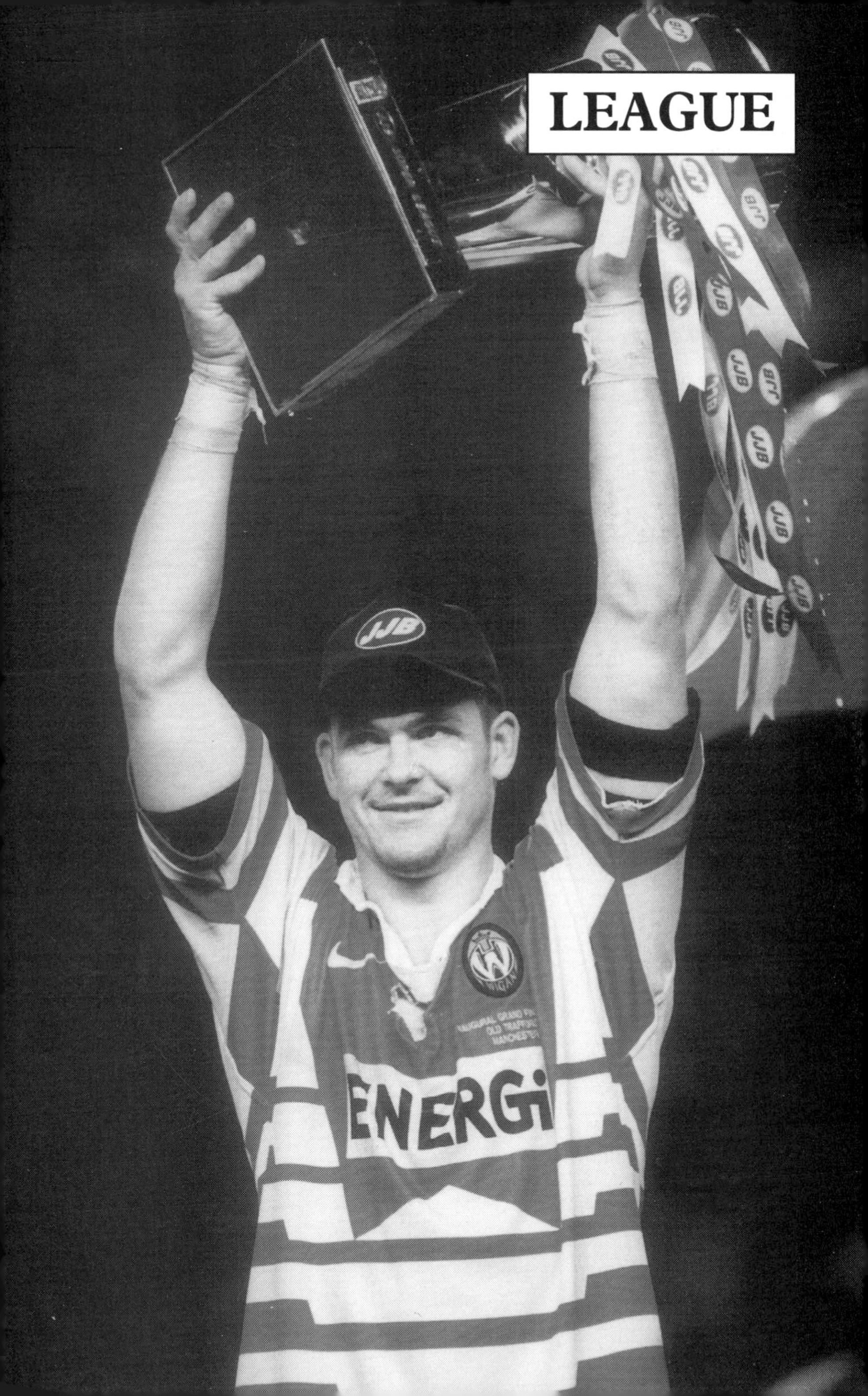

LEAGUE

JJB SUPER LEAGUE
1998 Grand Final

The inaugural Super League Grand Final was a huge success with Wigan Warriors beating Leeds Rhinos 10-4 in a tension-packed thriller that was in doubt right up to the last minute. And any fears that the public had not accepted the new play-off formula to decide the championship were allayed when a crowd of 43,553 defied heavy rain to make it a night to remember by creating an emotionally charged atmosphere at Manchester United's magnificent Old Trafford soccer stadium. The attendance surpassed the biggest for a Premiership final*, which the new format replaced, and produced record receipts of £637,105 for any club match outside Wembley.

Critics of the new format, who believed the championship should go to the club finishing at the top, would at least gain some satisfaction from Wigan's victory as they had finished four points clear of second-placed Leeds. But Wigan's only Super League defeats had both been against Leeds before beating them 17-4 in the qualifying semi-final.

That there was little to choose between the two teams was confirmed in the final as both scored just one try with Andrew Farrell's three goals proving the vital difference and completing his feat of scoring in all 30 of Wigan's matches throughout the season. Two of the goals were penalties and it was not until the last minute, when the Wigan captain banged over his second, that he could be sure of lifting the Super League trophy for the first time and a record cash prize of £275,000.

Despite Farrell's crucial kicking role, it was Jason Robinson who grabbed most of the headlines with a superb solo try that went a long way to earning him the Harry Sunderland Trophy as the man of the match. The try came out of nothing and against the run of play as Leeds had dominated the first half, which looked certain to finish with them 4-0 ahead until Robinson struck. From a play-the-ball near touch and 20 metres from Leeds' line, the

right winger shot forward in his unique style to leave a trail of defenders behind as he dodged his way between the posts. Farrell added the simple goal and Wigan went in at the interval 6-4 up.

Robinson continued to be a major threat to the Rhinos and was a popular winner of the man of the match award to become only the fifth player to win both the Harry Sunderland and Lance Todd trophies. His Lance Todd Trophy performance had also been against Leeds when he scored two tries in the 30-10 Silk Cut Challenge Cup final victory at Wembley in 1995.

This was Wigan's seventh successive appearance in an end of season final at Old Trafford, having won the Premiership six times in that period, including the last four in succession. But it was Leeds who made the first impact after the teams had entered the 'Theatre of Dreams' to a nerve-jangling roar and a rousing fanfare of classical music. They put Wigan under tremendous pressure and took the lead after 21 minutes when Richard Blackmore burst on to Ryan Sheridan's pass and charged in from close range.

With Super League player of the year Iestyn Harris by far the most impressive attacker in the first half, Leeds gave Wigan several more anxious moments without being able to add to their score and the turning point came with Robinson's stunning try. The only second-half scores were Farrell's two penalty goals, the first for a foul by Marc Glanville in the 47th minute and then the last minute clincher when Graham Holroyd struck out in frustration shortly after he lost the ball on Leeds' last desperate attack.

Wigan's victory completed a unique worldwide double for coach John Monie, who had also steered Parramatta to Grand Final success in Australia. A novelty for a British final was that they copied the Australian idea of presenting the winners with gold rings instead of medals.

In a game of ferocious defensive commitment, Leeds second row Anthony Farrell and Wigan hooker Robbie McCormack headed the tackle count with 38 each. Robinson was credited with most progress made on attack with 204 metres, followed by Harris's 158. Of the 20 penalties, seven were for fouls – five of them against Leeds.

* The record Premiership final attendance was 42,043 for the 1991 clash between Hull and Widnes, which was preceded by the Divisional Premiership final between Salford and Halifax.

QUOTES

JOHN MONIE (Wigan coach): This was as intense as any Australian Grand Final. There is the talent over here and the state of the game is good. I'm sure Wigan would give Brisbane [Australian Grand Final winners] a good rattle-up. The World Club Championship last year was a debacle for English clubs and you need the intensity of tonight's type of matches. The Grand Final system will lift the English game. We have played Leeds three times this season before tonight and could have won all three or lost all three. It does come down to a few points on the night. That is all there was in it.

GRAHAM MURRAY (Leeds coach): I'm proud of the fellas as they played their hearts out until the end. It's disappointing to lose - that's human nature - but you can't be disappointed with the attitude and commitment of this club. If we had taken a couple of opportunities it would have been a different ball game. The extra five minutes Wigan had the ball in the second half was crucial on that pitch. It calculates to about ten sets of six coming at you.

ANDREW FARRELL (Wigan captain): That was as tough a game as I have played in. It was just like Test football. It will help our game which will only get better. We didn't perform too well in the first half, but in the second half we were really desperate and showed we wanted it. We dug deep, moved up a lot faster in defence and started hitting harder. It made it very hard for Leeds to play. We've all pulled together and this win was for everybody at the club. But tonight really belongs to the players. They're the ones who make the sacrifices.

IESTYN HARRIS (Leeds captain): We didn't play the perfect game, but we gave it 100 per cent effort. Wigan played exceptionally well in the conditions and deserved to win on the night. We had them on the rack at times but let them back into the game when we had them dead and buried in the first half. The atmosphere was fantastic and probably the best I've experienced.

KRIS RADLINSKI (Wigan full back): To win is a fantastic feeling. I can't explain how good it is. The only feeling that is similar to this was beating the Aussies. We all realise that having played in the first Grand Final, we've been part of history. And in ten years' time this ring on my finger is going to be worth a lot of money.

ADRIAN MORLEY (Leeds second row): Losing in a Grand Final is probably the worst feeling in Rugby League. Worse, perhaps, than losing in the Cup Final at Wembley. Everyone in our dressing room is totally devastated. We are all gutted; everything we have worked for all year has come to nothing.

JASON ROBINSON (Wigan, man of the match): I haven't scored that many tries this season, so I was pleased to get one just when we needed it before half-time. I just kept looking for a gap and one opened up. Although I had always wanted to play for Leeds [his home town] I've never regretted signing for Wigan.

JJB SUPER LEAGUE GRAND FINAL
Saturday 24 October 1998   Old Trafford, Manchester

WIGAN WARRIORS 10

Kris Radlinski	Full back
Jason Robinson	Wing
Danny Moore	Centre
Gary Connolly	Centre
Mark Bell	Wing
Henry Paul	Stand off
Tony Smith	Scrum half
Terry O'Connor	Prop
Robbie McCormack	Hooker
Tony Mestrov	Prop
Lee Gilmour	Second row
Stephen Holgate	Second row
Andrew Farrell, Captain	Loose forward

Substitutes
Neil Cowie for O'Connor (18–48 min. blood bin)
Mick Cassidy for McCormack (27–33 min. blood bin)
Paul Johnson for Moore (37 min.)
Simon Haughton for Gilmour (27–33 min. blood bin)
Haughton for Holgate (33 min.)
Cowie for Mestrov (54 min.)
Cassidy for Haughton (64 min.)
Holgate for Cowie (68 min.)
Haughton for Gilmour (71–75 min. blood bin.)
Mestrov for O'Connor (75 min. blood bin)

T: Robinson
G: Farrell (3)

Coach: John Monie

Scrums: 11-7
Penalties: 13-7
Half-time: 6-4
Attendance: 43,553

LEEDS RHINOS 4

Iestyn Harris, Captain
Leroy Rivett
Richard Blackmore
Brad Godden
Francis Cummins
Daryl Powell
Ryan Sheridan
Martin Masella
Terry Newton
Darren Fleary
Adrian Morley
Anthony Farrell
Marc Glanville

Substitutes
Jamie Mathiou for Masella (25 min.)
Marcus St. Hilaire for Powell (half-time)
Graham Holroyd for Newton (49 min.)
Andy Hay for Fleary (54 min.)
Powell for Godden (58 min.)
Masella for Mathiou (71 min.)

T: Blackmore

Coach: Graham Murray

Referee: Russell Smith (Castleford)
Harry Sunderland Trophy for Man
of the Match: Jason Robinson (Wigan)
Receipts: £637,105

HOW THE SCORING WENT

21 min.	Blackmore (Leeds) try	0-4
38 min.	Robinson (Wigan) try, Farrell goal	6-4
47 min.	Farrell (Wigan) penalty goal	8-4
79 min.	Farrell (Wigan) penalty goal	10-4

Super try: Jason Robinson heads for the superb try that swung the final Wigan's way.

JJB SUPER LEAGUE 1998
PLAY-OFF FORMULA

Although the old one division championship had been decided by a top four play-off for over 60 years, this was the first time that the leaders of the top division had not automatically been awarded the title. The introduction of Super League play-off was similar to the Australian method which had decided their Premiership for many years.

The Super League play-off involves the top five clubs with the higher placed club in each match having home ground advantage apart from the final, which is played at a neutral venue. The formula greatly favours the top club as they have a bye at the first stage and then need to win only one match to the reach the final, while the fifth club would have to beat the other four to win the title.

(A) Elimination play-off
Fourth v Fifth (Losers eliminated)
(B) Qualifying play-off
Second v Third

(C) Elimination semi-final
B losers v A winners
(Losers eliminated)
(D) Qualifying semi-final
Leaders v B winners
(Winners through to final)

(E) Final eliminator
D losers v C winners

Elimination play-off
St. Helens 46 v Bradford B. 24

The inaugural Super League play-offs got off to an incident-packed and controversial start with Bradford losing a 12-6 lead after their captain Graeme Bradley was sent off in the 16th minute of his last match before retiring. Many thought that the alleged offence – illegal use of the elbow on St. Helens winger Chris Smith – did not warrant dismissal and this view was supported by the disciplinary committee who recorded a not guilty verdict. St. Helens took advantage of their extra man to race into a clear lead, but five minutes from the end referee Stuart Cummings came in for more criticism when he sent off Saints centre Paul Newlove for a high tackle. It seemed a harsh decision and again the disciplinary committee took a lenient view as they decided that the sending off was sufficient punishment.

Qualifying play-off
Leeds R. 13 v Halifax B. S. 6

Leeds gained revenge for a 42-0 defeat in their last Super League match of the season at Halifax a week earlier with a hard-earned victory in a match that lived up to all the predictions that the play-offs would be full of intensity. Rhinos coach Graham Murray had rested a few key players at Halifax, including captain Iestyn Harris, and they made all the difference when they returned for this showdown. But Halifax took a 6-0 interval before Marcus St. Hilaire went on to change the course of the game with a brilliant break that led to Anthony Farrell scoring Leeds' first try. The substitute full back then went through on his own for a superb solo try.

Elimination semi-final
Halifax B. S. 30 v St. Helens 37

St. Helens gained the only away victory of the play-offs, but almost threw it away as Halifax hit back from being 30-2 down going into the last 30 minutes. Halifax scored five tries in their desperate bid to overtake a lethargic Saints before time ran out for them. St. Helens looked unstoppable during the first half when they raced to a 24-2 interval lead, inspired by half backs Tommy Martyn and Sean Long. The Saints left wing partnership continued their outstanding run of form with centre Paul Newlove scoring one try and wing partner Anthony Sullivan adding two more.

Qualifying semi-final
Wigan W. 17 v Leeds R. 4

Wigan became the first club to win through to the inaugural Grand Final when the Super League leaders gained the victory over Leeds when it mattered most. Leeds had completed a League double over the Warriors during the season, but could not quite make it a hat-trick in another match of high intensity in pouring rain. The highlight of Wigan's victory was a spectacular 80-metre solo try by Lee Gilmour which must have gone a long way to earning the young forward a place in Great Britain's Test squad to face New Zealand.

Final eliminator
Leeds R. 44 v St. Helens 16

Leeds defied all the pre-match predictions that this would be a close, hard-fought battle by sweeping aside St. Helens with a seven-try onslaught. It was as good as all over by half-time as the Rhinos charged to a 24-4 lead and never relaxed their grip on the game. Victory was achieved in classic style with five of their tries going to wingers. Francis Cummins scored the only hat-trick of the play-offs and Leroy Rivett confirmed his increasing promise with two on the other flank.

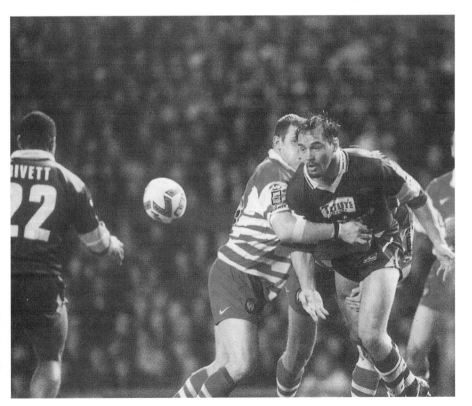

Moving on: Richard Blackmore keeps the Leeds Rhinos attack moving.

1998 JJB SUPER LEAGUE CHAMPIONSHIP

Wigan Warriors finished at the top of the JJB Super League Championship table, but there was no trophy or prize money for them until they had beaten Leeds Rhinos in the Grand Final. It was the first time that the top division title had been decided by a play-off.

Wigan equalled the record of the previous Super League leaders, St. Helens and Bradford Bulls, by losing only two matches and also matched the record they achieved three times themselves in the old Division One seasons of 1986-87, 1994-95 and 1995-96. Leeds were the only team to beat Wigan, 16-8 at home and 15-8 away, to complete their first League double over them since 1979-80.

Wigan captain Andrew Farrell became the first player to score in every Super League round throughout a season to finish with 254 points from six tries and a chart-topping 115 goals. The loose forward also maintained his record of being the only player to have appeared in every round of Super League since its launch in 1996, having been in Wigan's starting line-up 67 times. Other players to start every one of Wigan's 23 Super League matches in 1998 were full back Kris Radlinski, centre Gary Connolly, stand off Henry Paul and prop Tony Mestrov. Winger Jason Robinson also played in every match, including one as a substitute.

With Australian John Monie back as coach, Wigan were made 8-11 favourites to lift the title and they lived up to those odds by winning their first five matches before losing at Leeds in a tremendous encounter before a capacity crowd of 18,000. They strung together another 11 successive victories until Leeds again toppled them in another action-packed thriller. Wigan then won all five of their remaining matches to finish four points clear of Leeds. They had led from the third round apart from a four-round period in May-June when Leeds took over the leadership.

An innovation during the season was the staging of six 'On the Road' matches at venues outside the normal Rugby League strongholds, to test the ground for further expansion. Although the attendances were disappointing, totalling only 31,387, the venture was regarded as an overall success with the matches gaining favourable local media support in each area. The matches formed an extra round for Super League and were played over three weekends in July as follows: Leeds v Salford (at Gateshead), Halifax v Sheffield (at Northampton), Bradford v London (at Edinburgh), Huddersfield v Hull (Gateshead), Castleford v Warrington (at Cardiff) and St. Helens v Wigan (at Swansea).

Leeds Rhinos, with Australian coach Graham Murray in charge for the first time, showed a vast improvement on their two previous Super League seasons and won their first nine matches before going down to a shock 22-10 defeat at Hull Sharks. Captain Iestyn Harris was voted Super League's player of the season after finishing as the division's top scorer with 255 points. But he missed the chance of getting the three points to set a new Super League record when he was rested for the last match at Halifax Blue Sox. A few other players were also rested for that game as Leeds were already assured of second place and the two teams were due to meet in the play-off a week later. Leeds' weakened team were swept aside by Halifax and went down to a 42-0 defeat. Two weeks earlier Leeds had run up a record Super League away score with their 72-16 win at Huddersfield Giants.

Halifax Blue Sox and Castleford Tigers made the most progress over the year, both moving up four places. But it was Halifax who gained the most accolades as they made a strong bid for League honours to leap from seventh to third place after being rated among the outsiders at 80-1 in the pre-season betting. John Pendlebury's major role in the vast improvement earned him the Super League coach of the year award. Yet the players had to persuade him to stay at the club after he had quit early in the season over alleged interference in team matters by some members of the board. Halifax then went on to gain several impressive victories, including a double over the then reigning champions Bradford Bulls.

St. Helens had a troubled first half of the season with the departure of chief executive David Howes and an early decision not to retain coach Shaun McRae at the end of the season. They also transferred Bobbie Goulding to Huddersfield following disciplinary measures against the half back for off-the-field incidents. The trio had played a major role in Saints winning both the Super League title and the Challenge Cup (twice) in the previous two years. McRae agreed to see out the rest of the season and the players responded to lose only one of their last nine League matches. Anthony Sullivan finished as Super League's top tryscorer with 20, including a match record five at London Broncos.

Bradford Bulls, the defending champions, fell well below the high standard that they had set the season before and just managed to scrape into the top five play-offs. Surprisingly, four of their 11 defeats were at home although they still managed to pull in the season's best average crowd of more than 13,000.

Castleford Tigers, who had struggled against relegation in 1997, made steady progress throughout the season to move up from 10th to sixth place after being undefeated in their last four matches. The highlight of their season was a 22-16 home defeat of Leeds.

London Broncos were perhaps the biggest underachievers of the season. With so much expected of them after finishing second in 1997 they slumped to a disappointing seventh place. The Broncos had begun as joint 4-1 second favourites with Bradford, but like the Bulls they failed to match expectations and managed only one win in their first five matches. A major blow was an injury to Martin Offiah, which ruled out the free-scoring winger for most of the season.

Sheffield Eagles' season was dominated by their Silk Cut Challenge Cup run which culminated in the shock defeat of Wigan at Wembley and their League campaign seemed to be a lasting hangover. Following their Cup semi-final success, Sheffield lost their first three Super League matches and won only one of five matches after their Wembley triumph. Their top five hopes soon began to fade and they had to settle for equalling the previous season's eighth place finish.

Hull Sharks, promoted as First Division champions, did at least as well as expected in their first Super League season to finish a creditable ninth. They opened their campaign with a surprise win at Sheffield, followed by a home defeat of London, before being hit by a run of seven successive defeats which ended with the shock home success over League leaders Leeds.

Warrington Wolves never recovered from an opening sequence of four successive defeats and finished one below their 1997 ninth place. Home victories over Halifax and Bradford suggested that they should have been challenging for a top five place, but they lacked consistency and were always struggling to keep away from the bottom.

Salford Reds, who had done so well to finish sixth in their first Super League season of 1997, failed to maintain the pace this time and slumped to second off the bottom. The highlight of their season was an 11-10 home win over reigning champions Bradford, but defeats in their last four matches left them with only six wins and a draw.

Huddersfield Giants opened their first season in Super League with their biggest home League attendance (12,417) for 36 years, but the 38-6 defeat against Bradford was a warning of what was to follow. They finished with only two victories – the worst record in Super League history. Other unwanted Super League records were the run of 13 successive defeats and the most points conceded in a home match when they lost 72-16 to Leeds. Ironically, Huddersfield's two wins were while Garry Schofield was still in charge as coach and they never won another after he departed following a 48-6 13th round home defeat by Halifax. Schofield, in his first season as a coach, was the only one not to complete the season, although St. Helens gave Shaun McRae his notice in mid-term. Phil Veivers became Huddersfield's temporary coach until the end of the season, with Malcolm Reilly taking over for 1999.

● JJB Sports replaced Stones as the sponsors of the Super League Championship in 1998 with a two-year deal worth about £1.5m.

Sharks close in: Salford Reds centre Nathan McAvoy in the grip of Hull Sharks.

1998 JJB SUPER LEAGUE CHAMPIONSHIP

	P.	W.	D.	L.	Dg.	FOR			AGAINST				Pts.
						Gls.	Trs.	Pts.	Dg.	Gls.	Trs.	Pts.	
1. Wigan Warriors	23	21	0	2	0	123	129	762	6	34	37	222	42
2. Leeds Rhinos	23	19	0	4	8	103	112	662	5	62	60	369	38
3. Halifax Blue Sox	23	18	0	5	4	103	112	658	4	59	67	390	36
4. St. Helens	23	14	1	8	5	106	114	673	3	80	74	459	29
5. Bradford Bulls	23	12	0	11	4	77	85	498	6	66	78	450	24
6. Castleford Tigers	23	10	1	12	4	65	78	446	4	77	91	522	21
7. London Broncos	23	10	0	13	7	60	72	415	4	66	85	476	20
8. Sheffield Eagles	23	8	2	13	7	80	82	495	5	78	95	541	18
9. Hull Sharks	23	8	0	15	3	61	74	421	4	89	98	574	16
10. Warrington Wolves	23	7	1	15	5	59	72	411	7	97	111	645	15
11. Salford Reds	23	6	1	16	3	44	57	319	3	94	96	575	13
12. Huddersfield Giants	23	2	0	21	2	39	52	288	1	118	147	825	4

Fixture format: All clubs played each other home and away plus one 'On the Road' match at venues outside the traditional Rugby League area. The 'Road' matches were based on positions in the previous season: 1 v. 2; 3 v. 4, 5 v. 6 and so on. The top five clubs qualified for the Grand Final play-off to decide the championship. No relegation.

Totals: 138 matches; 52 drop goals; 920 goals; 1,039 tries; 6,048 points
1997: 132 matches; 45 drop goals; 948 goals; 1,056 tries; 6,165 points
1996: 132 matches; 32 drop goals; 1,090 goals; 1,288 tries; 7,364 points

1998 PRE-SEASON BETTING FOR SUPER LEAGUE CHAMPIONSHIP

Coral's pre-season odds:
8-11 Wigan W.; **4-1** Bradford B., London B.; **7-1** St. Helens; **14-1** Leeds R.; **33-1** Sheffield E.; **50-1** Castleford T.; **66-1** Salford R.; **80-1** Halifax B.S.; **100-1** Warrington W.; **150-1** Hull S., Huddersfield G.

Henry Paul: A key figure in Wigan Warriors' championship-winning season.

JJB SUPER LEAGUE TOP TEN SCORERS 1998
(League matches only. Not including Play-off matches)

TOP TEN TRIES
1. Anthony Sullivan (St. Helens) 20
2. Francis Cummins (Leeds Rhinos)....................17
3. Gary Connolly (Wigan Warriors)......................15
   Tony Smith (Wigan Warriors) 15
5. Keith Senior (Sheffield Eagles) 14
   Paul Newlove (St. Helens)...............................14
7. Iestyn Harris (Leeds Rhinos) 13
   Danny Arnold (Huddersfield Giants) 13
   Gavin Clinch (Halifax Blue Sox)......................13
10. Bright Sodje (Sheffield Eagles)........................12
    Sean Long (St. Helens) 12
    Paul Johnson (Wigan Warriors) 12
    Henry Paul (Wigan Warriors) 12
    Tevita Vaikona (Bradford Bulls) 12
    Martin Moana (Halifax Blue Sox)...................12

TOP TEN GOALS
1. Andrew Farrell (Wigan Warriors) 115
2. Iestyn Harris (Leeds Rhinos) ....(3) 103
3. Steve McNamara(Bradford Bulls).............(3) 76
   Sean Long (St. Helens) ....(3) 76
5. Martin Pearson (Halifax Blue Sox) 64
6. Bobbie Goulding (Huddersfield G.)...........(2) 46
   Lee Briers (Warrington Wolves).................(5) 46
8. Mark Aston (Sheffield Eagles) ....(2) 44
9. Terry Matterson (London Broncos)...........(4) 36
10. Brad Davis (Castleford Tigers) ....(2) 30
    Graeme Hallas (Hull Sharks)....................(1) 30
( ) *Drop goals included in total*

MOST DROP GOALS
Lee Briers (Warrington Wolves) 5

TOP TEN POINTS

	Trs.	Gls.	Dg.	Pts.
1. Iestyn Harris (Leeds Rhinos) 13		100	3	255
2. Andrew Farrell (Wigan Warriors) 6		115	0	254
3. Sean Long (St. Helens) 12		73	3	197
4. Steve McNamara (Bradford Bulls) 1		73	3	153
5. Martin Pearson (Halifax Blue Sox) 4		64	0	144
6. Lee Briers (Warrington Wolves) 4		41	5	103
7. Bobbie Goulding (Huddersfield Giants).. 2		44	2	98
8. Gavin Clinch (Halifax Blue Sox) 13		20	2	94
9. Mark Aston (Sheffield Eagles) 0		42	2	86
10. Danny Orr (Castleford Tigers) 10		21	0	82

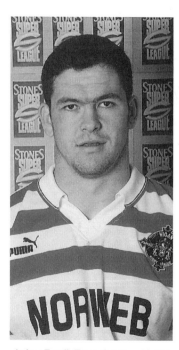

Anthony Sullivan: Top try scorer with 20.

Andrew Farrell: Top goals scorer with 115.

SUPER LEAGUE RECORDS

● League match records do not include scores in abandoned matches that were replayed. Super League records do not include play-off matches.

INDIVIDUAL

Match records

Most tries: 5 by Mike Umaga (Halifax B.S.) v. Workington T., 21 July 1996

Jason Robinson (Wigan) v. Leeds, 9 August 1996

Tony Smith (Wigan W.) v. Sheffield E., 29 June 1997

Anthony Sullivan (St. Helens) at London B., 18 September 1998

Most goals: 11 by Terry Matterson (London B.) v. Workington T., 21 April 1996

Bobbie Goulding (St. Helens) v. Castleford T., 27 May 1996

John Schuster (Halifax B.S.) v. Workington T., 21 July 1996

Andrew Farrell (Wigan W.) at St. Helens, 26 May 1997

Andrew Farrell (Wigan W.) v. Paris S.G., 30 May 1997

Most points: 28 (6g,4t) by Greg Barwick (London B.) v. Castleford T., 25 August 1996

Season records

Most tries: 28 by Paul Newlove (St. Helens) 1996

Most goals: 120 by Bobbie Goulding (St. Helens) 1996

Most points: 257 (5t,117g,3dg) by Bobbie Goulding (St. Helens) 1996

Scored in every round: Andrew Farrell (Wigan W.) 23 matches in 1998

Career records

Most tries: 52 by Paul Newlove (St. Helens)

Most goals: 327 by Andrew Farrell (Wigan W.)

Most points: 723 (324g,3dg,18t) by Andrew Farrell (Wigan W.)

Most appearances: Andrew Farrell is the only player to have played in all 67 rounds of Super League, having appeared in Wigan Warriors' starting line-up in every match from the start of the inaugural 1996 season.

Other records

Longest tryscoring sequence: 9 matches by Paul Newlove (St. Helens), 1996; Paul Sterling (Leeds R.), 1997

Longest goals and pointscoring sequence: 37 matches by Andrew Farrell (Wigan W.) 1997 - 1998

Youngest player: John Duffy (Warrington W.) was 16 years 262 days on his debut v. London B., 21 March 1997 (Born 2 July 1980)

Oldest player: Graham Steadman (Castleford T.) was 35 years 266 days when he made his last Super League appearance, as a substitute, v. Sheffield E., 31 August 1997 (Born 8 December 1961)

TEAM

Highest score and widest margin: Wigan 78 v. Workington T. 4, 24 August 1996

Highest away score: Huddersfield G. 16 v. Leeds R. 72, 13 September 1998

Widest away win margin: Workington T. 0 v. St. Helens 62, 31 March 1996

Lowest winning score and lowest points aggregate: Salford R. 4 v. Castleford T. 0, 16 March 1997

Highest points aggregate: (96) Leeds 68 v. Workington T. 28, 18 August 1996

Most points by losing team: Warrington W. 37 v. Paris S.G. 34, 27 April 1997

Highest score draw: St. Helens 32 v. Castleford T. 32, 13 September 1998

Longest winning run: 21 by Bradford B. Won last match of 1996 and first 20 of 1997 (Also longest unbeaten run)

Best opening sequence: 20 wins by Bradford B. 1997

Longest losing run and run without a win: 13 by Huddersfield G. 1998

Longest opening run of defeats: 10 by Castleford T. 1997 (Also longest opening run without a win)

Biggest attendance: 20,429 Wigan v. St. Helens, 21 June 1996

Lowest attendance: 500 Paris S.G. v. Salford R., 2 July 1997

Mike Umaga: Record five tries in a match.

COMBINED SUPER LEAGUE AND DIVISION ONE RECORDS

● Taking into account matches played in Super League, the old style Division One which ran from 1973-74 to 1994-95 inclusive, and the 1995–96 Centenary Championship

INDIVIDUAL

Match records

Most tries: 6 by Shane Cooper (St. Helens) v. Hull, 17 February 1988

Most goals: 13 by Geoff Pimblett (St. Helens) v. Bramley, 5 March 1978

Most points: 38 by (4t,11g) Bob Beardmore (Castleford) v. Barrow, 22 March 1987

Season records

Most tries: 44 by Ellery Hanley (Wigan) 1986-87

Most goals: 130 by Steve Hesford (Warrington) 1978-79

Most points: 326 by (18t,126g,2dg) John Schuster (Halifax) 1994-95

Steve Hesford: Record 130 goals in a season.

TEAM

Highest score and widest margin: Leeds 90 v. Barrow 0, 11 February 1990

Highest away score: Rochdale H. 12 v. Castleford 76, 3 March 1991

Widest away margin: Doncaster 0 v. Halifax 72, 9 October 1994

Most points by losing team: London B. 44 v. Castleford 50, 21 January 1996

Scoreless draw: Wigan 0 v. Castleford 0, 26 January 1974

Highest score draw: Leeds 46 v. Sheffield E. 46, 10 April 1994

Best opening sequence: 20 wins by Bradford B., 1997

Longest winning run: 25 by St. Helens. Won last 13 of 1985–86 and first 12 of 1986-87 (Also longest unbeaten run)

Longest losing run: 20 by Whitehaven 1983-84; Rochdale H. 1990-91

Longest losing run from start of season: 20 by Whitehaven 1983-84

Longest run without a win: 23, including 3 draws, by Whitehaven 1981-82 (Also longest opening run without a win)

Biggest attendance: 29,839 Wigan v. St. Helens, 9 April 1993

Top ten career tries

279 Ellery Hanley (Bradford N., Wigan, Leeds)
250 Martin Offiah (Widnes, Wigan, London B.)
194 Shaun Edwards (Wigan, London B., Bradford B.)
178 Phil Ford (Warrington, Wigan, Bradford N., Leeds, Salford)
175 Garry Schofield (Hull, Leeds, Huddersfield G.)
165 Keith Fielding (Salford)
154 Paul Newlove (Featherstone R., Bradford N., St. Helens)
144 David Smith (Wakefield T., Leeds, Bradford N.)
139 Stuart Wright (Wigan, Widnes)
136 Roy Mathias (St. Helens)

Most career goals

862 John Woods (Leigh, Bradford N., Warrington)

Most career points

2,150 John Woods (Leigh, Bradford N., Warrington)

20 tries in a season

1973-74	36	Keith Fielding (Salford)
	29	Roy Mathias (St. Helens)
	21	David Smith (Wakefield T.)
1974-75	21	Maurice Richards (Salford)
	21	Roy Mathias (St. Helens)
1975-76	26	Maurice Richards (Salford)
	20	David Smith (Wakefield T.)
1976-77	22	David Topliss (Wakefield T.)
	21	Keith Fielding (Salford)
	21	Ged Dunn (Hull K.R.)
	20	David Smith (Leeds)
	20	Stuart Wright (Widnes)
1977-78	26	Keith Fielding (Salford)
	25	Steve Fenton (Castleford)
	24	Stuart Wright (Widnes)
	20	David Smith (Leeds)
	20	Bruce Burton (Castleford)
	20	John Bevan (Warrington)
1978-79	28	Steve Hartley (Hull K.R.)
1979-80	24	Keith Fielding (Salford)

21 Roy Mathias (St. Helens)
21 Steve Hubbard (Hull K.R.)
20 David Smith (Leeds)
1980-81 20 Steve Hubbard (Hull K.R.)
1981-82 – David Hobbs (Featherstone R.) was top with 19
1982-83 22 Bob Eccles (Warrington)
20 Steve Evans (Hull)
1983-84 28 Garry Schofield (Hull)
23 John Woods (Leigh)
20 James Leuluai (Hull)
1984-85 40 Ellery Hanley (Bradford N.)
34 Gary Prohm (Hull K.R.)
23 Henderson Gill (Wigan)
22 Barry Ledger (St. Helens)
22 Mal Meninga (St. Helens)
1985-86 22 Ellery Hanley (Wigan)
1986-87 44 Ellery Hanley (Wigan)
24 Phil Ford (Bradford N.)
24 Henderson Gill (Wigan)
23 Garry Schofield (Hull)
21 John Henderson (Leigh)
1987-88 33 Martin Offiah (Widnes)
22 Ellery Hanley (Wigan)
1988-89 37 Martin Offiah (Widnes)
20 Grant Anderson (Castleford)
1989-90 28 Martin Offiah (Widnes)
25 Mark Preston (Wigan)
20 Steve Larder (Castleford)
1990-91 22 Martin Offiah (Widnes)
22 Les Quirk (St. Helens)
20 Ellery Hanley (Wigan)
1991-92 31 John Devereux (Widnes)
27 Greg Austin (Halifax)
25 Shaun Edwards (Wigan)
23 Mark Preston (Halifax)
1992-93 24 Shaun Edwards (Wigan)
23 Ellery Hanley (Leeds)
20 Martin Offiah (Wigan)
20 Alan Hunte (St. Helens)
1993-94 30 St. John Ellis (Castleford)
26 Martin Offiah (Wigan)
24 Jason Critchley (Salford)
23 Paul Newlove (Bradford N.)
21 John Bentley (Halifax)
20 Anthony Sullivan (St. Helens)
1994-95 33 Martin Offiah (Wigan)
29 Ellery Hanley (Leeds)
26 John Bentley (Halifax)
25 Alan Hunte (St. Helens)
23 Paul Newlove (Bradford N.)
21 Mark Preston (Halifax)
1995-96 20 Martin Offiah (Wigan)
1996 28 Paul Newlove (St. Helens)
24 Jason Robinson (Wigan)
21 John Bentley (Halifax B.S.)
20 Henry Paul (Wigan)
1997 – Nigel Vagana (Warrington W.) top with 17
1998 20 Anthony Sullivan (St. Helens)

Top goalscorers
1973-74 126 David Watkins (Salford)
1974-75 96 Sammy Lloyd (Castleford)
1975-76 118 Sammy Lloyd (Castleford)
1976-77 113 Steve Quinn (Featherstone R.)
1977-78 116 Steve Hesford (Warrington)
1978-79 130 Steve Hesford (Warrington)
1979-80 104 Steve Hubbard (Hull K.R.)
1980-81 96 Steve Diamond (Wakefield T.)
1981-82 110 Steve Quinn (Featherstone R.)
            John Woods (Leigh)
1982-83 105 Bob Beardmore (Castleford)
1983-84 106 Steve Hesford (Warrington)
1984-85 114 Sean Day (St. Helens)
1985-86 85 David Stephenson (Wigan)
1986-87 120 Paul Loughlin (St. Helens)
1987-88 95 John Woods (Warrington)
1988-89 95 David Hobbs (Bradford N.)
1989-90 96 Paul Loughlin (St. Helens)
1990-91 85 Paul Eastwood (Hull)
1991-92 86 Frano Botica (Wigan)
1992-93 107 Frano Botica (Wigan)
1993-94 123 Frano Botica (Wigan)
1994-95 128 John Schuster (Halifax)
1995-96 90 Bobbie Goulding (St. Helens)
1996 120 Bobbie Goulding (St. Helens)
1997 109 Andrew Farrell (Wigan W.)
1998 115 Andrew Farrell (Wigan W.)

Top points-scorers
1973-74 288 (12t, 126g)   David Watkins (Salford)
1974-75 191 (3t, 91g)   Steve Quinn (York)
1975-76 254 (6t, 118g)   Sammy Lloyd (Castleford)
1976-77 244 (6t, 113g)   Steve Quinn (Featherstone R.)
1977-78 244 (5t, 113g, 3dg)   Steve Hesford (Warrington)
1978-79 258 (3t, 119g 11dg)   Steve Hesford (Warrington)
1979-80 271 (21t, 104g)   Steve Hubbard (Hull K.R.)
1980-81 238 (5t, 95g,1dg)   Steve Diamond (Wakefield T.)
1981-82 261 (14t, 109g, 1dg) John Woods (Leigh)
1982-83 249 (13t, 105g)   Bob Beardmore (Castleford)
1983-84 295 (23t, 101g, 1dg) John Woods (Leigh)
1984-85 264 (9t, 114gt)   Sean Day (St. Helens)
1985-86 228 (15t, 83g, 2dg) David Stephenson (Wigan)
1986-87 252 (3t, 123g)   Paul Loughlin (St. Helens)
1987-88 218 (8t, 91g, 4dg) John Woods (Warrington)
1988-89 214 (7t, 91g, 4dg) David Hobbs (Bradford N.)
1989-90 238 (19t, 81g)   Paul Eastwood (Hull)
1990-91 214 (11t, 85g)   Paul Eastwood (Hull)
1991-92 199 (7t, 85g, 1dg) Frano Botica (Wigan)
1992-93 248 (23t, 2dg)   Frano Botica (Leigh)
1993-94 275 (8t, 119g, 5dg) Frano Botica (Wigan
1994-95 326 (18t, 126g, 2dg) John Schuster (Halifax)
1995-96 198 (11t, 77g)   Paul Cook (Bradford B.)
1996 257 (5t, 117g, 3dg) Bobbie Goulding (St. Helens)
1997 243 (7t, 106g, 3dg) Andrew Farrell (Wigan W.)
1998 255(13t, 100g, 3dg) Iestyn Harris (Leeds R.)

PLAYERS' SUPER LEAGUE CAREER RECORDS 1996-1998
Not including play-off matches

Player	Club	Period	App	T	G	D	Pts
Abram, Darren	Oldham Bears	1996-97	25+2	11	0	0	44
Adams, Darren	Paris St. Germain	1996	9+1	1	0	0	4
Adams, Guy	Huddersfield Giants	1998	1+2	0	0	0	0
Air, Glen	London Broncos	1998	15+1	9	0	0	36
Alexander, Neil	Salford Reds	1998	0+1	0	0	0	0
Alker, Malcolm	Salford Reds	1997-98	12+1	5	0	0	20
Allen, Chris	Castleford Tigers	1996	0+1	0	0	0	0
Allen, Gavin	London Broncos	1996	9	0	0	0	0
Allen, John	Workington Town	1996	20+1	6	0	0	24
Allen, Ray	London Broncos	1996	5+3	3	0	0	12
Amone, Asa	Halifax Blue Sox	1996-97	32+8	10	0	0	40
Anderson, Grant	Castleford Tigers	1996-97	15+6	3	0	0	12
Anderson, Paul	Bradford Bulls	1997	10+7	3	0	0	12
	Halifax Blue Sox	1996	5+1	1	0	0	4
Anderson, Paul	St. Helens	1996-98	2+28	4	1	0	18
Anselme, Eric	Halifax Blue Sox	1997	0+2	0	0	0	0
Armstrong, Colin	Workington Town	1996	11+2	1	0	0	4
Armswood, Richard	Workington Town	1996	5+1	1	0	0	4
Arnold, Danny	Huddersfield Giants	1998	23	13	0	0	52
	St. Helens	1996-97	40+1	33	0	0	132
Aston, Mark	Sheffield Eagles	1996-98	54+4	5	202	4	428
Atcheson, Paul	St. Helens	1998	23	7	0	0	28
	Oldham Bears	1996-97	40	21	0	0	84
Azema, Jerome	Paris St. Germain	1997	0+1	0	0	0	0
Baildon, David	Hull Sharks	1998	14+1	3	0	0	12
Baldwin, Simon	Halifax Blue Sox	1996-98	41+14	16	0	1	65
Ball, Rob	Wigan Warriors	1998	0+1	0	0	0	0
Banks, Michael	Bradford Bulls	1998	0+1	0	0	0	0
Banquet, Frederic	Paris St. Germain	1996	16+2	7	4	0	36
Bardauskas, Lee	Castleford Tigers	1996-97	0+2	0	0	0	0
Barker, Craig	Workington Town	1996	0+2	0	0	0	0
Barrow, Paul	Warrington Wolves	1996-97	1+10	1	0	0	4
Barrow, Scott	St. Helens	1997-98	1+2	0	0	0	0
Barrow, Steve	Hull Sharks	1998	1+1	0	0	0	0
	Wigan	1996	0+8	3	0	0	12
Barton, Ben	Huddersfield Giants	1998	1+6	1	0	0	4
Barwick, Greg	London Broncos	1996-97	30+4	21	110	2	306
Bastian, David	Halifax Blue Sox	1996	0+2	0	0	0	0
Bawden, Russell	London Broncos	1996-97	25+16	7	0	0	28
Baynes, Neil	Wigan Warriors	1996-98	0+10	1	0	0	4
Beazley, Robbie	London Broncos	1997-98	33+6	10	0	0	40
Bell, Dean	Leeds	1996	1	1	0	0	4
Bell, Mark	Wigan Warriors	1998	20	11	0	0	44
Bellamy, Troy	Paris St. Germain	1997	5+10	0	0	0	0
Belle, Adrian	Huddersfield Giants	1998	10+2	0	0	0	0
	Oldham Bears	1996	19	8	0	0	32
Benn, Jamie	Castleford Tigers	1998	0+3	0	4	0	8
Bennett, Andy	Warrington Wolves	1996	6+5	1	0	0	4
Bentley, John	Halifax Blue Sox	1996-98	22+3	24	0	0	96
Bergman, Phil	Paris St. Germain	1997	20+1	14	0	0	56
Berry, Joe	Huddersfield Giants	1998	6+12	1	0	0	4
Best, Roger	London Broncos	1997-98	1+5	1	0	0	4

Player	Club	Period	App	T	G	D	Pts
Bethwaite, Mike	Workington Town	1996	17+3	1	0	0	4
Betts, Denis	Wigan Warriors	1998	16+1	3	0	0	12
Bird, Deon	Paris St. Germain	1996-97	30	13	2	0	56
Blackmore, Richard	Leeds Rhinos	1997-98	38	16	0	0	64
Blakeley, Steve	Salford Reds	1997-98	30+1	8	91	1	215
Blease, Ian	Salford Reds	1997	0+1	0	0	0	0
Bloem, Jamie	Halifax Blue Sox	1998	11+8	8	5	0	42
Bloomfield, Vea	Paris St. Germain	1996	4+14	3	0	0	12
Bomati, Pascal	Paris St. Germain	1996	17+2	10	0	0	40
Booth, Simon	Hull Sharks	1998	12+3	1	0	0	4
	St. Helens	1996-97	10+4	1	0	0	4
Booth, Steve	Huddersfield Giants	1998	9+2	2	3	0	14
Boothroyd, Alan	Halifax Blue Sox	1997	2+3	0	0	0	0
Boslem, John	Paris St. Germain	1996	0+5	0	0	0	0
Botica, Frano	Castleford Tigers	1996	21	5	84	2	190
Boudebza, Hadj	Paris St. Germain	1996	0+2	0	0	0	0
Bouveng, David	Halifax Blue Sox	1997-98	40+1	16	0	0	64
Bowes, Tony	Huddersfield Giants	1998	3+2	0	0	0	0
Bradbury, David	Salford Reds	1997-98	11+3	5	0	0	20
	Oldham Bears	1996-97	19+6	9	0	0	36
Bradley, Graeme	Bradford Bulls	1996-98	61+1	29	0	0	116
Bretherton, Liam	Warrington Wolves	1997	0+2	0	0	0	0
Brewer, Johnny	Halifax Blue Sox	1996	4+2	2	0	0	8
Briers, Lee	Warrington Wolves	1997-98	35	7	76	11	191
	St. Helens	1997	3	0	11	0	22
Briggs, Carl	Halifax Blue Sox	1996	5+3	1	0	0	4
Broadbent, Gary	Salford Reds	1997-98	40	8	0	0	32
Broadbent, Paul	Sheffield Eagles	1996-98	63+1	6	0	0	24
Brown, Gavin	Leeds Rhinos	1996-97	5+2	1	2	0	8
Brown, Michael	London Broncos	1996	0+2	0	0	0	0
Brown, Todd	Paris St. Germain	1996	8+1	2	0	0	8
Bryant, Justin	London Broncos	1996	7+8	1	0	0	4
	Paris St. Germain	1996	4+1	0	0	0	0
Bunyan, James	Huddersfield Giants	1998	7+3	2	0	0	8
Burgess, Andy	Salford Reds	1997	3+12	0	0	0	0
Burns, Gary	Oldham Bears	1996	6	1	0	0	4
Burns, Paul	Workington Town	1996	5+2	1	0	0	4
Busby, Dean	Hull Sharks	1998	8+6	0	0	0	0
	St. Helens	1996-98	1+7	0	0	0	0
Butt, Ikram	London Broncos	1996	5+1	0	0	0	0
Byrne, Shane	Huddersfield Giants	1998	0+3	0	0	0	0
Cabestany, Didier	Paris St. Germain	1996-97	20+6	2	0	0	8
Calland, Matt	Bradford Bulls	1996-98	44+5	24	0	0	96
Cambres, Laurent	Paris St. Germain	1996	0+1	0	0	0	0
Campbell, Logan	Hull Sharks	1998	23	7	0	0	28
	Workington Town	1996	7+1	1	0	0	4
Cantillon, Phil	Leeds Rhinos	1997	0+1	0	0	0	0
Cardiss, Darryl	Wigan Warriors	1996-98	12+6	4	0	0	16
Cardoza, Dale	Sheffield Eagles	1998	0+3	1	0	0	4
Carney, Martin	Warrington Wolves	1997	0+1	0	0	0	0
Carr, Paul	Sheffield Eagles	1996-98	45+5	15	0	0	60
Carroll, Bernard	London Broncos	1996	2+1	1	0	0	4
Carroll, Mark	London Broncos	1998	15+3	1	0	0	4
Carter, Darren	Workington Town	1996	10+3	0	1	0	2
Cartwright, John	Salford Reds	1997	9	0	0	0	0
Carvell, Gareth	Leeds Rhinos	1997	0+1	0	0	0	0

Player	Club	Period	App	T	G	D	Pts
Cassidy, Mick	Wigan Warriors	1996-98	52+10	6	0	0	24
Causey, Chris	Warrington Wolves	1997-98	0+12	0	0	0	0
Cervello, Arnaud	Paris St. Germain	1996	4	4	0	0	16
Chambers, Gary	Warrington Wolves	1996-98	46+10	0	0	0	0
Chamorin, Pierre	Paris St. Germain	1996-97	27+3	8	3	0	38
Chapman, Damien	London Broncos	1998	6+2	3	4	1	21
Chapman, David	Castleford Tigers	1996-98	24+6	8	0	0	32
Chapman, Richard	Sheffield Eagles	1996	1	2	0	0	8
Cheetham, Andy	Huddersfield Giants	1998	11	1	0	0	4
Chesney, Kris	London Broncos	1998	1+2	0	0	0	0
Chester, Chris	Halifax Blue Sox	1996-98	37+12	12	15	1	79
Chilton, "James" Lee	Workington Town	1996	10+3	6	0	0	24
Christie, Gary	Bradford Bulls	1996-97	4+7	1	0	0	4
Clark, Dean	Leeds	1996	11+2	3	0	0	12
Clark, Des	Halifax Blue Sox	1998	15+8	5	0	0	20
Clarke, Greg	Halifax Blue Sox	1997	1+1	0	0	0	0
Clarke, John	Oldham Bears	1996-97	27+5	5	0	0	20
Clarke, Jonathan	Wigan Warriors	1997-98	3+9	0	0	0	0
Clinch, Gavin	Halifax Blue Sox	1998	21	13	20	2	94
Cochrane, Evan	London Broncos	1996	5+1	1	0	0	4
Collins, Wayne	Leeds Rhinos	1997	21	3	0	0	12
Connolly, Gary	Wigan Warriors	1996-98	63	41	4	0	172
Cook, Mick	Sheffield Eagles	1996	9+10	2	0	0	8
Cook, Paul	Huddersfield Giants	1998	10+6	2	13	0	34
	Bradford Bulls	1996-97	14+8	7	38	1	105
Cotton, Wes	London Broncos	1997-98	12	3	0	0	12
Coussons, Phil	Salford Reds	1997	7+2	3	0	0	12
Couttet, Alex	Paris St. Germain	1997	1	0	0	0	0
Couttet, Nicolas	Paris St. Germain	1997	1	0	0	0	0
Coventry, Jamie	Castleford Tigers	1996	1	0	0	0	0
Cowan, Jimmy	Oldham Bears	1996-97	2+8	0	0	0	0
Cowell, Will	Warrington Wolves	1998	1+4	0	0	0	0
Cowie, Neil	Wigan Warriors	1996-98	42+8	5	0	0	20
Craig, Andrew	Wigan	1996	5+5	2	0	0	8
Craven, Steve	Hull Sharks	1998	14+5	2	0	0	8
Crellin, Nicky	Workington Town	1996	0+2	0	0	0	0
Critchley, Jason	Castleford Tigers	1997-98	27+3	11	0	0	44
Crompton, Martin	Salford Reds	1998	8+2	3	6	1	25
	Oldham Bears	1996-97	36+1	16	0	3	67
Crook, Paul	Oldham Bears	1996	4+9	0	3	0	6
Crooks, Lee	Castleford Tigers	1996-97	27+2	2	14	0	36
Cross, Alan	St. Helens	1997	0+2	0	0	0	0
Crouthers, Kevin	Bradford Bulls	1997-98	3+8	1	0	0	4
Crowther, Matt	Sheffield Eagles	1996-98	25+3	16	9	0	82
Cullen, Paul	Warrington Wolves	1996	19	3	0	0	12
Cummins, Francis	Leeds Rhinos	1996-98	46+5	33	6	0	144
Cunningham, Keiron	St. Helens	1996-98	60+1	20	0	0	80
Currier, Andy	Warrington Wolves	1997	0+2	1	0	0	4
Dakuitoga, Joe	Sheffield Eagles	1996	6+3	0	0	0	0
Darbyshire, Paul	Warrington Wolves	1997	0+6	0	0	0	0
David, Maea	Hull Sharks	1998	1	0	0	0	0
Davidson, Paul	St. Helens	1998	13+9	5	0	0	20
	Oldham Bears	1996-97	16+19	14	0	1	57
Davies, Gareth	Warrington Wolves	1996-97	1+6	0	0	0	0
Davies, Wes	Wigan Warriors	1998	0+1	1	0	0	4
Davis, Brad	Castleford Tigers	1997-98	29	6	40	7	111

Player	Club	Period	App	T	G	D	Pts
Deacon, Paul	Bradford Bulls	1998	11+1	4	4	0	24
	Oldham Bears	1997	0+2	0	0	0	0
Dean, Craig	Halifax Blue Sox	1996-97	25+11	12	1	1	51
Dermott, Martin	Warrington Wolves	1997	1	0	0	0	0
Despin, David	Paris St. Germain	1996	0+1	0	0	0	0
Devecchi, Fabien	Paris St. Germain	1996-97	17+10	2	0	0	8
Dixon, Paul	Sheffield Eagles	1996-97	5+9	1	0	0	4
Dobson, Gareth	Castleford Tigers	1998	0+2	0	0	0	0
Donohue, Jason	Bradford Bulls	1996	0+4	0	0	0	0
Donougher, Jeremy	Bradford Bulls	1996-98	37+9	9	0	0	36
Doyle, Adam	Warrington Wolves	1998	9+3	4	0	0	16
Doyle, Rod	Sheffield Eagles	1997-98	34+5	3	0	1	13
Duffy, John	Warrington Wolves	1997-98	9+4	0	0	0	0
Duncan, Andrew	London Broncos	1997	2+4	2	0	0	8
	Warrington Wolves	1997	0+1	0	0	0	0
Dunford, Matt	London Broncos	1997-98	18+20	3	0	1	13
Durkin, James	Paris St. Germain	1997	0+5	0	0	0	0
Dwyer, Bernard	Bradford Bulls	1996-98	46+5	13	0	0	52
Dynevor, Leo	London Broncos	1996	8+11	5	7	0	34
Eade, Jason	Paris St. Germain	1997	9	4	0	0	16
Eagar, Michael	Warrington Wolves	1998	21	6	0	0	24
Eccles, Cliff	Salford Reds	1997-98	30+5	1	0	0	4
Eckersley, Chris	Warrington Wolves	1996	1	0	0	0	0
Edmed, Steve	Sheffield Eagles	1997	15+1	0	0	0	0
Edwards, Diccon	Castleford Tigers	1996-97	10+5	1	0	0	4
Edwards, Peter	Salford Reds	1997-98	35+2	4	0	0	16
Edwards, Shaun	London Broncos	1997-98	24+3	14	1	0	58
	Bradford Bulls	1998	8+2	4	0	0	16
	Wigan	1996	17+3	12	1	0	50
Ekoku, Abi	Bradford Bulls	1997-98	20+4	6	0	0	24
	Halifax Blue Sox	1996	15+1	5	0	0	20
El Khalouki, Abderazak	Paris St. Germain	1997	0+1	0	0	0	0
Ellison, Danny	Castleford Tigers	1998	5+4	2	0	0	8
	Wigan	1996-97	15+1	13	0	0	52
Entat, Patrick	Paris St. Germain	1996	22	2	0	0	8
Erba, Jason	Sheffield Eagles	1997	1+4	0	0	0	0
Evans, Paul	Paris St. Germain	1997	18	8	0	0	32
Eyres, Richard	Warrington Wolves	1997	2+5	0	0	0	0
	Sheffield Eagles	1997	2+3	0	0	0	0
Faimalo, Esene	Salford Reds	1997-98	23+19	2	0	0	8
	Leeds	1996	3+3	0	0	0	0
Faimalo. Joe	Salford Reds	1998	14+7	0	0	0	0
	Oldham Bears	1996-97	37+5	7	0	0	28
Fairbank, Karl	Bradford Bulls	1996	18+2	4	0	0	16
Fallon, Jim	Leeds	1996	10	5	0	0	20
Farrar, Danny	Warrington Wolves	1998	21	4	0	0	16
Farrell, Andrew	Wigan Warriors	1996-98	67	18	324	3	723
Farrell, Anthony	Leeds Rhinos	1997-98	40+5	8	0	0	32
	Sheffield Eagles	1996	14+5	5	0	0	20
Fatnowna, Abraham	London Broncos	1997-98	7+2	2	0	0	8
"Butch"	Workington Town	1997	5	2	0	0	8
Fawcett, Vince	Warrington Wolves	1998	4+8	1	0	0	4
	Oldham Bears	1997	5	3	0	0	12
Field, Jamie	Huddersfield Giants	1998	15+5	0	0	0	0
	Leeds Rhinos	1996-97	3+11	0	0	0	0
Fielden, Jamie	Huddersfield Giants	1998	2+3	0	0	0	0

Player	Club	Period	App	T	G	D	Pts
Fielden, Stuart	Bradford Bulls	1998	1+12	0	0	0	0
Filipo, Lafaele	Workington Town	1996	15+4	3	0	0	12
Finau, Salesi	Warrington Wolves	1996-97	16+15	8	0	0	32
Finney, Phil	Warrington Wolves	1998	1	0	0	0	0
Fleary, Darren	Leeds Rhinos	1997-98	20+2	0	0	0	0
Flowers, Jason	Castleford Tigers	1996-98	53+9	21	0	0	84
Flowers, Stuart	Castleford Tigers	1996	0+3	0	0	0	0
Flynn, Adrian	Castleford Tigers	1996-97	19+2	10	0	0	40
Flynn, Wayne	Sheffield Eagles	1997	3+4	0	0	0	0
Fogerty, Adam	Warrington Wolves	1998	4	0	0	0	0
	St. Helens	1996	13	1	0	0	4
Forber, Paul	Salford Reds	1997-98	19+12	4	0	0	16
Ford, Mike	Castleford Tigers	1997-98	25+12	5	0	3	23
	Warrington	1996	3	0	0	0	0
Forshaw, Mike	Bradford Bulls	1997-98	32+3	10	0	0	40
	Leeds	1996	11+3	5	0	0	20
Forster, Mark	Warrington Wolves	1996-98	64	25	0	0	100
Fozzard, Nick	Huddersfield Giants	1998	2+1	0	0	0	0
	Leeds Rhinos	1996-97	6+16	3	0	0	12
Fraisse, David	Workington Town	1996	8	0	0	0	0
Furness, David	Castleford Tigers	1996	0+1	0	0	0	0
Gamson, Mark	Sheffield Eagles	1996	3	0	0	0	0
Garcia, Jean-Marc	Sheffield Eagles	1996-97	35+3	22	0	0	88
Gartland, Steve	Oldham Bears	1996	1+1	0	1	0	2
Gay, Richard	Castleford Tigers	1996-98	36+9	14	0	0	56
Geritas, Sean	Warrington Wolves	1997	0+5	1	0	0	4
Gibbons, Anthony	Leeds	1996	9+4	2	0	1	9
Gibbons, David	Leeds	1996	3+4	2	0	0	8
Gibbs, Scott	St. Helens	1996	9	3	0	0	12
Gibson, Damian	Halifax Blue Sox	1998	20+1	6	0	0	24
	Leeds Rhinos	1997	18	3	0	0	12
Gildart, Ian	Oldham Bears	1996-97	31+7	0	0	0	0
Gill, Peter	London Broncos	1996-98	56+1	16	0	0	64
Gillespie, Carl	Halifax Blue Sox	1996-98	31+24	11	0	0	44
Gilmour, Lee	Wigan Warriors	1997-98	11+13	8	0	0	32
Glanville, Marc	Leeds Rhinos	1998	14+2	1	0	0	4
Glaze, Eddie	Castleford Tigers	1996	1	0	0	0	0
Gleadhill, Paul	Leeds	1996	4	0	0	0	0
Goddard, Richard	Castleford Tigers	1996-97	11+3	2	10	0	28
Godden, Brad	Leeds Rhinos	1998	19	8	0	0	36
Golden, Marvin	Leeds Rhinos	1996-98	20+8	10	0	0	36
Goldspink, Brett	St. Helens	1998	16+5	2	0	0	8
	Oldham Bears	1997	13+2	0	0	0	0
Goodwin, Luke	London Broncos	1998	9+2	3	1	1	15
	Oldham Bears	1997	16+4	10	17	2	76
Goulding, Bobbie	Huddersfield Giants	1998	5+1	0	11	2	24
	St. Helens	1996-98	42+2	9	210	4	460
Graham, Nathan	Bradford Bulls	1996-98	16+27	3	0	1	13
Greenwood, Brandon	Halifax Blue Sox	1996	1	0	0	0	0
Griffiths, Jonathan	Paris St. Germain	1996	0+4	1	0	0	4
Grima, Andrew	Workington Town	1996	2+9	2	0	0	8
Grimley, Danny	Sheffield Eagles	1996	4+1	1	0	0	4
Guy, Reece	Oldham Bears	1996	3+4	0	0	0	0
Haigh, Andy	St. Helens	1996-98	20+17	11	0	0	44
Hall, Carl	Leeds	1996	7+2	3	0	0	12

Player	Club	Period	App	T	G	D	Pts
Hall, Martin	Halifax Blue Sox	1998	2+8	0	0	0	0
	Castleford Tigers	1998	4	0	0	0	0
	Wigan Warriors	1996-97	31+5	7	6	0	40
Hallas, Graeme	Hull Sharks	1998	13+7	2	29	1	67
	Halifax Blue Sox	1996	11+4	5	0	0	20
Hamer, Jon	Bradford Bulls	1996	0+1	0	0	0	0
Hamilton, Andrew	London Broncos	1997	1+7	3	0	0	12
Hamilton, John	St. Helens	1998	3	0	0	0	0
Hammond, Karle	St. Helens	1996-98	59+5	28	0	4	116
Hancock, Anthony	Paris St. Germain	1997	8+6	1	0	0	4
Handley, Paddy	Leeds	1996	1+1	2	0	0	8
Hanger, Dean	Huddersfield Giants	1998	20+1	5	0	0	20
Hansen, Lee	Wigan Warriors	1997	10+5	0	0	0	0
Hargrave, Spencer	Castleford Tigers	1996-97	0+4	0	0	0	0
Harland, Lee	Castleford Tigers	1996-98	39+15	3	0	0	12
Harmon, Neil	Bradford Bulls	1998	8+1	1	0	0	4
	Huddersfield Giants	1998	12	1	0	0	4
	Leeds Rhinos	1996	10	1	0	0	4
Harris, Iestyn	Leeds Rhinos	1997-98	40+1	20	163	4	410
	Warrington Wolves	1996	16	4	63	2	144
Harrison, Karl	Halifax Blue Sox	1996-98	58+2	2	0	0	8
Hassan, Carlos	Bradford Bulls	1996	6+4	2	0	0	8
Hassan, Phil	Salford Reds	1998	15	2	0	0	8
	Leeds Rhinos	1996-97	38+4	12	0	0	48
Haughton, Simon	Wigan Warriors	1996-98	48+15	28	0	0	112
Hay, Andy	Leeds Rhinos	1997-98	20+11	11	0	0	44
	Sheffield Eagles	1996-97	17+3	5	0	0	20
Hayes, Joey	St. Helens	1996-98	11+6	7	0	0	28
Helliwell, Ricky	Salford Reds	1997	0+1	0	0	0	0
Henare, Richard	Warrington Wolves	1996-97	28+2	24	0	0	96
Hepi, Brad	Hull Sharks	1998	16+1	3	0	0	12
Higgins, Darren	London Broncos	1998	5+6	2	0	0	8
Higgins, "Iain" Robert	London Broncos	1997-98	1+7	2	0	0	8
Highton, Chris	Warrington Wolves	1997	1+1	0	0	0	0
Highton, David	Warrington Wolves	1998	6	1	0	0	4
Highton, Paul	Salford Reds	1998	10+3	1	0	0	4
	Halifax Blue Sox	1996-97	12+18	2	0	0	8
Hill, Howard	Oldham Bears	1996-97	22+12	4	0	0	16
Hilton, Mark	Warrington Wolves	1996-98	28+6	1	0	0	4
Hobson, Andy	Halifax Blue Sox	1998	0+6	0	0	0	0
Hodgson, Andy	Bradford Bulls	1997-98	8+2	4	0	0	16
Hogg, Darren	London Broncos	1996	0+1	0	0	0	0
Hogue, Michael	Paris St. Germain	1997	5+7	0	0	0	0
Holden, Chris	Warrington Wolves	1996-97	2+1	0	0	0	0
Holgate, Stephen	Wigan Warriors	1997-98	9+26	2	0	0	8
	Workington Town	1996	19	3	0	0	12
Holroyd, Graham	Leeds Rhinos	1996-98	40+24	22	101	8	298
Hough, John	Warrington Wolves	1996-97	9	2	0	0	8
Howard, Harvey	Bradford Bulls	1998	3+2	1	0	0	4
	Leeds	1996	8	0	0	0	0
Howard, Kim	London Broncos	1997	4+5	0	0	0	0
Howarth, Stuart	Workington Town	1996	0+2	0	0	0	0
Hudson, Ryan	Huddersfield Giants	1998	0+1	0	0	0	0
Hughes, Adam	Leeds Rhinos	1996-97	4+5	4	0	0	16
Hughes, Ian	Sheffield Eagles	1996	9+8	4	0	0	16

Player	Club	Period	App	T	G	D	Pts
Hulme, David	Salford Reds	1997-98	33+1	3	0	0	12
	Leeds	1996	8+1	2	0	0	8
Hulme, Paul	Warrington Wolves	1996-97	23+1	2	0	0	8
Hunte, Alan	Hull Sharks	1998	21	7	0	0	28
	St. Helens	1996-97	30+2	28	0	0	112
Hyde, Nicholas	Paris St. Germain	1997	5+5	1	0	0	4
Ireland, Andy	Hull Sharks	1998	10+8	0	0	0	0
	Bradford Bulls	1996	1	0	0	0	0
Iro, Kevin	Leeds	1996	16	9	0	0	36
Isherwood, Andrew	Wigan Warriors	1998	0+3	0	0	0	0
Jackson, Michael	Sheffield Eagles	1998	3+5	1	0	0	4
	Halifax Blue Sox	1996-97	27+6	11	0	0	44
Jackson, Paul	Huddersfield Giants	1998	0+11	0	0	0	0
Jackson, Wayne	Halifax Blue Sox	1996-97	17+5	2	0	0	8
James, Andy	Halifax Blue Sox	1996	0+4	0	0	0	0
Jampy, Pascal	Paris St. Germain	1996-97	3+2	0	0	0	0
Jennings, Ed	London Broncos	1998	0+1	0	0	0	0
Johnson, Andrew	Wigan	1996-97	24+16	18	0	0	72
Johnson, Jason	St. Helens	1997	1	0	0	0	0
Johnson, Mark	Hull Sharks	1998	10+1	4	0	0	16
	Workington Town	1996	12	4	0	0	16
Johnson, Paul	Wigan Warriors	1996-98	7+23	14	0	0	56
Jones, David	Oldham Bears	1997	14+1	5	0	0	20
Jones, Mark	Warrington Wolves	1996	9+11	2	0	0	8
Jowitt, Warren	Bradford Bulls	1996-98	3+10	2	0	0	8
Joynt, Chris	St. Helens	1996-98	55+1	14	0	0	56
Kacala, Gregory	Paris St. Germain	1996	7	1	0	0	4
Keating, Shaun	London Broncos	1996	1+3	0	0	0	0
Keenan, Mark	Workington Town	1996	3+4	1	0	0	4
Kemp, Tony	Leeds Rhinos	1996-98	23+2	5	0	2	22
Kenward, Shane	Salford Reds	1998	1	0	0	0	0
Keough, Jason	Paris St. Germain	1997	2	1	0	0	4
Ketteridge, Martin	Halifax Blue Sox	1996	7+5	0	0	0	0
Kettlewell, Ronnie	Warrington Wolves	1996	0+1	0	0	0	0
King, Dave	Huddersfield Giants	1998	11+6	2	0	0	8
Kitchin, Wayne	Workington Town	1996	11+6	3	17	1	47
Knott, Ian	Warrington Wolves	1996-98	22+24	12	16	0	80
Knowles, Matthew	Wigan	1996	0+3	0	0	0	0
Knowles, Phil	Salford Reds	1997	1	0	0	0	0
Knox, Simon	Salford Reds	1998	1+1	0	0	0	0
	Bradford Bulls	1996-98	9+19	7	0	0	28
Kohe-Love, Toa	Warrington Wolves	1996-98	42+1	17	0	0	68
Koloi, Paul	Wigan	1997	1+2	1	0	0	4
Krause, David	London Broncos	1996-97	22+1	7	0	0	28
Lane, Mark	Paris St. Germain	1996	0+2	0	0	0	0
Langer, Kevin	London Broncos	1996	12+4	1	0	0	4
Laughton, Dale	Sheffield Eagles	1996-98	29+16	4	0	0	16
Laurence, Jason	Salford Reds	1997	1	0	0	0	0
Law, Neil	Sheffield Eagles	1998	1+1	1	0	0	4
Lawford, Dean	Leeds Rhinos	1997-98	7+3	0	1	0	2
	Sheffield Eagles	1996	9+5	2	1	1	11
Lawless, Johnny	Sheffield Eagles	1996-98	46+4	10	0	0	40
Leapai, Faatni "Leroy"	London Broncos	1996	2	0	0	0	0
Leatham, Jim	Hull Sharks	1998	3+13	1	0	0	4
	Leeds Rhinos	1997	0+1	0	0	0	0
Leathem, Andy	St. Helens	1996-98	20+1	1	0	0	4

Player	Club	Period	App	T	G	D	Pts
Lee, Mark	Salford Reds	1997-98	16+6	1	0	4	8
Lester, Gary	Hull Sharks	1998	22	7	0	0	28
Lester, Stuart	Wigan	1997	1+3	0	0	0	0
Leuila, Peaufai "Afi"	Oldham Bears	1996-97	17+3	2	0	0	8
Lidden, Jason	Castleford Tigers	1997	15+1	7	0	0	28
Littler, Stuart	Salford Reds	1998	5	1	0	0	4
Livett, Peter	Workington Town	1996	3+1	0	0	0	0
Lomax, David	Paris St. Germain	1997	19+2	1	0	0	4
Long, Sean	St. Helens	1997-98	30+2	14	88	3	235
	Wigan Warriors	1996-97	1+5	0	0	0	0
Longo, Davide	Bradford Bulls	1996	1+3	0	0	0	0
Lord, Gary	Oldham Bears	1996-97	28+12	3	0	0	12
Loughlin, Paul	Huddersfield Giants	1998	12+1	1	4	0	12
	Bradford Bulls	1996-97	36+4	15	8	0	76
Lowes, James	Bradford Bulls	1996-98	61	31	0	0	124
Lucchese, Laurent	Paris St. Germain	1996	13+5	2	0	0	8
Mafi, Mateaki	Warrington Wolves	1996-97	7+8	7	0	0	28
Maguire, Mark	London Broncos	1996-97	11+4	7	13	0	54
Maher, Lee	Leeds	1996	4+1	0	0	0	0
Mahony, Shaun	Paris St. Germain	1997	5	0	0	0	0
Maloney, Francis	Castleford Tigers	1998	19+4	5	12	0	44
	Oldham Bears	1996-97	39+2	12	91	2	232
Mann, George	Warrington Wolves	1997	14+5	1	0	0	4
	Leeds	1996	11+4	2	0	0	8
Mardon, Nick	London Broncos	1997-98	14	2	0	0	8
Marns, Oliver	Halifax Blue Sox	1996-98	0+7	2	0	0	8
Marsh, Iain	Salford Reds	1998	1	0	0	0	0
Marshall, Richard	Halifax Blue Sox	1996-98	20+20	2	0	0	8
Martin, Jason	Paris St. Germain	1997	15+2	3	0	0	12
Martin, Scott	Salford Reds	1997-98	24+16	7	0	0	28
Martin, Tony	London Broncos	1996-97	26+1	8	0	1	33
Martindale, Mick	Halifax Blue Sox	1996	0+4	0	0	0	0
Martyn, Tommy	St. Helens	1996-98	26+11	20	2	0	84
Marwood, Dean	Workington Town	1996	9+6	0	22	0	44
Masella, Martin	Leeds Rhinos	1997-98	40+2	0	0	0	0
Maskill, Colin	Castleford Tigers	1996	8	1	1	0	6
Matautia, Vila	St. Helens	1996-98	18+25	6	0	0	24
Mather, Barrie-Jon	Castleford Tigers	1998	15	4	0	0	16
Mathiou, Jamie	Leeds Rhinos	1997-98	14+27	0	0	0	0
Matterson, Terry	London Broncos	1996-98	46	15	90	6	246
McAllister, Danny	Sheffield Eagles	1996-97	33+7	10	0	0	40
McAtee, John	St. Helens	1996	2+1	0	0	0	0
McAvoy, Nathan	Bradford Bulls	1998	6+1	1	0	0	4
	Salford Reds	1997-98	36	15	0	0	60
McCormack, Robbie	Wigan Warriors	1998	22	2	0	0	8
McCurrie, Steve	Warrington Wolves	1998	22+1	8	0	0	32
McDermott, Barrie	Leeds Rhinos	1996-98	29+17	10	0	0	40
McDermott, Brian	Bradford Bulls	1996-98	49+5	16	0	0	64
McGinty, Billy	Workington Town	1996	1	0	0	0	0
McGuirk, Gary	Workington Town	1996	0+4	0	0	0	0
McKell, Richard	Castleford Tigers	1997-98	22+7	2	0	0	8
McKenzie, Phil	Workington Town	1996	4	0	0	0	0
McKinney, Chris	Oldham Bears	1996-97	4+9	2	0	0	8
McNamara, Steve	Bradford Bulls	1996-98	64	9	249	6	540
McPherson, Neil	Salford Reds	1997	0+1	0	0	0	0
McRae, Duncan	London Broncos	1996	11+2	3	0	1	13

Player	Club	Period	App	T	G	D	Pts
McVey, Derek	St. Helens	1996-97	28+4	6	1	0	26
Mead, Dallas	Warrington Wolves	1997	2	0	0	0	0
Medley, Paul	Bradford Bulls	1996-98	6+34	9	0	0	36
Menkins, Craig	Paris St. Germain	1997	4+5	0	0	0	0
Mercer, Gary	Halifax Blue Sox	1998	22+1	7	0	0	28
	Leeds Rhinos	1996-97	34+2	9	0	0	36
Mestrov, Tony	Wigan Warriors	1998	23	1	0	0	4
	London Broncos	1996-97	42+1	4	0	0	16
Meyer, Keiran	London Broncos	1996	4	1	0	0	4
Middleton, Simon	Castleford Tigers	1996-97	19+3	8	0	0	32
Millard, Shane	London Broncos	1998	5+4	1	0	0	4
Minto, John	London Broncos	1996	13	4	0	0	16
Moana, Martin	Halifax Blue Sox	1996-98	49+8	32	0	0	128
Molloy, Steve	Sheffield Eagles	1998	6+15	2	0	0	8
Moore, Adrian	Huddersfield Giants	1998	0+4	0	0	0	0
Moore, Danny	Wigan Warriors	1998	18+2	8	0	0	32
Moore, Jason	Workington Town	1996	0+5	0	0	0	0
Morganson, Willie	Sheffield Eagles	1997-98	18+11	5	3	0	26
Moriarty, Paul	Halifax Blue Sox	1996	3+2	0	0	0	0
Morley, Adrian	Leeds Rhinos	1996-98	46+7	15	0	0	60
Morley, Chris	Warrington Wolves	1998	2+8	0	0	0	0
	St. Helens	1996-97	22+17	3	0	0	12
Moulinec, Wilfried	Paris St. Germain	1996	1	0	0	0	0
Moxon, Mark	Huddersfield Giants	1998	3	0	0	0	0
Munro, Damien	Halifax Blue Sox	1996-97	9+6	8	0	0	32
Munro, Matt	Oldham Bears	1996-97	26+5	8	0	0	32
Murdock, Craig	Hull Sharks	1998	15	6	0	2	26
	Wigan Warriors	1996	18+16	14	0	0	56
Murray, David "Doc"	Warrington Wolves	1997	0+2	0	0	0	0
	Wigan Warriors	1997	6+2	0	0	0	0
Mycoe, David	Sheffield Eagles	1996-97	12+13	1	0	0	4
Myler, Rob	Oldham Bears	1996-97	19+2	6	0	0	24
Nable, Matt	London Broncos	1997	2+1	1	0	0	4
Nairn, Brad	Workington Town	1996	14	4	0	0	16
Naylor, Scott	Salford Reds	1997-98	23+1	9	0	0	36
Neal, Mike	Salford Reds	1998	0+1	0	0	0	0
	Oldham Bears	1996-97	6+5	3	0	0	12
Neill, Jonathan	Huddersfield Giants	1998	8+1	0	0	0	0
	St. Helens	1996	1	0	0	0	0
Newlove, Paul	St. Helens	1996-98	59	52	0	0	208
Newton, Terry	Leeds Rhinos	1996-98	26+14	2	0	0	8
Nickle, Sonny	Bradford Bulls	1996-98	25+16	9	0	0	36
Nolan, Rob	Hull Sharks	1998	5+6	1	0	0	4
Norman, Paul	Oldham Bears	1996	0+1	0	0	0	0
Northey, Andy	St. Helens	1996-97	8+18	3	0	0	12
Nutley, Danny	Warrington Wolves	1998	23	0	0	0	0
Nuttall, Tony	Oldham Bears	1996-97	1+7	0	0	0	0
O'Connor, Matt	Paris St. Germain	1997	11+4	1	26	2	58
O'Connor, Terry	Wigan Warriors	1996-98	48+10	3	0	0	12
O'Donnell, David	Paris St. Germain	1997	21	3	0	0	12
O'Loughlin, Kevin	Halifax Blue Sox	1997-98	2+4	0	0	0	0
	St. Helens	1997	0+3	0	0	0	0
O'Neill, Julian	St. Helens	1997-98	40	2	0	0	8
Offiah, Martin	London Broncos	1996-98	20	16	0	0	64
	Wigan	1996	8	7	0	0	28
Okesene, Hitro	Hull Sharks	1998	21+1	0	0	0	0

Player	Club	Period	App	T	G	D	Pts
Okiwe, Anderson	Sheffield Eagles	1997	1	0	0	0	0
Olejnik, Jamie	Paris St. Germain	1997	11	8	0	0	32
Orr, Chris	Huddersfield Giants	1998	19+3	2	0	0	8
Orr, Danny	Castleford Tigers	1997-98	25+15	13	38	0	128
Palmada Jason	Workington Town	1996	12	2	0	0	8
Paramore, Peter "Junior"	Castleford Tigers	1996	5+6	3	0	0	12
Parker, Wayne	Halifax Blue Sox	1996-97	12+1	0	0	0	0
Parry, Jules	Paris St. Germain	1996	10+2	0	0	0	0
Pastre-Courtine, Regis	Paris St. Germain	1996	4+3	4	0	0	16
Patmore, Andrew	Oldham Bears	1996	8+5	3	0	0	12
Paul, Henry	Wigan Warriors	1996-98	58	36	23	0	190
Paul, Junior	London Broncos	1996	3	1	0	0	4
Paul, Robbie	Bradford Bulls	1996-98	53+3	36	0	0	144
Peacock, Danny	Bradford Bulls	1997-98	25+1	14	0	0	56
Pearson, Martin	Halifax Blue Sox	1997-98	37+4	14	113	0	282
Pech, Jacques	Paris St. Germain	1996	16	0	0	0	0
Pechey, Mike	Warrington Wolves	1998	6+3	2	0	0	8
Penni, Julian	Salford Reds	1998	3	0	0	0	0
Penny, Lee	Warrington Wolves	1996-98	47+1	15	0	0	60
Penrice, Paul	Workington Town	1996	11+2	2	0	0	8
Perelini, Apollo	St. Helens	1996-98	41+12	15	0	0	60
Perrett, Mark	Halifax Blue Sox	1996-97	15+4	4	0	0	16
Peters, Adam	Paris St. Germain	1997	16+3	0	0	0	0
Peters, Dominic	London Broncos	1998	1+2	0	0	0	0
Petrie, Adrian	Workington Town	1996	0+1	0	0	0	0
Phillips, Rowland	Workington Town	1996	22	1	0	0	4
Picchi, Nathan	Leeds	1996	0+1	0	0	0	0
Pickavance, Ian	St. Helens	1996-98	12+46	6	0	0	24
Pinkney, Nick	Sheffield Eagles	1997-98	33	10	0	0	40
Piscuonov, Michal	Paris St. Germain	1996	1+1	1	0	0	4
Pitt, Darryl	London Broncos	1996	2+17	4	0	1	17
Platt, Andy	Salford Reds	1997-98	20+3	1	0	0	4
Powell, Daio	Halifax Blue Sox	1997-98	28+3	16	0	0	64
Powell, Daryl	Leeds Rhinos	1998	11+10	5	0	0	20
Prescott, Steve	Hull Sharks	1998	19	7	20	0	68
	St. Helens	1996-97	32	15	17	0	94
Prest, Lee	Workington Town	1996	0+1	0	0	0	0
Price, Richard	Sheffield Eagles	1996	1+2	0	0	0	0
Priddle, Tony	Paris St. Germain	1997	11+7	3	0	0	12
Pryce, Leon	Bradford Bulls	1998	1	0	0	0	0
Quinnell, Scott	Wigan	1996	6+3	1	0	0	4
Radford, Lee	Hull Sharks	1998	0+8	2	0	0	8
Radlinski, Kris	Wigan Warriors	1996-98	62	26	0	0	104
Ramondou, Jean-Luc	Paris St. Germain	1996	1+1	1	0	0	4
Randall, Craig	Salford Reds	1997-98	12+19	4	0	0	16
Ranson, Scott	Oldham Bears	1996-97	19+2	7	0	0	28
Rea, Tony	London Broncos	1996	22	4	0	0	16
Reihana, Tahi	Bradford Bulls	1997-98	17+20	0	0	0	0
Retchless, Steele	London Broncos	1998	22+1	1	0	0	4
Ricard, Phillipe	Paris St. Germain	1996-97	2	0	0	0	0
Richards, Basil	Huddersfield Giants	1998	16+5	0	0	0	0
Richards, Craig	Oldham Bears	1996	1	0	0	0	0
Richardson, Sean	Castleford Tigers	1996	3+8	1	0	0	4
Rika, Craig	Halifax Blue Sox	1996-97	2	0	0	0	0
Riley, Peter	Workington Town	1996	7+5	0	0	0	0
Rivett, Leroy	Leeds Rhinos	1996-98	11+6	6	0	0	24

193

Player	Club	Period	App	T	G	D	Pts
Roach, Jason	Warrington Wolves	1998	16	5	0	0	20
	Castleford Tigers	1997	7	4	0	0	16
Robinson, Jason	Wigan Warriors	1996-98	63+1	47	0	1	189
Robinson, Jeremy	Paris St. Germain	1997	10+3	1	21	0	46
Roden, Carl	Warrington Wolves	1997	1	0	0	0	0
Rogers, Darren	Salford Reds	1997-98	42	16	0	0	64
Roper, Jon	Warrington Wolves	1996-98	39+4	20	25	0	130
Roskell, Scott	London Broncos	1996-97	29+2	16	0	0	64
Rosolen, Steve	London Broncos	1996-98	25+9	10	0	0	40
Ross, Adam	London Broncos	1996	0+1	0	0	0	0
Round, Paul	Castleford Tigers	1996	0+3	0	0	0	0
Rowley, Paul	Halifax Blue Sox	1996-98	60+3	14	0	1	57
Rudd, Chris	Warrington Wolves	1996-98	31+17	10	16	0	72
Rushforth, James	Halifax Blue Sox	1997	0+4	0	0	0	0
Russell, Danny	Huddersfield Giants	1998	22	4	0	0	16
Russell, Ian	Oldham Bears	1997	1+3	1	0	0	4
	Paris St. Germain	1996	3	0	0	0	0
Russell, Richard	Castleford Tigers	1996-98	37+4	2	0	0	8
Russell, Robert	Salford Reds	1998	2	0	1	0	2
Ryan, Chris	London Broncos	1998	21	9	10	0	56
Salter, Matt	London Broncos	1997-98	8+24	0	0	0	0
Sampson, Dean	Castleford Tigers	1996-98	45+9	8	0	0	32
Sands, Jason	Paris St. Germain	1996-97	28	0	0	0	0
Savelio, Lokeni	Salford Reds	1997-98	18+20	0	0	0	0
Scales, Jon	Bradford Bulls	1996-98	45+4	24	0	0	96
Schick, Andrew	Castleford Tigers	1996-98	45+13	9	0	0	36
Schofield, Garry	Huddersfield Giants	1998	0+2	0	0	0	0
Schubert, Gary	Workington Town	1996	0+1	0	0	0	0
Schultz, Matt	Hull Sharks	1998	12+5	2	0	0	8
	Leeds Rhinos	1996	2+4	0	0	0	0
Schuster, John	Halifax Blue Sox	1996-97	31	9	127	3	293
Sculthorpe, Paul	St. Helens	1998	19+1	5	0	0	20
	Warrington Wolves	1996-97	40	6	0	0	24
Seaby, Mick	London Broncos	1997	3+2	1	0	0	4
Seal, Danny	Halifax Blue Sox	1996	4+7	1	0	0	4
Senior, Keith	Sheffield Eagles	1996-98	61+2	34	0	0	136
Seru, Fili	Hull Sharks	1998	22	11	0	0	44
Shaw, Darren	Sheffield Eagles	1998	23	1	0	0	4
	London Broncos	1996	20+2	3	0	0	12
Shaw, Mick	Leeds	1996	12+2	7	0	0	28
Shead, Phil	Paris St. Germain	1996	3+2	0	0	0	0
Shelford, Kelly	Warrington Wolves	1996-97	26+3	4	0	2	18
Sheridan, Ryan	Leeds Rhinos	1997-98	35+3	10	0	0	40
	Sheffield Eagles	1996	9+3	5	0	1	21
Sherratt, Ian	Oldham Bears	1996	5+3	1	0	0	4
Shiel, Richard	St. Helens	1997	0+1	0	0	0	0
Simpson, Darren	Huddersfield Giants	1998	5	2	0	0	8
Sinfield, Kevin	Leeds Rhinos	1997-98	0+4	1	0	0	4
Sing, Wayne	Paris St. Germain	1997	18+1	2	0	0	8
Sini, Fata	Salford Reds	1997	22	7	0	0	28
Skerrett, Kelvin	Halifax Blue Sox	1997-98	19+6	2	0	0	8
	Wigan	1996	1+8	0	0	0	0
Slicker, Michael	Halifax Blue Sox	1997	2+5	0	0	0	0
Smales, Ian	Castleford Tigers	1996-97	10+8	5	0	0	20
Smith, Chris	St. Helens	1998	22	7	0	0	28
	Castleford Tigers	1996-97	36	12	0	0	48

Player	Club	Period	App	T	G	D	Pts
Smith, Damien	St. Helens	1998	18+1	5	0	0	20
Smith, Danny	Paris St. Germain	1996	10+2	1	15	0	34
	London Broncos	1996	2+1	1	0	0	4
Smith, Jamie	Hull Sharks	1998	8+4	3	12	0	36
	Workington Town	1996	5+3	0	1	0	2
Smith, Leigh	Workington Town	1996	9	4	0	0	16
Smith, Michael	Castleford Tigers	1998	14+6	6	0	0	24
Smith, Paul	Castleford Tigers	1997-98	1+13	1	0	0	4
Smith, Paul	London Broncos	1997	7+1	2	0	0	8
Smith, Peter	Oldham Bears	1996	2	0	0	0	0
Smith, Richard	Salford Reds	1997	0+1	1	0	0	4
Smith, Tony	Wigan Warriors	1997-98	35	30	0	0	120
	Castleford Tigers	1996-97	18+2	10	0	0	40
Smith, Tony	Workington Town	1996	9	1	0	0	4
Smyth, Rob	London Broncos	1998	16	5	0	0	20
	Wigan Warriors	1996	11+5	16	0	0	64
Sodje, Bright	Sheffield Eagles	1996-98	28	19	0	0	76
Sort, Romain	Paris St. Germain	1997	0+1	0	0	0	0
Southern, Paul	Salford Reds	1997-98	19+13	1	2	0	8
Southernwood, Roy	Halifax Blue Sox	1996	2	0	0	0	0
Sovatabua, Waisale	Sheffield Eagles	1996-98	45+7	16	0	1	65
Spencer, Adrian	London Broncos	1996-98	8+22	4	0	0	16
Spruce, Stuart	Bradford Bulls	1996-98	54+1	26	0	0	104
St. Hilaire, Lee	Castleford Tigers	1997	4+2	0	0	0	0
St. Hilaire, Marcus	Leeds Rhinos	1996-98	21+15	9	0	0	36
Stainton, Dylan	Workington Town	1996	2+3	0	0	0	0
Stamper, Mark	Workington Town	1996	0+1	0	0	0	0
Steadman, Graham	Castleford Tigers	1996-97	12+17	5	0	0	20
Stephens, Gareth	Sheffield Eagles	1997-98	9+5	1	0	0	4
Stephenson, David	Hull Sharks	1998	11+7	3	0	0	12
	Oldham Bears	1997	10+8	2	0	0	8
Sterling, Paul	Leeds Rhinos	1997-98	41+1	26	0	0	104
Stevens, Paul	Oldham Bears	1996	2+1	0	0	0	0
	London Broncos	1996	0+1	0	0	0	0
Stevens, Warren	Warrington Wolves	1996-98	14+16	0	0	0	0
Stewart, Tony	St. Helens	1997-98	1+5	1	0	0	4
Stott, Lynton	Sheffield Eagles	1996-98	40+5	15	0	0	60
Strutton, Graham	London Broncos	1996	9+1	2	0	0	8
Sturm, Matt	Huddersfield Giants	1998	23	6	0	0	24
Sullivan, Anthony	St. Helens	1996-98	60	51	0	0	204
Sumner, Phil	Warrington Wolves	1996	0+5	0	0	0	0
Svabic, Simon	Salford Reds	1998	7	0	12	0	24
Swann, Willie	Warrington Wolves	1996-97	25+2	6	0	0	24
Sykes, Nathan	Castleford Tigers	1996-98	41+5	2	0	0	8
Taewa, Whetu	Sheffield Eagles	1997-98	33+7	8	0	0	32
Tait, Alan	Leeds	1996	3+3	1	0	0	4
Talbot, Ian	Wigan	1997	3	1	0	0	4
Tallec, Gael	Castleford Tigers	1998	6+7	1	0	0	4
	Wigan Warriors	1996-97	8+12	3	0	0	12
Tamani, Joe	Bradford Bulls	1996	11+3	4	0	0	16
Tatupu, Shem	Wigan	1996	0+3	0	0	0	0
Tatupu, Tony	Warrington Wolves	1997	21+1	6	0	0	24
Taylor, Joe	Paris St. Germain	1997	9+5	2	0	0	8
Taylor, Lawrence	Sheffield Eagles	1996-97	0+2	0	0	0	0
Teixido, Frederic	Paris St. Germain	1996-97	2+3	1	0	0	4
Temu, Jason	Hull Sharks	1998	13+2	1	0	0	4
	Oldham Bears	1996-97	25+3	1	0	0	4

Player	Club	Period	App	T	G	D	Pts
Terry, Paul	London Broncos	1997	0+1	0	0	0	0
Thomas, Giles	London Broncos	1997-98	0+2	0	0	0	0
Thompson, Alex	Sheffield Eagles	1997	4+11	0	0	0	0
Thorniley, Tony	Warrington Wolves	1997	0+5	0	0	0	0
Timu, John	London Broncos	1998	17+1	6	0	0	24
Toby, Kerrod	London Broncos	1997	2+2	0	0	0	0
Tollett, Tulsen	London Broncos	1996-98	58+1	18	13	1	99
Tomlinson, Glen	Hull Sharks	1998	5	1	0	0	4
	Bradford Bulls	1996-97	27+13	12	0	0	48
Tonks, Ian	Castleford Tigers	1996-98	9+9	3	4	0	20
Topping, Paul	Oldham Bears	1996-97	23+10	1	19	0	42
Torreilles, Patrick	Paris St. Germain	1996	9+1	1	25	0	54
Toshack, Matt	London Broncos	1998	20+1	1	0	0	4
Tuigamala, Va'aiga	Wigan	1996	21	10	3	0	46
Tuilagi, Fereti	Halifax Blue Sox	1996-98	54+3	26	0	0	104
Tuipulotu, Sateki	Leeds	1996	6+3	1	2	0	8
Turner, Darren	Sheffield Eagles	1996-98	20+26	12	0	0	48
Turner, Ian	Paris St. Germain	1996	1+1	1	0	0	4
Tutard, Gregory	Paris St. Germain	1996	1+1	0	0	0	0
Tuuta, Brendon	Warrington Wolves	1998	18+2	4	0	0	16
	Castleford Tigers	1996-97	41+1	3	0	0	12
Umaga, Mike	Halifax Blue Sox	1996-97	38+1	16	5	0	74
Utoikamanu, Kava	Paris St. Germain	1996	6+3	0	0	0	0
Vagana, Nigel	Warrington Wolves	1997	20	17	0	0	68
Vaikona, Tevita	Bradford Bulls	1998	19	12	0	0	48
Van Brussell, Eric	Paris St. Germain	1996	2	0	0	0	0
Vassilakopoulos, Marcus	Sheffield Eagles	1997-98	15+9	3	10	1	33
	Leeds	1996-97	1+3	0	0	0	0
Veivers, Phil	Huddersfield Giants	1998	7+6	1	0	0	4
	St. Helens	1996	0+1	1	0	0	4
Vergniol, Eric	Paris St. Germain	1996	14+1	6	0	0	24
Vowles, Adrian	Castleford Tigers	1997-98	45	11	1	0	46
Wainwright, Mike	Warrington Wolves	1996-98	30+6	6	0	0	24
Wall, Anthony	Paris St. Germain	1997	9	2	3	0	14
Wallace, Mark	Workington Town	1996	14+1	3	0	0	12
Waring, Phil	Salford Reds	1997-98	1+6	1	0	0	4
Watson, Dave	Sheffield Eagles	1998	20+2	1	0	0	4
Watson, Ian	Salford Reds	1997	13+6	6	3	4	34
	Workington Town	1996	4+1	1	15	0	34
Watson, Kris	Warrington Wolves	1996	11+2	2	0	0	8
Wellens, Paul	St. Helens	1998	0+3	0	0	0	0
Wells, Jon	Castleford Tigers	1996-98	22+1	6	0	0	24
Weston, Craig	Huddersfield Giants	1998	18+1	5	8	0	36
Whalley, Andrew	Workington Town	1996	0+2	0	0	0	0
White, Josh	Salford Reds	1998	18+3	5	5	1	31
	London Broncos	1997	14+2	8	0	1	33
Whittle, Danny	Warrington Wolves	1998	0+2	0	0	0	0
Wilkes, Oliver	Sheffield Eagles	1998	0+1	0	0	0	0
Williams, Bart	London Broncos	1998	5+3	1	0	0	4
Wilson, George	Paris St. Germain	1996	7+2	3	0	0	12
Wilson, Richard	Hull Sharks	1998	0+10	0	0	0	0
Wilson, Scott	Warrington Wolves	1998	0+1	0	0	0	0
Wingfield, Paul	Warrington Wolves	1997	5+3	6	1	0	26
Wittenberg, Jeff	Huddersfield Giants	1998	18+1	1	0	0	4
	Bradford Bulls	1997	8+9	4	0	0	16

Player	Club	Period	App	T	G	D	Pts
Wood, Martin	Sheffield Eagles	1997-98	24+11	4	18	2	54
Wright, Nigel	Wigan	1996-97	5+5	2	0	1	9
Wright, Ricky	Sheffield Eagles	1997	2+5	0	0	0	0
Wulf, Vincent	Paris St. Germain	1996	13+5	4	0	0	16
Yaha, Bagdad	Paris St. Germain	1996	4+4	2	4	0	16
Yasa, Malakai	Sheffield Eagles	1996	1+3	0	0	0	0
Young, Grant	London Broncos	1998	20+2	2	0	0	8
Zenon, Ronel	Paris St. Germain	1996	0+4	0	0	0	0

Paul Newlove: Scorer of a record 52 Super League tries.

DIVISION ONE/SUPER LEAGUE CHAMPIONS'
AND RUNNERS-UP PLAYING RECORD

DIVISION ONE

		P	W	D	L	F	A	Pts
1902-03	**Halifax**	34	23	3	8	199	85	49
	Salford	34	20	5	9	244	130	45
1903-04	**Bradford**	34	25	2	7	303	96	52
	Salford	34	25	2	7	366	108	52
1904-05	**Oldham**	34	25	1	8	291	158	51
	Bradford	34	23	2	9	294	156	48
1962-63	**Swinton**	30	22	1	7	372	231	45
	St. Helens	30	19	1	10	525	260	39
1963-64	**Swinton**	30	25	0	5	401	202	50
	Wigan	30	21	2	7	530	294	44
1973-74	**Salford**	30	23	1	6	632	299	47
	St. Helens	30	22	2	6	595	263	46
1974-75	**St. Helens**	30	26	1	3	561	229	53
	Wigan	30	21	0	9	517	341	42
1975-76	**Salford**	30	22	1	7	555	350	45
	Featherstone Rovers	30	21	2	7	526	348	44
1976-77	**Featherstone Rovers**	30	21	2	7	568	334	44
	St. Helens	30	19	1	10	547	345	39
1977-78	**Widnes**	30	24	2	4	613	241	50
	Bradford Northern*	29	21	2	6	500	291	44
1978-79	**Hull Kingston Rvrs**	30	23	0	7	616	344	46
	Warrington	30	22	0	8	521	340	44
1979-80	**Bradford Northern**	30	23	0	7	448	272	46
	Widnes	30	22	1	7	546	293	45
1980-81	**Bradford Northern**	30	20	1	9	447	345	41
	Warrington	30	19	1	10	459	330	39
1981-82	**Leigh**	30	24	1	5	572	343	49
	Hull	30	23	1	6	611	273	47
1982-83	**Hull**	30	23	1	6	572	293	47
	Hull Kingston Rovers	30	21	1	8	496	276	43
1983-84	**Hull Kingston Rvrs**	30	22	2	6	795	421	46
	Hull	30	22	1	7	831	401	45
1984-85	**Hull Kingston Rvrs**	30	24	0	6	778	391	48
	St. Helens	30	22	1	7	920	508	45
1985-86	**Halifax**	30	19	6	5	499	365	44
	Wigan	30	20	3	7	776	300	43
1986-87	**Wigan**	30	28	0	2	941	193	56
	St. Helens	30	20	1	9	835	465	41
1987-88	**Widnes**	26	20	0	6	641	311	40

	St. Helens	26	18	0	8	672	337	36
1988-89	**Widnes**	26	20	1	5	726	345	41
	Wigan	26	19	0	7	543	434	38
1989-90	**Wigan**	26	20	0	6	699	349	40
	Leeds	26	18	0	8	704	383	36
1990-91	**Wigan**	26	20	2	4	652	313	42
	Widnes	26	20	0	6	635	340	40
1991-92	**Wigan**	26	22	0	4	645	307	44
	St. Helens	26	17	2	7	550	388	36
1992-93	**Wigan**	26	20	1	5	744	327	41
	St. Helens	26	20	1	5	632	345	41
1993-94	**Wigan**	30	23	0	7	780	403	46
	Bradford N.	30	23	0	7	784	555	46
	Warrington	30	23	0	7	628	430	46
1994-95	**Wigan**	30	28	0	2	1148	386	56
	Leeds	30	24	1	5	863	526	49
1995-96	**Wigan**	20	18	0	2	810	316	36
	Leeds	20	14	0	6	552	405	28

SUPER LEAGUE

1996	**St. Helens**	22	20	0	2	950	455	40
	Wigan	22	19	1	2	902	326	39
1997	**Bradford Bulls**	22	20	0	2	769	397	40
	London Broncos	22	15	3	4	616	418	33
1998	**Wigan Warriors★★**	23	21	0	2	762	222	42
	Leeds Rhinos	23	19	0	4	662	369	38

★ Bradford second on percentage as last game was cancelled following Featherstone Rovers players' strike.

★★ The title of champions went to the club winning the Grand Final after a top five play-off.

● The old Division One was the major league until it became the Centenary Championship in 1995-96 and the Stones European Super League in 1996. It became the JJB Super League in 1998. The old Division One was also known by its sponsorship title in the following seasons: Slalom Lager Championship 1980-81 to 1985-86; Stones Bitter Championship 1986-87 to 1994-95. It was the Stones Bitter Centenary Championship in 1995-96.

● In 1903-04 Salford had the same won 25, drew two, lost seven record as Bradford and had a better scoring ratio of 366 points against 188, but lost a play-off for the Championship 5-0 at Halifax.

On the two other occasions when the leading clubs have tied on points the title has gone to the club with the best For and Against points difference. This happened in 1992-93 and again in 1993-94 when Wigan, Bradford Northern and Warrington all finished with 46 points.

● Wigan (56 points) finished a record 15 points clear of second placed St. Helens (41) in 1986-87.

1998 FIRST DIVISION GRAND FINAL

Wakefield Trinity became the inaugural First Division Grand Final winners with a late 24-22 win over Featherstone Rovers after a pulsating game that lived up to the pre-match billing of 'A Night to Remember'. The League leaders snatched victory five minutes from the end when Francis Stephenson plunged over and Garen Casey kicked the match-winning goal just when it seemed Featherstone Rovers were going to complete their end of season surge by lifting the title from fourth place.

An action- and incident-packed final reached a tremendous climax with Featherstone coming from behind to take a 22-18 lead in the 68th minute and seeming to clinch victory with a spectacular long distance touchdown only for it to be disallowed. Wakefield then hit back to regain the lead and hold on to it in the last few frantic minutes.

Some consolation for Richard Chapman was that he became the first player from a losing side to receive the Tom Bergin Trophy as the man of the match ahead of some strong challengers. The hooker was involved in creating Featherstone's first two tries and kicked three goals.

Wakefield stand off Casey pushed him close for individual honours with one try, a big say in another and two goals, including the match winner landed under great pressure. It proved to be an impressive farewell to Trinity by the Australian who had already agreed to join Super League club Salford Reds.

The crucial moment of the game came just after Featherstone had taken their 22-18 lead 12 minutes from time. Wakefield were attacking deep inside the opposition's half when Featherstone forward substitute Asa Amone sent the ball spinning from Roy Southernwood's grasp with a shattering tackle. Amone snatched it up to break away and send Karl Pratt sprinting clear for a touchdown. Featherstone fans and players were in ecstatic mood until referee Nick Oddy was seen to consult a touch judge before ruling 'no try' because Amone had knocked on when making his tackle. Although the video screen was not in official use, TV recordings showed it was a correct decision.

Wakefield had dominated the first half after opening with two tries in six minutes and adding another in the 25th minute, but with Casey failing with all three conversion attempts Featherstone were only 12-6 down at the interval. Danny Baker scored Featherstone's first half try when he followed up Chapman's high kick to take advantage of a favourable bounce and touch down after wing colleague Pratt managed to get a hand to the ball.

Roy Southernwood had given Wakefield a flying start as he sneaked in from a play-the-ball after only two minutes and four minutes later Josh Bostock went in at the corner off Matt Fuller's pass. After Baker hit back with a Featherstone try, Bostock scored a second with the big Australian winger again using his strength to blast through the Rovers' defence.

Featherstone had stormed back from an 18-0 interval deficit to beat Wakefield earlier in the season and eight minutes into the second half of the Grand Final they were in front. Chapman inspired the comeback as he handled twice in a move close to Trinity's line before sending in Anthony Jackson at the corner. An angled goal from Chapman raised Rovers' hopes higher and he added an easier one when Ty Fallins broke away near the centre spot and Steve Collins backed up to go in between the posts.

Nine minutes later Wakefield were level again after Casey burst on to Roger Kenworthy's long pass to charge in from 20 metres and add the goal. But the match took another twist when Carl Hall's try in the corner made it 22-18 to Featherstone before Wakefield started their final surge for victory.

Although the attendance of just over 8000 was below expectations, the fans of both clubs gave vociferous support to create a tremendous traditional derby match atmosphere in a modern stadium. Despite their defeat, Featherstone earned just as much praise as the victors for their part in a highly entertaining game which reflected the fierce competition there had been throughout the First Division season.

Wakefield's victory earned them the right to apply to join Super League and after a careful study of their off-the-field qualifications they were promoted.

Roy Southernwood: Wakefield Trinity try scorer.

QUOTES

ANDY KELLY (Wakefield coach): I would like to pay tribute to Featherstone. I don't think as a team they could have done any more than they did and I thought Richard Chapman was a deserving man of the match. The turning point was our final try, because there were no certainties until then, with perhaps our spirit and strength of commitment eventually seeing us through. But I wouldn't have liked extra time. That would have been a nightmare.

STEVE SIMMS (Featherstone coach): I said to my players straight after the match that I was very proud of them, and that though they were losers in the game they were not losers as people. They put up an absolutely fantastic performance. I think if Wakefield get everything in order off the field they should be promoted. I shouldn't think they are too far behind the other Super League clubs if you take away the first half-dozen.

MATT FULLER (Wakefield captain): This was as intense as anything I experienced in Australia and as big as any game I've played in. After Featherstone's last try I had to give my players a bit of a blasting and ask them to lift their intensity for one more effort with something like ten minutes to go. We did that and held out like champions.

RICHARD CHAPMAN (Featherstone, man of the match): It was the most intense match I have played in this season. It went so fast with so much commitment from both sides. We were disappointed to let them get a big start on us. In the first half we tried to tackle too high, to big-hit them and it just didn't work. They are a bigger side than us and perhaps we should have leg tackled a bit more, because going high enabled them to offload the ball. But it was a great occasion and great performance in a great game.

FIRST DIVISION GRAND FINAL
Saturday 26 September 1998   Alfred McAlpine Stadium, Huddersfield

WAKEFIELD TRINITY 24

Martyn Holland	Full back	Steve Collins
Josh Bostock	Wing	Carl Hall
Adam Hughes	Centre	Shaun Irwin, Captain
Martin Law	Centre	Danny Baker
Kevin Gray	Wing	Karl Pratt
Garen Casey	Stand off	Jamie Coventry
Roger Kenworthy	Scrum half	Ty Fallins
Francis Stephenson	Prop	Anthony "Chico" Jackson
Roy Southernwood	Hooker	Richard Chapman
Gary Lord	Prop	Stuart Dickens
Ian Hughes	Second row	Gary Price
Sonny Whakarau	Second row	Neil Lowe
Matt Fuller, Captain	Loose forward	Richard Slater

FEATHERSTONE ROVERS 22

Substitutes
Sean Richardson for I. Hughes (32 min.)
Andy Fisher for Lord (26 min.)
David Mycoe (not used)
Wayne McDonald for Whakarau (70 min.)
Lord for Stephenson (40 min.)
Stephenson for Lord (70 min.)

Substitutes
Paddy Handley for Coventry (70 min.)
Asa Amone for Lowe (50 min.)
Micky Clarkson for Jackson (50 min.)
Steve Dooler (not used)

T: Bostock (2), Southernwood, Casey, Stephenson
G: Casey (2)

T: Baker, Jackson, Collins, Hall
G: Chapman (3)

Coach: Andy Kelly

Coach: Steve Simms

Penalties: 3-8
Half-time: 12-6
Tom Bergin Trophy for Man of the Match: Richard Chapman (Featherstone)

Referee: Nick Oddy (Halifax)
Attendance: 8224

HOW THE SCORING WENT

2 min. Southernwood (Wakefield) try		**4-0**
6 min. Bostock (Wakefield) try		**8-0**
14 min. Baker (Featherstone) try, Chapman goal		**8-6**
25 min. Bostock (Wakefield) try		**12-6**
44 min. Jackson (Featherstone) try, Chapman goal		**12-12**
48 min. Collins (Featherstone) try, Chapman goal		**12-18**
57 min. Casey (Wakefield) try, Casey goal		**18-18**
68 min. Hall (Featherstone) try		**18-22**
75 min. Stephenson (Wakefield) try, Casey goal		**24-22**

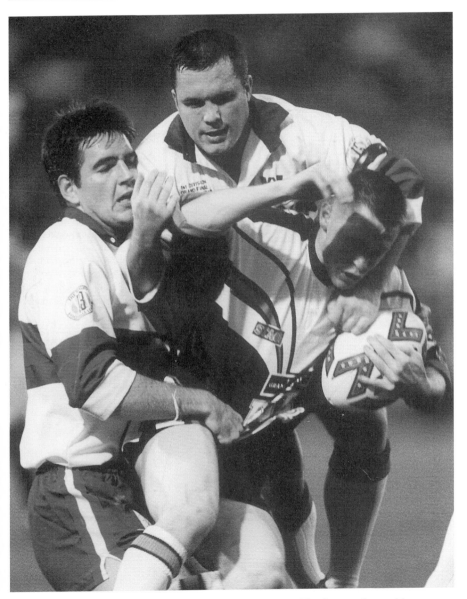

Grand defence: Wakefield Trinity players display the ferocious tackling that was a feature of the First Division Grand Final.

FIRST DIVISION 1998
PLAY-OFF MATCHES
The top five play-off formula was the same as for Super League.

Elimination Play-off
Featherstone R. 22 v Swinton L. 12
Featherstone snatched a play-off place with four wins in their last five matches taking them into fourth spot and they continued their late run of success by beating Swinton in a thrilling encounter at Post Office Road. A hat-trick of tries from second row Neil Lowe finished off Swinton, who had three tries disallowed. Australian scrum half Ty Fallins kept edging Featherstone ahead with four goals, including two drop goals.

Qualifying Play-off
Hull K. R. 18 v Dewsbury R. 2
Having beaten Hull K.R. twice in their three League meetings during the season, Dewsbury went to Craven Park full of confidence. But Rovers were well prepared this time and finished convincing winners despite being limited to only two tries. Mike Fletcher built up the score with four goals, while Chris Charles and Stanley Gene popped over drop goals.

Elimination semi-final
Dewsbury R. 10 v Featherstone R. 20
Featherstone's end-of-season snowball rolled on as they kept on course for the Grand Final by flattening Dewsbury at the Rams Stadium. Four tries to one give a truer reflection of Rovers' superiority with young winger Karl Pratt racing clear for two of them in a display that increased the interest being shown by Super League clubs. The defeat was a disappointing end to what remained Dewsbury's best season for over 20 years.

Qualifying semi-final
Wakefield T. 19 v Hull K.R. 16
Hull K.R. had piled up 98 points in beating Wakefield three times during the League season, but it all counted for nothing as Trinity gained the victory that mattered most to go through to the Grand Final. Four goals, includ-

ing a drop goal, by Garen Casey tipped the game Wakefield's way as both sides scored three tries. Casey also created an early try for Martyn Holland and went on to give an inspiring performance.

Final eliminator
Hull K.R. 6 v Featherstone R. 54
This was one of the most amazing scorelines of the season. Even Featherstone's late run of success prepared no one for the complete destruction of Hull K.R., who had been well fancied to reach the Grand Final. Featherstone had lost all three League matches to Hull K.R. during the League season, but their vast improvement was obvious as they raced to an 18-0 interval lead. Richard Chapman led the points spree with 24 points from two tries and eight goals in an impressive all-round display by the hooker. After struggling for much of the season to fulfil their expectations Featherstone were now through to the Grand Final with a great chance of winning the First Division championship from fourth place.

Mike Fletcher: Four goals for Hull K.R. in the defeat of Dewsbury Rams.

1998 FIRST DIVISION CHAMPIONSHIP

Wakefield Trinity finished at the top of the First Division and were awarded a League Leaders' trophy when FASDA clubs agreed to their request for one a few days before the last match of the season. This went against a pre-season decision by the RL Council not to award a trophy, but Trinity felt they should be rewarded for finishing four points ahead of their nearest rivals Hull Kingston Rovers. Ironically, Rovers had beaten Trinity in all three League matches before losing to them in the play-off. Coached by Andy Kelly with Matt Fuller as captain, Wakefield showed a big improvement after finishing fifth the previous season. They opened with five successive wins and led for most of the season. Stand off Garen Casey finished at the top of two First Division scoring charts with 112 goals and 281 points, including 15 tries. Despite finishing top, Wakefield had to win the Grand Final and then apply for Super League status before they were promoted.

Hull Kingston Rovers made the most progress over the year, rising from eighth in 1997 to finish second after leading for four rounds towards the end of the season. They were also the early season leaders following an opening run of six successive victories. Stanley Gene finished as the division's leading tryscorer with 28 and was elected player of the year.

Dewsbury Rams' rise from sixth to third place helped Neil Kelly take the FASDA coach of the year award. Highlights of their season were a win and a draw at Wakefield plus a double over Hull K.R.

Featherstone Rovers won their last three matches to jump from sixth to fourth place and continue their late surge right through to the Grand Final. Rovers went into their last match needing to win by at least 33 points to clinch a top five place and they achieved it with a 58-4 home defeat of Leigh Centurions.

Swinton Lions had home victories over all four teams who finished above them, but failed to produce their best form away. A top five place, however, was a big improvement on the previous year when they were always battling against relegation.

Hunslet Hawks challenged strongly for a top five spot after being promoted as Second Division champions and just missed out despite finishing the season with a 19-18 home victory over second placed Hull K.R. They had also beaten Rovers 31-30 at home earlier in the season to leap into the runners-up spot for a brief period.

Keighley Cougars began as 3-1 favourites for the title, but soon became outsiders after losing their first four matches. The run of defeats resulted in John Kain being replaced as coach by Lee Crooks, who started with a victory and saw the club make gradual improvement. A drop of four places to seventh, however, was still the biggest fall from the previous season.

Whitehaven Warriors shared Keighley's record of dropping four places and also parted company with their coach, Steve Martin. He was replaced by Colin Armstrong for their last five matches, which brought only one more victory and left them in eighth spot, before Kevin Tamati was appointed.

Widnes Vikings sacked Graeme West as coach following a 63-4 home defeat by Hull K.R. near the end of the season and replaced him with Colin Whitfield. A few weeks earlier Widnes had conceded a club record number of points with a 64-8 defeat at Wakefield.

Rochdale Hornets found it tough going after being promoted and finished second off bottom following an early season run of six successive defeats which led to the sacking of Shane Tupaea as coach. The run had been extended to 10 defeats when Deryck Fox ended it in his first match as player-coach with an extraordinary 46-18 win at Featherstone.

Leigh Centurions had only gained promotion after a revamping of the divisions and they were clearly not ready for it as they finished at the bottom. Norman Turley replaced Keith Latham as coach midway through the season in the early stages of an 11-match losing run.

1998 FIRST DIVISION CHAMPIONSHIP

	P.	W.	D.	L.	Dg.	FOR			AGAINST				
						Gls.	Trs.	Pts.	Dg.	Gls.	Trs.	Pts.	Pts.
1. Wakefield Trinity	30	22	1	7	4	115	139	790	8	83	83	506	45
2. Hull Kingston Rovers	30	20	1	9	6	125	123	748	12	74	80	480	41
3. Dewsbury Rams	30	19	2	9	5	121	119	723	5	74	82	481	40
4. Featherstone Rovers	30	17	1	12	11	124	130	779	7	87	108	613	35
5. Swinton Lions	30	17	1	12	14	102	121	702	6	85	92	544	35
6. Hunslet Hawks	30	17	1	12	13	105	124	719	7	90	97	575	35
7. Keighley Cougars	30	14	1	15	5	81	105	587	5	107	114	675	29
8. Whitehaven Warriors	30	13	0	17	2	93	112	636	7	99	113	657	26
9. Widnes Vikings	30	9	1	20	3	109	95	601	6	132	148	862	19
10. Rochdale Hornets	30	6	1	23	5	83	100	571	4	142	156	912	13
11. Leigh Centurions	30	6	0	24	1	80	86	505	2	165	181	1056	12

Totals: 165 matches; 69 drop goals; 1,138 goals; 1,254 tries; 7,361 points
Fixture format: Clubs played each other three times. The top five clubs qualified for the Grand Final play-off to decide the championship on the same lines as Super League.

1998 PRE-SEASON BETTING FOR THE FIRST DIVISION CHAMPIONSHIP
3-1 Keighley C.; **7-2** Featherstone R., Whitehaven W.; **9-2** Widnes V.; **6-1** Wakefield T.; **9-1** Hull K.R.; **10-1** Dewsbury R., Hunslet H.; **25-1** Rochdale H., Swinton L. , Leigh C.

FIRST DIVISION TOP TEN SCORERS

TOP TEN TRIES
1. Stanley Gene (Hull Kingston R.) 28
2. Matt Bramald (Dewsbury Rams) 20
3. Steve Collins (Featherstone Rovers)................19
4. Adam Hughes (Wakefield Trinity) 18
   Lee Kiddie (Whitehaven Warriors) 18
   Richard Baker (Hunslet Hawks) 18
7. Andy Craig (Swinton Lions) 16
   Jason Lee (Keighley Cougars) 16
9. Garen Casey (Wakefield Trinity) 15
10. Gavin Price-Jones (Swinton Lions) 14
    Karl Pratt (Featherstone Rovers) 14
    Richard Chapman (Featherstone Rovers).........14

TOP TEN GOALS
1. Garen Casey (Wakefield Trinity) ....(3) 112
2. Barry Eaton (Dewsbury Rams).......................109
3. Steve Gartland (Swinton Lions)...............(6) 103
4. Mike Fletcher (Hull Kingston R.) 91
5. Mark Hewitt (Widnes Vikings) ....(3) 86
6. Ty Fallins (Featherstone Rovers) ....(8) 70
7. St. John Ellis (Hunslet Hawks) ....(2) 67
8. Paul Wingfield (Leigh Centurions) 61
   Kevin Hetherington (Whitehaven W.) 61
   Richard Chapman (Featherstone R.)..........(1) 61
( ) *Drop goals included in total*

DROP GOALS

Ty Fallins (Featherstone Rovers).............................. 8
Steve Gartland (Swinton Lions) 6

TOP TEN POINTS

	Trs.	Gls.	Dg.	Pts.
1. Garen Casey (Wakefield Trinity)................	15	109	3	281
2. Steve Gartland (Swinton Lions).................	11	97	6	244
3. Barry Eaton (Dewsbury Rams)	6	109	0	242
4. Mike Fletcher (Hull Kingston R.)	2	91	0	190
5. Mark Hewitt (Widnes Vikings)	2	83	3	177
Richard Chapman (Featherstone Rovers) ...	14	60	1	177
7. St. John Ellis (Hunslet Hawks)...................	11	65	2	176
8. Ty Fallins (Featherstone Rovers)	6	62	8	156
9. Kevin Hetherington (Whitehaven W.)	6	61	0	146
10. Paul Wingfield (Leigh Centurions).............	4	61	0	138

Stanley Gene: Leading try scorer with 28.

1998 SECOND DIVISION CHAMPIONSHIP

Lancashire Lynx won the first trophy in their nine-year history when they became surprise winners of the Second Division championship after finishing only sixth a year earlier. There was no play-off for the title and captain Andy Ruane carried off the trophy after the last match of the season. Although Lancashire lost 31-22 at home to Batley Bulldogs to finish on the same 28 points mark as York, a superior scoring difference kept them at the top. On a tight budget and with a small squad of players, chief executive Kevin Tamati and coach Steve Hampson did a marvellous job in steering them to the championship. Stand off Phil Jones finished at the top of two Second Division scoring charts with 87 goals and 218 points, including 11 tries.

York had to win by a large margin in their last match and Lancashire lose for the Yorkshire club to lift the title. They made a big effort to achieve the near impossible with a 38-8 victory at Oldham, but even though Lancashire lost the title was theirs. It had been a tremendous late surge by York, who won their last five matches.

Batley Bulldogs also made a late charge for the title, ending the season with six successive victories but fell two points short of Lancashire and York, against whom they totalled five wins out of six meetings. But they finished at the top of the mid-season White Rose Championship, whose results were also included in the Second Division table, and beat Oldham in the final.

Bramley moved up from ninth in 1997 to fourth to share with Lancashire the record of making most progress over the year. But many regarded them as little more than a Leeds Rhinos reserve team as they took several of their players on loan, including Test forward Barrie McDermott.

Oldham took the Red Rose Championship in their first season after being re-born and placed in the Second Division following their demise as a Super League club. A modest fifth place was not enough to save Paddy Kirwan,

however, and he was replaced as coach by Mick Coates with three matches left.

Barrow Border Raiders made a promising start with only one defeat in their first five matches before a run of inconsistency was followed with just two wins in their last eight matches. Their sixth position was two places up on the previous year, but Stuart Wilkinson was sacked as coach at the end of the season and replaced by Paul Charlton.

Workington Town's disastrous decline continued. Bottom of Super League and the First Division in successive seasons, they just managed to avoid a basement hat-trick. Australian coach Robert Tew was not retained at the end of the season and former Great Britain forward Andy Platt was handed the job of restoring the club to its former glories.

Doncaster Dragons hit rock bottom only three years after their one season in the old Division One. Both of Doncaster's wins were against top three side Batley Bulldogs, while they managed draws against Bramley and Workington Town.

Steve Hampson: Coach of champions Lancashire Lynx.

1998 SECOND DIVISION CHAMPIONSHIP

	P.	W.	D.	L.	Dg.	Gls.	Trs.	Pts.	Dg.	Gls.	Trs.	Pts.	Pts.
						FOR				AGAINST			
1. Lancashire Lynx	20	13	2	5	7	85	96	561	9	45	60	339	28
2. York	20	14	0	6	12	64	84	476	6	49	44	280	28
3. Batley Bulldogs	20	13	0	7	9	70	72	437	14	44	63	354	26
4. Bramley	20	12	1	7	5	75	83	487	4	51	70	386	25
5. Oldham	20	10	1	9	3	52	73	399	5	59	65	383	21
6. Barrow Border Raiders	20	8	2	10	4	41	67	354	7	65	60	377	18
7. Workington Town	20	3	2	15	7	43	50	293	6	78	99	558	8
8. Doncaster Dragons	20	2	2	16	7	43	49	289	3	82	113	619	6

Totals: 80 matches; 54 drop goals; 473 goals; 574 tries; 3,296 points

Fixture format: Clubs played each other once before the division was split into two regions, East and West of the Pennines, for the Red Rose and White Rose championships. Each club played the three others in their region home and away with the two finishing on top meeting for the Trans-Pennine Cup. The normal Second Division programme then resumed. All regional matches, apart from the final, also counted in the Second Division championship with the leaders becoming champions.

SECOND DIVISION TOP TEN SCORERS 1998

TOP TEN TRIES

1. Chris Eckersley (Oldham) 15
2. Leigh Deakin (York) 13
3. Neil Parsley (Lancashire Lynx) 11
   Dan Potter (Bramley) 11
   Phil Jones (Lancashire Lynx) 11
   Paul Gleadhill (Batley Bulldogs) 11
7. Chris Kelly (Lancashire Lynx) 9
   Darren Abram (Lancashire Lynx) 9
   Shaun Austerfield (York) 9
10. Gary Ruddy (Barrow Border R.) 8
    David Murray (Lancashire Lynx) 8
    Afi Leuila (Oldham).................................... 8
    Alex Godfrey (York) 8

TOP TEN GOALS

1. Phil Jones (Lancashire Lynx)..........................87
2. Richard Price (Batley Bulldogs)......................67
3. Kris Smith (Bramley)......................................52
4. Chris Wilkinson (Oldham)...................... (3) 35
5. Craig Booth (York)..25
6. Dean Marwood (Barrow Border R.).........(2) 23
   John Edwards (Doncaster Dragons) ....(6) 23
8. Craig Fisher (Workington Town) 20
9. Chris Hopcutt (York) ... .19
10. Paul Branthwaite (Workington T.) ... .17
( ) *Drop goals included in total*

DROP GOALS

Gary Barnett (Batley Bulldogs)................... 6
John Edwards (Doncaster Dragons)............ 6
Andy Ruane (Lancashire Lynx) 5
Steve Maguire (Workington Town) 5

TOP TEN POINTS

	Trs.	Gls.	Dg.	Pts.
1. Phil Jones (Lancashire Lynx)	11	87	0	218
2. Richard Price (Batley Bulldogs)	7	67	0	162
3. Kris Smith (Bramley)	2	52	0	112
4. Craig Booth (York)	5	25	0	70
5. Chris Wilkinson (Oldham)	0	32	3	67
6. Chris Eckersley (Oldham)	15	0	0	60
7. Phil Atkinson (Barrow Border R.)	6	15	1	55
8. Leigh Deakin (York)	13	0	0	52
Dean Marwood (Barrow Border R.)	2	21	2	52
10. Chris Hopcutt (York)	3	19	0	50

Andy Ruane: Captain of Second Division champions Lancashire Lynx.

TRANS-PENNINE CUP

1998 Final

Batley Bulldogs lifted their first trophy for 74 years when they beat Oldham 28-12 in the Trans-Pennine Cup final on their own Mount Pleasant ground. They had reached the final after losing only one of their six White Rose Championship matches, while Oldham just scraped through on points difference after dropping three points in the Red Rose Championship. The one-off competition for Second Division teams provided a touch of glory for two clubs who had been struggling for many years. In fact, Oldham were in their first year of re-birth after the old club had folded, while Batley were appearing in their first final since losing to Huddersfield in the 1952 Yorkshire Cup final.

Incessant rain failed to dampen the enthusiasm of the fans with Oldham's large following boosting the attendance to 2696 – Batley's biggest for three years. But the match nearly ended in tragedy after only 20 minutes when Batley captain Roy Powell swallowed his tongue and was near to losing his life before medical attention brought him round. The incident followed a scrum and play had continued before Powell was seen lying flat out. When referee Steve Nicholson realised the seriousness of the situation he waved the teams off the pitch and it was 15 minutes before play resumed as Powell was led to the dressing room. Powell had suffered a similar collapse nine years earlier while playing for Leeds.

The 33-year-old forward was playing again four weeks after the Cup final, but died tragically of a heart attack during training with his new club Rochdale Hornets on 27 December.

Batley were leading 6-0 when play was interrupted by the Powell incident and within three minutes of the restart they went 12 points ahead. They never looked like being caught from that moment as they took full advantage of the notorious Mount Pleasant slope to dominate the first half. It was 26-6 at the interval and though

Oldham made a big second half fight back they had left themselves with far too much to do.

Gary Barnett took the sponsors' man of the match award with an influential game at scrum half, scoring two tries and creating another before blotting his performance by spending the last few minutes of the game in the sin bin for dissent. Roger Simpson had Barnett to thank for the 100th try of his career, including 25 for Batley, as the scrum half drew Oldham's defence to one side before sending the centre in the opposite direction for a touchdown near the posts. Oldham pulled back to 12-6 only for Barnett to virtually finish them off with two tries in the last 11 minutes of the half.

A quick dummy from close range took him in for his first and he rounded off a superb attacking raid to go over for his second. Paul Harrison sparked off the 80-metre attack to launch the centre-wing partnership of Simpson and Paul Gleadhill down the left before Barnett took over to touch down. It was a top quality score and confirmed Batley's superiority although they added only a third penalty goal from Richard Price in the second half.

Stand off Price also made a big contribution to Batley's victory with a try and six goals to emphasise their big advantage at half back. Price had opened the scoring in the sixth minute when he exchanged passes with Harrison to go over for a well-worked try.

Oldham's performance was epitomised by Mick Martindale, who made some unforced handling errors, but kept battling away to score one try and have a hand in another. Ironically, his 27th minute try followed a dropped ball by Batley on their own line when the loose forward pounced for the touchdown. His involvement in Oldham's other try followed within minutes of returning to the field after being substituted, combining with Neil Flanagan to send Ian Sinfield over in the 54th minute.

Oldham were getting on top at this stage and would have put Batley under greater pressure had not Afi Leuila and Sean Cooper touchdowns been disallowed. They also went close to scoring when Chris Eckersley went hard for the corner and was crashed into touch by Jeremy Dyson's desperate tackle. It was typical of Batley's all-out effort which earned them the Cup and a much needed £20,000 cash prize.

With the First and Second Divisons combining for 1999, there was no place for the Red and White Rose championships or the Trans-Pennine Cup final in the new fixture format.

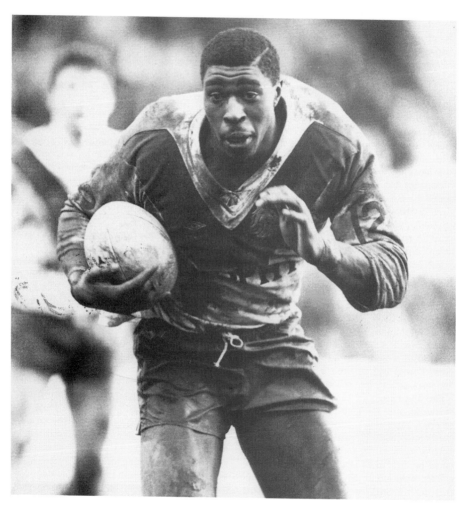

Roy Powell: Batley Bulldogs captain and former Great Britain forward, who died tragically of a heart attack in December.

TRANS-PENNINE CUP FINAL
Sunday 19 July 1998   Mount Pleasant, Batley

BATLEY BULLDOGS 28		OLDHAM 12
Jeremy Dyson	Full back	Stephen Wilde
Lee Bargate	Wing	Richard Darkes
Darren Hughes	Centre	Afi Leuila
Roger Simpson	Centre	Sean Cooper
Paul Gleadhill	Wing	Chris Eckersley
Richard Price	Stand off	Chris Wilkinson
Gary Barnett	Scrum half	Neil Flanagan, Captain
Roy Powell, Captain	Prop	Andrew Proctor
Mark Cass	Hooker	John Hough
Chris McWilliam	Prop	Michael Edwards
Grant Miers	Second row	Graeme Shaw
Phil Mirfin	Second row	Joe Naidole
Paul Harrison	Loose forward	Mick Martindale

Substitutes
Steve Walker – (not used)
Graham Middleton for Mifin (55 min.)
Andy Wray for Powell (20 min.)
Neil Bradbrook – (not used)
Mirfin for Wray (68 min.)

Substitutes
Adrian Mead for Wilde (13 min. blood bin)
Ian Sinfield for Martindale (50 min.)
Nathan Varley for Shaw (half-time)
Paul Round for Proctor (43 min.)
Martindale for Hough (53–64 min. blood bin)
Shaw for Naidole (58 min.)
Martindale for Varley (71 min.)
Proctor for Edwards (78 min.)

T: Barnett (2), Price, Simpson
G: Price (6)

T: Martindale, Sinfield
G: Wilkinson (2)

Coach: David Ward

Coach: Paddy Kirwan

Sin bin: Gary Barnett (77 min.)
Penalties: 10-13
Half-time: 26-6
Attendance: 2696

Referee: Steve Nicholson (Whitehaven)
Sponsors' man of the match: Gary Barnett (Batley)
Cup presented by Lord Lofthouse

HOW THE SCORING WENT

6 min. Price (Batley) try	4-0
8 min. Price (Batley) penalty goal	6-0
23 min. Simpson (Batley) try, Price goal	12-0
27 min. Martindale (Oldham) try, Wilkinson goal	12-6
29 min. Barnett (Batley) try, Price goal	18-6
35 min. Price (Batley) penalty goal	20-6
39 min. Barnett (Batley) try, Price goal	26-6
47 min. Price (Batley) penalty goal	28-6
54 min. Sinfield (Oldham) try, Wilkinson goal	28-12

QUOTES

DAVID WARD (Batley coach): I've played at Wembley and in Test matches, but I still get a big thrill out of occasions like this. This is massive, working with a bunch of guys like these. They are really 'roll up your sleeves' type of guys and they've got their reward today. I know the commitment they put in and I'm proud to be with them. They don't get great financial rewards, but hopefully they will now get some recognition. This is what Rugby League is all about. It was terrific. You don't need 100,000 people; there was still a great atmosphere.

PADDY KIRWAN (Oldham coach): We thought we were in the game until the stoppage for the Roy Powell incident. We felt that Batley had thrown everything at us and were starting to blow a little bit after about 20 minutes into the game. But they came out better after that break. We also made too many unforced errors and I thought the pass for Simpson's try was two yards forward. A couple of other decisions went against us.

RED ROSE/WHITE ROSE CHAMPIONSHIP

The Trans-Pennine Cup final involved the teams finishing at the top of the Red Rose and White Rose Championship tables after a mid-season competition for the eight Second Division clubs. These additional home and away matches between clubs from the same county were also incorporated in the normal Second Division table. A toss of a coin decided which club would be at home in the final. The competition was introduced to give Second Division clubs a larger programme of matches.

RED ROSE CHAMPIONSHIP TABLE

	P	W	D	L	F	A	Pts
Oldham	6	4	1	1	160	83	9
Lancashire L.	6	4	1	1	166	106	9
Barrow B.R.	6	2	0	4	100	116	4
Workington T.	6	1	0	5	83	204	2

WHITE ROSE CHAMPIONSHIP TABLE

	P	W	D	L	F	A	Pts
Batley B.	6	5	0	1	132	91	10
Bramley	6	4	0	2	185	119	8
York	6	3	0	3	118	99	6
Doncaster D.	6	0	0	6	102	228	0

Roger Simpson: Former Bradford Northern player who scored his 100th career try in Batley Bulldogs' Trans-Pennine Cup final victory.

Celebrations: Trans-Pennine Cup winners Batley Bulldogs were still celebrating at the end of the season after clinching promotion. The Second Division was later scrapped and all clubs moved up to the First Division.

DIVISION CHAMPIONS

	FIRST DIVISION*	SECOND DIVISION
1902-03	Halifax	Keighley
1903-04	Bradford	Wakefield Trinity
1904-05	Oldham	Dewsbury

1962-63	Swinton	Hunslet
1963-64	Swinton	Oldham

1973-74	Salford	Bradford Northern
1974-75	St. Helens	Huddersfield
1975-76	Salford	Barrow
1976-77	Featherstone Rovers	Hull
1977-78	Widnes	Leigh
1978-79	Hull Kingston Rovers	Hull
1979-80	Bradford Northern	Featherstone Rovers
1980-81	Bradford Northern	York
1981-82	Leigh	Oldham
1982-83	Hull	Fulham
1983-84	Hull Kingston Rovers	Barrow
1984-85	Hull Kingston Rovers	Swinton
1985-86	Halifax	Leigh
1986-87	Wigan	Hunslet
1987-88	Widnes	Oldham
1988-89	Widnes	Leigh
1989-90	Wigan	Hull Kingston Rovers
1990-91	Wigan	Salford
1991-92	Wigan	Sheffield Eagles
1992-93	Wigan	Featherstone Rovers
1993-94	Wigan	Workington Town
1994-95	Wigan	Keighley Cougars

Salford captain Ian Blease holds aloft the old Second Division Championship trophy in 1991.

THIRD DIVISION

1991-92 Huddersfield
1992-93 Keighley Cougars
—
—

CENTENARY SEASON

A shortened League programme was introduced for the 1995-96 Centenary Championship season to bridge the gap between the change over from winter to summer rugby and the new Super League era. It also heralded a new three-division format with the two lower divisions becoming the First and Second.

1995-96 **Centenary Championship*** - Wigan; **First Division** - Salford Reds; **Second Division** - Hull Kingston Rovers

	SUPER LEAGUE*	FIRST DIVISION	SECOND DIVISION
1996	St. Helens	Salford Reds	Hull Kingston Rovers
1997	Bradford Bulls	Hull Sharks	Hunslet Hawks
1998	Wigan Warriors	Wakefield Trinity	Lancashire Lynx

*Major championship

RELEGATION AND PROMOTION

Since reintroduction of two divisions in 1973-74.

● Figure in brackets indicates position in division.

	RELEGATED	PROMOTED
1973-74	Oldham (13) Hull K.R. (14) Leigh (15) Whitehaven (16)	Bradford Northern (1) York (2) Keighley (3) Halifax (4)
1974-75	York (13) Bramley (14) Rochdale Hornets (15) Halifax (16)	Huddersfield (1) Hull K.R. (2) Oldham (3) Swinton (4)
1975-76	Dewsbury (13) Keighley (14) Huddersfield (15) Swinton (16)	Barrow (1) Rochdale Hornets (2) Workington Town (3) Leigh (4)
1976-77	Rochdale Hornets (13) Leigh (14) Barrow (15) Oldham (16)	Hull (1) Dewsbury (2) Bramley (3) New Hunslet (4)
1977-78	Hull (13) New Hunslet (14) Bramley (15) Dewsbury (16)	Leigh (1) Barrow (2) Rochdale Hornets (3) Huddersfield (4)
1978-79	Barrow (13) Featherstone Rovers (14) Rochdale Hornets (15) Huddersfield (16)	Hull (1) New Hunslet (2) York (3) Blackpool Borough (4)
1979-80	Wigan (13) Hunslet (14) York (15) Blackpool Borough (16)	Featherstone Rovers (1) Halifax (2) Oldham (3) Barrow (4)
1980-81	Halifax (13) Salford (14) Workington Town (15) Oldham (16)	York (1) Wigan (2) Fulham (3) Whitehaven (4)
1981-82	Fulham (13) Wakefield Trinity (14) York (15) Whitehaven (16)	Oldham (1) Carlisle (2) Workington Town (3) Halifax (4)
1982-83	Barrow (13) Workington Town (14) Halifax (15) Carlisle (16)	Fulham (1) Wakefield Trinity (2) Salford (3) Whitehaven (4)

1983-84	Fulham (13)	Barrow (1)	
	Wakefield Trinity (14)	Workington Town (2)	
	Salford (15)	Hunslet (3)	
	Whitehaven (16)	Halifax (4)	
1984-85	Barrow (13)	Swinton (1)	
	Leigh (14)	Salford (2)	
	Hunslet (15)	York (3)	
	Workington Town (16)	Dewsbury (4)	
1985-86	York (14)	Leigh (1)	
	Swinton (15)	Barrow (2)	
	Dewsbury (16)	Wakefield Trinity (3)	
1986-87	Oldham (13)	Hunslet (1)	
	Featherstone Rovers (14)	Swinton (2)	
	Barrow (15)		
	Wakefield Trinity (16)		
1987-88	Leigh (12)	Oldham (1)	
	Swinton (13)	Featherstone Rovers (2)	
	Hunslet (14)	Wakefield Trinity (3)	
1988-89	Oldham (12)	Leigh (1)	
	Halifax (13)	Barrow (2)	
	Hull K.R. (14)	Sheffield Eagles (3)	
1989-90	Leigh (12)	Hull K.R. (1)	
	Salford (13)	Rochdale Hornets (2)	
	Barrow (14)	Oldham (3)	
1990-91	Oldham (12)	Salford (1)	
	Sheffield Eagles (13)	Halifax (2)	
	Rochdale Hornets (14)	Swinton (3)	

	FIRST DIVISION	SECOND DIVISION	THIRD DIVISION
1991-92	Down: Featherstone R. (13)	Up: Sheffield E. (1)	Up: Huddersfield (1)
	Swinton (14)	Leigh (2)	Bramley (2)
		Down: Ryedale-York (7)	
		Workington Town (8)	
1992-93	Salford (13)	Up: Featherstone R. (1)	Keighley C. (1)
	Hull K.R. (14)	Oldham (2)	Workington T. (2)

● Reverted to two divisions with only Featherstone and Oldham moving divisions.

	RELEGATED	PROMOTED
1993-94	Hull K.R. (15)	Workington Town (1)
	Leigh (16)	Doncaster (2)
1994-95	Hull (15)	Keighley Cougars (1)
	Doncaster (16)	Batley (2)

● Promotion and relegation not carried out following formation of Super League and two other divisions.

1995-96: Interim season before changeover from winter to summer rugby. No promotion or relegation. Wigan won the Stones Bitter Centenary Championship; Salford Reds the new First Division Championship and Hull Kingston Rovers the new Second Division Championship.

	SUPER LEAGUE	FIRST DIVISION	SECOND DIVISION
1996	Down: Workington T. (12)	Up: Salford R. (1) Down: Rochdale H. (10) Batley B. (11)	Up: Hull K.R. (1) Swinton L. (2)
1997	Down: Oldham B. (12) *Oldham Bears were wound up at the end of the season, but were reformed as Oldham and admitted to the Second Division*	Up: Hull S. (1) Down: Widnes V. (10) Workington T. (11) *Huddersfield G. (2) were also promoted after Paris S.G dropped out of Super League. Widnes remained in the First Division following a revamp of the lower divisions*	Up: Hunslet H. (1) Rochdale H. (2) *Leigh C. (3) were also promoted following a revamp of the lower divisions after Carlisle B.R. merged with Barrow and Prescot P. dropped out.*
1998	No relegation	Up: Wakefield T. No relegation	Lancashire L. (1) York (2) Batley B. (3)

● Reverted to two divisions for 1999 with First and Second Division combining.

Going up: Doncaster's Audley Pennant on the attack as the Dons clinch promotion to the top division with the defeat of Batley in 1994.

Eric Prescott scores St. Helens' last try as they beat Leeds in the 1970 Championship final at Bradford's Odsal Stadium.

CHAMPIONSHIP PLAY-OFFS
1907-1973

Following the breakaway from the English Rugby Union, 22 clubs formed the Northern Rugby Football League. Each club played 42 matches and Manningham won the first championship as League leaders in 1895-96.

This format was then abandoned and replaced by the Yorkshire Senior and Lancashire Senior Combination Leagues until 1901-02 when 14 clubs broke away to form the Northern Rugby League with Broughton Rangers winning the first championship.

The following season two divisions were formed with the Division One title going to Halifax (1902-03), Bradford (1903-04), who won a play-off against Salford 5-0 at Halifax after both teams tied with 52 points, and Oldham (1904-05).

In 1905-06 the two divisions were merged with Leigh taking the championship as League leaders. They won the title on a percentage basis as the 31 clubs did not play the same number of matches. The following season the top four play-off was introduced as a fairer means of deciding the title.

The top club played the fourth, the second meeting the third, with the higher club having home advantage. A final was staged at a neutral venue.

It was not until 1930-31 that all clubs played the same number of matches, but not all against each other, the top four play-off being a necessity until the re-introduction of two divisions in 1962-63.

This spell of two division rugby lasted only two seasons and the restoration of the one League championship table brought about the introduction of a top-16 play-off, this format continuing until the re-appearance of two divisions in 1973-74.

A play-off to decide the Super League championship returned in 1998, involving the top five clubs.

CHAMPIONSHIP PLAY-OFF FINALS

Season	Winners		Beaten finalists		Venue	Attendance	Receipts
1906-07	Halifax	18	Oldham	3	Huddersfield	13,200	£722
1907-08	Hunslet	7	Oldham	7	Salford	14,000	£690
Replay	Hunslet	12	Oldham	2	Wakefield	14,054	£800
1908-09	Wigan	7	Oldham	3	Salford	12,000	£630
1909-10	Oldham	13	Wigan	7	Broughton	10,850	£520
1910-11	Oldham	20	Wigan	7	Broughton	15,543	£717
1911-12	Huddersfield	13	Wigan	5	Halifax	15,000	£591
1912-13	Huddersfield	29	Wigan	2	Wakefield	17,000	£914
1913-14	Salford	5	Huddersfield	3	Leeds	8091	£474
1914-15	Huddersfield	35	Leeds	2	Wakefield	14,000	£750

COMPETITION SUSPENDED DURING WAR-TIME

Season	Winners		Beaten finalists		Venue	Attendance	Receipts
1919-20	Hull	3	Huddersfield	2	Leeds	12,900	£1,615
1920-21	Hull	16	Hull K.R.	14	Leeds	10,000	£1,320
1921-22	Wigan	13	Oldham	2	Broughton	26,000	£1,825
1922-23	Hull K.R.	15	Huddersfield	5	Leeds	14,000	£1,370
1923-24	Batley	13	Wigan	7	Broughton	13,729	£968
1924-25	Hull K.R.	9	Swinton	5	Rochdale	21,580	£1,504
1925-26	Wigan	22	Warrington	10	St. Helens	20,000	£1,100
1926-27	Swinton	13	St. Helens Recs.	8	Warrington	24,432	£1,803
1927-28	Swinton	11	Featherstone R.	0	Oldham	15,451	£1,136
1928-29	Huddersfield	2	Leeds	0	Halifax	25,604	£2,028
1929-30	Huddersfield	2	Leeds	2	Wakefield	32,095	£2,111
Replay	Huddersfield	10	Leeds	0	Halifax	18,563	£1,319
1930-31	Swinton	14	Leeds	7	Wigan	31,000	£2,100
1931-32	St. Helens	9	Huddersfield	5	Wakefield	19,386	£943
1932-33	Salford	15	Swinton	5	Wigan	18,000	£1,053
1933-34	Wigan	15	Salford	3	Warrington	31,564	£2,114
1934-35	Swinton	14	Warrington	3	Wigan	27,700	£1,710
1935-36	Hull	21	Widnes	2	Huddersfield	17,276	£1,208
1936-37	Salford	13	Warrington	11	Wigan	31,500	£2,000
1937-38	Hunslet	8	Leeds	2	Leeds U. FC	54,112	£3,572
1938-39	Salford	8	Castleford	6	Man. C. FC	69,504	£4,301

WAR-TIME EMERGENCY PLAY-OFF FINALS

For the first two seasons the Yorkshire League and Lancashire champions met in a two-leg final as follows:

Season	Winners		Beaten finalists		Venue	Attendance	Receipts
1939-40	Swinton	13	Bradford N.	21	Swinton	4800	£237
	Bradford N.	16	Swinton	9	Bradford	11,721	£570
1940-41	Wigan	6	Bradford N.	17	Wigan	11,245	£640
	Bradford N.	28	Wigan	9	Bradford	20,205	£1,148

For the remainder of the war the top four in the War-time League played off, resulting in the following finals:

Season	Winners		Beaten finalists		Venue	Attendance	Receipts
1941-42	Dewsbury	13	Bradford N.	0	Leeds	18,000	£1,121
1942-43	Dewsbury	11	Halifax	3	Dewsbury	7000	£400
	Halifax	13	Dewsbury	22	Halifax	9700	£683

Dewsbury won 33-16 on aggregate, but the Championship was declared null and void because they had fielded an ineligible player

1943-44	Wigan	13	Dewsbury	9	Wigan	14,000	£915
	Dewsbury	5	Wigan	12	Dewsbury	9000	£700
1944-45	Halifax	9	Bradford N.	2	Halifax	9426	£955
	Bradford N.	24	Halifax	11	Bradford	16,000	£1,850
1945-46	Wigan	13	Huddersfield	4	Man. C. FC	67,136	£8,387
1946-47	Wigan	13	Dewsbury	4	Man. C. FC	40,599	£5,895
1947-48	Warrington	15	Bradford N.	5	Man. C. FC	69,143	£9,792
1948-49	Huddersfield	13	Warrington	12	Man. C. FC	75,194	£11,073
1949-50	Wigan	20	Huddersfield	2	Man. C. FC	65,065	£11,500
1950-51	Workington T.	26	Warrington	11	Man. C. FC	61,618	£10,993
1951-52	Wigan	13	Bradford N.	6	Hudd'field T. FC	48,684	£8,215
1952-53	St. Helens	24	Halifax	14	Man. C. FC	51,083	£11,503
1953-54	Warrington	8	Halifax	7	Man. C. FC	36,519	£9,076
1954-55	Warrington	7	Oldham	3	Man. C. FC	49,434	£11,516
1955-56	Hull	10	Halifax	9	Man. C. FC	36,675	£9,179
1956-57	Oldham	15	Hull	14	Bradford	62,199	£12,054
1957-58	Hull	20	Workington T.	3	Bradford	57,699	£11,149
1958-59	St. Helens	44	Hunslet	22	Bradford	52,650	£10,146
1959-60	Wigan	27	Wakefield T.	3	Bradford	83,190	£14,482
1960-61	Leeds	25	Warrington	10	Bradford	52,177	£10,475
1961-62	Huddersfield	14	Wakefield T.	5	Bradford	37,451	£7,979

TWO DIVISIONS 1962-63 and 1963-64
Top 16 Plays-Offs

1964-65	Halifax	15	St. Helens	7	Swinton	20,786	£6,141
1965-66	St. Helens	35	Halifax	12	Swinton	30,634	£8,750
1966-67	Wakefield T.	7	St. Helens	7	Leeds	20,161	£6,702
Replay	Wakefield T.	21	St. Helens	9	Swinton	33,537	£9,800
1967-68	Wakefield T.	17	Hull K.R.	10	Leeds	22,586	£7,697
1968-69	Leeds	16	Castleford	14	Bradford	28,442	£10,130
1969-70	St. Helens	24	Leeds	12	Bradford	26,358	£9,791
1970-71	St. Helens	16	Wigan	12	Swinton	21,745	£10,200
1971-72	Leeds	9	St. Helens	5	Swinton	24,055	£9,513
1972-73	Dewsbury	22	Leeds	13	Bradford	18,889	£9,479

*Happy duo: Lance Todd Trophy winner Mark Aston
(left) and captain Paul Broadbent hold aloft the Silk Cut
Challenge Cup after Sheffield Eagles' shock defeat of
Wigan Warriors in the 1998 final.*

CHALLENGE CUP

CHALLENGE CUP

1998 Final

Sheffield Eagles achieved the biggest Challenge Cup final shock of all time with a stunning 17-8 defeat of red-hot favourites Wigan Warriors on a memorable 'I was there' afternoon at Wembley. Although Sheffield should never have been written off as no-hopers after their impressive Cup run, bookmakers William Hill made Wigan record 14-1 *on* favourites with Sheffield at 13-2 against. The handicap coupons gave Sheffield 22 points start. Wigan had been firm favourites to lift the Cup since before the first round, but Sheffield had made this their target and chairman Tim Adams backed them with a £1,000 bet at 33-1.

Most critics thought it was a waste of money even when Sheffield reached the quarter-finals for the first time in their 14-year history and went on to beat Salford Reds in the semi-finals. Fears of Sheffield being overwhelmed at Wembley grew as they lost their first three Super League matches before winning at bottom club Huddersfield Giants a week prior to Wembley, which lifted them to eighth place. In contrast, Wigan were the leaders after winning all four matches to extend their Cup and League victory run to 14 matches stretching back to August 1997.

History was also against Sheffield as, while they were appearing in their first Challenge Cup final, Wigan were making a record-extending 26th appearance including a record 21 victories. And Wigan coach John Monie was aiming to maintain his record of never having lost a Challenge Cup-tie in five seasons at the club.

The only people who thought Sheffield had a chance of becoming the first Yorkshire club to win at Wembley since 1987 were their players and John Kear, who was aiming to be the first English coach for 12 years to get his hands on the Cup. With so many having written off Sheffield it was no surprise that ticket sales were slow and the attendance of 60,669 was the lowest for a Wembley final since 1946. But the ones who stayed away were the losers as

Sheffield's victory was acclaimed as one of sport's biggest upsets, achieved in a game full of passion and drama.

Although it was essentially a great team effort that won the Cup, Sheffield scrum half Mark Aston took the Lance Todd Trophy as man of the match. Sheffield players dominated the voting with Aston receiving 10 nominations; Dave Watson 8; Paul Broadbent 7; Dale Laughton, Matt Crowther 2 and Johnny Lawless 1. The only Wigan player to be nominated was Tony Smith with two votes.

Aston took the prestigious award after playing a major role in the victory, starting with his perfectly-placed high crossfield kick into Wigan's in-goal which Nick Pinkney plucked out of the air for a shock fourth-minute touchdown. Aston missed with the conversion attempt but hit a superb touchline goal after Matt Crowther went over in the corner 24 minutes later. That made it 10-0 to the Eagles and though Andrew Farrell pulled back two points with a penalty goal, Aston took another stab at wounded Wigan with a drop goal just before half-time.

Aston stretched Sheffield's lead to an amazing 17-2 by adding the goal to a dubious 52nd minute try by substitute Darren Turner. But Aston's biggest effort in the second half was a try-saving tackle on Farrell, which proved to be Wigan's last chance of turning the game round. It came in the 64th minute after Wigan had recovered to close the gap to nine points following a try by Mark Bell, superbly goaled by Farrell.

Wigan continued to pile on so much pressure that it seemed they must score again. In fact, Farrell did get over the line but Aston got under the big forward to prevent him getting the ball down. Farrell clearly thought he had scored and when he protested to referee Stuart Cummings the Wigan captain was penalised for dissent. They were costly words as Sheffield were able to relieve the pressure with a penalty kick to touch and an unlikely victory now looked a certainty.

Turner's dubious try was given only after Cummings had consulted his in-goal judge. After viewing the incident later on TV, referees' coaching director Geoff Berry said he would have disallowed the try because of a double movement by Turner. Following debatable decisions in the previous final it had been suggested that a video referee would be used at Wembley for the first time, but the idea was not taken up.

No one disputed Sheffield's victory, however, as their players stuck to Kear's master plan to outthink and outplay the Cup kings. The Sheffield props, captain Paul Broadbent and Dale Laughton, laid the foundations with a ground-gaining barrage up the middle. Behind them Aston and half-back partner Dave Watson were always in control, although scrum half Smith was Wigan's most penetrative runner.

Apart from the doubt about Turner's try, Berry was full of praise for Cummings, who was making a record-equalling third successive appearance at Wembley as a Cup final referee.

Another record was the appearance of 11 overseas players in a Challenge Cup final. Sheffield had a record-equalling six in one side with Australians Paul Carr, Darren Shaw and Rod Doyle; New Zealanders Whetu Taewa and Dave Watson plus Fijian Waisale Sovatabua. Wigan's overseas five were Australians Mark Bell, Robbie McCormack, Tony Mestrov and Danny Moore plus New Zealander Henry Paul. The previous record number of overseas players was 10 in the 1985 final between Wigan and Hull, the latter totalling six Australians and New Zealanders.

Lynton Stott must have had mixed feelings about the victory as the Sheffield player was the first substitute not to get on the field for a Wembley final since Paul Forber of St. Helens in 1987.

There was record prize money for both finalists with the winners receiving £100,000 and the losers half as much.

QUOTES

JOHN KEAR (Sheffield coach): This is a great day for British coaches. Hopefully, other clubs might begin to look inwards and not outwards now it's been proved that British is not necessarily second best. We played some very clever football today. My players are very intelligent players. They not only played with heart; they also played with the grey matter. It just shows what the mind can do and make the body achieve.

JOHN MONIE (Wigan coach): Sheffield played to their potential and got the big prize. They had us on the back foot from the start. If anything, we looked liked the team who had the Wembley nerves. They put us off our stride and deserved to win.

MARK ASTON (Sheffield scrum half): I never heard the announcement that I had won the Lance Todd Trophy. I blocked it out of my mind – the crowd, the Tannoy, everything. I was just focusing on 80 minutes of do or die. We stuck to the plan we discussed at our team meeting on Friday night. At that meeting you could have cut the atmosphere with a knife. It was an incredible feeling.

ANDREW FARRELL (Wigan captain): No matter what I think about my disallowed try, Sheffield thoroughly deserved to win and that's the bottom line. Usually we don't get frustrated and just play our normal game, but we went away from what we had worked on all week.

TIM ADAMS (Sheffield chairman): They said that we were the underdogs. They didn't realise we had a pack full of rottweilers, backs who were Yorkshire terriers, 13 bulldogs and every one could run like a bloody greyhound.

SILK CUT CHALLENGE CUP FINAL

Saturday 2 May 1998   **Wembley**

SHEFFIELD EAGLES   17

Waisale Sovatabua	Full back
Nick Pinkney	Wing
Whetu Taewa	Centre
Keith Senior	Centre
Matt Crowther	Wing
Dave Watson	Stand off
Mark Aston	Scrum half
Paul Broadbent, Captain	Prop
Johnny Lawless	Hooker
Dale Laughton	Prop
Paul Carr	Second row
Darren Shaw	Second row
Rod Doyle	Loose forward

WIGAN WARRIORS   8

Kris Radlinski
Mark Bell
Danny Moore
Gary Connolly
Jason Robinson
Henry Paul
Tony Smith
Stephen Holgate
Robbie McCormack
Tony Mestrov
Denis Betts
Simon Haughton
Andrew Farrell, Captain

Substitutes

Lynton Stott – not used
Michael Jackson for Carr (25 min.)
Darren Turner for Lawless (47 min.)
Martin Wood for Watson (74 min.)
Carr for Laughton (58 min.)
Laughton for Broadbent (68 min.)
Lawless for Jackson (72 min.)

Substitutes

Lee Gilmour for Mestrov (26min.)
Neil Cowie for Holgate (26 min.)
Mick Cassidy for Haughton (46min.)
Terry O'Connor for Cowie (68 min.)
Haughton for Gilmour (68 min.)

T: Pinkney, Crowther, Turner
G: Aston (2, dg)

T: Bell
G: Farrell (2)

Coach: John Kear

Coach: John Monie

Scrums: 9-11
Penalties: 4-6
Lance Todd Trophy for Man of the Match:
Mark Aston (Sheffield)

Half-time: 11-2
Referee: Stuart Cummings (Widnes)
Attendance: 60,669
Receipts: £1,557,150

Cup presented by Chris Smith MP, Secretary of State for Culture, Media and Sport

HOW THE SCORING WENT

4 min.	Pinkney (Sheffield) try	**4-0**
28 min.	Crowther (Sheffield) try, Aston goal	**10-0**
33 min.	Farrell (Wigan) penalty goal	**10-2**
39 min.	Aston (Sheffield) drop goal	**11-2**
52 min.	Turner (Sheffield) try, Aston goal	**17-2**
56 min.	Bell (Wigan) try, Farrell goal	**17-8**

Wigan Warriors full back Kris Radlinski looks for support.

Sheffield Eagles centre Keith Senior falls to a two-man tackle.

1998 Round-by-Round

First and Second Rounds

A record 73 amateur clubs entered for the 1998 competition plus Alliance side Blackpool Gladiators, who withdrew after failing with their application to rejoin the Rugby Football League. The first round was marred further by the failure of three other clubs to fulfil their fixtures: West London Colonials at Charleston, Westfield Hotel at Norland, and Kells at Wigan Rose Bridge. All three clubs, who each claimed that they were unable to raise a team, were banned from the competition for three years and fined £250 (£200 suspended). Their opponents were given a bye into round two.

The 14 National Conference Premier Division clubs were exempt from the all-amateur random first round draw which included an Irish entry for the first time – Dublin Blues, who lost 32-7 at Dewsbury Moor.

National Conference Division Two side Ovenden caused one of the second round upsets when they won 30-22 at home to Wigan St. Patricks of the Premier Division after trailing 18-4 at half-time. It was one of five defeats sustained by National Conference Premier sides against opposition from outside the division. Leeds University's hopes of being the first student team to face professionals were dashed by a 40-8 defeat at Eastmoor Dragons.

Play-off Tie

Reborn Oldham were originally left out of the Challenge Cup because they were not in existence when the format for the 1998 competition was drawn up. But after a strong protest by the club, which had risen from the old Oldham Bears outfit, it was agreed that they would compete in a play-off tie for the right to join other First and Second Division professionals in the third round. Nine second round amateur victors volunteered to enter a special preliminary draw to decide Oldham's opponents 30 minutes before the main third round

draw was made. Oldham were given automatic home advantage and Heworth were drawn out of the bag to become the new club's first opponents in a competitive match on 18 January. The York amateurs took a shock 14-12 interval lead at Boundary Park before going down 36-14.

Third Round

The First and Second Division professional clubs entered at this stage with each assured of a home tie against amateur opposition, apart from late entrants Oldham. There were also two all-amateur ties with Egremont Rangers winning 20-14 at Eastmoor Dragons, and Ovenden 20-10 at Moldgreen. Added to victories by Ellenborough Rangers and Featherstone Lions this resulted in four amateurs clubs going through to the last 32 for the first time in 50 years.

Ellenborough stunned Bramley with a 16-10 victory at Headingley, taking an early lead and finishing with a three tries to two advantage. Featherstone Lions added a professional team to their record of not having lost all season when they beat Doncaster Dragons 23-18 at Wakefield with six goals, including a drop, by Nick Frankland tipping the scales after both sides had scored three tries. Despite these upsets, the professional clubs generally proved too powerful for their amateur foes with Swinton Lions' 74-6 defeat of Folly Lane the most emphatic thrashing. In the only all-professional tie, reborn Oldham went out 48-8 in the first competitive match to be played at Widnes Vikings' new Halton Community Stadium.

Fourth Round

The Super League clubs entered at this stage, but it was another historic round for the amateurs with two non-League clubs going through to the last 16 for the first time in over 90 years. Both were from Cumbria with Egremont stunning county neighbours Second Division Workington Town at Whitehaven 18-0, while Ellenborough pulled off an even bigger shock by beating First Division Hunslet Hawks 14-12 at Workington. Egremont also became the first amateur side to nil professionals in the Cup for over 90 years. The other two amateur clubs both took a hammering, however, as Featherstone Lions went down 56-20 to Hull Kingston Rovers at Post Office Road and Ovenden crashed 74-0 to Salford Reds at Halifax's Thrum Hall.

The BBC were televising two weekend Cup-ties for the first time and they began with a Saturday afternoon thriller at Headingley, where visitors Castleford Tigers pulled off a last minute 15-12 victory over Leeds Rhinos when Andrew Schick touched down Adrian Vowles' high kick. Featherstone Rovers also staged a comeback in the televised Sunday tie, but it was never going to succeed as they trailed 50-0 to visiting Cup-holders St. Helens after an hour before going out 56-24. Sheffield Eagles began their first ever trip to Wembley with a 66-11 romp at Leigh Centurions, while their destined final opponents Wigan Warriors had it even easier at Keighley Cougars where they won 76-0. Halifax Blue Sox played their last competitive game at Thrum Hall and made it a fond farewell with a 28-8 defeat of Huddersfield Giants. Shaun Edwards starred on his debut for Bradford Bulls after being transferred from London Broncos and helped his new club to a 48-10 win at Rochdale Hornets.

After trailing 14-15 at home to York, Swinton recovered to race to a 39-21 victory with Steve Gartland collecting 18 points from seven goals and a try. Second Division Batley Bulldogs were on course for a shock defeat of Super League's London Broncos when they led 18-14 at half-time, only to fade in the later stages and go down to 44-20 home defeat. Barrow Border Raiders put up a tremendous battle against visiting Widnes Vikings before going out 36-22. Barry Eaton snatched Dewsbury Rams a 28-28 draw at Lancashire Lynx with a penalty goal three minutes from the end of a rousing Cup-tie. He then added

seven more goals in the replay to help the Rams to a 31-14 victory. Warrington Wolves were never in danger at Wakefield Trinity despite some early resistance and finished comfortable 42-6 winners. It was a much tougher inter-division tie at Whitehaven Warriors, who put up a great fight before losing 26-12 to Hull Sharks.

Fifth Round

Castleford played the major role in another TV thriller when they came from behind again to beat Bradford 26-21. Bradford had staged their own fightback to take a one-point lead after trailing 20-8 at half-time, before Jason Flowers came up with the match-winning try eight minutes from the end. St. Helens and Warrington made it a double TV treat as they followed up with a high-scoring but intensely fought battle that finished with the home side not so convincing winners as the 35-22 scoreline suggests. London's 21-18 home defeat of Halifax was full of controversy and the visitors made an official protest over referee Steve Presley's handling of the game. There was no disputing Salford's win at Widnes as they coasted to a 48-6 triumph nor Wigan's 50-0 runaway victory at Dewsbury. The amateurs' run of success came to an abrupt end with Ellenborough crashing 78-0 at Hull and Egremont being on the receiving end of Sheffield's biggest ever victory, 84-6, which included a club record-equalling 12 goals from Mark Aston. In the only all First Division clash Hull K.R. won 46-24 at home to Swinton.

Quarter-Finals

Castleford made it a hat-trick of TV appearances, but this time it was Sheffield who took the glory with a 32-22 victory in their first ever quarter-final appearance. Controversy surrounded the win as Keith Senior scored two of Sheffield's tries after he had been put on report for punching Castleford's Barrie-Jon Mather who was led off injured. The other TV tie produced a classic encounter with Wigan ending St. Helens' two-year hold on the Cup after finishing strongly to gain a 22-10 home success. Salford reached the semi-finals for a second successive season with a convincing 41-10 home victory over Hull. The last of the non-Super League clubs went out when Hull K.R. fell 46-18 to London, who reached the semi-finals for the first time.

Semi-Finals

Sheffield stormed to their first Wembley appearance with a thrilling 22-18 defeat of Salford at Headingley. They were losing 18-10 going into the last 13 minutes, but produced a tremendous rally that finished with Dale Laughton crashing over for the 71st minute match-winning try. A highly entertaining game ended on a sour note when referee Stuart

Cummings was attacked by a spectator who ran onto the field as the full-time hooter sounded, with play continuing and Salford's Steve Blakeley going close to scoring an amazing last-second try. Another dismal note was a gate of only 6,961 – the lowest for a semi-final during the Wembley era which began in 1929.

London's first semi-final proved to be a big disappointment as they were completely outplayed 38-8 by a Wigan side that was returning to Wembley for the first time since completing a record run of eight successive appearances and victories at the stadium in 1995. Wigan were never in serious trouble from the time Jason Robinson went in for the first of their six tries in the second minute.

Sheffield Eagles players in jubilant mood immediately after their 1998 final triumph.

231

1998 RESULTS

First Round

Blackbrook	17	Haydock	23
Broughton Red R.	14	Hull Dockers	24
Charleston	w/o	W. London Colonials	
Dewsbury Moor	32	Dublin Blues	7
Eccles	12	Featherstone Lions	26
Ellenborough R.	40	Crosfields	14
Farnworth ROB	26	Lowca	12
Ideal ABI	5	Hunslet Warriors	30
John Moores Univ.	16	Eastmoor Dragons	40
Leigh East	18	East Hull	4
London Skolars	10	Myton Warriors	12
Milford	6	Queens	16
Millom	22	York Acorn	2
Moldgreen	18	Barrow Island	8
New Earswick A.B.	6	B.R.K	34
Norland	w/o	Westfield Hotel	
Normanton Knights	14	Folly Lane	14
Oulton Raiders	36	Loughborough Univ.	16
Ovenden	18	Dodworth	16
Queensbury	24	East Leeds	16
Redhill	36	Wigan St. Judes	12
Shaw Cross Sharks	0	Clayton	20
Siddal	40	Lindley Swifts	6
Skirlaugh	w/o	Blackpool Gladiators	
Stanningley	50	Nottingham Crus.	16
Teesside Steelers	10	Leeds University	48
Waterhead	28	Westgate Redoubt	4
West Bowling	18	Thornhill	24
Wigan Rose B.	w/o	Kells	
Worth Village	32	Fulham Travellers	4

Replay

Folly Lane	22	Normanton Knights	15

w/o: home side given a walkover into next round after their opponents withdrew

Second Round

B.R.K.	20	Leigh East	18
Charleston	8	Saddleworth Rangers	34
Dewsbury Moor	8	Oulton Raiders	27
Dudley Hill	14	Skirlaugh	42
Eastmoor Dragons	40	Leeds University	8
Egremont Rangers	24	Hull Dockers	12
Ellenbrough R.	28	Queensbury	22
Folly Lane	37	Askam	14
Haydock	11	Waterhead	0
Heworth	12	Clayton	4
Hunslet Warriors	14	Millom	6
Mayfield	4	Featherstone Lions	28
Moldgreen	22	Siddal	20
Myton Warriors	0	Norland	52
Ovenden	30	Wigan St. Patricks	22
Queens	42	Beverley	18
Redhill	14	Lock Lane	19
Stanningley	10	Farnworth ROB	37
Walney Central	12	Leigh Miners R.	12
Wigan Rose B.	8	West Hull	37
Woolston Rovers	22	Oldham St. Annes	0
Worth Village	4	Thornhill	52

Replay

Leigh Miners R.	46	Walney Central	4

Second Round Play-off

Oldham	36	Heworth	14

Third Round

Barrow B.R.	52	Farnworth ROB	8
Batley B.	44	Oulton Raiders	2
Bramley	10	Ellenborough R.	16
Dewsbury R.	40	Thornhill	2
Doncaster D.	18	Featherstone Lions	23
Eastmoor Dragons	14	Egremont Rangers	20
Featherstone R.	56	Woolston Rovers	0
Hull K.R.	34	Queens	16
Hunslet H.	44	Skirlaugh	12
Keighley C.	66	Saddleworth Rangers	16
Lancashire L.	46	West Hull	0
Leigh C.	44	Hunslet Warriors	4
Moldgreen	10	Ovenden	20
Rochdale H.	44	Leigh Miners R.	4
Swinton L.	74	Folly Lane	6
Wakefield T.	44	B.R.K.	6
Whitehaven W.	48	Lock Lane	7
Widnes V.	48	Oldham	8
Workington T.	12	Haydock	8
York	37	Norland	5

Fourth Round

Barrow B.R.	22	Widnes V.	36
Batley B.	20	London B.	44
Egremont Rangers	18	Workington T.	0
Ellenborough R.	14	Hunslet H.	12
Featherstone Lions	20	Hull K.R.	56
Featherstone R.	24	St. Helens	56
Halifax B.S.	28	Huddersfield G.	8
Keighley C.	0	Wigan W.	76
Lancashire L.	28	Dewsbury R.	28
Leeds R.	12	Castleford T.	15
Leigh C.	11	Sheffield E.	66
Ovenden	0	Salford R.	74

Rochdale H.	10	Bradford B.	48
Swinton L.	39	York	21
Wakefield T.	6	Warrington W.	42
Whitehaven W.	12	Hull S.	26

Replay

| Dewsbury R. | 31 | Lancashire L. | 14 |

Fifth Round

Castleford T.	26	Bradford B.	21
Dewsbury R.	0	Wigan W.	56
Hull S.	78	Ellenborough R.	0
Hull K.R.	46	Swinton L.	24
London B.	21	Halifax B.S.	18
Sheffield E.	84	Egremont Rangers	6
St. Helens	35	Warrington W.	22
Widnes V.	6	Salford R.	48

Quarter-Finals

Castleford T.	22	Sheffield E.	32
London B.	46	Hull K.R.	18
Salford R.	41	Hull S.	10
Wigan W.	22	St. Helens	10

Semi-Finals

Sheffield E.	22	Salford R.	18
(at Leeds)			
Wigan W.	38	London B.	8
(at Huddersfield)			

Final

| Sheffield E. | 17 | Wigan W. | 8 |
| (at Wembley) | | | |

1998 Prize money

Third Round losers
 (First and Second Division clubs) £4,000
Third Round losers (Amateur clubs)............. £1,000
Fourth Round losers £5,000
Fifth Round losers £8,000
Quarter-Final losers £15,000
Semi-Final losers...................................... £20,000
Runners-up... £50,000
Winners.. £100,000

| **Projected Prize Fund** | £486,000 |
| **Capital Development Fund** | £214,000 |

| **Grand Total** | £700,000 |

*Dave Watson: Outstanding for Sheffield Eagles
in 1998 Cup final victory.*

CHALLENGE CUP FINALS

Year	Winners		Runners-up		Venue	Attendance	Receipts
1897	Batley	10	St. Helens	3	Leeds	13,492	£624.17.7
1898	Batley	7	Bradford	0	Leeds	27,941	£1,586.3.0
1899	Oldham	19	Hunslet	9	Manchester	15,763	£946.16.0
1900	Swinton	16	Salford	8	Manchester	17,864	£1,100.0.0
1901	Batley	6	Warrington	0	Leeds	29,563	£1,644.16.0
1902	Broughton R.	25	Salford	0	Rochdale	15,006	£846.11.0
1903	Halifax	7	Salford	0	Leeds	32,507	£1,834.8.6
1904	Halifax	8	Warrington	3	Salford	17,041	£936.5.0
1905	Warrington	6	Hull K.R.	0	Leeds	19,638	£1,271.18.0
1906	Bradford	5	Salford	0	Leeds	15,834	£920.0.0
1907	Warrington	17	Oldham	3	Broughton	18,500	£1,010.0.0
1908	Hunslet	14	Hull	0	Huddersfield	18,000	£903.0.0
1909	Wakefield T.	17	Hull	0	Leeds	23,587	£1,490.0.0
1910	Leeds	7	Hull	7	Huddersfield	19,413	£1,102.0.0
Replay	Leeds	26	Hull	12	Huddersfield	11,608	£657.0.0
1911	Broughton R.	4	Wigan	0	Salford	8,000	£376.0.0
1912	Dewsbury	8	Oldham	5	Leeds	15,271	£853.0.0
1913	Huddersfield	9	Warrington	5	Leeds	22,754	£1,446.9.6
1914	Hull	6	Wakefield T.	0	Halifax	19,000	£1,035.5.0
1915	Huddersfield	37	St. Helens	3	Oldham	8,000	£472.0.0
1920	Huddersfield	21	Wigan	10	Leeds	14,000	£1,936.0.0
1921	Leigh	13	Halifax	0	Broughton	25,000	£2,700.0.0
1922	Rochdale H.	10	Hull	9	Leeds	32,596	£2,964.0.0
1923	Leeds	28	Hull	3	Wakefield	29,335	£2,390.0.0
1924	Wigan	21	Oldham	4	Rochdale	41,831	£3,712.0.0
1925	Oldham	16	Hull K.R.	3	Leeds	28,335	£2,879.0.0
1926	Swinton	9	Oldham	3	Rochdale	27,000	£2,551.0.0
1927	Oldham	26	Swinton	7	Wigan	33,448	£3,170.0.0
1928	Swinton	5	Warrington	3	Wigan	33,909	£3,158.1.11
1929	Wigan	13	Dewsbury	2	Wembley	41,500	£5,614.0.0
1930	Widnes	10	St. Helens	3	Wembley	36,544	£3,102.0.0
1931	Halifax	22	York	8	Wembley	40,368	£3,908.0.0
1932	Leeds	11	Swinton	8	Wigan	29,000	£2,479.0.0
1933	Huddersfield	21	Warrington	17	Wembley	41,874	£6,465.0.0
1934	Hunslet	11	Widnes	5	Wembley	41,280	£6,686.0.0
1935	Castleford	11	Huddersfield	8	Wembley	39,000	£5,533.0.0
1936	Leeds	18	Warrington	2	Wembley	51,250	£7,070.0.0
1937	Widnes	18	Keighley	5	Wembley	47,699	£6,704.0.0
1938	Salford	7	Barrow	4	Wembley	51,243	£7,174.0.0
1939	Halifax	20	Salford	3	Wembley	55,453	£7,681.0.0
1940	*No competition*						
1941	Leeds	19	Halifax	2	Bradford	28,500	£1,703.0.0
1942	Leeds	15	Halifax	10	Bradford	15,250	£1,276.0.0
1943	Dewsbury	16	Leeds	9	Dewsbury	10,470	£823.0.0
	Dewsbury	0	Leeds	6	Leeds	16,000	£1,521.0.0
	Dewsbury won on aggregate 16-15						
1944	Bradford N.	0	Wigan	3	Wigan	22,000	£1,640.0.0
	Bradford N.	8	Wigan	0	Bradford	30,000	£2,200.0.0
	Bradford won on aggregate 8-3						
1945	Huddersfield	7	Bradford N.	4	Huddersfield	9,041	£1,184.3.7
	Huddersfield	6	Bradford N.	5	Bradford	17,500	£2,050.0.0
	Huddersfield won on aggregate13-9						

Year	Winners		Runners-up		Venue	Attendance	Receipts
1946	Wakefield T.	13	Wigan	12	Wembley	54,730	£12,013.13.6
1947	Bradford N.	8	Leeds	4	Wembley	77,605	£17,434.5.0
1948	Wigan	8	Bradford N.	3	Wembley	91,465	£21,121.9.9
1949	Bradford N.	12	Halifax	0	Wembley	*95,050	£21,930.5.0
1950	Warrington	19	Widnes	0	Wembley	94,249	£24,782.13.0
1951	Wigan	10	Barrow	0	Wembley	94,262	£24,797.19.0
1952	Workington T.	18	Featherstone R.	10	Wembley	72,093	£22,374.2.0
1953	Huddersfield	15	St. Helens	10	Wembley	89,588	£30,865.12.3
1954	Warrington	4	Halifax	4	Wembley	81,841	£29,706.7.3
Replay	Warrington	8	Halifax	4	Bradford	102,569	£18,623.7.0
1955	Barrow	21	Workington T.	12	Wembley	66,513	£27,453.16.0
1956	St. Helens	13	Halifax	2	Wembley	79,341	£29,424.7.6
1957	Leeds	9	Barrow	7	Wembley	76,318	£32,671.14.3
1958	Wigan	13	Workington T.	9	Wembley	66,109	£33,175.17.6
1959	Wigan	30	Hull	13	Wembley	79,811	£35,718.19.9
1960	Wakefield T.	38	Hull	5	Wembley	79,773	£35,754.16.0
1961	St. Helens	12	Wigan	6	Wembley	94,672	£38,479.11.9
1962	Wakefield T.	12	Huddersfield	6	Wembley	81,263	£33,390.18.4
1963	Wakefield T.	25	Wigan	10	Wembley	84,492	£44,521.17.0
1964	Widnes	13	Hull K.R.	5	Wembley	84,488	£44,840.19.0
1965	Wigan	20	Hunslet	16	Wembley	89,016	£48,080.4.0
1966	St. Helens	21	Wigan	2	Wembley	*98,536	£50,409.0.0
1967	Featherstone R.	17	Barrow	12	Wembley	76,290	£53,465.14.0
1968	Leeds	11	Wakefield T.	10	Wembley	87,100	£56,171.16.6
1969	Castleford	11	Salford	6	Wembley	*97,939	£58,848.1.0
1970	Castleford	7	Wigan	2	Wembley	95,255	£89,262.2.0
1971	Leigh	24	Leeds	7	Wembley	85,514	£84,452.15
1972	St. Helens	16	Leeds	13	Wembley	89,495	£86,414.30
1973	Featherstone R.	33	Bradford N.	14	Wembley	72,395	£125,826.40
1974	Warrington	24	Featherstone R.	9	Wembley	77,400	£132,021.05
1975	Widnes	14	Warrington	7	Wembley	85,098	£140,684.45
1976	St. Helens	20	Widnes	5	Wembley	89,982	£190,129.40
1977	Leeds	16	Widnes	7	Wembley	80,871	£241,488.00
1978	Leeds	14	St. Helens	12	Wembley	*96,000	£330,575.00
1979	Widnes	12	Wakefield T.	3	Wembley	94,218	£383,157.00
1980	Hull K.R.	10	Hull	5	Wembley	*95,000	£448,202.90
1981	Widnes	18	Hull K.R.	9	Wembley	92,496	£591,117.00
1982	Hull	14	Widnes	14	Wembley	92,147	£684,500.00
Replay	Hull	18	Widnes	9	Elland Rd, L'ds	41,171	£180,525.00
1983	Featherstone R.	14	Hull	12	Wembley	84,969	£655,510.00
1984	Widnes	19	Wigan	6	Wembley	80,116	£686,171.00
1985	Wigan	28	Hull	24	Wembley	*97,801	£760,322.00
1986	Castleford	15	Hull K.R.	14	Wembley	82,134	£806,676.00
1987	Halifax	19	St. Helens	18	Wembley	91,267	£1,009,206.00
1988	Wigan	32	Halifax	12	Wembley	*94,273	£1,102,247.00
1989	Wigan	27	St. Helens	0	Wembley	*78,000	£1,121,293.00
1990	Wigan	36	Warrington	14	Wembley	*77,729	£1,360,000.00
1991	Wigan	13	St. Helens	8	Wembley	75,532	£1,610,447.00
1992	Wigan	28	Castleford	12	Wembley	77,286	£1,877,564.00
1993	Wigan	20	Widnes	14	Wembley	*77,684	£1,981,591.00
1994	Wigan	26	Leeds	16	Wembley	*78,348	£2,032,839.00
1995	Wigan	30	Leeds	10	Wembley	*78,550	£2,040,000.00
1996	St. Helens	40	Bradford B.	32	Wembley	75,994	£1,893,000.00
1997	St. Helens	32	Bradford B.	22	Wembley	*78,022	£2,033,426.00
1998	Sheffield E.	17	Wigan W.	8	Wembley	60,699	£1,557,150.00

*Indicates a capacity attendance, the limit being fixed annually taking into account variable factors.

CUP FINAL TEAMS FROM 1979

*Captain

1978-79

Widnes 12 Eckersley (1dg); S. Wright (1t), Aspey, George (Hull), Burke (2g); Hughes (1t), Bowden*; Mills, Elwell (1dg), Shaw, Adams, Dearden (M. O'Neill), Laughton
Coach: Doug Laughton

Wakefield T. 3 Sheard; Fletcher (1t), K. Smith, Diamond, Juliff; Topliss*, Lampkowski; Burke, McCurrie, Skerrett, Ashurst, Keith Rayne, Idle
Coach: Bill Kirkbride
Referee: Joe Jackson (Pudsey)

1979-80

Hull K.R. 10 Hall; Hubbard (1t, 3g) (Hogan), M. Smith, Hartley, Sullivan; Millward* (1dg), Agar; Holdstock, Watkinson, Lockwood, Lowe, Rose (Millington), Casey
Player-coach: Roger Millward

Hull 5 Woods; Bray, Walters, Wilby (1t), Prendiville; Newlove (Hancock), Pickerill; Tindall, Wileman, Stone (Farrar), Birdsall, Lloyd (1g), Norton*
Coach: Arthur Bunting
Referee: Fred Lindop (Wakefield)

1980-81

Widnes 18 Burke (1t, 4g); S. Wright, George (1t), Cunningham (J. Myler), Bentley; Hughes, Gregory (1t); M. O'Neill (Shaw), Elwell, Lockwood, L. Gorley, E. Prescott, Adams* (1dg)
Coach: Doug Laughton

Hull K.R. 9 Hall; Hubbard (3g), M. Smith, Hogan, Muscroft; Hartley, Harkin; Holdstock (Millington), Watkinson, Crooks (Proctor), Lowe, Burton (1t), Casey*
Coach: Roger Millward
Referee: Gerry Kershaw (Easingwold)

1981-82

Hull 14 Kemble; O'Hara (1t), Day, S. Evans, Prendiville; Topliss*, Harkin; Skerrett, Wileman, Stone, Crane (L. Crooks), Lloyd (4g), Norton (1t)
Coach: Arthur Bunting

Widnes 14 Burke (1g) (A. Myler); S. Wright (1t), Keiron O'Loughlin, Cunningham (2t), Basnett; Hughes, Gregory (1g); M. O'Neill, Elwell (1dg), Lockwood (S. O'Neill), L. Gorley, E. Prescott, Adams*
Coach: Doug Laughton
Referee: Fred Lindop (Wakefield)

Replay

Hull 18 Kemble (1t); Sullivan, Leuluai, S. Evans, Prendiville; Topliss* (2t), Dean; Tindall, Duke, Stone, Skerrett, L. Crooks (1t, 3g), Norton (Crane)
Coach: Arthur Bunting

Widnes 9 Burke (3g); S. Wright (1t), Keiron O'Loughlin, Cunningham, Basnett; Hughes, Gregory; M. O'Neill, Elwell, Lockwood, L. Gorley, E. Prescott, Adams*
Coach: Doug Laughton
Referee: Fred Lindop (Wakefield)

1982-83

Featherstone R. 14 N. Barker; Marsden, Quinn (4g), Gilbert (Lyman), K. Kellett; A. Banks, Hudson*; Gibbins,

Handscombe, Hankins, D. Hobbs (2t), Slatter (Siddall), P. Smith
Coach: Allan Agar

Hull 12 Kemble; O'Hara, S. Evans, Leuluai (1t), Prendiville; Topliss*, Harkin (Day) (Crane); Skerrett, Bridges, Stone, Rose, L. Crooks (1t, 3g), Norton
Coach: Arthur Bunting
Referee: Robin Whitfield (Widnes)

1983-84

Widnes 19 Burke (3g); S. Wright, Hughes* (D. Hulme), Lydon (2t), Basnett; Keiron O'Loughlin (1t), Gregory; S. O'Neill (1dg), Elwell, K. Tamati, L. Gorley, M. O'Neill (Whitfield), Adams
Coach: Vince Karalius

Wigan 6 Edwards; Ramsdale, Stephenson, Whitfield (1g) (Elvin), Gill; Cannon, Stephens; Hemsley (1t), H. Tamati, Case (Juliff), West*, Scott, Pendlebury
Coach: Alex Murphy
Referee: Billy Thompson (Huddersfield)

1984-85

Wigan 28 Edwards (1t); Ferguson (2t), Stephenson (1g), Donlan, Gill (1t, 3g); Kenny (1t), M. Ford; Courtney, Kiss, Case (Campbell), West*, Dunn, Potter
Coach: Colin Clarke/Alan McInnes

Hull 24 Kemble; James (1t), S. Evans (1t), Leuluai (2t), O'Hara (Schofield); Ah Kuoi, Sterling; L. Crooks* (2g), Patrick, Puckering (Divorty 1t), Muggleton, Rose, Norton
Coach: Arthur Bunting
Referee: Ron Campbell (Widnes)

1985-86

Castleford 15 Lord (Roockley); Plange, Marchant (1t), Hyde, Sandy (1t), Joyner*; R. Beardmore (1t, 1dg); Ward, K. Beardmore (Horton), B. Johnson, England, Ketteridge (1g), I. French
Coach: Malcolm Reilly

Hull K.R. 14 Fairbairn; Clark, M. Smith, Prohm (2t), Laws; Dorahy (1g), Harkin; P. Johnston, Watkinson*, Ema, Kelly (G. Smith), Des Harrison (Lydiat 1t), Miller
Coach: Roger Millward
Referee: Robin Whitfield (Widnes)

1986-87

Halifax 19 Eadie (1t); S. Wilson, Whitfield (3g), Rix, George (1t), C. Anderson* (Juliff), Stephens; Beevers (James), McCallion (1t), Neller, Dixon, Scott, Pendlebury (1dg)
Player-coach: Chris Anderson

St. Helens 18 Veivers; Ledger, Loughlin (1t, 3g), Elia (1t), McCormack; Clark, Holding; Burke, Liptrot, Fieldhouse, Platt, Haggerty (Round 1t), Arkwright*
Coach: Alex Murphy
Referee: John Holdsworth (Kippax)

1987-88

Wigan 32 Lydon (1t, 1g); T. Iro (1t), K. Iro (2t), Bell (1t), Gill (1t); Edwards* (Byrne), Gregory (1g); Case, Kiss, Shelford, Goodway, Potter (Wane), Hanley (1t)
Coach: Graham Lowe

Halifax 12 Eadie*; Meredith, T. Anderson (1t), Wilkinson,

Whitfield (2g); Grogan, S. Robinson (Fairbank); James (1t), McCallion, Neller, Holliday (Scott), Dixon, Pendlebury
Coach: Chris Anderson
Referee: Fred Lindop (Wakefield)
1988-89
Wigan 27 Hampson (1t); T. Iro, K. Iro (2t), Bell, Lydon (3g); Edwards, Gregory (1t, 1dg); Lucas, Kiss (Betts), Shelford, Platt, Potter (Goodway), Hanley* (1t)
Coach: Graham Lowe
St. Helens 0 Connolly; O'Connor, Veivers, Loughlin (Bloor), Quirk; Cooper, Holding; Burke, Groves, Forber, Dwyer (Evans), Haggerty, Vautin*
Coach: Alex Murphy
Referee: Ray Tennant (Castleford)
1989-90
Wigan 36 Hampson; Lydon (6g); K. Iro (2t), Bell, Preston (2t) (Gildart); Edwards, Gregory; Shelford, Dermott (Goulding), Platt, Betts (1t), Goodway, Hanley* (1t)
Coach: John Monie
Warrington 14 Lyon (1t); Drummond, Mercer, Darbyshire (1g), Forster; Crompton, Bishop (2g) (McGinty); Burke, Mann, Harmon, Jackson (Thomas), Sanderson, M. Gregory* (1t)
Coach: Brian Johnson
Referee: John Holdsworth (Kippax)
1990-91
Wigan 13 Hampson; Myers (1t), K. Iro, Bell, Botica (1t, 2g); Edwards, Gregory (1dg); Lucas, Dermott (Goulding), Platt, Betts, Clarke (Goodway), Hanley*
Coach: John Monie
St. Helens 8 Veivers (Connolly); Hunte (1t), Ropati, Loughlin, Quirk; Griffiths, Bishop (2g); Neill (Groves), Dwyer, Ward, Harrison, Mann, Cooper*
Coach: Mike McClennan
Referee: Jim Smith (Halifax)
1991-92
Wigan 28 Lydon (2dg); Botica (5g), Bell*, Miles, Offiah (2t); Edwards (1t), Gregory; Skerrett, Dermott, Platt, Betts, McGinty (Hampson 1t) (Cowie), Clarke
Coach: John Monie
Castleford 12 Steadman; Wray, Ellis, Blackmore (1t), Nelson; Anderson (T. Smith), Ford; Crooks* (Sampson), Southernwood, England (1t), Bradley, Ketteridge (2g), Nikau
Coach: Darryl Van De Velde
Referee: Robin Whitfield (Widnes)
1992-93
Wigan 20 Hampson; Robinson, Lydon (Panapa 1t), Farrar, Offiah; Botica (4g), Edwards; Skerrett (1t) (Farrell), Dermott, Platt, Betts, Clarke, Bell* (1t)
Coach: John Monie
Widnes 14 Spruce; Devereux, Currier (McCurrie), D. Wright, Myers; Davies (3g), Goulding; Sorensen (1t), P. Hulme*, Howard, R. Eyres (1t), Faimalo (J. O'Neill), D. Hulme
Coach: Phil Larder
Referee: Russell Smith (Castleford)

1993-94
Wigan 26 Connolly; Tuigamala, Bell*, Mather, Offiah (2t); Botica (5g), Edwards; Skerrett, Dermott, Platt (Panapa 1t), Betts, Farrell (1t) (Cassidy), Clarke
Coach: John Dorahy
Leeds 16 Tait; Fallon (1t), Iro, Innes, Cummins (1t); Holroyd (2g), Schofield (1t); Harmon (M. O'Neill), Lowes, Howard, Mercer, Eyres, Hanley* (Vassilakopoulos)
Coach: Doug Laughton
Referee: David Campbell (Widnes)
1994-95
Wigan 30 Paul (1t); Robinson (2t), Tuigamala (1t), Connolly, Offiah; Botica (5g), Edwards*; Skerrett (Atcheson), Hall (1t), Cowie, Betts, Cassidy (Farrell), Clarke
Coach: Graeme West
Leeds 10 Tait; Fallon, Iro, Innes, Cummins; Schofield, Holroyd (3g); Howard (Mann), Lowes (1t), Faimalo (Harmon), Mercer, Eyres, Hanley*
Coach: Doug Laughton
Referee: Russell Smith (Castleford)
1996
St. Helens 40 Prescott (2t); Arnold (2t), Gibbs, Newlove, Sullivan; Hammond, Goulding* (4g); Perelini (1t) (Hunte), Cunningham (1t), Leathem (Matautia), Joynt, Booth (1t), Northey (Martyn) (Pickavance 1t)
Coach: Shaun McRae
Bradford B. 32 Graham (Hassan); Cook (6g), Calland, Loughlin, Scales (1t); Bradley, Paul* (3t); McDermott, Dwyer (1t), Hamer (Fairbank), Donougher, Nickle (Medley), Knox (Donohue)
Coach: Brian Smith
Referee: Stuart Cummings (Widnes)
1997
St. Helens 32 Prescott; Arnold, Haigh (Matautia), Newlove, Sullivan (1t); Martyn (2t), Goulding* (6g); Perelini (Northey), Cunningham, O'Neill (Pickavance), Joynt (1t), McVey (Morley), Hammond (1t)
Coach: Shaun McRae
Bradford B. 22 Spruce; Ekoku, Peacock (1t), Loughlin (1t) (Calland), Cook; Bradley, Paul* (Tomlinson 1t); McDermott, Lowes (1t), Reihana (Medley), Nickle, Dwyer (Knox), McNamara (3g)
Coach: Matthew Elliott
Referee: Stuart Cummings (Widnes)
1998
Sheffield E. 17 Sovatabua; Pinkney (1t), Taewa, Senior, Crowther (1t); Watson (Wood), Aston (2g, dg); Broadbent*, Lawless (Turner), Laughton, Carr (Jackson), Shaw, Doyle
Coach: John Kear
Wigan W. 8 Radlinski; Bell (1t), Moore, Connolly, Robinson; Paul, Smith; Holgate (Cowie) (O'Connor), McCormack, Mestrov (Gilmour), Betts, Haughton (Cassidy), Farrell* (2g)
Coach: John Monie
Referee: Stuart Cummings (Widnes)

RUGBY LEAGUE CHALLENGE CUP FINAL PLAYERS' REGISTER FROM 1979

The following is an index of players who have appeared in the Rugby League Challenge Cup final in the last 20 seasons. It also includes the pre-1979 record of any listed player. W — winners, L — losers, D — draw. Substitute appearances in lower case letters. The year denotes the second half of the season. *denotes replay.

ADAMS, Mick: Widnes 75W, 76L, 77L, 79W, 81W, 82DL*, 84W
AGAR, Allan: Hull K.R. 80W
AH KUOI, Fred: Hull 85L
ANDERSON, Chris: Widnes 75W; Halifax 87W
ANDERSON, Grant: Castleford 92L
ANDERSON, Tony: Halifax 88L
ARKWRIGHT, Chris: St. Helens 87L
ARNOLD, Danny: St. Helens 96W, 97W
ASHURST, Bill: Wigan 70L; Wakefield T. 79L
ASPEY, Malcolm: Widnes 75W, 77L, 79W
ASTON, Mark: Sheffield E. 98W
ATCHESON, Paul: Wigan 95w

BANKS, Alan: Featherstone R. 83W
BARKER, Nigel: Featherstone R. 83W
BASNETT, John: Widnes 82DL*, 84W
BEARDMORE, Kevin: Castleford 86W
BEARDMORE, Bob: Castleford 86W
BEEVERS, Graham: Halifax 87W
BELL, Dean: Wigan 88W, 89W, 90W, 91W, 92W, 93W, 94W
BELL, Mark: Wigan W. 98L
BENTLEY, Keith: Widnes 81W
BETTS, Denis: Wigan 89W, 90W, 91W, 92W, 93W, 94W, 95W, 98L
BIRDSALL, Charlie: Hull 80L
BISHOP, Paul: Warrington 90L; St. Helens 91L
BLACKMORE, Richard: Castleford 92L
BLOOR, Darren: St. Helens 89l
BOOTH, Simon: St.Helens 96W
BOTICA, Frano: Wigan 91W, 92W, 93W, 94W, 95W
BOWDEN, Reg: Widnes 75W, 76L, 77L, 79W
BRADLEY, Graeme: Castleford 92L; Bradford B. 96L, 97L
BRAY, Graham: Featherstone R. 74L; Hull 80L
BRIDGES, John "Keith": Featherstone R. 73W, 74L; Hull 83L
BROADBENT, Paul: Sheffield E. 98W
BURKE, John: Leeds 71L; Wakefield T. 79L
BURKE, Mick: Widnes 79W, 81W, 82DL*, 84W
BURKE, Tony: St. Helens 87L, 89L; Warrington 90L
BURTON, Chris: Hull K.R. 81L
BYRNE, Ged: Wigan 88w

CALLAND, Matt: Bradford B. 96L, 97l
CAMPBELL, Danny: Wigan 85w
CANNON, Mark: Wigan 84L
CARR, Paul: Sheffield E. 98W
CASE, Brian: Wigan 84L, 85W, 88W
CASEY, Len: Hull K.R. 80W, 81L
CASSIDY, Mick: Wigan 94w, 95W, 98l
CLARK, Brett: St. Helens 87L
CLARK, Garry: Hull K.R. 86L
CLARKE, Phil: Wigan 91W, 92W, 93W, 94W, 95W
CONNOLLY, Gary: St. Helens 89L, 91l; Wigan 94W, 95W, 98L
COOK, Paul: Bradford B. 96L, 97L
COOPER, Shane: St. Helens 89L, 91L
COURTNEY, Neil: Wigan 85W
COWIE, Neil: Wigan 92w, 95W, 98l
CRANE, Mick: Leeds 78W; Hull 82Dw*, 83l

CROMPTON, Martin: Warrington 90L
CROOKS, Lee: Hull 82dW*, 83L, 85L; Castleford 92L
CROOKS, Steve: Hull K.R. 81L
CROWTHER, Matt: Sheffield E. 98W
CUMMINS, Francis: Leeds 94L, 95L
CUNNINGHAM, Eddie: St. Helens 76W, 78L; Widnes 81W, 82DL*
CUNNINGHAM, Keiron: St. Helens 96W, 97W
CURRIER, Andy: Widnes 93L

DARBYSHIRE, Paul: Warrington 90L
DAVIES, Jonathan: Widnes 93L
DAY, Terry: Hull 82D, 83l
DEAN, Tony: Hull 82W*
DEARDEN, Alan: Widnes 77L, 79W
DERMOTT, Martin: Wigan 90W, 91W, 92W, 93W, 94W
DEVEREUX, John: Widnes 93L
DIAMOND, Steve: Wakefield T. 79L
DIVORTY, Gary: Hull 85l
DIXON, Paul: Halifax 87W, 88L
DONLAN, Steve: Wigan 85W
DONOHUE, Jason: Bradford B. 96l
DONOUGHER, Jeremy: Bradford B. 96L
DORAHY, John: Hull K.R. 86L
DOYLE. Rod: Sheffield E. 98W
DRUMMOND, Des: Warrington 90L
DUKE, Tony: Hull 82W*
DUNN, Brian: Wigan 85W
DWYER, Bernard: St. Helens 89L, 91L; Bradford B. 96L, 97L

EADIE, Graham: Halifax 87W, 88L
ECKERSLEY, David: Leigh 71W; Widnes 76L, 77L, 79W
EDWARDS, Shaun: Wigan 84L, 85W, 88W, 89W, 90W, 91W, 92W, 93W, 94W, 95W
EKOKU, Abi: Bradford B. 97L
ELIA, Mark: St. Helens 87L
ELLIS, St. John: Castleford 92L
ELVIN, Wayne: Wigan 84l
ELWELL, Keith: Widnes 75W, 76L, 77L, 79W, 81W, 82DL*, 84W
EMA, Asuquo: Hull K.R. 86L
ENGLAND, Keith: Castleford 86W, 92L
EVANS, Steve: Hull 82DW*, 83L, 85L
EVANS, Stuart: St. Helens 89l
EYRES, Richard: Widnes 93L; Leeds 94L, 95L

FAIMALO, Esene: Widnes 93L; Leeds 95L
FAIRBAIRN, George: Hull K.R. 86L
FAIRBANK, Dick: Halifax 88l
FAIRBANK, Karl: Bradford B. 96l
FALLON, Jim: Leeds 94L, 95L
FARRAR, Andrew: Wigan 93W
FARRAR, Vince: Featherstone R. 73W; Hull 80l
FARRELL, Andrew: Wigan 93w, 94W, 95w, 98L
FERGUSON, John: Wigan 85W
FIELDHOUSE, John: St. Helens 87L
FLETCHER, Andrew: Wakefield T. 79L
FORBER, Paul: St. Helens 89L
FORD, Mike: Wigan 85W, Castleford 92L
FORSTER, Mark: Warrington 90L

238

FRENCH, Ian: Castleford 86W

GEORGE, Derek "Mick": Widnes 75W, 76L, 77l, 79W, 81W

GEORGE, Wilf: Halifax 87W

GIBBINS, Mick: Featherstone R. 83W

GIBBS, Scott: St. Helens 96W

GILBERT, John: Featherstone R. 83W

GILDART, Ian: Wigan 90w

GILL, Henderson: Wigan 84L, 85W, 88W

GILMOUR, Lee: Wigan W. 98l

GOODWAY, Andy: Wigan 88W, 89w, 90W, 91w

GORLEY, Les: Widnes 81W, 82DL*, 84W

GOULDING, Bobbie: Wigan 90w, 91w; Widnes 93L; St. Helens 96W, 97W

GRAHAM, Nathan: Bradford B. 96L

GREGORY, Andy: Widnes 81W, 82DL*, 84W; Wigan 88W, 89W, 90W, 91W, 92W

GREGORY, Mike: Warrington 90L

GRIFFITHS, Jonathan: St. Helens 91L

GROGAN, Bob: Halifax 88L

GROVES, Paul: St. Helens 89L, 91l

HAGGERTY, Roy: St. Helens 87L, 89L

HAIGH, Andy: St. Helens 97W

HALL, David: Hull K.R. 80W, 81L

HALL, Martin: Wigan 95W

HAMER, Jon: Bradford B. 96L

HAMMOND, Karle: St. Helens 96W, 97W

HAMPSON, Steve: Wigan 89W, 90W, 91W, 92w, 93W

HANCOCK, Brian: Hull 80l

HANDSCOMBE, Ray: Featherstone R. 83W

HANKINS, Steve: Featherstone R. 83W

HANLEY, Ellery: Wigan 88W, 89W, 90W, 91W; Leeds 94L, 95L

HARKIN, Kevin: Hull 82D, 83L

HARKIN, Paul: Hull K.R. 81L, 86L

HARMON, Neil: Warrington 90L; Leeds 94L, 95l

HARRISON, Des: Hull K.R. 86L

HARRISON, John: St. Helens 91L

HARTLEY, Steve: Hull K.R. 80W, 81L

HASSAN, Carlos: Bradford B. 96l

HAUGHTON, Simon: Wigan W. 98L

HEMSLEY, Kerry: Wigan 84L

HOBBS, David: Featherstone R. 83W

HOGAN, Phil: Hull K.R. 80w, 81L

HOLDING, Neil: St. Helens 87L, 89L

HOLDSTOCK, Roy: Hull K.R. 80W, 81L

HOLGATE, Stephen: Wigan W. 98L

HOLLIDAY, Les: Halifax 88L

HOLROYD, Graham: Leeds 94L, 95L

HORTON, Stuart: Castleford 86w

HOWARD, Harvey: Widnes 93L; Leeds 94L, 95L

HUBBARD, Steve: Hull K.R. 80W, 81L

HUDSON, Terry: Featherstone R. 83W

HUGHES, Eric: Widnes 75W, 76L, 77L, 79W, 81W, 82DL*, 84W

HULL, David: St. Helens 76W; Widnes 79w

HULME, David: Widnes 84w, 93L

HULME, Paul: Widnes 93L

HUNTE, Alan: St. Helens 91L, 96w

HYDE, Gary: Castleford 86W

IDLE, Graham: Wakefield T. 79L

INNES, Craig: Leeds 94L, 95L

IRO, Kevin: Wigan 88W, 89W, 90W, 91W; Leeds 94L, 95L

IRO, Tony: Wigan 88W, 89W

JACKSON, Bob: Warrington 90L

JACKSON, Michael: Sheffield E. 98w

JAMES, Kevin: Hull 85L

JAMES, Neil: Halifax 87w, 88L

JOHNSON, Barry: Castleford 86W

JOHNSTON, Peter: Hull K.R. 86L

JOYNER, John: Castleford 86W

JOYNT, Chris: St. Helens 96W, 97W

JULIFF, Brian: Wakefield T. 79L; Wigan 84l; Halifax 87w

KELLETT, Ken: Featherstone R. 73W, 83W

KELLY, Andy: Hull K.R. 86L

KEMBLE, Gary: Hull 82DW*, 83L, 85L

KENNY, Brett: Wigan 85W

KETTERIDGE, Martin: Castleford 86W, 92L

KISS, Nicky: Wigan 85W, 88W, 89W

KNOX, Simon: Bradford B. 96L, 97l

LAMPKOWSKI, Mike: Wakefield T. 79L

LAUGHTON, Dale: Sheffield E. 98W

LAUGHTON, Doug: Wigan 70L; Widnes 75W, 76L, 77L, 79W

LAWLESS, Johnny: Sheffield E. 98W

LAWS, David: Hull K.R. 86L

LEATHEM, Andy: St. Helens 96W

LEDGER, Barry: St. Helens 87L

LEULUAI, James: Hull 82W*, 83L, 85L

LIPTROT, Graham: St. Helens 78L, 87L

LLOYD, Geoff "Sammy": Hull 80L, 82D

LOCKWOOD, Brian: Castleford 69W, 70W; Hull K.R. 80W; Widnes 81W, 82DL*

LORD, Gary: Castleford 86W

LOUGHLIN, Paul: St. Helens 87L, 89L, 91L; Bradford B. 96L, 97L

LOWE, Phil: Hull K.R. 80W, 81L

LOWES, James: Leeds 94L, 95L; Bradford B. 97L

LUCAS, Ian: Wigan 89W, 91W

LYDIAT, John: Hull K.R. 86l

LYDON, Joe: Widnes 84W; Wigan 88W, 89W, 90W, 92W, 93W

LYMAN, Paul: Featherstone R. 83w

LYON, David: Warrington 90L

McCALLION, Seamus: Halifax 87W, 88L

McCORMACK, Kevin: St. Helens 87L

McCORMACK, Robbie: Wigan W. 98L

McCURRIE, Alan: Wakefield T. 79L

McCURRIE, Steve: Widnes 93l

McDERMOTT, Brian: Bradford B. 96L, 97L

McGINTY, Billy: Warrington 90l; Wigan 92W

McNAMARA, Steve: Bradford B. 97L

McVEY, Derek: St. Helens 97W

MANN, Duane: Warrington 90L

MANN, George: St. Helens 91L; Leeds 95L

MARCHANT, Tony: Castleford 86W

MARSDEN, John: Featherstone R. 83W

MARTYN, Tommy: St. Helens 96w, 97W

MATAUTIA, Vila: St. Helens 96w, 97w

MATHER, Barrie-Jon: Wigan 94W

MEDLEY, Paul: Bradford B. 96l, 97l

MERCER, Gary: Warrington 90L; Leeds 94L, 95L

MEREDITH, Martin: Halifax 86L

MESTROV, Tony: Wigan W. 98L

MILES, Gene: Wigan 92W

MILLER, Gavin: Hull K.R. 86L

MILLINGTON, John: Hull K.R. 80w, 81l

239

MILLS, Jim: Widnes 75W, 77L, 79W
MILLWARD, Roger: Hull K.R. 80W
MOORE, Danny: Wigan W. 98L
MORLEY, Chris: St. Helens 97w
MUGGLETON, John: Hull 85L
MUSCROFT, Peter: Hull K.R. 81L
MYERS, David: Wigan 91W; Widnes 93L
MYLER, John: Widnes 81w
MYLER, Tony: Widnes 82d

NEILL, Jonathan: St. Helens 91L
NELLER, Keith: Halifax 87W, 88L
NELSON, David: Castleford 92L
NEWLOVE, John: Featherstone R. 73W, 74L; Hull 80L
NEWLOVE, Paul: St. Helens 96W, 97W
NICKLE, Sonny: Bradford B. 96L, 97L
NIKAU, Tawera: Castleford 92L
NORTHEY, Andy: St. Helens 96W, 97w
NORTON, Steve: Hull 80L, 82DW*, 83L, 85L

O'CONNOR, Michael: St. Helens 89L
O'CONNOR, Terry: Wigan W. 98l
OFFIAH, Martin: Wigan 92W, 93W, 94W, 95W
O'HARA, Dane: Hull 82D, 83L, 85L
O'LOUGHLIN, Keiron: Widnes 82DL*, 84W
O'NEILL, Julian (Aust.): Widnes 93l
O'NEILL, Julian (NZ): St. Helens 97W
O'NEILL, Mike: Widnes 79w, 81W, 82DL*, 84W; Leeds 94l
O'NEILL, Steve: Widnes 82d, 84W

PANAPA, Sam: Wigan 93w, 94w
PATRICK, Shaun: Hull 85L
PAUL, Henry: Wigan 95W, 98L
PAUL, Robbie: Bradford B. 96L, 97L
PEACOCK, Danny: Bradford B. 97L
PENDLEBURY, John: Wigan 84L; Halifax 87W, 88L
PERELINI, Apollo: St. Helens 96W, 97W
PICKAVANCE, Ian: St. Helens 96w, 97w
PICKERILL, Clive: Hull 80L
PINKNEY, Nick: Sheffield E. 98W
PLANGE, David: Castleford 86W
PLATT, Andy: St. Helens 87L; Wigan 89W, 90W, 91W, 92W, 93W, 94W
POTTER, Ian: Wigan 85W, 88W, 89W
PRENDIVILLE, Paul: Hull 80L, 82DW*, 83L
PRESCOTT, Eric: Widnes 81W, 82DL*
PRESCOTT, Steve: St. Helens 96W, 97W
PRESTON, Mark: Wigan 90W
PROCTOR, Paul: Hull K.R. 81l
PROHM, Gary: Hull K.R. 86L
PUCKERING, Neil: Hull 85L

QUINN, Steve: Featherstone R. 83W
QUIRK, Les: St. Helens 89L, 91L

RADLINSKI, Kris: Wigan W. 98L
RAMSDALE, Denis: Wigan 84L
RAYNE, Keith: Wakefield T. 79L
REIHANA, Tahi: Bradford B. 97L
RIX, Grant: Halifax 87W
ROBINSON, Jason: Wigan 93W, 95W, 98L
ROBINSON, Steve: Halifax 88L
ROOCKLEY, David: Castleford 86w
ROPATI, Tea: St. Helens 91L
ROSE, Paul: Hull K.R. 80W; Hull 83L, 85L
ROUND, Paul: St. Helens 87l

SAMPSON, Dean: Castleford 92L

SANDERSON, Gary: Warrington 90L
SANDY, Jamie: Castleford 86W
SCALES, Jon: Bradford B. 96L
SCHOFIELD, Garry: Hull 85l; Leeds 94L, 95L
SCOTT, Mick: Wigan 84L; Halifax 87W, 88l
SENIOR, Keith: Sheffield E. 98W
SHAW, Darren: Sheffield E. 98W
SHAW, Glyn: Widnes 79W, 81w
SHEARD, Les: Wakefield T. 79L
SHELFORD, Adrian: Wigan 88W, 89W, 90W
SIDDALL, Gary: Featherstone R. 83w
SKERRETT, Kelvin: Wigan 92W, 93W, 94W, 95W
SKERRETT, Trevor: Wakefield T. 79L; Hull 82DW*, 83L
SLATTER, Tim: Featherstone R. 83W
SMITH, Gordon: Hull K.R. 86l
SMITH, Keith: Wakefield T. 79L
SMITH, Mike: Hull K.R. 80W, 81L, 86L
SMITH, Peter: Featherstone R. 83W
SMITH, Tony: Castleford 92l; Wigan W. 98L
SORENSEN, Kurt: Widnes 93L
SOUTHERNWOOD, Graham: Castleford 92L
SOVATABUA, Waisale: Sheffield E. 98W
SPRUCE, Stuart: Widnes 93L; Bradford B. 97L
STEADMAN, Graham: Castleford 92L
STEPHENS, Gary: Wigan 84L; Halifax 87W
STEPHENSON, David: Wigan 84L, 85W
STERLING, Peter: Hull 85L
STONE, Richard "Charlie": Featherstone R. 73W, 74l; Hull 80L, 82DW*, 83L
SULLIVAN, Anthony: St. Helens 96W, 97W
SULLIVAN, Clive: Hull K.R. 80W; Hull 82W*

TAIT, Alan: Leeds 94L, 95L
TAMATI, Howie: Wigan 84L
TAMATI, Kevin: Widnes 84W
TAEWA, Whetu: Sheffield E. 98W
THOMAS, Mark: Warrington 90l
TINDALL, Keith: Hull 80L, 82W*
TOMLINSON, Glen: Bradford B. 97l
TOPLISS, David: Wakefield T. 79L; Hull 82DW*, 83L
TUIGAMALA, Va'aiga: Wigan 94W, 95W
TURNER, Darren: Sheffield E. 98w

VASSILAKOPOULOS, Marcus: Leeds 94l
VAUTIN, Paul: St. Helens 89L
VEIVERS, Phil: St. Helens 87L, 89L, 91L

WALTERS, Graham: Hull 80L
WANE, Shaun: Wigan 88w
WARD, Kevin: Castleford 86W; St. Helens 91L
WATKINSON, David: Hull K.R. 80W, 81L, 86L
WATSON, Dave: Sheffield E. 98W
WEST, Graeme: Wigan 84L, 85W
WHITFIELD, Colin: Wigan 84L; Halifax 87W, 88L
WHITFIELD, Fred: Widnes 84w
WILBY, Tim: Hull 80L
WILEMAN, Ron: Hull 80L, 82D
WILKINSON, Ian: Halifax 88L
WILSON, Scott: Halifax 87W
WOOD, Martin: Sheffield E. 98w
WOODS, Paul: Hull 80L
WRAY, Jon: Castleford 92L
WRIGHT, Darren: Widnes 93L
WRIGHT, Stuart: Widnes 77L, 79W, 81W, 82DL*, 84W

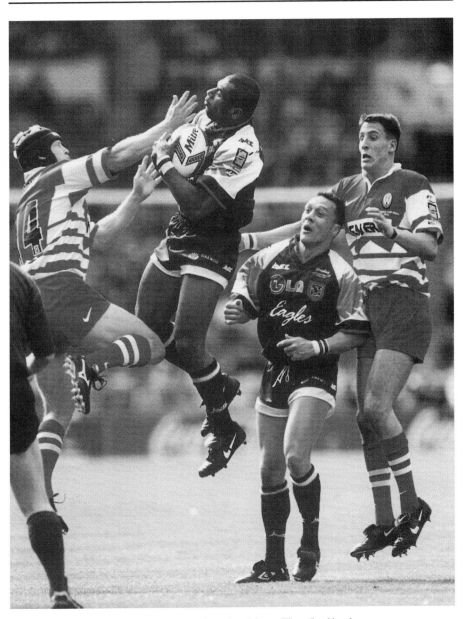

Sheffield Eagles full back Waisale Sovatabua defuses a Wigan 'bomb' under pressure.

THE LANCE TODD TROPHY

The Lance Todd Trophy is presented to the Man of the Match in the Rugby League Challenge Cup final, the decision being reached by a ballot of members of the Rugby League Writers' Association present at the game.

Lance Todd made his name in Britain as a player with Wigan and as manager of Salford. His untimely death in a road accident on the return journey from a game at Oldham in 1942 was commemorated by the introduction of the Lance Todd Trophy.

The award was instituted by Australian-born Harry Sunderland, Warrington director Bob Anderton and Yorkshire journalist John Bapty.

Around 1950, the Red Devils' Association at Salford, comprising players and officials who had worked with Todd, raised sufficient funds to provide a trophy and replica for each winner.

Hull's Tommy Harris is the only hooker to earn the title; and Ray Ashby and Brian Gabbitas the only players to share the honour.

Following the 1954 replay, it was decided by the Red Devils that in the future the trophy would be awarded for the Wembley game. In 1954, Gerry Helme had received the trophy for his performance in the Odsal replay. In the 1982 replay at Elland Road, Leeds, the Man of the Match award went to Hull skipper David Topliss, the Lance Todd Trophy having been awarded to Eddie Cunningham, of Widnes, in the drawn Wembley tie.

In 1990 Andy Gregory, of Wigan, became the first player to win the trophy twice at Wembley, having also won it two years earlier, a feat emulated by Martin Offiah in 1992 and 1994.

Peter Ramsden is the youngest player to win the award, receiving it on his 19th birthday after scoring two tries for Huddersfield in the 15-10 defeat of St. Helens in 1953.

Frank Whitcombe is the oldest winner, the Bradford Northern prop being 29 days short of his 35th birthday in 1948 when he became the first player of a beaten team to receive the award after losing 8-3 to Wigan.

THE LANCE TODD TROPHY WINNERS

Year	Winner	Team	Position
1946	Billy Stott	Wakefield Trinity (v Wigan)	Centre
1947	Willie Davies	Bradford Northern (v Leeds)	Stand off
1948	Frank Whitcombe	Bradford Northern* (v Wigan)	Prop
1949	Ernest Ward	Bradford Northern (v Halifax)	Centre
1950	Gerry Helme	Warrington (v Widnes)	Scrum half
1951	Cec Mountford	Wigan (v Barrow)	Stand off
1952	Billy Ivison	Workington T. (v Featherstone R.)	Loose forward
1953	Peter Ramsden	Huddersfield (v St. Helens)	Stand off
1954	Gerry Helme	Warrington (v Halifax)	Scrum half
1955	Jack Grundy	Barrow (v Workington Town)	Second row
1956	Alan Prescott	St. Helens (v Halifax)	Prop
1957	Jeff Stevenson	Leeds (v Barrow)	Scrum half
1958	Rees Thomas	Wigan (v Workington Town)	Scrum half
1959	Brian McTigue	Wigan (v Hull)	Second row
1960	Tommy Harris	Hull* (v Wakefield Trinity)	Hooker
1961	Dick Huddart	St. Helens (v Wigan)	Second row
1962	Neil Fox	Wakefield Trinity (v Huddersfield)	Centre
1963	Harold Poynton	Wakefield Trinity (v Wigan)	Stand off
1964	Frank Collier	Widnes (v Hull K.R.)	Prop

1965	Ray Ashby	Wigan	Full back
	Brian Gabbitas	Hunslet*	Stand off
1966	Len Killeen	St. Helens (v Wigan)	Winger
1967	Carl Dooler	Featherstone Rovers (v Barrow)	Scrum half
1968	Don Fox	Wakefield Trinity* (v Leeds)	Prop
1969	Malcolm Reilly	Castleford (v Salford)	Loose forward
1970	Bill Kirkbride	Castleford (v Wigan)	Second row
1971	Alex Murphy	Leigh (v Leeds)	Scrum half
1972	Kel Coslett	St. Helens (v Leeds)	Loose forward
1973	Steve Nash	Featherstone R. (v Bradford N.)	Scrum half
1974	Derek Whitehead	Warrington (v Featherstone Rovers)	Full back
1975	Ray Dutton	Widnes (v Warrington)	Full back
1976	Geoff Pimblett	St. Helens (v Widnes)	Full back
1977	Steve Pitchford	Leeds (v Widnes)	Prop
1978	George Nicholls	St. Helens* (v Leeds)	Second row
1979	David Topliss	Wakefield Trinity* (v Widnes)	Stand off
1980	Brian Lockwood	Hull K.R. (v Hull)	Prop
1981	Mick Burke	Widnes (v Hull K.R.)	Full back
1982	Eddie Cunningham	Widnes (v. Hull)	Centre
1983	David Hobbs	Featherstone Rovers (v Hull)	Second row
1984	Joe Lydon	Widnes (v Wigan)	Centre
1985	Brett Kenny	Wigan (v Hull)	Stand off
1986	Bob Beardmore	Castleford (v Hull K.R.)	Scrum half
1987	Graham Eadie	Halifax (v St. Helens)	Full back
1988	Andy Gregory	Wigan (v Halifax)	Scrum half
1989	Ellery Hanley	Wigan (v St. Helens)	Loose forward
1990	Andy Gregory	Wigan (v Warrington)	Scrum half
1991	Denis Betts	Wigan (v St. Helens)	Second row
1992	Martin Offiah	Wigan (v Castleford)	Winger
1993	Dean Bell	Wigan (v Widnes)	Loose forward
1994	Martin Offiah	Wigan (v Leeds)	Winger
1995	Jason Robinson	Wigan (v Leeds)	Winger
1996	Robbie Paul	Bradford B.* (v St. Helens)	Scrum half
1997	Tommy Martyn	St. Helens (v Bradford B.)	Stand off
1998	Mark Aston	Sheffield E. (v Wigan W.)	Scrum half

* Losing team

CUP FINAL RECORDS
(Wembley records in italics)

TEAM
Most finals: 26 by Wigan
           22 by Wigan

Most wins: 16 by Wigan
          15 by Wigan

Consecutive finals and wins: *8 by Wigan 1988-1995*

Highest score:
St. Helens 40 v. Bradford B. 32 1996
(Also most points by losers)

Lowest winning score:
Broughton Rangers 4 v. Wigan 0 1911
Salford 7 v. Barrow 4 . . . . *1938*
Castleford 7 v. Wigan 2 . . . . *1970*

Widest margin:
Huddersfield 37 v. St. Helens 3 1915
Wakefield Trinity 38 v. Hull 5 . . . . *1960*

Most points aggregate:
(72) St. Helens 40 v. Bradford B. 32 . . . . *1996*

Least points aggregate:
(4) Broughton Rangers 4 v. Wigan 0 1911
(8) Halifax 4 v. Warrington 4 . . . . *1954*

Most tries aggregate:
(13) St. Helens 8 v. Bradford B. 5 . . . . *1996*

Most tries by one team:
9 by Huddersfield v. St. Helens 1915
8 by Wakefield T. v. Hull *1960*
St. Helens v. Bradford B. *1996*

Lowest placed winners:
Leigh (20th) beat Halifax (3rd) 13-0 in 1921
Widnes (20th) beat Keighley (18th) 18-5 in 1937
Featherstone R. (20th) beat Barrow (15th) 17-12 in 1967

Lowest placed finalists:
Halifax (25th) lost to Bradford N. (10th) 12-0 in 1949

Widest gulf between finalists:
Featherstone R. (2nd) beat Bradford N. (23rd) 33-14 in 1973

Biggest attendance:
102,569 Warrington v. Halifax
(Replay at Bradford) 1954
98,536 St. Helens v. Wigan *1966*
Record receipts: *£2,040,000 Wigan v. Leeds* . . . *1995*

INDIVIDUAL

Most appearances:
10 by Shaun Edwards (Wigan 1984, 85, 88, 89, 90, 91, 92, 93, 94, 95)

Most wins:
9 by Shaun Edwards (Wigan as above except 1984)

Most tries in all finals:
6 by Kevin Iro (Wigan 1988 2t, 1989 2t, 1990 2t; also played for Wigan in 1991 final and Leeds 1994, 95)

Most goals in all finals:
21 by Frano Botica (Wigan 1991 2g, 1992 5g, 1993 4g, 1994 5g, 1995 5g)

Most points in all finals:
46 by Frano Botica (Wigan 1991 8pts, 1992 10pts, 1993 8pts, 1994 10pts, 1995 10pts)

Most tries in a final:
3 by Bob Wilson (Broughton R.) v. Salford . . . 1902
Stan Moorhouse (Huddersfield) v. Warrington
. . . . 1913
Tom Holliday (Oldham) v. Swinton 1927
Robbie Paul (Bradford B.) v. St. Helens *1996*

Most goals in a final:
8 by Cyril Kellett (Featherstone) v. Bradford N. . . *1973*

Most points in a final:
20 (2t,7g) by Neil Fox (Wakefield T.) v. Hull ... *1960*

CUP RECORDS – ALL ROUNDS

TEAM
Highest score:
Huddersfield 119 v. Swinton Park★ 2 1914

INDIVIDUAL

Most tries in a match:
11 by George West (Hull K.R.) v. Brookland
Rovers★ 1905

Most goals in a match:
22 by Jim Sullivan (Wigan) v. Flimby and Fothergill*
. . . . 1925

Most points in a match:
53 by George West (Hull K.R.) v. Brookland
Rovers* 1905

*Amateur clubs

WIGAN'S RECORD CUP RUN

Wigan's 26-16 fifth round defeat at Salford Reds in 1996 ended a record Challenge Cup run of 43 successive ties unbeaten, including one draw – against St. Helens – which followed 36 successive wins. Only 12 of the ties were at home, with 15 on opposition grounds and 16 at neutral venues. They won the Cup a record eight successive times and Shaun Edwards was the only player to appear in all 43 ties, including one as a substitute.

OTHER WEMBLEY FACTS

Radio and TV

The first radio broadcast of a Cup final was in 1927 for the Oldham v. Swinton match from Central Park, Wigan. Two years later the first Wembley final, between Wigan and Dewsbury, was also broadcast.

The first full live national television coverage of a Cup final came in 1952 when the BBC showed Workington Town's defeat of Featherstone Rovers at Wembley. The 1948 final between Wigan and Bradford Northern was televised in the London area only and the 1950 Warrington v. Widnes final was shown in the Midlands, although it was picked up by some Northwest viewers. Every final has been televised live by the BBC since 1958 when Wigan beat Workington.

Captains

Eric Ashton captained a record six teams at Wembley – Wigan in 1958, 59, 61, 63, 65 and 66, being a record three times winner and

loser. His record of three wins (in 1958, 59, 65) is shared with Derek Turner (Wakefield Trinity 1960, 62, 63), Alex Murphy (St. Helens 1966, Leigh 1971 and Warrington 1974), Ellery Hanley (Wigan 1989, 90, 91) and Dean Bell (Wigan 1992, 93, 94). Murphy is the only captain to lead three different clubs to victory at Wembley, while Hanley and Bell are the only ones to lift the Cup in three successive seasons.

Gus Risman led two different clubs to victory – a record 14 years apart. He was captain of Salford in 1938 and of Workington Town in 1952 when he became the oldest player at 41 years 29 days. Risman was also captain when Salford lost in 1939. Robbie Paul of Bradford Bulls became Wembley's youngest captain when he led them in defeat against St. Helens in 1996 at the age of 20 years three months. Shaun Edwards of Wigan is the youngest winning captain, leading them to victory over Halifax in 1988 when he was 21 years six months.

Coaches and player-coaches

Alex Murphy has been a coach at Wembley a record six times. He won as player-coach with Leigh (1971) and Warrington (1974), but lost each time when confined to the bench with Warrington (1975), Wigan (1984) and St. Helens (1987 and 1989). John Monie has the best winning record, taking Wigan to victory in four successive seasons from 1990. Murphy is the only player-coach to win twice at Wembley.

Willie Horne went a record three times as player-coach with Barrow – in 1951 (lost), 1955 (won) and 1957 (lost). There have been two finals in which both teams had a player-coach: 1952 Gus Risman (Workington T.) beat Eric Batten (Featherstone R.); 1965 Eric Ashton (Wigan) beat Fred Ward (Hunslet). Chris Anderson of Halifax was the last player-coach at Wembley, leading his side to victory in 1987.

Captain, coach and chairman

Eric Ashton is the only person to have captained, coached and been the chairman of a

Wembley team – and he has been a winner in each category. He captained Wigan six times (see **Captains**), also coaching in two of the finals including 1965 (won) and 1966 (lost) as player-coach. He was coach only when Wigan lost in 1970. Ashton then coached St. Helens in 1976 (won) and 1978 (lost), before leading out Saints as chairman in 1996 and 1997 for further victories.

Referees

The record of most appearances as a referee at Wembley is shared by George Phillips of Widnes (1939, 1948, 1949 and 1953), Ron Gelder of Wakefield (1954, 1955, 1956 and 1958) and Fred Lindop of Wakefield (1970, 1980, 1982 and 1988). Gelder (1954 Odsal, Bradford) and Lindop (1980 Elland Road, Leeds) also had charge of replayed finals.

Gelder and Stuart Cummings of Widnes (1996, 1997 and 1998) hold the record of three successive Wembley appearances.

Youngest player

Francis Cummins was 17 years 200 days when he played on the wing for Leeds when they lost to Wigan in 1994. Marcus Vassilakopoulos of Leeds went on as a substitute in the same final to become the youngest ever Wembley forward at 17 years seven months. The youngest winner at Wembley is Andrew Farrell, a Wigan forward substitute at 17 years 11 months when they beat Widnes in 1993.

Oldest player

Gus Risman was 41 years 29 days when the full back led Workington Town to victory over Featherstone Rovers in 1952.

Debut at Wembley

Many great players have gone through an entire career without achieving their ambition of playing at Wembley. Hull's Mike Smith achieved it in his first senior game! Smith made one of the most remarkable debuts in sporting history when he played in the second row of an injury-hit Hull side against Wakefield Trinity in 1960.

In contrast, Freddie Miller signed for Hull in 1932 and did not play at Wembley until 1952 – two years after signing for Featherstone Rovers.

Longest playing span

Mike O'Neill holds the record for the longest playing span at Wembley of 15 years. He was a playing substitute forward for Widnes in the 1979 victory and had the same role for Leeds when they lost in 1994. O'Neill made three full appearances in between.

Substitutes

Substitutes were allowed from the 1964-65 season, but the first was not used at Wembley until 1970 when Wigan's Cliff Hill replaced Colin Tyrer in the 16th minute after the full back suffered a broken jaw following a high tackle by Castleford's Keith Hepworth. It was not until the 1973 Featherstone Rovers v. Bradford Northern final that all four substitutes – two from each team – played. Four substitutes each were introduced in 1996 and all eight were used in that year's final between St. Helens and Bradford Bulls. The last non-playing substitute at Wembley was Sheffield Eagles back Lynton Stott in 1998 when they beat Wigan Warriors.

David Hartley of Featherstone became the first substitute to score at Wembley when he grabbed the last try in their 33-14 defeat of Bradford in 1973. He had replaced injured centre Mick Smith in the 72nd minute. Peter Glynn of St. Helens is the only substitute to score two tries in a Wembley final, against Widnes in 1976. He went on in the 44th minute for injured centre Billy Benyon with Saints leading 6-4 and scored the last two tries in a 20-5 victory.

Most overseas players

A record 11 overseas players trod the Wembley turf in 1998. Sheffield Eagles fielded a record-equalling six from one club – Australians Paul Carr, Darren Shaw and Rod Doyle; New Zealanders Taewa Whetu and Dave Watson plus Fijian Waisale Sovatabua. Wigan's five were Australians Mark Bell, Danny Moore, Robbie McCormack and Tony Mestrov plus New Zealander Henry Paul.

In 1985 Hull were the first to field six overseas players in a Wembley final. Australians

Peter Sterling and John Muggleton, plus New Zealanders Gary Kemble, James Leuluai, Dane O'Hara and Fred Ah Kuoi. Wigan had Australians John Ferguson and Brett Kenny with New Zealanders Graeme West and Danny Campbell, who went on as a substitute. South African Nick Du Toit was also a Wigan substitute but did not play.

The last team to play at Wembley without an overseas player was Featherstone Rovers, who beat a Hull side including three New Zealanders, 14-12 in 1983. The last final without either side fielding an overseas player was in 1981 when Widnes beat Hull K.R. 18-9.

Most locals

Widnes fielded a team of 13 local-born players when they lost 11-5 to Hunslet in 1934. They had 12 local-born players when beating St. Helens in 1930 and Keighley in 1937. Featherstone Rovers had 12 players who lived within five miles of their ground when they beat Hull in 1983.

Unluckiest players

Paul Loughlin has played at Wembley five times and been a loser on each occasion. He lost with St. Helens in 1987, 1989 and 1991, then with Bradford Bulls in 1996 and 1997 when they were beaten – by St. Helens!

Dai Davies played at Wembley with three different clubs and was never a winner. He lost with Warrington (1933), Huddersfield (1935) and Keighley (1937). He was also in Warrington's beaten team in the pre-Wembley year of 1928.

Tallest and smallest

The tallest players at Wembley were St. Helens second row John Harrison in 1991 and Wigan centre Barrie-Jon Mather in 1994. Both were 6ft 7in.

The smallest were scrum halves Harry Anderson (Widnes) in 1950 and Gerald Smith (Barrow) in 1967. Both were 5ft 1in.

Schoolboys

Schoolboys who have appeared in an Under-11 curtain-raiser at Wembley and returned to play in the major final are: Joe Lydon, David Hulme, Mike Ford, Neil Puckering, David Plange, Denis Betts, Bobbie Goulding, Phil Clarke, Danny Arnold, Terry O'Connor and Darren Turner. Lydon became the first to achieve the feat, with Widnes in the 1984 final defeat of Wigan. He was followed by team-mate Hulme, who went on as a 72nd minute substitute. Both had played in the first schoolboys' curtain-raiser in 1975 – Lydon for Wigan and Hulme for Widnes.

Best recovery

St. Helens staged the best recovery ever seen at Wembley when they came back from being 26-12 down going into the last 23 minutes and beat Bradford Bulls 40-32 in 1996.

Fastest scores

The fastest try scored at Wembley went to Graham Rees of St. Helens well inside a minute against Leeds in 1972. Newspaper reports at the time varied between 30 and 90 seconds with 35 seconds now accepted as the record. St. Helens had kicked off and after Leeds had been tackled three times Keith Hewporth attempted a clearance because a scrum then followed a fourth tackle. The kick was charged down by Rees close to the line and he crashed over. Kel Coslett added the goal to put St. Helens on the way to a 16-13 victory

The fastest goal was kicked by Wigan's Laurie Gilfedder, whose penalty soared over the bar 54 seconds after Hunslet had kicked off the 1965 final. The penalty was awarded because Alan Marchant's kick off went into touch on the full. A TV video recording gives the precise time of the goal which put Wigan on the way to a 20-16 victory.

Sent off

Although several players had been sent off in pre-1929 finals, Syd Hynes became the first at Wembley in 1971 when referee Billy Thompson dismissed the Leeds captain for an alleged butt on Leigh captain Alex Murphy after 65 minutes. Leigh were leading 17-2 and finished 24-7 winners. Hynes was later suspended for six matches.

Richard Eyres is the only other player to be

sent off at Wembley, the Widnes forward being dismissed by referee Russell Smith after 65 minutes of the 1993 final for a high tackle on Wigan winger Martin Offiah. Wigan were leading 20-14 and there was no further score. Eyres was later suspended for six matches. In addition to the coincidences of each player being sent off in the 65th minute and receiving a six-match ban, they were both dismissed following the referee's consultation with a touch judge.

Although Widnes scrum half Bobbie Goulding was only penalised and warned for a foul near the end of the 1993 final, he was later charged with misconduct by the League's Board of Directors and fined £1,000, half suspended for 12 months.

Sin bin

The sin bin was introduced in January 1983 and was occupied for the first time at Wembley that year when Hull forward Paul Rose was dismissed for 10 minutes by referee Robin Whitfield for a high tackle on Featherstone Rovers centre John Gilbert in the 35th minute. Featherstone captain Terry Hudson was also sent off for 10 minutes in the 58th minute for kneeing Hull captain David Topliss.

Favourites

Favourites have won 36 finals at Wembley and lost 25 with two drawn. Wigan Warriors were the hottest favourites to lose at Wembley when Sheffield Eagles beat them 17-8 in 1998. Wigan were 14-1 *on* to win the final and Sheffield 13-2.

Dates

The earliest date for a Cup final at Wembley is 18 April 1936 for Leeds v. Warrington, while the latest is 21 May 1966 for St. Helens v. Wigan.

Still hoping

Nine of last season's clubs have never appeared at Wembley – Batley Bulldogs, Bramley, Doncaster Dragons, Lancashire Lynx, London Broncos, Oldham, Rochdale Hornets, Swinton Lions and Whitehaven Warriors.

Fate seems to be against Swinton and Oldham. In each of the five years preceding the move to Wembley in 1929 one or the other appeared in the final, twice meeting. Oldham played in four successive finals in that period, while Swinton's run of three successive finals ended during the first Wembley era season. Swinton did get through to the final three years later – only for it to be played at Wigan! Of the non-Wembley clubs, Oldham hold the record for being beaten semi-finalists seven times. Swinton have lost two semi-finals.

Although Hull have appeared at Wembley six times they have yet to win there. They lost in 1959, 60, 80, 83 and 85. They drew in 1982 and won the replay – at Elland Road, Leeds. Wigan have lost a record seven times at Wembley, but have also won a record 15 finals there.

Jeff Grayshon: Never played at Wembley in a 24-year career.

WEMBLEY ERA SEMI-FINALS

It is generally felt that is better to have played at Wembley and lost than never to have played there at all. This makes the semi-final stage of the RL Challenge Cup almost as important as the final, with no consolation for the losers.

Of last season's nine clubs who have never appeared at Wembley, five have been beaten semi-finalists. They are Oldham (seven times), Rochdale Hornets (twice), Swinton (twice) and Whitehaven Warriors and London Broncos.

Probably the unluckiest are Oldham. They have reached the penultimate stage seven times without being able to realise their ambition. Oldham almost made it in 1964. After drawing 5-5 with Hull K.R., they were winning 17-14 in extra time of the replay when bad light stopped play and they were beaten in the third game.

Swinton did win a semi-final in 1932 but the final that year was switched from Wembley to Wigan!

There have been three occasions when Yorkshire has provided all four semi-finalists in one year – in 1962, 1973 and 1983. Four times have all four semi-finalists come from west of the Pennines – in 1930, 1989, 1990 and 1991.

Until 1962 the two semi-finals were always played on the same Saturday, but with four Yorkshire clubs competing for the first time it was decided to play one midweek. Both matches were played at Odsal Stadium, Bradford. The first was on a Wednesday evening – without floodlights – when 43,625 saw Wakefield Trinity beat Featherstone Rovers and on the following Saturday there were 31,423 to see Huddersfield beat Hull K.R.

The following year both semi-finals were again played on the same Saturday, but since then they have been staged on different days.

Some semi-final facts during the Wembley era are:

Biggest attendance: 69,898 Warrington v. Leeds at Bradford in 1950

Biggest aggregate: 104,453 in 1939 (Only other six-figure aggregate was 102,080 in 1951)

Record receipts: £206,555 Bradford B. v. Leeds R. at the McAlpine Stadium, Huddersfield, in 1997.

Lowest attendance: 6,961 Sheffield E. v. Salford R. at Leeds in 1998

Highest score and widest margin:
Wigan 71 v. Bradford N. 10 in 1992

CHALLENGE CUP SEMI-FINALS

Year	Winners		Runners-up		Venue	Attendance	Receipts
1929	Dewsbury	9	Castleford	3	Huddersfield	25,000	£1,562
	Wigan	7	St. Helens Recs.	7	Swinton	31,000	£2,209
Replay	Wigan	13	St. Helens Recs.	12	Leigh	21,940	£1,437
1930	Widnes	10	Barrow	3	Warrington	25,500	£1,630
	St. Helens	5	Wigan	5	Swinton	37,169	£2,666
Replay	St. Helens	22	Wigan	10	Leigh	24,000	£1,657
1931	Halifax	11	St. Helens	2	Rochdale	21,674	£1,498
	York	15	Warrington	5	Leeds	32,419	£2,329
1932*	Leeds	2	Halifax	2	Huddersfield	31,818	£2,456
Replay	Leeds	9	Halifax	2	Wakefield	21,000	£1,417
	Swinton	7	Wakefield T.	4	Rochdale	21,273	£1,369
Final was played at Wigan, not Wembley							
1933	Huddersfield	30	Leeds	8	Wakefield	36,359	£2,299
	Warrington	11	St. Helens	5	Swinton	30,373	£2,055
1934	Hunslet	12	Huddersfield	7	Wakefield	27,450	£1,797
	Widnes	7	Oldham	4	Swinton	17,577	£1,050
1935	Castleford	11	Barrow	5	Swinton	24,469	£1,534
	Huddersfield	21	Hull	5	Leeds	37,111	£2,753

Year	Winners		Runners-up		Venue	Attendance	Receipts
1936	Leeds	10	Huddersfield	5	Wakefield	37,906	£2,456
	Warrington	7	Salford	2	Wigan	41,538	£2,796
1937	Keighley	0	Wakefield T.	0	Leeds	39,998	£2,793
Replay	Keighley	5	Wakefield T.	3	Huddersfield	14,400	£1,052
	Widnes	13	Wigan	9	Warrington	29,260	£1,972
1938	Barrow	4	Halifax	2	Huddersfield	31,384	£2,431
	Salford	6	Swinton	0	Belle Vue, Manchester	31,664	£2,396
1939	Halifax	10	Leeds	4	Bradford	64,453	£3,645
	Salford	11	Wigan	2	Rochdale	40,000	£2,154

● *During the war the semi-finals were two-legged and the finals were not played at Wembley*

Year	Winners		Runners-up		Venue	Attendance	Receipts
1946	Wakefield T.	7	Hunslet	3	Leeds	33,000	£4,991
	Wigan	12	Widnes	5	Swinton	36,976	£4,746
1947	Bradford N.	11	Warrington	7	Swinton	33,474	£4,946
	Leeds	21	Wakefield T.	0	Huddersfield	35,136	£6,339
1948	Bradford N.	14	Hunslet	7	Leeds	38,125	£7,437
	Wigan	11	Rochdale H.	0	Swinton	26,004	£4,206
1949	Bradford N.	10	Barrow	0	Swinton	26,572	£4,646
	Halifax	11	Huddersfield	10	Bradford	61,875	£8,638
1950	Warrington	16	Leeds	4	Bradford	69,898	£9,861
	Widnes	8	Bradford N.	0	Wigan	25,390	£3,936
1951	Barrow	14	Leeds	14	Bradford	57,459	£8,248
Replay	Barrow	28	Leeds	13	Huddersfield	31,078	£5,098
	Wigan	3	Warrington	2	Swinton	44,621	£7,358
1952	Featherstone R.	6	Leigh	2	Leeds	35,621	£6,494
	Workington T.	5	Barrow	2	Wigan	31,206	£4,782
1953	Huddersfield	7	Wigan	0	Bradford	58,722	£10,519
	St. Helens	9	Warrington	3	Swinton	38,059	£7,768
1954	Halifax	18	Hunslet	3	Bradford	46,961	£8,243
	Warrington	8	Leeds	4	Swinton	36,993	£7,596
1955	Barrow	9	Hunslet	6	Wigan	25,493	£4,671
	Workington T.	13	Featherstone R.	2	Leeds	33,499	£7,305
1956	Halifax	11	Wigan	10	Bradford	51,889	£9,054
	St. Helens	5	Barrow	5	Swinton	38,897	£7,793
Replay	St. Helens	10	Barrow	5	Wigan	44,731	£7,750
1957	Barrow	2	Leigh	2	Wigan	34,628	£6,340
Replay	Barrow	15	Leigh	10	Swinton	28,081	£5,695
	Leeds	10	Whitehaven	9	Bradford	49,094	£8,987
1958	Wigan	5	Rochdale H.	3	Swinton	28,597	£6,354
	Workington T.	8	Featherstone R.	2	Bradford	31,517	£6,325
1959	Wigan	5	Leigh	0	Swinton	27,906	£6,068
	Hull	15	Featherstone R.	5	Bradford	52,131	£9,776
1960	Wakefield T.	11	Featherstone R.	2	Bradford	55,935	£10,390
	Hull	12	Oldham	9	Swinton	27,545	£6,093
1961	St. Helens	26	Hull	9	Bradford	42,935	£9,231
	Wigan	19	Halifax	10	Swinton	35,118	£7,557
1962	Wakefield T.	9	Featherstone R.	0	Bradford	43,625	£8,496
	Huddersfield	6	Hull K.R.	0	Bradford	31,423	£6,685
1963	Wakefield T.	5	Warrington	2	Swinton	15,565	£3,530
	Wigan	18	Hull K.R.	4	Leeds	21,420	£6,029

Year	Winners		Runners-up		Venue	Attendance	Receipts
1964	Widnes	7	Castleford	7	Swinton	25,603	£5,541
Replay	Widnes	7	Castleford	5	Wakefield	28,739	£5,313
	Hull K.R.	5	Oldham	5	Leeds	28,823	£7,411
Replay	Hull K.R.	14	Oldham	17	Swinton	27,209	£5,929

● *Score after 80 minutes was 14-14, then bad light caused match to be abandoned after 12 minutes of extra time with Oldham winning 17-14*

Year	Winners		Runners-up		Venue	Attendance	Receipts
Second Replay	Hull K.R.	12	Oldham	2	Huddersfield	28,732	£6,183
1965	Wigan	25	Swinton	10	St. Helens	26,658	£6,384
	Hunslet	8	Wakefield T.	0	Leeds	21,262	£6,090
1966	St. Helens	12	Dewsbury	5	Swinton	13,046	£3,102
	Wigan	7	Leeds	2	Huddersfield	22,758	£5,971
1967	Featherstone R.	16	Leeds	8	Huddersfield	20,052	£6,276
	Barrow	14	Dewsbury	9	Swinton	13,744	£4,560
1968	Leeds	25	Wigan	4	Swinton	30,058	£9,845
	Wakefield T.	0	Huddersfield	0	Bradford	21,569	£6,196
Replay	Wakefield T.	15	Huddersfield	10	Leeds	20,983	£6,425
1969	Castleford	16	Wakefield T.	10	Leeds	21,497	£8,477
	Salford	15	Warrington	8	Wigan	20,600	£7,738
1970	Castleford	6	St. Helens	3	Swinton	18,913	£7,171
	Wigan	19	Hull K.R.	8	Leeds	18,495	£7,862
1971	Leeds	19	Castleford	8	Bradford	24,464	£9,120
	Leigh	10	Huddersfield	4	Wigan	14,875	£5,670
1972	St. Helens	10	Warrington	10	Wigan	19,300	£8,250
Replay	St. Helens	10	Warrington	6	Wigan	32,380	£12,604
	Leeds	16	Halifax	3	Bradford	16,680	£6,851
1973	Featherstone R.	17	Castleford	3	Leeds	15,369	£9,454
	Bradford N.	23	Dewsbury	7	Leeds	14,028	£9,221
1974	Warrington	17	Dewsbury	7	Wigan	11,789	£6,821
	Featherstone R.	21	Leigh	14	Leeds	7,971	£4,461
1975	Widnes	13	Wakefield T.	7	Bradford	9,155	£5,856
	Warrington	11	Leeds	4	Wigan	13,168	£9,581
1976	Widnes	15	Featherstone R.	9	Swinton	13,019	£9,078
	St. Helens	5	Keighley	4	Huddersfield	9,829	£6,113
1977	Leeds	7	St. Helens	2	Wigan	12,974	£11,379
	Widnes	14	Hull K.R.	5	Leeds	17,053	£16,068
1978	Leeds	14	Featherstone R.	9	Bradford	12,824	£11,322
	St. Helens	12	Warrington	8	Wigan	16,167	£13,960
1979	Widnes	14	Bradford N.	11	Swinton	14,324	£16,363
	Wakefield T.	9	St. Helens	7	Leeds	12,393	£14,195
1980	Hull K.R.	20	Halifax	7	Leeds	17,910	£31,650
	Hull	10	Widnes	5	Swinton	18,347	£29,415
1981	Widnes	17	Warrington	9	Wigan	12,624	£20,673
	Hull K.R.	22	St. Helens	5	Leeds	17,073	£30,616
1982	Hull	15	Castleford	11	Leeds	21,207	£41,867
	Widnes	11	Leeds	8	Swinton	13,075	£25,796
1983	Featherstone R.	11	Bradford N.	6	Leeds	10,784	£22,579
	Hull	14	Castleford	7	Elland Rd, L'ds	26,031	£65,498
1984	Wigan	14	York	8	Elland Rd, L'ds	17,156	£52,888
	Widnes	15	Leeds	4	Swinton	14,046	£37,183
1985	Wigan	18	Hull K.R.	11	Elland Rd, L'ds	19,275	£70,192
	Hull	10	Castleford	10	Leeds	20,982	£64,163
Replay	Hull	22	Castleford	16	Leeds	20,968	£65,005

Year	Winners		Runners-up		Venue	Attendance	Receipts
1986	Castleford	18	Oldham	7	Wigan	12,430	£38,296
	Hull K.R.	24	Leeds	24	Elland Rd, L'ds	23,866	£83,757
Replay	Hull K.R.	17	Leeds	0	Elland Rd, L'ds	32,485	£113,345
1987	St. Helens	14	Leigh	8	Wigan	13,105	£48,627
	Halifax	12	Widnes	8	Leeds	16,064	£61,260
1988	Wigan	34	Salford	4	Bolton W. FC	20,783	£95,876
	Halifax	0	Hull	0	Leeds	20,534	£82,026
Replay	Halifax	4	Hull	3	Elland Rd, L'ds	25,117	£113,679
1989	St. Helens	16	Widnes	14	Wigan	17,119	£70,411
	Wigan	13	Warrington	6	Man. C. FC	26,529	£144,056
1990	Wigan	20	St. Helens	14	Man. U. FC	26,489	£177,161
	Warrington	10	Oldham	6	Wigan	15,631	£80,500
1991	Wigan	30	Oldham	16	Bolton W. FC	19,057	£116,937
	St. Helens	19	Widnes	2	Wigan	16,109	£81,342
1992	Castleford	8	Hull	4	Leeds	14,636	£91,225
	Wigan	71	Bradford N.	10	Bolton W. FC	18,027	£131,124
1993	Widnes	39	Leeds	4	Wigan	13,823	£83,914
	Wigan	15	Bradford N.	6	Elland Rd, L'ds	20,085	£150,167
1994	Wigan	20	Castleford	6	Leeds	17,049	£115,842
	Leeds	20	St. Helens	8	Wigan	20,771	£135,722
1995	Wigan	48	Oldham	20	Huddersfield	12,749	£115,705
	Leeds	39	Featherstone R.	22	Elland Rd, L'ds	21,485	£175,245
1996	St. Helens	24	Widnes	14	Wigan	13,424	£89,760
	Bradford B.	28	Leeds	6	Huddersfield	17,139	£166,597
1997	St. Helens	50	Salford R.	20	Wigan	12,580	£101,957
	Bradford B.	24	Leeds R.	10	Huddersfield	18,193	£206,555
1998	Sheffield E.	22	Salford R.	18	Leeds	6,961	£48,380
	Wigan W.	38	London B.	8	Huddersfield	11,058	£122,960

Les Gorley scores Widnes' only try in the 1980 RL Challenge Cup semi-final defeat by Hull.

AMATEUR CLUBS IN THE CHALLENGE CUP

In the early years of the Northern Union Challenge Cup the line between professional and amateur clubs was not clearly defined. A variety of Leagues also made it difficult to set non-League clubs apart and the complications continued until 1904. By then the League format had settled down and non-League clubs had to qualify for round one. So it is from 1904 that the progress and records of non-League clubs in the Challenge Cup can be established and they can all be referred to as amateurs from that period.

The number of amateur entrants has varied over the years, usually depending on how many were needed to make up a mathematically suitable first round of 32 clubs. When the number of professional clubs exceeded 32 from 1982 to 1985 there was no place for amateurs in the Cup. This was remedied with the introduction of a small preliminary round involving two to four amateur clubs until 1992. The following year there was no invitation to the amateurs because of a dispute with the British Amateur RL Association.

In 1994 came the biggest revamp for 90 years when the much criticised preliminary round was scrapped and amateur clubs only were involved in the first two rounds, with a starting line-up of 64. The 32 National Conference League clubs had automatic home advantage in round one followed by a random draw for round two. Those 16 winners then played away to the professional Second Division clubs before the First Division clubs entered a round four random draw.

The 1996 Challenge Cup began the previous December when the first two rounds were again limited to amateurs, starting with a reduced total of 36. The survivors were drawn away to the 1995-96 Division Two professionals in round three before the Centenary Championship and First Division clubs entered round four for a random draw.

The 1997 competition got underway with a record 70 amateur clubs plus Alliance teams

Blackpool Gladiators and Hemel Hempstead entering the first round, which was split into two regional groups to minimise travel costs. The two Alliance clubs and all except the bottom two of the 36 National Conference League entrants were guaranteed home draws against leading amateur teams from the regional leagues plus two universities.

The second round involved 36 clubs in a random draw before the professionals from 11 First Division and 11 Second Division clubs entered round three. The professional clubs were favoured with home draws against amateur opposition with the exception of Bramley and Prescot Panthers, who had filled the bottom two places of Division Two in 1996.

A record 73 amateur clubs entered for the 1998 competition plus Alliance side Blackpool Gladiators, who withdrew after failing with their application to rejoin the Rugby Football League. The first round was marred further by the failure of three other clubs to fulfil their fixtures: West London Colonials at Charleston, Westfield Hotel at Norland, and Kells at Wigan Rose Bridge. All three clubs, who each claimed they were unable to raise a team, were banned from the competition for three years and fined £250 (£200 suspended). Their opponents were given a bye into round two.

The 14 National Conference Premier Division clubs were exempt from the all-amateur random first round draw which included an Irish entry for the first time – Dublin Blues, who lost 32-7 at Dewsbury Moor.

FIRST NON-LEAGUE SUCCESSES OVER SENIOR CLUBS

The inaugural 1897 Challenge Cup saw EASTMOOR become the first club outside the major leagues to avoid defeat when facing senior opposition, drawing 3-3 at home to Stockport of the Lancashire Senior Competition (LSC) in the second round. Eastmoor, who had beaten OLDHAM JUNIORS in the first round, lost the replay at Stockport 28-8.

The first victories by non-League sides against senior opposition came in 1899 when it was achieved by three clubs in round one. In their last season before gaining senior status, HULL KINGSTON ROVERS had an 11-2 home win over Manningham from the Yorkshire Senior Competition (YSC). Rovers lost 10-2 at Lancashire's Broughton Rangers in round two.

YORK, who did not gain senior status until 1901-02, won 4-0 at Liversedge of the YSC before losing 29-5 at Batley in round two. Two years before gaining senior status, DEWS-BURY had a 2-0 home victory over Tyldesley of the LSC and lost 28-3 at Widnes in round two. NORMANTON also beat senior opposition in 1899 after first winning at fellow non-League side RADCLIFFE. In round two they had a 7-2 home win over Holbeck of the YSC before losing 23-2 at Huddersfield in round three.

AMATEUR CLUB VICTORIES OVER SENIOR CLUBS SINCE 1904
(Amateur clubs in capitals)

1903-04   Preliminary round
           Millom 7 v. PARTON 8
           (Lost 26-0 at Broughton R. in first round)

1905-06   Second round
           FEATHERSTONE ROVERS 23 v. Widnes 2
           (Lost 3-0 to Keighley in third round, having
           beaten BROOKLAND ROVERS 16-5 in first
           round. Featherstone remain the last amateur
           club to reach the last eight)

1906-07   Preliminary round
           SAVILLE GREEN 10 v. Bramley 0
           (Lost 10-0 at WHITEHAVEN RECREATION
           in first round)

1907-08   First round
           WHITEHAVEN RECREATION 13 v.
           St. Helens 8
           (Lost 33-5 at Merthyr Tydfil in second round)

1908-09   First round
           BEVERLEY 7 v. Ebbw Vale 2
           (Lost 53-2 at Halifax in second round)

1945-46   First round, first leg
           SHARLSTON ROVERS 12 v. Workington T. 7
           (Lost second leg 2-16)

1947-48   First round, second leg
           RISEHOW & GILLHEAD 10 v. Keighley 2
           (Had lost first leg 11-0)

1994-95   Third round
           Highfield 4 v. BEVERLEY 27
           (Lost 20-30 to Batley in fourth round)

1996   Third round
           Chorley 12 v. THATTO HEATH 27
           (Lost 54-8 at Rochdale H. in fourth round)
           Highfield 20 v. WEST HULL 35
           Fourth round
           WEST HULL 10 v. York 6
           (Lost 8-40 to Wakefield T. in fifth round)

1997   Third round
           York 14 v. DUDLEY HILL 21
           (Lost 62-2 at Carlisle B.R. in fourth round)

1998   Third round
           Bramley 10 v. ELLENBOROUGH RANGERS 16
           Doncaster D. 18 v. FEATHERSTONE LIONS 23
           (Lost 20-56 to Hull K.R. in fourth round)

           Fourth round
           ELLENBOROUGH RANGERS 14 v. Hunslet 12
           (Lost 78-0 at Hull S. in fifth round)
           EGREMONT RANGERS 18 v. Workington T. 0
           (Lost 84-6 at Sheffield E. in fifth round)

Draws against senior clubs

1905-06   First round
           VICTORIA RANGERS 0 v. Widnes 0
           (Lost replay 8-3)

1906-07   Preliminary round
           HULL NEWINGTON ROVERS 3 v. York 3
           (Replay 13-13; lost second replay 14-5 at Hull)
           WORKINGTON 3 v. Wakefield T. 3
           (Lost replay 16-5)

1907-8   First round
           WIGAN HIGHFIELD 3 v. Bramley 3
           (Lost replay 8-6)

1911-12   First round
           NORMANTON ST. JOHN'S 6 v. Warrington 6
           (Lost replay 75-0)

1921-22   First round
           Widnes 5 v. WIGAN HIGHFIELD 5
           (Lost replay 4-9)

1951-52   First round, second leg
           RYLAND RECREATION 9 v. Whitehaven 9
           (Had lost first leg 16-0)

1986-87   First round
             KELLS 4 v. Fulham 4
             (Lost replay 22-14)

RECORDS

TEAM

Highest score (and widest margin):
Huddersfield 119 v. SWINTON PARK 2   1914

Highest amateur score:
Highfield 20 v. WEST HULL 35   1996

Widest amateur margin:
Highfield 4 v. BEVERLEY 27   1995

Lowest senior club score:
VICTORIA RANGERS 0 v. Widnes 0   1906
SAVILLE GREEN 10 v. Bramley 0   1907
EGREMONT RANGERS 18 v. Workington T. 0   1998

INDIVIDUAL

Most tries and points: 11* tries (10g) 53* points by George West (Hull K.R.) v. BROOKLAND ROVERS 1905
Most goals: 22* by Jim Sullivan (Wigan) v. FLIMBY & FOTHERGILL 1925
* Records for any competitive match in Britain

Most amateur tries: 3 by Ray Waring (THATTO HEATH) at Chorley......................................1996

Most amateur goals and points: 7 goals 14 points by Dave Roe (WEST HULL) at Highfield 1996

Former Great Britain forward Len Casey was coach of Beverley when they scored a record 27–4 victory over Highfield in 1995.

255

CHALLENGE CUP PROGRESS CHART

A 20-year review . . . .

Key: W — Winners. F — Beaten finalists. SF — Semi-final. P — Preliminary round.

	1998	1997	1996	1994-95	1993-94*	1992-93	1991-92	1990-91	1989-90	1988-89	1987-88	1986-87	1985-86	1984-85	1983-84	1982-83	1981-82	1980-81	1979-80	1978-79	1977-78
BARROW B.	4	4	4	4	4	1	2	2	1	2	1	2	2	P	1	2	2	1	2	3	1
BATLEY B.	4	4	4	5	4	2	1	1	1	1	1	1	1	1	1	1	2	1	1	1	1
BRADFORD B.	5	F	F	4	6	SF	SF	3	3	2	1	2	3	3	3	SF	3	1	3	SF	3
BRAMLEY	3	3	4	4	4	1	P	1	1	P	P	1	2	3	1	1	1	1	1	2	1
CASTLEFORD T.	6	4	4	4	SF	3	F	1	P	2	1	1	W	SF	3	SF	SF	2	2	3	3
DEWSBURY R.	5	5	5	4	4	1	2	1	2	1	1	1	1	1	1	1	1	2	1	2	1
DONCASTER D.	3	4	3	4	6	1	2	1	P	1	3	1	2	P	2	1	1	1	1	1	1
FEATHERSTONE R.	4	6	4	SF	6	1	3	1	1	3	2	1	1	P	1	W	P	3	1	1	SF
HALIFAX B. S.	5	5	6	4	3	3	3	3	1	1	F	W	1	2	1	2	3	2	SF	1	1
HUDDERSFIELD G.	4	4	4	6	4	2	P	P	P	1	P	1	1	1	1	1	1	1	2	3	3
HULL S.	6	5	6	4	5	P	SF	P	2	1	SF	3	1	F	2	F	W	2	F	3	2
HULL K.R.	6	4	4	5	5	3	1	1	1	3	3	3	F	SF	3	1	2	F	W	2	1
HUNSLET H.	4	4	4	4	4	2	2	1	1	P	1	2	1	3	2	3	1	1	1	1	2
KEIGHLEY C.	4	6	5	5	5	2	1	2	2	2	2	2	1	1	1	1	1	2	1	2	1
LANCASHIRE L.	4	4	3	(3)	(2)	1	P	1	1												
LEEDS R.	4	SF	SF	F	F	SF	2	2	P	3	2	3	SF	1	SF	2	SF	1	2	1	W
LEIGH C.	4	4	5	5	4	1	1	1	1	1	1	SF	3	2	1	1	3	2	1	2	1
LONDON B.	SF	5	4	4	4	1	2	1	2	1	1	1	1	1	2	2	2	1			
OLDHAM	3	6	4	SF	5	3	1	SF	SF	3	1	2	SF	1	2	1	2	3	2	2	2
ROCHDALE H.	4	4	5	4	4	2	1	2	2	1	2	1	2	2	1	1	2	1	2	2	1
ST. HELENS	6	W	W	4	SF	2	3	F	SF	F	3	F	2	1	3	3	1	SF	2	SF	F
SALFORD R.	SF	SF	6	5	4	1	1	3	2	1	SF	1	1	2	1	2	1	3	3	1	2
SHEFFIELD E.	W	5	5	5	5	2	2	2	2	2	2	1	1	1							
SWINTON L.	5	4	4	4	P	1	1	1	1	P	P	1	P	2	1	1	1	1	2		
WAKEFIELD T.	4	5	6	4	4	2	1	2	3	2	1	2	1	2	2	2	3	3	3	F	2
WARRINGTON W.	5	6	5	5	5	1	2	3	F	SF	2	1	2	2	2	3	1	SF	3	1	SF
WHITEHAVEN W.	4	4	4	6	5	1	1	2	3	1	P	3	1	1	1	1	1	1	1	1	1
WIDNES V.	5	4	SF	6	6	F	1	SF	3	SF	3	SF	3	3	W	1	F	W	SF	W	3
WIGAN W.	F	4	5	W	W	W	W	W	W	W	1	3	W	F	1	2	1	1	2	2	
WORKINGTON T.	4	4	4	6	5	1	3	2	1	P	1	P	1	2	2	3	2	2	1	1	2
YORK	4	3	4	5	4	1	1	1	1	1	1	P	2	1	SF	1	1	2	2	1	1

* From 1993-94, clubs from the top division were exempt until round four with all other senior clubs having joined non-League clubs in round three. This resulted in six rounds before the semi-finals.

( ) Entered as non-League side.

Final farewell: Veteran Lancashire Lynx forward Carl Briscoe takes the ball up in the Treize Tournoi final against Villeneuve - his last match of a long career.

TREIZE TOURNOI

TREIZE TOURNOI

1998 Final

Lancashire Lynx remained the surprise success of the inaugural EMAP Treize Tournoi despite going down 16-10 to Villeneuve in the final at the Stade De Toulouse. Many thought that the English Second Division champions were only making up the numbers in the six-club tournament, but they did much better than the First Division Grand Finalists, champions Wakefield Trinity and Featherstone Rovers. They also completed a double over French champions St. Esteve and led for much of the final before Villeneuve stormed to victory in the closing stages.

All this was achieved after Lancashire's players had agreed to play in the tournament without payment when the club explained that they had not budgeted for reaching the competition. Their small squad of players was also hit by injuries and they often struggled to field 17 fit players, starting the final without six who had played in most of their Second Division championship-winning matches. The players' response to the challenge was magnificent with coach Steve Hampson deserving much of the credit for repeatedly upsetting the odds.

Lancashire appeared to be heading for another shock victory in the final when they led 10-0 going into the last half hour. It was a remarkable reversal of form, for though Lancashire had beaten Villeneuve 28-24 at home, they were thrashed 39-0 away in the return match. Villeneuve continued their domination in the first half of the final, but it was Lancashire who took a six-point interval lead after opening the scoring three minutes before half-time. Andy Ruane, returning after being injured in Lynx's previous match against Villeneuve two weeks earlier, set up the try when he turned the ball inside to give Steve Taylor a simple touchdown between the posts. Phil Jones added the conversion to extend his club records to 101 goals and 254 points for the season.

Within two minutes of the restart Lancashire had gone further ahead with David Jones going over for a try. Villeneuve looked to be in trouble. They had lost Paul Sironen, the powerful former Australian Test forward, with a knee injury midway through the first half and were finding it difficult to pierce Lancashire's determined defence. Then a long hard season suddenly caught up with injury-hit Lancashire as they conceded three tries in the last 30 minutes.

The French breakthrough came in the 50th minute when a sustained attacked finished with Gilles Cornut squeezing in at the corner. Eleven minutes later Villeneuve were level after player-coach Grant Doorey, the former Keighley Cougars forward, went in between the posts from fellow Australian Steve Plath's pass and Frederic Banquet added the goal. Plath was hurt making his tryscoring dash and was carried off on a stretcher, but Villeneuve continued to pile on the pressure.

Lancashire were tiring rapidly and when they failed to cover Fabien Devecchi's high kick in the 69th minute Laurent Frayssinous pounced to score the winning try, leaving Banquet to complete the scoring with a simple goal. Former Wakefield and Featherstone player Banquet's goal crowned a series of impressive displays in the tournament.

Fabien Devecchi: Villeneuve's captain.

QUOTES

STEVE HAMPSON (Lancashire coach): I was very pleased with our all round performance. To be Second Division champions and to get to the final of the Treize Tournoi is brilliant. And our guys aren't even getting paid for this competition. They've made a lot of sacrifices and agreed to play without the usual match payment. I think the whole thing has been great.

PAUL SIRONEN (Villeneuve prop): It was very disappointing to have to go off with a knee injury halfway through the first half. I guess it is old age. My knee just jarred and I couldn't get it right. We all want to play finals and it was still nil-nil at that stage. But the guys were real-ly patient and did well to come back like that. We looked at Lancashire Lynx's other matches and they seemed to score all their points in the first half and then run out of puff.

SIR RODNEY WALKER (RFL chairman): Lancashire Lynx have been an outstanding success and should be proud of their achievements. It has been an outstanding competition all round and I certainly want to see us build on this as one way of promoting the game outside Super League.

BOB SCOTT (FASDA general manager): This competition has proved a fabulous advance for Rugby League at our level. And it has been played in the right spirit with not one player sent off in the 13 matches.

Steve Taylor: Played in all five Treize Tournoi matches for Lancashire Lynx.

TREIZE TOURNOI FINAL
Sunday 1 November 1998   Stade De Toulouse

VILLENEUVE 16

		LANCASHIRE LYNX 10
Frederic Banquet	Full back	David "Doc" Murray
Daniel Calvert	Wing	David Jones
Laurent Minut	Centre	Milton Finney
Laurent Frayssinous	Centre	Craig Campbell
Gilles Cornut	Wing	Neil Parsley
Fabien Devecchi, Captain	Stand off	Phil Jones
Steve Plath	Scrum half	Chris Kelly
David Collado	Prop	Steve Taylor
Vincent Wulf	Hooker	Andy Ruane, Captain
Paul Sironen	Prop	Carl Briscoe
Laurent Carrasco	Second row	Steve Gee
Pierre Sabatie	Second row	Simon Smith
Grant Doorey	Loose forward	Joe Walsh

Substitutes
Vea Bloomfield for Sironen (19 min.)
Emmanuel Peralta for Collado (55 min.)
Christophe Canal for Plath (61 min.)
Julien Rinaldi for Wulf (74 min.)
Collado for Peralta (77 min.)

Substitutes
Lee Prest for Gee (half-time)
Paul Norton for Solomon (half-time)
Neil Briscoe for Smith (17 min.)
Pehi J. Solomon for Walsh (17 min.)
Smith for Ruane (66 min.)

T: Cornut, Doorey, Frayssinous
G: Banquet (2)

T: Taylor, D. Jones
G: P. Jones

Coach: Grant Doorey

Coach: Steve Hampson

Penalties: 7-6
Half-time: 0-6

Referee: Graham Shaw (Wigan)
Attendance: 10,283

HOW THE SCORING WENT

37 min. Taylor (Lancs.) try, P. Jones goal	**0-6**
42 min. D. Jones (Lancs.) try	**0-10**
50 min. Cornut (Villeneuve) try	**4-10**
61 min. Doorey (Villeneuve) try, Banquet goal	**10-10**
69 min. Frayssinous (Villeneuve) try, Banquet goal	**16-10**

TREIZE TOURNOI 1998
ROUND BY ROUND REVIEW

The first Treize Tournoi featured the two 1998 English First Division Grand Finalists (Wakefield Trinity and Featherstone Rovers) and the Second Division champions Lancashire Lynx plus France's top three teams of 1997-98: League leaders Villeneuve, second placed Limoux and St. Esteve, who won the French Championship Final from third place.

Each club played two teams from the opposing country home and away, giving them a total of four matches. The leaders of the English and French groups then met in the final at Toulouse to decide the winners of the tournament which was sponsored by EMAP, a publishing and radio company.

Round One – in France

Lancashire Lynx pulled off the first of their series of shock wins in the tournament when they crossed the Channel and beat French champions St. Esteve 40-26 with a superb performance of hard and fast rugby. Full back David "Doc" Murray stood out in a great team effort with a club record-equalling four tries.

A week after winning the First Division Grand Final, a weakened Wakefield Trinity appeared to be still in party mood when they faced Villeneuve and were emphatically beaten 34-12. Former Australian Test forward Paul Sironen made his French club debut for Villeneuve when he went on as a substitute only a few hours after a 26-hour flight. Winger Ludovic Perolari led the French tryscoring with a hat-trick.

Beaten First Division finalists Featherstone Rovers also took a well below full strength side to Limoux and went down 19-10. It was Kevin Hobbs' first match in charge of Featherstone after the departure of coach Steve Simms the day before the squad set off for France.

Round Two – in England

The Lancashire Lynx shock waves continued as they beat Villeneuve 28-24 at the Preston Grasshoppers RU ground. Lynx led 22-10 at half-time and then had to dig deep when Villeneuve made a late bid for victory. A few of Lancashire's players were still recovering from heavy colds and others carried injuries, but they held out for another impressive victory.

Wakefield seemed determined to make up for their poor showing in France and led 26-4 early in the second half against Limoux, but had to withstand a late rally before finishing 38-36 victors. Australian centre Josh Bostock was Trinity's main attacking force, going in for a hat-trick of tries before Limoux started their fightback. Then Limoux centre Lawrence Raleigh went one better to complete an impressive display with four tries.

St. Esteve regained their French-Championship winning form to sweep aside Featherstone and race through for eight tries in their 42-4 victory. Although Featherstone were still without three or four first team players, they were expected to improve on their Cross-Channel performance a week earlier. In fact, they were even less impressive apart from some determined running by Carl Hall.

Round Three – in France

The Lancashire Lynx bubble appeared to have burst when they were swamped by 39-0 by Villeneuve on a rain-lashed pitch. Only a week after upsetting Villeneuve at home, Lancashire just could not raise themselves for another mighty effort. Their injury problems continued right to the last seconds when captain Andy Ruane suffered damaged ribs in an off-the-ball incident as the final hooter sounded.

Featherstone's dismal French venture continued as a third successive defeat ended any chance of appearing in the final. Their young and inexperienced side was no match for St. Esteve, who scored eight tries in a 48-24 victory.

The most bitterly fought match of the tournament ended with Wakefield returning to something like their championship form to beat

Limoux 24-10 at Carcassonne. Halifax referee Nick Oddy came in for much local criticism after sending two players from each side to the sin bin for fighting.

Round Four – in England
Lancashire Lynx made it through to the final with yet another surprise victory, while Wakefield lost. The final round had begun with Lancashire and Wakefield leading the English group with two wins each, but the latter were favoured as they had a superior points difference of 15.

Lancashire's injury-hit squad rose to the occasion yet again to beat St. Esteve 26-18 and complete a double over the French champions. With their match kicking off 30 minutes earlier than Wakefield's, Lancashire increased the pressure on their English rivals by racing to a 26-4 interval before their lead was whittled away.

Lynx then listened anxiously in their dressing room to telephone reports from Wakefield to find out who would be going to Toulouse for the final. It was nail-biting listening as Wakefield hit back from being 24-10 down going into the last half hour before time ran out and they lost 25-22. Villeneuve's victory also meant they pipped St. Esteve to be France's representative in the final.

Featherstone finally gained a victory in their last match by running up the highest score of the tournament with a 54-10 defeat of Limoux.

TREIZE TOURNOI 1998 - ROUND BY ROUND SUMMARY

ROUND ONE

Saturday 3 October

Limoux	(12)	**19**	
T: Puso (2), Raleigh			
G: Alberola (3), Bourrel (dg)			

Featherstone R.	(4)	**10**	
T: Lowe, Baker			
G: Chapman			
Att: 2112			

Referee: Peter Taberner (Wigan)

St. Esteve (16) **26**
T: Brown, Couttet, E. Van Brussel, Thompson, Doyle
G: Couttet (3)

Lancashire L. (24) **40**
T: Murray (4), Walsh, Mawdsley, D. Jones
G: P. Jones (6)
Att: 2000

Referee: Ron Laughton (Barnsley)

Villenueve (14) **34**
T: Perolari (3), Despin, Banquet, Devecchi
G: Banquet (5)
Referee: Paul Lee (Tyldesley)

Wakefield T. (8) **12**
T: Stephenson, A. Hughes
G: A. Hughes (2)
Att: 2000

ROUND TWO

Sunday 11 October

Featherstone R.	(0)	**4**	**St. Esteve**	(16)	**42**

T: Hall

T: Guisset (2), Verges, E. Van Brussel,
Lockwood, Doyle, Torreilles, Garcia
G: Couttet (4), Torreilles
Att: 1130

Referee: Thierry Alibert (France)

Lancashire L.	(22)	**28**	**Villeneuve**	(10)	**24**

T: Parsley, Donno, Gee, Kelly, Taylor
G: P. Jones (4)
Referee: Claude Alba (France)

T: Carrasco (2), Perolari, Doorey, Wulf
G: Banquet (2)
Att: 372 (At Preston Grasshoppers RU)

Wakefield T.	(16)	**38**	**Limoux**	(4)	**36**

T: Bostock (3), Gray (2), Mycoe,
P. March
G: A. Hughes (5)
Referee: David Segura (France)

T: Raleigh (4), Hebert, Puso, Alonso
G: Alberola (4)
Att: 1506

ROUND THREE

Saturday 17 October

Villeneuve	(17)	**39**	**Lancashire L.**	(0)	**0**

T: Perolari (2), Cornut (2),
Frayssinous (2), Devecchi
G: Banquet (5, dg)
Referee: Ian McGregor (Huddersfield)

Att: 2000

Limoux	(10)	**10**	**Wakefield T.**	(8)	**24**

T: Rossel, Gonzales
G: Masson
Referee: Nick Oddy (Halifax)

T: McDonald (2), Wray, Briggs, A. Hughes
G: Gray (2)
Att: 2000 (At Carcassonne)

St. Esteve	(24)	**48**	**Featherstone R.**	(6)	**24**

T: Torreilles (2), Gomez (2), Couttet,
Verges, Thompson, Durand
G: Couttet (8)
Referee: Alan Bates (Workington)

T: Handley, Chapman, Riley, Peacock
G: Chapman (2), Rooney (2)
Att: 1500

ROUND FOUR

Sunday 25 October

Featherstone R. (16)   54   **Limoux** (10)   10
T: Pratt (2), Dickens (2), Spurr (2),   T: Lacans, Rossel
Chapman, Swinson, Stokes   G: Masson
G: Chapman (9)   Att: 804
Referee: Richard Frileux (France)

Lancashire L. (26)   26   **St. Esteve** (4)   18
T: Gee (2), Parsley, Campbell, Murray   T: Verges, Garcia, Guisset, Boudebza
G: P. Jones (3)   G: Couttet
Referee: Claude Alba (France)   Att: 247 (At Preston Grasshoppers RU)

Wakefield T. (10)   22   **Villeneuve** (20)   25
T: Fisher, Bostock, P. March, Mycoe   T: Collado (2), Devecchi, Banquet, Carrasco
G: A. Hughes (3)   G: Banquet (2), Frayssinous (dg)
Referee: Thierry Alibert (France)   Att: 1270

ENGLISH GROUP

	P	W	D	L	F	A	Pts
Lancashire L.	4	3	0	1	94	107	6
Wakefield T.	4	2	0	2	96	105	4
Featherstone R.	4	1	0	3	92	119	2

FRENCH GROUP

	P	W	D	L	F	A	Pts
Villeneuve	4	3	0	1	122	62	6
St. Esteve	4	2	0	2	134	94	4
Limoux	4	1	0	3	75	126	2

FINAL (at Stade De Toulouse)

Sunday 1 November

Villeneuve (0)   16   **Lancashire L.** (6)   10
T: Cornut, Doorey, Frayssinous   T: Taylor, D. Jones
G: Banquet (2)   G: P. Jones
     Att: 10,283

OUTSTANDING FEATS

Biggest attendance: In England: 1506 Wakefield T. v. Limoux
                     In France: 10,283 Villeneuve v. Lancashire L. (Final at Toulouse)
Highest score and widest margin: Featherstone R. 54 v. Limoux 10
Most tries in a match: 4 by David "Doc" Murray (Lancashire L.) at St. Esteve
                                  Lawrence Raleigh (Limoux) at Wakefield T.
Most goals in a match: 9 by Richard Chapman (Featherstone R.) v. Limoux
Most points in a match: 22 (9g, 1t) by Richard Chapman (Featherstone R.) v. Limoux
Most tries in the tournament: 6 by Ludovic Perolari (Villeneuve)
Most goals in the tournament: 17 (inc.1dg) by Frederic Banquet (Villeneuve)
Most points in the tournament: 41 (2t, 16g, 1dg) by Frederic Banquet (Villeneuve)

Premiers: Widnes captain Kurt Sorensen holds aloft the
old Premiership Trophy after the defeat of Bradford
Northern in the 1990 final.

PREMIERSHIP

PREMIERSHIP HISTORY

With the reintroduction of two divisions in 1973-74 there was no longer a need for a play-off to decide the championship. However, it was decided to continue the tradition of an end-of-season competition, the winners to receive the new Premiership Trophy.

In the first season of the Premiership, 1974-75, the top 12 Division One clubs and the top four from Division Two went into a first round draw, the luck of the draw operating through to the final which was played at a neutral venue.

The following season the competition was reduced to the top eight clubs in Division One, the ties being decided on league positions; i.e. 1st v 8th, 2nd v 7th etc. At the semi-final stage the highest placed clubs had the option of when to play at home in a two-legged tie.

In 1978-79 the two-leg system was suspended because of fixture congestion and the higher-placed clubs had home advantage right through to the neutrally staged final. Two legs returned the following season, but were finally abolished from 1980-81.

At the end of the first Super League season of 1996, the Premiership entrants was reduced to just the top four clubs with the leaders playing against the fourth, and second meeting third with the higher clubs having home advantage.

The following year it was expanded to all 12 Super League clubs. The top four were exempt from a preliminary round based on the familiar league placings format. The quarter-finals gave the top four clubs home advantage against the preliminary round winners with the usual league placings format carried through to the semi-finals.

The 1997 Premiership was the last as it was replaced by a complicated Australian-style Grand Final play-off to decide the Super League championship.

Platt attack: St. Helens forward Andy Platt on the attack against Hull Kingston Rovers in the 1985 Premiership final.

PREMIERSHIP FINALS

Year	Winners		Runners-up		Venue	Attendance	Receipts
1975	Leeds (3)	26	St. Helens (1)	11	Wigan	14,531	£7,795
1976	St. Helens (4)	15	Salford (1)	2	Swinton	18,082	£13,138
1977	St. Helens (2)	32	Warrington (5)	20	Swinton	11,178	£11,626
1978	Bradford N. (2)	17	Widnes (1)	8	Swinton	16,813	£18,677
1979	Leeds (4)	24	Bradford N. (8)	2	Fartown, Huddersfield	19,486	£21,291
1980	Widnes (2)	19	Bradford N. (1)	5	Swinton	10,215	£13,665
1981	Hull K.R. (3)	11	Hull (7)	7	Leeds	29,448	£47,529
1982	Widnes (3)	23	Hull (2)	8	Leeds	12,100	£23,749
1983	Widnes (5)	22	Hull (1)	10	Leeds	17,813	£34,145
1984	Hull K.R. (1)	18	Castleford (4)	10	Leeds	12,515	£31,769
1985	St. Helens (2)	36	Hull K.R. (1)	16	Elland Rd, Leeds	15,518	£46,950
1986	Warrington (4)	38	Halifax (1)	10	Elland Rd, Leeds	13,683	£50,879
1987	Wigan (1)	8	Warrington (3)	0	Old Trafford, Man'r	38,756	£165,166
1988	Widnes (1)	38	St. Helens (2)	14	Old Trafford, Man'r	35,252	£202,616
1989	Widnes (1)	18	Hull (4)	10	Old Trafford, Man'r	40,194	£264,242
1990	Widnes (3)	28	Bradford N. (4)	6	Old Trafford, Man'r	40,796	£273,877
1991	Hull (3)	14	Widnes (2)	4	Old Trafford, Man'r	42,043	£384,300
1992	Wigan (1)	48	St. Helens (2)	16	Old Trafford, Man'r	33,157	£389,988
1993	St. Helens (2)	10	Wigan (1)	4	Old Trafford, Man'r	36,598	£454,013
1994	Wigan (1)	24	Castleford (4)	20	Old Trafford, Man'r	35,644	£475,000
1995	Wigan (1)	69	Leeds (2)	12	Old Trafford, Man'r	30,160	£351,038
1996	Wigan (2)	44	St. Helens (1)	14	Old Trafford, Man'r	35,013	£404,000
1997	Wigan (4)	33	St. Helens (3)	20	Old Trafford, Man'r	33,389	£359,303

( ) denotes final League position

PREMIERSHIP RECORDS

ALL ROUNDS
TEAM
Highest score (and widest margin):
Wigan 74 v. Leeds 6 ....Semi-final 1992
Biggest attendance: 42,043
Hull v. Widnes (at Old Trafford, Manchester).   Final 1991

INDIVIDUAL
Most goals: 11 by Mark Aston
(Sheffield E.) at London B. .... Quarter-final 1997
Most tries: by 10 by Martin Offiah
(Wigan) v. Leeds .... Semi-final 1992
Most points: 40 by Martin Offiah
(Wigan) v. Leeds .... Semi-final 1992

FINAL ONLY
TEAM
Most final appearances: 9 by St. Helens
Most wins: 6 by Widnes, Wigan W.
Highest score (and widest margin):
Wigan 69 v. Leeds 12 1995
Biggest attendance: 42,043
Hull v. Widnes (At Old Trafford) 1991
Record receipts: £475,000
Wigan v. Castleford (at Old Trafford) 1994
INDIVIDUAL
Most finals: 8 by Martin Offiah (Widnes 1988, 89, 90, 91 and
Wigan 1992, 93, 94, 95)
Most wins: 6 by Martin Offiah (Widnes 1988, 89, 90) and
Wigan 1992, 94, 95)
Mike O'Neill (Widnes 1980, 82, 83, 88, 89, 90)
Most tries: 3 by Kris Radlinski (Wigan) v. Leeds 1995
Gary Connolly (Wigan) v. Leeds 1995
Danny Ellison (Wigan) v. St. Helens 1996
Most goals: 10 by Frano Botica (Wigan) v. St. Helens ... 1992
Frano Botica (Wigan) v. Leeds.................. 1995
Most points: 20 (10g) by Frano Botica
(Wigan) v. St. Helens 1992
Frano Botica (Wigan) v. Leeds 1995

PREMIERSHIP FINAL TEAMS

*Captain

1974-75

Leeds 26 Holmes (2g) (Marshall 3g); Alan Smith (1t), Hynes* (1t, 1dg) (Eccles), Dyl, Atkinson (2t); Mason (1t), Hepworth; Dickinson, Ward, Pitchford, Cookson, Batten, Haigh
Coach: Roy Francis
St. Helens 11 G. Pimblett; L. Jones (1t), Wilson, Hull, Mathias (1t); Walsh, Heaton (1t); Warlow (Cunningham), A. Karalius, Mantle (K. Gwilliam), E. Chisnall, Nicholls, Coslett* (1g)
Coach: Eric Ashton
Referee: W.H. Thompson (Huddersfield)

1975-76

St. Helens 15 G. Pimblett (3g); L. Jones, Glynn (1t), Noonan, Mathias; Benyon, Heaton (K. Gwilliam); Mantle, A. Karalius (1t), James, Nicholls, E. Chisnall (1t), Coslett*
Coach: Eric Ashton
Salford 2 Watkins (2dg); Fielding, Richards, Hesketh*, Graham; Butler, Nash; Coulman, Raistrick, Sheffield, Knighton (Turnbull), Dixon, E. Prescott
Coach: Les Bettinson
Referee: M.J. Naughton (Widnes)

1976-77

St. Helens 32 G. Pimblett (1t, 7g); L. Jones, Benyon* (1t), Cunningham (1t), Mathias (1t); Glynn (Ashton), K. Gwilliam (1t); D. Chisnall, Liptrot, James (1t), Nicholls (A. Karalius), E. Chisnall, Pinner
Coach: Eric Ashton
Warrington 20 Finnegan; Curling, Bevan (Cunliffe), Hesford (4g), M. Kelly; A. Gwilliam (1t), Gordon* (1t); Weavill (1t), Price, Case, Martyn (Peers), Lester, B. Philbin (1t)
Coach: Alex Murphy
Referee: G.F. Lindop (Wakefield)

1977-78

Bradford N. 17 Mumby (2g); Barends (1t), Roe (1t), Austin, D. Redfearn (1t); Wolford (1dg), A. Redfearn; I. Van Bellen (N. Fox), Raistrick, Thompson, Joyce (Forsyth), Trotter, Haigh* (1t)
Coach: Peter Fox
Widnes 8 Eckersley; S. Wright, Hughes, Aspey (2t); Woods (1g); Gill, Bowden*; Mills, Elwell, Shaw (Ramsey) (George), Adams, Hull, Laughton
Coach: Frank Myler
Referee: J.E. Jackson (Pudsey)

1978-79

Leeds 24 Hague; Alan Smith (1t), D. Smith (1t), Dyl

(Fletcher), Atkinson; Dick (7g, 1dg), J. Sanderson; Harrison, Ward* (1t), Pitchford, Joyce, Eccles (Adams), Cookson
Coach: Syd Hynes
Bradford N. 2 Mumby; D. Parker, Okulicz, Gant, Spencer; Ferres (1g), A. Redfearn; Thompson*, Bridges, Forsyth (I. Van Bellen), Trotter (Mordue), J. Grayshon, Casey
Coach: Peter Fox
Referee: W.H. Thompson (Huddersfield)

1979-80

Widnes 19 Burke (1g); S. Wright (1t), George, Aspey (1t), Bentley (1t); Eckersley (1dg), Bowden*; Shaw, Elwell (1t, 1dg), M. O'Neill, L. Gorley (1t), Hull (Hogan), Adams
Coach: Doug Laughton
Bradford N. 5 Mumby (1g); MacLean (Ferres), D. Redfearn (1t), D. Parker, Gant; Stephenson, A. Redfearn; Thompson*, Bridges, Forsyth, Clarkson (G. Van Bellen), J. Grayshon, Hale
Coach: Peter Fox
Referee: W.H. Thompson (Huddersfield)

1980-81

Hull K.R. 11 Proctor; Hubbard (1g), M. Smith (1t), Hogan (1t), Muscroft; Hartley (1t), Harkin; Holdstock, Watkinson, Millington, Lowe, Casey*, Hall (Burton)
Coach: Roger Millward
Hull 7 Woods (2g); Peacham, Elliott, Wilby, Prendiville; Banks, Dean; Tindall, Wileman, Stone*, Skerrett (Madley), Crane (1t), Norton
Coach: Arthur Bunting
Referee: J. Holdsworth (Kippax)

1981-82

Widnes 23 Burke (1t, 4g); S. Wright (1t), Kieron O'Loughlin, Cunningham (A. Myler), Basnett (1t); Hughes (1t), Gregory; M. O'Neill, Elwell, Lockwood (Whitfield), L. Gorley, Prescott, Adams* (1t)
Coach: Doug Laughton
Hull 8 Kemble; O'Hara (Day), Leuluai, S. Evans, Prendiville; Topliss*, Harkin; Tindall, Wileman (Lloyd), Stone, Skerrett, L. Crooks (1t, 2g, 1dg), Norton
Coach: Arthur Bunting
Referee: S. Wall (Leigh)

1982-83

Widnes 22 Burke; Linton, Hughes*, Lydon (5g), Basnett (2t); A. Myler (1t), Gregory (1t) (D. Hulme); M. O'Neill, Elwell, L. Gorley, Whitfield (S. O'Neill), Prescott, Adams
Coach: Harry Dawson/Colin Tyrer
Hull 10 Kemble; O'Hara (1t), Day (Solal), Leuluai, S. Evans; Topliss* (1t), Dean; Skerrett, Bridges, Stone,

Rose, L. Crooks (2g), Norton (Crane)
Coach: Arthur Bunting
Referee: G.F. Lindop (Wakefield)
1983-84
Hull K.R. 18 Fairbairn; G. Clark, M. Smith (1t),
Prohm (1t), Laws (1t); Dorahy (1t, 1g), Harkin;
Holdstock, Rudd, Millington (Robinson), Burton
(Lydiat), Broadhurst, Hall*
Coach: Roger Millward
Castleford 10 Roockley; Coen, Marchant, Hyde, Kear
(1t); Robinson, R. Beardmore* (3g); Ward, Horton,
Connell, Crampton, B. Atkins, Joyner
Coach: Malcolm Reilly
Referee: R. Campbell (Widnes)
1984-85
St. Helens 36 Veivers (1t); Ledger (2t), Peters,
Meninga (2t) (Allen), Day (4g); Arkwright, Holding;
Burke (Forber), Ainsworth (1t), P. Gorley, Platt,
Haggerty, Pinner* (1t)
Coach: Billy Benyon
Hull K.R. 16 Fairbairn (1t, 2g); G. Clark, Robinson (1t),
Prohm, Laws (1t); M. Smith, G. Smith (Harkin);
Broadhurst, Watkinson*, Ema (Lydiat), Kelly, Hogan,
Hall
Coach: Roger Millward
Referee: S. Wall (Leigh)
1985-86
Warrington 38 Paul Ford (Johnson 1t); Forster (1t),
Cullen, R. Duane, Carbert; Bishop (1t, 5g), A. Gregory;
Boyd* (2t), Tamati (1t), Jackson (1t), Sanderson
(McGinty), Roberts, M. Gregory
Coach: Tony Barrow
Halifax 10 Whitfield (3g) (Smith); Riddlesden,
T. Anderson, C. Anderson* (1t), S. Wilson; Crossley,
Stephens; Scott, McCallion, G. Robinson, Juliff, James
(Bond), Dixon
Player-Coach: Chris Anderson
Referee: G.F. Lindop (Wakefield)
1986-87
Wigan 8 Hampson; Gill (1g), Stephenson (1g), Bell,
Lydon (1t) (Russell); Edwards, Gregory; Case, Kiss,
Wane (West), Goodway, Potter, Hanley*
Coach: Graham Lowe
Warrington 0 Johnson; Drummond, Ropati, B. Peters,
Forster; Cullen, Bishop; Tamati, Roberts (Eccles),
Jackson*, Humphries (M. Gregory), Sanderson,
R. Duane
Coach: Tony Barrow
Referee: K. Allatt (Southport)
1987-88
Widnes 38 Platt (1g); Thackray (Tait 1t), Currier (4g),

D. Wright (2t), Offiah; Dowd, D. Hulme (2t);
Sorensen* (1t), McKenzie (1t), Grima (S. O'Neill),
M. O'Neill, P. Hulme, R. Eyres
Coach: Doug Laughton
St. Helens 14 Loughlin (3g); Ledger (1t), Tanner, Elia,
Quirk; Bailey, Holding; Burke, Groves*, Evans (Dwyer),
Forber, Fieldhouse (Allen), Haggerty (1t)
Coach: Alex Murphy
Referee: J. Holdsworth (Kippax)
1988-89
Widnes 18 Tait; Davies (3g), Currier (1t) (Pyke),
D. Wright (1t), Offiah (1t); D. Hulme (A. Myler),
P. Hulme; Sorensen*, McKenzie, Grima, M. O'Neill,
Koloto, R. Eyres
Coach: Doug Laughton
Hull 10 Fletcher; Eastwood, Blacker, Price (Wilby),
O'Hara*; Pearce (3g), Windley (R. Nolan); Dannatt,
L. Jackson, S. Crooks, Welham (1t), Sharp, Divorty
Coach: Brian Smith
Referee: J. Holdsworth (Kippax)
1989-90
Widnes 28 Tait (2t); Davies (4g), Currier (2t),
D. Wright, Offiah; D. Hulme, P. Hulme; Sorensen* (A.
Myler), McKenzie, M. O'Neill, Koloto (Grima),
R. Eyres, Holliday (1t)
Coach: Doug Laughton
Bradford N. 6 Wilkinson; Cordle, McGowan (Cooper),
Marchant (1t), Francis; Simpson, Harkin; Skerrett, Noble
(Richards), Hobbs*, Medley, Fairbank, Mumby (1g)
Player-Coach: David Hobbs
Referee: C. Morris (Huddersfield)
1990-91
Hull 14 Gay (1t); Eastwood (1g), McGarry (G. Nolan
1t), Webb, Turner; Mackey*, Entat; Harrison,
L. Jackson, Dannatt, Marlow (Busby), Walker (1t),
Sharp
Coach: Noel Cleal
Widnes 4 Tait; Devereux, Currier, Davies*, Offiah (1t);
Dowd, D. Hulme; Sorensen, McKenzie (D. Wright),
Grima, P. Hulme, Koloto (Howard), McCurrie
Coach: Doug Laughton
Referee: J. Holdsworth (Kippax)
1991-92
Wigan 48 Hampson (Myers 1t); Lydon, Bell*, Miles
(1t), Offiah (2t); Botica (10g), Edwards; Cowie,
Dermott, Platt (1t), Betts (2t), McGinty (Panapa),
P. Clarke
Coach: John Monie
St. Helens 16 Veivers; Hunte, Connolly (Griffiths),
Loughlin (1t, 2g), Sullivan (2t); Ropati, Bishop; Neill
(Groves), Dwyer, Ward, Nickle, Mann, Cooper*

269

Coach: Mike McClennan
Referee: J. Holdsworth (Kippax)
1992-93
St. Helens 10 Lyon; Riley, Connolly (1t), Loughlin (1t), Hunte; Ropati, O'Donnell (2dg); Neill, Dwyer, Mann (Griffiths), Joynt, Nickle, Cooper*
Coach: Mike McClennan
Wigan 4 Atcheson; Robinson, Panapa, Farrar, Offiah; Botica, Edwards*; Cowie, Dermott, Skerrett (Gildart), Cassidy (Forshaw 1t), Farrell, P. Clarke
Coach: John Monie
Referee: J. Holdsworth (Kippax)
1993-94
Wigan 24 Atcheson; Robinson, Panapa (1t) (Lydon), Connolly, Offiah; Botica (1t, 4g), Edwards*; Skerrett, Hall, Cowie (Cassidy), Betts (1t), Farrell (1t), P. Clarke
Coach: Graeme West
Castleford 20 Ellis; C. Smith, Blackmore, T. Smith, Middleton; Steadman (1t, 2g), Ford; Crooks* (2g) (Sykes, 1t), Russell, Sampson (1t), Ketteridge (Smales), Hay, Nikau
Coach: John Joyner
Referee: S. Cummings (Widnes)
1994-95
Wigan 69 Paul (1t); Robinson, Radlinski (3t), Connolly (3t), Offiah; Botica (10g), Edwards* (1t); Skerrett (1t) (Cassidy), Hall (1t), Cowie, Betts (1t), Farrell (dg) (Haughton 1t), P. Clarke
Coach: Graeme West
Leeds 12 Tait; Fallon, Iro*, Hassan (Vassilakopoulos), Cummins; Innes (1t), Holroyd (2g); Howard (Harmon), Lowes, Faimalo, Mann, Eyres (1t), Mercer
Coach: Doug Laughton
Referee: S. Cummings (Widnes)
1996
Wigan 44 Radlinski; Ellison (3t), Connolly (1t), Tuigamala, Robinson (1t); Paul (1t), Edwards (1t) (Murdock 1t); Skerrett (Cowie), Hall, O'Connor, Haughton (1t) (S. Barrow), Cassidy (A. Johnson), Farrell* (4g)
Coach: Graeme West
St Helens 14 Prescott; Hayes (Arnold), Hunte, Newlove (1t), Sullivan; Martyn (1t), Goulding* (3g); Perelini, Cunningham, Fogerty (Pickavance), McVey (Booth), Morley (Haigh), Hammond
Coach: Shaun McRae
Referee: D. Campbell (Widnes)
1997
Wigan W. 33 Robinson (1t); Ellison, Connolly (Wright dg), Radlinski (1t), A. Johnson (1t); Paul, T. Smith (Tallec); Cowie (O'Connor), J. Clarke, Hansen

(Holgate), Haughton (1t), Cassidy, Farrell* (1t, 6g)
Coach: Eric Hughes
St. Helens 20 Arnold; Stewart, Hunte, Newlove (1t), Sullivan; Hammond (1t), Long (2g); Leathem (Pickavance), Cunningham, O'Neill (Booth), McVey (1t) (Anderson 1t), Perelini (Morley), Joynt*
Coach: Shaun McRae
Referee: S. Cummings (Widnes)

PREMIERSHIP TROPHY FINAL PLAYERS' REGISTER

The following is an index of players who appeared in a Premiership final. W — winners, L — losers. Substitute appearances in lower case letters.

ADAMS, Bryan: Leeds 79w
ADAMS, Mick: Widnes 78L, 80W, 82W, 83W
AINSWORTH, Gary: St. Helens 85W
ALLEN, Shaun: St. Helens 85w, 88l
ANDERSON, Chris: Halifax 86L
ANDERSON, Paul: St. Helens 97l
ANDERSON, Tony: Halifax 86L
ARKWRIGHT, Chris: St. Helens 85W
ARNOLD, Danny: St. Helens 96l, 97L
ASHTON, Alan: St. Helens 77l
ASPEY, Malcolm: Widnes 78L, 80W
ATCHESON, Paul: Wigan 93L, 94W
ATKINS, Brett: Castleford 84L
ATKINSON, John: Leeds 75W, 79W
AUSTIN, Jack: Bradford N. 78W

BAILEY, Mark: St. Helens 88L
BANKS, Barry: Hull 81L
BARENDS, David: Bradford N. 78W
BARROW, Steve: Wigan 96w
BASNETT, John: Widnes 82W, 83W
BATTEN, Ray: Leeds 75W
BEARDMORE, Bob: Castleford 84L
BELL, Dean: Wigan 87W, 92W
BENTLEY, Keith: Widnes 80W
BENYON, Billy: St. Helens 76W, 77W
BETTS, Denis: Wigan 92W, 94W, 95W
BEVAN, John: Warrington 77L
BISHOP, Paul: Warrington 86W, 87L; St. Helens 92L
BLACKER, Brian: Hull 89L
BLACKMORE, Richard: Castleford 94L
BOND, Steve: Halifax 86l
BOOTH, Simon: St. Helens 96l, 97l
BOTICA, Frano: Wigan 92W, 93L, 94W, 95W
BOWDEN, Reg: Widnes 78L, 80W
BOYD, Les: Warrington 86W
BRIDGES, John "Keith": Bradford N. 79L, 80L; Hull 83L

BROADHURST, Mark: Hull K.R. 84W, 85L
BURKE, Mick: Widnes 80W, 82W, 83W
BURKE, Tony: St. Helens 85W, 88L
BURTON, Chris: Hull K.R. 81w, 84W
BUSBY, Dean: Hull 91w
BUTLER, John: Salford 76L

CARBERT, Brian: Warrington 86W
CASE, Brian: Warrington 77L; Wigan 87W
CASEY, Len: Bradford N. 79L; Hull K.R. 81W
CASSIDY, Mick: Wigan 93L, 94w, 95w, 96W, 97W
CHISNALL, Dave: St. Helens 77W
CHISNALL, Eric: St. Helens 75L, 76W, 77W
CLARK, Garry: Hull K.R. 84W, 85L
CLARKE, Jon: Wigan 97W
CLARKE, Phil: Wigan 92W, 93L, 94W, 95W
CLARKSON, Geoff: Bradford N. 80L
COEN, Darren: Castleford 84L
CONNELL, Gary: Castleford 84L
CONNOLLY, Gary: St. Helens 92L, 93W; Wigan 94W, 95W, 96W, 97W
COOKSON, Phil: Leeds 75W, 79W
COOPER, David: Bradford N. 90l
COOPER, Shane: St. Helens 92L, 93W
CORDLE, Gerald: Bradford N. 90L
COSLETT, Kel: St. Helens 75L, 76W
COULMAN, Mike: Salford 76L
COWIE, Neil: Wigan 92W, 93L, 94W, 95W, 96w, 97W
CRAMPTON, Jimmy: Castleford 84L
CRANE, Mick: Hull 81L, 83l
CROOKS, Lee: Hull 82L, 83L; Castleford 94L
CROOKS, Steve: Hull 89L
CROSSLEY, John: Halifax 86L
CULLEN, Paul: Warrington 86W, 87L
CUMMINS, Francis: Leeds 95L
CUNLIFFE, Dave: Warrington 77l
CUNNINGHAM, Eddie: St. Helens 75l, 77W; Widnes 82W
CUNNINGHAM, Kieron: St. Helens 96L, 97L
CURLING, Denis: Warrington 77L
CURRIER, Andy: Widnes 88W, 89W, 90W, 91L

DANNATT, Andy: Hull 89L, 91W
DAVIES, Jonathan: Widnes 89W, 90W, 91L
DAY, Sean: St. Helens 85W
DAY, Terry: Hull 82l, 83L
DEAN, Tony: Hull 81L, 83L
DERMOTT, Martin: Wigan 92W, 93L
DEVEREUX, John: Widnes 91L
DICK, Kevin: Leeds 79W
DICKINSON, Roy: Leeds 75W
DIVORTY, Gary: Hull 89L
DIXON, Colin: Salford 76L
DIXON, Paul: Halifax 86L
DORAHY, John: Hull K.R. 84W
DOWD, Barry: Widnes 88W, 91L

DRUMMOND, Des: Warrington 87L
DUANE, Ronnie: Warrington 86W, 87L
DWYER, Bernard: St. Helens 88l, 92L, 93W
DYL, Les: Leeds 75W, 79W

EASTWOOD, Paul: Hull 89L, 91W
ECCLES, Bob: Warrington 87l
ECCLES, Graham: Leeds 75w, 79W
ECKERSLEY, David: Widnes 78L, 80W
EDWARDS, Shaun: Wigan 87W, 92W, 93L, 94W, 95W, 96W
ELIA, Mark: St. Helens 88L
ELLIOTT, David: Hull 81L
ELLIS, St. John: Castleford 94L
ELLISON, Danny: Wigan 96W, 97W
ELWELL, Keith: Widnes 78L, 80W, 82W, 83W
EMA, Asuquo: Hull K.R. 85L
ENTAT, Patrick: Hull 91W
EVANS, Steve: Hull 82L, 83L
EVANS, Stuart: St. Helens 88L
EYRES, Richard: Widnes 88W, 89W, 90W; Leeds 95L

FAIMALO, Esene: Leeds 95L
FAIRBAIRN, George: Hull K.R. 84W, 85L
FAIRBANK, Karl: Bradford N. 90L
FALLON, Jim: Leeds 95L
FARRAR, Andrew: Wigan 93L
FARRELL, Andrew: Wigan 93L, 94W, 95W, 96W, 97W
FERRES, Steve: Bradford N. 79L, 80l
FIELDHOUSE, John: St. Helens 88L
FIELDING, Keith: Salford 76L
FINNEGAN, Derek: Warrington 77L
FLETCHER, Paul: Hull 89L
FLETCHER, Paul: Leeds 79w
FOGERTY, Adam: St. Helens 96L
FORBER, Paul: St. Helens 85w, 88L
FORD, Mike: Castleford 94L
FORD, Paul: Warrington 86W
FORSHAW, Mike: Wigan 93l
FORSTER, Mark: Warrington 86W, 87L
FORSYTH, Colin: Bradford N. 78w, 79L, 80L
FOX, Neil: Bradford N. 78w
FRANCIS, Richard: Bradford N. 90L

GANT, Les: Bradford N. 79L, 80L
GAY, Richard: Hull 91W
GEORGE, Derek "Mick": Widnes 78l, 80W
GILDART, Ian: Wigan 93l
GILL, Henderson: Wigan 87W
GILL, Ken: Widnes 78L
GLYNN, Peter: St. Helens 76W, 77W
GOODWAY, Andy: Wigan 87W
GORDON, Parry: Warrington 77L
GORLEY, Les: Widnes 80W, 82W, 83W
GORLEY, Peter: St. Helens 85W

GOULDING, Bobbie: St. Helens 96L
GRAHAM, Gordon: Salford 76L
GRAYSHON, Jeff: Bradford N. 79L, 80L
GREGORY, Andy: Widnes 82W, 83W; Warrington 86W; Wigan 87W
GREGORY, Mike: Warrington 86W, 871
GRIFFITHS, Jonathan: St. Helens 92l, 93w
GRIMA, Joe: Widnes 88W, 89W, 90w, 91L
GROVES, Paul: St. Helens 88L, 921
GWILLIAM, Alan: Warrington 77L
GWILLIAM, Ken: St. Helens 75l, 76w, 77W

HAGGERTY, Roy: St. Helens 85W, 88L
HAGUE, Neil: Leeds 79W
HAIGH, Andy: St. Helens 96l
HAIGH, Bob: Leeds 75W; Bradford N. 78W
HALE, Gary: Bradford N. 80L
HALL, David: Hull K.R. 81W, 84W, 85L
HALL, Martin: Wigan 94W, 95W, 96W
HAMMOND, Karle: St. Helens 96L, 97L
HAMPSON, Steve: Wigan 87W, 92W
HANLEY, Ellery: Wigan 87W
HANSEN, Lee: Wigan 97W
HARKIN, Kevin: Hull 82L
HARKIN, Paul: Hull K.R. 81W, 84W, 85l; Bradford N. 90L
HARMON, Neil: Leeds 95l
HARRISON, Karl: Hull 91W
HARRISON, Mick: Leeds 79W
HARTLEY, Steve: Hull K.R. 81W
HASSAN, Phil: Leeds 95L
HAUGHTON, Simon: Wigan 95w, 96W, 97W
HAY, Andy: Castleford 94L
HAYES, Joey: St. Helens 96L
HEATON, Jeff: St. Helens 75L, 76W
HEPWORTH, Keith: Leeds 75W
HESFORD, Steve: Warrington 77L
HESKETH, Chris: Salford 76L
HOBBS, David: Bradford N. 90L
HOGAN, Brian: Widnes 80w
HOGAN, Phil: Hull K.R. 81W, 85L
HOLDING, Neil: St. Helens 85W, 88L
HOLDSTOCK, Roy: Hull K.R. 81W, 84W
HOLGATE, Stephen: Wigan 97w
HOLLIDAY, Les: Widnes 90W
HOLROYD, Graham: Leeds 95L
HOLMES, John: Leeds 75W
HORTON, Stuart: Castleford 84L
HOWARD, Harvey: Widnes 91l; Leeds 95L
HUBBARD, Steve: Hull K.R. 81W
HUGHES, Eric: Widnes 78L, 82W, 83W
HULL, David: St. Helens 75L; Widnes 78L, 80W
HULME, David: Widnes 83w, 88W, 89W, 90W, 91L
HULME, Paul: Widnes 88W, 89W, 90W, 91L
HUMPHRIES, Tony: Warrington 87L
HUNTE, Alan: St. Helens 92L, 93W, 96L, 97L

HYDE, Gary: Castleford 84L
HYNES, Syd: Leeds 75W

INNES, Craig: Leeds 95L
IRO, Kevin: Leeds 95L

JACKSON, Bob: Warrington 86W, 87L
JACKSON, Lee: Hull 89L, 91W
JAMES, Mel: St. Helens 76W, 77W
JAMES, Neil: Halifax 86L
JOHNSON, Andy: Wigan 96w, 97W
JOHNSON, Brian: Warrington 86w, 87L
JONES, Les: St. Helens 75L, 76W, 77W
JOYCE, Graham: Bradford N. 78W; Leeds 79W
JOYNER, John: Castleford 84L
JOYNT, Chris: St. Helens 93W, 97L
JULIFF, Brian: Halifax 86L

KARALIUS, Tony: St. Helens 75L, 76W, 77w
KEAR, John: Castleford 84L
KELLY, Andy: Hull K.R. 85L
KELLY, Mike: Warrington 77L
KEMBLE, Gary: Hull 82L, 83L
KETTERIDGE, Martin: Castleford 94L
KISS, Nicky: Wigan 87W
KNIGHTON, John: Salford 76L
KOLOTO, Emosi: Widnes 89W, 90W, 91L

LAUGHTON, Doug: Widnes 78L
LAWS, David: Hull K.R. 84W, 85L
LEATHEM, Andy: St. Helens 97L
LEDGER, Barry: St. Helens 85W, 88L
LESTER, Roy: Warrington 77L
LEULUAI, James: Hull 82L, 83L
LINTON, Ralph: Widnes 83W
LIPTROT, Graham: St. Helens 77W
LLOYD, Geoff "Sammy": Hull 82l
LOCKWOOD, Brian: Widnes 82W
LONG, Sean: St. Helens 97L
LOUGHLIN, Paul: St. Helens 88L, 92L, 93W
LOWE, Phil: Hull K.R. 81W
LOWES, James: Leeds 95L
LYDIAT, John: Hull K.R. 84w, 85l
LYDON, Joe: Widnes 83W; Wigan 87W, 92W, 94w
LYON, David: St. Helens 93W

McCALLION, Seamus: Halifax 86L
McCURRIE, Steve: Widnes 91L
McGARRY, Damien: Hull 91W
McGINTY, Billy: Warrington 86w; Wigan 92W
McGOWAN, Steve: Bradford N. 90L
McKENZIE, Phil: Widnes 88W, 89W, 90W, 91L
McVEY, Derek: St. Helens 96L, 97L
MACKEY, Greg: Hull 91W
MacLEAN, Ian: Bradford N. 80L
MADLEY, Ian: Hull 811
MANN, George: St. Helens 92L, 93W; Leeds 95L

MANTLE, John: St. Helens 75L, 76W
MARCHANT, Tony: Castleford 84L; Bradford
N. 90L
MARLOW, Ian: Hull 91W
MARSHALL, David: Leeds 75w
MARTYN, (Snr) Tommy: Warrington 77L
MARTYN (Jnr), Tommy: St. Helens 96L
MASON, Mel: Leeds 75W
MATHIAS, Roy: St. Helens 75L, 76W, 77W
MEDLEY, Paul: Bradford N. 90L
MENINGA, Mal: St. Helens 85W
MERCER, Gary: Leeds 95L
MIDDLETON, Simon: Castleford 94L
MILES, Gene: Wigan 92W
MILLINGTON, John: Hull K.R. 81W, 84W
MILLS, Jim: Widnes 78L
MORDUE, David: Bradford N. 79l
MORLEY, Chris: St. Helens 96L, 97l
MUMBY, Keith: Bradford N. 78W, 79L, 80L, 90L
MURDOCK, Craig: Wigan 96w
MUSCROFT, Peter: Hull K.R. 81W
MYERS, David: Wigan 92w
MYLER, Tony: Widnes 82w, 83W, 89w, 90w

NASH, Steve: Salford 76L
NEILL, Jonathan: St. Helens 92L, 93W
NEWLOVE, Paul: St. Helens 96L, 97L
NICHOLLS, George: St. Helens 75L, 76W, 77W
NICKLE, Sonny: St. Helens 92L, 93W
NIKAU, Tawera: Castleford 94L
NOBLE, Brian: Bradford N. 90L
NOLAN, Gary: Hull 91w
NOLAN, Rob: Hull 89l
NOONAN, Derek: St. Helens 76W
NORTON, Steve: Hull 81L, 82L, 83L

O'CONNOR, Terry: Wigan 96W, 97w
O'DONNELL, Gus: St. Helens 93W
OFFIAH, Martin: Widnes 88W, 89W, 90W, 91L;
 Wigan 92W, 93L, 94W, 95W
O'HARA, Dane: Hull 82L, 83L, 89L
OKULICZ, Eddie: Bradford N. 79L
O'LOUGHLIN, Kieron: Widnes 82W
O'NEILL, Julian: St. Helens 97L
O'NEILL, Mike: Widnes 80W, 82W, 83W, 88W,
 89W, 90W
O'NEILL, Steve: Widnes 83w, 88w

PANAPA, Sam: Wigan 92w, 93L, 94W
PARKER, Derek: Bradford N. 79L, 80L
PAUL, Henry: Wigan 95W, 96W, 97W
PEACHAM, Gary: Hull 81L
PEARCE, Gary: Hull 89L
PEERS, Mike: Warrington 77l
PERELINI, Apollo: St. Helens 96L, 97L
PETERS, Barry: Warrington 87L
PETERS, Steve: St. Helens 85W

PHILBIN, Barry: Warrington 77L
PICKAVANCE, Ian: St. Helens 96l, 97l
PIMBLETT, Geoff: St. Helens 75L, 76W, 77W
PINNER, Harry: St. Helens 77W, 85W
PITCHFORD, Steve: Leeds 75W, 79W
PLATT, Andy: St. Helens 85W; Wigan 92W
PLATT, Duncan: Widnes 88W
POTTER, Ian: Wigan 87W
PRENDIVILLE, Paul: Hull 81L, 82L
PRESCOTT, Eric: Salford 76L; Widnes 82W, 83W
PRESCOTT, Steve: St. Helens 96L
PRICE, Joe: Warrington 77L
PRICE, Richard: Hull 89L
PROCTOR, Paul: Hull K.R. 81W
PROHM, Gary: Hull K.R. 84W, 85L
PYKE, Derek: Widnes 89w

QUIRK, Les: St. Helens 88L

RADLINSKI, Kris: Wigan 95W, 96W, 97W
RAISTRICK, Dean: Salford 76L; Bradford N. 78W
RAMSEY, Bill: Widnes 78l
REDFEARN, Alan: Bradford N. 78W, 79L, 80L
REDFEARN, David: Bradford N. 78W, 80L
RICHARDS, Craig: Bradford N. 90l
RICHARDS, Maurice: Salford 76L
RIDDLESDEN, Eddie: Halifax 86L
RILEY, Mike: St. Helens 93W
ROBERTS, Mark: Warrington 86W, 87L
ROBINSON, Geoff: Halifax 86L
ROBINSON, Ian: Hull K.R. 84w, 85L
ROBINSON, Jason: Wigan 93L, 94W, 95W, 96W,
 97W
ROBINSON, Steve: Castleford 84L
ROE, Peter: Bradford N. 78W
ROOCKLEY, David: Castleford 84L
ROPATI, Joe: Warrington 87L
ROPATI, Tea: St. Helens 92L, 93W
ROSE, Paul: Hull 83L
RUDD, Chris: Hull K.R. 84W
RUSSELL, Richard: Wigan 87w; Castleford 94L

SAMPSON, Dean: Castleford 94L
SANDERSON, Gary: Warrington 86W, 87L
SANDERSON, John "Sammy": Leeds 79W
SCOTT, Mick: Halifax 86L
SHARP, Jon: Hull 89L, 91W
SHAW, Glyn: Widnes 78L, 80W
SHEFFIELD, Bill: Salford 76L
SIMPSON, Roger: Bradford N. 90L
SKERRETT, Kelvin: Bradford N. 90L; Wigan 93L,
 94W, 95W, 96W
SKERRETT, Trevor: Hull 81L, 82L, 83L
SMALES, Ian: Castleford 94l
SMITH, Alan: Leeds 75W, 79W
SMITH, Chris: Castleford 94L

273

SMITH, David: Leeds 79W
SMITH, Gordon: Hull K.R. 85L
SMITH, Mike: Hull K.R. 81W, 84W, 85L
SMITH, Steve: Halifax 86l
SMITH, Tony: Castleford 94L; Wigan 97W
SOLAL, Patrick: Hull 83l
SORENSEN, Kurt: Widnes 88W, 89W, 90W, 91L
SPENCER, Alan: Bradford N. 79L
STEADMAN, Graham: Castleford 94L
STEPHENS, Gary: Halifax 86L
STEPHENSON, David: Wigan 87W
STEPHENSON, Nigel: Bradford N. 80L
STEWART, Anthony: St. Helens 97L
STONE, Richard "Charlie": Hull 81L, 82L, 83L
SULLIVAN, Anthony: St. Helens 92L, 96L, 97L
SYKES, Nathan: Castleford 94l

TAIT, Alan: Widnes 88w, 89W, 90W, 91L; Leeds 95L
TALLEC, Gael: Wigan 97w
TAMATI, Kevin: Warrington 86W, 87L
TANNER, David: St. Helens 88L
THACKRAY, Rick: Widnes 88W
THOMPSON, Jimmy: Bradford N. 78W, 79L, 80L
TINDALL, Keith: Hull 81L, 82L
TOPLISS, David: Hull 82L, 83L
TROTTER, Dennis: Bradford N. 78W, 79L
TUIGAMALA, Va'aiga: Wigan 96W
TURNBULL, Sam: Salford 76l
TURNER, Neil: Hull 91W

VAN BELLEN, Gary: Bradford N. 80l
VAN BELLEN, Ian: Bradford N. 78W, 79l
VASSILAKOPOULOS, Marcus: Leeds 95l
VEIVERS, Phil: St. Helens 85W, 92L

WALKER, Russ: Hull 91W
WALSH, John: St. Helens 75L
WANE, Shaun: Wigan 87W
WARD, David: Leeds 75W, 79W
WARD, Kevin: Castleford 84L; St. Helens 92L
WARLOW, John: St. Helens 75L
WATKINS, David: Salford 76L
WATKINSON, David: Hull K.R. 81W, 85L
WEAVILL, Dave: Warrington 77L
WEBB, Brad: Hull 91W
WELHAM, Paul: Hull 89L
WEST, Graeme: Wigan 87w
WHITFIELD, Colin: Halifax 86L
WHITFIELD, Fred: Widnes 82w, 83W
WILBY, Tim: Hull 81L, 89l
WILEMAN, Ronnie: Hull 81L, 82L
WILKINSON, Ian: Bradford N. 90L
WILSON, Frank: St. Helens 75L
WILSON, Scott: Halifax 86L
WINDLEY, Phil: Hull 89L
WOLFORD, John: Bradford N. 78W
WOODS, Paul: Widnes 78L; Hull 81L
WRIGHT, Darren: Widnes 88W, 89W, 90W, 91l
WRIGHT, Nigel: Wigan 97w
WRIGHT, Stuart: Widnes 78L, 80W, 82W

Wright way: Darren Wright of Widnes goes over for a try against St. Helens in the 1988 Premiership final.

THE HARRY SUNDERLAND TROPHY

The trophy, in memory of the famous Queenslander, a former Australian tour manager, broadcaster and journalist, is presented to the Man of the Match in the end-of-season Championship or Premiership final. The award is donated and judged by the Rugby League Writers' Association.

Year	Winner	Team	Position
Championship			
1965	Terry Fogerty	Halifax (v. St. Helens)	Second row
1966	Albert Halsall	St. Helens (v. Halifax)	Prop
1967	Ray Owen	Wakefield T. (v. St. Helens)	Scrum half
1968	Gary Cooper	Wakefield T. (v. Hull K.R.)	Full back
1969	Bev Risman	Leeds (v. Castleford)	Full back
1970	Frank Myler	St. Helens (v. Leeds)	Stand off
1971	Bill Ashurst	*Wigan (v. St. Helens)	Second row
1972	Terry Clawson	Leeds (v. St. Helens)	Prop
1973	Mick Stephenson	Dewsbury (v. Leeds)	Hooker
Club Merit Championship			
1974	Barry Philbin	Warrington (v. St. Helens)	Loose forward
Premiership			
1975	Mel Mason	Leeds (v. St. Helens)	Stand off
1976	George Nicholls	St. Helens (v. Salford)	Second row
1977	Geoff Pimblett	St. Helens (v. Warrington)	Full back
1978	Bob Haigh	Bradford N. (v. Widnes)	Loose forward
1979	Kevin Dick	Leeds (v. Bradford N.)	Stand off
1980	Mal Aspey	Widnes (v. Bradford N.)	Centre
1981	Len Casey	Hull K.R. (v. Hull)	Second row
1982	Mick Burke	Widnes (v. Hull)	Full back
1983	Tony Myler	Widnes (v. Hull)	Stand off
1984	John Dorahy	Hull K.R. (v. Castleford)	Stand off
1985	Harry Pinner	St. Helens (v. Hull K.R.)	Loose forward
1986	Les Boyd	Warrington (v. Halifax)	Prop
1987	Joe Lydon	Wigan (v. Warrington)	Winger
1988	David Hulme	Widnes (v. St. Helens)	Scrum half
1989	Alan Tait	Widnes (v. Hull)	Full back
1990	Alan Tait	Widnes (v. Bradford N.)	Full back
1991	Greg Mackey	Hull (v. Widnes)	Stand off
1992	Andy Platt	Wigan (v. St. Helens)	Prop
1993	Chris Joynt	St. Helens (v. Wigan)	Second row
1994	Sam Panapa	Wigan (v. Castleford)	Centre
1995	Kris Radlinski	Wigan (v. Leeds)	Centre
1996	Andrew Farrell	Wigan (v. St. Helens)	Loose forward
1997	Andrew Farrell	Wigan W. (v. St. Helens)	Loose forward
Grand Final			
1998	Jason Robinson	Wigan W. (v. Leeds R.)	Winger

*Losing team

DIVISIONAL PREMIERSHIP HISTORY

The Divisional Premiership began in 1987 to provide the first stage of a double-header when the major Premiership final moved to Manchester United's Old Trafford soccer ground. It was then the Second Division Premiership (there were only two divisions) and restricted to the top eight clubs. The top four clubs had home advantage in the first round which was based on league positions: 1st v. 8th; 2nd v. 7th, 3rd v. 6th and 4th v. 5th. The formula continued for the semi-finals.

With the introduction of three divisions in 1991-92, a new-style Divisional Premiership began with a top eight Division Three play-off based on the familiar league placings formula. In the second round, the top four clubs in Division Two had home advantage against Division Three opposition, the highest again playing the lowest qualifier and so on.

In 1993-94 there was a return to two divisions and a top eight battle for the Second Division Premiership.

The arrival of Super League in 1996 and another return to three divisions brought a further change for the Divisional Premiership with only four clubs involved. This time the champions of Division One (now the second of three divisions) played at home to the Division Two champions, while Division One's second club entertained the third.

One year later it was all change. All but the bottom two clubs in Division Two were divided into four regional leagues of five clubs – Cumbria, Lancashire, East Yorkshire and West Yorkshire. The top two from each league then went into a random draw for a four-tie quarter-final followed by the semi-finals.

The Divisional Premiership was scrapped after the 1997 final and replaced by a First Division top five play-off to decide the championship and right to apply for promotion. The final was no longer the first stage of a double-header at Old Trafford and was moved to the Alfred McAlpine Stadium, Huddersfield.

DIVISIONAL PREMIERSHIP RECORDS
(Including Second Division Premiership)

ALL ROUNDS
(Not including regional pool matches)
TEAM
Highest score (and widest margin):
Sheffield E. 72 v. Keighley C. 14 1992
Biggest attendance (not including final): 5,885 Halifax v. Leigh
....Semi-final 1991

INDIVIDUAL
Most goals: 12 by Mark Aston (Sheffield E.) v. Keighley C.
.... 1992
Most tries: 4 by Martin Wood (Halifax) v. Fulham 1991
Most points: 26 (3t, 7g) by Martin Pearson (Featherstone R.) v. Ryedale-York 1993

FINAL ONLY
TEAM
Most final appearances: 3 by Oldham
Most wins: 2 by Oldham, Sheffield Eagles, Salford
Highest score (and widest margin):
Sheffield E. 43 v. Swinton 18 1989

INDIVIDUAL
Most finals: 4 by Daryl Powell (Sheffield E. 1989, 1992; Keighley C. 1995, 1996)
Most wins: 3 by Daryl Powell (Sheffield E., 1989, 1992; Keighley C. 1995) and Charlie McAlister (Oldham 1988, 1990; Sheffield E. 1992)
Most tries: 3 by Daryl Powell (Sheffield E.) v. Swinton . 1989
Daryl Powell (Sheffield E.) v. Oldham 1992
Mark Johnson (London C.) v. Workington T. 1994
Most goals: 8 by Mark Aston (Sheffield E.) v. Swinton 1989
Most points: 19 (1t,7g,1dg) by Mark Aston (Sheffield E.) v. Swinton 1989

Daryl Powell: Star of four finals.

SECOND DIVISION/DIVISIONAL FINALS

Year	Winners		Runners-up		Venue
1987	Swinton (2)	27	Hunslet (1)	10	Old Trafford, Manchester
1988	Oldham (1)	28	Featherstone R. (2)	26	Old Trafford, Manchester
1989	Sheffield E. (3)	43	Swinton (5)	18	Old Trafford, Manchester
1990	Oldham (3)	30	Hull K.R. (1)	29	Old Trafford, Manchester
1991	Salford (1)	27	Halifax (2)	20	Old Trafford, Manchester
† 1992	Sheffield E. (1)	34	Oldham (3)	20	Old Trafford, Manchester
† 1993	Featherstone R. (1)	20	Workington T. (*2)	16	Old Trafford, Manchester
1994	Workington T. (1)	30	London C. (3)	22	Old Trafford, Manchester
1995	Keighley C. (1)	26	Huddersfield (3)	6	Old Trafford, Manchester
† 1996	Salford R. (1)	19	Keighley C. (2)	6	Old Trafford, Manchester
† 1997	Huddersfield (2)	18	Hull S. (1)	0	Old Trafford, Manchester

( ) Denotes Second Grade position   (*) Denotes Third Grade position
† Divisional Premiership, three divisions

THE TOM BERGIN TROPHY

The trophy, in honour of the late president of the Rugby League Writers' Association and former editor of the *Salford City Reporter*, was presented to the Man of the Match in the end-of-season Second Division, later Divisional Premiership final. It then became the top individual award in the First Division Grand final. The award is donated and judged by the Association.

Year	Winner	Team	Position
Second Division/Divisional Premiership			
1987	Gary Ainsworth	Swinton (v. Hunslet)	Hooker
1988	Des Foy	Oldham (v. Featherstone R.)	Centre
1989	Mark Aston	Sheffield E. (v. Swinton)	Stand off
1990	Mike Ford	Oldham (v. Hull K.R.)	Scrum half
1991	Steve Kerry	Salford (v. Halifax)	Scrum half
1992	Daryl Powell	Sheffield E. (v. Oldham)	Centre
1993	Paul Newlove	Featherstone R. (v. Workington T.)	Centre
1994	Dean Marwood	Workington T. (v. London C.)	Scrum half
1995	Martin Wood	Keighley C. (v. Huddersfield)	Loose forward
1996	Cliff Eccles	Salford R. (v. Keighley C.)	Prop
1997	Craig Weston	Huddersfield G. (v. Hull S.)	Stand off
Grand final			
1998	Richard Chapman	*Featherstone R. (v. Wakefield T.)	Hooker

*Losing team

SECOND DIVISION/DIVISONAL PREMIERSHIP FINAL TEAMS

*Captain

1986-87

Swinton 27 Viller; Bate (1t), Topping (Ratcliffe), Brown, Rippon (3g); Snape, Lee (1t); Grima (1t), Ainsworth (1t), Muller, Derbyshire (1t), M. Holliday (Allen), L. Holliday* (1dg)
Coach: Bill Holliday/Mike Peers
Hunslet 10 Kay; Tate, Penola, Irvine, Wilson; Coates, King; Sykes, Gibson (Senior), Bateman (2t), Platt (1g) (Mason), Bowden, Jennings*
Coach: Peter Jarvis/David Ward
Referee: J. McDonald (Wigan)

1987-88

Oldham 28 Burke (Irving); Round, D. Foy (2t), McAlister (4g), Meadows (1t); Walsh (1t), Ford; Sherratt (Warnecke), Sanderson, Waddell, Hawkyard, Graham*, Flanagan (1t)
Coach: Eric Fitzsimons
Featherstone R. 26 Quinn (5g); Bannister (1t), Sykes (1t), Banks, Marsh (Crossley); Steadman (2t), Fox*; Siddall (Bastian), K. Bell, Harrison, Hughes, Smith, Lyman
Coach: Peter Fox
Referee: R. Whitfield (Widnes)

1988-89

Sheffield E. 43 Gamson; Cartwright, Dickinson, Powell* (3t), Young; Aston (1t, 7g, 1dg), Close (Evans); Broadbent (1t), Cook (1t), Van Bellen, Nickle, Fleming (McDermott 1t), Smiles
Coach: Gary Hetherington
Swinton 18 Topping; Ranson (1t), Viller (Maloney), Snape, Bate; Frodsham (1t), Hewitt; Mooney, Melling (1t), S. O'Neill, Ainsworth, Allen (Horrocks), J. Myler* (3g)
Coach: Frank Barrow
Referee: R. Whitfield (Widnes)

1989-90

Oldham 30 Platt (1g) (Martyn 1t); Irving (1t), Hyde (2g), Henderson (1t), Lord (1t); Brett Clark, Ford* (1t); Casey (Newton), Ruane (1t), Fieldhouse, Round, McAlister, Russell
Coach: Tony Barrow
Hull K.R. 29 Lightfoot; G. Clark (1t), M. Fletcher (4g), Austin, Sullivan; Parker (2t, 1dg), Bishop (Irvine); Niebling*, Rudd, Ema, Des Harrison (1t) (Armstrong), Thompson, Lyman (1t)
Coach: Roger Millward
Referee: R. Whitfield (Widnes)

1990-91

Salford 27 Gibson; Evans (1t), Gilfillan (1t), Birkett, Hadley (Dean); Cassidy (1dg), Kerry (2t, 4g, 1dg); Worrall, Lee (1dg), Hansen, Bradshaw (Sherratt), Blease*, Burgess
Coach: Kevin Tamati
Halifax 20 Smith; Wood (1t), W. Wilson (1t), Austin, Silva (Platt 2g); Lyons, R. Southernwood (1t); Hill* (1t), Ramshaw, Bell (Scott), Brown, Milner, Keebles
Coach: Peter Roe
Referee: B. Galtress (Bradford)

1991-92

Sheffield E. 34 Mycoe (1t); Gamson, McAlister, Powell (3t), Plange; Price, Aston (5g); Broadbent, Cook*, Waddell, Laughton (Lumb 1t), Hughes (Mumby 1t), Farrell
Coach: Gary Hetherington
Oldham 20 Platt (1t); Ranson (1t), Nicklin, Ropati, Tyrer; Russell* (Warburton), Martyn (2g); Sherratt, Pachniuk, Newton (1t), Joynt, Tupaea (Street), Byrne (1t)
Coach: Peter Tunks
Referee: S. Cummings (Widnes)

1992-93

Featherstone R. 20 Pearson (4g); Butt, Manning, Newlove (2t), Simpson (Roebuck); Maloney (1t), Daunt; Casey (Gunn), Wilson*, Taekata, G.S. Price, Smales, Tuuta
Coach: Steve Martin
Workington T. 16 Mulligan; Drummond, Kay, Hepi, Smith; Byrne, Marwood (4g); Pickering, McKenzie (1t), Riley (Schubert), Scott, Armstrong*, Kitchin (Oglanby 1t)
Coach: Peter Walsh
Referee: J. Connolly (Wigan)

1993-94

Workington T. 30 Mulligan (1t); Drummond (1t), Kay (1t), Burns, Cocker (2t); Kitchin, Marwood (3g); Pickering (Riley), McKenzie, Armstrong*, Hepi, Oglanby, Byrne (1t) (Penrice)
Coach: Peter Walsh
London C. 22 Stoop; Gallagher (3g), Roskell, Campbell (1t), Johnson (3t); McIvor, Riley (Luxon); Whiteley, Carter (Smith), Rotheram, Rosolen, Stewart*, Ramsey
Coach: Tony Gordon
Referee: J. Connolly (Wigan)

1994-95

Keighley C. 26 Stoop; Eyres (1t), Pinkney (1t), Irving* (4g), Dixon; Powell (1t), Appleby; Hill (Tupaea) (Larder), Ramshaw (2dg), Gately, Fleary, Cochrane, Wood (1t)
Coach: Phil Larder

Huddersfield 6 Hellewell; Barton, Shelford, Austin* (dg), Reynolds; Hanger, Kerry (dg); King, L. St. Hilaire, Pucill, Richards (Coulter), Senior (Taylor), Pearce (2g)
Coach: George Fairbairn
Referee: R. Smith (Castleford)

1996
Salford R. 19 Hampson; Sini, Naylor (2t), McAvoy, Rogers; Blakeley* (1t,3g,dg), Lee; Blease (Burgess), Edwards (Watson), Eccles, Forber (Martin), Savelio (Randall), Panapa
Coach: Andy Gregory
Keighley C. 6 Dixon; Wray, Milner, Irving (1g), Critchley; Powell*, Robinson; Parsons, Cantillon (1t), Hall (Larder) (Ramshaw) (Tawhai), Fleary (Doorey), Whakarau, Wood
Coach: Phil Larder
Referee: S. Cummings (Widnes)

1997
Huddersfield G. 18 Veivers*; Cook (3g), Bunyan (1t) (Booth), Hanger, Cheetham (1t); Weston, Davys (1t); Harmon, Russell, Fozzard (Richards), Bowes (Berry), King (Dixon), Sturm
Coach: Steve Ferres
Hull S. 0 Holmes (Campbell); Hallas, Gray, Vaikona, Johnson; R. Nolan, Hewitt (Danby); Wilson (A. Jackson), Dixon, Ireland, Boyd* (David), Schultz, Hepi
Coach: Peter Walsh
Referee: J. Connolly (Wigan)

Rovers raid: Paul Lyman leads a Featherstone Rovers attack against Oldham in the 1988 Second Division Premiership final.

SECOND DIVISION/DIVISIONAL PREMIERSHIP TROPHY FINAL PLAYERS' REGISTER

The following is an index of players who appeared in a Divisional Premiership final.
W — winners, L — losers. Substitute appearances in lower case letters.

AINSWORTH, Gary: Swinton 87W, 89L
ALLEN, John: Swinton 87w, 89L
APPLEBY, Darren: Keighley C. 95W
ARMSTRONG, Colin: Hull K.R. 90l; Workington T. 93L, 94W
ASTON, Mark: Sheffield E. 89W, 92W
AUSTIN, Greg: Hull K.R. 90L; Halifax 91L; Huddersfield 95L

BANKS, Alan: Featherstone R. 88L
BANNISTER, Andy: Featherstone R. 88L
BARTON, Ben: Huddersfield 95L
BASTIAN, John: Featherstone R. 88l
BATE, Derek: Swinton 87W, 89L
BATEMAN, Andy: Hunslet 87L
BELL, Keith: Featherstone R. 88L
BELL, Peter: Halifax 91L
BERRY, Joe: Huddersfield G. 97w
BIRKETT, Martin: Salford 91W
BISHOP, David: Hull K.R. 90L
BLAKELEY, Steve: Salford R. 96W
BLEASE, Ian: Salford 91W, 96W
BOOTH, Steve: Huddersfield G. 97w
BOWDEN, Chris: Hunslet 87L
BOWES, Tony: Huddersfield G. 97W
BOYD, David: Hull S. 97L
BRADSHAW, Arthur: Salford 91W
BROADBENT, Paul: Sheffield E. 89W, 92W
BROWN, Jeff: Swinton 87W
BROWN, Peter: Halifax 91L
BUNYAN, James: Huddersfield G. 97W
BURGESS, Andy: Salford 91W, 96w
BURKE, Mick: Oldham 88W
BURNS, Paul: Workington T. 94W
BUTT, Ikram: Featherstone R. 93W
BYRNE, Ged: Oldham 92L; Workington T. 93L, 94W

CAMPBELL, Logan: London C. 94L; Hull S. 97l
CANTILLON, Phil: Keighley C. 96L
CARTER, Scott: London C. 94L
CARTWRIGHT, Phil: Sheffield E. 89W
CASEY, Leo: Oldham 90W; Featherstone R. 93W
CASSIDY, Frank: Salford 91W
CHEETHAM, Andy: Huddersfield G. 97W
CLARK, Brett: Oldham 90W
CLARK, Garry: Hull K.R. 90L
CLOSE, David: Sheffield E. 89W

COATES, Ged: Hunslet 87L
COCHRANE, Gareth: Keighley C. 95W
COCKER, Stuart: Workington T. 94W
COOK, Mick: Sheffield E. 89W, 92W
COOK, Paul: Huddersfield G. 97W
COULTER, Gary: Huddersfield 95l
CRITCHLEY, Jason: Keighley C. 96L
CROSSLEY, John: Featherstone R. 88l

DANBY, Rob: Hull S. 97l
DAUNT, Brett: Featherstone R. 93W
DAVID, Maea: Hull S. 97l
DAVYS, Ali: Huddersfield G. 97W
DEAN, Mick: Salford 91w
DERBYSHIRE, Alan: Swinton 87W
DICKINSON, Andy: Sheffield E. 89W
DIXON, Keith: Keighley C. 95W, 96L
DIXON, Mike: Hull S. 97L
DIXON, Paul: Huddersfield G. 97w
DOOREY, Grant: Keighley C. 96l
DRUMMOND, Des: Workington T. 93L, 94W

ECCLES, Cliff: Salford R. 96W
EDWARDS, Peter: Salford R. 96W
EMA, Asuquo: Hull K.R. 90L
EVANS, Steve: Sheffield E. 89w
EVANS, Tex: Salford 91W
EYRES, Andy: Keighley C. 95W

FARRELL, Anthony: Sheffield E. 92W
FIELDHOUSE, John: Oldham 90W
FLANAGAN, Terry: Oldham 88W
FLEARY, Darren: Keighley C. 95W, 96L
FLEMING, Mark: Sheffield E. 89W
FLETCHER, Mike: Hull K.R. 90L
FORBER, Paul: Salford R. 96W
FORD, Mike: Oldham 88W, 90W
FOX, Deryck: Featherstone R. 88L
FOY, Des: Oldham 88W
FOZZARD, Nick: Huddersfield G. 97W
FRODSHAM, Tommy: Swinton 89L

GALLAGHER, John: London C. 94L
GAMSON, Mark: Sheffield E. 89W, 92W
GATELY, Ian: Keighley C. 95W
GIBSON, Phil: Hunslet 87L
GIBSON, Steve: Salford 91W
GILFILLAN, John: Salford 91W
GRAHAM, Mal: Oldham 88W
GRAY, Kevin: Hull S. 97L
GRIMA, Joe: Swinton 87W
GUNN, Richard: Featherstone R. 93w

HADLEY, Adrian: Salford 91W
HALL, Steve: Keighley C. 96L
HALLAS, Graeme: Hull S. 97L
HAMPSON, Steve: Salford R. 96W

HANSEN, Shane: Salford 91W
HANGER, Dean: Huddersfield 95L, 97W
HARMON, Neil: Huddersfield G. 97W
HARRISON, Des: Hull K.R. 90L
HARRISON, Karl: Featherstone R. 88L
HAWKYARD, Colin: Oldham 88W
HELLEWELL, Phil: Huddersfield 95L
HENDERSON, John: Oldham 90W
HEPI, Brad: Workington T. 93L, 94W; Hull S. 97L
HEWITT, Mark: Hull S. 97L
HEWITT, Tony: Swinton 89L
HILL, Brendan: Halifax 91L; Keighley C. 95W
HOLLIDAY, Les: Swinton 87W
HOLLIDAY, Mike: Swinton 87W
HOLMES, Steve: Hull S. 97L
HORROCKS, John: Swinton 89l
HUGHES, Ian: Sheffield E. 92W
HUGHES, Paul: Featherstone R. 88L
HYDE, Gary: Oldham 90W

IRELAND, Andy: Hull S. 97L
IRVINE, Jimmy: Hunslet 87L; Hull K.R. 90l
IRVING, Richard: Oldham 88w, 90W
IRVING, Simon: Keighley C. 95W, 96L

JACKSON, Anthony: Hull S. 97l
JENNINGS, Graeme: Hunslet 87L
JOHNSON, Mark: London C. 94L; Hull S. 97L
JOYNT, Chris: Oldham 92L

KAY, Andy: Hunslet 87L
KAY, Tony: Workington T. 93L, 94W
KEEBLES, Mick: Halifax 91L
KERRY, Steve: Salford 91W; Huddersfield 95L
KING, Graham: Hunslet 87L
KING, Dave: Huddersfield 95L, 97W
KITCHIN, Wayne: Workington T. 93L, 94W

LAUGHTON, Dale: Sheffield E. 92W
LARDER, David: Keighley C. 95w, 96l
LEE, Mark: Salford 91W, 96W
LEE, Martin: Swinton 87W
LORD, Paul: Oldham 90W
LIGHTFOOT, David: Hull K.R. 90L
LUMB, Tim: Sheffield E. 92w
LUXON, Geoff: London C. 94l
LYMAN, Paul: Featherstone R. 88L; Hull K.R. 90L
LYONS, John: Halifax 91L

McALISTER, Charlie: Oldham 88W, 90W;
    Sheffield E. 92W
McAVOY, Nathan: Salford R. 96W
McDERMOTT, Paul: Sheffield E. 89w
McIVOR, Dixon: London C. 94L
McKENZIE, Phil: Workington T. 93L, 94W
MALONEY, Dave: Swinton 89l
MALONEY, Francis: Featherstone R. 93W

MANNING, Terry: Featherstone R. 93W
MARSH, Richard: Featherstone R. 88L
MARTIN, Scott: Salford R. 96w
MARTYN, Tommy: Oldham 90w, 92L
MARWOOD, Dean: Workington T. 93L, 94W
MASON, Keith: Hunslet 87l
MEADOWS, Kevin: Oldham 88W
MELLING, Alex: Swinton 89L
MILNER, Mark: Keighley C. 96L
MILNER, Richard: Halifax 91L
MOONEY, Frank: Swinton 89L
MULLER, Roby: Swinton 87W
MULLIGAN, Mark: Workington T. 93L, 94W
MUMBY, Keith: Sheffield E. 92w
MYCOE, David: Sheffield E. 92W
MYLER, John: Swinton 89L

NAYLOR, Scott: Salford R. 96W
NEWLOVE, Paul: Featherstone R. 93W
NEWTON, Keith: Oldham 90w, 92L
NICKLE, Sonny: Sheffield E. 89W
NICKLIN, Vince: Oldham 92L
NIEBLING, Bryan: Hull K.R. 90L
NOLAN, Rob: Hull S. 97L

OGLANBY, Martin: Workington T. 93l, 94W
O'NEILL, Steve: Swinton 89L

PACHNIUK, Richard: Oldham 92L
PANAPA, Sam: Salford R. 96W
PARKER, Wayne: Hull K.R. 90L
PARSONS, Steve: Keighley C. 96L
PEARCE, Greg: Huddersfield 95L
PEARSON, Martin: Featherstone R. 93W
PENOLA, Colin: Hunslet 87L
PENRICE, Paul: Workington T. 94w
PICKERING, James: Workington T. 93L, 94W
PINKNEY, Nick: Keighley C. 95W
PLANGE, David: Sheffield E. 92W
PLATT, Alan: Hunslet 87L; Halifax 91l
PLATT, Duncan: Oldham 90W, 92L
POWELL, Daryl: Sheffield E. 89W, 92W; Keighley C. 95W,
    96L
PRICE, Gary S.: Featherstone R. 93W
PRICE, Richard: Sheffield E. 92W
PUCILL, Andy: Huddersfield 95L

QUINN, Steve: Featherstone R. 88L

RAMSEY, Neville: London C. 94L
RAMSHAW, Jason: Halifax 91L; Keighley C. 95W, 96l
RANDALL, Craig: Salford R. 96w
RANSON, Scott: Swinton 89L; Oldham 92L
RATCLIFFE, Alan: Swinton 87w
REYNOLDS, Simon: Huddersfield 95L
RICHARDS, Basil: Huddersfield 95L, 97w
RILEY, Mark: London C. 94L

RILEY, Peter: Workington T. 93L, 94w
RIPPON, Andy: Swinton 87W
ROBINSON, Chris: Keighley C. 96L
ROEBUCK, Neil: Featherstone R. 93w
ROGERS, Darren: Salford R. 96W
ROPATI, Iva: Oldham 92L
ROSKELL, Scott: London C. 94L
ROSOLEN, Steve: London C. 94L
ROTHERAM, Dave: London C. 94L
ROUND, Paul: Oldham 88W, 90W
RUANE, Andy: Oldham 90W
RUDD, Chris: Hull K.R. 90L
RUSSELL, Danny: Huddersfield G. 97W
RUSSELL, Richard: Oldham 90W, 92L

ST. HILAIRE, Lee: Huddersfield 95L
SANDERSON, Ian: Oldham 88W
SAVELIO, Lokeni: Salford R. 96W
SCHUBERT, Gary: Workington T. 93l
SCHULTZ, Matt: Hull S. 97L
SCOTT, Ian: Workington T. 93L
SCOTT, Mick: Halifax 91l
SENIOR, Gary: Hunslet 87l; Huddersfield 95L
SHERRATT, Ian: Oldham 88W, 92L; Salford 91w
SHELFORD, Darrall: Huddersfield 95L
SIDDALL, Gary: Featherstone R. 88L
SILVA, Matthew: Halifax 91L
SIMPSON, Owen: Featherstone R. 93W
SINI, Fata: Salford R. 96W
SMALES, Ian: Featherstone R. 93W
SMILES, Warren: Sheffield E. 89W
SMITH, Gary: Workington T. 93L
SMITH, Kris: London C. 94l
SMITH, Peter: Featherstone R. 88L
SMITH, Steve: Halifax 91L
SNAPE, Steve: Swinton 87W, 89L
SOUTHERNWOOD, Roy: Halifax 91L
STEADMAN, Graham: Featherstone R. 88L
STEWART, Sam: London C. 94L

STOOP, Andre: London C. 94L; Keighley C. 95W
STREET, Tim: Oldham 92l
STURM, Matt: Huddersfield G. 97W
SULLIVAN, Anthony: Hull K.R. 90L
SYKES, Andy: Hunslet 87L
SYKES, David: Featherstone R. 88L

TAEKATA, Wayne: Featherstone R. 93W
TATE, Phil: Hunslet 87L
TAWHAI, Latham: Keighley C. 96l
TAYLOR, Mick: Huddersfield 95l
THOMPSON, Andy: Hull K.R. 90L
TOPPING, Paul: Swinton 87W, 89L
TUPAEA, Shane: Oldham 92L; Keighley C. 95w
TUUTA, Brendon: Featherstone R. 93W
TYRER, Sean: Oldham 92L

VAIKONA, Tevita: Hull S. 97L
VAN BELLEN, Gary: Sheffield E. 89W
VEIVERS, Phil: Huddersfield G. 97W
VILLER, Mark: Swinton 87W, 89L

WADDELL, Hugh: Oldham 88W; Sheffield E. 92W
WALSH, Peter: Oldham 88W
WARBURTON, Steve: Oldham 92l
WARNECKE, Gary: Oldham 88w
WATSON, Ian: Salford R. 96w
WESTON, Craig: Huddersfield G. 97W
WHAKARAU, Sonny: Keighley C. 96L
WHITELEY, Chris: London C. 94L
WILSON, Mark: Featherstone R. 93W
WILSON, Richard: Hull S. 97L
WILSON, Warren: Hunslet 87L; Halifax 91L
WOOD, Martin: Halifax 91L; Keighley C. 95W, 96L
WORRALL, Mick: Salford 91W
WRAY, Simon: Keighley C. 96L

YOUNG, Andy: Sheffield E. 89W

Tough Test: Great Britain captain Andrew Farrell found it tough going against the 1998 New Zealand Test team.

GREAT BRITAIN

GREAT BRITAIN

1998 LINCOLN TEST SERIES

New Zealand set a number of records while winning a Test series in Great Britain for the first time since 1971 with an entertaining brand of teamwork allied to some outstanding individual performances.

• By winning two of the three Lincoln Tests with one drawn they became the first New Zealand side to remain unbeaten in a series in Britain.

• They extended their unbeaten run of Tests against Britain to a record-breaking six, including the last one drawn. The previous best was four successive wins in 1984-85.

• The 36-16 second Test victory at Bolton produced New Zealand's highest score against Britain and equalled the widest winning margin. It beat the 32-16 win in the third Test at Auckland in 1984 and the 32-12 third Test win at Christchurch in 1996, while equalling the winning margin in the latter match. New Zealand's previous highest score and winning margin in Britain was their 29-11 first Test victory at Headingley, Leeds, in 1961.

• Their total of 81 points was the most by New Zealand in a Test series against Britain, beating the 72 at home in 1984.

• Daryl Halligan equalled two New Zealand records in a series against Britain with 14 goals and 28 points. Full back Doug Ladner set the records in the 1970 series at home.

• Sean Hoppe became New Zealand's all-time top tryscorer with one try taking his career total to a record-breaking 17.

Against this set of New Zealand records, Great Britain's Jason Robinson became the first British player to score a try in every Test of a three-match series against both Australia Super League and New Zealand. He also equalled the Great Britain record of touching down in six successive Test matches. The record was set by Wigan scrum half Johnny Thomas 90 years ago and equalled by fellow Welshman Clive Sullivan, Hull's winger, in the 1970s.

Apart from his try-a-match sequence, Robinson also impressed with several darting runs to be a clear winner of the Press-nominated Great Britain player of the series award, while scrum half Stacey Jones was voted the best of several impressive New Zealand players.

Britain's failure to win even one Test was a big disappointment after claims that three years of Super League had raised standards, with the epic inaugural Grand Final between Wigan Warriors and Leeds Rhinos given as apparent proof of the perceived progress. The top two clubs provided 14 of Great Britain's 23-man squad – nine from Wigan – and the final was thought to be ideal preparation for the first Test played a week later.

Whatever progress had been made, however, still left them some way behind a New Zealand squad that included 11 players from an Auckland Warriors side who had finished 15th of 20 clubs in the Australian National League. Ironically, Auckland sacked Frank Endacott as coach before he steered New Zealand to triumph in Britain. The gap between the two hemispheres becomes even more clearer when it is noted that Australia had just beaten New Zealand 30-12 and 36-16 after losing 22-16 earlier in the year.

Matthew Ridge, New Zealand's captain, full back and goalkicker, was injured against Australia and announced his retirement from international rugby, leaving the Test selectors needing to find three players to cover all his vital roles. And they came up with a trio who were to prove huge successes. Quentin Pongia took over the captaincy and set a great example up front; Richard Barnett was an outstanding success at full back and Daryl Halligan equalled the New Zealand record of 14 goals in a series against Great Britain. Injury also ruled Leeds Rhinos centre Richard Blackmore out of their 22-man squad.

Great Britain suffered a double blow when injury cost them their powerful second row pair. Wigan's Denis Betts was ruled out before coach Andy Goodway named his 23-man squad and Adrian Morley of Leeds fought a losing battle to be fit for any of the Tests.

Injuries continued to disrupt the Britain squad and with Goodway making the occasional tactical change Morley was the only player not appear in the series. It meant six players made their Test debut: Francis Cummins, Darren Fleary, Terry Newton, Lee Gilmour, Harvey Howard and Dale Laughton.

In contrast, New Zealand were able to name an unchanged starting line-up for all three Tests and made only one substitute change. The squad's main surprise was the inclusion of Nathan Cayless, who was born and raised in Sydney and had played for Australian Schoolboys before signing for ARL club Parramatta Eels. But both his parents were New Zealanders and he considered himself a Kiwi. Lesley Vainikolo, Ali Lauitiiti and Craig Smith were the only non-Test players with Smith making his New Zealand debut as substitute in the last match.

The major surprise when Goodway announced his full squad six days before the first Test was the omission of St. Helens winger Anthony Sullivan, who had been in outstanding tryscoring form alongside Great Britain centre Paul Newlove. Although Sullivan had already announced his intention to have a three-month spell with Cardiff Rugby Union club, Goodway said he had been left out for tactical reasons. St. Helens stand off Tommy Martyn and Sheffield Eagles prop Paul Broadbent were also considered unlucky not to be selected.

Sheffield Eagles' John Kear relinquished his role as coach of France's national squad to replace Australian Shaun McRae as Britain's assistant coach. McCrae had just left St. Helens for new club Gateshead Thunder and wished to concentrate on his new job.

A £120,000 sponsorship deal for the series was announced four weeks before the first Test with American company Lincoln Financial Group, a major provider of pensions, life assurance and unit trusts.

The three Saturday night Tests were all televised live on Sky TV with an hour's highlights being shown on BBC's *Sunday Grandstand* the following day.

Record-breaker: Sean Hoppe races away in the second Test for his record-breaking 17th career try for New Zealand.

285

GREAT BRITAIN TEST SQUAD
Coach: Andy Goodway
Manager: Phil Lowe
Captain: Andrew Farrell
Gary Connolly (Wigan Warriors)
Neil Cowie (Wigan Warriors)
Francis Cummins (Leeds Rhinos)
Keiron Cunningham (St. Helens)
Andrew Farrell (Wigan Warriors)
Darren Fleary (Leeds Rhinos)
Mike Forshaw (Bradford Bulls)
Lee Gilmour (Wigan Warriors)
Iestyn Harris (Leeds Rhinos)
Simon Haughton (Wigan Warriors)
Harvey Howard (Bradford Bulls)*
Chris Joynt (St. Helens)
Dale Laughton (Sheffield Eagles)
Sean Long (St. Helens)
Adrian Morley (Leeds Rhinos)
Paul Newlove (St. Helens)
Terry Newton (Leeds Rhinos)
Terry O'Connor (Wigan Warriors)
Kris Radlinski (Wigan Warriors)
Jason Robinson (Wigan Warriors)
Paul Sculthorpe (St. Helens)
Keith Senior (Sheffield Eagles)
Tony Smith (Wigan Warriors)
On loan from Western Suburbs (Australia)

NEW ZEALAND TEST SQUAD
Coach: Frank Endacott
Manager: Gary Cooksley
Captain: Quentin Pongia
Richard Barnett (Sydney C. Roosters)
Nathan Cayless (Parramatta Eels)
Syd Eru (Auckland Warriors)
Daryl Halligan (Canterbury Bulldogs)
Sean Hoppe (Auckland Warriors)
Kevin Iro (Auckland Warriors)
Tony Iro (Adelaide Rams)
Stacey Jones (Auckland Warriors)
Stephen Kearney (Auckland Warriors)
Ali Lauitiiti (Auckland Warriors)
Jarrod McCracken (Parramatta Eels)
Gene Ngamu (Auckland Warriors)
Henry Paul (Wigan Warriors)
Robbie Paul (Bradford Bulls)
Quentin Pongia (Auckland Warriors)
Tony Puletua (Penrith Panthers)
Craig Smith (Illawarra Steelers)
Logan Swann (Auckland Warriors)
Joe Vagana (Auckland Warriors)
Nigel Vagana (Auckland Warriors)
Lesley Vainikolo (Canberra Raiders)
Ruben Wiki (Canberra Raiders)

Kiwi caught: New Zealand winger Sean Hoppe is well held by Great Britain's Gary Connolly.

*Great Britain's 1998 Test squad. Back row left to right: Morley, O'Connor, Sculthorpe, Laughton, Newlove, Joynt, Senior, Howard.
Middle row: Pinkerton (physio), Radlinski, Smith, Cowie, Cummins, Forshaw, Fleary, Gilmour, Cunningham, Newton, Robinson, Tomlinson (physio),
Miles (Asst. coach).
Front row: Haughton, Connolly, Kear (Asst. coach), Farrell, Goodway (coach), Harris, Long.*

FIRST LINCOLN TEST

Two controversial decisions by Australian referee Bill Harrigan went against Great Britain and caused much post-match debate, but New Zealand were still worthy 22-16 winners of the first Test at the Alfred McAlpine Stadium, Huddersfield. It gave them a record-equalling fourth successive defeat of Britain.

The first controversial decision came when the hooter blasted out to end the first half. But as British players relaxed and prepared to walk off, Harrigan allowed play to continue and New Zealand prop Joe Vagana took full advantage to canter 30 metres past a bemused home defence for a try near the posts. Daryl Halligan added the goal to give the Kiwis a 12-2 interval lead. Repeated TV recording showed that the hooter sounded just after New Zealander Richard Barnett had risen to his feet but had not put the ball down to play it back to Vagana. Although many believed the referee should have stopped play, the British players were also criticised for failing to 'play to the whistle'.

The second controversial decision happened just before the end of the game with Britain having rallied to be only 22-16 behind. They continued to pile on the pressure and when Britain's captain Andrew Farrell sent a high kick over to the left hand corner Keith Senior leaped to take it near the goal line. But Kiwi stand off Robbie Paul drove him into touch by tackling him a split second before he caught the ball and also while the British winger had his feet off the ground.

It was an illegal tackle on both counts, but though Halligan gave Britain a penalty many believed he should have awarded them a penalty try. That would have resulted in a simple kick from in front of the posts which Farrell would almost certainly have converted to produce a 22-22 draw. The referee later explained, however, that he was not certain Senior would have touched down and therefore could not award a penalty try. Harrigan was also criticised in the media for not making more use of the video referee, especially when Tony Iro crashed over the line and was ruled not to have got the ball down.

Harrigan's decisions were not the only ones to be questioned as Great Britain coach Andy Goodway also had a lot of explaining to do after leaving Iestyn Harris, Super League's outstanding player in 1998, on the substitutes' bench for the first 22 minutes. Goodway had added to the pre-match debate by naming St. Helens back row forward Paul Sculthorpe at No.6 with Wigan loose forward Farrell wearing his usual No.13 shirt. It was Sculthorpe who packed down at loose forward for the first scrum, however, with Farrell at stand off. Then after 22 minutes Harris went on for second row Lee Gilmour and took over at stand off with Farrell going to loose forward. Britain's coach later explained that he wanted seven forwards on the field to withstand what he expected would be a furious opening onslaught by the New Zealand pack.

The explosive start never came, however, as New Zealand relied on a more restrained approach which still brought them an early lead after Stephen Kearney opened the scoring with a try when he touched down Stacey Jones' kick. Harrigan handed the decision over to the video referee and there was a long wait before he ruled in New Zealand's favour. Britain hit back early in the second half with Senior scoring a try on his debut and Paul Newlove going in off Harris' pass. Although Farrell missed with both kicks, he scored a 57th minute penalty goal to level the scores before New Zealand pulled away again with Henry Paul sending Jones away for a try and Robbie Paul touching down after taking a superb pass out of a tackle from Kearney.

Halligan added a goal to open a ten-point lead, which was soon cut when Gilmour put in a kick to the corner and Jason Robinson won the chase to touch down. Britain went all out to salvage the game, but were foiled by Robbie Paul's desperate tackle on Senior.

QUOTES

Both teams agreed before the series not to criticise the referee, but were still free to explain their roles in controversial incidents.

FRANK ENDACOTT (New Zealand coach): I didn't think that there was a problem with the hooter sounding or that the half was over. As a ten-year-old you are taught to play to the whistle. These guys are at first-class level. They slackened off for half a second and paid the price. I wouldn't be blaming the referee; I would be blaming the players.

I've no idea what Andy Goodway was thinking about starting with Farrell at stand off and Harris on the bench. It's not for me to comment, but they might play one of their props there next week and I'll be quite happy. When you start doing that you lose your cohesion. I hope he does it again. Our half backs Stacey Jones and Robbie Paul took over the whole show.

I just knew we had a chance to make the most of Harris's absence for as long as we could; I feel that a stand off should play at stand off because they are there to create and the longer they left Harris off the field the better it would be for us. That was crucial and it was where I think the battle was won.

But I agree with Andy Goodway that it was probably a Test that Great Britain lost, rather than we won. With the amount of ball we gave Britain in the second half they should have won the game in that period.

Robbie Paul's tackle on Keith Senior was marvellous and I just saw it as a great defensive moment to not only save a try, but save a Test match. I never expected a penalty, never mind anything else and I thought a penalty try would have been a really tough call.

ANDY GOODWAY (Great Britain coach): You have to go with the referee's decisions and his interpretation of the rules. There are two things you can do nothing about: the weather and referees' decisions. I still think referee Bill Harrigan is the best in the world.

We probably paid New Zealand too much respect. I was expecting their forwards to really hit us in the opening quarter. They never did and we were surprised at the lack of intensity. We were asleep in the first half, woke up in the second and did what we had to do for a large part.

ANDREW FARRELL (Great Britain captain): I've no complaints abut the referee's decisions. That's the way rugby is. You take the bad decisions with the good and I am sure we had a few good decisions too. We are all disappointed that we lost, but we can see where we can improve. And we will improve. There were a lot of good things to come out of the game; a lot of positives.

ROBBIE PAUL (New Zealand stand off): After making that tackle on Keith Senior it did flash in my mind that maybe I had given away a penalty try. In the split second I had to think about it I thought this guy is six-foot four, I'm five-foot nothing and in those circumstances you've got to do whatever it takes to stop the try being scored.

KEITH SENIOR (Great Britain winger): Robbie Paul made no attempt for the ball when he tackled me. He took me out in mid-air. The rule says he interfered in the act of scoring a try. It probably cost us the game.

IESTYN HARRIS (Great Britain substitute): Andy Goodway decided I would be a substitute and he had a quiet word with me about it. We went in with a big set of forwards to soak up the pressure early on. I was determined to take the decision the right way and make the most of my opportunity when it came, although as a substitute it's difficult to catch up to the pace of the game.

FIRST LINCOLN TEST

Saturday 31 October 1998 Alfred McAlpine Stadium, Huddersfield

GREAT BRITAIN 16

NEW ZEALAND 22

Kris Radlinski (Wigan W.)	Full back	Richard Barnett (Sidney City R.)
Jason Robinson (Wigan W.)	Wing	Sean Hoppe (Auckland W.)
Gary Connolly (Wigan W.)	Centre	Kevin Iro (Auckland W.)
Paul Newlove (St. Helens)	Centre	Ruben Wiki (Canberra R.)
Keith Senior (Sheffield E.)	Wing	Daryl Halligan (North Sydney B.)
Andrew Farrell (Wigan W.),* Captain	Stand off	Robbie Paul (Bradford B.)
Tony Smith (Wigan W.)	Scrum half	Stacey Jones (Auckland W.)
Neil Cowie (Wigan W.)	Prop	Joe Vagana (Auckland W.)
Keiron Cunningham (St. Helens)	Hooker	Syd Eru (Auckland W.)
Darren Fleary (Leeds R.)	Prop	Quentin Pongia (Auckland W.), Captain
Chris Joynt (St. Helens)	Second row	Jarrod McCracken (Parramatta E.)
Lee Gilmour (Wigan W.)	Second row	Stephen Kearney (Auckland W.)
Paul Sculthorpe (St. Helens)*	Loose forward	Logan Swann (Auckland W.)

Substitutes
Iestyn Harris (Leeds W.)
for Gilmour (22 min.)
Dale Laughton (Sheffield E.)
for Fleary (19 min.)
Simon Haughton (Wigan W.)
for Cunningham (61 min. blood bin)
Terry O'Connor (Wigan W.)
for Cowie (31 min.)
Fleary for Laughton (56 min.)
Gilmour for Joynt (67 min.)
Cowie for Fleary (73 min.)

Substitutes
Henry Paul (Wigan W.)
for Eru (31 min.)
Tony Iro (Adelaide R.)
for Swann (53 min.)
Tony Puletua (Penrith P.)
for McCracken (59 min.)
Nathan Cayless (Parramatta E.)
for Vagana (26-38 min. blood bin)
Cayless for Vagana (62 min. blood bin)
McCracken for T. Iro (73 min.)

* *Sculthorpe wore No.6 and Farrell No.13 and were announced as stand off and loose forward respectively, but their positions were reversed from the kick-off*

T: Senior, Newlove, Robinson
G: Farrell (2)

T: Kearney, Vagana, Jones, R. Paul
G: Halligan (3)

Coach: Andy Goodway

Coach: Frank Endacott

Scrums: 9-3
Penalties: 9-3
Half-time: 2-12
Attendance: 18,509

Referee: Bill Harrigan (Australia)
Man of the Match: Stacey Jones (NZ)
Receipts:£208,295

HOW THE SCORING WENT

15 min. Kearney (NZ) try, Halligan goal	**0-6**
38 min. Farrell (GB) penalty goal	**2-6**
40 min. Vagana (NZ) try, Halligan goal	**2-12**
48 min. Senior (GB) try,	**6-12**
51 min. Newlove (GB) try	**10-12**
57 min. Farrell (GB) penalty goal	**12-12**
61 min. Jones (NZ) try	**12-16**
71 min. R. Paul (NZ) try, Halligan goal	**12-22**
76 min. Robinson (GB) try	**16-22**

Well held: Great Britain scrum half Tony Smith cannot break free in the third Test.

THIRD LINCOLN TEST

Great Britain won back their pride when Tony Smith kicked an equalising drop goal five seconds from the end at Vicarage Road to snatch a 23-23 draw that prevented New Zealand achieving their first 3-0 series whitewash on British soil. The Watford soccer ground can have seen few more dramatic late goals than the one that completed a remarkable last two minutes in which New Zealand squandered a 23-16 lead.

It seemed that Stacey Jones had sealed New Zealand's victory in the 71st minute when he landed a 20-metre drop goal to open a vital seven-point lead. But, as in the first Test, Britain again showed their best form when they had nothing to lose by going on all out attack. It resulted in them scoring a superb 78th minute try following a sweeping move, which began with Sean Long's searching crossfield run from the centre spot and finished with left wing pair Keith Senior and Francis Cummins sending Smith racing 20 metres for the touchdown. Andrew Farrell added the goal and then produced a short kick off which enabled Britain to retain possession and have a last-minute fling to salvage something from another generally disappointing performance.

After failing with a desperate attempt to score a match-winning try, Britain decided to go for a draw only for Farrell's drop goal attempt to rebound off an opposing player. The ball went to Senior, who was 10 metres in front of Farrell, and the centre made a dash for the line before being brought down. With the seconds ticking away, Smith then moved up and as first receiver at the play-the-ball coolly kicked the equalising drop goal from 20 metres – incredibly the first of his career. The hooter sounded almost immediately and British players reacted as if they had won, while the New Zealanders expressed great disappointment at letting slip their golden chance of a series whitewash.

It had all been so different less than 20 minutes earlier when the game seemed to be heading for a repeat of New Zealand's runaway second Test victory. The Kiwis again trailed by eight points at the interval before making another startling recovery to take a 22-10 lead in the 63rd minute. Jones led the fightback with a hand in all three of the converted tries that swept them ahead to confirm his rating as the player of the series. The scrum-half was involved in the build up to Henry Paul's try, which was scored while Britain's Senior was in the sin bin for a play-the-ball infringement. Jones combined superbly with Robbie Paul to send his half-back partner through for two identical touchdowns. And when Great Britain stand off Long replied with a well-taken solo try, goaled by Farrell, Jones came up with the drop goal that seemed to have assured New Zealand of victory.

Although Jones certainly stamped his authority on the game, Smith pushed him close for match honours with an almost identical contribution for Britain, having a say in all three of their tries and snatching a draw with his drop goal. It was Smith's clever inside kick which led to Jason Robinson winning the scramble to score the opening try and equal the Great Britain record of touching down in six successive Tests in addition to becoming the first player to score a try in each match of a three-Test series against both Australia Super League and New Zealand. Smith also pulled in the Kiwi defence before slipping out the pass to send Long on the way to his touch down before Britain's No.7 scored the try and drop goal that produced only the fourth draw involving the two countries.

Great Britain coach Andy Goodway expressed general satisfaction with the performance after injuries robbed him of four of his squad's best players. Iestyn Harris was replaced by Long at stand off; Paul Newlove failed another fitness test to leave Senior at centre and Keiron Cunningham's hooking role went to Terry Newton on his Test debut. Morley was also ruled out yet again.

An attendance of 13,278 on a rain-lashed night was regarded as satisfactory considering the series had already been decided and kept alive the possibility of a Super League club joining the Saracens Rugby Union outfit at the soccer ground.

QUOTES

ANDY GOODWAY (Great Britain coach): It's the first time I've been able to smile all week. For an inexperienced team we performed magnificently and although the results have not gone our way in this series we are only eight months into a three-year programme. Sean Long's try was fantastic. That's what he was there for. He's done everything we asked of him, even if he has us tearing our hair out at times, and there are a few more things we can show him over the next couple of years. And Tony Smith has been a revelation for us. He's learned and been willing to push other players, which he's never done before. So that bodes well for the future. Looking back, I still have to say that lack of preparation is the reason why we have not won the series. People may say that is just an excuse, but it is a fact.

FRANK ENDACOTT (New Zealand coach): I'm disappointed we didn't win the series 3-0 but I can live with the fact we're the best New Zealand side for 91 years. Australia are still No.1, but I don't believe we are too far away from them now. We have got a young side and it is getting better. Great Britain have a side they can build on for the World Cup, but if they are going to improve they've got to be playing us or Australia on a regular basis.

TONY SMITH (Great Britain scrum half): That was my first ever drop goal. I had one eye on the clock and I knew there were only a few seconds left. I could see the clock and Faz (Farrell) had not managed to get his chance, so it was up to me. I knew the pressure was on, but in a situation like that you don't have time

to think. We've been doing drop goal practice with trainer David Miles and it paid off. I didn't have time to really think about it. You just do what you have to do.

ANDREW FARRELL (Great Britain captain): When the ball went back to Tony Smith for the drop goal attempt we thought 'Oh no, anyone but him'. I have never seen him hit the mark in training. It surprised me a little, but it was a good drop goal and I was glad to see it go over. I am proud that we came back, but I am still disappointed that we let them take the initiative after we had controlled the game in the first half. Of course we wanted to win at least one game in the series, but to get a draw was an improvement. It was nice to snatch something at the end and we showed that we were desperate, that we wanted to get something from the game. We had gone away from the game plan again for a spell, but we gave our best and our commitment has never been in question.

QUENTIN PONGIA (New Zealand captain): I have loved the series. Playing the full 80 minutes in the first two Tests was probably the first full 80 minutes I have played all year. I looked at the sideline occasionally to see if the coach would bring me off, but he never did. Having said that, I was disappointed to be kept off at the start of the second half tonight. I would have preferred to have kept on the park for what I knew was going to be big hit.

SEAN LONG (Great Britain stand off): My try came when Tony Smith threw a ball back and I saw a little gap and went for it. They have players like Stacey Jones and the Paul brothers who are very quick off the mark, so why not play them at their own game? Andy Goodway had faith in me and put me in the team and I'm grateful for that. I had my chance and like to think I took it. In the first half I was perhaps a little bit quiet and we kept to the game plan. But when we trailed in the second half I decided to have a go and the try was a bonus.

THIRD LINCOLN TEST

Saturday 14 November 1998   Vicarage Road, Watford

GREAT BRITAIN   23   **NEW ZEALAND   23**

Great Britain	Position	New Zealand
Kris Radlinski (Wigan W.)	Full back	Richard Barnett (Sydney City R.)
Jason Robinson (Wigan W.)	Wing	Sean Hoppe (Auckland W.)
Gary Connolly (Wigan W.)	Centre	Kevin Iro (Auckland W.)
Keith Senior (Sheffield E.)	Centre	Ruben Wiki (Canberra R.)
Francis Cummins (Leeds R.)	Wing	Daryl Halligan (North Sydney B.)
Sean Long (St. Helens)	Stand off	Robbie Paul (Bradford B.)
Tony Smith (Wigan W.)	Scrum half	Stacey Jones (Auckland W.)
Terry O'Connor (Wigan W.)	Prop	Joe Vagana (Auckland W.)
Terry Newton (Leeds Rhinos)	Hooker	Syd Eru (Auckland W.)
Dale Laughton (Sheffield E.)	Prop	Quentin Pongia (Auckland W.), Captain
Chris Joynt (St. Helens)	Second row	Jarrod McCracken ((Parramatta E.)
Paul Sculthorpe (St. Helens)	Second row	Stephen Kearney (Auckland W.)
Andrew Farrell (Wigan W.), Captain	Loose forward	Logan Swann (Auckland W.)

Substitutes:
Lee Gilmour (Wigan W.) (not used)
Mike Forshaw (Bradford B.)
for Newton (44 min.)
Simon Haughton (Wigan W.)
for O'Connor (60 min.)
Darren Fleary (Leeds Rhinos)
for O'Connor (18-27 min. blood bin)
Fleary for Laughton (31 min.)
Laughton for Fleary (64 min.)
Newton for Joynt (70 min.)

Substitutes:
Henry Paul (Wigan W.)
for Eru (34 min.)
Craig Smith (Illawarra Steelers)
for Pongia (40 min.)
Tony Puletua (Penrith Panthers)
for Swann (50 min.)
Nathan Cayless (Parramatta E.)
for Vagana (25-34 min. blood bin)
Pongia for Smith (56 min.)
Cayless for Vagana (50-63 min.
blood bin)
Swann for McCracken (71 min.)
McCracken for Barnett (78 min.)

*T:*Robinson, Long, Smith
G: Farrell (5), Smith (dg)
Sin bin: Sculthorpe (32 min.); Senior (38 min.)

T: R. Paul (2), H. Paul
G: Halligan (5), Jones (dg)
Sin bin: McCracken (32 min.)

Coach: Andy Goodway

Coach: Frank Endacott

Scrums: 6-3
Penalties: 7-13
Half-time: 10-2
Attendance: 13,278

Referee: Bill Harrigan (Australia)
Man of the Match:
Stacey Jones (NZ)
Receipts:£154,944

HOW THE SCORING WENT

13 min. Farrell (GB) penalty goal		**2-0**
18 min. Halligan (NZ) penalty goal		**2-2**
25 min. Robinson (GB) try, Farrell goal		**8-2**
38 min. Farrell (GB) penalty goal		**10-2**
43 min. H. Paul (NZ) try, Halligan goal		**10-8**
50 min. Harrigan (NZ) penalty goal		**10-10**
55 min. R. Paul (NZ) try, Halligan goal		**10-16**
63 min. R. Paul (NZ) try, Halligan goal		**10-22**
66 min. Long (GB) try, Farrell goal		**16-22**
71 min. Jones (NZ) drop goal		**16-23**
78 min. Smith (GB) try, Farrell goal		**22-23**
80 min. Smith (GB) drop goal		**23-23**

TESTS

● Although early Tests were played under the titles of Northern Union or England, it is acceptable to regard them as Great Britain.

W - Won, D - Drawn, L - Lost refer to Great Britain.

ASHES SERIES TESTS
GREAT BRITAIN v. AUSTRALIA (Also see v. AUSTRALIA SUPER LEAGUE)

12	Dec.	1908	D	22-22	QPR, London	2,000	22 Jul.	1950	L	2-5	Sydney	47,178
23	Jan.	1909	W	15-5	Newcastle	22,000	4 Oct.	1952	W	19-6	Leeds	34,505
15	Feb.	1909	W	6-5	Birmingham	9,000	8 Nov.	1952	W	21-5	Swinton	32,421
18	Jun.	1910	W	27-20	Sydney	42,000	13 Dec.	1952	L	7-27	Bradford	30,509
2	Jul.	1910	W	22-17	Brisbane	18,000	12 Jun.	1954	L	12-37	Sydney	65,884
8	Nov.	1911	L	10-19	Newcastle	6,500	3 Jul.	1954	W	38-21	Brisbane	46,355
16	Dec.	1911	D	11-11	Edinburgh	6,000	17 Jul.	1954	L	16-20	Sydney	67,577
1	Jan.	1912	L	8-33	Birmingham	4,000	17 Nov.	1956	W	21-10	Wigan	22,473
27	Jun.	1914	W	23-5	Sydney	40,000	1 Dec.	1956	L	9-22	Bradford	23,634
29	Jun.	1914	L	7-12	Sydney	55,000	15 Dec.	1956	W	19-0	Swinton	17,542
4	Jul.	1914	W	14-6	Sydney	34,420	14 Jun.	1958	L	8-25	Sydney	68,777
26	Jun.	1920	L	4-8	Brisbane	28,000	5 Jul.	1958	W	25-18	Brisbane	32,965
3	Jul.	1920	L	8-21	Sydney	40,000	19 Jul.	1958	W	40-17	Sydney	68,720
10	Jul.	1920	W	23-13	Sydney	32,000	17 Oct.	1959	L	14-22	Swinton	35,224
1	Oct.	1921	W	6-5	Leeds	32,000	21 Nov.	1959	W	11-10	Leeds	30,184
5	Nov.	1921	L	2-16	Hull	21,504	12 Dec.	1959	W	18-12	Wigan	26,089
14	Jan.	1922	W	6-0	Salford	21,000	9 Jun.	1962	W	31-12	Sydney	70,174
23	Jun.	1924	W	22-3	Sydney	50,000	30 Jun.	1962	W	17-10	Brisbane	34,766
28	Jun.	1924	W	5-3	Sydney	33,842	14 Jul.	1962	L	17-18	Sydney	42,104
12	Jul.	1924	L	11-21	Brisbane	36,000	16 Oct.	1963	L	2-28	Wembley	13,946
23	Jun.	1928	W	15-12	Brisbane	39,200	9 Nov.	1963	L	12-50	Swinton	30,833
14	Jul.	1928	W	8-0	Sydney	44,548	30 Nov.	1963	W	16-5	Leeds	20,497
21	Jul.	1928	L	14-21	Sydney	37,000	25 Jun.	1966	W	17-13	Sydney	57,962
5	Oct.	1929	L	8-31	Hull K.R.	20,000	16 Jul.	1966	L	4-6	Brisbane	45,057
9	Nov.	1929	W	9-3	Leeds	31,402	23 Jul.	1966	L	14-19	Sydney	63,503
4	Jan.	1930	D	0-0	Swinton	34,709	21 Oct.	1967	W	16-11	Leeds	22,293
15	Jan.	1930	W	3-0	Rochdale	16,743	3 Nov.	1967	L	11-17	White City, London	17,445
6	Jun.	1932	W	8-6	Sydney	70,204	9 Dec.	1967	L	3-11	Swinton	13,615
18	Jun.	1932	L	6-15	Brisbane	26,500	6 Jun.	1970	L	15-37	Brisbane	42,807
16	Jul.	1932	W	18-13	Sydney	50,053	20 Jun.	1970	W	28-7	Sydney	60,962
7	Oct.	1933	W	4-0	Belle Vue, Manchester	34,000	4 Jul.	1970	W	21-17	Sydney	61,258
11	Nov.	1933	W	7-5	Leeds	29,618	3 Nov.	1973	W	21-12	Wembley	9,874
16	Dec.	1933	W	19-16	Swinton	10,990	24 Nov.	1973	L	6-14	Leeds	16,674
29	Jun.	1936	L	8-24	Sydney	63,920	1 Dec.	1973	L	5-15	Warrington	10,019
4	Jul.	1936	W	12-7	Brisbane	29,486	15 Jun.	1974	L	6-12	Brisbane	30,280
18	Jul.	1936	W	12-7	Sydney	53,546	6 Jul.	1974	W	16-11	Sydney	48,006
16	Oct.	1937	W	5-4	Leeds	31,949	20 Jul.	1974	L	18-22	Sydney	55,505
13	Nov.	1937	W	13-3	Swinton	31,724	21 Oct.	1978	L	9-15	Wigan	17,644
18	Dec.	1937	L	3-13	Huddersfield	9,093	5 Nov.	1978	W	18-14	Bradford	26,447
17	Jun.	1946	D	8-8	Sydney	64,527	18 Nov.	1978	L	6-23	Leeds	29,627
6	Jul.	1946	W	14-5	Brisbane	40,500	16 Jun.	1979	L	0-35	Brisbane	23,051
20	Jul.	1946	W	20-7	Sydney	35,294	30 Jun.	1979	L	16-24	Sydney	26,837
9	Oct.	1948	W	23-21	Leeds	36,529	14 Jul.	1979	L	2-28	Sydney	16,844
6	Nov.	1948	W	16-7	Swinton	36,354	30 Oct.	1982	L	4-40	Hull C. FC	26,771
29	Jan.	1949	W	23-9	Bradford	42,000	20 Nov.	1982	L	6-27	Wigan	23,216
12	Jun.	1950	W	6-4	Sydney	47,215	28 Nov.	1982	L	8-32	Leeds	17,318
1	Jul.	1950	L	3-15	Brisbane	35,000	9 Jun.	1984	L	8-25	Sydney	30,190

26 Jun.	1984	L	6-18	Brisbane	26,534		
7 Jul.	1984	L	7-20	Sydney	18,756		
25 Oct.	1986	L	16-38	Man U. FC	50,583		
8 Nov.	1986	L	4-34	Elland Rd,			
				Leeds	30,808		
* 22 Nov.	1986	L	15-24	Wigan	20,169		
11 Jun.	1988	L	6-17	Sydney	24,202		
28 Jun.	1988	L	14-34	Brisbane	27,103		
* 9 Jul.	1988	W	26-12	Sydney	15,994		
27 Oct.	1990	W	19-12	Wembley	54,569		
10 Nov.	1990	L	10-14	Man U. FC	46,615		

* 24 Nov.	1990	L	0-14	Elland Rd,	
				Leeds	32,500
12 Jun.	1992	L	6-22	Sydney	40,141
26 Jun.	1992	W	33-10	Melbourne	30,257
* 3 Jul.	1992	L	10-16	Brisbane	32,313
22 Oct.	1994	W	8-4	Wembley	57,034
5 Nov.	1994	L	8-38	Man U. FC	43,930
20 Nov.	1994	L	4-23	Elland Rd,	
				Leeds	39,468

* Also World Cup match.

	Played	Won	Drawn	Lost	Tries	Goals	Dr	Pts for
Great Britain	111	53	4	54	264	276	7	1382
Australia	111	54	4	53	320	343	7	1718

GREAT BRITAIN-AUSTRALIA TEST MATCH RECORDS

Britain
Highest score: 40-17 Third Test at Sydney, 19 July 1958
Widest margin win: As above and
     33-10 Second Test at Melbourne, 26 June 1992
Most tries in a match: 4 by Jim Leytham (Wigan) Second Test at Brisbane, 2 July 1910
Most goals in a match: 10 by Lewis Jones (Leeds) Second Test at Brisbane, 3 July 1954
Most points in a match: 20 by Lewis Jones (as above)
     20 (2t, 7g) by Roger Millward (Hull K.R.) Second Test at Sydney,
     20 June 1970
Biggest attendance: 57,034 First Test at Wembley, London, 22 October 1994
● For the World Cup final at Wembley on 24 October 1992, there was an attendance of 73,631.

Australia
Highest score: 50-12 Second Test at Swinton, 9 Nov 1963 (Also widest margin win)
Most tries in a match: 3 by Jimmy Devereux, First Test at QPR, London, 12 December 1908
     3 by Reg Gasnier, First Test at Swinton, 17 October 1959
     3 by Reg Gasnier, First Test at Wembley, 16 October 1963
     3 by Ken Irvine, Second Test at Swinton, 9 November 1963
     3 by Ken Irvine, Third Test at Sydney, 23 July 1966
     3 by Gene Miles, First Test at Manchester U. FC, 25 October 1986
     3 by Michael O'Connor, First Test at Manchester U. FC, 25 October
     1986
Most goals in a match: 10 by Mick Cronin, First Test at Brisbane, 16 June 1979
Most points in a match: 22 (3t, 5g) by Michael O'Connor, First Test at Manchester U. FC,
     25 October 1986
Biggest attendance: 70,204 First Test at Sydney, 6 June 1932
● In a World Cup match at Perpignan, France, on 29 October 1972, Bobby Fulton scored 3 tries.

GREAT BRITAIN v. AUSTRALIA IN WORLD CUP

Not including matches which doubled as Tests

31 Oct. 1954	W	28-13	Lyon	10,250
17 Jun. 1957	L	6-31	Sydney	57,955
8 Oct. 1960	W	10-3	Bradford	32,773
25 May 1968	L	10-25	Sydney	62,256
24 Oct. 1970	W	11-4	Leeds	15,084
7 Nov.1970*	L	7-12	Leeds	18,776
29 Oct. 1972	W	27-21	Perpignan	6,324
11 Nov.1972*	D	10-10†	Lyon	4,231
18 Jun. 1977	L	5-19	Brisbane	27,000
25 Jun. 1977*	L	12-13	Sydney	24,457
24 Oct. 1992*	L	6-10	Wembley	73,631

* Final
† After extra time. 10-10 after 80 min. Britain awarded World Cup because of higher position in table.

Snowbound: Great Britain centre Malcolm Price is tackled by Australia's Johnny Greaves at a snow covered Station Road, Swinton, in 1967.

GREAT BRITAIN v. AUSTRALIA SUPER LEAGUE TESTS

1 Nov. 1997	L	14-38	Wembley	41,135
8 Nov. 1997	W	20-12	Man U. FC	40,324
16 Nov. 1997	L	20-37	Elland Rd, Leeds	39,337

	Played	Won	Drawn	Lost	Tries	Goals	Dr.	Pts. for
Great Britain	3	1	0	2	7	13	0	54
Australia SL	3	2	0	1	16	11	1	87

GREAT BRITAIN-AUSTRALIA SUPER LEAGUE TEST MATCH RECORDS

Britain

Most tries in a match:	No player has scored 3 or more
Most goals in a match:	6 by Andrew Farrell (Wigan W.) Second Test at Manchester U. FC, 8 November 1997
Most points in a match:	16 (6g, 1t) by Andrew Farrell as above

Australia SL

Most tries in a match:	3 by Laurie Daley, First Test at Wembley, 1 November 1997
Most goals in a match:	5 by Ryan Girdler, First Test at Wembley, 1 November 1997
Most points in a match:	12 (3t) by Laurie Daley, First Test at Wembley, 1 November 1997

GREAT BRITAIN v. NEW ZEALAND
TESTS

25 Jan.	1908	W	14-6	Leeds	8,182
8 Feb.	1908	L	6-18	Chelsea	14,000
15 Feb.	1908	L	5-8	Cheltenham	4,000
30 Jul.	1910	W	52-20	Auckland	16,000
1 Aug.	1914	W	16-13	Auckland	15,000
31 Jul.	1920	W	31-7	Auckland	34,000
7 Aug.	1920	W	19-3	Christchurch	10,000
14 Aug.	1920	W	11-10	Wellington	4,000
2 Aug.	1924	L	8-16	Auckland	22,000
6 Aug.	1924	L	11-13	Wellington	6,000
9 Aug.	1924	W	31-18	Dunedin	14,000
2 Oct.	1926	W	28-20	Wigan	14,500
13 Nov.	1926	W	21-11	Hull	7,000
15 Jan.	1927	W	32-17	Leeds	6,000
4 Aug.	1928	L	13-17	Auckland	28,000
18 Aug.	1928	W	13-5	Dunedin	12,000
25 Aug.	1928	W	6-5	Christchurch	21,000
30 Jul.	1932	W	24-9	Auckland	25,000
13 Aug.	1932	W	25-14	Christchurch	5,000
20 Aug.	1932	W	20-18	Auckland	6,500
8 Aug.	1936	W	10-8	Auckland	25,000
15 Aug.	1936	W	23-11	Auckland	17,000
10 Aug.	1946	L	8-13	Auckland	10,000
4 Oct.	1947	W	11-10	Leeds	28,445
8 Nov.	1947	L	7-10	Swinton	29,031
20 Dec.	1947	W	25-9	Bradford	42,680
29 Jul.	1950	L	10-16	Christchurch	10,000
12 Aug.	1950	L	13-20	Auckland	20,000
6 Oct.	1951	W	21-15	Bradford	37,475
10 Nov.	1951	W	20-19	Swinton	29,938
15 Dec.	1951	W	16-12	Leeds	18,649
24 Jul.	1954	W	27-7	Auckland	22,097
31 Jul.	1954	L	14-20	Greymouth	4,240
14 Aug.	1954	W	12-6	Auckland	6,186
8 Oct.	1955	W	25-6	Swinton	21,937
12 Nov.	1955	W	27-12	Bradford	24,443
17 Dec.	1955	L	13-28	Leeds	10,438
26 Jul.	1958	L	10-15	Auckland	25,000
9 Aug.	1958	W	32-15	Auckland	25,000
30 Sep.	1961	L	11-29	Leeds	16,540
21 Oct.	1961	W	23-10	Bradford	19,980
4 Nov.	1961	W	35-19	Swinton	22,536
28 Jul.	1962	L	0-19	Auckland	14,976
11 Aug.	1962	L	8-27	Auckland	16,411
25 Sep.	1965	W	7-2	Swinton	8,541
23 Oct.	1965	W	15-9	Bradford	15,740
6 Nov.	1965	D	9-9	Wigan	7,919
6 Aug.	1966	W	25-8	Auckland	14,494
20 Aug.	1966	W	22-14	Auckland	10,657
11 Jul.	1970	W	19-15	Auckland	15,948
19 Jul.	1970	W	23-9	Christchurch	8,600
25 Jul.	1970	W	33-16	Auckland	13,137
25 Sep.	1971	L	13-18	Salford	3,764
16 Oct.	1971	L	14-17	Castleford	4,108
6 Nov.	1971	W	12-3	Leeds	5,479
27 Jul.	1974	L	8-13	Auckland	10,466
4 Aug.	1974	W	17-8	Christchurch	6,316
10 Aug.	1974	W	20-0	Auckland	11,574
21 Jul.	1979	W	16-8	Auckland	9,000
5 Aug.	1979	W	22-7	Christchurch	8,500
11 Aug.	1979	L	11-18	Auckland	7,000
18 Oct.	1980	D	14-14	Wigan	7,031
2 Nov.	1980	L	8-12	Bradford	10,946
15 Nov.	1980	W	10-2	Leeds	8,210
14 Jul.	1984	L	0-12	Auckland	10,238
22 Jul.	1984	L	12-28	Christchurch	3,824
28 Jul.	1984	L	16-32	Auckland	7,967
19 Oct.	1985	L	22-24	Leeds	12,591
2 Nov.	1985	W	25-8	Wigan	15,506
* 9 Nov.	1985	D	6-6	Elland Rd, Leeds	22,209
* 17 Jul.	1988	L	10-12	Christchurch	8,525
21 Oct.	1989	L	16-24	Man U. FC	18,273
28 Oct.	1989	W	26-6	Elland Rd, Leeds	13,073
* 11 Nov.	1989	W	10-6	Wigan	20,346
24 Jun.	1990	W	11-10	Palmerston N.	8,073
8 Jul.	1990	W	16-14	Auckland	7,843
* 15 Jul.	1990	L	18-21	Christchurch	3,133
12 Jul.	1992	L	14-15	Palmerston N.	11,548
19 Jul.	1992	W	19-16	Auckland	10,223
16 Oct.	1993	W	17-0	Wembley	36,131
30 Oct.	1993	W	29-12	Wigan	16,502
6 Nov.	1993	W	29-10	Leeds	15,139
18 Oct.	1996	L	12-17	Auckland	7,400
25 Oct.	1996	L	15-18	Palmerston N.	9,000
1 Nov.	1996	L	12-32	Christchurch	9,000
31 Oct.	1998	L	16-22	Huddersfield	18,509
7 Nov.	1998	L	16-36	Bolton W. FC	27,884
14 Nov.	1998	D	23-23	Watford FC	13,278

* Also World Cup match.

	Played	Won	Drawn	Lost	Tries	Goals	Dr	Pts for
Great Britain	88	51	4	33	305	254	10	1495
New Zealand	88	33	4	51	209	257	4	1210

GREAT BRITAIN-NEW ZEALAND TEST MATCH RECORDS

Britain

Highest score:	52-20 First Test at Auckland, 30 July 1910 (Also widest margin win)
Most tries in a match:	4 by Billy Boston (Wigan) First Test at Auckland, 24 July 1954
	4 by Garry Schofield (Hull) Second Test at Wigan, 2 November 1985
Most goals in a match:	7 by Eric Fraser (Warrington) Second Test at Auckland, 9 August 1958
	7 by Neil Fox (Wakefield T.) Third Test at Swinton, 4 November 1961
Most points in a match:	16 (4t) by Garry Schofield (Hull) Second Test at Wigan, 2 November 1985
Biggest attendance:	42,680 Third Test at Bradford, 20 December 1947

● In a World Cup Match at Pau, France, on 4 November 1972, Britain won 53-19 with John Holmes (Leeds) scoring 26 points from 10 goals and two tries.
In a World Cup match at Sydney on 8 June 1968, Bev Risman (Leeds) scored seven goals.

New Zealand

Highest score:	36-16 Second Test at Bolton W. FC, 7 November 1998
	Widest margin win: Above and
	32-12 Third Test at Christchurch, 1 November 1996
	(Also widest margin win)
No player has scored three tries or more in a Test.	
Most goals and points:	7g-14pts by Des White, Second Test at Greymouth, 31 July 1954
	Jack Fagan, First Test at Headingley, 30 September 1961
	Ernie Wiggs, Second Test at Auckland, 20 August 1966
Biggest attendance:	34,000 First Test at Auckland, 31 July 1920

● In a World Cup match at Sydney, Australia, on 25 June 1957, Bill Sorensen also scored seven goals, 14 points.

GREAT BRITAIN v. NEW ZEALAND IN WORLD CUP

Not including matches which doubled as Tests

11 Nov. 1954	W	26-6	Bordeaux	14,000
25 Jun. 1957	L	21-29	Sydney	14,263
24 Sep. 1960	W	23-8	Bradford	20,577
8 Jun. 1968	W	38-14	Sydney	14,105
31 Oct. 1970	W	27-17	Swinton	5,609
4 Nov. 1972	W	53-19	Pau	7,500
12 Jun. 1977	W	30-12	Christchurch	7,000

GREAT BRITAIN v. FRANCE TESTS

● **Results since France were given Test match status.**

26 Jan. 1957	W	45-12	Leeds	20,221
3 Mar. 1957	D	19-19	Toulouse	16,000
10 Apr. 1957	W	29-14	St. Helens	23,250
3 Nov. 1957	W	25-14	Toulouse	15,000

23 Nov. 1957	W	44-15	Wigan	19,152
2 Mar. 1958	W	23-9	Grenoble	20,000
14 Mar. 1959	W	50-15	Leeds	22,000
5 Apr. 1959	L	15-24	Grenoble	8,500
6 Mar. 1960	L	18-20	Toulouse	15,308
26 Mar. 1960	D	17-17	St. Helens	14,000
11 Dec. 1960	W	21-10	Bordeaux	8,000
28 Jan. 1961	W	27-8	St. Helens	18,000
17 Feb. 1962	L	15-20	Wigan	17,277
11 Mar. 1962	L	13-23	Perpignan	14,000
2 Dec. 1962	L	12-17	Perpignan	5,000
3 Apr. 1963	W	42-4	Wigan	19,487
8 Mar. 1964	W	11-5	Perpignan	4,326
18 Mar. 1964	W	39-0	Leigh	4,750
6 Dec. 1964	L	8-18	Perpignan	15,000
23 Jan. 1965	W	17-7	Swinton	9,959
16 Jan. 1966	L	13-18	Perpignan	6,000
5 Mar. 1966	L	4-8	Wigan	14,004

22 Jan.	1967	W	16-13	Carcassonne	10,650		17 Mar.	1985	L	16-24	Perpignan	5,000
4 Mar.	1967	L	13-23	Wigan	7,448	*	16 Feb.	1986	D	10-10	Avignon	4,000
11 Feb.	1968	W	22-13	Paris	8,000		1 Mar.	1986	W	24-10	Wigan	8,112
2 Mar.	1968	W	19-8	Bradford	14,196	*	24 Jan.	1987	W	52-4	Leeds	6,567
30 Nov.	1968	W	34-10	St. Helens	6,080		8 Feb.	1987	W	20-10	Carcassonne	2,000
2 Feb.	1969	L	9-13	Toulouse	10,000		24 Jan.	1988	W	28-14	Avignon	6,500
7 Feb.	1971	L	8-16	Toulouse	14,960		6 Feb.	1988	W	30-12	Leeds	7,007
17 Mar.	1971	W	24-2	St. Helens	7,783		21 Jan.	1989	W	26-10	Wigan	8,266
6 Feb.	1972	W	10-9	Toulouse	11,508		5 Feb.	1989	W	30-8	Avignon	6,500
12 Mar.	1972	W	45-10	Bradford	7,313		18 Mar.	1990	W	8-4	Perpignan	6,000
20 Jan.	1974	W	24-5	Grenoble	5,500		7 Apr.	1990	L	18-25	Leeds	6,554
17 Feb.	1974	W	29-0	Wigan	10,105	*	27 Jan.	1991	W	45-10	Perpignan	3,965
6 Dec.	1981	W	37-0	Hull	13,173		16 Feb.	1991	W	60-4	Leeds	5,284
20 Dec.	1981	L	2-19	Marseilles	6,500		16 Feb.	1992	W	30-12	Perpignan	5,688
20 Feb.	1983	W	20-5	Carcassonne	3,826	*	7 Mar.	1992	W	36-0	Hull	5,250
6 Mar.	1983	W	17-5	Hull	6,055		7 Mar.	1993	W	48-6	Carcassonne	5,500
29 Jan.	1984	W	12-0	Avignon	4,000		2 Apr.	1993	W	72-6	Leeds	8,196
17 Feb.	1984	W	10-0	Leeds	7,646		20 Mar.	1994	W	12-4	Carcassonne	7,000
1 Mar.	1985	W	50-4	Leeds	6,491							

* Also World Cup match.

	Played	Won	Drawn	Lost	Tries	Goals	Dr	Pts for
Great Britain	59	42	3	14	282	258	1	1473
France	59	14	3	42	106	137	4	625

GREAT BRITAIN-FRANCE TEST MATCH RECORDS

Britain

Highest score:	72-6 at Leeds, 2 April 1993 (Also widest margin win)
Most tries in a match:	5 by Martin Offiah (Widnes) at Leeds, 16 February 1991
Most goals in a match:	10 by Bernard Ganley (Oldham) at Wigan, 23 November 1957
	10 by Jonathan Davies (Widnes) at Leeds, 2 April 1993
Most points in a match:	21 (1t, 9g) by Lewis Jones (Leeds) at Leeds, 26 January 1957
	21 (1t, 9g) by Neil Fox (Wakefield T.) at Wigan, 3 April 1963
	21 (1t, 9g) by Neil Fox (Wakefield T.) at Leigh, 18 March 1964
Biggest attendance:	23,250 at St. Helens, 10 April 1957

France

Highest score:	25-18 at Leeds, 7 April 1990
Widest margin win:	19-2 at Marseilles, 20 December 1981
Most tries in a match:	3 by Didier Couston at Perpignan, 17 March 1985
Most goals in a match:	7 by Pierre Lacaze at Wigan, 4 March 1967
Most points in a match:	14 by Pierre Lacaze (as above)
	14 (2t, 4g) by Gilbert Benausse at Wigan, 17 February 1962
Biggest attendance:	20,000 at Grenoble, 2 March 1958

● In a World Cup match at Toulouse on 7 November 1954, there were 37,471 spectators.

GREAT BRITAIN v. FRANCE IN WORLD CUP

Not including matches which doubled as Tests

	7 Nov.	1954	D	13-13	Toulouse	37,471
*	13 Nov.	1954	W	16-12	Paris	30,368
	15 Jun.	1957	W	23-5	Sydney	50,007
	1 Oct.	1960	W	33-7	Swinton	22,923
	2 Jun.	1968	L	2-7	Auckland	15,760
	28 Oct.	1970	W	6-0	Castleford	8,958
	1 Nov.	1972	W	13-4	Grenoble	5,321
	5 Jun.	1977	W	23-4	Auckland	10,000

* *Play-off*

GREAT BRITAIN v. PAPUA NEW GUINEA

	5 Aug.	1984	W	38-20	Mt. Hagen	7,510
*	24 Oct.	1987	W	42-0	Wigan	9,121
*	22 May	1988	W	42-22	Port Moresby	12,107
	27 May	1990	L	18-20	Goroka	11,598

Additional Great Britain v. France

Pre-Test status

22 May	1952	L	12-22	Paris	16,466
24 May	1953	L	17-28	Lyons	
27 Apr.	1954	W	17-8	Bradford	14,153
11 Dec.	1955	L	5-17	Paris	18,000
11 Apr.	1956	W	18-10	Bradford	10,453

Other match

31 July	1982	L	7-8	Venice	1,500

*	2 Jun.	1990	W	40-8	Port Moresby	5,969
*	9 Nov.	1991	W	56-4	Wigan	4,193
	31 May	1992	W	20-14	Port Moresby	7,294
	28 Sep.	1996	W	32-30	Lae	10,000

*Also World Cup match.

	Played	Won	Lost	Tries	Goals	Dr	Pts for
Great Britain	8	7	1	50	44	0	288
Papua New Guinea	8	1	7	20	18	2	118

GREAT BRITAIN-PAPUA NEW GUINEA TEST MATCH RECORDS

Britain

Highest score:	56-4 at Wigan, 9 November 1991 (Also widest margin win)
Most tries in a match:	No player has scored 3 or more
Most goals in a match:	8 by Jonathan Davies (Widnes) at Wigan, 9 November 1991
Most points in a match:	16 by Jonathan Davies (Widnes) as above
	by Bobbie Goulding (St. Helens) at Lae, 28 September 1996
Biggest attendance:	9,121 at Wigan, 24 October 1987

Papua New Guinea

Highest score:	30-32 lost at Lae, 28 September 1996
Only win:	20-18 at Goroka, 27 May 1990
Most tries in a match:	No player has scored 3 or more
Most goals in a match:	6 by Bal Numapo at Goroka, 27 May 1990
Most points in a match:	11 (5g, 1dg) by Bal Numapo as above
Biggest attendance:	12,107 at Port Moresby, 22 May 1988

GREAT BRITAIN-FIJI TEST MATCH RECORDS

5 Oct. 1996 W 72-4   Nadi 5,000

Britain

Most tries, goals and points: Bobbie Goulding 3t, 10g, 32pts.

CLUB REPRESENTATION

Wigan hold the record for most players supplied by one club for a Test or World Cup match. They have had eight in Great Britain's starting line-up on four occasions as follows:

v. Papua New Guinea at Wigan on 24 October 1987. Won 42-0: Steve Hampson, David Stephenson, Joe Lydon, Shaun Edwards, Andy Gregory, Brian Case, Andy Goodway and Ellery Hanley (capt).

v. Australia at Melbourne on 26 June 1992. Won 33-10: Martin Offiah, Shaun Edwards, Kelvin Skerrett, Martin Dermott, Andy Platt, Denis Betts, Billy McGinty and Phil Clarke.

v. Australia at Brisbane on 3 July 1992. Lost 10-16: As above.

v. Australia at Elland Road, Leeds, on 20 November 1994. Lost 4-23: Gary Connolly, Jason Robinson, Martin Offiah, Phil Clarke, Shaun Edwards (capt.), Barrie McDermott, Denis Betts and Andrew Farrell.

In the second and third Tests of 1992 Wigan became the only club to provide all six forwards.

Wigan had a record 10 players on duty for the first 1992 Test against Australia, seven in the starting line-up plus three substitutes, all of whom played. For a brief period, there were a record nine Wigan players in action.

Wigan also hold the record for the total of players selected from one club over the years with 93.

Only three of last season's clubs have not had a player selected for Great Britain – Bramley, Lancashire Lynx and Doncaster Dragons.

*A register of each club's representation for Great Britain is featured in the CLUBS section.

Brian Case: One of eight Wigan players in Great Britain's team that met Papua New Guinea in 1987.

GREAT BRITAIN TEAMS

The following is a compendium of Great Britain Test and World Cup teams since 1978.

Initials are included where more than one player shared a surname in the same era. Only playing substitutes are included on the teamsheet.

(WC): World Cup   t: try   g: goal
dg: drop goal   * captain

1978 Australia
Wigan: 21 Oct.
Lost 9-15
Fairbairn (Wigan) 3g
Wright, S. (Widnes)
Hughes (Widnes)
Cunningham (St. Helens)
Bevan, J. (Warrington) 1t
*Millward (Hull K.R.)
Nash (Salford)
Thompson, J. (Bradford N.)
Ward, D. (Leeds)
Rose, P. (Hull K.R.)
Nicholls (St. Helens)
Casey (Hull K.R.)
Norton (Hull)
Sub: Holmes (Leeds)
　　Hogan (Barrow)

1979 Australia
Brisbane: 16 June
Lost 0-35
Woods, J. (Leigh)
Barends (Bradford N.)
Joyner (Castleford)
Hughes (Widnes)
Mathias (St. Helens)
Holmes (Leeds)
Stephens (Castleford)
Mills (Widnes)
Ward, D. (Leeds)
Skerrett, T. (Wakefield T.)
Nicholls (St. Helens)
*Laughton (Widnes)
Norton (Hull)
Sub: Evans, S. (Featherstone R.)
　　Hogan (Hull K.R.)

1979 New Zealand
Auckland: 21 July
Won 16-8
Fairbairn (Wigan) 1t, 2g
Evans, S. (Featherstone R.) 1t
Joyner (Castleford)
Smith, M. (Hull K.R.) 1t
Hughes (Widnes) 1t
Holmes (Leeds)
Stephens (Castleford)
Casey (Bradford N.)
Ward, D. (Leeds)
*Nicholls (St. Helens)
Hogan (Hull K.R.)
Grayshon (Bradford N.)
Adams, M. (Widnes)
Sub: Lockwood (Hull K.R.)

1978 Australia
Bradford: 5 Nov.
Won 18-14
Fairbairn (Wigan) 6g
Wright, S. (Widnes) 2t
Joyner (Castleford)
Dyl (Leeds)
Atkinson, J. (Leeds)
*Millward (Hull K.R.)
Nash (Salford)
Mills (Widnes)
Fisher (Bradford N.)
Lockwood (Hull K.R.)
Nicholls (St. Helens)
Lowe, P. (Hull K.R.)
Norton (Hull)
Sub: Holmes (Leeds)
　　Rose, P. (Hull K.R.)

1979 Australia
Sydney: 30 June
Lost 16-24
Fairbairn (Wigan)
Barends (Bradford N.)
Joyner (Castleford) 1t
Woods, J. (Leigh) 5g
Hughes (Widnes) 1t
Holmes (Leeds)
Stephens (Castleford)
*Nicholls (St. Helens)
Ward, D. (Leeds)
Skerrett, T. (Wakefield T.)
Casey (Bradford N.)
Grayshon (Bradford N.)
Adams, M. (Widnes)
Sub: Evans, S. (Featherstone R.)
　　Watkinson (Hull K.R.)

1979 New Zealand
Christchurch: 5 Aug.
Won 22-7
Fairbairn (Wigan) 5g
Evans, S. (Featherstone R.) 1t
Joyner (Castleford)
Smith, M. (Hull K.R.)
Hughes (Widnes) 1t
Holmes (Leeds)
Stephens (Castleford)
*Nicholls (St. Helens)
Ward, D. (Leeds)
Skerrett, T. (Wakefield T.)
Casey (Bradford N.) 1t
Grayshon (Bradford N.) 1t
Adams, M. (Widnes)

1978 Australia
Leeds: 18 Nov.
Lost 6-23
Fairbairn (Wigan)
Wright, S. (Widnes)
Joyner (Castleford)
Bevan, J. (Warrington) 1t
Atkinson, J. (Leeds)
*Millward (Hull K.R.) 1t
Nash (Salford)
Mills (Widnes)
Fisher (Bradford N.)
Farrar (Hull)
Nicholls (St. Helens)
Lowe, P. (Hull K.R.)
Norton (Hull)
Sub: Holmes (Leeds)
　　Rose, P. (Hull K.R.)

1979 Australia
Sydney: 14 July
Lost 2-28
Fairbairn (Wigan) 1g
Evans, S. (Featherstone R.)
Joyner (Castleford)
Woods, J. (Leigh)
Hughes (Widnes)
Topliss (Wakefield T.)
Redfearn, A. (Bradford N.)
*Nicholls (St. Helens)
Ward, D. (Leeds)
Casey (Bradford N.)
Hogan (Hull K.R.)
Grayshon (Bradford N.)
Norton (Hull)
Sub: Holmes (Leeds)
　　Adams, M. (Widnes)

1979 New Zealand
Auckland: 11 Aug.
Lost 11-18
Fairbairn (Wigan) 1g
Evans, S. (Featherstone R.)
Joyner (Castleford)
Smith, M. (Hull K.R.) 1t
Hughes (Widnes) 1t
Holmes (Leeds)
Stephens (Castleford) 1t
Skerrett, T. (Wakefield T.)
Ward, D. (Leeds)
*Nicholls (St. Helens)
Casey (Bradford N.)
Grayshon (Bradford N.)
Adams, M. (Widnes)
Sub: Woods, J. (Leigh)
　　Hogan (Hull K.R.)

1980 New Zealand
Wigan: 18 Oct.
Drew 14-14
*Fairbairn (Wigan) 4g
Camilleri (Barrow) 1t
Joyner (Castleford)
Smith, M. (Hull K.R.) 1t
Bentley, K. (Widnes)
Hartley, S. (Hull K.R.)
Dick (Leeds)
Holdstock (Hull K.R.)
Watkinson (Hull K.R.)
Skerrett, T. (Hull)
Gorley, L. (Widnes)
Grayshon (Bradford N.)
Casey (Hull K.R.)
Sub: Pinner (St. Helens)

1980 New Zealand
Bradford: 2 Nov.
Lost 8-12
*Fairbairn (Wigan) 4g
Drummond (Leigh)
Joyner (Castleford)
Smith, M. (Hull K.R.)
Camilleri (Barrow)
Kelly, K. (Warrington)
Dick (Leeds)
Holdstock (Hull K.R.)
Elwell (Widnes)
Shaw, G. (Widnes)
Casey (Hull K.R.)
Grayshon (Bradford N.)
Pinner (St. Helens)
Sub: Evans, S. (Featherstone R.)
Gorley, L. (Widnes)

1980 New Zealand
Leeds: 15 Nov.
Won 10-2
Burke (Widnes) 2g
Drummond (Leigh) 2t
Joyner (Castleford)
Evans, S. (Featherstone R.)
Atkinson, J. (Leeds)
Woods, J. (Leigh)
Walker (Whitehaven)
Skerrett, T. (Hull)
Elwell (Widnes)
*Casey (Hull K.R.)
Gorley, P. (St. Helens)
Adams, M. (Widnes)
Norton (Hull)

Harry Pinner.

1981 France
Hull: 6 Dec.
Won 37-0
Fairbairn (Hull K.R.) 1g
Drummond (Leigh) 2t
Smith, M. (Hull K.R.)
Woods, J. (Leigh) 1t, 7g
Gill, H. (Wigan) 3t
Hartley, S. (Hull K.R.) 1t
Gregory, A. (Widnes)
Grayshon (Bradford N.)
*Ward, D. (Leeds)
Skerrett, T. (Hull)
Gorley, L. (Widnes)
Gorley, P. (St. Helens)
Norton (Hull)
Sub: Burke (Widnes)
Szymala (Barrow)

1981 France
Marseilles: 20 Dec.
Lost 2-19
Burke (Widnes)
Drummond (Leigh)
Smith, M. (Hull K.R.)
Woods, J. (Leigh) 1g
Gill, H. (Wigan)
Hartley, S. (Hull K.R.)
Gregory, A. (Widnes)
*Grayshon (Bradford N.)
Watkinson (Hull K.R.)
Skerrett, T. (Hull)
Gorley, L. (Widnes)
Szymala (Barrow)
Norton (Hull)
Sub: Gorley, P. (St. Helens)

1982 Australia
Hull City FC: 30 Oct.
Lost 4-40
Fairbairn (Hull K.R.)
Drummond (Leigh)
Hughes (Widnes)
Dyl (Leeds)
Evans, S. (Hull)
Woods, J. (Leigh)
*Nash (Salford)
Grayshon (Bradford N.)
Ward, D. (Leeds)
Skerrett, T. (Hull)
Gorley, L. (Widnes)
Crooks, L. (Hull) 2g
Norton (Hull)
Sub: Heron, D. (Leeds)

1982 Australia
Wigan: 20 Nov.
Lost 6-27
Mumby (Bradford N.) 3g
Drummond (Leigh)
Smith, M. (Hull K.R.)
Stephenson (Wigan)
Gill, H. (Wigan)
Holmes (Leeds)
Kelly, K. (Warrington)
*Grayshon (Bradford N.)
Dalgreen (Fulham)
Skerrett, T. (Hull)
Eccles (Warrington)
Burton (Hull K.R.)
Heron, D. (Leeds)
Sub: Woods, J. (Leigh)
Rathbone (Bradford N.)

1982 Australia
Leeds: 28 Nov.
Lost 8-32
Fairbairn (Hull K.R.)
Drummond (Leigh)
Stephenson (Wigan)
Smith, M. (Hull K.R.)
Evans, S. (Hull) 1t
*Topliss (Hull)
Gregory, A. (Widnes)
O'Neill, M. (Widnes)
Noble (Bradford N.)
Rose, P. (Hull)
Smith, P. (Featherstone R.)
Crooks, L. (Hull) 2g, 1dg
Crane (Hull)
Sub: Courtney (Warrington)

1983 France
Carcassonne: 20 Feb.
Won 20-5
Burke (Widnes) 1g
Drummond (Leigh)
Joyner (Castleford) 1t
Duane, R. (Warrington)
Lydon (Widnes) 1t, 3g
Myler, A. (Widnes)
Gregory, A. (Widnes)
O'Neill, M. (Widnes)
Noble (Bradford N.) 1t
Goodway (Oldham) 1t
*Casey (Hull K.R.)
Rathbone (Bradford N.)
Flanagan (Oldham)
Sub: Woods, J. (Leigh)
　　　Smith, P. (Featherstone R.)

1983 France
Hull: 6 Mar.
Won 17-5
Mumby (Bradford N.) 4g
Drummond (Leigh)
Joyner (Castleford)
Duane, R. (Warrington) 1t
Lydon (Widnes)
Myler, A. (Widnes)
Gregory, A. (Widnes) 1t
O'Neill, M. (Widnes)
Noble (Bradford N.)
Goodway (Oldham)
*Casey (Hull K.R.)
Rathbone (Bradford N.)
Flanagan (Oldham)
Sub: Smith, P. (Featherstone R.) 1t

Andy Gregory.

1984 France
Avignon: 29 Jan.
Won 12-0
*Mumby (Bradford N.)
Drummond (Leigh)
Duane, R. (Warrington)
Foy, D. (Oldham) 1t
Clark (Hull K.R.)
Lydon (Widnes)
Cairns (Barrow)
Rayne, Keith (Leeds)
Watkinson (Hull K.R.)
Goodway (Oldham) 1t
Worrall, M. (Oldham)
Hobbs, D. (Featherstone R.)
Hall (Hull K.R.)
Sub: Hanley (Bradford N.)
　　　Crooks, L. (Hull) 2g

1984 France
Leeds: 17 Feb.
Won 10-0
Mumby (Bradford N.)
Clark (Hull K.R.)
Joyner (Castleford)
Schofield (Hull)
Basnett (Widnes)
Hanley (Bradford N.)
Cairns (Barrow)
Rayne, Keith (Leeds)
*Noble (Bradford N.)
Ward, K. (Castleford)
Jasiewicz (Bradford N.)
Hobbs, D. (Featherstone R.) 5g
Hall (Hull K.R.)
Sub: Smith, M. (Hull K.R.)
　　　Smith, P. (Featherstone R.)

Andy Goodway.

1984 Australia
Sydney: 9 June
Lost 8-25
Burke (Widnes) 2g
Drummond (Leigh)
Schofield (Hull) 1t
Mumby (Bradford N.)
Hanley (Bradford N.)
Foy, D. (Oldham)
Holding (St. Helens)
Crooks, L. (Hull)
*Noble (Bradford N.)
Goodway (Oldham)
Burton (Hull K.R.)
Worrall, M. (Oldham)
Adams, M. (Widnes)
Sub: Lydon (Widnes)
　　　Hobbs, D. (Featherstone R.)

1984 Australia
Brisbane: 26 June
Lost 6-18
Burke (Widnes) 1g
Drummond (Leigh)
Schofield (Hull) 1t
Mumby (Bradford N.)
Hanley (Bradford N.)
Myler, A. (Widnes)
Holding (St. Helens)
Rayne, Keith (Leeds)
*Noble (Bradford N.)
Crooks, L. (Hull)
Burton (Hull K.R.)
Goodway (Oldham)
Worrall, M. (Oldham)
Sub: Gregory, A. (Widnes)
　　　Adams, M. (Widnes)

1984 Australia
Sydney: 7 July
Lost 7-20
Burke (Widnes) 1g
Drummond (Leigh)
Schofield (Hull)
Mumby (Bradford N.)
Hanley (Bradford N.) 1t
Myler, A. (Widnes)
Holding (St. Helens) 1dg
Hobbs, D. (Featherstone R.)
*Noble (Bradford N.)
Case (Wigan)
Burton (Hull K.R.)
Goodway (Oldham)
Adams, M. (Widnes)

1984 New Zealand
Auckland: 14 July
Lost 0-12
Burke (Widnes)
Drummond (Leigh)
Schofield (Hull)
Mumby (Bradford N.)
Hanley (Bradford N.)
Smith, M. (Hull K.R.)
Holding (St. Helens)
Hobbs, D. (Featherstone R.)
*Noble (Bradford N.)
Case (Wigan)
Burton (Hull K.R.)
Goodway (Oldham)
Adams, M. (Widnes)

1984 Papua New Guinea
Mount Hagen: 5 Aug.
Won 38-20
Burke (Widnes) 1t, 5g
Drummond (Leigh) 2t
Hanley (Bradford N.) 1t
Mumby (Bradford N.) 1t
Lydon (Widnes)
Myler, A. (Widnes)
Gregory, A. (Widnes)
Rayne, Keith (Leeds) 1t
*Noble (Bradford N.)
Goodway (Oldham)
Flanagan (Oldham)
Hobbs, D. (Featherstone R.) 1t
Adams, M. (Widnes)
Sub: Donlan (Leigh)
    Proctor (Hull)

1985 New Zealand
Leeds: 19 Oct.
Lost 22-24
Burke (Widnes) 3g
Drummond (Leigh)
Schofield (Hull)
Hanley (Wigan) 1t
Lydon (Widnes) 1t, 2g
Myler, A. (Widnes)
Fox (Featherstone R.)
Crooks, L. (Hull)
Watkinson (Hull K.R.)
Fieldhouse (Widnes)
Goodway (Wigan) 1t
Potter (Wigan)
*Pinner (St. Helens)
Sub: Arkwright (St. Helens)

1984 New Zealand
Christchurch: 22 July
Lost 12-28
Burke (Widnes) 2g
Drummond (Leigh)
Hanley (Bradford N.) 1t
Mumby (Bradford N.)
Lydon (Widnes)
Myler, A. (Widnes) 1t
Gregory, A. (Widnes)
Hobbs, D. (Featherstone R.)
*Noble (Bradford N.)
Case (Wigan)
Burton (Hull K.R.)
Goodway (Oldham)
Adams, M. (Widnes)
Sub: Joyner (Castleford)
    Beardmore, K. (Castleford)

1985 France
Leeds: 1 Mar.
Won 50-4
Edwards (Wigan)
Ledger (St. Helens)
Creasser (Leeds) 8g
Gribbin (Whitehaven) 1t
Gill, H. (Wigan) 1t
Hanley (Bradford N.) 2t
Fox (Featherstone R.) 2t, 1g
Dickinson (Leeds)
Watkinson (Hull K.R.) 1t
Dannatt (Hull)
*Goodway (Oldham)
Rathbone (Bradford N.)
Divorty (Hull) 1t
Sub: Gibson (Batley)
    Platt (St. Helens)

1985 New Zealand
Wigan: 2 Nov.
Won 25-8
Burke (Widnes)
Drummond (Leigh)
Schofield (Hull) 4t
Hanley (Wigan)
Lydon (Widnes) 4g
Myler, A. (Widnes)
Fox (Featherstone R.)
Grayshon (Leeds)
Watkinson (Hull K.R.)
Fieldhouse (Widnes)
Goodway (Wigan)
Potter (Wigan)
*Pinner (St. Helens) 1dg
Sub: Edwards (Wigan)
    Burton (Hull K.R.)

1984 New Zealand
Auckland: 28 July
Lost 16-32
Burke (Widnes) 4g
Drummond (Leigh)
Hanley (Bradford N.) 1t
Mumby (Bradford N.) 1t
Lydon (Widnes)
Myler, A. (Widnes)
Gregory, A. (Widnes)
Hobbs, D. (Featherstone R.)
*Noble (Bradford N.)
Case (Wigan)
Adams, M. (Widnes)
Goodway (Oldham)
Flanagan (Oldham)
Sub: Donlan (Leigh)
    Joyner (Castleford)

1985 France
Perpignan: 17 Mar.
Lost 16-24
Johnson, C. (Leigh)
Clark (Hull K.R.)
Creasser (Leeds) 1g
Foy, D. (Oldham) 1t
Ford, P. (Wigan) 2t
*Hanley (Bradford N.)
Fox (Featherstone R.)
Dickinson (Leeds)
Kiss (Wigan)
Wane (Wigan)
Dannatt (Hull)
Rathbone (Bradford N.)
Divorty (Hull) 1g
Sub: Harkin, P. (Hull K.R.)
    Powell, R. (Leeds)

1985 New Zealand (Also WC)
Elland Rd, Leeds: 9 Nov.
Drew 6-6
Burke (Widnes)
Drummond (Leigh)
Schofield (Hull)
Edwards (Wigan)
Lydon (Widnes)
Hanley (Wigan)
Fox (Featherstone R.)
Grayshon (Leeds)
Watkinson (Hull K.R.)
Fieldhouse (Widnes)
Goodway (Wigan)
Potter (Wigan)
*Pinner (St. Helens)
Sub: Arkwright (St. Helens)
    Crooks, L. (Hull) 3g

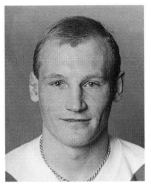

Deryck Fox.

1986 France (Also WC)
Avignon: 16 Feb.
Drew 10-10
Burke (Widnes)
Drummond (Leigh)
Schofield (Hull)
Hanley (Wigan) 1t
Gill, H. (Wigan)
Myler, A. (Widnes)
Fox (Featherstone R.)
Crooks, L. (Hull) 3g
Watkinson (Hull K.R.)
Wane (Wigan)
Potter (Wigan)
Fieldhouse (Widnes)
*Pinner (St. Helens)

1986 France
Wigan: 1 Mar.
Won 24-10
Lydon (Wigan)
Drummond (Leigh) 1t
Schofield (Hull) 1t, 2g
Marchant (Castleford) 1t
Laws (Hull K.R.)
Myler, A. (Widnes)
Fox (Featherstone R.)
Crooks, L. (Hull) 2g
*Watkinson (Hull K.R.)
Fieldhouse (Widnes)
Rayne, Kevin (Leeds)
James (Halifax) 1t
Potter (Wigan)
Sub: Platt (St. Helens)

1986 Australia
Man U. FC: 25 Oct.
Lost 16-38
Lydon (Wigan) 1t
Marchant (Castleford)
Schofield (Hull) 2t
Hanley (Wigan)
Gill, H. (Wigan) 1g
Myler, A. (Widnes)
Fox (Featherstone R.)
Ward K. (Castleford)
*Watkinson (Hull K.R.)
Fieldhouse (Widnes)
Crooks, L. (Hull) 1g
Potter (Wigan)
Goodway (Wigan)

1986 Australia
Elland Rd, Leeds: 8 Nov.
Lost 4-34
Lydon (Wigan)
Ledger (St. Helens)
Schofield (Hull) 1t
Marchant (Castleford)
Gill, H. (Wigan)
Myler, A. (Widnes)
Fox (Featherstone R.)
Ward, K. (Castleford)
*Watkinson (Hull K.R.)
Fieldhouse (St. Helens)
Crooks, L. (Hull)
Potter (Wigan)
Goodway (Wigan)
Sub: Edwards (Wigan)
Platt (St. Helens)

1986 Australia (Also WC)
Wigan: 22 Nov.
Lost 15-24
Lydon (Wigan) 2g
Gill, H. (Wigan) 1g
Schofield (Hull) 2t, 1dg
Stephenson (Hull)
Basnett (Widnes)
Myler, A. (Widnes)
Gregory, A. (Warrington)
Ward, K. (Castleford)
*Watkinson (Hull K.R.)
Crooks, L. (Hull)
Burton (Hull K.R.)
Goodway (Wigan)
Pinner (Widnes)
Sub: Potter (Wigan)

1987 France (Also WC)
Leeds: 24 Jan.
Won 52-4
Lydon (Wigan) 1t, 8g
Forster (Warrington) 1t
Schofield (Hull)
Stephenson (Wigan)
Gill, H. (Wigan)
*Hanley (Wigan) 2t
Edwards (Wigan) 2t
Hobbs, D. (Oldham)
Beardmore, K. (Castleford)
Crooks, L. (Hull)
Goodway (Wigan) 1t
Haggerty (St. Helens)
Gregory, M. (Warrington) 2t
Sub: Creasser (Leeds)
England (Castleford)

1987 France
Carcassonne: 8 Feb.
Won 20-10
Lydon (Wigan) 4g
Forster (Warrington)
Schofield (Hull)
*Hanley (Wigan) 1t
Gill, H. (Wigan) 1t
Edwards (Wigan)
Gregory, A. (Wigan)
Hobbs, D. (Oldham)
Beardmore, K. (Castleford) 1t
England (Castleford)
Burton (Hull K.R.)
Haggerty (St. Helens)
Gregory, M. (Warrington)
Sub: Dixon (Halifax)

1987 Papua New Guinea (Also WC)
Wigan: 24 Oct.
Won 42-0
Hampson (Wigan)
Drummond (Warrington)
Stephenson (Wigan) 7g
Lydon (Wigan) 1t
Ford, P. (Bradford N.) 1t
Edwards (Wigan) 2t
Gregory, A. (Wigan) 1t
Ward, K. (Castleford)
Groves (St. Helens)
Case (Wigan)
Medley (Leeds) 1t
Goodway (Wigan)
*Hanley (Wigan) 1t
Sub: Woods, J. (Warrington)
Fairbank (Bradford N.)

311

1988 France
Avignon: 24 Jan.
Won 28-14
Hampson (Wigan)
Drummond (Warrington) 1t
Schofield (Leeds) 2t
Loughlin (St. Helens) 3g
Offiah (Widnes) 1t
*Hanley (Wigan) 1t
Edwards (Wigan)
Ward, K. (Castleford)
Beardmore, K. (Castleford)
Waddell (Oldham)
Powell, R. (Leeds)
Medley (Leeds)
Platt (St. Helens)
Sub: Creasser (Leeds) 1g
　　　Dixon (Halifax)

1988 France
Leeds: 6 Feb.
Won 30-12
Hampson (Wigan)
Plange (Castleford) 1t
Schofield (Leeds) 1t, 5g
*Hanley (Wigan) 2t
Ford, P. (Bradford N.)
Edwards (Wigan)
Gregory, A. (Wigan) 1t
Ward, K. (Castleford)
Beardmore, K. (Castleford)
Waddell (Oldham)
Powell, R. (Leeds)
Dixon (Halifax)
Platt (St. Helens)
Sub: Stephenson (Leeds)
　　　Medley (Leeds)

1988 Papua New Guinea (Also WC)
Port Moresby: 22 May
Won 42-22
Loughlin (St. Helens) 7g
Ford, P. (Bradford N.)
Schofield (Leeds) 2t
Stephenson (Leeds) 1t
Gill, H. (Wigan) 2t
Edwards (Wigan)
Gregory, A. (Wigan)
Ward, K. (Castleford)
Beardmore, K. (Castleford)
Case (Wigan)
Medley (Leeds) 1t
Gregory, M. (Warrington) 1t
*Hanley (Wigan)
Sub: Hulme, D. (Widnes)
　　　Dixon (Halifax)

1988 Australia
Sydney: 11 June
Lost 6-17
Loughlin (St. Helens) 1g
Ford, P. (Bradford N.)
Schofield (Leeds)
Stephenson (Leeds)
Offiah (Widnes)
Hulme, D. (Widnes)
Gregory, A. (Wigan)
Ward, K. (Castleford)
Beardmore, K. (Castleford)
Dixon (Halifax)
Gregory, M. (Warrington)
Platt (St. Helens)
*Hanley (Wigan) 1t
Sub: Gill, H. (Wigan)
　　　Powell, R. (Leeds)

1988 Australia
Brisbane: 28 June
Lost 14-34
Loughlin (St. Helens) 3g
Gill, H. (Wigan)
Ford, P. (Bradford N.) 1t
*Hanley (Wigan)
Offiah (Widnes) 1t
Hulme, D. (Widnes)
Gregory, A. (Wigan)
Ward, K. (Castleford)
Beardmore, K. (Castleford)
Powell, R. (Leeds)
Dixon (Halifax)
Platt (St. Helens)
Gregory, M. (Warrington)
Sub: Wright, D. (Widnes)
　　　Hulme, P. (Widnes)

1988 Australia (Also WC)
Sydney: 9 July
Won 26-12
Ford, P. (Bradford N.) 1t
Gill, H. (Wigan) 2t
Stephenson (Leeds)
Loughlin (St. Helens) 3g
Offiah (Widnes) 1t
Hulme, D. (Widnes)
Gregory, A. (Wigan)
Ward, K. (Castleford)
Hulme, P. (Widnes)
Waddell (Oldham)
Gregory, M. (Warrington) 1t
Powell, R. (Leeds)
*Hanley (Wigan)
Sub: Case (Wigan)

1988 New Zealand (Also WC)
Christchurch: 17 July
Lost 10-12
Ford, P. (Bradford N.)
Gill, H. (Wigan)
Stephenson (Leeds)
Loughlin (St. Helens) 1t, 1g
Offiah (Widnes)
Hulme, D. (Widnes) 1t
Gregory, A. (Wigan)
Ward, K. (Castleford)
Beardmore, K. (Castleford)
Waddell (Oldham)
Gregory, M. (Warrington)
Powell, R. (Leeds)
*Hanley (Wigan)
Sub: Hulme, P. (Widnes)

1989 France
Wigan: 21 Jan.
Won 26-10
Tait (Widnes)
Ford, P. (Leeds) 1t
Loughlin (St. Helens) 3g
Lydon (Wigan) 1t
Offiah (Widnes) 1t
Edwards (Wigan) 1t
Gregory, A. (Wigan)
Ward, K. (Castleford)
Beardmore, K. (Castleford)
Waddell (Leeds)
Gregory, M. (Warrington)
Powell, R. (Leeds)
*Hanley (Wigan) 1t
Sub: Williams, P. (Salford)
　　　Eyres (Widnes)

1989 France
Avignon: 5 Feb.
Won: 30-8
Tait (Widnes) 1t
Ford, P. (Leeds) 2t
Williams, P. (Salford) 1t
Lydon (Wigan) 3g
Offiah (Widnes)
Edwards (Wigan) 1t
Gregory, A. (Wigan)
Ward, K. (Castleford)
Beardmore, K. (Castleford)
Crooks, L. (Leeds)
Gregory, M. (Warrington)
Powell, R. (Leeds)
*Hanley (Wigan) 1t
Sub: Hampson (Wigan)
　　　England (Castleford)

1989 New Zealand
Man U. FC: 21 Oct.
Lost 16-24
Tait (Widnes) 1t
Ford, P. (Leeds) 1t
Currier (Widnes)
Loughlin (St. Helens) 2g
Offiah (Widnes) 1t
Hulme, D. (Widnes)
Gregory, A. (Wigan)
Skerrett, K. (Bradford N.)
Beardmore, K. (Castleford)
Hobbs, D. (Bradford N.)
Goodway (Wigan)
Platt (Wigan)
*Gregory, M. (Warrington)
Sub: Edwards (Wigan)
    Newlove (Featherstone R.)

1989 New Zealand
Elland Rd, Leeds: 28 Oct.
Won 26-6
Hampson (Wigan)
Ford, P. (Leeds)
Newlove (Featherstone R.)
Loughlin (St. Helens) 5g
Offiah (Widnes) 1t
Edwards (Wigan) 1t
Hulme, D. (Widnes)
Skerrett, K. (Bradford N.)
Hulme, P. (Widnes)
Platt (Wigan)
Goodway (Wigan) 2t
Powell, R. (Leeds)
*Gregory, M. (Warrington)
Sub: Hobbs, D. (Bradford N.)
    Fox (Featherstone R.)

1989 New Zealand (Also WC)
Wigan: 11 Nov.
Won 10-6
Tait (Widnes) 1t
Ford, P. (Leeds)
Newlove (Featherstone R.)
Loughlin (St. Helens) 1g
Offiah (Widnes) 1t
Edwards (Wigan)
Hulme, D. (Widnes)
Skerrett, K. (Bradford N.)
Hulme, P. (Widnes)
Platt (Wigan)
Goodway (Wigan)
Powell, R. (Leeds)
*Gregory, M. (Warrington)
Sub: Lydon (Wigan)
    England (Castleford)

1990 France
Perpignan: 18 Mar.
Won 8-4
Tait (Widnes)
Lydon (Wigan)
Schofield (Leeds) 2g
Loughlin (St. Helens)
Offiah (Widnes) 1t
Edwards (Wigan)
Gregory, A. (Wigan)
Skerrett, K. (Bradford N.)
Beardmore, K. (Castleford)
Platt (Wigan)
Gregory, M. (Warrington)
Goodway (Wigan)
*Hanley (Wigan)
Sub: Powell, D. (Sheffield E.)
    Betts (Wigan)

1990 France
Leeds: 7 Apr.
Lost 18-25
Tait (Widnes) 1t
Cordle (Bradford N.) 1t
Schofield (Leeds)
Gibson (Leeds)
Offiah (Widnes) 1t
Steadman (Castleford) 3g
*Edwards (Wigan)
Skerrett, K. (Bradford N.)
Beardmore, K. (Castleford)
England (Castleford)
Betts (Wigan)
Fairbank (Bradford N.)
Gregory, M. (Warrington)
Sub: Irwin (Castleford)
    Bishop (Hull K.R.)

Phil Ford.

1990 Papua New Guinea
Goroka: 27 May
Lost 18-20
Tait (Widnes)
Eastwood (Hull) 1t
Powell, D. (Sheffield E.)
Davies (Widnes) 1t, 3g
Gibson (Leeds)
Schofield (Leeds)
Goulding (Wigan) 1t
Powell, R. (Leeds)
Jackson, L. (Hull)
Dixon (Leeds)
Betts (Wigan)
Fairbank (Bradford N.)
*Gregory, M. (Warrington)
Sub: Irwin (Castleford)
    England (Castleford)

1990 Papua New Guinea (Also WC)
Port Moresby: 2 June
Won 40-8
Tait (Widnes)
Eastwood (Hull) 1t
Davies (Widnes) 6g
Powell, D. (Sheffield E.) 1t
Gibson (Leeds) 2t
Schofield (Leeds) 1t
Goulding (Wigan) 1t
Powell, R. (Leeds)
Jackson, L. (Hull)
England (Castleford)
Betts (Wigan)
Dixon (Leeds) 1t
*Gregory, M. (Warrington)
Sub: Fox (Featherstone R.)
    Clarke (Wigan)

Mike Gregory.

313

1990 New Zealand
Palmerston North: 24 June
Won 11-10
Bibb (Featherstone R.)
Davies (Widnes) 1t, 1g
Lydon (Wigan)
Gibson (Leeds) 1t
Offiah (Widnes)
Schofield (Leeds) 1dg
Goulding (Wigan)
Skerrett, K. (Bradford N.)
Dermott (Wigan)
England (Castleford)
Betts (Wigan)
Dixon (Leeds)
*Gregory, M. (Warrington)
Sub: Powell, D. (Sheffield E.)
    Powell, R. (Leeds)

1990 Australia
Wembley: 27 Oct.
Won 19-12
Hampson (Wigan)
Eastwood (Hull) 2t, 3g
Powell, D. (Sheffield E.)
Gibson (Leeds)
Offiah (Widnes) 1t
Schofield (Leeds) 1dg
Gregory, A. (Wigan)
Harrison (Hull)
Jackson, L. (Hull)
Dixon (Leeds)
Betts (Wigan)
Powell, R. (Leeds)
*Hanley (Wigan)
Sub: Fairbank (Bradford N.)
    Ward, K. (St. Helens)

Carl Gibson.

1990 New Zealand
Auckland: 8 July
Won 16-14
Lydon (Wigan)
Davies (Widnes) 2g
Powell, D. (Sheffield E.)
Gibson (Leeds)
Offiah (Widnes) 1t
Schofield (Leeds) 1t
Goulding (Wigan)
Skerrett, K. (Bradford N.)
Jackson, L. (Hull)
England (Castleford)
Betts (Wigan) 1t
Dixon (Leeds)
*Gregory, M. (Warrington)
Sub: Irwin (Castleford)
    Powell, R. (Leeds)

1990 Australia
Man U. FC: 10 Nov.
Lost 10-14
Hampson (Wigan)
Eastwood (Hull) 1g
Powell, D. (Sheffield E.)
Gibson (Leeds)
Offiah (Widnes)
Schofield (Leeds)
Gregory, A. (Wigan)
Harrison (Hull)
Jackson, L. (Hull)
Platt (Wigan)
Betts (Wigan)
Dixon (Leeds) 1t
*Hanley (Wigan)
Sub: Loughlin (St. Helens) 1t
    Ward, K. (St. Helens)

1991 France (Also WC)
Perpignan: 27 Jan.
Won 45-10
Hampson (Wigan)
Eastwood (Hull) 6g
Powell, D. (Sheffield E.)
Gibson (Leeds)
Offiah (Widnes) 2t
Schofield (Leeds) 2t, 1dg
Edwards (Wigan) 2t
Lucas (Wigan)
Jackson, L. (Hull)
Platt (Wigan) 1t
Betts (Wigan) 1t
Holliday (Widnes)
*Hanley (Wigan)
Sub: Aston (Sheffield E.)
    Ellis, S. (Castleford)
    Fairbank (Bradford N.)
    Eyres (Widnes)

1990 New Zealand (Also WC)
Christchurch: 15 July
Lost 18-21
Lydon (Wigan)
Davies (Widnes) 3g
Gibson (Leeds)
Powell, D. (Sheffield E.)
Offiah (Widnes) 1t
Schofield (Leeds) 1t
Goulding (Wigan)
Skerrett, K. (Bradford N.)
Dermott (Wigan)
England (Castleford)
Betts (Wigan)
Powell, R. (Leeds) 1t
*Gregory, M. (Warrington)
Sub: Irwin (Castleford)
    Dixon (Leeds)

1990 Australia (Also WC)
Elland Rd, Leeds: 24 Nov.
Lost 0-14
Hampson (Wigan)
Eastwood (Hull)
Powell, D. (Sheffield E.)
Gibson (Leeds)
Offiah (Widnes)
Schofield (Leeds)
Gregory, A. (Wigan)
Harrison (Hull)
Jackson, L. (Hull)
Platt (Wigan)
Betts (Wigan)
Dixon (Leeds)
*Hanley (Wigan)
Sub: Davies (Widnes)
    Gregory, M. (Warrington)
    Powell, R. (Leeds)

1991 France
Leeds: 16 Feb.
Won 60-4
Hampson (Wigan) 1t
Eastwood (Hull) 1t, 8g
Powell, D. (Sheffield E.)
Loughlin (St. Helens)
Offiah (Widnes) 5t
Schofield (Leeds) 3t
Edwards (Wigan) 1t
Dannatt (Hull)
Jackson, L. (Hull)
Platt (Wigan)
Eyres (Widnes)
Fairbank (Bradford N.)
*Hanley (Wigan)
Sub: Ellis, K. (Warrington)
    Ellis, S. (Castleford)
    England (Castleford)
    Powell, R. (Leeds)

1991 Papua New Guinea (Also WC)
Wigan: 9 Nov.
Won 56-4
Hampson (Wigan)
Newlove (Featherstone R.) 1t
Powell, D. (Sheffield E.) 1t
Davies (Widnes) 8g
Sullivan, A. (St. Helens) 1t
*Schofield (Leeds) 1t
Edwards (Wigan)
Harrison (Halifax)
Dermott (Wigan)
Platt (Wigan)
Betts (Wigan) 1t
Moriarty (Widnes) 2t
Jackson, M. (Wakefield T.) 2t
Sub: Connolly (St. Helens)
　　 Fox (Featherstone R.)
　　 Fairbank (Bradford N.) 1t
　　 Price, G.H. (Wakefield T.)

1992 France
Perpignan: 16 Feb.
Won 30-12
Tait (Widnes)
Devereux (Widnes) 1t
Connolly (St. Helens)
*Davies (Widnes) 3g
Bentley, J. (Leeds) 1t
Griffiths (St. Helens) 1t
Goulding (Leeds)
Crooks, L. (Castleford)
Jackson, L. (Hull)
Dixon (Leeds)
Fairbank (Bradford N.)
Jackson, M. (Wakefield T.)
Holliday (Widnes)
Sub: Powell, D. (Sheffield E.)
　　 Steadman (Castleford) 2t
　　 Jones, M. (Hull)
　　 Eyres (Widnes) 1t

1992 France (Also WC)
Hull: 7 Mar.
Won 36-0
Steadman (Castleford)
Eastwood (Hull) 1t, 6g
Connolly (St. Helens)
Bateman (Warrington)
Hunte (St. Helens) 1t
Powell, D. (Sheffield E.)
*Edwards (Wigan)
Crooks, L. (Castleford)
Dermott (Wigan) 1t
Skerrett, K. (Wigan)
Betts (Wigan)
Fairbank (Bradford N.)
Holliday (Widnes) 1t
Sub: Fox (Featherstone R.) 1t
　　 Platt (Wigan) 1t
　　 McNamara (Hull)

1992 Papua New Guinea
Port Moresby: 31 May
Won 20-14
Hampson (Wigan)
Eastwood (Hull) 1t
*Schofield (Leeds)
Loughlin (St. Helens) 2g
Offiah (Wigan) 2t
Powell, D. (Sheffield E.)
Edwards (Wigan)
Crooks, L. (Castleford)
Dermott (Wigan)
Platt (Wigan)
Betts (Wigan)
Fairbank (Bradford N.)
Clarke (Wigan) 1t
Sub: Lydon (Wigan)
　　 Skerrett, K. (Wigan)
　　 Newlove (Featherstone R.)
　　 Nickle (St. Helens)

Paul Moriarty.

Billy McGinty.

1992 Australia
Sydney: 12 June
Lost 6-22
Steadman (Castleford)
Newlove (Featherstone R.)
Powell, D. (Sheffield E.)
Loughlin (St. Helens)
Offiah (Wigan)
*Schofield (Leeds)
Gregory, A. (Wigan)
Skerrett, K. (Wigan)
Dermott (Wigan)
Crooks, L. (Castleford) 1g
Betts (Wigan)
Platt (Wigan)
Clarke (Wigan)
Sub: Edwards (Wigan)
　　 Jackson, M. (Wakefield T.)
　　 Lydon (Wigan) 1t
　　 Lucas (Wigan)

1992 Australia
Melbourne: 26 June
Won 33-10
Steadman (Castleford) 1t
Eastwood (Hull) 6g
Newlove (Featherstone R.) 1t
Powell, D. (Sheffield E.)
Offiah (Wigan) 1t
*Schofield (Leeds) 1t, 1dg
Edwards (Wigan)
Skerrett, K. (Wigan)
Dermott (Wigan)
Platt (Wigan)
Betts (Wigan)
McGinty (Wigan)
Clarke (Wigan) 1t
Sub: Connolly (St. Helens)
　　 Hulme, P. (Widnes)
　　 Lydon (Wigan)
　　 Harrison (Halifax)

1992 Australia
Brisbane: 3 July
Lost 10-16
Steadman (Castleford) 3g
Eastwood (Hull)
Powell, D. (Sheffield E.)
Newlove (Featherstone R.)
Offiah (Wigan) 1t
*Schofield (Leeds)
Edwards (Wigan)
Skerrett, K. (Wigan)
Dermott (Wigan)
Platt (Wigan)
Betts (Wigan)
McGinty (Wigan)
Clarke (Wigan)
Sub: Connolly (St. Helens)
　　 Hulme, P. (Widnes)
　　 Lydon (Wigan)
　　 Harrison (Halifax)

1992 New Zealand
Palmerston North: 12 July
Lost 14-15
Steadman (Castleford)
Eastwood (Hull) 3g
Powell, D. (Sheffield E.)
Connolly (St. Helens)
Offiah (Wigan)
*Schofield (Leeds)
Edwards (Wigan) 1t
Skerrett, K. (Wigan)
Jackson, L. (Hull)
Platt (Wigan)
Betts (Wigan)
McGinty (Wigan)
Clarke (Wigan) 1t
Sub: Lydon (Wigan)
    Hulme, P. (Widnes)
    Harrison (Halifax)

Mike Ford.

1993 New Zealand
Wembley: 16 Oct.
Won 17-0
Davies (Warrington) 2g, 1dg
Robinson (Wigan) 2t
Newlove (Bradford N.)
Connolly (Wigan)
Devereux (Widnes) 1t
*Schofield (Leeds)
Edwards (Wigan)
Harrison (Halifax)
Dermott (Wigan)
Fairbank (Bradford N.)
Betts (Wigan)
Joynt (St. Helens)
Clarke (Wigan)
Sub: Powell, D. (Sheffield E.)
    Eyres (Leeds)
    Tait (Leeds)
    Nickle (St. Helens)

1992 New Zealand
Auckland: 19 July
Won 19-16
Steadman (Castleford)
Eastwood (Hull) 3g
Powell, D. (Sheffield E.)
Connolly (St. Helens)
Offiah (Wigan) 1t
*Schofield (Leeds) 1dg
Edwards (Wigan)
Harrison (Halifax)
Jackson, L. (Hull) 1t
Platt (Wigan)
Betts (Wigan) 1t
McGinty (Wigan)
Clarke (Wigan)
Sub: Newlove (Featherstone R.)
    Jackson, M. (Wakefield T.)
    Devereux (Widnes)
    Fairbank (Bradford N.)

1993 France
Carcassonne: 7 Mar.
Won 48-6
Spruce (Widnes)
Devereux (Widnes) 1t
Currier (Widnes) 6g
Connolly (St. Helens)
Hunte (St. Helens)
*Schofield (Leeds) 3t
Edwards (Wigan) 1t
Cowie (Wigan)
McCurrie (Widnes)
Molloy (Leeds)
Eyres (Widnes) 1t
Clarke (Wigan)
Hanley (Leeds) 2t
Sub: Ford, M. (Castleford) 1t
    Joynt (St. Helens)
    Bateman (Warrington)
    McNamara (Hull)

1993 New Zealand
Wigan: 30 Oct.
Won 29-12
Davies (Warrington) 4g
Devereux (Widnes) 2t
Connolly (Wigan)
Newlove (Bradford N.) 1t
Offiah (Wigan) 1t
*Schofield (Leeds) 1t, 1dg
Edwards (Wigan)
Harrison (Halifax)
Jackson, L. (Sheffield E.)
Fairbank (Bradford N.)
Nickle (St. Helens)
Joynt (St. Helens)
Clarke (Wigan)
Sub: Powell, D. (Sheffield E.)
    Eyres (Leeds)
    Tait (Leeds)
    Jackson, M. (Halifax)

1992 Australia (WC Final)
Wembley: 24 Oct.
Lost 6-10
Lydon (Wigan)
Hunte (St. Helens)
Connolly (St. Helens)
*Schofield (Leeds)
Offiah (Wigan)
Edwards (Wigan)
Fox (Bradford N.) 3g
Ward, K. (St. Helens)
Dermott (Wigan)
Platt (Wigan)
Betts (Wigan)
Clarke (Wigan)
Hanley (Leeds)
Sub: Devereux (Widnes)
    Tait (Leeds)
    Skerrett, K. (Wigan)
    Eyres (Widnes)

1993 France
Leeds: 2 Apr.
Won 72-6
Tait (Leeds) 2t
Devereux (Widnes) 1t
Newlove (Featherstone R.) 3t
Connolly (St. Helens)
Hunte (St. Helens) 2t
Davies (Widnes) 10g
Edwards (Wigan) 2t
Harrison (Halifax)
Dermott (Wigan)
*Platt (Wigan)
Betts (Wigan) 1t
Eyres (Widnes)
Clarke (Wigan)
Sub: Ford, M. (Castleford) 1t
    Fairbank (Bradford N.)
    Powell, D. (Sheffield E.) 1t
    Nickle (St. Helens)

1993 New Zealand
Leeds: 6 Nov.
Won 29-10
Davies (Warrington) 1t, 4g, 1dg
Devereux (Widnes)
Connolly (Wigan)
Newlove (Bradford N.)
Offiah (Wigan) 1t
*Schofield (Leeds)
Edwards (Wigan)
Skerrett, K. (Wigan)
Jackson, L. (Sheffield E.)
Fairbank (Bradford N.) 1t
Farrell (Wigan) 1t
Joynt (St. Helens)
Clarke (Wigan) 1t
Sub: Powell, D. (Sheffield E.)
    Nickle (St. Helens)
    Tait (Leeds)
    Jackson, M. (Halifax)

1994 France
Carcassonne: 20 Mar.
Won 12-4
Steadman (Castleford)
Bentley, J. (Halifax)
Connolly (Wigan)
Newlove (Bradford N.) 1t
Offiah (Wigan)
*Schofield (Leeds)
Edwards (Wigan) 1t
Crooks, L. (Castleford) 1g
Jackson, L. (Sheffield E.)
Molloy (Featherstone R.)
Farrell (Wigan) 1g
Fairbank (Bradford N.)
Joynt (St. Helens)
Sub: Ellis, S. (Castleford)
    Moriarty (Widnes)
    Powell, D. (Sheffield E.)
    Mather (Wigan)

1994 Australia
Wembley: 22 Oct.
Won 8-4
Davies (Warrington) 1t, 1g
Robinson (Wigan)
Connolly (Wigan)
Hunte (St. Helens)
Offiah (Wigan)
Powell, D. (Sheffield E.)
*Edwards (Wigan)
Harrison (Halifax)
Jackson, L. (Sheffield E.)
Joynt (St. Helens)
Betts (Wigan)
Farrell (Wigan)
Clarke (Wigan)
Sub: Goulding (St. Helens) 1g
    McDermott, Barrie (Wigan)
    Bateman (Warrington)
    Cassidy (Wigan)

Barrie McDermott.

Graham Steadman.

1994 Australia
Man. U. FC: 5 Nov.
Lost 8-38
Steadman (Castleford)
Robinson (Wigan)
Connolly (Wigan)
Hunte (St. Helens)
Offiah (Wigan)
Powell, D. (Sheffield E.)
Goulding (St. Helens) 2g
Harrison (Halifax)
Jackson, L. (Sheffield E.)
Joynt (St. Helens)
Betts (Wigan)
Farrell (Wigan)
*Clarke (Wigan)
Sub: Schofield (Leeds)
    McDermott, Barrie (Wigan)
    Newlove (Bradford N.) 1t
    Cassidy (Wigan)

1996 Papua New Guinea
Lae: 28 Sept.
Won: 32-30
Spruce (Bradford B.)
Hayes (St. Helens)
Radlinski (Wigan) 2t
Hunte (St. Helens)
Sullivan, A. (St. Helens) 1t
Harris (Warrington)
Goulding (St. Helens) 1t, 6g
Broadbent (Sheffield E.)
Cunningham, K. (St. Helens) 1t
O'Connor (Wigan)
Betts (Auckland W.)
Joynt (St. Helens)
*Farrell (Wigan)
Sub: Smith, T. (Castleford)
    Phillips (Workington T.)
    Powell, D. (Keighley C.)
    Sculthorpe (Warrington)

Lee Crooks.

1994 Australia
Elland Rd, Leeds: 20 Nov.
Lost 4-23
Connolly (Wigan)
Robinson (Wigan)
Hunte (St. Helens)
Newlove (Bradford N.)
Offiah (Wigan)
Clarke (Wigan)
*Edwards (Wigan)
Harrison (Halifax)
Jackson, L. (Sheffield E.)
McDermott, Barrie (Wigan)
Betts (Wigan)
Farrell (Wigan) 2g
Joynt (St. Helens)
Sub: Goulding (St. Helens)
    Powell, D. (Sheffield E.)
    Schofield (Leeds)
    Nickle (St. Helens)

1996 Fiji
Nadi: 5 Oct.
Won: 72-4
Spruce (Bradford B.) 2t
Hunte (St. Helens) 2t
Radlinski (Wigan)
Powell, D. (Keighley C.) 2t
Sullivan, A. (St. Helens) 1t
Harris (Warrington)
Goulding (St. Helens) 3t, 10g
Broadbent (Sheffield E.)
Cunningham, K. (St. Helens)
McDermott, Brian (Bradford B.)
Betts (Auckland W.)
Sculthorpe (Warrington)
*Farrell (Wigan) 1t
Sub: Smith, T. (Castleford)
    Senior (Sheffield E.) 1t
    Molloy (Featherstone R.)
    Cassidy (Wigan) 1t

1996 New Zealand
Auckland: 18 Oct.
Lost 12-17
Spruce (Bradford B.)
Hunte (St. Helens) 1t
Radlinski (Wigan)
Powell, D. (Keighley C.)
Sullivan, A. (St. Helens)
Harris (Warrington)
Goulding (St. Helens) 2g
Broadbent (Sheffield E.)
Cunningham, K. (St. Helens)
O'Connor (Wigan)
Betts (Auckland W.) 1t
Sculthorpe (Warrington)
*Farrell (Wigan)
  Sub: Joynt (St. Helens)
        Morley, A. (Leeds)
        Senior (Sheffield E.)

1997 Australia SL
Wembley: 1 Nov.
Lost 14-38
Robinson (Wigan W.) 1t
Hunte (St. Helens)
Radlinski (Wigan W.)
Newlove (St. Helens)
Sullivan (St. Helens)
*Farrell (Wigan W.) 3g
Goulding (St. Helens)
McDermott, Brian (Bradford B.)
Lowes (Bradford B.) 1t
Broadbent (Sheffield E.)
Joynt (St. Helens)
Cassidy (Wigan W.)
Sculthorpe (Warrington W.)
Sub: McNamara (Bradford B.)
      Atcheson (St. Helens)
      Morley, A. (Leeds R.)
      Sampson (Castleford T.)

1998 New Zealand
Huddersfield: 31 October
Lost 16-22
Radlinski (Wigan W.)
Robinson (Wigan W.) 1t
Connolly (Wigan W.)
Newlove (St. Helens) 1t
Senior (Sheffield E.) 1t
*Farrell (Wigan W.) 2g
Smith, T. (Wigan W.)
Cowie (Wigan W.)
Cunningham, K. (St. Helens)
Fleary (Leeds R.)
Joynt (St. Helens)
Gilmour (Wigan W.)
Sculthorpe (St. Helens)
Sub: Harris (Leeds R.)
      Haughton (Wigan W.)
      O'Connor (Wigan W.)
      Laughton (Sheffield E.)

1996 New Zealand
Palmerston North: 25 Oct.
Lost 15-18
Spruce (Bradford B.)
Hunte (St. Helens) 1t
Radlinski (Wigan)
Powell, D. (Keighley C.)
Sullivan, A. (St. Helens)
Harris (Warrington)
Goulding (St. Helens) 3g, dg
Broadbent (Sheffield E.)
Cunningham, K. (St. Helens)
O'Connor (Wigan)
Betts (Auckland W.) 1t
Sculthorpe (Warrington)
*Farrell (Wigan)
  Sub: Mather (Perth Western
        Reds)
        Molloy (Featherstone R.)
        Hammond (St. Helens)
        Joynt (St. Helens)

1997 Australia SL
Man. U. FC: 8 Nov.
Won 20-12
Atcheson (St. Helens)
Robinson (Wigan W.) 1t
Radlinski (Wigan W.)
Newlove (St. Helens)
Hunte (St. Helens)
*Farrell (Wigan W.) 6g, 1t
Goulding (St. Helens)
McDermott, Brian (Bradford B.)
Lowes (Bradford B.)
Broadbent (Sheffield E.)
Joynt (St. Helens)
Morley, A. (Leeds R.)
Sculthorpe (Warrington W.)
Sub: Haughton (Wigan W.)
      Forshaw (Bradford B.)

1998 New Zealand
Bolton: 7 November
Lost 16-36
Radlinski (Wigan W.)
Robinson (Wigan W.) 1t
Connolly (Wigan W.)
Senior (Sheffield E.)
Cummins (Leeds R.)
Harris (Leeds R.) 1t
Smith, T. (Wigan W.)
Cowie (Wigan W.)
Cunningham, K. (St. Helens)
Laughton (Sheffield E.)
Joynt (St. Helens)
Sculthorpe (St. Helens)
*Farrell (Wigan W.) 4g
Sub: O'Connor (Wigan W.)
      Haughton (Wigan W.)
      Howard (Bradford B.)
      Gilmour (Wigan W.)

1996 New Zealand
Christchurch: 1 Nov.
Lost 12-32
Spruce (Bradford B.)
Hunte (St. Helens)
Radlinski (Wigan)
Powell, D. (Keighley C.)
Mather (Perth Western Reds)
Hammond (St. Helens)
Goulding (St. Helens) 2g
Broadbent (Sheffield E.)
Cunningham, K. (St. Helens)
O'Connor (Wigan)
Betts (Auckland W.) 1t
Sculthorpe (Warrington)
*Farrell (Wigan)
  Sub: Harris (Warrington)
        Morley, A. (Leeds) 1t
        Joynt (St. Helens)
        Dwyer (Bradford B.)

1997 Australia SL
Elland Rd, Leeds: 16 Nov.
Lost 20-37
Atcheson (St. Helens)
Robinson (Wigan W.) 1t
Radlinski (Wigan W.)
Newlove (St. Helens)
Hunte (St. Helens)
*Farrell (Wigan W.) 4g
Goulding (St. Helens)
McDermott, Brian (Bradford B.)
Lowes (Bradford B.)
Broadbent (Sheffield E.)
Joynt (St. Helens)
Morley, A. (Leeds R.)
Sculthorpe (Warrington W.)
Sub: McNamara (Bradford B.)
      Haughton (Wigan W.) 2t
      Long (St. Helens)
      Forshaw (Bradford B.)

1998 New Zealand
Watford: 14 November
Drew 23-23
Radlinski (Wigan W.)
Robinson (Wigan W.) 1t
Connolly (Wigan W.)
Senior (Sheffield E.)
Cummins (Leeds R.)
Long (St. Helens) 1t
Smith, T. (Wigan W.) 1t, 1dg
O'Connor (Wigan W.)
Newton (Leeds R.)
Laughton (Sheffield E.)
Joynt (St. Helens)
Sculthorpe (St. Helens)
*Farrell (Wigan W.) 5g
Sub: Forshaw (Bradford B.)
      Haughton (Wigan W.)
      Fleary (Leeds R.)

GREAT BRITAIN REGISTER

The following is a record of the 643 players who have appeared for Great Britain in 296 Test and World Cup matches.

It does not include matches against France before 1957, the year they were given official Test match status.

Figures in brackets are the total of appearances, with the plus sign indicating substitute appearances, e.g. (7+3).

For matches against touring teams, the year given is for the first half of the season.

World Cup matches are in bold letters except when also classified as Test matches. Substitute appearances are in lower case letters.

Key: A - Australia; ASL – Australia Super League; F - France; NZ - New Zealand; P - Papua New Guinea.

ACKERLEY, Alvin (2) Halifax: 1952 A; 1958 NZ
ADAMS, Les (1) Leeds: 1932 A
ADAMS, Mick (11+2) Widnes: 1979 Aa,NZ3; 1980 NZ; 1984 A2a,NZ3,P
ARKWRIGHT, Chris (+2) St. Helens: 1985 nz2
ARKWRIGHT, Jack (6) Warrington: 1936 A2,NZ; 1937 A3
ARMITT, Tom (8) Swinton: 1933 A; 1936 A2,NZ2; 1937 A3
ASHBY, Ray (2) Liverpool: 1964 F; Wigan: 1965 F
ASHCROFT, Ernest (11) Wigan: 1947 NZ2; 1950 A3,NZ; 1954 A3,NZ2
ASHCROFT, Kevin (5+1) Leigh: **1968 A**; 1968 F; 1969 F; **1970 F,NZ**; Warrington: 1974 nz
ASHTON, Eric (26) Wigan: **1957 A,NZ**; 1958 A2,NZ2; 1959 F,A3; 1960 F2; **1960 NZ,A**; 1961 NZ3; 1962 F3,A3; 1963 F,A2
ASHURST, Bill (3) Wigan: 1971 NZ; 1972 F2
ASKIN, Tommy (6) Featherstone R: 1928 A3,NZ3
ASPINALL, Willie (1) Warrington: 1966 NZ
ASTON, Len (3) St. Helens: 1947 NZ3
ASTON, Mark (+1) Sheffield E: 1991 f
ATCHESON, Paul (2+1) St. Helens 1977 asl, ASL2
ATKINSON, Arthur (11) Castleford: 1929 A3; 1932 A3,NZ3; 1933 A; 1936 A
ATKINSON, John (26) Leeds: **1968 F,NZ**; 1970 A3,NZ3; **1970 A2,F,NZ**; 1971 F2,NZ; 1972 F2; **1972 A2,F,NZ**; 1973 A2; 1978 A2; 1980 NZ
AVERY, Albert (4) Oldham: 1910 A,NZ; 1911 A2

BACON, Jim (11) Leeds: 1920 A3,NZ3; 1921 A3; 1924 A; 1926 NZ
BARENDS, David (2) Bradford N: 1979 A2
BARTON, Frank (1) Wigan: 1951 NZ

BARTON, John (2) Wigan: 1960 F; 1961 NZ
BASNETT, John (2) Widnes: 1984 F; 1986 A
BASSETT, Arthur (2) Halifax: 1946 A2
BATEMAN, Allan (1+2) Warrington: 1992 F; 1993 f; 1994 a
BATES, Alan (2+2) Dewsbury: 1974 F2, nz2
BATTEN, Billy (10) Hunslet: 1907 NZ; 1908 A3; 1910 A2, NZ; 1911 A2; Hull: 1921 A
BATTEN, Eric (4) Bradford N: 1946 A2,NZ; 1947 NZ
BATTEN, Ray (3) Leeds: 1969 F; 1973 A2
BAXTER, Johnnie (1) Rochdale H: 1907 NZ
BEAMES, Jack (2) Halifax: 1921 A2
BEARDMORE, Kevin (13+1) Castleford: 1984 nz; 1987 F2; 1988 F2,P,A2,NZ; 1989 F2,NZ; 1990 F2
BELSHAW, Billy (8) Liverpool S: 1936 A3,NZ2; 1937 A; Warrington: 1937 A2
BENNETT, Jack (7) Rochdale H: 1924 A3,NZ3; Wigan: 1926 NZ
BENTHAM, Billy (2) Broughton R: 1924 NZ2
BENTHAM, Nat (10) Wigan H: 1928 A3,NZ3; Halifax: 1929 A2; Warrington: 1929 A2
BENTLEY, John (2) Leeds: 1992 F; Halifax: 1994 F
BENTLEY, Keith (1) Widnes: 1980 NZ
BENYON, Billy (5+1) St. Helens: 1971 F2,NZnz; 1972 F2
BETTS, Denis (29+1) Wigan: 1990 fF,P2,NZ3,A3; 1991 F,P; 1992 F,P,A3,NZ2, **A**; 1993 F,NZ; 1994 A3; 1996 Auckland W: P,Fiji,NZ3
BEVAN, Dai (1) Warrington: 1952 A
BEVAN, John (6) Warrington: 1974 A2,NZ2; 1978 A2
BEVERLEY, Harry (6) Hunslet: 1936 A3; 1937 A; Halifax: 1937 A2
BIBB, Chris (1) Featherstone R: 1990 NZ
BIRCH, Jim (1) Leeds: 1907 NZ
BISHOP, David (+1) Hull KR: 1990 f
BISHOP, Tommy (15) St. Helens: 1966 A3,NZ2; 1967 A3; 1968 F3; **1968 A,F,NZ**; 1969 F
BLAN, Billy (3) Wigan: 1951 NZ3
BLINKHORN, Tom (1) Warrington: 1929 A
BOLTON, Dave (23) Wigan: 1957 F3; 1958 F,A2; 1959 F,A3; 1960 F2; 1961 NZ3; 1962 F2,A,NZ2; 1963 F,A2
BOSTON, Billy (31) Wigan: 1954 A2,NZ3; 1955 NZ; 1956 A3; 1957 F5; **1957 F,A**; 1958 F; 1959 A; 1960 F; **1960 A**; 1961 F,NZ3; 1962 F2,A3,NZ; 1963 F
BOTT, Charlie (1) Oldham: 1966 F
BOWDEN, Jim (3) Huddersfield: 1954 A2,NZ
BOWEN, Frank (3) St. Helens Recs: 1928 NZ3
BOWERS, Joe (1) Rochdale H: 1920 NZ
BOWMAN, Eddie (4) Workington T: **1977 F,NZ,A2**
BOWMAN, Harold (8) Hull: 1924 NZ2; 1926 NZ2; 1928 A2,NZ; 1929 A
BOWMAN, Ken (3) Huddersfield: 1962 F; 1963 F,A
BOYLEN, Frank (1) Hull: 1908 A
BRADSHAW, Tommy (6) Wigan: 1947 NZ2; 1950 A3,NZ
BRIDGES, John "Keith" (3) Featherstone R: 1974 F2,A
BRIGGS, Brian (1) Huddersfield: 1954 NZ
BROADBENT, Paul (8) Sheffield E.: 1996 P,Fiji,NZ3; 1997 ASL3

BROGDEN, Stan (16) Huddersfield: 1929 A; 1932 A3, NZ3; 1933 A2; Leeds: 1936 A3,NZ2; 1937 A2

BROOKE, Ian (13) Bradford N: 1966 A3, NZ2; Wakefield T: 1967 A3; 1968 F2; **1968 A,F,NZ**

BROOKS, Ernie (3) Warrington: 1908 A3

BROUGH, Albert (2) Oldham: 1924 A,NZ

BROUGH, Jim (5) Leeds: 1928 A2,NZ2; 1936 A

BROWN, Gordon (6) Leeds: **1954 F2,NZ,A**; 1955 NZ2

BRYANT, Bill (4+1) Castleford: 1964 F2; 1966 Aa; 1967 F

BUCKLEY, Alan (7) Swinton: 1963 A; 1964 F; 1965 NZ; 1966 F,A2,NZ

BURGESS, Bill (16) Barrow: 1924 A3,NZ3; 1926 NZ3; 1928 A3,NZ2; 1929 A2

BURGESS, Bill (14) Barrow: 1962 F; 1963 A; 1965 NZ2; 1966 F,A3,NZ2; 1967 F,A; 1968 F; Salford: 1969 F

BURGHAM, Oliver (1) Halifax: 1911 A

BURKE, Mick (14+1) Widnes: 1980 NZ; 1981 fF; 1983 F; 1984 A3,NZ3,P; 1985 NZ3; 1986 F

BURNELL, Alf (3) Hunslet: 1951 NZ2; 1954 NZ

BURTON, Chris (8+1) Hull KR: 1982 A; 1984 A3,NZ2; 1985 nz; 1986 A; 1987 F

BURWELL, Alan (7+1) Hull KR: 1967 a; 1968 F3; **1968 A,F,NZ**; 1969 F

BUTTERS, Fred (2) Swinton: 1929 A2

CAIRNS, David (2) Barrow: 1984 F2

CAMILLERI, Chris (2) Barrow: 1980 NZ2

CARLTON, Frank (2) St. Helens: 1958 NZ; Wigan: 1962 NZ

CARR, Charlie (7) Barrow: 1924 A2,NZ2; 1926 NZ3

CARTWRIGHT, Joe (7) Leigh: 1920 A,NZ3; 1921 A3

CASE, Brian (6+1) Wigan: 1984 A,NZ3; 1987 P; 1988 P,a

CASEY, Len (12+2) Hull KR: **1977 f,nz,A**; 1978 A; Bradford N: 1979 A2,NZ3; Hull KR: 1980 NZ3; 1983 F2

CASSIDY, Mick (1+3) Wigan: 1994 a2; 1996 fiji; 1997 ASL

CASTLE, Frank (4) Barrow: 1952 A3; 1954 A

CHALLINOR, Jim (3) Warrington: 1958 A,NZ; **1960 F**

CHARLTON, Paul (18+1) Workington T: 1965 NZ; Salford: **1970 nz**; 1972 F2; **1972 A2,F,NZ**; 1973 A3; 1974 F2,A3,NZ3

CHERRINGTON, Norman (1) Wigan: 1960 F

CHILCOTT, Jack (3) Huddersfield: 1914 A3

CHISNALL, Dave (2) Leigh: 1970 A; **1970 NZ**

CHISNALL, Eric (4) St. Helens: 1974 A2,NZ2

CLAMPITT, Jim (3) Broughton R: 1907 NZ; 1911 A; 1914 NZ

CLARK, Doug (11) Huddersfield: 1911 A2; 1914 A3; 1920 A3,NZ3

CLARK, Garry (3) Hull KR: 1984 F2; 1985 F

CLARK, Mick (5) Leeds: 1968 F2; **1968 A,F,NZ**

CLARKE, Colin (7) Wigan: 1965 NZ; 1966 F,NZ; 1967 F; 1973 A3

CLARKE, Phil (15+1) Wigan: 1990 p; 1992 P,A3,NZ2, **A**; 1993 F2,NZ3; 1994 A3

CLAWSON, Terry (14) Featherstone R: 1962 F2; Leeds:

1972 A2,F; Oldham: 1973 A3; 1974 F2,A2,NZ2

CLOSE, Don (1) Huddersfield: 1967 F

COLDRICK, Percy (4) Wigan: 1914 A3,NZ

COLLIER, Frank (2) Wigan: 1963 A; Widnes: 1964 F

CONNOLLY, Gary (17+3) St. Helens: 1991 p; 1992 F2,a2,NZ2,**A**; 1993 F2; Wigan: 1993 NZ3; 1994 F,A3; 1998 NZ3

CORDLE, Gerald (1) Bradford N: 1990 F

COULMAN, Mike (2+1) Salford: 1971 f,NZ2

COURTNEY, Neil (+1) Warrington: 1982 a

COVERDALE, Bob (4) Hull: **1954 F2,NZ,A**

COWIE, Neil (3) Wigan: 1993 F; 1998 NZ2

CRACKNELL, Dick (2) Huddersfield: 1951 NZ2

CRANE, Mick (1) Hull: 1982 A

CREASSER, David (2+2) Leeds: 1985 F2; 1987 f; 1988 f

CROOKS, Lee (17+2) Hull: 1982 A2; 1984 f,A2; 1985 NZnz; 1986 F2,A3; 1987 F; Leeds: 1989 F; Castleford: 1992 F2,P,A; 1994 F

CROSTON, Jim (1) Castleford: 1937 A

CROWTHER, Hector (1) Hunslet: 1929 A

CUMMINS, Francis (2) Leeds R.: 1998 NZ2

CUNLIFFE, Billy (11) Warrington: 1920 A,NZ2; 1921 A3; 1924 A3,NZ; 1926 NZ

CUNLIFFE, Jack (4) Wigan: 1950 A,NZ; 1951 NZ; 1954 A

CUNNIFFE, Bernard (1) Castleford: 1937 A

CUNNINGHAM, Eddie (1) St. Helens: 1978 A

CUNNINGHAM, Keiron (7) St. Helens: 1996 P,Fiji,NZ3; 1998 NZ2.

CURRAN, George (6) Salford: 1946 A,NZ; 1947 NZ; 1948 A3

CURRIER, Andy (2) Widnes: 1989 NZ; 1993 F

CURZON, Ephraim (1) Salford: 1910 A

DAGNALL, Bob (4) St. Helens: 1961 NZ2; 1964 F; 1965 F

DALGREEN, John (1) Fulham: 1982 A

DANBY, Tom (3) Salford: 1950 A2,NZ

DANIELS, Arthur (3) Halifax: 1952 A2; 1955 NZ

DANNATT, Andy (3) Hull: 1985 F2; 1991 F

DARWELL, Joe (5) Leigh: 1924 A3,NZ2

DAVIES, Alan (20) Oldham: 1955 NZ; 1956 A3; **1957 F,A**; 1957 F2; 1958 F,A2,NZ2; 1959 F2,A; **1960 NZ,F,A**; 1960 F

DAVIES, Billy (1) Swinton: 1968 F

DAVIES, Billy J (1) Castleford: 1933 A

DAVIES, Evan (3) Oldham: 1920 NZ3

DAVIES, Jim (2) Huddersfield: 1911 A2

DAVIES, Jonathan (12+1) Widnes: 1990 P2,NZ3,a; 1991 P; 1992 F; 1993 F; Warrington: 1993 NZ3; 1994 A

DAVIES, Will T (1) Halifax: 1911 A

DAVIES, Willie A (2) Leeds: 1914 A,NZ

DAVIES, Willie T.H. (3) Bradford N: 1946 NZ; 1947 NZ2

DAWSON, Edgar (1) York: 1956 A

DERMOTT, Martin (11) Wigan: 1990 NZ2; 1991 P; 1992 F,P,A3,**A**; 1993 F,NZ

DEVEREUX, John (6+2) Widnes: 1992 F,nz,a; 1993 F2,NZ3

DICK, Kevin (2) Leeds: 1980 NZ2

DICKENSON, George (1) Warrington: 1908 A
DICKINSON, Roy (2) Leeds: 1985 F2
DINGSDALE, Billy (3) Warrington: 1929 A2; 1933 A
DIVORTY, Gary (2) Hull: 1985 F2
DIXON, Colin (12+2) Halifax: 1968 F; Salford: 1969 F; 1971 NZ; **1972 F**; 1973 a2; 1974 F2,A3,NZ3
DIXON, Malcolm (2) Featherstone R: 1962 F; 1964 F
DIXON, Paul (11+4) Halifax: 1987 f; 1988 fF,p,A2; Leeds: 1990 P2,NZ2nz,A3; 1992 F
DOCKAR, Alec (1) Hull KR: 1947 NZ
DONLAN, Steve (+2) Leigh: 1984 nz,p
DRAKE, Bill (1) Hull: 1962 F
DRAKE, Jim (1) Hull: 1960 F
DRUMMOND, Des (24) Leigh: 1980 NZ2; 1981 F2; 1982 A3; 1983 F2; 1984 F,A3,NZ3,P; 1985 NZ3; 1986 F2; Warrington: 1987 P; 1988 F
DUANE, Ronnie (3) Warrington: 1983 F2; 1984 F
DUTTON, Ray (6) Widnes: 1970 NZ2; **1970 A2,F,NZ**
DWYER, Bernard (+1) Bradford B.: 1996 nz
DYL, Les (11) Leeds: 1974 A2,NZ3; **1977 F,NZ,A2**; 1978 A; 1982 A
DYSON, Frank (1) Huddersfield: 1959 A

EASTWOOD, Paul (13) Hull: 1990 P2,A3; 1991 F2; 1992 F,P,A2,NZ2
ECCLES, Bob (1) Warrington: 1982 A
ECCLES, Percy (1) Halifax: 1907 NZ
ECKERSLEY, David (2+2) St. Helens: 1973 Aa; 1974 Aa
EDGAR, Brian (11) Workington T: 1958 A,NZ; 1961 NZ; 1962 A3,NZ; 1965 NZ; 1966 A3
EDWARDS, Alan (7) Salford: 1936 A3,NZ2; 1937 A2
EDWARDS, Derek (3+2) Castleford: 1968 f; 1970 A; 1971 NZ2nz
EDWARDS, Shaun (32+4) Wigan: 1985 F,nzNZ; 1986 a; 1987 F2,P; 1988 F2,P; 1989 F2,nzNZ2; 1990 F2; 1991 F2,P; 1992 F,P,aA2,NZ2,A; 1993 F2,NZ3; 1994 F,A2
EGAN, Joe (14) Wigan: 1946 A3; 1947 NZ3; 1948 A3; 1950 A3,NZ2
ELLABY, Alf (13) St. Helens: 1928 A3,NZ2; 1929 A2; 1932 A3,NZ2; 1933 A
ELLIS, Kevin (+1) Warrington: 1991 f
ELLIS, St. John (+3) Castleford: 1991 f2; 1994 f
ELWELL, Keith (3) Widnes: **1977 A**; 1980 NZ2
ENGLAND, Keith (6+5) Castleford: 1987 fF; 1989 f,nz; 1990 F,pP,NZ3; 1991 f
EVANS, Bryn (10) Swinton: 1926 NZ; 1928 NZ; 1929 A; 1932 A2,NZ3; 1933 A2
EVANS, Frank (4) Swinton: 1924 A2,NZ2
EVANS, Jack (4) Hunslet: 1951 NZ; 1952 A3
EVANS, Jack (3) Swinton: 1926 NZ3
EVANS, Roy (4) Wigan: 1961 NZ2; 1962 F,NZ
EVANS, Steve (7+3) Featherstone R: 1979 Aa2,NZ3; 1980 NZnz; Hull: 1982 A2
EYRE, Ken (1) Hunslet: 1965 NZ
EYRES, Richard (3+6) Widnes: 1989 f; 1991 fF; 1992 f,a; 1993 F2; Leeds: 1993 nz2

FAIRBAIRN, George (17) Wigan: **1977 F,NZ,A2**; 1978 A3; 1979 A2,NZ3; 1980 NZ2; Hull KR: 1981 F; 1982 A2
FAIRBANK, Karl (10+6) Bradford N: 1987 p; 1990 F,P,a; 1991 fF,p; 1992 F2,P,nz; 1993 f,NZ3; 1994 F
FAIRCLOUGH, Les (6) St. Helens: 1926 NZ; 1928 A2,NZ2; 1929 A
FARRAR, Vince (1) Hull: 1978 A
FARRELL, Andrew (16) Wigan: 1993 NZ; 1994 F, A3; 1996 P,Fiji,NZ3; 1997 ASL3; 1998 NZ3
FEATHERSTONE, Jim (6) Warrington: 1948 A; 1950 NZ2; 1952 A3
FEETHAM, Jack (8) Hull KR: 1929 A; Salford: 1932 A2,NZ2; 1933 A3
FIELD, Harry (3) York: 1936, A,NZ2
FIELD, Norman (1) Batley: 1963 A
FIELDHOUSE, John (7) Widnes: 1985 NZ3; 1986 F2,A; St. Helens: 1986 A
FIELDING, Keith (3) Salford: 1974 F2; **1977 F**
FILDES, Alec (15) St. Helens Recs: 1926 NZ2; 1928 A3,NZ3; 1929 A3; St. Helens: 1932, A,NZ3
FISHER, Tony (11) Bradford N: 1970 A2,NZ3; **1970 A;** Leeds: **1970 A;** 1971 F2; Bradford N: 1978 A2
FLANAGAN, Peter (14) Hull KR: 1962 F; 1963 F2; 1966 A3,NZ; 1967 A3; 1968 F2; **1968 F,NZ;** 1970 A
FLANAGAN, Terry (4) Oldham: 1983 F2; 1984 NZ,P
FLEARY, Darren (1+1) Leeds R.: 1998 NZnz
FOGERTY, Terry (2+1) Halifax: 1966 nz; Wigan: 1967 F; Rochdale H: 1974 F
FORD, Mike (+2) Castleford: 1993 f2
FORD, Phil (13) Wigan: 1985 F; Bradford N: 1987 P; 1988 F,P,A3, NZ; Leeds: 1989 F2,NZ3
FORSHAW, Mike (+3) Bradford B.: 1997 asl2; 1998 nz
FORSTER, Mark (2) Warrington: 1987 F2
FOSTER, Frank (1) Hull KR: 1967 A
FOSTER, Peter (3) Leigh: 1955 NZ3
FOSTER, Trevor (3) Bradford N: 1946 NZ; 1948 A2
FOX, Deryck (10+4) Featherstone R: 1985 F2, NZ3; 1986 F2,A2; 1989 nz; 1990 p; 1991 p; 1992 f; Bradford N: 1992 **A**
FOX, Don (1) Featherstone R: 1963 A
FOX, Neil (29) Wakefield T: 1959 F,A2; 1960 F3; 1961 NZ2; 1962 F3,A3,NZ2; 1963 A2,F; 1964 F; 1965 F; 1966 F; 1967 F2,A; 1968 F3; 1969 F
FOY, Des (3) Oldham: 1984 F,A; 1985 F
FRANCIS, Bill (4) Wigan: 1967 A; **1977 NZ,A2**
FRANCIS, Roy (1) Barrow: 1947 NZ
FRASER, Eric (16) Warrington: 1958 A3,NZ2; 1959 F2,A; 1960 F3; **1960 F,NZ;** 1961 F,NZ2
FRENCH, Ray (4) Widnes: 1968 F2; **1968 A,NZ**
FRODSHAM, Alf (3) St. Helens: 1928 NZ2; 1929 A

GABBITAS, Brian (1) Hunslet: 1959 F
GALLAGHER, Frank (12) Dewsbury: 1920 A3; 1921 A; Batley: 1924 A3,NZ3; 1926 NZ2
GANLEY, Bernard (3) Oldham: 1957 F2; 1958 F
GARDINER, Danny (1) Wigan: 1965 NZ

GEE, Ken (17) Wigan: 1946 A3,NZ; 1947 NZ3; 1948 A3; 1950 A3,NZ2; 1951 NZ2

GEMMELL, Dick (3) Leeds: 1964 F; Hull: 1968 F; 1969 F

GIBSON, Carl (10+1) Batley: 1985 f; Leeds: 1990 F,P2,NZ3,A3; 1991 F

GIFFORD, Harry (2) Barrow: 1908 A2

GILFEDDER, Laurie (5) Warrington: 1962 A,NZ2,F; 1963 F

GILL, Henderson (14+1) Wigan: 1981 F2; 1982 A; 1985 F; 1986 F,A3; 1987 F2; 1988 P,A2a,NZ

GILL, Ken (5+2) Salford: 1974 F2,A2,NZ; **1977 f,a**

GILMOUR, Lee (1+1) Wigan W.: 1998 NZnz

GOODWAY, Andy (23) Oldham: 1983 F2; 1984 F,A3,NZ3,P; 1985 F; Wigan: 1985 NZ3; 1986 A3; 1987 F,P; 1989 NZ3; 1990 F

GOODWIN, Dennis (5) Barrow: 1957 F2; 1958 F,NZ2

GORE, Jack (1) Salford: 1926 NZ

GORLEY, Les (4+1) Widnes: 1980 NZnz; 1981 F2; 1982 A

GORLEY, Peter (2+1) St. Helens: 1980 NZ; 1981 Ff

GOULDING, Bobbie (15+2) Wigan: 1990 P2,NZ3; Leeds: 1992 F; St. Helens: 1994 Aa2; 1996 P,Fiji,NZ3; 1997 ASL3

GOWERS, Ken (14) Swinton: 1962 F; 1963 F,A3; 1964 F2; 1965 NZ2; 1966 F2,A,NZ2

GRAY, John (5+3) Wigan: 1974 f2,A2a,NZ3

GRAYSHON, Jeff (13) Bradford N: 1979 A2, NZ3; 1980 NZ2; 1981 F2; 1982 A2; Leeds: 1985 NZ2

GREENALL, Doug (6) St. Helens: 1951 NZ3; 1952 A2; 1954 NZ

GREENALL, Johnny (1) St. Helens Recs: 1921 A

GREENOUGH, Bobby (1) Warrington: **1960 NZ**

GREGORY, Andy (25+1) Widnes: 1981 F2; 1982 A; 1983 F2; 1984 a,NZ2,P; Warrington: 1986 A; Wigan: 1987 F,P; 1988 F,P,A3,NZ; 1989 F2,NZ; 1990 F,A3; 1992 A

GREGORY, Mike (19+1) Warrington: 1987 F2; 1988 P,A3,NZ; 1989 F2,NZ3; 1990 F2,P2,NZ3,a

GRIBBIN, Vince (1) Whitehaven: 1985 F

GRIFFITHS, Jonathan (1) St. Helens: 1992 F

GRONOW, Ben (7) Huddersfield: 1911 A2; 1920 A2,NZ3

GROVES, Paul (1) St. Helens: 1987 P

GRUNDY, Jack (12) Barrow: 1955 NZ3; 1956 A3; 1957 F3; **1957 F,A,NZ**

GUNNEY, Geoff (11) Hunslet: 1954 NZ3; 1956 A; 1957 F3; **1957 F,NZ**; 1964 F; 1965 F

GWYNNE, Emlyn (3) Hull: 1928 A,NZ; 1929 A

GWYTHER, Elwyn (6) Belle Vue R: 1947 NZ2; 1950 A3; 1951 NZ

HAGGERTY, Roy (2) St. Helens: 1987 F2

HAIGH, Bob (5+1) Wakefield T: **1968 A,F**; Leeds: **1970 NZ,a**; 1971 F,NZ

HALL, Billy (4) Oldham: 1914 A3,NZ

HALL, Dave (2) Hull KR: 1984 F2

HALLAS, Derek (2) Leeds: 1961 F,NZ

HALMSHAW, Tony (1) Halifax: 1971 NZ

HALSALL, Hector (1) Swinton: 1929 A

HAMMOND, Karle (1+1) St. Helens: 1996 nzNZ

HAMPSON, Steve (11+1) Wigan: 1987 P; 1988 F2; 1989

f,NZ; 1990 A3; 1991 F2,P; 1992 P

HANLEY, Ellery (35+1) Bradford N: 1984 fF,A3,NZ3,P; 1985 F2; Wigan: 1985 NZ3; 1986 F,A; 1987 F2,P; 1988 F2,P,A3,NZ; 1989 F2; 1990 F,A3; 1991 F2; Leeds: 1992 **A**; 1993 F

HARDISTY, Alan (12) Castleford: 1964 F3; 1965 F,NZ; 1966 A3,NZ; 1967 F2; 1970 A

HARE, Ian (1) Widnes: 1967 F

HARKIN, Paul (+1) Hull KR: 1985 f

HARRIS, Iestyn (5+2) Warrington: 1996 P,Fiji,NZ2nz; Leeds R.: 1998 NZnz

HARRIS, Tommy (25) Hull: 1954 NZ2; 1956 A3; 1957 F5; **1957 F,A**; 1958 A3,NZ,F; 1959 F2,A3; 1960 F2; **1960 NZ**

HARRISON, Fred (3) Leeds: 1911 A3

HARRISON, Karl (11+3) Hull: 1990 A3; Halifax: 1991 P; 1992 a2,nzNZ; 1993 F,NZ2; 1994 A3

HARRISON, Mick (7) Hull: 1967 F2; 1971 NZ2; 1972 F2; 1973 A

HARTLEY, Dennis (11) Hunslet: 1964 F2; Castleford: 1968 F; 1969 F; 1970 A2,NZ2; **1970 A2,F**

HARTLEY, Steve (3) Hull KR: 1980 NZ; 1981 F2

HAUGHTON, Simon (+5) Wigan W.: 1997 asl2; 1998 nz3

HAYES, Joey (1) St. Helens: 1996 P

HELME, Gerry (12) Warrington: 1948 A3; 1954 A3,NZ2; **1954 F2,A,NZ**

HEPWORTH, Keith (11) Castleford: 1967 F2; 1970 A3,NZ2; **1970 A2,F,NZ**

HERBERT, Norman (6) Workington T: 1961 NZ; 1962 F,A3,NZ

HERON, David (1+1) Leeds: 1982 aA

HESKETH, Chris (21+2) Salford: 1970 NZ; **1970 NZ,a**; 1971 Ff,NZ3; **1972 A2,F,NZ**; 1973 A3; 1974 F2,A3,NZ3

HICKS, Mervyn (1) St. Helens: 1965 NZ

HIGGINS, Fred (6) Widnes: 1950 A3,NZ2; 1951 NZ

HIGGINS, Harold (2) Widnes: 1937 A2

HIGSON, John (2) Hunslet: 1908 A2

HILL, Cliff (1) Wigan: 1966 F

HILL, David (1) Wigan: 1971 F

HILTON, Herman (7) Oldham: 1920 A3,NZ3; 1921 A

HILTON, Jack (4) Wigan: 1950 A2,NZ2

HOBBS, David (10+2) Featherstone R: 1984 F2,Aa,NZ3,P; Oldham: 1987 F2; Bradford N: 1989 NZnz

HODGSON, Martin (16) Swinton: 1929 A2; 1932 A3,NZ3; 1933 A3; 1936 A3,NZ3; 1937 A

HOGAN, Phil (6+3) Barrow: **1977 F,NZ,A2**; 1978 a; Hull KR: 1979 Aa,NZnz

HOGG, Andrew (1) Broughton R: 1907 NZ

HOLDEN, Keith (1) Warrington: 1963 A

HOLDER, Billy (1) Hull: 1907 NZ

HOLDING, Neil (2) St. Helens: 1984 A3,NZ

HOLDSTOCK, Roy (2) Hull KR: 1980 NZ2

HOLLAND, Dave (4) Oldham: 1914 A3,NZ

HOLLIDAY, Bill (9+1) Whitehaven: 1964 F; Hull KR: 1965 F,NZ3; 1966 Ff; 1967 A3

HOLLIDAY, Les (3) Widnes: 1991 F; 1992 F2

HOLLINDRAKE, Terry (1) Keighley: 1955 NZ
HOLMES, John (14+6) Leeds: 1971 NZ; 1972 F2; **1972 Aa,NZ; 1977 F,NZ,Aa**; 1978 a3; 1979 A2a,NZ3;1982 A
HORNE, Willie (8) Barrow: 1946 A3; 1947 NZ; 1948 A; 1952 A3
HORTON, Bill (14) Wakefield T: 1928 A3,NZ3; 1929 A; 1932 A3,NZ; 1933 A3
HOWARD, Harvey (+1) Bradford B.: 1998 nz
HOWLEY, Tommy (6) Wigan: 1924 A3,NZ3
HUDDART, Dick (16) Whitehaven: 1958 A2,NZ2; St. Helens: 1959 A; 1961 NZ3; 1962 F2,A3,NZ2; 1963 A
HUDSON, Barney (8) Salford: 1932 NZ, 1933 A2; 1936 A,NZ2; 1937 A2
HUDSON, Bill (1) Wigan: 1948 A
HUGHES, Eric (8) Widnes: 1978 A; 1979 A3,NZ3; 1982 A
HULME, David (7+1) Widnes: 1988 p,A3,NZ; 1989 NZ3
HULME, Paul (3+5) Widnes: 1988 aa,nz; 1989 NZ2; 1992 a2,nz
HUNTE, Alan (15) St. Helens: 1992 F,**A**; 1993 F2; 1994 A3; 1996 P,Fiji,NZ3; 1997 ASL3
HURCOMBE, Danny (8) Wigan: 1920 A2,NZ; 1921 A; 1924 A2,NZ2
HYNES, Syd (12+1) Leeds: 1970 A2,NZ2nz; **1970 A2,F,NZ**; 1971 F; 1973 A3

IRVING, Bob (8+3) Oldham: 1967 F2,A3; 1970 a,NZ; 1971 NZ; 1972 f; **1972 NZ,a**
IRWIN, Shaun (+4) Castleford: 1990 f,p,nz2

JACKSON, Ken (2) Oldham: 1957 F2
JACKSON, Lee (17) Hull: 1990 P2,NZ,A3; 1991 F2; 1992 F,NZ2; Sheffield E: 1993 NZ2; 1994 F,A3
JACKSON, Michael (2+4) Wakefield T: 1991 P; 1992 F,a,nz; Halifax: 1993 nz2
JACKSON, Phil (27) Barrow: 1954 A3,NZ3; **1954 F2,A,NZ**; 1955 NZ3; 1956 A3; **1957 F,NZ**; 1957 F5; 1958 F,A2,NZ
JAMES, Neil (1) Halifax: 1986 F
JARMAN, Billy (2) Leeds: 1914 A2
JASIEWICZ, Dick (1) Bradford N: 1984 F
JEANES, David (8) Wakefield T: 1971 F,NZ2; 1972 F2; Leeds: **1972 A2,NZ**
JENKINS, Bert (12) Wigan: 1907 NZ3; 1908 A3; 1910 A,NZ; 1911 A2; 1914 A,NZ
JENKINS, Dai (1) Hunslet: 1929 A
JENKINS, Dai (1) Leeds: 1947 NZ
JENKINS, Emlyn (9) Salford: 1933 A; 1936 A3,NZ2; 1937 A3
JENKINSON, Albert (2) Hunslet: 1911 A2
JOHNSON, Albert (4) Widnes: 1914 A,NZ; 1920 A2
JOHNSON, Albert (6) Warrington: 1946 A2,NZ; 1947 NZ3
JOHNSON, Chris (1) Leigh: 1985 F
JOLLEY, Jim (3) Runcorn: 1907 NZ3
JONES, Berwyn (3) Wakefield T: 1964 F; 1965 F; 1966 F
JONES, Dai (2) Merthyr: 1907 NZ2
JONES, Ernest (4) Rochdale H: 1920 A,NZ3
JONES, Joe (1) Barrow: 1946 NZ
JONES, Keri (2) Wigan: **1970 F,NZ**

JONES, Les (1) St. Helens: 1971 NZ
JONES, Lewis (15) Leeds: 1954 A3,NZ3; 1955 NZ3; 1957 F3; **1957 F,A,NZ**
JONES, Mark (+1) Hull: 1992 f
JORDAN, Gary (2) Featherstone R: 1964 F; 1967 A
JOYNER, John (14+2) Castleford: 1978 A2; 1979 A3,NZ3; 1980 NZ3; 1983 F2; 1984 F,nz2
JOYNT, Chris (14+4) St. Helens: 1993 f,NZ3; 1994 F,A3; 1996 P,nz3; 1997 ASL3; 1998 NZ3
JUBB, Ken (2) Leeds: 1937 A2
JUKES, Bill (6) Hunslet: 1908 A3; 1910 A2,NZ

KARALIUS, Tony (4+1) St. Helens: 1971 NZ3; 1972 F; **1972 nz**
KARALIUS, Vince (12) St. Helens: 1958 A2,NZ2; 1959 F; **1960 NZ,F,A**; 1960 F; 1961 F; Widnes: 1963 A2
KEEGAN, Arthur (9) Hull: 1966 A2; 1967 F2,A3; 1968 F; 1969 F
KELLY, Ken (4) St. Helens: 1972 F2; Warrington: 1980 NZ; 1982 A
KEMEL, George (2) Widnes: 1965 NZ2
KERSHAW, Herbert (2) Wakefield T: 1910 A,NZ
KINNEAR, Roy (1) Wigan: 1929 A
KISS, Nicky (1) Wigan: 1985 F
KITCHEN, Frank (2) Leigh: **1954 A,NZ**
KITCHIN, Phil (1) Whitehaven: 1965 NZ
KITCHING, Jack (1) Bradford N: 1946 A
KNAPMAN, Ernest (1) Oldham: 1924 NZ
KNOWELDEN, Bryn (1) Barrow: 1946 NZ

LAUGHTON, Dale (2+1) Sheffield E.: 1998 NZ2nz
LAUGHTON, Doug (15) Wigan: 1970 A3,NZ2; **1970 A2,F,NZ**; 1971 F2; Widnes: 1973 A; 1974 F2; 1979 A
LAWRENSON, John (3) Wigan: 1948 A3
LAWS, David (1) Hull KR: 1986 F
LEDGARD, Jim (11) Dewsbury: 1947 NZ2; Leigh: 1948 A; 1950 A2,NZ; 1951 NZ; **1954 F2,A,NZ**
LEDGER, Barry (2) St. Helens: 1985 F; 1986 A
LEWIS, Gordon (1) Leigh: 1965 NZ
LEYTHAM, Jim (5) Wigan: 1907 NZ2; 1910 A2,NZ
LITTLE, Syd (10) Oldham: 1956 A; 1957 F5; **1957 F,A,NZ**; 1958 F
LLEWELLYN, Tom (2) Oldham: 1907 NZ2
LLOYD, Robbie (1) Halifax: 1920 A
LOCKWOOD, Brian (8+1) Castleford: **1972 A2,F,NZ**; 1973 A2; 1974 F; Hull KR: 1978 A; 1979 nz
LOMAS, Jim (7) Salford: 1908 A2; 1910 A2,NZ; Oldham: 1911 A2
LONG, Sean (1+1) St. Helens: 1997 asl; 1998 NZ
LONGSTAFF, Fred (2) Huddersfield: 1914 A,NZ
LONGWORTH, Bill (3) Oldham: 1908 A3
LOUGHLIN, Paul (14+1) St. Helens: 1988 F,P,A3,NZ; 1989 F,NZ3; 1990 P,a; 1991 F; 1992 P,A
LOWE, John (1) Leeds: 1932 NZ
LOWE, Phil (12) Hull KR: 1970 NZ; 1972 F2; **1972 A2,F,NZ**; 1973 A3; 1978 A2
LOWES, James (3) Bradford B.: 1997 ASL3
LOXTON, Ken (1) Huddersfield: 1971 NZ

LUCAS, Ian (1+1) Wigan: 1991 F; 1992 a
LYDON, Joe (23+7) Widnes: 1983 F2; 1984 F,a,NZ2,P; 1985 NZ3; Wigan: 1986 F,A3; 1987 F2,P; 1989 F2,nz; 1990 F,NZ3; 1992 p,a3,nz,**A**

McCORMICK, Stan (3) Belle Vue R: 1948 A2; St. Helens: 1948 A
McCUE, Tommy (6) Widnes: 1936 A; 1937 A; 1946 A3,NZ
McCURRIE, Steve (1) Widnes: 1993 F
McDERMOTT, Barrie (1+2) Wigan: 1994 A,a2
McDERMOTT, Brian (4) Bradford B.: 1996 Fiji; 1997 ASL3
McGINTY, Billy (4) Wigan: 1992 A2,NZ2
McINTYRE, Len (1) Oldham: 1963 A
McKEATING, Vince (2) Workington T: 1951 NZ2
McKINNEY, Tom (11) Salford: 1951 NZ; 1952 A2; 1954 A3,NZ; Warrington: 1955 NZ3; St. Helens: **1957 NZ**
McNAMARA, Steve (+4) Hull: 1992 f; 1993 f; Bradford B.: 1997 asl2
McTIGUE, Brian (25) Wigan: 1958 A2,NZ2; 1959 F2,A3; 1960 F2; **1960 NZ,F,A**; 1961 F,NZ3; 1962 F,A3,NZ2; 1963 F
MANN, Arthur (2) Bradford N: 1908 A2
MANTLE, John (13) St. Helens: 1966 F2,A3; 1967 A2; 1969 F; 1971 F2,NZ2; 1973 A
MARCHANT, Tony (3) Castleford: 1986 F,A2
MARTIN, Billy (1) Workington T: 1962 F
MARTYN, Mick (2) Leigh: 1958 A; 1959 A
MATHER, Barrie-Jon (1+2) Wigan: 1994f; Perth Western Reds: 1996 nzNZ
MATHIAS, Roy (1) St. Helens: 1979 A
MEASURES, Jim (2) Widnes: 1963 A2
MEDLEY, Paul (3+1) Leeds: 1987 P; 1988 Ff,P
MIDDLETON, Alf (1) Salford: 1929 A
MILLER, Joe (1) Wigan: 1911 A
MILLER, Joe "Jack" (6) Warrington: 1933 A3; 1936 A,NZ2
MILLS, Jim (6) Widnes: 1974 A2,NZ; 1978 A2; 1979 A
MILLWARD, Roger (28+1) Castleford: 1966 F; Hull KR: 1967 A3; 1968 F2; **1968 A,F,NZ**; 1970 A2,NZ3; 1971 F,NZ3; 1973 A; 1974 A2a; **1977 F,NZ,A2**; 1978 A3
MILNES, Alf (2) Halifax: 1920 A2
MOLLOY, Steve (2+2) Leeds: 1993 F; Featherstone R: 1994 F; 1996 fiji,nz
MOONEY, Walter (2) Leigh: 1924 NZ2
MOORHOUSE, Stan (2) Huddersfield: 1914 A,NZ
MORGAN, Arnold (4) Featherstone R: 1968 F2; **1968 F,NZ**
MORGAN, Edgar (2) Hull: 1921 A2
MORGAN, Ron (2) Swinton: 1963 F,A
MORIARTY, Paul (1+1) Widnes: 1991 P; 1994 f
MORLEY, Adrian (2+3) Leeds: 1996 nz2; 1997 asl, ASL2
MORLEY, Jack (2) Wigan: 1936 A; 1937 A
MORTIMER, Frank (2) Wakefield T: 1956 A2
MOSES, Glyn (9) St. Helens: 1955 NZ2; 1956 A; 1957 F3; **1957 F,A,NZ**

MUMBY, Keith (11) Bradford N: 1982 A; 1983 F; 1984 F2,A3,NZ3,P
MURPHY, Alex (27) St. Helens: 1958 A3,NZ; 1959 F2,A; **1960 NZ,F,A**; 1960 F; 1961 F,NZ3; 1962 F,A3; 1963 A2; 1964 F; 1965 F,NZ; 1966 F2; Warrington: 1971 NZ
MURPHY, Harry (1) Wakefield T: 1950 A
MYLER, Frank (23+1) Widnes: **1960 NZ,F,A**; 1960 F; 1961 F; 1962 F; 1963 A; 1964 F; 1965 F,NZ; 1966 A,NZnz; 1967 F2; St. Helens: 1970 A3,NZ3; **1970 A2,F**
MYLER, Tony (14) Widnes: 1983 F2; 1984 A2,NZ2,P; 1985 NZ2; 1986 F2,A3

NASH, Steve (24) Featherstone R: 1971 F,NZ; 1972 F2; **1972 A2,F,NZ**; 1973 A2; 1974 A3,NZ3; Salford: **1977 F,NZ,A2**; 1978 A3; 1982 A
NAUGHTON, Albert (2) Warrington: **1954 F2**
NEWBOULD, Tommy (1) Wakefield T: 1910 A
NEWLOVE, Paul (16+4) Featherstone R: 1989 nzNZ2; 1991 P; 1992 p,A3,nz; 1993 F; Bradford N: 1993 NZ3; 1994 F,Aa; St. Helens: 1997 ASL3; 1998 NZ
NEWTON, Terry (1) Leeds R.: 1998 NZ
NICHOLLS, George (29) Widnes: 1971 NZ; 1972 F2; **1972 A2,F,NZ**; St. Helens: 1973 A2; 1974 F2,A3,NZ3; **1977 F,NZ,A**; 1978 A3; 1979 A3,NZ3
NICHOLSON, Bob (3) Huddersfield: 1946 NZ; 1948 A2
NICKLE, Sonny (1+5) St. Helens: 1992 p; 1993 f,NZnz2; 1994 a
NOBLE, Brian (11) Bradford N: 1982 A; 1983 F2; 1984 F,A3,NZ3,P
NORTON, Steve (11+1) Castleford: 1974 a,NZ2; Hull: 1978 A3; 1979 A2; 1980 NZ; 1981 F2; 1982 A

O'CONNOR, Terry (5+2) Wigan: 1996 P,NZ3; 1998 NZnz2
OFFIAH, Martin (33) Widnes: 1988 F,A3,NZ; 1989 F2,NZ3; 1990 F2,NZ3,A3; 1991 F2; Wigan: 1992 P,A3,NZ2,**A**; 1993 NZ2; 1994 F,A3
O'GRADY, Terry (6) Oldham: 1954 A2,NZ3; Warrington: 1961 NZ
OLIVER, Joe (4) Batley: 1928 A3,NZ
O'NEILL, Dennis (2+1) Widnes: 1971 nz; **1972 A,F**
O'NEILL, Mike (3) Widnes: 1982 A; 1983 F2
OSTER, Jack (1) Oldham: 1929 A
OWEN, Jim (1) St. Helens Recs: 1921 A
OWEN, Stan (1) Leigh: 1958 F
OWENS, Ike (4) Leeds: 1946 A3,NZ

PADBURY, Dick (1) Runcorn: 1908 A
PALIN, Harold (2) Warrington: 1947 NZ2
PARKER, Dave (2) Oldham: 1964 F2
PARKIN, Jonty (17) Wakefield T: 1920 A2,NZ3; 1921 A2; 1924 A3,NZ; 1926 NZ2; 1928 A,NZ; 1929 A2
PARR, Ken (1) Warrington: 1968 F
PAWSEY, Charlie (7) Leigh: 1952 A3; 1954 A2,NZ2
PEPPERELL, Albert (2) Workington T: 1950 NZ; 1951 NZ
PHILLIPS, Doug (4) Oldham: 1946 A3; Belle Vue R: 1950 A

PHILLIPS, Rowland (+1) Workington T: 1996 p
PIMBLETT, Albert (3) Warrington: 1948 A3
PINNER, Harry (6+1) St. Helens: 1980 nzNZ; 1985 NZ3;
1986 F; Widnes: 1986 A
PITCHFORD, Frank (2) Oldham: 1958 NZ; 1962 F
PITCHFORD, Steve (4) Leeds: 1977 **F,NZ,A2**
PLANGE, David (1) Castleford: 1988 F
PLATT, Andy (21+4) St. Helens: 1985 f; 1986 f,a; 1988
F2,A2; Wigan: 1989 NZ3; 1990 F,A2; 1991 F2,P;
1992 f,P,A3,NZ2,**A**; 1993 F
POLLARD, Charlie (1) Wakefield T: 1924 NZ
POLLARD, Ernest (2) Wakefield T: 1932 A2
POLLARD, Roy (1) Dewsbury: 1950 NZ
POOLE, Harry (3) Hull KR: 1964 F; Leeds: 1966 NZ2
POTTER, Ian (7+1) Wigan: 1985 NZ3; 1986 F2,A2a
POWELL, Daryl (23+10) Sheffield E: 1990
f,P2,nzNZ2,A3; 1991 F2,P; 1992 fF,P,A3,NZ2; 1993
f,nz3; 1994 f,A2a; Keighley C.: 1996 p,Fiji,NZ3
POWELL, Roy (13+6) Leeds: 1985 f; 1988 F2,A2a,NZ;
1989 F2,NZ2; 1990 P2,nz2NZ,Aa; 1991 f
POYNTON, Harold (3) Wakefield T: 1962 A2,NZ
PRESCOTT, Alan (28) St. Helens: 1951 NZ2; 1952 A3;
1954 A3,NZ3; 1955 NZ3; 1956 A3; 1957 F5; **1957
F,A,NZ**; 1958 F,A2
PRICE, Gary H (+1) Wakefield T: 1991 p
PRICE, Jack (6) Broughton R: 1921 A2; Wigan: 1924 A2,NZ2
PRICE, Malcolm (2) Rochdale H: 1967 A2
PRICE, Ray (9) Warrington: 1954 A,NZ2; 1955 NZ; 1956
A3; 1957 F2
PRICE, Terry (1) Bradford N: 1970 A
PRIOR, Bernard (1) Hunslet: 1966 F
PROCTOR, Wayne (+1) Hull: 1984 p
PROSSER, Dai (1) Leeds: 1937 A
PROSSER, Stuart (1) Halifax: 1914 A

RADLINSKI, Kris (11) Wigan 1996 P,Fiji,NZ3; 1997
ASL3; 1998 NZ3
RAE, Johnny (1) Bradford N: 1965 NZ
RAMSDALE, Dick (8) Wigan: 1910 A2; 1911 A2; 1914
A3,NZ
RAMSEY, Bill (7+1) Hunslet: 1965 NZ2; 1966 F,A2,NZ2;
Bradford N; 1974 nz
RATCLIFFE, Gordon (3) Wigan: 1947 NZ; 1950 A2
RATHBONE, Alan (4+1) Bradford N: 1982 a; 1983 F2;
1985 F2
RAYNE, Keith (4) Leeds: 1984 F2,A,P
RAYNE, Kevin (1) Leeds: 1986 F
REDFEARN, Alan (1) Bradford N: 1979 A
REDFEARN, David (6+1) Bradford N: **1972 nz**; 1974
F2,A,NZ3
REES, Billo (11) Swinton: 1926 NZ2; 1928 A3,NZ3; 1929
A3
REES, Dai (1) Halifax: 1926 NZ
REES, Tom (1) Oldham: 1929 A
REILLY, Malcolm (9) Castleford: 1970 A3,NZ3; **1970
A2,F**
RENILSON, Charlie (7+1) Halifax: 1965 NZ; 1967 a; 1968

F3; **1968 A,F,NZ**
RHODES, Austin (4) St. Helens: **1957 NZ; 1960 F,A;** 1961
NZ
RICHARDS, Maurice (2) Salford: 1974 A,NZ
RILEY, Joe (1) Halifax: 1910 A
RING, Johnny (2) Wigan: 1924 A; 1926 NZ
RISMAN, Bev (5) Leeds: 1968 F2; **1968 A,F,NZ**
RISMAN, Gus (17) Salford: 1932 A,NZ3; 1933 A3; 1936
A2,NZ2; 1937 A3; 1946 A3
RIX, Sid (9) Oldham: 1924 A3,NZ3; 1926 NZ3
ROBERTS, Ken (10) Halifax: 1963 A; 1964 F2; 1965
F,NZ3; 1966 F,NZ2
ROBINSON, Asa (3) Halifax: 1907 NZ; 1908 A2
ROBINSON, Bill (2) Leigh: 1963 F,A
ROBINSON, Dave (13) Swinton: 1965 NZ; 1966
F2,A3,NZ2; 1967 F2,A2; Wigan: 1970 A
ROBINSON, Don (10) Wakefield T: **1954 F2,NZ,A;** 1955
NZ; Leeds: 1956 A2; 1959 A2; 1960 F
ROBINSON, Jack (2) Rochdale H: 1914 A2
ROBINSON, Jason (10) Wigan: 1993 NZ; 1994 A3; 1997
ASL3; 1998 NZ3
ROGERS, Johnny (7) Huddersfield: 1914 A; 1920 A3; 1921
A3
ROSE, David (4) Leeds: **1954 F2,A,NZ**
ROSE, Paul (2+3) Hull KR: 1974 a; 1978 Aa2; Hull: 1982
A
ROUND, Gerry (8) Wakefield T: 1959 A; 1962
F2,A3,NZ2
RUDDICK, George (3) Broughton R: 1907 NZ2; 1910 A
RYAN, Bob (5) Warrington: 1950 A,NZ2; 1951 NZ; 1952
A
RYAN, Martin (4) Wigan: 1947 NZ; 1948 A2; 1950 A
RYDER, Ron (1) Warrington: 1952 A

SAMPSON, Dean (+1) Castleford T.: 1997 asl
SAYER, Bill (7) Wigan: 1961 NZ; 1962 F,A3,NZ; 1963 A
SCHOFIELD, Derrick (1) Halifax: 1955 NZ
SCHOFIELD, Garry (44+2) Hull: 1984 F,A3,NZ; 1985
NZ3; 1986 F2,A3; 1987 F2; Leeds: 1988 F2,P,A; 1990
F2,P2,NZ3,A3; 1991 F2,P; 1992 P,A3,NZ2,**A;** 1993
F,NZ3; 1994 F,a2
SCULTHORPE, Paul (10+1) Warrington 1996:p,Fiji, NZ3;
1997 ASL3; St. Helens: 1998 NZ3
SEABOURNE, Barry (1) Leeds: 1970 NZ
SENIOR, Keith (3+2) Sheffield E: 1996 fiji, nz 1998 NZ3
SENIOR, Ken (2) Huddersfield: 1965 NZ; 1967 F
SHARROCK, Jim (4) Wigan: 1910 A2,NZ; 1911 A
SHAW, Brian (6) Hunslet: 1956 A2; **1960 F,A;** 1960 F;
Leeds: 1961 F
SHAW, Glyn (1) Widnes: 1980 NZ
SHAW, John (5) Halifax: **1960 F,A;** 1960 F; 1961 F; 1962
NZ
SHELTON, Geoff (7) Hunslet: 1964 F2; 1965 NZ3; 1966
F2
SHOEBOTTOM, Mick (10+2) Leeds: **1968 A,nz;** 1969 F;
1970 A2a,NZ; **1970 A2,F,NZ;** 1971 F
SHUGARS, Frank (1) Warrington: 1910 NZ

SILCOCK, Dick (1) Wigan: 1908 A

SILCOCK, Nat (12) Widnes: 1932 A2,NZ2; 1933 A3; 1936 A3; 1937 A2

SILCOCK, Nat (3) Wigan: 1954 A3

SIMMS, Barry (1) Leeds: 1962 F

SKELHORNE, George "Jack" (7) Warrington: 1920 A,NZ3; 1921 A3

SKERRETT, Kelvin (14+2) Bradford N: 1989 NZ3; 1990 F2,NZ3; Wigan: 1992 F,p,A3,NZ,a; 1993 NZ

SKERRETT, Trevor (10) Wakefield T: 1979 A2, NZ2; Hull: 1980 NZ2; 1981 F2; 1982 A2

SLOMAN, Bob (5) Oldham: 1928 A3,NZ2

SMALES, Tommy (8) Huddersfield: 1962 F; 1963 F,A; 1964 F2; Bradford N: 1965 NZ3

SMALL, Peter (1) Castleford: 1962 NZ

SMITH, Alan (10) Leeds: 1970 A2,NZ3; **1970 A2**; 1971 F2; 1973 A

SMITH, Arthur (6) Oldham: 1907 NZ3; 1908 A3

SMITH, Bert (2) Bradford N: 1926 NZ2

SMITH, Fred (9) Hunslet: 1910 A,NZ; 1911 A3; 1914 A3,NZ

SMITH, Geoff (3) York: 1963 A; 1964 F2

SMITH, Mike (10+1) Hull KR: 1979 NZ3; 1980 NZ2; 1981 F2; 1982 A2; 1984 f,NZ

SMITH, Peter (1+5) Featherstone R: **1977 a2**; 1982 A; 1983 f2; 1984 f

SMITH, Sam (4) Hunslet: **1954 A,NZ,F2**

SMITH, Stanley (11) Wakefield T: 1929 A; Leeds: 1929 A2; 1932 A3,NZ3; 1933 A2

SMITH, Tony (3+2) Castleford T: 1996 p,fiji; Wigan W: 1998 NZ3

SOUTHWARD, Ike (11) Workington T: 1958 A3,NZ; Oldham: 1959 F2,A2; 1960 F2; 1962 NZ

SPENCER, Jack (1) Salford: 1907 NZ

SPRUCE, Stuart (6) Widnes: 1993 F; Bradford B: 1996 P, Fiji,NZ3

STACEY, Cyril (1) Halifax: 1920 NZ

STEADMAN, Graham (9+1) Castleford: 1990 F; 1992 fF,A3,NZ2; 1994 F,A

STEPHENS, Gary (5) Castleford: 1979 A2,NZ3

STEPHENSON, David (9+1) Wigan: 1982 A2; 1986 A; 1987 F,P; Leeds: 1988 f,P,A2,NZ

STEPHENSON, Mick (5+1) Dewsbury: 1971 nz; 1972 F; **1972 A2,F,NZ**

STEVENSON, Jeff (19) Leeds: 1955 NZ3; 1956 A3; 1957 F5; **1957 F,A,NZ**; 1958 F; York: 1959 A2; 1960 F2

STOCKWELL, Squire (3) Leeds: 1920 A; 1921 A2

STONE, Billy (8) Hull: 1920 A3,NZ3; 1921 A2

STOPFORD, John (12) Swinton: 1961 F; 1963 F,A2; 1964 F2; 1965 F,NZ2; 1966 F2,A

STOTT, Jim (1) St. Helens: 1947 NZ

STREET, Harry (4) Dewsbury: 1950 A3,NZ

SULLIVAN, Anthony (6) St. Helens: 1991 P; 1996 P,Fiji, NZ2; 1997 ASL

SULLIVAN, Clive (17) Hull: 1967 F; **1968 A,F,NZ**; 1970 A; 1971 NZ3; 1972 F2; **1972 A2,F,NZ**; 1973 A3

SULLIVAN, Jim (25) Wigan: 1924 A3,NZ; 1926 NZ3; 1928 A3,NZ3; 1929 A3; 1932 A3,NZ3; 1933 A3

SULLIVAN, Mick (46) Huddersfield: **1954 F2,NZ,A**; 1955 NZ3; 1956 A3; 1957 F3; **1957 F,A,NZ**; Wigan: 1957 F2; 1958 F,A3,NZ2; 1959 F2,A3; 1960 F3; **1960 F,NZ,A**; St. Helens: 1961 F,NZ2; 1962 F3,A3,NZ; York: 1963 A

SZYMALA, Eddie (1+1) Barrow: 1981 fF

TAIT, Alan (10+4) Widnes: 1989 F2,NZ2; 1990 F2,P2; 1992 F; Leeds: 1992 **a**; 1993 F,nz3

TAYLOR, Bob (2) Hull: 1921 A; 1926 NZ

TAYLOR, Harry (3) Hull: 1907 NZ3

TEMBEY, John (2) St. Helens: 1963 A; 1964 F

TERRY, Abe (11) St. Helens: 1958 A2; 1959 F2,A3; 1960 F; 1961 F,NZ; Leeds: 1962 F

THOMAS, Arthur "Ginger" (4) Leeds: 1926 NZ2; 1929 A2

THOMAS, George (1) Warrington: 1907 NZ

THOMAS, Gwyn (9) Wigan: 1914 A; Huddersfield: 1920 A3,NZ2; 1921 A3

THOMAS, Johnny (8) Wigan: 1907 NZ; 1908 A3; 1910 A2,NZ; 1911 A

THOMAS, Les (1) Oldham: 1947 NZ

THOMAS, Phil (1) Leeds: 1907 NZ

THOMPSON, Cecil (2) Hunslet: 1951 NZ2

THOMPSON, Jim (20+1) Featherstone R: 1970 A2,NZ2; **1970 F2,F,NZ**; 1971 Ff; 1974 A3,NZ3; **1977 F,NZ,A2**; Bradford N: 1978 A

THOMPSON, Joe (12) Leeds: 1924 A,NZ2; 1928 A,NZ; 1929 A; 1932 A3,NZ3

THORLEY, John (4) Halifax: **1954 F2,NZ,A**

TOOHEY, Ted (3) Barrow: 1952 A3

TOPLISS, David (4) Wakefield T: 1973 A2; 1979 A; Hull: 1982 A

TRAILL, Ken (8) Bradford N: 1950 NZ2; 1951 NZ; 1952 A3; 1954 A,NZ

TROUP, Alec (2) Barrow: 1936 NZ2

TURNBULL, Andrew (1) Leeds: 1951 NZ

TURNER, Derek (24) Oldham: 1956 A2; 1957 F5; **1957 F,A,NZ**; 1958 F; Wakefield T: 1959 A; 1960 F3; **1960 NZ,A**; 1961 F,NZ; 1962 A2,NZ2,F

TYSON, Brian (3) Hull KR: 1963 A; 1965 F; 1967 F

TYSON, George (4) Oldham: 1907 NZ; 1908 A3

VALENTINE, Dave (15) Huddersfield: 1948 A3; 1951 NZ; 1952 A2; 1954 A3, NZ2; **1954 F2,NZ,A**

VALENTINE, Rob (1) Huddersfield: 1967 A

VINES, Don (3) Wakefield T: 1959 F2,A

WADDELL, Hugh (5) Oldham: 1988 F2,A,NZ; Leeds: 1989 F

WAGSTAFF, Harold (12) Huddersfield: 1911 A2; 1914 A3,NZ; 1920 A2,NZ2; 1921 A2

WALKER, Arnold (1) Whitehaven: 1980 NZ

WALLACE, Jim (1) St. Helens Recs: 1926 NZ

WALSH, Joe (1) Leigh: 1971 NZ

WALSH, John (4+1) St. Helens: 1972 f; **1972 A2,F,NZ**

WALTON, Doug (1) Castleford: 1965 F
WANE, Shaun (2) Wigan: 1985 F; 1986 F
WARD, Billy (1) Leeds: 1910 A
WARD, David (12) Leeds: **1977 F,NZ,A**; 1978 A; 1979 A3,NZ3; 1981 F; 1982 A
WARD, Ted (3) Wigan: 1946 A2; 1947 NZ
WARD, Ernest (20) Bradford N: 1946 A3,NZ; 1947 NZ2; 1948 A3; 1950 A3,NZ2; 1951 NZ3; 1952 A3
WARD, Johnny (4) Castleford: 1963 A; 1964 F2; Salford: 1970 NZ
WARD, Kevin (15+2) Castleford: 1984 F; 1986 A3; 1987 P; 1988 F2,P,A3,NZ; 1989 F2; St. Helens: 1990 a2; 1992 **A**
WARLOW, John (6+1) St. Helens: 1964 F; **1968 f,NZ**; 1968 F; Widnes: 1971 F2,NZ
WARWICK, Silas (2) Salford: 1907 NZ2
WATKINS, Billy (7) Salford: 1933 A; 1936 A2,NZ2; 1937 A2
WATKINS, David (2+4) Salford: 1971 f,NZ; 1973 a; 1974 f2,A
WATKINSON, David (12+1) Hull KR: 1979 a; 1980 NZ; 1981 F; 1984 F; 1985 F,NZ3; 1986 F2,A3
WATSON, Cliff (29+1) St. Helens: 1963 A2; 1966 F2,A3,NZ2; 1967 F,A3; 1968 F2; **1968 A,F,nz**; 1969 F; 1970 A3,NZ3; **1970 A2,F,NZ**; 1971 F
WATTS, Basil (5) York: **1954 F2,NZ,A**; 1955 NZ
WEBSTER, Fred (3) Leeds: 1910 A2,NZ
WHITCOMBE, Frank (2) Bradford N: 1946 A2
WHITE, Les (7) Hunslet: 1932 A3,NZ2; 1933 A2
WHITE, Les (6) York: 1946 A3,NZ; Wigan: 1947 NZ2
WHITE, Tommy (1) Oldham: 1907 NZ
WHITEHEAD, Derek (3) Warrington: 1971 F2,NZ
WHITELEY, Johnny (15) Hull: **1957 A**; 1958 A3,NZ; 1959

F2,A2; 1960 F; **1960 NZ,F**; 1961 NZ2; 1962 F
WILKINSON, Jack (13) Halifax: 1954 A,NZ2; 1955 NZ3; Wakefield T: 1959 A; 1960 F2; **1960 NZ,F,A**; 1962 NZ
WILLIAMS, Billy (2) Salford: 1929 A; 1932 A
WILLIAMS, Dickie (12) Leeds: 1948 A2; 1950 A2,NZ2; 1951 NZ3; Hunslet: 1954 A2,NZ
WILLIAMS, Frank (2) Halifax: 1914 A2
WILLIAMS, Peter (1+1) Salford: 1989 fF
WILLICOMBE, David (3) Halifax: 1974 F; Wigan: 1974 F,NZ
WILSON, George (3) Workington T: 1951 NZ3
WILSON, Harry (3) Hunslet: 1907 NZ3
WINSLADE, Charlie (1) Oldham: 1959 F
WINSTANLEY, Billy (5) Leigh: 1910 A,NZ; Wigan: 1911 A3
WOOD, Alf (4) Oldham: 1911 A2; 1914 A,NZ
WOODS, Harry (6) Liverpool S: 1936 A3,NZ2; Leeds: 1937 A
WOODS, Jack (1) Barrow: 1933 A
WOODS, John (7+4) Leigh: 1979 A3,nz; 1980 NZ; 1981 F2; 1982 Aa; 1983 f; Warrington: 1987 p
WOODS, Tommy (2) Rochdale H: 1911 A2
WORRALL, Mick (3) Oldham: 1984 F,A2
WRIGHT, Darren (+1) Widnes: 1988 a
WRIGHT, Joe (1) Swinton: 1932 NZ
WRIGHT, Stuart (7) Widnes: **1977 F,NZ,A2**; 1978 A3
WRIGLESWORTH, Geoff (5) Leeds: 1965 NZ; 1966 A2,NZ2

YOUNG, Chris (5) Hull KR: 1967 A3; 1968 F2
YOUNG, Frank (1) Leeds: 1908 A
YOUNG, Harold (1) Huddersfield: 1929 A

LONGEST TEST CAREERS

14 years   —   Gus Risman
1932 to 1946 (17 appearances)
13 years 9 months   —   Billy Batten
1908 to 1921 (10 appearances)
13 years 6 months   —   Alex Murphy
1958 to 1971 (27 appearances)
12 years 9 months   —   Roger Millward
1966 to 1978 (28+1 appearances)
12 years 6 months   —   John Atkinson
1968 to 1980 (26 appearances)
12 years 6 months   —   Terry Clawson
1962 to 1974 (14 appearances)

YOUNGEST TEST PLAYER

Paul Newlove was 18 years 72 days old when he made his Great Britain Test debut as a 76th-minute substitute in the first Test against New Zealand at Old Trafford, Manchester, on 21 October 1989, making his full debut a week later. Born on 10 August 1971, he beat the previous record held by Shaun Edwards (born 17 October 1966) who was 18 years 135 days old when capped against France at Leeds on 1 March 1985.

Roger Millward (born 16 September 1947) was 18 years 37 days old when he was a non-playing substitute for the second Test against New Zealand at Bradford on 23 October 1965.

OLDEST TEST PLAYER

Jeff Grayshon (born 4 March 1949) was 36 years eight months when he played in his last Test for Britain, against New Zealand at Elland Road, Leeds, on 9 November 1985.

RECORD TEAM CHANGES

The record number of team changes made by the Great Britain selectors were, on three occasions, all against Australia.

In 1929, Britain crashed 31-8 to Australia in the first Test at Hull KR and retained only three players for the second Test at Leeds, where they won 9-3.

After their biggest ever defeat of 50-12 in the 1963 second Test at Swinton, Britain dropped nine players and were forced to make another change when Vince Karalius was injured and replaced by Don Fox. Britain stopped Australia making a clean sweep of the series by winning 16-5 at Leeds in the last Test.

Following the 40-4 first Test defeat at Hull City's soccer ground in 1982, the selectors again made 10 changes, not including substitutes, Britain going down 27-6 in the second Test at Wigan.

Britain have never fielded the same team for three or more successive Tests.

GREAT BRITAIN RECORDS

● In Test and World Cup matches.

MOST TRIES IN CAREER

*41	Mick Sullivan (Huddersfield, Wigan, St. Helens, York)	1954-63
31	Garry Schofield (Hull, Leeds)	1984-94
26	Martin Offiah (Widnes, Wigan)	1988-94
24	Billy Boston (Wigan)	1954-63
20	Ellery Hanley (Bradford N., Wigan, Leeds)	1984-93
17	Roger Millward (Cas'd, Hull K.R.)	1966-78
16	Alex Murphy (St. Helens, Warrington)	1958-71
15	Shaun Edwards (Wigan)	1985-94
14	Eric Ashton (Wigan)	1957-63
14	Neil Fox (Wakefield T.)	1959-69
13	Clive Sullivan (Hull)	1967-73
12	John Atkinson (Leeds)	1968-80
10	Jim Leytham (Wigan)	1907-10

* Mick Sullivan also scored two tries for Great Britain against France before the matches were given Test status.
● Most tries by a forward is eight by Derek Turner (Oldham, Wakefield T.) 1956-62; Phil Lowe (Hull K.R.) 1970-78 and Denis Betts (Wigan, Auckland W.) 1990-.

MOST GOALS IN CAREER

93	Neil Fox (Wakefield T.)	1959-69
66	Lewis Jones (Leeds)	1954-57
64	Jim Sullivan (Wigan)	1924-33
53	Eric Fraser (Warrington)	1958-61
49	Jonathan Davies (Widnes, Warrington)	1990-94
44	George Fairbairn (Wigan, Hull K.R.)	1977-82
39	Paul Eastwood (Hull)	1990-92
31	Paul Loughlin (St. Helens)	1988-92
27	Bobbie Goulding (Wigan, Leeds, St. Helens)	1990-97
27	Andrew Farrell (Wigan W.)	1993-98
26	Joe Lydon (Widnes, Wigan)	1983-92
25	Terry Clawson (Featherstone R., Leeds, Oldham)	1962-74
22	Ray Dutton (Widnes)	1970
22	John Holmes (Leeds)	1971-82
22	Ernest Ward (Bradford N.)	1946-52
21	Mick Burke (Widnes)	1980-86
21	Ken Gowers (Swinton)	1962-66

MOST POINTS IN CAREER

228	Neil Fox (Wakefield T.)	1959-69
149	Garry Schofield (Hull, Leeds)	1984-94
147	Lewis Jones (Leeds)	1954-57
128	Jim Sullivan (Wigan)	1924-33
123	Mick Sullivan (Huddersfield, Wigan, St. Helens, York)	1954-63
112	Jonathan Davies (Widnes, Warrington)	1990-94
109	Eric Fraser (Warrington)	1958-61
106	Paul Eastwood (Hull)	1990-92
104	Martin Offiah (Widnes, Wigan)	1988-94
91	George Fairbairn (Wigan, Hull K.R.)	1977-82
81	Roger Millward (Castleford, Hull K.R.)	1966-78
80	Ellery Hanley (Bradford N., Wigan, Leeds)	1984-93

MOST TRIES IN A MATCH

5 by Martin Offiah (Widnes) v. France at Leeds
16 February, 1991
4 by Jim Leytham (Wigan) v. Australia at Brisbane
2 July, 1910
Billy Boston (Wigan) v. New Zealand at Auckland
24 July, 1954
Alex Murphy (St. Helens) v. France at Leeds
14 March, 1959
Garry Schofield (Hull) v. New Zealand at Wigan
2 November, 1985
3 by Bill Jukes (Hunslet) v. Australia at Sydney
18 June, 1910
Bert Avery (Oldham) v. New Zealand at Auckland
30 July, 1910
Billy Stone (Hull) v. New Zealand at Auckland
31 July, 1920
Jonty Parkin (Wakefield T.) v. New Zealand at Auckland 31 July, 1920
Charlie Carr (Barrow) v. New Zealand at Leeds
15 January, 1927
Stan Smith (Leeds) v. Australia at Sydney
16 July, 1932
Arthur Bassett (Halifax) v. Australia at Brisbane
6 July, 1946
George Wilson (Workington T.) v. New Zealand at Bradford 6 October, 1951
Mick Sullivan (Huddersfield) v. New Zealand at Bradford 12 November, 1955
Dave Bolton (Wigan) v. France at Wigan
23 November, 1957
Mick Sullivan (Wigan) v. Australia at Sydney
19 July, 1958
Mick Sullivan (Wigan) v. New Zealand at Auckland
9 August, 1958
Mick Sullivan (Wigan) v. France at Leeds
14 March, 1959
Clive Sullivan (Hull) v. New Zealand at Sydney
(World Cup) 8 June, 1968
Bill Burgess (Barrow) v. France at St. Helens
30 November, 1968
Keith Fielding (Salford) v. France at Grenoble
20 January, 1974
Henderson Gill (Wigan) v. France at Hull
6 December, 1981
Garry Schofield (Leeds) v. France at Leeds
16 February, 1991
Garry Schofield (Leeds) v. France at Carcassonne
7 March, 1993
Paul Newlove (Featherstone R.) v. France at Leeds
2 April, 1994
Bobbie Goulding (St. Helens) v. Fiji at Nadi
5 October, 1996

● Bill Jukes and Bert Avery are the only forwards to have scored hat tricks for Great Britain, both on tour in 1910.

MOST GOALS IN A MATCH

10 by Lewis Jones (Leeds) v. Australia at Brisbane
3 July, 1954
Bernard Ganley (Oldham) v. France at Wigan
23 November, 1957
John Holmes (Leeds) v. New Zealand at Pau
(World Cup) 4 November, 1972
Jonathan Davies (Widnes) v. France at Leeds
2 April, 1993
Bobbie Goulding (St. Helens) v. Fiji at Nadi
5 October, 1996

9 by Lewis Jones (Leeds) v. France at Leeds
26 January, 1957
Neil Fox (Wakefield T.) v. France at Wigan
3 April, 1963
Neil Fox (Wakefield T.) v. France at Leigh
18 March, 1964

8 by Eric Fraser (Warrington) v. Australia at Sydney
19 July, 1958
David Creasser (Leeds) v. France at Leeds
1 March, 1985
Joe Lydon (Wigan) v. France at Leeds
24 January, 1987
Paul Eastwood (Hull) v. France at Leeds
16 February, 1991
Jonathan Davies (Widnes) v. Papua New Guinea at
Wigan 9 November, 1991

7 by Lewis Jones (Leeds) v. France at St. Helens
10 April, 1957
Eric Fraser (Warrington) v. New Zealand at Auckland
9 August, 1958
Eric Fraser (Warrington) v. France at Leeds
14 March, 1959
Neil Fox (Wakefield T.) v. New Zealand at Swinton
4 November, 1961
Neil Fox (Wakefield T.) v. France at Swinton
23 January, 1965
Bev Risman (Leeds) v. New Zealand at Sydney
(World Cup) 8 June, 1968
Roger Millward (Hull K.R.) v. Australia at Sydney
20 June, 1970
George Fairbairn (Wigan) v. France at Auckland
(World Cup) 5 June, 1977
John Woods (Leigh) v. France at Hull
6 December, 1981
David Stephenson (Wigan) v. Papua New Guinea at
Wigan 24 October, 1987
Paul Loughlin (St. Helens) v. Papua New Guinea at
Port Moresby 22 May, 1988

MOST POINTS IN A MATCH

32 (3t, 10g) by Bobbie Goulding (St. Helens) v. Fiji at
Nadi 5 October, 1996

26 (2t, 10g) by John Holmes (Leeds) v. New Zealand at
Pau (World Cup) 4 November, 1972

21 (1t, 9g) by Lewis Jones (Leeds) v. France at Leeds
26 January, 1957
Neil Fox (Wakefield T.) v. France at
Wigan 3 April, 1963
Neil Fox (Wakefield T.) v. France at Leigh
18 March, 1964

20 (10g) by Lewis Jones (Leeds) v. Australia at
Brisbane 3 July, 1954

(10g) Bernard Ganley (Oldham) v. France at
Wigan 23 November, 1957

(2t, 7g) Roger Millward (Hull K.R.) v. Australia at
Sydney 20 June, 1970

(1t, 8g) Joe Lydon (Wigan) v. France at Leeds 24
February, 1987

(5t) Martin Offiah (Widnes) v. France at Leeds
16 February, 1991

(1t, 8g) Paul Eastwood (Hull) v. France at Leeds
16 February, 1991

(10g) Jonathan Davies (Widnes) v. France at
Leeds 2 April, 1993

MOST APPEARANCES

46	Mick Sullivan*
46(2)	Garry Schofield
36(1)	Ellery Hanley
36(4)	Shaun Edwards
33	Martin Offiah
33(10)	Daryl Powell
31	Billy Boston
30(1)	Cliff Watson
30(1)	Denis Betts
30(7)	Joe Lydon
29	George Nicholls
29	Neil Fox
29(1)	Roger Millward
28	Alan Prescott
27	Phil Jackson
27	Alex Murphy
26	Eric Ashton
26	John Atkinson
26(1)	Andy Gregory
25	Brian McTigue
25	Jim Sullivan
25	Tommy Harris
25(4)	Andy Platt
( )	Indicates substitute appearance included in total

* Mick Sullivan's joint record number of appearances includes a record run of 36 successive matches. In addition he played in two matches against France before they were given Test status.

ALL TIME TOUR RECORDS

IN AUSTRALIA
Highest score: 101-0 v. South Australia in 1914

Biggest defeat: 42-6 v. New South Wales in 1920
(Also *widest margin*)

Fewest defeats: 1 (and 1 draw) from 21 matches in 1958 and
from 17 matches in 1970

Most defeats: 9 from 22 matches in 1966

Biggest attendances: 70,419 v. New South Wales (Sydney) in
1950

IN NEW ZEALAND
Highest score: 81-14 v. Bay of Plenty in 1962

Widest margin win: 72-3 v. Buller in 1928
72-3 v. North Island in 1958

Biggest defeat: 46-13 v. Auckland in 1962 (Also *widest margin*)

Fewest defeats: The tourists have won all their matches in the
following years: 1910 (4 matches), 1914 (6), 1932 (8), 1936
(8), 1966 (8), 1970 (7).

Most defeats: 5 from 6 in 1996 (1 draw)

Biggest attendance: 35,000 v. Auckland in 1920

PLAYERS' FULL TOUR RECORDS
Most full appearances: 24 by Dick Huddart in 1958

Most tries: 38 by Mick Sullivan in 1958

Most goals and points: 127g, 278 pts by Lewis Jones in 1954

Most tours: 4 by Garry Schofield (1984, 1988, 1990, 1992)

Biggest club representation: 13+1 replacement by Wigan in
1992 — Denis Betts, Phil Clarke, Neil Cowie, Martin
Dermott, Shaun Edwards, Andy Gregory, Steve Hampson,
Ian Lucas, Joe Lydon, Billy McGinty, Martin Offiah, Andy
Platt, Kelvin Skerrett, plus David Myers as a replacement

Brothers touring together: Bryn and Jack Evans (1928), Don
and Neil Fox (1962), Alan and John Bates (1974), David
and Paul Hulme (1988, Paul as replacement)

Youngest tourist: Bobbie Goulding 18 years 4 months in 1990

*Three-to-one: Wales forward Neil Cowie charges into a
three-man Emerging England tackle.*

ENGLAND AND WALES
Ireland and Scotland

ENGLAND AND WALES

THOMSON ESG INTERNATIONAL
Emerging England v. Wales
The 1998 international season saw the introduction of an Emerging England team for the first time, comprising mainly of players on the fringe of Test honours. Great Britain coach Andy Goodway, who was also in charge of the Emerging England side, did not select players he regarded as almost certain to be in his Test squad to face New Zealand at the end of the season. Instead, for the match against Wales on 19 July, he named an initial squad of 21 players of varying experience. The youngest was 19-year-old Bradford half back Paul Deacon, who had made only four senior appearances, and the oldest 33-year-old Leeds winger Paul Sterling. The only players with any Test experience were Steve Molloy, Keith Senior and Sean Long.

Phil Lowe continued his partnership with Goodway as a manager of both Emerging England and Great Britain.

EMERGING ENGLAND SQUAD (Announced 3 June): Steve Blakeley (Salford, Capt.), David Bradbury (Salford), Gary Broadbent (Salford), Francis Cummins (Leeds), Paul Davidson (St. Helens), Paul Deacon (Bradford), Darren Fleary (Leeds), Lee Gilmour (Wigan), Andy Hay (Leeds), Mark Hilton (Warrington), Graham Holroyd (Leeds), Paul Johnson (Wigan), Sean Long (St. Helens), Steve Molloy (Sheffield), Nathan McAvoy (Salford), Steve Naylor (Salford), Danny Orr (Castleford), Jonathan Roper (Warrington), Paul Rowley (Halifax), Keith Senior (Sheffield), Paul Sterling (Leeds).

Injuries ruled out Blakeley, Naylor and Roper. Blakeley had been named as captain and the leadership was handed over to Molloy. Wigan forward Simon Haughton, who had played in two Tests, was added to the squad along with Chris Chester (Halifax) and Darren Turner (Sheffield).

Following the return of nearly all Welsh-born players to Rugby Union, Wales had to rely almost entirely on English-born players with a Welsh-born parent or grandparent plus Australian Damian Gibson. Dean Busby, Jason Critchley and Richard Eyres had already played for England. Clive Griffiths was retained as coach despite now being in charge of Rugby Union club London Welsh and his original 23-man squad included two former RL players who were playing for Rugby Union clubs – Rowland Phillips, from his own club, and Paul Moriarty of Swansea. They were the only Welsh-born players in the squad, which had Mike Nicholas as manager.

WALES SQUAD (Announced 16 June): Paul Atcheson (St. Helens), Lee Briers (Warrington), Dean Busby (Hull, on loan from St. Helens), Neil Cowie (Wigan), Jason Critchley (Castleford), Keiron Cunningham (St. Helens), Barry Eaton (Dewsbury), Richard Eyres (Rochdale), Martin Hall (Wigan, later Halifax), Karle Hammond (St. Helens), Iestyn Harris (Leeds), Jason Lee (Keighley), Paul Moriarty (Swansea RU), Chris Morley (Warrington), Mark Perrett (Halifax), Rowland Phillips (London Welsh RU), Gavin Price-Jones (Swinton), Daio Powell (Halifax), Kelvin Skerrett (Halifax, Capt.), Gareth Stephens (Sheffield), Anthony Sullivan (St. Helens), Ian Watson (Swinton), Barry Williams (Workington).

Injury caused the withdrawal of Morley and Perrett; Williams was dropped after not attending training and Moriarty was refused permission to play by his new RU club Bristol. Into the squad came Andrew Grundy (Leigh), Craig Dean (Halifax player on loan to Featherstone), Martin Pearson (Halifax) and Welsh-born Steve Thomas (Bradford).

Both the Emerging England squad and the match were sponsored by global securities firm Thomson Electronic Settlements Group with the game to be known as the Thomson ESG International. Wales were sponsored by Brannigans, the live entertainment venues group.

● Although the match was billed as England v Wales, RFL chief executive Neil Tunnicliffe said that the home side was, in fact, Emerging England and the game was not awarded full international status. The *Rothmans RL Yearbook*, therefore does not credit the players with having played for England or Wales in a full international match, although appearances and any points scored are included in their overall career record.

THOMSON ESG INTERNATIONAL

Emerging England 15 v. Wales 12

St. Helens forward Paul Davidson came off the bench to snatch a late converted try that gave Emerging England an unconvincing victory over Wales at the Auto Quest Stadium, Widnes. Wales were leading 12-8 when Davidson replaced earlier tryscorer Andy Hay in the 57th minute and 12 minutes later he cut through for the equalising touchdown, to which Graham Holroyd added the winning goal. Sean Long capped the victory with a drop goal soon after that to leave Wales regretting their lack of goal-kicking success as both teams finished with two tries.

England and Great Britain coach Andy Goodway had looked on the game as a trial match to access the qualifications of players he needed to strengthen his squad for the Test series against New Zealand at the end of the season. He had chosen none of his near Test certainties for England, but few of those who played in a scrappy game made a strong claim for the Great Britain team. Salford Reds' Gary Broadbent was one exception at full back and St. Helens half back Long had his moments, too.

The outstanding player was in the Wales team, however, with Wigan Warriors prop Neil Cowie taking the sponsors' man of the match award with a powerful game up front. Wales, who selected their strongest possible team, also had the most impressive back as Iestyn Harris confirmed he would be one of Goodway's first choices for the Test. Having been a major star in the first half of the season at full back for Leeds Rhinos, Harris reverted impressively to stand off for Wales. He was involved in the build up to their first try, kicked two goals and combined well with young scrum half partner Lee Briers.

Referee John Connolly was criticised by Goodway for being too ready to blow his whistle and not letting the game flow, but both sides could also be blamed for the stop-start tempo as they made a succession of handling errors in wet conditions. Penalties went 11-8 to Wales, while Wales winger Jason Critchley was sent to the sin bin in the 30th minute for obstruction and the Welshmen did well not to concede a point in his absence. Wales substitute forward Rowland Phillips was placed on report for allegedly leading with his elbow and as he was registered with London Welsh Rugby Union club it raised an interesting point about what disciplinary action could be taken if he were found guilty. The situation never developed, however, as the RFL executive decided that he had no case to answer.

Until England's late victory surge, most of the excitement came in the first 16 minutes when the lead changed hands four times. Holroyd put England ahead with the first of his three goals after Karle Hammond was penalised for a high tackle on Simon Haughton. Wales hit back immediately and went in front after nine minutes with a well-worked try for Daio Powell. Half backs Harris and Briers linked up to bring Paul Atcheson charging through from full back before Powell finished off the move in fine style. Harris added the goal to give a further boost to Wales's rising confidence only for England to regain the lead within four minutes.

Paul Rowley and Holroyd combined to work the ball out to Keith Senior and his inside pass saw Hay cleave through for the touchdown. Holroyd's goal pushed England ahead, but the game took another sudden twist only three minutes later when Keiron Cunningham sneaked in from close range off Hammond's pass and Harris tagged on the goal to make it 12-8 to Wales after 16 minutes. And that's how it stayed for almost an hour as both teams failed to maintain their early promise.

England made the vital break through when Holroyd and Long set up Davidson for a strong burst to the line for his first try of the season, not having scored for St. Helens since moving from Oldham in 1997. Wales tried desperately to snatch back the lead in the closing stages, but they lacked the finishing touch and England hung on for a victory that had a hollow ring about it.

QUOTES

ANDY GOODWAY (England coach): The result wasn't that important. Everybody likes to win, but what is more important is that the public see quality players playing with freedom. We wanted the referee to let the game flow and get an entertaining, fast game. But the response of the crowd showed what they thought. Perhaps we should have an Emerging Referees' team. I still learned a lot, though. Not just from the game, but from the things we tried to do and the way players reacted to being outside their normal club environment.

CLIVE GRIFFITHS (Wales coach): At half-time I couldn't see us losing. But we made too many mistakes. That is why we lost the game. It's as simple as that. There were some good individual performances, particularly by Neil Cowie. I planned to take him off at some stage, but he was a dynamo and showed that he is the number one prop in this country at the moment.

KEITH SENIOR (England centre): The Welsh came out with all guns firing and really set about us. I was a bit surprised about how fierce they came, but we stuck to our guns to win it in the last 10 minutes. We won through sheer determination and this badge on our chest means a lot. We were also playing for Test places at the end of the season.

JOE LYDON (RFL technical director): As a contest it was excellent. The passion and commitment was there from both sides. The tackling was furious and we had no complaints. We wanted a close game, so one of the key areas we focused on was to try and balance the teams, which is why we ended up with a very experienced Wales side and an emerging young England side. If I was truthful, I would say Wales lost the game rather than England won it.

Harassed: Wales stand off Iestyn Harris gets to grips with Simon Haughton of Emerging England.

THOMSON ESG INTERNATIONAL MATCH

Sunday 19 July 1998   **Auto Quest Stadium, Widnes**

EMERGING ENGLAND   15   **WALES   12**

Gary Broadbent (Salford Reds)	Full back	Paul Atcheson (St. Helens)
Paul Sterling (Leeds Rhinos)	Wing	Jason Critchley (Castleford Tigers)
Nathan McAvoy (Salford Reds)	Centre	Damian Gibson (Halifax Blue Sox)
Keith Senior (Sheffield Eagles)	Centre	Daio Powell (Halifax Blue Sox)
Francis Cummins (Leeds Rhinos)	Wing	Anthony Sullivan (St. Helens)
Graham Holroyd (Leeds Rhinos)	Stand off	Iestyn Harris (Leeds Rhinos)
Sean Long (St. Helens)	Scrum half	Lee Briers (Warrington Wolves)
Steve Molloy (Sheffield Eagles), Captain	Prop	Kelvin Skerrett (Halifax Blue Sox), Captain
Paul Rowley (Halifax Blue Sox)	Hooker	Keiron Cunningham (St. Helens)
Darren Fleary (Leeds Rhinos)	Prop	Neil Cowie (Wigan Warriors)
Simon Haughton (Wigan Warriors)	Second row	Dean Busby (Hull Sharks)
Andy Hay (Leeds Rhinos)	Second row	Richard Eyres (Rochdale Hornets)
Lee Gilmour (Wigan Warriors)	Loose forward	Karle Hammond (St. Helens)

Substitutes
Mark Hilton (Warrington Wolves)
for Fleary (22 min.)
Paul Davidson (St. Helens)
for Hay (57 min.)
Paul Johnson (Wigan Warriors)
for McAvoy (45 min.)
Danny Orr (Castleford Tigers)
for Rowley (67 min.)
Fleary for Molloy (51 min.)
Molloy for Hilton (69 min.)

Substitutes
Gareth Stephens (Sheffield Eagles)
for Hall (77 min.)
Martin Hall (Halifax Blue Sox)
for Eyres (22 min.)
Rowland Phillips (London Welsh RU)
for Skerrett (27 min.)
Martin Pearson (Halifax Blue Sox)
for Powell (22 min.)
Skerrett for Phillips (52 min.)

T: Hay, Davidson
G: Holroyd (3), Long (dg)

T: Powell, Cunningham
G: Harris (2)

Coach: Andy Goodway

Coach: Clive Griffiths

Sin bin: Critchley (30 min.)
Penalties: 8-11
Half-time: 8-12

Attendance: 5154
Referee: John Connolly (Wigan)
Sponsors' man of the match: Neil Cowie

HOW THE SCORING WENT

6 min. Holroyd (England) penalty goal	2-0
9 min. Powell (Wales) try, Harris goal	2-6
13 min. Hay (England) try, Holroyd goal	8-6
16 min. Cunningham (Wales) try, Harris goal	8-12
69 min. Davidson (England) try, Holroyd goal	14-12
75 min. Long (England) drop goal	15-12

Kelvin Skerrett: Wales prop.

TRI-NATIONS CHAMPIONSHIP

France won the Tri-Nations Championship after beating the other two countries, Ireland and Scotland, to top the table in the end of season tournament. The new championship was introduced to provide more international matches and give Ireland and Scotland their first taste of competition rugby. It was also a chance for France to continue their steady progress after being withdrawn from Test matches against the more powerful Great Britain in 1994.

With so few Irish or Scottish-born professionals players, both countries relied almost entirely on established professionals whose parents or grandparents qualified them for selection.

The qualification rule was of particular benefit to Ireland and coach Steve O'Neill included the following Great Britain Test players when he named a 24-man squad on 16 September: Mick Cassidy (Wigan), Gary Connolly (Wigan), Bernard Dwyer (Bradford), Shaun Edwards (London), Mark Forster (Warrington), Joey Hayes (St. Helens), James Lowes (Bradford), Barrie McDermott (Leeds), Adrian Morley (Leeds) and Terry O'Connor (Wigan).

The rest of the squad was: Andy Burgess (Salford), Lee Child (Featherstone), Martin Crompton (Salford), Cliff Eccles (Salford), Neil Harmon (Bradford), Tommy Martyn (St. Helens), Ian Pickavance (St. Helens, later Huddersfield), Steve Prescott (Hull) and Richard Smith (Hull K.R.) plus five players from Irish clubs: Innes Gray (Bangor Vikings); Brian Carney, Sean Cleary, Connor O'Sullivan and Neil Ryan (Dublin Blues). Johnny Lawless (Sheffield) later replaced injured Lowes as hooker.

Scotland did not have one Test player in their 24-man squad when coach Billy McGinty and manager George Fairbairn announced it on 22 July, although prop Dale Laughton made his Great Britain debut against New Zealand later in the year. Nick Mardon and Iain Higgins were the only Scottish-born players in the original squad. The full squad, with country of birth, was:

England: Danny Arnold (Huddersfield), Joe Berry (Huddersfield), John Duffy (Warrington), Jason Flowers (Castleford), Nathan Graham (Bradford), Gareth Hewitt (Leeds), Dale Laughton (Sheffield), Jonathan Neill (Huddersfield), Lee Penny (Warrington), Jason Roach (Warrington), Graeme Shaw (Oldham), Jamie Smith (Hull), Mike Wainwright (Warrington); **Scotland:** Iain Higgins (London), Nick Mardon (London); **Australia:** Terry Matterson (London), Chris Orr (Huddersfield), Danny Russell (Huddersfield), Darren Shaw (Sheffield), Phil Veivers (Huddersfield); **New Zealand:** Logan Campbell (Hull), Brad Hepi (Hull), Pehi J. Solomon (Lancashire); **South Africa:** Jamie Bloem (Halifax). Later additions to the squad were English-born Mike Dixon (Hull K.R.) and Simon Knox (Bradford) plus Scottish-born Colin Wilson from amateur club Linlithgow Lions of Scotland.

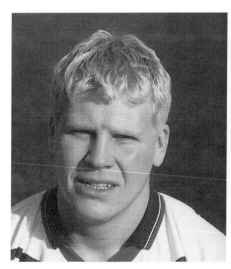

Mick Cassidy: Ireland forward.

TRI-NATIONS CHAMPIONSHIP

Ireland 22 v. France 24

The new Tri-Nations Championship opened with France snatching a dramatic victory in the last few seconds when Frederic Banquet converted his own try with a magnificent touchline goal at Tolka Park, Dublin. The former Wakefield Trinity, Featherstone Rovers and Sheffield Eagles player also kicked three other goals to finish with half of the French points in an outstanding full back display.

Two tries from Ireland scrum half Shaun Edwards took him into the top 20 all-time list of tryscorers with a club and representative career total of 321. He is now in joint 20th place with Johnny Lawrenson, the former Wigan, Workington Town and Swinton winger. The veteran still had hopes of regaining his long-held Great Britain place in the series against New Zealand and his first try was typical of many he scored at his peak. Edwards sent Richard Smith on a 40-metre break and kept up in support to take the return pass and go in for the 19th minute touchdown.

Another classic piece of vintage Edwards brought him his second try and led to Ireland taking the lead for the first time in the 42nd minute when he dummied through. Tommy Martyn, who made a confident international return after suffering a serious knee injury against France over a year earlier, added the goal to make it 16-14.

Ireland continued to pile on the pressure and when captain Martin Crompton went over in the 62nd minute for a try, goaled again by Martyn, they seemed to be heading for victory with an eight-point lead. But another exciting finish was building up. Eighteen months earlier it had been Ireland who battled back to earn a 30-30 draw in the closing minutes of the first ever meeting between the two countries. Now France were to do even better.

A try from Claude Sirvent began the fightback in the 73rd minute after Fabien Devicchi threw out a long pass which dropped short of its target, but bobbed up for Banquet to send in the substi-tute at the left hand corner. Ireland were still holding out with only two minutes left when Jean-Marc Garcia, who had been carried off on a stretcher in the 51st minute, sprung to life shortly after returning.

France's captain appeared to have scored a vital try when a snappy dummy opened the way for him to go round behind the posts only for a touch judge to report an obstruction and the touchdown was disallowed. But it was only a brief reprieve for Ireland as, with the seconds ticking away, France's last fling brought them victory with Banquet stretching out for the try to which he added the winning goal.

France had finished as they had begun, for they opened the tryscoring in the sixth minute when Garcia made the first of his many contribu-tions. The former Sheffield Eagles player put in a kick towards the home line and when the ball bounced off a defender's leg Garcia was there to touch down. Banquet added the goal and a penal-ty in the 23rd minute to put France back in front after Edwards had scored his first converted try.

They surged further ahead when the impres-sive Jerome Guisset squeezed out a pass close to the Irish line for Patrice Benausse to touch down and Banquet's goal made it 6-14. Ireland were in need of a boost and they got it when Cliff Eccles replaced Barrie McDermott. The prop made an immediate impact when he charged forward and hooked out a pass for Richard Smith to score to leave Ireland four points behind at the interval. They maintained their improvement in the sec-ond half to lead 22-14 with less than 10 minutes left when France made their late bid for victory.

'We got we deserved really,' said Ireland's coach Steve O'Neill. 'They've come over and done a good job on us tonight. We lacked match fitness because several of our players had not played for quite a few weeks. But you can't detract from a good French performance.'

France's manager Ivan Greseque said: 'The level in France has risen so much. We've been learning a lot from looking at Super League stan-dards. The team has worked hard and now we are ready for Super League.'

TRI-NATIONS CHAMPIONSHIP
Wednesday 4 November 1998   Tolka Park, Dublin

IRELAND 22		FRANCE 24
Steve Prescott (Hull Sharks)	Full back	Frederic Banquet (Villeneuve)
Lee Child (Featherstone R.)	Wing	Patrice Benausse (Carcassonne)
Mark Forster (Warrington W.)	Centre	Eric Vergniol (Tonneins)
Richard Smith (Hull K.R.)	Centre	Arnaud Dulac (St. Gaudens)
Brian Carney (Dublin Blues)	Wing	Gilles Gironella (XIII Catalan)
Tommy Martyn (St. Helens)	Stand off	Jean-Marc Garcia (St. Esteve), Captain
Shaun Edwards (London Broncos)	Scrum half	Fabien Devecchi (Villeneuve)
Neil Harmon (Bradford Bulls)	Prop	Jason Sands (Villefranche)
Johnny Lawless (Sheffield Eagles)	Hooker	Vincent Wulf (Villeneuve)
Barrie McDermott (Leeds Rhinos)	Prop	Jerome Guisset (St. Esteve)
Mick Cassidy (Wigan Warriors)	Second row	Romain Sort (Carpentras)
Ian Pickavance (Huddersfield Giants)	Second row	Gael Tallec (Castleford Tigers)
Martin Crompton (Salford Reds), Captain	Loose forward	Pascal Jampy (XIII Catalan)

Substitutes
Innes Gray (Bangor Vikings)
for Prescott (71 min.)
Cliff Eccles (Salford Reds)
for McDermott (28 min.)
Sean Cleary (Dublin Blues)
for Carney (25 min.)
Andy Burgess (Salford Reds)
for Harmon (55 min.)
McDermott for Pickavance (46 min.)

Substitutes
Claude Sirvent (St. Gaudens)
for Benausse (35-40 min. blood bin)
Abderazak El Khalouki (Toulouse)
for Sands (55 min.)
Frederic Teixido (Limoux)
for Tallec (28 min.)
Vea Bloomfield (Villeneuve)
for Teixido (60 min.)
Sirvent for Garcia (51 min.)
Sands for Guisset (70 min. blood bin)
Garcia for Benausse (74 min.)

T: Edwards (2), Smith, Crompton
G: Martyn (3)

T: Garcia, Benausse, Sirvent, Banquet
G: Banquet (4)

Coach: Steve O'Neill

Coaches: Patrick Pedrazzani, Gilles Dumas

Penalties: 5-11
Half-time: 10-14

Attendance: 1511
Referee: Claude Alba (France)

HOW THE SCORING WENT

6 min.	Garcia (France) try, Banquet goal	**0-6**
19 min.	Edwards (Ireland) try, Martyn goal	**6-6**
23 min.	Banquet (France) penalty goal	**6-8**
27 min.	Benausse (France) try, Banquet goal	**6-14**
30 min.	Smith (Ireland) try	**10-14**
42 min.	Edwards (Ireland) try, Martyn goal	**16-14**
63 min.	Crompton (Ireland) try, Martyn goal	**22-14**
73 min.	Sirvent (France) try	**22-18**
80 min.	Banquet (France) try and goal	**22-24**

Mark Forster: Ireland centre.

TRI-NATIONS CHAMPIONSHIP

France 26 v. Scotland 22

France became the first winners of the new Tri-Nations Championship by following up their 24-22 victory in Ireland with a similar scoreline defeat of Scotland at Perpignan. It was a further sign of France's progress as they overcame another side with plenty of experienced Super League players.

They again owed much to two players with British club experience, Frederic Banquet and captain Jean-Marc Garcia. Banquet totalled 10 points from a try and three goals, while Garcia scored the 55th minute try that put France in front for the first time and clinched victory with the final touchdown 10 minutes from the end.

But it was Scotland who dominated early on to score three unconverted tries in the first half hour and take a 16-12 interval lead. Their first try came after only six minutes when Lee Penny linked up from full back to send Jason Flowers over for a well-worked try. France hit back when their full back, Banquet, joined the attack to touch down four minutes later.

The duel between two enterprising full backs continued and Penny struck again as he sent Danny Arnold on a long run for Scotland's second try. Pehi J. Solomon then opened the way for Jason Roach to score the first of his two tries as Scotland grew in confidence.

But eight minutes before the interval France gave an indication of what was to follow when Claude Sirvent got them back into the game by touching down Banquet's kick ahead. Scotland's 16-12 half-time lead did not look too secure and within 15 minutes of the restart it had gone after a near length of the field run by French winger Gilles Gironella set up the position for Garcia to go in for his first try and Banquet added a goal.

Scotland snatched back the lead with Roach's second try but they could not last the pace and France finished much stronger with two tries in the last 10 minutes. Eric Vergniol went over in the 63rd minute and Garcia completed an impressive display with his second try.

France's late flourish was sparked off by key positional switches after they had gone 16-14 down in the 50th minute. Substitute Vincent Banet took over at scrum half with Fabien Devecchi moving to stand off and Garcia going into the centre. Although France missed a couple of scoring chances they began to play with some of their old traditional flair and Scotland were unable to match their free-flowing play.

They were more evenly matched in the forwards where France missed the power of injured Jerome Guisset and Castleford Tigers' Gael Tallec, who had both been such a force against Ireland. Although several of Scotland's players had not played since their club season ended a few weeks earlier, it is debatable whether that was a bigger handicap than France fielding players who were playing their fourth match in 10 days.

France's official man of the match award went to Garcia for an impressive all-round display, while Penny took the visitors' award on his debut for Scotland.

Garcia said: 'We've been working together as a national squad for two years now and I think we've proved that we're capable of competing with Super League players. There's more work still to do, but since Paris St. Germain, which gave a big boost to the game here, players have been more aware of what they need to do. Increased television coverage through Eurosport, who broadcast the Ireland match, has also made players and coaches want to do their best to present the best image of the game.'

Scotland coach Billy McGinty said: 'Many of the Scottish lads had not played any rugby for over two months and they were tired in that vital final quarter of the match. But I don't think we really lost the game there. We made too many mistakes early on and they capitalised on them. But it was a very closely matched game and the tournament is proving a huge success for all three countries.'

TRI-NATIONS CHAMPIONSHIP
Wednesday 11 November 1998 Stade Jean Laffon, Perpignan

FRANCE   26

Frederic Banquet (Villeneuve)	Full back
Claude Sirvent (St. Gaudens)	Wing
Eric Vergniol (Tonneins)	Centre
Arnaud Dulac (St. Gaudens)	Centre
Gilles Gironella (XIII Catalan)	Wing
Jean-Marc Garcia (St. Esteve), Captain	Stand off
Fabien Devecchi (Villeneuve)	Scrum half
Jason Sands (Villefrance)	Prop
Vincent Wulf (Villeneuve)	Hooker
Abderazak El Khalouki (Toulouse)	Prop
Romain Sort (Carpentras)	Second row
Eric Frayssinet (Toulouse)	Second row
Pascal Jampy (XIII Catalan)	Loose forward

SCOTLAND   22

Lee Penny (Warrington Wolves)	
Jason Roach (Warrington Wolves)	
Logan Campbell (Hull Sharks)	
Danny Arnold (Huddersfield Giants)	
Jason Flowers (Castleford Tigers)	
Chris Orr (Huddersfield Giants)	
John Duffy (Warrington Wolves)	
Darren Shaw (Sheffield Eagles)	
Danny Russell (Huddersfield G.), Captain	
Joe Berry (Huddersfield Giants)	
Mike Wainwright (Warrington Wolves)	
Pehi J. Solomon (Lancashire Lynx)	
Nathan Graham (Bradford Bulls)	

Substitutes
Vincent Banet (Limoux)
for Sirvent (40 min.)
Laurent Carrasco (Villeneuve)
for Frayssinet (40 min.)
Amar Tamghart (Carpentras)
for Jampy (74 min.)
Frederic Teixido (Limoux)
for Sands (62 min.)

T: Garcia (2), Banquet, Sirvent, Vergniol,
G: Banquet (3)

Coaches: Patrick Pedrazzani, Gilles Dumas

Half-time: 12-16
Attendance: 3,700

Substitutes
Gareth Hewitt (Leeds Rhinos)
for Campbell (20-30 min. blood bin)
Graeme Shaw (Oldham)
for Solomon (69 min.)
Simon Knox (Salford Reds)
for Wilson (57 min.)
Colin Wilson (Linlithgow Lions)
for Berry (31 min.)

T: Roach (2), Flowers, Arnold
G: Duffy (3)

Coach: Billy McGinty

Referee: Robert Connolly (Wigan)

HOW THE SCORING WENT

6 min.	Flowers (Scotland) try, Duffy goal	**0-6**
10 min.	Banquet (France) try and goal	**6-6**
12 min.	Banquet (France) penalty goal	**8-6**
18 min.	Arnold (Scotland) try, Duffy goal	**8-12**
25 min.	Roach (Scotland) try	**8-16**
32 min.	Sirvent (France) try	**12-16**
50 min.	Banquet (France) penalty goal	**14-16**
55 min.	Garcia (France) try	**18-16**
60 min.	Roach (Scotland) try, Duffy goal	**18-22**
63 min.	Vergniol (France) try	**22-22**
70 min.	Garcia (France) try	**26-22**

Lee Penny: Scotland full back.

TRI-NATIONS CHAMPIONSHIP

Scotland 10 v. Ireland 17

Ireland gained their first ever international victory after a tough battle at Firhill Park, Glasgow, to leave Scotland with the Tri-Nations wooden spoon on a cold, wet November night. It was Ireland's fourth match since they were given full international status in 1996 and their record now reads one win and a draw against two defeats.

They were strengthened considerably for the trip to Scotland by the inclusion of Wigan Warriors stars centre Gary Connolly and Terry O'Connor, who made their Ireland debuts after missing the match against France because they were with the Great Britain squad preparing for the Test series against New Zealand. O'Connor, in particular, stood out with a tremendous front row performance to take the *Open Rugby* man of the match award only four days after playing in the final Test.

Tommy Martyn was another key figure for Ireland at stand off, overcoming his disappointment at being left out of the Great Britain squad to score one try and have a hand in others by Richard Smith and Mark Forster. He also kicked two goals, including a second minute penalty which gave Ireland the lead they never lost. Sixteen minutes later Martyn instigated the move that led to Smith's try after Steve Prescott had linked up from full back.

Martyn tagged on the goal to give Ireland their 6-0 interval lead and early in the second half he continued his domination to add another six points with a try and goal. Scotland should have been prepared for Martyn's try as it was a copy of many he has scored for St. Helens, kicking through and winning the 15-metre chase to touch down.

Scotland scrum half John Duffy halted the Martyn show briefly when he nipped in for a try and added the goal in the 61st minute. But Martyn was back again four minutes later, shaping to drop a goal and then moving the ball wide for Mick Cassidy and Smith to send in Forster. Martin Crompton was not fooling a few minutes later when he did drop a goal to complete Ireland's scoring before Logan Campbell scored a last minute consolation try for Scotland.

Brian Carney, the only player from outside the English Leagues in either starting line-up, gained more encouraging reports after his eye-catching display against France. The Dublin Blues winger made up for his lack of top level experience with a determination that makes him one of Ireland's most promising prospects.

Scotland, who had beaten Ireland 26-6 in their only other encounter two years earlier, were always struggling this time despite a succession of penalties giving them plenty of possession. They again owed much to another good all-round performance by Lee Penny at full back, while Duffy produced some neat touches at half back just over a year after becoming the youngest international of all time at 17 years and a week.

There is no doubt, however, that Ireland have a stronger squad of top class players than Scotland. In addition to Connolly, Forster, O'Connor, Barrie McDermott and Mick Cassidy, who have all played for Great Britain, they were without other Test players Shaun Edwards, Adrian Morley, James Lowes and Bernard Dwyer. Dale Laughton, the only player with Great Britain experience in Scotland's squad did not play against Ireland.

Although the attendance of just over 1000 was down on Scotland's previous two matches in Glasgow, officials were not discouraged by the turn out on a cold, wet night and pointed out that these were still early days in the development of Rugby League in the country.

Coach Billy McGinty also thought Scotland's playing prospects looked good despite a second defeat leaving them at the bottom of the Tri-Nations table. 'Ireland took their opportunities and we didn't take ours,' said McGinty. 'But it was still a great performance by my lads and I'm proud of them all.'

Ireland's coach Steve O'Neill said: 'We are sowing the seeds and raising the awareness of the game in both countries. We will keep chiselling away and are determined to show people that Rugby League will not go away in Ireland and Scotland.'

TRI-NATIONS CHAMPIONSHIP
Wednesday 18 November 1998 Firhill Park, Partick Thistle FC, Glasgow

SCOTLAND 10		IRELAND 17
Lee Penny (Warrington Wolves)	Full back	Steve Prescott (Hull Sharks)
Jason Roach (Warrington Wolves)	Wing	Brian Carney (Dublin Blues)
Nathan Graham (Bradford Bulls)	Centre	Gary Connolly (Wigan Warriors)
Logan Campbell (Hull Sharks)	Centre	Richard Smith (Hull K.R.)
Danny Arnold (Huddersfield Giants)	Wing	Mark Forster (Warrington Wolves)
Chris Orr (Huddersfield Giants)	Stand off	Tommy Martyn (St. Helens)
John Duffy (Warrington Wolves)	Scrum half	Martin Crompton (Salford Reds), Captain
Darren Shaw (Sheffield Eagles)	Prop	Terry O'Connor (Wigan Warriors)
Danny Russell (Huddersfield G.), Captain	Hooker	Johnny Lawless (Sheffield Eagles)
Joe Berry (Huddersfield Giants)	Prop	Barrie McDermott (Leeds Rhinos)
Simon Knox (Salford Reds)	Second row	Neil Harmon (Bradford Bulls)
Pehi J. Solomon (Lancashire Lynx)	Second row	Mick Cassidy (Wigan Warriors)
Mike Wainwright (Warrington Wolves)	Loose forward	Andy Burgess (Salford Reds)

Substitutes
Mike Dixon (Hull K.R.)
for Russell (53 min.)
Graeme Shaw (Oldham)
for Berry (30 min.)
Jason Flowers (Castleford Tigers)
for Arnold (73 min.)
Colin Wilson (Linlithgow Lions)
Wainwright (31 min.)
Berry for Wilson (55 min.)
Wainwright for Shaw (59 min. blood bin)
Shaw for Knox (69 min.)

Substitutes
Lee Child (Featherstone Rovers)
for Forster (71 min.)
Cliff Eccles (Salford Reds)
for McDermott (30 min.)
Connor O'Sullivan (Dublin Blues)
for Burgess (75 min.)
Innes Gray (Bangor Vikings)
for Smith (77 min.)
McDermott for O'Connor (58 min.)
O'Connor for Eccles (71 min.)

T: Duffy, Campbell
G: Duffy

T: Smith, Martyn, Forster
G: Martyn (2), Crompton (dg)

Coach: Billy McGinty

Coach: Steve O'Neill

Penalties: 8-3
Half-time: 0-6

Attendance: 1028
Referee: John Connolly (Wigan)

HOW THE SCORING WENT

2 min.	Martyn (Ireland) penalty goal	0-2
18 min.	Smith (Ireland) try	0-6
46 min.	Martyn (Ireland) try and goal	0-12
61 min.	Duffy (Scotland) try and goal	6-12
65 min.	Forster (Ireland) try	6-16
72 min.	Crompton (Ireland) drop goal	6-17
80 min.	Campbell (Scotland) try	10-17

Steve Prescott: Ireland full back.

TRI-NATIONS CHAMPIONSHIP TABLE

	P	W	D	L	F	A	Pts
France	2	2	0	0	50	44	4
Ireland	2	1	0	1	39	34	2
Scotland	2	0	0	2	32	43	0

IRELAND INTERNATIONAL MATCHES

Date						Venue	Attendance
6 August 1996	Scotland	26	Ireland	6		Glasgow	1147
13 May 1997	France	30	Ireland	30		Paris	4250
4 November 1998	Ireland	22	France	24		Dublin	1511
18 November 1998	Scotland	10	Ireland	17		Glasgow	1028

SCOTLAND INTERNATIONAL MATCHES

Date						Venue	Attendance
6 August 1996	Scotland	26	Ireland	6		Glasgow	1147
9 July 1997	Scotland	20	France	22		Glasgow	2233
11 November 1998	France	26	Scotland	22		Perpignan	3700
18 November 1998	Scotland	10	Ireland	17		Glasgow	1028

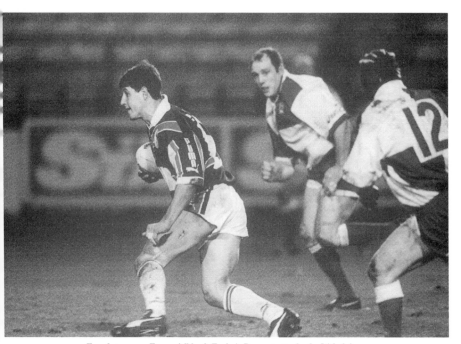

French pressure: France full back Frederic Banquet attacks the Irish defence.

IRELAND REGISTER

Includes only matches since Ireland were given full international status in 1996.
Substitute appearances are in lower case letters and are indicated in the player's total by a plus sign, e.g. (1+1).
Key: F - France; S - Scotland

BURGESS, Andy (3+1) Salford R: 1996 S; 1997 F; 1998 f,S

CARNEY, Brian (2) Dublin Blues: 1998 F,S
CASEY, Leo (2) Swinton L: 1996 S; 1997 F
CASSIDY, Mick (2) Wigan W: 1998 F,S
CHILD, Lee (2+1) Wakefield T: 1996 S; Featherstone R: 1998 F,s
CLEARY, Sean (+3) Dublin Blues: 1996 s; 1997 f; 1998 f
COMERFORD, Phelim (2) Dublin Blues:1996 S; 1997 F
CONNOLLY, Gary (1) Wigan W: 1998 S
CROMPTON, Martin (4) Oldham B: 1996 S; 1997 F; Salford R: 1998 F,S

DOYLE, Eric (+1) Dublin Blues: 1996 s
DWYER, Bernard (1) Bradford B: 1996 S

ECCLES, Cliff (1+2) Salford R: 1997 F; 1998 f,s
EDWARDS, Shaun (1) London B.: 1998 F

FORSTER, Mark (3) Warrington W: 1997 F; 1998 F,S
FOY, Des (1) Killarney: 1996 S

GARTH, Jonathan (1) Dublin Blues: 1996 S
GORDON, Gavin (2) Bangor Vikings 1996 S; London B: 1997 F
GRAY, Innes (+2) Bangor Vikings: 1998 f,s

HANLAN, Lee (2) Hunslet H: 1996 S; Keighley C: 1997 F
HARMON, Neil (3) Huddersfield G: 1997 F; Bradford B: 1998 F,S

KENNEDY, Phillip (+1) Belfast Buccaneers: 1996 s

LAWLESS, Johnny (2) Sheffield E: 1998 F,S
LOWES, James (2) Bradford B: 1996 S; 1997 F

McCALLION, Seamus (1) Bramley: 1996 S
McDERMOTT, Barrie (3) Leeds R: 1997 F; 1998 F,S
McELHATTON, Craig (+1) Bradford B: 1997 f
MARTYN, Tommy (3) St. Helens: 1997 F; 1998 F,S
MOFFAT, Dave (1) Hull: 1996 S

NUTTALL, Tony (+1) Oldham B: 1997 f

O'CONNOR, Terry (1) Wigan W: 1998 S
O'SULLIVAN, Conor (+1) Dublin Blues 1998 s

PICKAVANCE, Ian (1) Huddersfield G: 1998 F
PRESCOTT, Steve (2) Hull S: 1998 F,S

SMITH, Richard (3) Bradford B: 1997 F; Hull K.R: 1998 F,S

WYVILL, Shaun (+1) Skirlaugh ARL: 1996 s

Martin Crompton: Ireland captain.

SCOTLAND REGISTER

Includes only matches since Scotland were given full international status in 1996.
Substitute appearances are in lower case letters and are indicated in the player's total by a plus sign, e.g. (1+1).
Key: F - France; I - Ireland

ARNOLD, Danny (2) Huddersfield G: 1998 F,I

BELL, Glenn (1) Dewsbury R: 1997 F
BERRY, Joe (2) Huddersfield G: 1998 F,I
BLEE, Alisdair (+1) Loughborough: 1996 i

CAMPBELL, Logan (2) Hull S: 1998 F,I
CARR, Paul (1) Sheffield E: 1997 F
CHRISTIE, Gary (1) Bradford B: 1997 F
COWAN, Jim (1) Oldham B: 1996 I
CROWTHER, Matt (2) Sheffield E: 1996 I; 1997 F
CUSACK, Sean (1) Carlisle: 1996 I

DIXON, Mike (+2) Hull S: 1997 f; Hull K.R: 1998 i
DUFFY, John (3) Warrington W: 1997 F; 1998 F,I
DUNCAN, Andrew (+1) London B: 1997 f

FLOWERS, Jason (1+1) Castleford T: 1998 F,i

GAMBA, Billy (1) Aberdeen: 1996 I
GILMOUR, Scott (+1) Dundee Inst: 1996 i
GRAHAM, Nathan (2) Bradford B: 1998 F,I

HEWITT, Gareth (+1) Leeds R: 1998 f
HIGGINS, Robert "Iain" (+1) London B: 1997 f

KEENAN, Mark (1) Workington T: 1996 I
KETTERIDGE, Martin (1) Halifax B.S: 1996 I
KNOX, Simon (1+1) Bradford B: 1998 f,I

LAUGHTON, Dale (1) Wakefield T: 1997 F

McCARTHY, Stuart (1) Scottish Students: 1997 F
McKELVIE, Danny (+1) Dewsbury R: 1997 f
McLAREN, Jim (1) Wakefield T: 1997 F
MARDON, Nick (2) Boroughmuir: 1996 I; London B: 1997 F
MILNER, Lee (1) Huddersfield G: 1996 I
MURDOCK, Gary (+1) Ellenborough ARL: 1996 i

NEILL, Jon (1) Huddersfield G: 1997 F

ORR, Chris (2) Huddersfield G: 1998 F,I

PENNY, Lee (2) Warrington W: 1998 F,I

ROACH, Jason (2) Warrington W: 1998 F,I

RUSSELL, Danny (4) Carlisle: 1996 I; Huddersfield G: 1997 F; 1998 F,I

SHAW, Darren (3) London B: 1996 I; Sheffield E: 1998 F,I
SHAW, Graeme (+2) Oldham: 1998 f,i
SHELFORD, Darrall (1) Huddersfield G: 1996 I
SIMES, Jason (+1) Heriots: 1996 i
SOLOMON, Pehi James (3) Lancashire L: 1997 F; 1998 F,I

TAIT, Alan (1) Leeds: 1996 I
THOMPSON, Graeme (1) Edinburgh: 1996 I

VEIVERS, Phil (1) Huddersfield G: 1997 F

WAINWRIGHT, Mike (2) Warrington W: 1998 F,I
WILSON, Colin (+2) Linlithgow Lions: 1998 f,i

Danny Arnold: Two appearances for Scotland.

ENGLAND REGISTER
● Since 1975

The following is a register of England appearances since the reintroduction of European and World Championship matches in 1975, but does not include the challenge match against Australia played after the 1975 World Championship.

Figures in brackets are the total appearances for England since 1975, with the plus sign indicating substitute appearances, e.g. (7+3).

A few players also played in the 1969-70 European Championship and this is shown as an additional total outside bracket, e.g. (11)2.

World Championship matches are in bold letters. Substitute appearances are in lower case letters.

Key: A - Australia; Fi - Fiji; F - France; NZ - New Zealand; SA - South Africa; W - Wales

ADAMS, Mick (3+2) Widnes: 1975 NZ, a; 1978 F; 1979 W; 1981 w
ARKWRIGHT, Chris (+1) St. Helens: 1984 w
ATKINSON, John (7)4 Leeds: 1975 W, F, W, NZ, W; 1978 F, W

BALDWIN, Simon (1+1) Halifax: 1995 w, F
BANKS, Barry (+1) York: 1979 f
BEARDMORE, Kevin (1) Castleford: 1984 W
BENTLEY, John (5) Halifax: 1995 F, A, Fi, SA; 1996W
BETTS, Denis (4) Auckland W.: 1995 A, A, Fi, W
BEVERLEY, Harry (1) Workington T: 1979 W
BLAKELEY, Steve (1+1) Salford R.: 1996 F, w
BRIDGES, John "Keith" (7) Featherstone R: 1975 NZ, A, W, F, NZ, A; 1977 W
BROADBENT, Paul (4+1) Sheffield E.: 1995 F, Fi, sa; 1996 F, W
BURKE, Mick (1) Widnes: 1984 W
BUSBY, Dean (+1) Hull: 1992 w
BUTT, Ikram (1) Featherstone R.: 1995 W

CAIRNS, David (1) Barrow: 1984 W
CALLAND, Matt (+1) Bradford B.: 1996 f
CASE, Brian (1) Warrington: 1981 F
CASEY, Len (5) Hull KR: 1978 F, W; 1980 W; 1981 F, W
CASSIDY, Mick (2+4) Wigan: 1995 w, a, Fi, SA, w, 1996w
CHARLTON, Paul (1) Salford: 1975 F
CHISNALL, Dave (3+1) Warrington: 1975 w, F, W, NZ
CHISNALL, Eric (3+1) St. Helens: 1975 F, W, NZ, a
CLARK, Garry (1) Hull KR: 1984 W

CLARKE, Phil (6) Wigan: 1992 W; 1995 W; Sydney C.R.: A, A, SA, W
CONNOLLY, Gary (4) St. Helens: 1992 W; Wigan: 1996 F, W; 1995 A
COOK, Paul (1+1) Leeds: 1995 fi, SA
COOKSON, Phil (2) Leeds: 1975 NZ, A
COULMAN, Mike (5) Salford: 1975 F, W, W, A; 1977 F
CRITCHLEY, Jason (+1) Salford: 1992 w
CROOKS, Lee (1) Castleford: 1992 W
CUMMINS, Francis (1) Leeds: 1995 F
CUNNINGHAM, John (2) Barrow: 1975 F, W

DONLAN, Steve (1) Leigh: 1984 W
DRUMMOND, Des (5) Leigh: 1980 W, F; 1981 F, W; 1984 W
DUNN, Ged (6) Hull KR: 1975 W, A, F, NZ, A; 1977 F
DYL, Les (12+1) Leeds: 1975 W, F, F, W, NZ, A, nz, A; 1977 W, F; 1978 F, W; 1981 W

ECKERSLEY, Dave (+5) St. Helens: 1975 f, w, f; Widnes: 1977 w; 1978 w
EDWARDS, Shaun (3) Wigan: 1995 A; 1996 F, W
ELWELL, Keith (2) Widnes: 1978 F, W
EVANS, Steve (3) Featherstone R: 1979 F; 1980 W, F
EYRES, Richard (1) Widnes: 1992 W

FAIRBAIRN, George (15) Wigan: 1975 W, NZ, A, W, F, NZ, A; 1977 W, F; 1978 F; 1980 W, F; 1981 F, W; Hull KR: 1981 W
FARRAR, Vince (1) Featherstone R: 1977 F
FARRELL, Andrew (5) Wigan: 1995 A, A, Fi, W; 1996 W
FARRELL, Anthony (1) Sheffield E.: 1995 W
FENTON, Steve (2) Castleford: 1981 F, W
FIELDING, Keith (7) Salford: 1975 F, F, W, NZ, A, W, F
FORD, Mike (1) Castleford: 1992 W
FORSYTH, Colin (3) Bradford N: 1975 W, F, NZ
FOX, Deryck (2) Bradford N.: 1995 W, F

GAY, Richard (2) Hull: 1995 W, F
GILL, Henderson (1) Wigan: 1981 W
GILL, Ken (9+2) Salford: 1975 W, F, w, NZ, a, W, F, NZ, A; 1977 W, F
GLYNN, Peter (2) St. Helens: 1979 W, F
GODDARD, Richard (1) Castleford: 1995 F
GOODWAY, Andy (1) Oldham: 1984 W
GORLEY, Les (1+1) Workington T: 1977 W; Widnes: 1981 w
GORLEY, Peter (2+1) St. Helens: 1980 W, f; 1981 W
GOULDING, Bobbie (4+1) St. Helens: 1995 A, Fi, SA, W; 1996 w
GRAY, John (3) Wigan: 1975 F, W, F
GRAYSHON, Jeff (9+1) Dewsbury: 1975 W, F, NZ, A; 1977 W; Bradford N: 1979 W, F; 1980 w, F; 1981 W
HANLEY, Ellery (2) Bradford N: 1984 W; Leeds: 1992 W
HARRISON, Karl (6) Halifax: 1995 W, A, A, SA, W; 1996 F

HARRISON, Mick (2) Leeds: 1978 F, W
HAUGHTON, Simon (1+3) Wigan: 1995 **a, fi, SA, w**
HILTON, Mark (+1) Warrington, 1995 f
HOBBS, David (1) Featherstone R: 1984 W
HOGAN, Brian (5) Wigan: 1975 **W, F, NZ, A**; 1977 W
HOGAN, Phil (1) Hull KR: 1979 F
HOLDING, Neil (1) St. Helens: 1980 W
HOLDSTOCK, Roy (3) Hull KR: 1980 W, F; 1981 W
HOLGATE, Stephen (1) Workington T.: 1995 F
HOLMES, John (5+2) Leeds: 1975 **W, F, NZ, A**; 1977 W,
   f; 1978 f
HOWARD, Harvey (1) Leeds: 1995 W
HUDDART, Milton (1) Whitehaven: 1984 W
HUGHES, Eric (8+1) Widnes: 1975 **W, F, NZ, a**; 1977 F;
   1978 F, W; 1979 W, F
HUNTE, Alan (1) St. Helens: 1992 W

IRVING, Bob (3) Wigan: 1975 **W, F, A**

JACKSON, Lee (6) Hull: 1992 W; Sheffield E.: 1995 F, **A,
   A, Fi, W**
JACKSON, Phil (2) Bradford N: 1975 W, F
JONES, Les (1) St. Helens: 1977 W
JOYNER, John (4) Castleford: 1980 W, F; 1981 F, W
JOYNT, Chris (3+3) St. Helens: 1992 w; 1995 **a, a, SA**;
   1996 F, W

KELLY, Andy (1) Hull KR: 1984 W
KELLY, Ken (3) Warrington: 1979 W; 1981 F, W

LAUGHTON, Doug (1) Widnes: 1977 W
LAWLESS, Johnny (2) Sheffield E.: 1996 F, W
LEDGER, Barry (+1) St. Helens: 1984 w
LIPTROT, Graham (2) St. Helens: 1979 W, F
LOCKWOOD, Brian (2)+1 Hull KR: 1979 W, F
LOWE, Phil (3)2 Hull KR: 1977 F; 1978 F; 1981 W

McAVOY, Nathan (1) Salford R.: 1996 W
McCURRIE, Steve (+3) Widnes: 1995 w, f, **fi**
McDERMOTT, Barrie (+1) Leeds: 1996 w
McNAMARA Steve (2+1) Hull: 1995, w, f; Bradford B.:
   1996 F
MARTYN, Tommy (4+1) Warrington: 1975 W, **F, w**; 1979
   W, F
MATHER, Barrie-Jon (2) Wigan: 1995 **A, SA**
MILLINGTON, John (2) Hull KR: 1975 F; 1981 W
MILLWARD, Roger (13)3+1 Hull KR: 1975 F, W, **F, W,
   A, W, F, NZ, A**; 1977 W, F; 1978 F, W
MOLLOY, Steve (2+1) Leeds: 1992 W; Featherstone R.:
   1996 f, W
MORGAN, Mick (3+3) Wakefield T: 1975 f, W, **f, W, nz,
   A**
MORLEY, Adrian (+1) Leeds: 1996 f
MUMBY, Keith (2) Bradford N: 1979 W, F
MURPHY, Martin (1) Oldham: 1975 F

NASH, Steve (7) Featherstone R: 1975 **W, NZ, A**; Salford:

NEWLOVE, Paul (7) Featherstone R: 1992 W;
   Bradford N.: 1995 **W, A, A, Fi, W**; St. Helens: 1996 F
NICHOLLS, George (7+4) St. Helens: 1975 F, **F, W, NZ,
   A, w, nz, f;** 1977 f; 1978 F, W
NICKLE, Sonny (1) St. Helens: 1995 W
NOONAN, Derek (3) Warrington: 1975 W, **F, W**
NORTON, Steve (11) Castleford: 1975 **W, NZ, A, W, F,
   NZ, A;** 1977 F; Hull: 1978 W; 1981 W, W

OFFIAH, Martin (5) Wigan: 1992 W; 1995 **A, SA, W;** 1996 F
O'NEILL, Steve (1) Wigan: 1981 F

PATTINSON, Bill (1+1) Workington T: 1981 f, W
PHILBIN, Barry (1) Warrington: 1975 **F**
PIMBLETT, Geoff (1) St. Helens: 1978 W
PINKNEY, Nick (4) Keighley C.: 1995 F, **Fi, SA, W**
PINNER, Harry (3) St. Helens: 1980 W, F; 1981 F
PLATT, Andy (4) Widnes/Auckland W.: 1995 **A, A, SA, W**
POTTER, Ian (2) Warrington: 1981 F, W
POWELL, Daryl (5+1) Sheffield E: 1992 w; Keighley C.:
   1995 W, F, **A, SA;** 1996 W
PRESCOTT, Steve (2) St. Helens: 1996 F, W

RADLINSKI, Kris (4+1) Wigan: 1995 **A, A, sa, W, Fi**
RAYNE, Keith (2) Wakefield T: 1980 W, F
REDFEARN, Alan (2) Bradford N: 1979 F; 1980 F
REDFEARN, Dave (2) Bradford N: 1975 F, **A**
REILLY, Malcolm (+1)2 Castleford: 1977 w
RICHARDSON, Terry (1) Castleford: 1981 W
ROBINSON, Jason (7) Wigan: 1995 W, **A, A, Fi, W;** 1996
   F, W
ROSE, Paul (2) Hull KR: 1977 F; 1978 W
ROWLEY, Paul (+1) Halifax B. S.: 1996 f
RUSSELL, Richard (1) Castleford: 1995 W

SAMPSON, Dean (1+2) Castleford: 1995 **Fi, sa, w**
SCHOFIELD, Garry (3) Hull: 1984 W; Leeds: 1992 W;
   1995 W
SCULTHORPE, Paul (2) Warrington: 1996 F,W
SHEARD, Les (1) Wakefield T: 1975 W
SIMPSON, Roger (+1) Bradford N.: 1995 f
SMITH, David (1) Leeds: 1977 F
SMITH, Keith (1) Wakefield T: 1979 W
SMITH, Mike (5) Hull KR: 1980 W, F; 1981 F, W, W
SMITH, Peter (1) Featherstone R: 1980 F
SMITH, Tony (3+2) Castleford: 1995 f, **A, Fi, sa, W**
SPRUCE, Stuart (1) Widnes: 1992 W
STEPHENS, Gary (1) Castleford: 1979 W
SZYMALA, Eddie (+1) Barrow: 1979 f

THOMPSON, Jimmy (2+1)1 Featherstone R: 1975 **A;**
   1977 W; Bradford N: 1978 w
TINDALL, Keith (1) Hull: 1979 F
TOPLISS, David (1) Wakefield T: 1975 F

WADDELL, Hugh (1) Blackpool B: 1984 W

WALKER, Arnold (1) Whitehaven: 1981 F
WALSH, John (3) St. Helens: 1975 F, **NZ**, **A**
WARD, David (6) Leeds: 1977 F; 1980 W, F; 1981 F, W, W
WATKINSON, David (+1) Hull KR: 1977 w
WOODS, John (3+4) Leigh: 1979 w, F; 1980 w, F; 1981 f, w, W
WRIGHT, Nigel (1) Wakefield T.: 1995 F
WRIGHT, Stuart (7) Wigan: 1975 **NZ**; Widnes: 1977 W; 1978 F, W; 1979 W, F; 1980 W

WALES REGISTER

● Since 1975
Figures in brackets are the total appearances for Wales since 1975, with the plus sign indicating substitute appearances, e.g. (7+3).

A few players also played in the 1969-70 European Championship and this is shown as an additional total outside bracket, e.g. (11)2.

Appearances against Emerging England are not included.

World Championship matches are in bold letters. Substitute appearances are in lower case letters. Key: A - Australia; E - England; F - France; NZ - New Zealand; P - Papua New Guinea; WS - Western Samoa

ACKERMAN, Rob (4+1) Carlisle: 1991 P; 1992 F; Salford: 1992 E, F; Cardiff I. ARL: 1993 nz

ATCHESON, Paul (4+1) Wigan: 1995 E, F; Oldham: **ws**; 1996 F, E

BANNER, Peter (9) Salford: 1975 F, E, **F**, **E**, **NZ**; Featherstone R: 1975 **E**, **A**, **NZ**, **F**

BATEMAN, Allan (12) Warrington: 1991 P; 1992 F, E, F; 1993 NZ; 1994 F; 1995 E, F, **F**, **WS**, **E**; 1996 Cronulla: E

BAYLISS, Steve (1) St. Helens: 1981 E

BEVAN, John (17) Warrington: 1975 F, E, **E**, **A**, **NZ**, **F**; 1977 E, F; 1978 A; 1979 F, E; 1980 F, E; 1981 F, E, E; 1982 A

BISHOP, David (4) Hull KR: 1991 P; 1992 F; London C: 1992 E, F

BOX, Harold (5) Featherstone R: 1979 F, E; 1980 F, E; Wakefield T: 1981 F

BUTLER, Brian (2+2) Swinton: 1975 **F**, **nz**; Warrington: 1975 **f**; 1977 F

CAMBRIANI, Adrian (3) Fulham: 1981 F, E, E

CAMILLERI, Chris (3) Barrow: 1980 F; Widnes: 1982 A; Bridgend: 1984 E

CORDLE, Gerald (4+2) Bradford N: 1991 p; 1992 E; 1993 NZ; 1994 F, a; S. Wales: 1996 F

COSLETT, Kel (8)2 St. Helens: 1975 F, E, **F**, **E**, **A**, **NZ**, E, A

COWIE, Neil (1+3) Wigan: 1995 e, f, **ws**; 1996 E

CRITCHLEY, Jason (2) Keighley C.: 1996 F, E

CUNNINGHAM, Eddie (8) St. Helens: 1975 **E**, **A**, **E**, **A**; 1977 E; 1978 F, E, A

CUNNINGHAM, Keiron (2+3) St. Helens: 1995 **f**, **ws**, **e**; 1996 F, E

CUNNINGHAM, Tommy (2) Warrington: 1979 F, E

CURLING, Dennis (+1) Warrington: 1977 f

DAVID, Tommy (2) Cardiff C: 1981 E; 1982 A

DAVIES, Frank (1) New Hunslet: 1978 E

DAVIES, Gareth (2) Warrington: 1996 F, E

DAVIES, Jonathan (9) Widnes: 1991 P; 1992 F; Warrington: 1993 NZ; 1994 F; 1995 E, F, **F**, **WS**, **E**

DAVIES, Mike (1) Bridgend: 1984 E

DEVEREUX, John (10) Widnes: 1991 P; 1992 F, E, F; 1993 NZ; 1994 A; 1995 F, **F**, **WS**, **E**

DIAMOND, Steve (2+1) Wakefield T: 1980 F, e; 1981 F

DIXON, Colin (10)3 Salford: 1975 F, E, **F**, **E**, **NZ**, **A**; 1977 E, F; 1978 F; Hull KR: 1981 E

EDWARDS, Diccon (1) Castleford T.: 1996 E

ELLIS, Kevin (12) Warrington: 1991 P; 1992 F, E, F; 1993 NZ; 1994 F, A; 1995 **F**, **WS**, **E**; Workington T.: 1995 F, F

EVANS, Richard (5) Swinton: 1975 E, **F**, **F**; 1978 F; Salford: 1978 E

EYRES, Richard (5) Leeds: 1995 E, F, **F**, **WS**, **E**

FENWICK, Steve (2) Cardiff C: 1981 E; 1982 A

FISHER, Tony (10)4 Leeds: 1975 F, **E**, **A**, **NZ**; Castleford: 1975 **E**, **A**, **NZ**; 1977 E, F; Bradford N: 1978 A

FLOWERS, Ness (4) Wigan: 1980 F, E; 1981 E; Bridgend: 1984 E

FORD, Phil (9+1) Warrington: 1984 E; Leeds: 1991 P; 1992 F; Salford: 1992 E, F; 1993 NZ; 1994 F, A; 1995 E, f

FRANCIS, Bill (19) Wigan: 1975 F, E, **F**, **E**, **A**, **NZ**, **E**, **A**, **NZ**, **F**; 1977 E, F; St. Helens: 1978 F, E, A; 1979 F, E; Oldham: 1980 F, E

GALLACHER, Stuart (3+1) Keighley: 1975 f, E, **NZ**, **F**

GIBBS, Scott (3) St. Helens: 1994 A, 1995 F, **E**

GREGORY, Brian (3) Wigan: 1975 **E**, **NZ**, **F**

GRIFFITHS, Clive (+2) St. Helens: 1980 f; 1981 f

GRIFFITHS, Jonathan (6) St. Helens: 1991 P; 1992 F, E; 1993 NZ; 1994 F, A

HADLEY, Adrian (3+6) Salford: 1991 p; 1992 f; Widnes: 1992 e, F; 1993 nz; 1994 A; 1995 f, **f**, **WS**

HALL, Martin (5+2) Wigan: 1995 E, F, **WS**, **E**; 1996 f, e

HALLETT, Lynn (2) Cardiff C: 1982 A; Bridgend: 1984 E

HARRIS, Iestyn (8) Warrington: 1994 A, 1995 E, F, **F**, **WS**, **E**; 1996 F, E

HERDMAN, Martin (2+1) Fulham: 1981 e, E; 1982 A

HOPKINS, Lyn (1) Workington T: 1982 A

JAMES, Mel (11) St. Helens: 1975 **E**; 1978 F, E, A; 1979 F, E; 1980 F, E; 1981 F, E, E

JOHNS, Graeme (+2) Salford: 1979 f; Blackpool B: 1984 e

JONES, Clive (1+3) Leigh: 1975 **nz**, **F**; 1978 f, e

JONES, Mark (7+2) Hull: 1991 P; 1992 F, E; 1993 NZ; 1994 F; Warrington: **f**, **e**; 1996 F, E

JULIFF, Brian (8) Wakefield T: 1979 F, E; 1980 F, E; 1981 F, E; Wigan: 1982 A; 1984 E

KENNETT, Paul (+1) Swinton: 1992 f

LEE, Jason (+2) Warrington: 1994 a; 1996 f

McJENNETT, Mark (2+1) Barrow: 1980 F; 1982 a; 1984 E

MANTLE, John (11+1)3 St. Helens: 1975 F, E, **F**, **e**, **A**, **NZ**, **E**, **A**, **NZ**, **F**; 1977 E; 1978 E

MARLOW, Ian (5+1) Hull: 1992 F, E, F; Wakefield T: 1993 NZ; 1994 f, A

MATHIAS, Roy (20) St. Helens: 1975 F, E, **F**, **E**, **A**, **NZ**, **A**, **NZ**, **F**; 1977 E, F; 1978 F, E, A; 1979 F, E; 1980 F, E; 1981 F, E

MILLS, Jim (13)4 Widnes: 1975 F, E, **E**, **A**, **NZ**, **A**, **NZ**; 1977 E, F; 1978 F, E, A; 1979 E

MORAN, Mark (+2) Leigh: 1992 e, f

MORIARTY, Paul (12) Widnes: 1991 P; 1992 E, F; 1994 F; Halifax: 1994 A; 1995 E, **F**, **WS**, **E**; 1996 S. Wales: F, E

MORLEY, Chris (1+1) St. Helens: 1996 f, E

MURPHY, Mick (4+1) Bradford N: 1975 **F**, **NZ**, **F**; 1977 f; St. Jacques, France: 1979 F

NICHOLAS, Mike (4+2) Warrington: 1975 F, e; 1977 E, F; 1978 F; 1979 e

O'BRIEN, Chris (1) Bridgend: 1984 E

OWEN, Gareth (2) Oldham: 1981 E, F

OWEN, Roger (+2) St. Helens: 1981 f, e

PARRY, Donald (6) Blackpool B: 1980 F, E; 1981 F, E, E; 1982 A

PEARCE, Gary (1+3) Scarborough P: 1991 p; Ryedale-York: 1992 f, e, F

PERRETT, Mark (7) Halifax: 1994 F, A; 1995 E, F, **F**; 1996 F, E

PHILLIPS, Rowland (5+9) Warrington: 1991 p; 1992 f, e, F; 1993 NZ; 1994 F, A; Workington T.: 1995 e, f, **f**, **ws**, **e**; 1996 F, e

POWELL, Daio (+2) Bradford N: 1994 f, a

PREECE, Chris (1) Bradford N: 1984 E

PRENDIVILLE, Paul (4+2) Hull: 1979 e; 1980 E; 1981 F, e; 1982 A; 1984 E

PRITCHARD, Gordon (1+2) Barrow: 1978 f, e; Cardiff C: 1981 E

QUINNELL, Scott (2) Wigan: 1995 **WS**, **E**

RICHARDS, Maurice (2)1 Salford: 1975 **F**; 1977 E

RINGER, Paul (2) Cardiff C: 1981 E; 1982 A

RISMAN, John (2+1) Workington T: 1978 F; 1979 f, E

ROWE, Peter (4+3)2 Blackpool B: 1975 **a**, **e**, **a**; Huddersfield: 1977 E, F; 1979 F, E

RULE, Steve (1) Salford: 1981 E

SELDON, Chris (1+1) St. Helens: 1980 f, E

SHAW, Glyn (7) Widnes: 1978 F, A; 1980 F, E; 1981 E; Wigan: 1982 A; 1984 E

SILVA, Matthew (+1) Halifax: 1991 p

SKERRETT, Kelvin (5) Wigan: 1995 E, F, **F**, **WS**, **E**

SKERRETT, Trevor (7) Wakefield T: 1978 A; 1979 F, E; 1980 F; Hull: 1981 F, E; 1984 E

STEPHENS, Gareth (+1) Hull: 1996 e

STEVENS, Ian (+1) Hull: 1992 f

Tommy David: Two appearances for Wales.

349

SULLIVAN, Anthony (13) St. Helens: 1991 P; 1992 F, E, F; 1993 NZ; 1994 F, A: 1995 E, F, **F**, **WS**, E; 1996 F
SULLIVAN, Clive (10)4 Hull KR: 1975 **E**, **A**, **NZ**, **E**; 1977 F; 1978 F, E, A; 1979 F, E

TREASURE, David (5) Oldham: 1975 **E**, **A**, **NZ**, **E**; 1977 F
TURNER, Glyn (3+3) Hull KR: 1975 **e**, **A**, **e**, **A**, **f**; Hull: 1978 E

WALLACE, Richard (+1) York: 1975 **f**
WALTERS, Graham (2+1) Hull: 1980 E; 1981 E; Bridgend 1984 e
WANBON, Bobby (3)3+1 Warrington: 1975 **E**, **A**, **NZ**
WATKINS, David (14) Salford: 1975 F, E, **F**, **E**, **A**, **NZ**, **E**, **A**, **NZ**, **F**; 1977 E; 1978 E, A; 1979 F
WATSON, Ian (2) Salford R: 1996 F, E
WEBSTER, Richard (+4) Salford: 1994 f, a; 1996 f, e

WILKINS, Ray (1+1) Workington T: 1977 e, F
WILLIAMS, Barry (4) Carlisle: 1991 P; 1992 F; 1993 NZ; 1994 F
WILLIAMS, Brynmor (1) Cardiff C: 1982 A
WILLIAMS, Peter (+1) Salford: 1992 f
WILLICOMBE, David (11)+2 Wigan: 1975 F, E, **F**, **E**, **A**, **NZ**, **NZ**, **F**; 1978 F, E, A
WILSON, Danny (4) Swinton: 1981 F, E, E; 1984 E
WILSON, Frank (7+2)4 St. Helens: 1975 F, E, **F**, **e**, **a**, **E**, **A**, **NZ**, **F**
WOODS, Paul (10) Widnes: 1977 E, F; 1978 F, E, A; Rochdale H: 1979 F, E; Hull: 1980 E; 1981 F, E

YOUNG, David (13) Salford: 1991 P; 1992 F, E, F; 1993 NZ; 1994 F, A; 1995 E, F, **F**, **WS**, E; 1996 F

ENGLAND RECORDS

Highest score:	73-6 v. France at Gateshead, 12 June 1996 (Also widest margin win)
Highest score against:	63-13* v. Australia at Paris, 31 December 1933

*England included Welshmen. Highest score against All-England side 42-13 v. France at Marseilles, 25 November 1951 (Also widest margin defeat)

Most tries in a match:	4 by Jim Leytham (Wigan) v. Other Nationalities at Bradford, 2 January 1905
	4 by Stan Moorhouse (Huddersfield) v. Wales at Plymouth, 15 February 1913
	4 by Peter Norburn (Swinton) v. Other Nationalities at Wigan, 28 November 1953
	4 by Keith Fielding (Salford) v. France at Bordeaux, 11 October 1975
	4 by Stuart Wright (Widnes) v. Wales at St. Helens, 28 May 1978
	4 by Martin Offiah (Wigan) v. France at Gateshead, 12 June 1996
Most goals in a match:	9 by Geoff Pimblett (St. Helens) v. Wales at St. Helens, 28 May 1978
Most points in a match:	22 by Steve Prescott (St. Helens) v. France at Gateshead, 12 June 1996
Biggest home attendance:	27,500 v. Wales at Wigan, 1 March 1950

WALES RECORDS

Highest score:	68-0 v. Papua New Guinea at Swansea C. FC, 27 October 1991 (Also widest margin win)
Highest score against:	60-13 v. England at St. Helens, 28 May 1978 (Also widest margin defeat)
Most tries in a match:	4 by Will (W.T.) Davies (Halifax) v. Australia at Ebbw Vale, 7 October 1911
Most goals and points in a match:	8g-24pts by Jonathan Davies (Widnes) v. Papua New Guinea at Swansea C. FC, 27 October 1991
Biggest home attendance:	30,000 v. England at Swansea, 24 November 1945

ENGLAND SYNOPSIS

	P	W	D	L	F	A
v. FRANCE						
Euro'n Championship	28	19	2	7	414	313
World Cup	2	2	0	0	68	4
Other matches	1	1	0	0	18	6
Totals	31	22	2	7	500	323
v. WALES						
Euro'n Championship	27	17	0	10	485	261
World Championship	3	2	0	1	54	38
Other matches	32	25	2	5	670	429
Totals	62	44	2	16	1,209	728
v. AUSTRALIA						
World Championship	4	2	1	1	54	55
Other matches	9	5	1	3	93	153
Totals	13	7	2	4	147	208
v. NEW ZEALAND						
World Championship	2	1	1	0	44	29
Others	1	1	0	0	18	16
Totals	3	2	1	0	62	45
v. PAPUA NEW GUINEA						
Other matches	1	1	0	0	40	12
v. FIJI						
World Championship	1	1	0	0	46	0
v. SOUTH AFRICA						
World Championship	1	1	0	0	46	0
v. OTHER NATIONALITIES						
Euro'n Championship	6	2	0	4	106	152
Other matches	10	6	1	3	230	173
Totals	16	8	1	7	336	325
GRAND TOTALS	128	86	8	34	2,386	1,641

WALES SYNOPSIS

	P	W	D	L	F	A
v. ENGLAND						
Euro'n Championship	27	10	0	17	261	485
World Championship	3	1	0	2	38	54
Other matches	32	5	2	25	429	670
Totals	62	16	2	44	728	1,209
v. FRANCE						
Euro'n Championship	27	11	0	16	390	391
World Championship	3	2	0	1	58	22
Other matches	6	3	0	3	91	101
Totals	36	16	0	20	539	514
v. AUSTRALIA						
World Championship	2	0	0	2	19	48
Other matches	8	0	0	8	84	229
Totals	10	0	0	10	103	277
v. NEW ZEALAND						
World Championship	2	1	0	1	33	37
Other matches	5	2	0	3	85	83
Totals	7	3	0	4	118	120
v. PAPUA NEW GUINEA						
Other matches	1	1	0	0	68	0
v. WESTERN SAMOA						
World Championship	1	1	0	0	22	10
v. OTHER NATIONALITIES						
Euro'n Championship	5	1	0	4	60	101
GRAND TOTALS	122	38	2	82	1,638	2,231
Also						
v. EMERGING ENGLAND						
Other match	1	0	0	1	12	15

Ward off: England hooker David Ward breaks clear against Wales in 1981.

UNDER-21s

GREAT BRITAIN
UNDER-21s RESULTS

25 Nov.	1984	W	24-8	v. F	Castleford
16 Dec.	1984	W	8-2	v. F	Albi
9 Oct.	1985	L	12-16	v. NZ	Bradford
19 Jan.	1986	L	6-19	v. F	St. Esteve
2 Feb.	1986	W	6-2	v. F	Whitehaven
8 Mar.	1987	W	40-7	v. F	St. Jean de Luz
21 Mar.	1987	W	54-6	v. F	St. Helens
6 Mar.	1988	L	13-14	v. F	Ausillon
19 Mar.	1988	L	4-8	v. F	St. Helens
20 Jan.	1989	W	30-0	v. F	Leeds
4 Feb.	1989	L	8-16	v. F	Carpentras
20 Jan.	1990	W	22-0	v. F	Villeneuve
16 Feb.	1990	W	20-6	v. F	Doncaster
26 Jan.	1991	W	48-2	v. F	Limoux
15 Feb.	1991	L	6-16	v. F	Wigan
30 Oct.	1991	W	58-0	v. P	Leeds
6 Mar.	1992	W	56-2	v. F	Halifax
20 Mar.	1992	W	34-2	v. F	Albi
17 Feb.	1993	W	46-10	v. F	Rochdale
26 Oct.	1993	L	24-37	v. NZ	Workington
2 Dec.	1993	W	28-16	v. F	Warrington
15 Nov.	1994	L	10-54	v. A	Gateshead
4 Mar.	1995	L	16-17	v. F	Albi

Key: A – Australia; F – France;
NZ – New Zealand; P – Papua New Guinea

UNDER-24s RESULTS

3 Apr.	1965	W	17-9	v. F	Toulouse
20 Oct.	1965	W	12-5	v. F	Oldham
26 Nov.	1966	L	4-7	v. F	Bayonne
17 Apr.	1969	W	42-2	v. F	Castleford
14 Nov.	1976	W	19-2	v. F	Hull K.R.
5 Dec.	1976	W	11-9	v. F	Albi
12 Nov.	1977	W	27-9	v. F	Hull
18 Dec.	1977	W	8-4	v. F	Tonneins
4 Oct.	1978	L	8-30	v. A	Hull K.R.
14 Jan.	1979	W	15-3	v. F	Limoux
24 Nov.	1979	W	14-2	v. F	Leigh
13 Jan.	1980	W	11-7	v. F	Carcassonne
5 Nov.	1980	L	14-18	v. NZ	Fulham
10 Jan.	1981	W	9-2	v. F	Villeneuve
16 Jan.	1982	W	19-16	v. F	Leeds
21 Feb.	1982	W	24-12	v. F	Tonneins
16 Jan.	1983	W	19-5	v. F	Carpentras
11 Nov.	1983	W	28-23	v. F	Villeneuve
4 Dec.	1983	W	48-1	v. F	Oldham

UNDER-21s RECORDS

Highest score:	58-0 v. Papua New Guinea at Leeds, 30 October 1991
Highest against:	10-54 v. Australia at Gateshead 15 November 1994
Most tries in a match:	3 by Neil Puckering (Hull) v. France at St. Helens, 21 March 1987
	David Myers (Wigan) v. PNG at Leeds, 30 October 1991
	David Myers (Wigan) v. France at Halifax, 6 March 1992
	Martin Pearson (Featherstone R.) v. France at Halifax, 6 March 1992
	David Myers (Wigan) v. France at Albi, 20 March 1992
Most goals in a match:	8 by Chris Rudd (Warrington) v. France at Limoux, 26 January 1991
	Martin Pearson (Featherstone R.) v. PNG at Leeds, 30 October 1991
Most points in a match:	24 (3t,6g) by Martin Pearson (Featherstone R.) v. France at Halifax, 6 March 1992
Biggest attendance:	4,596 v. France at Doncaster, 16 February 1990

Gary Divorty: Six appearances.

GREAT BRITAIN UNDER-21s REGISTER

The following is a register of appearances for Great Britain Under-21s since classification of match was introduced in 1984. The Under-21s last played in March 1995.

Figures in brackets are the total appearances, with the plus sign indicating substitute appearances, e.g. (3+1).

Away matches are in bold letters. Substitute appearances are in lower case letters.

ALLEN, Shaun (1) St. Helens: 1984 F
ANDERSON, Grant (4) Castleford: 1989 F, F; 1990 F, F
ANDERSON, Paul (2) Leeds: 1992 F, 1993 F
ATCHESON, Paul (1) Wigan: 1993 F

BALDWIN, Simon (1) Halifax: 1995 F
BECKWITH, Mark (1+1) Whitehaven: 1986 f, F
BETTS, Denis (4) Wigan: 1989 F, F; 1990 F, F
BIBB, Chris (5) Featherstone R.: 1987 F, F; 1988 F; 1989 F, F
BISHOP, Paul (1+1) Warrington: 1987 F, f
BONSON, Paul (2) Featherstone R.: 1992 F, F
BOOTHROYD, Giles (1) Castleford: 1989 F
BURGESS, Andy (+1) Salford: 1991 f
BUSBY, Dean (2+1) Hull: 1991 P; 1992 F, f

CARBERT, Brian (3) Warrington: 1985 NZ; 1986 F, F
CASSIDY, Frank (1+1) Swinton: 1988 f, F
CASSIDY, Jez (+3) Hull: 1993 nz, f; 1994a
CASSIDY, Mick (2+1) Wigan: 1993 f, NZ, F
CHAMBERLAIN, Richard (1+1) Hull K.R.: 1993 f, F
CHAMBERS, Gary (2) Warrington: 1991 F, F
CHRISTIE, Gary (1) Oldham: 1993 F
CLARK, Garry (2) Hull K.R.: 1984 F, F
CLARKE, John (1) Oldham: 1994 A
CLARKE, Phil (5) Wigan: 1990 F; 1991 F, F; 1992 F, F
COCHRANE, Gareth (+1) Keighley C.: 1995 f
CONNOLLY, Gary (4) St. Helens: 1990 F; 1991 F, P; 1992 F
CONWAY, Mark (1) Leeds: 1984 F
CREASSER, David (5) Leeds: 1984 F, F; 1985 NZ; 1986 F, F
CRITCHLEY, Jason (+1) Widnes: 1990 f
CROOKS, Lee (2) Hull: 1984 F, F
CUMMINS, Francis (2) Leeds: 1994 A, 1995 F
CURRIER, Andy (2) Widnes: 1984, F, F

DALTON, James (3) Whitehaven: 1985 NZ; 1986 F, F
DANBY, Rob (2) Hull: 1993 NZ, F
DANNATT, Andy (6) Hull: 1984 F, F; 1985 NZ; 1986 F; 1987 F, F
DARBYSHIRE, Paul (1+1) Warrington: 1991 f, F
DELANEY, Paul (+2) Leeds: 1990 f, f
DERMOTT, Martin (5) Wigan: 1987 F, F; 1988 F, F; 1989 F

DISLEY, Gary (+1) Salford: 1987 f
DIVORTY, Gary (6) Hull: 1984 F; 1985 NZ; 1986 F, F; 1987 F, F
DIXON, Mike (1) Hull: 1991 P
DONOHUE, Jason (+2) Leigh: 1992 f; 1993 f

EASTWOOD, Paul (2) Hull: 1987 F, F
EDWARDS, Shaun (4) Wigan: 1984 F; 1985 NZ; 1987 F, F

FARRELL, Andrew (1) Wigan: 1993 NZ
FARRELL, Anthony (1+1) Huddersfield: 1989 f, F
FAWCETT, Vince (3) Leeds: 1990 F, F; 1991 F
FLETCHER, Mike (2) Hull K.R.: 1988 F, F
FLYNN, Adrian (1) Wakefield T.: 1995 F
FORD, Mike (3+1) Wigan: 1985 NZ; 1986 F; Leigh: 1987 f, F
FORSHAW, Michael (+2) Wigan: 1991 f, f
FORSTER, Mark (3) Warrington: 1985 NZ; 1986 F, F
FOX, Deryck (1) Featherstone R.: 1984 F

GILDART, Ian (6) Wigan: 1988 F, F; 1989 F, F; 1990 F, F
GODDARD, Richard (4) Wakefield T.: 1993 NZ, F; Castleford: 1994 A; 1995 F
GOULDING, Bobbie (5) Wigan: 1990 F, F; 1991 F, F; Leeds: 1991 P
GREGORY, Mike (1) Warrington: 1984 F
GRIBBIN, Vince (1+1) Whitehaven: 1984 f, F
GROVES, Paul (3) Salford: 1984 F, F; 1985 NZ

HALLAS, Graeme (1+2) Hull K.R.: 1991 P; 1992 f, f
HAMMOND, Karle (1+1) Widnes: 1994 A; 1995 f
HARCOMBE, Kevin (1) Rochdale H.: 1986 F
HARLAND, Lee (2 +1) Halifax: 1993 NZ, f; 1994 A
HARMON, Neil (1+3) Warrington: 1988 f, F; 1989 f, f
HARRIS, Iestyn (2) Warrington: 1993 NZ, F
HAY, Andy (1) Castleford: 1995 F
HEWITT, Mark (1+1) Hull: 1994 a; 1995 F
HILL, Brendan (+1) Leeds: 1986 f
HILL, Kenny (3) Castleford: 1988 F, F; 1989 F
HILTON, Mark (2) Warrington: 1994 A; 1995 F
HOLROYD, Graham (+1) Leeds: 1993 f
HUGHES, Gary (1) Leigh: 1986 F
HUGHES, Ian (1) Sheffield E.: 1993 F
HULME, David (2+1) Widnes: 1985 nz; 1986 F, F
HUNTE, Alan (2) St. Helens: 1990 F; 1991 F

IRWIN, Shaun (4) Castleford: 1988 F; 1989 F, F; 1990 F

JACKSON, Michael (+1) Hunslet: 1991 f
JOHNSON, Errol (2) Leeds: 1988 F, F
JOYNT, Chris (4) Oldham: 1991 P; 1992 F, F; St. Helens: 1993 F

LAY, Steve (+1) Hunslet: 1989 f
LEATHAM, Jim (+1) Leeds: 1994 f
LORD, Gary (1) Castleford: 1988 F

LOUGHLIN, Paul (2) St. Helens: 1987 **F**, F
LUCAS, Ian (4) Wigan: 1988 **F**, F; 1989 F, **F**
LUMB, Tim (+1) Hunslet: 1991 **f**
LYMAN, Paul (3) Featherstone R.: 1985 NZ; 1986 **F**, F
LYON, David (2) Widnes: 1985 NZ; 1986 **F**

McAVOY, Nathan (+1) Salford: 1994 a
McCORMACK, Kevin (2) St. Helens: 1987 **F**, F
McCURRIE, Steve (4+1) Widnes: 1991 P; 1992 f; 1993 F, NZ, F
McNAMARA, Steve (5) Hull: 1991 **F**, F, P; 1992 **F**; 1993 F
MAKIN, Craig (+1) Widnes: 1993 nz
MALONEY, Francis (2) Featherstone R.: 1993 NZ, F
MARTIN, Scott (2+2) Leigh: 1993 nz, f, Sheffield E.: 1994 A; Leigh: 1995 **F**
MARTYN, Tommy (1+3) Oldham: 1991 **F**, f, p; 1992 **f**
MATHER, Barrie-Jon (3+1) Wigan: 1992 f; 1993 F, NZ, F
MEDLEY, Paul (2) Leeds: 1987 **F**, F
MOLLOY, Steve (2) Warrington: 1990 **F**, F
MOSLEY, James (1) Wakefield T.: 1993 F
MOUNTAIN, Dean (+1) Castleford: 1987 **f**
MOXON, Darren (1) Bradford N.: 1991 **F**
MYCOE, David (4) Sheffield E.: 1990 **F**; 1991 P; 1992 F, **F**
MYERS, David (5) Wigan: 1991 **F**, F, P; 1992 F, **F**

NEWLOVE, Paul (8) Featherstone R.: 1989 F, **F**; 1990 F, **F**; 1991 **F**, P; 1992 F, **F**
NICKLE, Sonny (1) Sheffield E.: 1990 **F**

O'DONNELL, Gus (2) Wigan: 1992 F, **F**

PARKER, Wayne (2) Hull K.R.: 1988 **F**, F
PARR, Chris (1) Huddersfield: 1991 P
PEARSON, Martin (4) Featherstone R.: 1991 P; 1992 F, **F**; 1993 F
PENNY, Lee (3) Warrington: 1993 F, NZ, F
PERRETT, Mark (2) Halifax: 1993 F, 1994 A
PICKSLEY, Richard (1) Sheffield E.: 1992 F
PINKNEY, Nick (+1) Ryedale-York: 1991 p
POWELL, Daio (2) Bradford N.: 1993 NZ, F
POWELL, Roy (5) Leeds: 1984 F, **F**; 1985 NZ; 1986 **F**, F
PRATT, Richard (2) Leeds: 1988 **F**, F
PRECIOUS, Andy (+1) Hunslet: 1991 p
PRESCOTT, Steve (2) St. Helens: 1994 A; 1995 **F**
PRICE, Gary H. (5+1) Wakefield T.: 1988 f; 1989 F, **F**; 1990 F; 1991 **F**, F
PRICE, Richard (2) Hull: 1989 F, **F**
PROCTOR, Wayne (+1) Hull: 1984 f
PUCKERING, Neil (4) Hull: 1986 **F**, F; 1987 **F**, F

REYNOLDS, Simon (+1) Huddersfield: 1995 **f**
RICHARDS, Craig (2) Bradford N.: 1991 **F**, F
RILEY, Mike (2) St. Helens: 1992 F, **F**
RIPPON, Andy (1) Swinton: 1984 F
ROBINSON, Jason (1) Wigan: 1993 F
ROBINSON, Steve (1) Halifax: 1988 F
ROEBUCK, Neil (+1) Castleford: 1990 f
ROUND, Paul (1+1) St. Helens: 1984 F, **f**
ROWLEY, Paul (1) Halifax: 1995 **F**

RUDD, Chris (2) Warrington: 1991 **F**, F
RUSSELL, Richard (1+1) Wigan: 1987 **F**; 1988 f

SAMPSON, Dean (1) Castleford: 1988 **F**
SANDERSON, Gary (4) Warrington: 1987 **F**, F; 1988 **F**, F
SCHOFIELD, Garry (2) Hull: 1984 **F**, F
SHERIDAN, Ryan (1) Sheffield E.: 1994 A
SLATER, Richard (+1) Wakefield T.: 1992 **f**
SMITH, Chris (2) Castleford: 1994 A; 1995 **F**
SMITH, Tony (1) Castleford: 1991 **F**
SOUTHERNWOOD, Graham (6) Castleford: 1990 **F**, F; 1991 **F**, F; 1992 F, **F**
SOUTHERNWOOD, Roy (2) Castleford: 1989 F, **F**
SPRUCE, Stuart (+1) Widnes: 1991 f
STEPHENS, Gareth (2+1) Leeds: 1993 f, NZ, F
STREET, Tim (2) Leigh: 1989 F, **F**
SULLIVAN, Anthony (1) Hull K.R.: 1990 F
SUMNER, Phil (3) Warrington: 1990 F; 1991 P; 1992 F
SYKES, Nathan (1+1) Castleford: 1993 F; 1994 a

THOMPSON, Alex (3) Sheffield E.: 1993 NZ; 1994 A; 1995 **F**
TURNER, Robert (1) Warrington: 1990 F

WANE, Shaun (3) Wigan: 1984 **F**; 1985 NZ; 1986 **F**
WESTHEAD, John (1+2) Leigh: 1985 nz; 1986 **f**, F
WRIGHT, Darren (2) Widnes: 1987 **F**; 1988 **F**
WRIGHT, Nigel (3+1) Wakefield T.: 1993 F; Wigan 1993 nz; Wakefield T.: 1994 A, 1995 **F**

GREAT BRITAIN UNDER-24s REGISTER

The following is a register of appearances by current players, who played at least one club game in 1998, for Great Britain Under-24s since this classification of match was reintroduced in 1976, until it was replaced by the new Under-21 level in 1984.

Figures in brackets are the total appearances, with the plus sign indicating substitute appearances, e.g. (7+3).

Away matches are in bold letters. Substitute appearances are in lower case letters.

FIELDHOUSE, John (1+1) Warrington: 1983 **F**, f
MASKILL, Colin (1) Wakefield T.: 1983 **F**
SCHOFIELD, Garry (+2) Hull: 1983 **f**, f

GREAT BRITAIN ACADEMY

The Rugby League Academy was introduced in 1991-92 for players under 19 at midnight 31 August of the new season. In 1996 this criteria was changed to midnight on 31 December of the year preceding the new season.

● Academy players' scores and appearances are not included in their senior records.

1998 INTERNATIONAL MATCHES

31 October   At South Leeds Stadium, Hunslet

Great Britain Academy 56	France Under-21s 16
T: Sinfield (2), Isherwood (2),	*T:* Guisset (2), Gironella
Pratt (2), Fielden, Radford,	*G:* Dekkiche, Durand
Clarke, Stewart	
G: Sinfield (8)	
Half-time: 38-2	Attendance: 500

Great Britain Academy: Paul Wellens (St. Helens); Steve Hall (St. Helens), Tony Stewart (St. Helens), Dwayne West (Wigan W.), Karl Pratt (Featherstone R.); Scott Barrow (St. Helens), Paul Deacon (Bradford B.); Stuart Fielden (Bradford B.), Jon Clarke (Wigan W., Capt.), Stuart Dickens (Featherstone R.), Andrew Isherwood (Wigan W.), Lee Radford (Bradford B.), Kevin Sinfield (Leeds R.). **Playing subs:** Chris Chapman (Leeds R.), David Highton (Warrington W.), Jamie Jones-Buchanan (Leeds R.), Gareth Carvell (Leeds R.). **Coach:** Mike Gregory

France Under-21s: Julien Gerin (St. Gaudens); Franck Durand (St. Esteve), Yacine Dekkiche (Avignon), Gilles Gironella (XIII Catalan), Sebastien Terrado (Pia); Nicolas Piccolo (Limoux), Jean-Emmanuel Cassin (Toulouse); Philippe Laurent (Limoux), Cedric Lacans (Limoux), Romain Gagliazzo (Carcassonne), Jerome Guisset (St. Esteve, Capt.), Ludovic Pena (St. Esteve), Guillaume Knecht (Pia). **Playing subs:** Alexandre Dufour (Carpentras), Raphael Musichini (Avignon), Florien Chautard (Carpentras), Olivier Pramil (St. Esteve). **Coaches:** Jean Eric Ducuing, Mathieu Khedimi
Referee: Steve Ganson (St. Helens)

11 November   At Stade Jean Laffon, Perpignan
(Curtain-raiser to France v. Scotland)

France Under-21s 8	Great Britain Academy 28
T: Dufour, Knecht	*T:* Pratt, Sinfield, Isherwood, Hall, Wellens
	G: Sinfield (4)
Half-time: 8-0	

France Under-21s: Julien Gerin (St. Gaudens); Alexandre Dufour (Carpentras), Yacine Dekkiche (Avignon), Renaud Guigue (Avignon), Sylvain Houles (XIII Catalan); Laurent Frayssinous (Villeneuve, Capt.), Julien Rinaldi (Villeneuve); David Ferriol (Limoux), Jean-Emmanuel Cassin (Toulouse), Romain Gagliazzo (Carcassonne), Guillaume Knecht (Pia), Pierre Sabatie (Villeneuve), Sebastien Gauffre (Villeneuve). **Playing subs:** Florien Chautard (Carpentras), Ludovic Pena (St. Esteve), Olivier Pramil (St. Esteve), Cedric Lacans (Limoux). **Coaches:** Jean Eric Ducuing, Matheiu Khedimi

Great Britain Academy: Paul Wellens (St. Helens); Steve Hall (St. Helens), Tony Stewart (St. Helens), Dwayne West (Wigan Warriors), Karl Pratt (Featherstone R.); Scott Barrow (St. Helens), Paul Deacon (Bradford B.); Stuart Fielden (Bradford B.), Jon Clarke (Wigan W., Capt.), Stuart Dickens (Featherstone R.), Andrew Isherwood (Wigan W.), Lee Radford (Bradford B.), Kevin Sinfield (Leeds R.). **Playing subs:** Chris Chapman (Leeds R.), David Highton (Warrington W.), Jamie Jones-Buchanan (Leeds R.), Dave Wrench (Leeds R.). **Coach:** Mike Gregory
Referee: Thierry Alibert (France)

1994 TOUR OF AUSTRALIA

P7   W1   L6   F99   A219

TESTS: Lost 8-46 and 10-647

Squad: Simon Baldwin (Leigh), Phil Cantillon (Wigan), Paul Cook (Leeds), Andrew Craig (Wigan), Francis Cummins (Leeds), Jason Flowers (Castleford), Adrian Flynn (Wakefield T.), Iestyn Harris (Warrington), Simon Haughton (Wigan), Mark Hilton (Warrington), Graham Holroyd (Leeds), Matthew Knowles (Wigan), Sean Long (Wigan), Scott Martin (Leigh), Carl Pearson (Leeds), Lee Penny (Warrington), Jonathan Roper (Warrington), Paul Rowley (Leigh), Ryan Sheridan (Sheffield E.), Chris Smith (Castleford). **Paul Stevens (Wigan, Capt.),** Nathan Sykes (Castleford), Marcus Vassilakopoulos (Leeds), Michael Wainwright (Warrington), Phil Waring (St. Helens), Johan Windley (Hull)

Coach: John Kear

1996 TOUR OF NEW ZEALAND

P7   W3   L4   F232   A176

TESTS: Lost 14-35, 24-27 and 36-37

Squad: Paul Anderson (St. Helens), Danny Arnold (St. Helens), Neil Baynes (Wigan), Gary Broadbent (Widnes), Gavin Brown (Leeds), Darryl Cardiss (Wigan), Jonathan Clarke (Wigan), Craig Dean (Halifax B.S.), Jamie Field (Leeds), Wayne Flynn (Wakefield T.), Nick Fozzard (Leeds), Lee Gilmour (Wigan), Marvin Golden (Leeds), Paul Highton (Halifax B.S.), Paul Johnson (Wigan), Chris Kitching (Hull), Ian Knott (Warrington), **Nathan McAvoy (Salford R., Capt.),** Chris McKinney (Oldham B.), Lee Milner (Huddersfield G.), Damien Munro (Halifax B.S.), Terry Newton (Leeds R.), Kevin O'Loughlin (St. Helens), Marcus St. Hilaire (Leeds), Matthew Salter (London B.), Jamies Stokes (Featherstone R.), Ian Talbot (Wigan), Ian Watson (Salford R.)

Coach: Ray Unsworth

GREAT BRITAIN ACADEMY RESULTS

16 Feb. 1992	France	Won	28-7	Perpignan
25 Feb. 1992	France	Drew	14-14	Wigan
16 Feb. 1993	France	Won	33-12	Wigan
7 Mar.1993	France	Won	25-18	Carcassonne
16 Oct. 1993	Junior Kiwis	Lost	22-30	Wembley
21 Oct. 1993	Junior Kiwis	Won	34-12	Wigan
8 Feb. 1994	France	Won	22-6	York
20 Mar. 1994	France	Lost	8-10	Carcassonne
6 July 1994	Australia	Lost	8-46	Parramatta
16 July 1994	Australia	Lost	10-64	Brisbane
31 Jan. 1995	France	Won	36-0	Leigh
5 Mar. 1995	France	Won	48-4	Carcassonne
6 Feb. 1996	France	Won	64-10	Hull
5 Jun. 1996	France	Won	72-10	Carcassonne
18 Oct. 1996	Junior Kiwis	Lost	14-35	Auckland
25 Oct. 1996	Junior Kiwis	Lost	24-27	Palmerston North
1 Nov. 1996	Junior Kiwis	Lost	36-37	Christchurch
16 Nov. 1997	France	Won	36-9	Elland Rd, Leeds

| 31 Oct. 1998 | France | Won | 56-16 | Hunslet |
| 11 Nov. 1998 | France | Won | 28-8 | Perpignan |

SUMMARY

	P	W	D	L	F	A
Australia	2	0	0	2	18	110
France*	13	11	1	1	470	124
Junior Kiwis	5	1	0	4	130	141
Totals	**20**	**12**	**1**	**7**	**618**	**375**

*Academy and Under-21s

GREAT BRITAIN ACADEMY REGISTER

A register of players' appearances in international matches since the inauguration of Great Britain Academy in 1991-92.

Figures in brackets are the total appearances, with the plus sign indicating substitute appearances, e.g. (3+1). Substitute appearances are in lower case letters.

Key: A - Australia; F - France; K - Junior Kiwis

ALLEN, Kieran (1+1) Wakefield T.: 1994 Ff
ANDERSON, Paul (2+1) St. Helens: 1996 f,K2
ARNOLD, Danny (5) St. Helens 1996 F2,K3
ATCHESON, Paul (1) Widnes: 1992 F

BALDWIN, Simon (6+1) Leigh: 1993 F2,k; 1994 F2,A2
BARRATT, Anthony (1) Leeds: 1992 F
BARROW, Scott (2) St. Helens: 1998 F2
BARROW, Steve (2) Wigan: 1995 F2
BAYNES, Neil (5) Wigan: 1996 F2,K3
BRIERS, Lee (1) Warrington W.: 1997 F
BROADBENT, Gary (2+2) Widnes: 1996 f,K2k
BROWN, Gavin (2) Leeds: 1996 F,K
BUSBY, Dean (2) Hull: 1992 F2

CANTILLON, Phil (2) Wigan: 1995 F2
CARDISS, Darryl (6) Wigan W.: 1996 F2,K3; 1997 F
CARVELL, Gareth (+1) Leeds R.: 1998: f
CASSIDY, Mick (+2) Wigan: 1992 f2
CHAMBERLAIN, Richard (2) Hull K.R.: 1992 F2
CHAPMAN, Chris (+2) Leeds R.: 1998 f2
CHESTER, Chris (1) Halifax B.S.: 1997 F
CLARKE, Jonathan (5+1) Wigan W.: 1996 F,Kk; 1997 F; 1998 F2
COCHRANE, Gareth (+2) Hull: 1993 f; 1994 f
COOK, Paul (2+1) Leeds: 1994 a; 1995 F2

COUSSONS, Phil (2) Salford: 1992 F2
COVENTRY, Jamie (+1) Castleford: 1996 f
COX, Mark (1) Whitehaven W.: 1997 F
CRAIG, Andrew (1) Wigan: 1994 F
CUMMINS, Francis (2) Leeds: 1994 A2
CUNNINGHAM, Keiron (+1) St. Helens: 1995 f

DEACON, Paul (2) Bradford B.: 1998 F2
DEAN, Craig (3) Halifax B.S.: 1996 K3
DICKENS, Stuart (2) Featherstone R.: 1998 F2
DUSHER, Mark (1) Warrington: 1992 F

FARRELL, Andrew (5) Wigan: 1992 F2; 1993 F2,K
FIELD, Jamie (5+1) Leeds: 1995 f; 1996 F2,K3
FIELDEN, Stuart (2) Bradford B.: 1998 F2
FLOWERS, Jason (2) Castleford: 1994 F,A
FLYNN, Adrian (6) Wakefield T.: 1993 K2; 1994 F2,A2
FLYNN, Wayne (1+2) Wakefield T. 1996 Ff,k
FOZZARD, Nick (4) Leeds: 1995 F2; 1996 F,K
GILMOUR, Lee (1+1) Wigan W.: 1996 f; 1997 F
GODDARD, Richard (2) Wakefield T.: 1993 F2
GOLDEN, Marvin (3+1) Leeds: 1995 f; 1996 K3

HALL, Steve (2) St. Helens: 1998 F2
HARRIS, Iestyn (4+1) Warrington: 1993 K2; 1994 F2,a
HAUGHTON, Simon (8+1) Wigan: 1993 F2,Kk; 1994 F2,A2; 1995 F
HAYES, Joey (1) St. Helens: 1995 F
HIGHTON, David (+2) Warrington W.: 1998 f2
HIGHTON, Paul (2) Halifax B.S.: 1996 F,K
HILTON, Mark (7) Warrington: 1992 F2; 1993 F2,K; 1994 A2
HODKINSON, Colin (2) Warrington: 1993 F2
HOLROYD, Graham (3+1) Leeds: 1993 K2; 1994 Aa
HOPE, Mark (+2) Wigan 1993 f; 1994 f
HUGHES, Darren (+2) Leeds: 1993 f2

ISHERWOOD, Andrew (2+1) Wigan W.: 1997 f; 1998 F2

JONES-BUCHANAN, Jamie (+2) Leeds R.: 1998 f2
JOHNSON, Andy (2) Wigan: 1993 F2
JOHNSON, Paul (5) Wigan W.: 1996 F,K3; 1997 F

KITCHING, Chris (2) Hull: 1996 F2
KNOTT, Ian (4) Warrington: 1996 F,K3
KNOWLES, Matthew (1+1) Wigan: 1994 a; 1995 F

LAWFORD, Dean (1) Sheffield E.: 1996 F
LAWLESS, John (+3) Halifax: 1993 k2; 1994 f
LEATHEM, Andy (+1) St. Helens: 1996 f
LEIGHTON, Jamie (+1) Hull K.R. 1992 f
LONG, Sean (4) Wigan: 1994 A2; 1995 F2
LONGO, Davide (2) Dewsbury: 1995 F2
LOWE, Neil (1) Featherstone R.: 1997 F

McATEE, John (5) St. Helens 1993 F2; 1993 K;
1994 F2
McAVOY, Nathan (7) Salford: 1995 F2; 1996
F2,K3
McCURRIE, Steve (2) Widnes: 1992 F2
McDONALD, Wayne (+1) Wakefield T.: 1995 f
McKINNEY, Chris (1) Oldham: 1996 F
MAHER, Lee (+2) Leeds: 1995 f2
MARNS, Oliver (+1) Halifax B.S.: 1997 f
MARTIN, Scott (4+1) Leigh: 1993 f; 1993 K2;
1994 A2
MATHER, Barrie-Jon (2) Wigan: 1992 F2
MILNER, Lee (1+1) Huddersfield G.: 1996 Kk
MORLEY, Adrian (2) Leeds: 1996 F2
MUNRO, Damien (+1) Halifax B.S.: 1996 k
MYLER, Danny (+1) Widnes V.: 1997 f

NEWTON, Terry (2+2) Leeds R.: 1996 Kk2; 1997 F

O'LOUGHLIN, Kevin (+2) St. Helens: 1996 k2
ORR, Danny (1) Castleford T.: 1997 F

PEARSON, Carl (3+1) Leeds: 1993 K; 1994 F2,a
PENNY, Lee (4) Warrington: 1993 K2; 1994 F,A
POWELL, Daio (2) Bradford N.: 1992 F2
PRATT, Karl (2) Featherstone R.: 1998 F2

RADFORD, Lee (2) Bradford B.: F2
RADLINSKI, Kris (2+1) Wigan: 1994 f; 1995 F2

ROBINSON, Jason (2) Wigan: 1992 F2
RODGERS, Darren (2) Dewsbury: 1993 F2
ROPER, Jonathan (7) Warrington: 1993 K2; 1994
F,A2; 1995 F2
ROWLEY, Paul (6) Leigh: 1993 K2; 1994 F2,A2

SCHULTZ, Matthew (1+1) Leeds: Kk
SCULTHORPE, Paul (2) Warrington: 1995 F2
SENIOR, Lee (2) Featherstone R.: 1993 F2
SHERIDAN, Ryan (2+2) Sheffield E. 1993 f2,K;
1994 F
SINFIELD, Kevin (2) Leeds R.: 1998 F2
SMITH, Chris (4+3) Castleford: 1993 k2; 1994
Ff,A2; 1995 F
SMITH, Kris (+1) Leeds R.: 1997 f
SMITH, Simon (2) Wigan: 1993 F2
SMYTH, Rob (1) Wigan: 1996 F2
SOUTHERN, Paul (1+1) Salford: 1995 Ff
STEPHENS, Gareth (1+1) Leeds: 1992 f F
STEVENS, Paul (9) Wigan: 1992 F2; 1993 F2,K2;
1994 F,A2
STEVENS, Warren (1) Warrington W.: 1997 F
STEWART, Tony (3) St. Helens: 1997 F; 1998 F2
ST. HILAIRE, Marcus (+1) Huddersfield G.: 1996 f
STOKES, Jamie (1) Featherstone R.: 1997 F
SULLIVAN, Scott (+1) Hull: 1992 f
SYKES, Nathan (4+2) Castleford: 1993 f; 1993 K2;
1994 F2,a

TALBOT, Ian (3) Wigan 1996 F,K2
THOMPSON, Alex (2+2) Sheffield E.: 1992 f2;
1993 F2
TONKS, Ian (1+1) Castleford: 1995 Ff
TYRER, Christian (2) Widnes: 1992 F2

VASSILAKOPOULOS, Marcus: (+3) Leeds 1994
f2; 1996 f

WAINWRIGHT, Michael (3+3) Warrington 1993
Kk; 1994 F2,a2
WARING, Phil (1) St. Helens; 1994 A
WATSON, Ian (+3) Salford R.: 1996 k3
WELLENS, Paul (2) St. Helens: 1998 F2
WEST, Dwayne (2) Wigan W.: 1998 F2
WRENCH, Dave (+1) Leeds R. 1998 f
WRIGHT, Nigel (+1) Wakefield T.: 1992 f

John Pendlebury: Super League Coach of the Year.

COACHES

COACHES

INDEX OF COACHES

The following is an index of the 324 coaches who have held first team coaching posts since the start of the 1974-75 season to 1 January 1999.

It includes the alphabetical listing of British clubs they coached in the period plus French Super League club Paris St. Germain.

Thirteen new coaches were added to the list during the period when 14 clubs made at least one change.

Although some clubs appoint team managers with a coach as his assistant, the list refers only to the man generally recognised as being in overall charge of team affairs.

A caretaker coach, who stands in while the club is seeking a permanent appointment, is listed if he takes charge for more than a few matches.

Overseas coaches are in bold: A – Australian; NZ – New Zealander.

For a list of each club's appointments since 1974 see CLUBS section.

Ray Abbey (Dewsbury)
Jack Addy (Dewsbury, Huddersfield B.)
Allan Agar (Bramley, Carlisle, Featherstone R., Rochdale H.)
Gary Ainsworth (Trafford B.)
Dave Alred (Bridgend)
Chris Anderson – A (Halifax)
Harry Archer (Workington T.)
Chris Arkwright (Highfield)
Colin Armstrong (Whitehaven W.)
Kevin Ashcroft (Leigh, Salford, Warrington)
Eric Ashton (St. Helens)
Ray Ashton (Bramley, Workington T.)
Bill Ashurst (Runcorn H., Wakefield T.)
Mal Aspey (Salford)
Peter Astbury (Doncaster D.)
John Atkinson (Carlisle)
Jack Austin (Hunslet)
Warren Ayres (Prescot P.)

Trevor Bailey (Scarborough P., Wakefield T.)
Maurice Bamford (Bramley, Dewsbury, Halifax, Huddersfield, Leeds, Prescot P., Wigan, Workington T.)
Frank Barrow (Oldham, Swinton)
Tony Barrow (Oldham, Swinton, Warrington)

Ray Batten (Wakefield T.)
Jeff Bawden (Whitehaven)
Mel Bedford (Huddersfield)
Cameron Bell – NZ (Carlisle)
Dean Bell – NZ (Leeds)
Billy Benyon (Leigh, St. Helens, Warrington)
Les Bettinson (Salford)
Charlie Birdsall (Rochdale H.)
Alan Bishop (Runcorn H.)
Tommy Bishop (Barrow, Leigh, Workington T.)
Mick Blacker (Halifax, Huddersfield, Mansfield M.)
Tommy Blakeley (Blackpool B.)
Dick Bonser (Rochdale H.)
Reg Bowden (Fulham, Warrington)
Mitch Brennan – A (Wakefield T.)
Carl Briscoe (Chorley B.)
Drew Broatch (Hunslet)
Ian Brooke (Bradford N., Doncaster, Huddersfield, Wakefield T.)
Arthur Bunting (Hull, Hull K.R.)
Mark Burgess (Nottingham C.)
Dave Busfield (Dewsbury)

Len Casey (Hull, Scarborough P., Wakefield T.)
Jim Challinor (Oldham)
Paul Charlton (Barrow B.R., Carlisle, Workington T.)
Eddie Cheetham (Leigh)
Dave Chisnall (Runcorn H.)
Colin Clarke (Leigh, Wigan)
Terry Clawson (Featherstone R.)
Noel Cleal – A (Hull)
Malcolm Clift – A (Leeds)
Joe Coan (Wigan)
Mick Coates (Oldham)
John Cogger – A (Runcorn H.)
Gary Cooper (York)
Kel Coslett (Rochdale H., St. Helens, Wigan)
Gordon Cottier (Whitehaven)
Keith Cotton (Featherstone R.)
Mike Coulman (Salford)
Les Coulter (Keighley)
Dave Cox (Batley, Castleford, Dewsbury, Huyton, Oldham, Workington T.)
Jim Crellin (Blackpool B., Halifax, Highfield, Leigh, Mansfield M., Rochdale H., Swinton)
Terry Crook (Batley, Dewsbury)
Lee Crooks (Keighley C.)
Steve Crooks (Hull K.R., Ryedale-York)
Tony Currie – A (London B.)

Arthur Daley (Runcorn H.)

Paul Daley (Batley, Featherstone R., Hunslet, York)
Jackie Davidson (Whitehaven, Workington T.)
Keith Davies (Workington T.)
Tommy Dawes (Barrow, Carlisle, Whitehaven)
Harry Dawson (Widnes)
Tony Dean (Hull, Wakefield T.)
Henry Delooze (Rochdale H.)
Steve Dennison (Mansfield M.)
Robin Dewhurst (Leeds)
Bakary Diabira (Blackpool B., Keighley)
Tommy Dickens (Blackpool B., Leigh)
Roy Dickinson (Bramley)
Colin Dixon (Halifax, Keighley, Salford)
Mal Dixon (York)
John Dorahy – A (Halifax, Warrington, Wigan)
David Doyle-Davidson (Hull, York)
Ray Dutton (Whitehaven)

Graham Eadie – A (Halifax)
Bob Eccles (Blackpool G., Chorley)
Derek Edwards (Doncaster)
Joe Egan Jnr. (Blackpool B.)
Matthew Elliott – A (Bradford B.)

George Fairbairn (Huddersfield, Hull K.R., Wigan)
Vince Farrar (Featherstone R.)
Albert Fearnley (Batley, Blackpool B., Keighley)
Steve Ferres (Huddersfield G., Hunslet)
John Fieldhouse (Oldham)
Tony Fisher (Bramley, Dewsbury, Doncaster, Keighley)
Eric Fitzsimons (Oldham, Rochdale H., Whitehaven)
Bob Fleet (Swinton)
Geoff Fletcher (Huyton, Runcorn H.)
Paul Fletcher (Bramley)
Terry Fogerty (Rochdale H.)
Mike Ford (Bramley)
Chris Forster (Bramley, Huddersfield B.)
Derek Foster (Ryedale-York)
Frank Foster (Barrow, Whitehaven)
Kenny Foulkes (Hull)
Deryck Fox (Rochdale H.)
Don Fox (Batley)
Harry Fox (Halifax)
Neil Fox (Huddersfield)
Peter Fox (Bradford N., Bramley, Featherstone R., Leeds, Wakefield T.)
Bill Francis (Oldham)
Roy Francis (Bradford N., Leeds)
Tommy Frodsham (Highfield/Prescot P.)

Paul Gamble (Blackpool G.)
Bill Gardner – A (Sheffield E.)

Brian Gartland (Oldham)
Andy Gascoigne (Doncaster D.)
Steve Gibson – A (Rochdale H.)
Stan Gittins (Blackpool B., Chorley, Rochdale H., Springfield B.)
Andy Goodway (Oldham, Paris St. Germain)
Bill Goodwin (Fulham, Kent/Southend Invicta)
Tony Gordon – NZ (Hull, London C.)
Terry Gorman (Huyton, Swinton)
Keith Goulding (Featherstone R., Huddersfield, York)
Mal Graham – A (Oldham)
Tom Grainey (Leigh, Swinton)
Jeff Grayshon (Batley, Dewsbury)
Lee Greenwood (Keighley, Mansfield M./Nottingham C.)
Andy Gregory (Salford)
Gary Grienke – A (London B.)
Clive Griffiths (South Wales)
Geoff Gunney (Wakefield T.)

Bob Haigh (Wakefield T.)
Derek Hallas (Halifax)
Ken Halliwell (Swinton)
Steve Hampson (Lancashire L.)
Ellery Hanley (St. Helens)
Alan Hardisty (Dewsbury, Halifax, York)
Paul Harkin (Wakefield T.)
Dave Harrison (Hull K.R.)
Arnold Hema – NZ (Nottingham C.)
Graham Heptinstall (Doncaster)
Alan Hepworth (Batley)
Keith Hepworth (Bramley, Hull)
Gary Hetherington (Sheffield E.)
Ron Hill (Dewsbury)
David Hobbs (Bradford N., Wakefield T.)
Kevin Hobbs (Featherstone R.)
Steve Hogan (Barrow B.)
Neil Holding (Rochdale H.)
Bill Holliday (Swinton)
Les Holliday (Swinton L.)
Stewart Horton (Ryedale-York)
Eric Hughes (Leigh C., Rochdale H., St. Helens, Widnes, Wigan W.)
Syd Hynes (Leeds)

Bob Irving (Blackpool B.)
Keith Irving (Workington T.)

Garry Jack – A (Salford)
Dennis Jackson (Barrow)
Francis Jarvis (Huddersfield)
Peter Jarvis (Bramley, Hunslet)

Graeme Jennings – A (Hunslet)
Barry Johnson (Bramley)
Brian Johnson – A (Warrington)
Willie Johnson (Highfield)
Allen Jones (Huddersfield B.)
Lewis Jones (Dewsbury)
John Joyner (Castleford)

John Kain (Keighley C.)
Vince Karalius (Widnes, Wigan)
Paul Kavanagh (Barrow)
John Kear (Bramley, Sheffield E.)
Arthur Keegan (Bramley)
Ivor Kelland (Barrow)
Alan Kellett (Carlisle, Halifax, Keighley)
Andy Kelly (Wakefield T.)
Neil Kelly (Dewsbury)
Bill Kenny (Doncaster)
Bill Kindon (Leigh)
Bill Kirkbride (Mansfield M., Rochdale H.,
    Wakefield T., York)
Paddy Kirwan (Oldham)
Phil Kitchin (Whitehaven, Workington T.)
Mike Kuiti – NZ (Batley B.)

Dave Lamming (Wakefield T.)
Steve Lane (Kent Invicta)
Phil Larder (Keighley C., Sheffield E., Widnes)
Keith Latham (Leigh C.)
Doug Laughton (Leeds, Widnes)
Roy Lester (Carlisle, Fulham)
Bob Lindner – A (Oldham)
Alan Lockwood (Dewsbury)
Brian Lockwood (Batley, Huddersfield,
    Wakefield T.)
Paul Longstaff (Rochdale H.)
Graham Lowe – NZ (Wigan)
Phil Lowe (York)
Trevor Lowe (Batley, Doncaster)
Ken Loxton (Bramley)
Ian Lucas (Leigh)
Geoff Lyon (Blackpool B.)

Mike McClennan – NZ (St. Helens)
Stan McCormick (Salford)
John McFarlane (Whitehaven)
Alan McInnes (Salford, Wigan)
Shaun McRae – A (Gateshead T., St. Helens)
John Mantle (Blackpool B., Cardiff C., Leigh)
Stan Martin – NZ (Whitehaven)
Steve Martin – A (Featherstone R.)
Colin Maskill (Doncaster D.)

Michel Mazare (Paris St. Germain)
Jack Melling (Blackpool G.)
Ian Millward – A (Leigh C.)
Roger Millward (Halifax, Hull K.R., Ryedale-York)
John Monie – A (Wigan)
Mick Morgan (Carlisle)
Geoff Morris (Doncaster)
Dave Mortimer (Huddersfield)
Peter Mulholland – A (Paris St. Germain)
Alex Murphy (Huddersfield, Leigh, St. Helens,
    Salford, Warrington, Wigan)
Graham Murray – A (Leeds R.)
Frank Myler (Oldham, Rochdale H., Swinton,
    Widnes)
Tony Myler (Widnes)

Steve Nash (Mansfield M.)
Steve Norton (Barrow)

Ross O'Reilly – A (Workington T.)
Chris O'Sullivan – A (Swinton)

Les Pearce (Bramley, Halifax)
Mike Peers (Blackpool G., Springfield B./Chorley
    B./Trafford B., Highfield, Swinton)
Geoff Peggs (Keighley)
John Pendlebury (Halifax B.S.)
George Pieniazek (Batley, Featherstone R.)
David Plange (Hunslet H.)
Andy Platt (Workington T.)
Billy Platt (Mansfield M.)
Harry Poole (Hull K.R.)
Daryl Powell (Keighley C.)

Dennis Ramsdale (Barrow, Leigh)
Bill Ramsey (Hunslet)
Terry Ramshaw (Oldham)
Stuart Raper – A (Castleford T.)
Keith Rayne (Batley)
Rod Reddy – A (Barrow)
Graham Rees (Blackpool B.)
Peter Regan – A (Batley B., Doncaster D.,
    Rochdale H.)
Malcolm Reilly (Castleford, Halifax, Huddersfield
    G., Leeds)
Alan Rhodes (Doncaster, Sheffield E.)
Austin Rhodes (Swinton)
Bev Risman (Fulham)
Ken Roberts (Halifax)
Dean Robinson (York)
Don Robinson (Bramley)
Don Robson (Doncaster)

Peter Roe (Barrow, Halifax, Keighley, Swinton)
Sol Roper (Workington T.)

Roy Sabine (Keighley)
Dave Sampson (Castleford, Doncaster,
    Nottingham C.)
Garry Schofield (Huddersfield G.)
Gary Schubert – A (Barrow B.)
Barry Seabourne (Bradford N., Huddersfield,
    Keighley)
Les Sheard (Huddersfield)
Danny Sheehan (York)
John Sheridan (Doncaster)
Phil Sigsworth – A (Hull)
Royce Simmons – A (Hull)
Steve Simms – A (Featherstone R., Halifax B.S.,
    Leigh)
Tommy Smales [*Scrum half*] (Featherstone R.)
Tommy Smales [*Forward*] (Batley, Bramley,
    Dewsbury, Doncaster, Featherstone R.)
Peter Smethurst (Leigh, Oldham)
Barry Smith (Whitehaven)
Bill Smith (Whitehaven, Workington T.)
Brian Smith (Huddersfield)
Brian Smith – A (Bradford B., Hull)
Norman Smith (Dewsbury)
Kurt Sorensen – NZ (Whitehaven, Workington T.)
Ike Southward (Whitehaven, Workington T.)
Dan Stains – A (London B.)
Graham Starkey (Oldham, Rochdale H.)
Gary Stephens (York)
Nigel Stephenson (Huddersfield, Hunslet)
Dave Stockwell (Batley, Bramley)
John Stopford (Swinton)
Ted Strawbridge (Doncaster)
Ross Strudwick – A (Fulham/London C., Halifax)
Clive Sullivan (Doncaster, Hull)
Phil Sullivan – A (Fulham)

Kevin Tamati – NZ (Chorley/Lancashire L.,
    Salford, Whitehaven W.)
John Taylor (Chorley B.)
Robert Tew – A (Workington T.)
Bob Tomlinson (Huddersfield)
Ted Toohey (Wigan)
David Topliss (Wakefield T.)
Peter Tunks – A (Oldham)
Shane Tupaea – NZ (Rochdale H.)
Norman Turley (Leigh C., Trafford B., Whitehaven,
    Workington T.)
Derek Turner (Wakefield T.)

Colin Tyrer (Widnes)

Phil Veivers – A (Huddersfield G.)
Darryl Van de Velde – A (Castleford,
    Huddersfield, Warrington W.)
Don Vines (Doncaster)

Hugh Waddell (Carlisle)
Arnold Walker (Whitehaven)
Russ Walker (Hull)
Trevor Walker (Batley)
Peter Walsh – A (Hull S., Workington T.)
David Ward (Batley, Featherstone R., Hunslet,
    Leeds)
John Warlow (Bridgend)
David Watkins (Cardiff C.)
Bernard Watson (Dewsbury)
Graeme West – NZ (Widnes V., Wigan)
Colin Whitfield (Widnes V.)
Neil Whittaker (Huddersfield B.)
Mel Wibberley (Nottingham C.)
Stuart Wilkinson (Barrow B.)
Ron Willey – A (Bradford N.)
Dean Williams – NZ (Workington T.)
Frank Wilson (Runcorn H.)
Phil Windley (Hull)
John Wolford (Hunslet)
Jeff Woods (Bridgend)
John Woods (Leigh)
Paul Woods (Runcorn H.)
Geoff Worrall (Barrow)
Geoff Wraith (Wakefield T.)

Billy Yates (Doncaster)

Norman Smith: Former Dewsbury coach.

DOSSIER OF 1998 COACHES

The following is a dossier of the British coaching and playing careers of coaches holding first team posts in 1998. Overseas details are not included.

● BF — beaten finalist; GF — Grand Final.

COLIN ARMSTRONG

Whitehaven W: July 98 - Oct. 98
Played for: Carlisle, Workington T., Hull K.R., Swinton L., Whitehaven W.

PAUL CHARLTON

Workington T.:   June 75 - June 76 (Promotion)
Workington T.:   July 82 - Dec. 82
Carlisle: Dec. 94 - Oct. 97
Barrow B.R.   Sept. 98 -
Played for: Workington T., Salford, Blackpool B.

MICK COATES

Oldham: Aug. 98 -
Played for: Rochdale H., Swinton

LEE CROOKS

Keighley C: Mar. 98 -
Played for: Hull, Leeds, Castleford

TONY CURRIE (Australian)

London B.:   Jan. 96 - Oct. 98
Played for: Leeds

MATTHEW ELLIOTT (Australian)

Bradford B.:   Sep. 96 - (Super League champs, RL Cup BF (2))

PAUL FLETCHER

Bramley: Jan. 97 - Nov. 98
Played for: Leeds, Bramley

MIKE FORD

Bramley: Nov. 98 -
Played for: Wigan, Leigh, Oldham, Castleford, Warrington W., Wakefield T.

DERYCK FOX

Rochdale H: May 1998 -
Played for: Featherstone R., Bradford N., Batley B., Rochdale H.

Lee Crooks: Former international forward began his coaching career at Keighley Cougars.

ANDY GREGORY
Salford: Mar. 95 - (Div. 1 champs - new division (2))
Played for: Widnes, Warrington, Wigan, Leeds, Salford

STEVE HAMPSON
Lancashire L: Oct. 97* - (Div.2 champs., Treize Tournoi BF)
Played for: Wigan, Halifax, Salford R., Widnes V.
* Appointed coach with Kevin Tamati remaining as manager. Hampson became full-time coach in September 1998 following Tamati's departure.

ELLERY HANLEY
St. Helens: Oct. 98 -
Great Britain: Aug. 94 - May 95
Played for: Bradford N., Wigan, Leeds

DAVE HARRISON
Hull K.R.: May 97 -
Played for: Hull K.R., St. Helens

KEVIN HOBBS
Featherstone R: Oct. 98 -
Played for: Featherstone R.

LES HOLLIDAY
Swinton L.: Mar. 97 -
Played for: Halifax, Widnes, Dewsbury, Swinton

JOHN KAIN
Keighley C.: July 97 - Mar. 98
Played for: Castleford, York, Bramley

JOHN KEAR
Bramley: Dec. 90 - Jan. 91
Sheffield E.: May 97 - (RL Cup winners)
France: Sep. 97 - Oct. 98
Also took charge of Paris St. Germain for several weeks in 1996
Played for: Castleford

ANDY KELLY
Wakefield T.: Jan. 95 - Jan. 96
Wakefield T.: June 97 - (Div. 1 champs - new division)
Played for: Wakefield T., Huddersfield, Hull K.R.

NEIL KELLY
Dewsbury: Feb. 96 -
Played for: Dewsbury, Wakefield T., Featherstone R.

John Kear: Sheffield Eagles coach.

365

PADDY KIRWAN
Oldham: Nov. 97 - Aug. 98 (Trans-
                    Pennine Cup BF)
Played for: Oldham, Leigh

KEITH LATHAM
Leigh C.:   Nov. 96 - May 98
Played for: Salford, Blackpool B.

SHAUN McRAE (Australian)
St. Helens: Jan. 96 - Oct. 98
                    (RL Cup winners (2), Super
                    League champs, Premier BF (2)),
Gateshead T.:   Nov. 98 -

STAN MARTIN (New Zealander)
Whitehaven: Oct. 95 - July 98

COLIN MASKILL
Doncaster D.:   May 97 -
Played for: Wakefield T., Leeds, Doncaster,
Castleford, Featherstone R.

IAN MILLWARD (Australian)
Leigh C.:   Sep. 98 -

JOHN MONIE (Australian)
Wigan: Sep. 89 - May 93
                    (Div. 1 champs (4), RL Cup
                    winners (4), Regal Trophy
                    winners (2),
                    Premier winners & BF, Lancs.
                    Cup winners, World Club
                    Challenge winners & BF, Charity
                    Shield winners & BF (2))
                    Nov. 97 - (Super League champs,
                    RL Cup BF)

GRAHAM MURRAY (Australian)
Leeds R.:   Dec. 97 - (Super League GF BF)

JOHN PENDLEBURY
Halifax B.S.:   Mar. 97 -
Played for: Wigan, Halifax, Bradford N., Leigh,
Salford

DAVID PLANGE
Hunslet H.:   Nov. 96 - (Div. 2 champs - new
                    division)
Played for: Doncaster, Castleford, Hull K.R., Hunslet

ANDY PLATT
Workington T.:   Oct. 98 -
Played for: St. Helens, Wigan, Widnes, Salford R.

STUART RAPER (Australian)
Castleford T.:   Apr. 97 -
Played for: Oldham

MALCOLM REILLY
Castleford: Dec. 74 - May 87
                    (RL Cup winners, John Player
                    winners, Premier BF, Yorks. Cup
                    winners (3) & BF (2), Charity
                    Shield BF, Floodlit Trophy
                    winners)
Leeds: Aug. 88 - Sep. 89
                    (Yorks. Cup winners)
Halifax: Jan. 93 - Sep. 94
Huddersfield G.:   Oct. 98 -
Great Britain: Jan. 87 - Aug. 94
GB Under-21s: 1986-87, 1987-88, 1989-90,
                    1991-92, 1992-93
Played for: Castleford

DEAN ROBINSON
York: Dec. 96 -
Played for: Wakefield T.

GARRY SCHOFIELD
Huddersfield G.:   Nov. 97 - July 98
Played for: Hull, Leeds, Huddersfield G.

STEVE SIMMS (Australian)
Leigh: Nov. 92 - Sep. 94
Halifax: Sep. 94 - Feb. 97
Featherstone R.:   Apr. 97 - Oct. 98 (First Div. GF
                    BF)

DAN STAINS
London B.:   Nov. 98 -
Played for: Halifax

KEVIN TAMATI (New Zealander)
Salford: Oct. 89 - July 93
Chorley/   Feb. 96 - Sep. 98 (Div. 2 champs
Lancashire L.:   - new division)
Whitehaven W.:   Nov. 98 -
Played for: Widnes, Warrington, Salford, Lancashire L.
* *Tamati became manager in October 1997 with Steve
Hampson as coach. Tamati left Lancashire in September
1998*

ROBERT TEW (Australian)
Workington T.:   Apr. 97 - Oct. 98

SHANE TUPAEA (New Zealander)
Rochdale H.:   May 96 - April 98 (Promotion)
Played for: Mansfield M., Rochdale H., Swinton, Oldham, Keighley C.

NORMAN TURLEY
Workington T.:   Mar. 87 - Apr. 88
Whitehaven: June 90 - Apr. 91
Trafford B.:   June 91 - Dec. 91
Leigh C.:   May 98 - Sep. 98
Played for: Warrington, Rochdale H., Blackpool B., Trafford B., Swinton, Runcorn H., Barrow, Workington T., Whitehaven

DARRYL VAN DE VELDE (Australian)
Castleford: July 88 - May 93 (Yorks. Cup winners (2) & BF, Challenge Cup (BF)
Huddersfield: Dec. 95 - Sep. 96
Warrington W.:   Apr. 97 -

PHIL VEIVERS
Huddersfield G.:   July 98 - Sep. 98
Played for: St. Helens, Huddersfield G.

PETER WALSH (Australian)
Workington T.:   Apr. 92 - July 95 (Div. 2 champs, Div. 2 Premier winners, Divisional Premiership BF)
Hull S.:   July 97 - (Divisional Premiership BF)
Cumbria: 1994-95
Played for: Oldham

DAVID WARD
Hunslet: July 86 - Apr. 88 (Div. 2 champs, Div. 2 Premier BF)
Hunslet: Jan. 89 - May 89
Leeds: Sep. 89 - May 91
Batley: May 91 - Oct. 94
Featherstone R.:   Oct. 94 - Apr. 97
Batley B.:   Sep. 97 - (Trans-Pennine Cup winners)
Played for: Leeds, Workington T.

GRAEME WEST (New Zealander)
Wigan: May 94 - Feb. 97 (Premier winners (3), World Club Challenge winners, Div. 1 champs (2*), Regal Trophy winners (2), RL Cup winners, Charity Shield winners)
          Including Centenary Championship
Widnes V.:   May 97 - Aug 98
Played for: Wigan

COLIN WHITFIELD
Widnes V.   Aug. 98 -
Played for: Salford, Wigan, Halifax, Rochdale H.

STUART WILKINSON
Barrow: Apr. 97 - Sep 98
Played for: Barrow

Colin Whitfield: New Widnes Vikings coach.

REPRESENTATIVE REGISTER

The following is a list of international and county coaches since 1974-75.

GREAT BRITAIN

Jim Challinor	Dec. 71 - Aug. 74 (Inc. tours)
David Watkins	1977 World Championship
Peter Fox	1978
Eric Ashton	1979 tour
Johnny Whiteley	Aug. 80 - Nov. 82
Frank Myler	Dec. 82 - Aug. 84 (Inc. tour)
Maurice Bamford	Oct. 84 - Dec. 86
Malcolm Reilly	Jan. 87 - Aug. 94 (Inc. tours)
Ellery Hanley	Aug. 94 - May 95
Phil Larder	Jan. 96 - Nov. 96 (Inc. 1996 tour)
Andy Goodway	Sep. 97 -

ENGLAND

Alex Murphy	Jan. 75 - Nov. 75 (Inc. World Championship tour)
Peter Fox	1976-77
Frank Myler	1977-78
Eric Ashton	1978-79, 1979-80
Johnny Whiteley	1980-81, 1981-82
Reg Parker (Mgr)	1984-85
Malcolm Reilly	1992-93
Ellery Hanley	1994-95
Phil Larder	1995-96, 1996

EMERGING ENGLAND

Andy Goodway	1998

IRELAND

Niel Wood/Mick Slicker	1996
Steve O'Neill	1997, 1998

SCOTLAND

George Fairbairn	1996, 1997
Billy McGinty	1998

WALES

Les Pearce	Jan. 75 - Nov. 75 (Inc. World Championship tour)
David Watkins } Bill Francis }	1976-77
Kel Coslett } Bill Francis }	1977-78

Kel Coslett	1978-79 to 1981-82
David Watkins	1982-83, 1984-85
Clive Griffiths	1991-92, 1992-93, 1993-94, 1994-95, 1995-96, 1996, 1998

GREAT BRITAIN UNDER-24s

Johnny Whiteley	1976-82
Frank Myler	1983-84

GREAT BRITAIN UNDER-21s

Maurice Bamford	Oct. 84 - Dec. 86
Malcolm Reilly	1986-87, 1987-88, 1989-90, 1991-92, 1992-93, 1993-94
David Topliss	1988-89
Phil Larder	1990-91, 1991-92
Gary Hetherington	1994-95
Phil Larder	1995-96

CUMBRIA

Ike Southward	1975-76
Frank Foster	1976-77 to 1977-78
Sol Roper	1978-79
Frank Foster	1979-80
Phil Kitchin	1980-81 to 1981-82
Frank Foster	1982-83
Jackie Davidson	1985-86
Phil Kitchin	1986-87 to 1991-92
Gordon Cottier	1992-93
Peter Walsh } Kurt Sorensen }	1994-95

LANCASHIRE

Alex Murphy	1973-74 to 1977-78
Eric Ashton	1978-79 to 1979-80
Tom Grainey	1980-81 to 1981-82
Doug Laughton	1982-83
Alex Murphy	1985-86 to 1987-88
Doug Laughton	1988-89 to 1989-90
Ray Ashton	1991-92

YORKSHIRE

Johnny Whiteley	1970-71 to 1979-80
Arthur Keegan	1980-81
Johnny Whiteley	1981-82 to 1982-83
Peter Fox	1985-86 to 1991-92

OTHER NATIONALITIES

Dave Cox	1974-75 to 1975-76

Bobbie Goulding: Surprise transfer from St. Helens to Huddersfield Giants.

TRANSFERS

1998 TRANSFER REVIEW

A radical change to the transfer system was agreed at an RL Council meeting on 24 June. From 1 January 1999 there will be no transfer fees for players over 24 years of age. The age limit is believed necessary to give clubs who produce and develop their own young players some degree of protection and the chance of compensation if they are lured away before they reach the age of 24.

The change was virtually forced on to the RFL to bring it in line with European Law following the Bosman case in soccer two years earlier. Belgian player Jean-Marc Bosman won a court case which changed soccer's transfer system and granted players freedom of movement.

Even before the rule was introduced into Rugby League, it had its effect on the old transfer system in 1998 as clubs were reluctant to pay large fees for players who would become free agents in the new year. Conversely, selling clubs were eager to get what they could for players before it became too late to cash in. Allied to clubs manoeuvring to keep within the salary cap, it all resulted in a flurry of transfer activity as the year drew to a close.

There was also an increasing reluctance by clubs to reveal the exact fee involved in transfers and 'substantial' was often no more than they would be prepared to disclose. The biggest reported transfer fee during 1998 was the estimated £140,000 Bradford Bulls paid Salford Reds for 21-year-old centre Nathan McAvoy on 29 July. On the same day, Bradford also signed Huddersfield Giants prop Neil Harmon for a 'nominal' fee.

Bradford continued their recruiting drive by signing McAvoy's wing partner at Salford, Scott Naylor, for an undisclosed fee, and New Zealand international Henry Paul from Wigan Warriors. Both signings followed an increasing trend of transfers being announced before the current

contract had been completed and the players continued to play for the selling club until the end of the season.

Leeds Rhinos were reported to have agreed to pay over £100,000 in stages for Featherstone Rovers' 18-year-old winger or stand off Karl Pratt, the full amount depending on how much club and international progress he makes.

Halifax were involved in a late flurry of transfer activity when they signed stand off Graham Holroyd from Leeds just before completing a big exchange deal. They took Test prop Paul Broadbent and international centre Nick Pinkney from Sheffield Eagles, who collected backs Martin Pearson and Daio Powell plus forward Simon Baldwin. Holroyd had been listed at £195,000 in June 1997, but one report suggested that his transfer fee was less than £50,000 when he moved to Halifax. This was a clear example of the impending free transfer rule already affecting the market, as Holroyd's contract had only a another year to run at Leeds and then he could have moved for nothing as he would be over 24 years old. Leeds had also calculated that releasing Holroyd from his contract would give them more scope within the salary cap.

Bobbie Goulding, who had been involved in three deals ranging from £90,000 to £160,000 over the years, joined Huddersfield Giants on a free transfer from St. Helens. The 26-year-old Test scrum half had been suspended in a disciplinary measure by Saints, who appeared glad to release Goulding from his highly lucrative contract.

Steve Molloy's transfer from Featherstone Rovers to Sheffield Eagles in February ended the forward's threat to take Rovers to court if they did not grant him a free transfer. Molloy, backed by the RL Players' Association, sought to be released after the club had offered him a much reduced contract. Featherstone, who had bought Molloy from Leeds for a tribunal fixed fee of

£100,000 in 1993, sought half that amount from Sheffield but eventually let him go for much less.

Leeds were accused of abusing the loan system by lending several promising young players to Bramley, their Second Division tenants at Headingley. Critics accused Leeds, who had disbanded their Alliance team, of using Bramley as a reserve side to give the Super League club's fringe players match practice.

The criticism increased when Leeds loaned international forward Barrie McDermott to Bramley for four matches to help him regain full fitness after completing a five-match suspension. Terry Newton also had a two-match loan spell with Bramley following injury before regaining his Leeds place and making a Test debut for Great Britain at the end of the season. Leeds defended themselves by saying that they had not broken any rules.

LEAGUE-UNION LINK

Leeds Rhinos were involved in two extraordinary movements of players linked with their partners at Headingley, the Leeds Tykes Rugby Union Club. Wendell Sailor, the outstanding Brisbane Broncos and Australia Test winger, joined the Tykes as an 'amateur' after failing to gain a permit from the Rugby Football Union to play as a professional because he had not played a sufficient number of RU matches. Sailor had initially been reported to have joined Leeds Rugby Club – the parent company of the two clubs – for almost £100,000. The deal was for Sailor to play regularly for the Tykes during a 16-week stay plus two friendly matches for the Rhinos over the Christmas-New Year holiday period.

Wigan Warriors viewed the 'amateur' arrangement with some anger and cynicism as Sailor had agreed a two-year deal with them back in January reckoned to be worth about £500,000. But Brisbane had refused to release him.

In November, Adam Hughes became the first player to sign a joint contract with the Leeds Rugby Club to play for both the Rhinos and the Tykes. The 21-year-old centre had just returned to Leeds RL after a season's loan to Wakefield Trinity.

Elsewhere the movement between the two codes was mostly one way, with no major Rugby Union player having joined a Rugby League club since the 15-a-side game went professional in 1996. Among those who left League for Union, perhaps the greatest loss was that of international centre Barrie-Jon Mather, who left Castleford Tigers for Sale RU.

St. Helens' international winger Anthony Sullivan headed several players who had a temporary winter stint in Rugby Union when he joined Cardiff and he was soon selected for Wales B.

OVERSEAS PLAYERS

With three fewer clubs than in 1997, the total of overseas players making at least one first- team appearance during the season fell from the previous year's record 206 to 174. But the numbers in Super League alone remained at 96.

Australia again provided the most overseas players with 101 in all three divisions, against 108 in 1997. They included two Test players, both making their British club debuts – Danny Moore at Wigan Warriors and Mark Carroll with London Broncos.

London Broncos, who remain exempt from quota restrictions, again had most overseas players with 22, mostly Australians.

The total number of New Zealanders playing in Britain dropped from 56 to 45. They included 13 Tests players, one more than in 1997.

There were 24 players from the other South Pacific countries, plus three South Africans and a Frenchman.

OVERSEAS REGISTER 1998

Players from overseas who made at least one first-team appearance for British clubs in 1998.
*Test or World Cup players as at 1 January 1998

AUSTRALIA (101)

Air, Glen	London B.
Antonik, Nathan	Keighley C.
Appleby, Darren	Rochdale H.
Baildon, David	Hull S.
Baker, Danny	Featherstone R.
Beauchamp, Keith	Hull K.R.
Beazley, Robbie	London B.
Bell, Mark	Wigan W.
Best, Roger	London B.
Bostock, Joshua	Wakefield T.
Bouveng, David	Halifax B.S.
Bradley, Graeme	Bradford B.
Brown, Danny	Hull K.R.
Byrne, Steve	Lancashire L.
Carr, Paul	Sheffield E.
*Carroll, Mark	London B.
Casey, Garen	Wakefield T.
Chapman, Damien	London B.
Chapman, David	Castleford T.
Clark, Des	Halifax B.S.
Clinch, Gavin	Halifax B.S.
Collins, Steve	Featherstone R.
Collins, Wayne	Dewsbury R.
Davis, Brad	Castleford T.
Donougher, Jeremy	Bradford B.
Doyle, Adam	Warrington W.
Doyle, Rod	Sheffield E.
Driscoll, Steve	Leigh C.
Dunford, Matt	London B.
Eagar, Michael	Warrington W.
Eldershaw, Justin	Bramley
Evans, Paul	Dewsbury R.
Fallins, Tyron	Featherstone R.
Farrar, Danny	Warrington W.
Fatnowna, Abraham	London B.
Fitzgerald, Peter	Rochdale H.
Fuller, Matt	Wakefield T.
Garces, Steve	Leigh C.
Gibson, Damian	Halifax B.S.
Gill, Peter	London B.
Glanville, Marc	Leeds R.
Godden, Brad	Leeds R.
Goldspink, Brett	St. Helens
Goodwin, Luke	London B.

Hanger, Dean	Huddersfield G.
Higgins, Darren	London B.
Jenkins, Nick	Leigh C.
Kennedy, Jamie	Hull K.R.
Kenward, Shane	Salford R.
Kenworthy, Roger	Wakefield T.
Kerr, Ken	Rochdale H.
King, David	Huddersfield G.
Lambert, Matt	York
Laurence, Jason	Keighley C.
Lester, Gary	Hull S.
Maher, Adam	Rochdale H.
Mathiou, Jamie	Leeds R.
Matterson, Terry	London B.
McCormack, Robbie	Wigan W.
McDonald, Brock	Keighley C.
McKell, Richard	Castleford T.
McKelleher, John	Barrow B.R.
McKelvie, Danny	Dewsbury R.
McWilliam, Chris	Batley B.
Mestrov, Tony	Wigan W.
Miers, Grant	Batley B.
Millard, Shane	London B.
*Moore, Danny	Wigan W.
Moore, Martin	Widnes V.
Morganson, Willie	Sheffield E.
Nixon, Matt	Leigh C.
Nutley, Danny	Warrington W.
O'Donnell, David	Dewsbury R.
Orr, Chris	Huddersfield G.
Patterson, Brett	Dewsbury R.
Peacock, Danny	Bradford B.
Pechey, Mike	Hunslet H., Warrington W.
Price-Jones, Gavin	Swinton L.
Retchless, Steele	London B.
Rosolen, Steve	London B.
Russell, Danny	Huddersfield G.
Ryan, Chris	London B.
Schick, Andrew	Castleford T.
Shaw, Darren	Sheffield E.
Smith, Damien	St. Helens
Smith, Duncan	Keighley C.
Strange, John	York
Sullivan, Chris	Workington T.
Tomlinson, Glen	Hull S.
Toshack, Matt	London B.
Veivers, Phil	Huddersfield G.
Vowles, Adrian	Castleford T.
Wallis, Shaun	Barrow B.R.
Weston, Craig	Huddersfield G.
White, Josh	Salford R.

White, Kyle — Widnes V.
Williams, Bart — London B.
Williams, Brendan — Dewsbury R.
Wilson, Scott — Warrington W.
Wilson, Shane — Widnes V.
Wittenberg, Jeff — Huddersfield G.

NEW ZEALAND (45)
Adams, Gareth — Swinton L.
Bell, Glen — Doncaster D.
*Blackmore, Richard — Leeds R.
Campbell, Logan — Hull S.
Cooksley, Jayson *see* Pekepo
David, Maea — Hull S.
*Edwards, Peter — Salford R.
*Faimalo, Esene — Salford R.
Faimalo, Joe — Salford R.
Fatialofa, David — Whitehaven W.
Hall, Carl — Featherstone R.
Henare, Richard — Workington T.
Hepi, Brad — Hull S.
Howell, Paul — Widnes V.
Joe, Leroy — Whitehaven W.
*Kemp, Tony — Leeds R.
Kini, Troy — Doncaster D.
Kohe-Love, Toa — Warrington W.
Lester, Aaron — Whitehaven W.
Manihera, Tane — Widnes V., Barrow B.R.
Mansson, Paul — Hunslet H.
*Mercer, Gary — Halifax B.S.
Moana, Martin — Halifax B.S.
Murray, David "Doc" — Lancashire L.
*Okesene, Hitro — Hull S.
O'Neill, Julian — St. Helens
Opetaia, Scott — Rochdale H.
*Paul, Henry — Wigan W.
*Paul, Robbie — Bradford B.
Pekepo, Jayson — Lancashire L.
Reihana, Tahi — Bradford B.
Samuel, Anthony — Workington T.
Smith, Michael — Castleford T.
Smits, Alex — Keighley C.
Solomon, Pehi James — Lancashire L.
Sturm, Matt — Huddersfield G.
*Taewa, Whetu — Sheffield E.
Tawhai, Latham — Hunslet H.
Temu, Jason — Hull S.
Terry, Taniora — Bramley

*Timu, John — London B.
Tupaea, Shane — Rochdale H.
*Tuuta, Brendon — Warrington W.
*Watson, Dave — Sheffield E.
Whakarau, Sonny — Wakefield T.
*Young, Grant — London B.

FIJI (2)
*Seru, Fili — Hull S.
*Sovatabua, Waisale — Sheffield E.

FRANCE (1)
*Tallec, Gael — Castleford T.

PAPUA NEW GUINEA (2)
*Gene, Stanley — Hull K.R.
*Okul, John — Hull K.R., Doncaster D.

SOUTH AFRICA (3)
*Ballot, Andrew — Hunslet H.
*Bloem, Jamie — Widnes V., Halifax B.S.
*Johnson, Mark — Hull S.

TONGA (9)
*Amone, Asa — Featherstone R.
*Hansen, Liuaki "Lee" — Wigan W., Keighley C.
Leuila, Peaufai "Afi" — Oldham
*Liku, Tau'alupe — Leigh C.
Mafi, Mateaki — Workington T.
**Mann, George — Keighley C., Swinton L.
*Masella, Martin — Leeds R.
*Vaikona, Tevita — Bradford B.
*Veikoso, Jimmy — Swinton L.
** *Also played for New Zealand*

WESTERN SAMOA (11)
Filipo, Lafaele — Hunslet H.
*Malietoa-Brown, Gus — Whitehaven W.
*Matautia, Vila — St. Helens
Muliumu, Siose — Whitehaven W.
*Perelini, Apollo — St. Helens
*Poching, Willie — Hunslet H.
Sapatu, Fred — Keighley C.
Savelio, Lokeni — Salford R.
Sini, Iefata "Fata" — York
*Swann, Willie — Rochdale H.
Tuilagi, Fereti — Halifax B.S.

TOP CASH-ONLY TRANSFERS

Fee	Player	Position	From	To	Date
£440,000	Martin Offiah	Winger	Widnes	Wigan	January 1992
£325,000*	Iestyn Harris	Stand off	Warrington W.	Leeds R.	April 1997
£300,000***	Paul Sculthorpe	Loose forward	Warrington W.	St. Helens	December 1997
£250,000**	Paul Newlove	Centre	Bradford N.	St. Helens	November 1995
£250,000	Gary Connolly	Centre	St. Helens	Wigan	August 1993
£250,000	Ellery Hanley	Loose forward	Wigan	Leeds	September 1991
£250,000	Alan Hunte	Centre	St. Helens	Hull S.	December 1997
£245,000	Paul Newlove	Centre	Featherstone R.	Bradford N.	July 1993
£170,000	Graham Steadman	Stand off	Featherstone R.	Castleford	June 1989
£160,000	Bobbie Goulding	Scrum half	Widnes	St. Helens	July 1994
£155,000	Garry Schofield	Centre	Hull	Leeds	October 1987
£150,000	Tony Smith	Scrum half	Castleford T.	Wigan W.	March 1997
£150,000	Andy Currier	Centre	Widnes	Featherstone R.	August 1993
£150,000	Lee Crooks	Prop	Leeds	Castleford	January 1990
£150,000	Lee Crooks	Prop/2nd row	Hull	Leeds	June 1987

* Part of an estimated £350,000 deal with Warrington also receiving Danny Sculthorpe from Leeds.
** Part of an estimated £500,000 deal with Bradford also receiving St. Helens players Bernard Dwyer, Paul Loughlin and Sonny Nickle.
*** Part of a £370,000 deal with Warrington also receiving Chris Morley from St. Helens.

RECORD TRANSFERS

The first £1,000 transfer came in 1921 when Harold Buck joined Leeds from Hunslet, although there were reports at the time that another player was involved in the deal to make up the four-figure transfer. Other claims for the first £1,000 transfer are attached to Stan Brogden's move from Bradford Northern to Huddersfield in 1929. The following list shows how transfer fees have grown this century in straight cash deals only:

Fee	Player	Position	From	To	Season
£100	Jim Lomas	Centre	Bramley	Salford	1901-02
£300	Jim Lomas	Centre	Salford	Oldham	1910-11
£600	Billy Batten	Centre	Hunslet	Hull	1912-13
£1,000	Harold Buck	Wing	Hunslet	Leeds	1921-22
£1,075	Stanley Smith	Wing	Wakefield T.	Leeds	1929-30
£1,200	Stanley Brogden	Wing/Centre	Huddersfield	Leeds	1933-34
£1,450	Billy Belshaw	Full back	Liverpool S.	Warrington	1937-38
£1,650	Bill Davies	Full back/Centre	Huddersfield	Dewsbury	1946-47
£2,000	Bill Hudson	Forward	Batley	Wigan	1947-48
£2,650	Jim Ledgard	Full back	Dewsbury	Leigh	1947-48
£2,750	Ike Owens	Forward	Leeds	Castleford	1948-49
£2,750	Ike Owens	Forward	Castleford	Huddersfield	1948-49
£4,000	Stan McCormick	Wing	Belle Vue R.	St. Helens	1948-49
£4,600	Albert Naughton	Centre	Widnes	Warrington	1949-50
£4,750	Bruce Ryan	Wing	Hull	Leeds	1950-51
£5,000	Joe Egan	Hooker	Wigan	Leigh	1950-51
£5,000	Harry Street	Forward	Dewsbury	Wigan	1950-51
£9,500	Mick Sullivan	Wing	Huddersfield	Wigan	1957-58
£10,650	Ike Southward	Wing	Workington T.	Oldham	1958-59

£11,000	Mick Sullivan	Wing	Wigan	St. Helens	1960-61
£11,002 10s	Ike Southward	Wing	Oldham	Workington T.	1960-61
£12,000	Colin Dixon	Forward	Halifax	Salford	1968-69
£12,500	Paul Charlton	Full back	Workington T.	Salford	1969-70
£13,000	Eric Prescott	Forward	St. Helens	Salford	1972-73
£15,000	Steve Nash	Scrum half	Featherstone R.	Salford	1975-76
£18,000	Bill Ashurst	Forward	Wigan	Wakefield T.	1977-78
£20,000	Clive Pickerill	Scrum half	Castleford	Hull	1978-79
£35,000	Phil Hogan	Forward	Barrow	Hull K.R.	1978-79
£38,000	Len Casey	Forward	Bradford N.	Hull K.R.	1979-80
£40,000	Trevor Skerrett	Forward	Wakefield T.	Hull	1980-81
£72,500	George Fairbairn	Full back	Wigan	Hull K.R.	1980-81
£85,000	Ellery Hanley	Centre/Stand off	Bradford N.	Wigan	1985-86
£100,000	Joe Lydon	Centre	Widnes	Wigan	1985-86
£130,000	Andy Gregory	Scrum half	Warrington	Wigan	1986-87
£150,000	Lee Crooks	Forward	Hull	Leeds	1987-88
£155,000	Garry Schofield	Centre	Hull	Leeds	1987-88
£170,000	Graham Steadman	Stand off	Featherstone R.	Castleford	1989-90
£250,000	Ellery Hanley	Forward	Wigan	Leeds	1991-92
£440,000	Martin Offiah	Winger	Widnes	Wigan	1991-92

Record cash plus player exchange deal: Paul Newlove's transfer from Bradford Bulls to St. Helens in November 1995 was reckoned to be worth £500,000. The centre moved in exchange for St. Helens forwards Bernard Dwyer and Sonny Nickle, centre Paul Loughlin plus £250,000.

Joint transfer: Martin Offiah was involved in a unique joint transfer when he left Wigan to sign for both London Broncos and Bedford Rugby Union club in August 1996. The total fee was reported to be £300,000, with Bedford paying the larger amount, but it was never confirmed. The international winger signed a three-year contract with London and a four-year deal with Bedford, but gave up his Rugby Union career in August 1997.

Record fee fixed by Transfer Tribunal: Paul Newlove's transfer fee when he moved from Featherstone Rovers to Bradford Northern in July 1993 was fixed by the tribunal at £245,000. Bradford had offered £150,000 after Featherstone listed the centre at a then record £750,000.

Record transfer list fee: Iestyn Harris was listed at a world record £1,350,000 by Warrington on 23 July 1996 after the 20-year-old international utility back had made it clear that he did not wish to play for them. Leeds Rhinos signed Harris in a £350,000 deal in April 1997.

Record transfer fee for teenager: Nineteen-year-old utility back Nigel Wright was transferred from Wakefield Trinity to Wigan for £140,000 on 1 July 1993.

Record transfer fee paid by lower division club: £135,000 by Keighley Cougars and Huddersfield Giants, both non-top division clubs. Keighley, of the old Second Division, set the record when they signed Great Britain stand-off Daryl Powell from First Division Sheffield Eagles in April 1995. Huddersfield, of the new First Division, equalled the record to sign Garry Schofield, another Test stand-off, from Super League club Leeds in February 1996.

Record fee for each position: Full back: £120,000 Stuart Spruce (Widnes to Bradford

Bulls) May 1996; **Wing:** £440,000 Martin Offiah (Widnes to Wigan) January 1992; **Centre:** £250,000 Gary Connolly (St. Helens to Wigan) August 1993; Paul Newlove (Bradford Bulls to St. Helens) November 1995 as part of a £500,000 exchange deal; Alan Hunte (St. Helens to Hull Sharks) December 1997; **Stand off:** £325,000 Iestyn Harris (Warrington Wolves to Leeds Rhinos) April 1997 with Warrington also receiving £25,000 rated Danny Sculthorpe; **Scrum half:** £160,000 Bobbie Goulding (Widnes to St. Helens) July 1994; **Prop/Second row:** £150,000 Lee Crooks (Hull to Leeds) June 1987 and (Leeds to Castleford) January 1990; Wigan Warriors signed Widnes Vikings prop Lee Hansen in April 1997 in an estimated £160,000 deal, including £80,000-rated Sean Long; **Hooker:** £83,000 Lee Jackson (Hull to Sheffield Eagles) September 1993; **Loose forward:** £300,000 Paul Sculthorpe (Warrington Wolves to St. Helens) December 1997. Warrington also received £70,000 rated Chris Morley.

Record RU signing: Putting a figure on contracts signed by Rugby Union players can only be speculative, because neither club nor players reveal the exact amounts. It is no more than probable that the best deal was signed by Welsh international forward Scott Quinnell when he moved from Llanelli RU to Wigan in September 1994 for a reported basic £50,000 per season rising to a potential £500,000 over four years. But as Quinnell returned to Rugby Union with Richmond in a reported £300,000 transfer two years later it is unlikely he received anything like the full amount.

Before Quinnell's move to Rugby League, the British record deal for a Rugby Union player was generally accepted as the £350,000 five-year contract for New Zealand international full back John Gallagher when he signed for Leeds in 1990 and a similar amount over four

years that Wigan handed to another All Black, winger Va'aiga Tuigamala in 1993.

Record fee for a non-Test player: Graham Steadman had still not made his Test debut when Castleford signed the stand off from Featherstone Rovers for £145,000 in June 1989. The fee was fixed by the transfer tribunal, who ruled that Castleford should pay an extra £25,000 if he played for Great Britain, which he did the following April.

Record fee by an RU club for an RL player: When Va'aiga Tuigamala left Wigan Warriors for Newcastle RU in February 1997 it was said to have been for a £750,000 transfer fee spread over five years as part of a £2m deal. The deal also included payment to the winger or centre of the £250,000 loyalty bonus that had tied him to Super League at the start of the dispute with the Australian RL.

Most moves: Geoff Clarkson was involved in a record 12 transfers in his 17-year career. He played for 10 different English clubs, including two spells at Wakefield Trinity, Leigh and Bradford Northern, and also had a brief period in Australia. The back row forward joined Wakefield Trinity in 1966 from Wakefield Rugby Union club and was 40 years old when he finished playing regular first team rugby in 1983-84.

Clarkson's club career in England was as follows:

1966 – Wakefield T.
1968 – Bradford N.
1970 – Leigh
1971 – Warrington
1972 – Leeds
1975 – York
1976 – Bramley
1978 – Wakefield T. and Hull K.R.
1980 – Bradford N. and Oldham
1981 – Leigh
1983 – Featherstone R.

Iestyn Harris: Picked up three top individual awards, including Man of Steel.

AWARDS

IESTYN HARRIS of Leeds Rhinos won the three major individual awards in 1998. The Leeds full back and occasional stand off was named the JJB Super League Players' Player of the Year; the Rugby League Writers' Association Player of the Year; and Man of Steel as the personality to have made the most impact on the season.

All the awards were made before he played in the Grand Final and for Great Britain in the Test series against New Zealand, but Harris had long left his mark on the season with a series of outstanding performances. He headed the Super League points chart with 255 from 13 tries and 103 goals, including three drop goals.

In his first year as Leeds' captain, Harris led them in great style to a place in the inaugural Grand Final and finished with a Cup and League total of 283 points from 13 tries and 117 goals, including three drop goals.

Harris also played for Wales against Emerging England in mid season.

For the first time since its inception in 1977, the major awards evening came under the sole control of Super League Europe and did not include the First and Second Division Players of the Year, which were run separately by FASDA.

Launched in 1976-77, the Rugby Football League's official awards were presented at a Man of Steel evening until it became the Stones Gold Awards Dinner at the end of the first Super League season of 1996 and since then has been held at the Holiday Inn Crowne Plaza, Manchester.

The original official awards and ceremony were sponsored by Trumanns Steel from 1977 to 1983, with brewers Greenall Whitley taking over until Stones Bitter became the sponsors in 1990. JJB Sports became the sponsors in 1998 when the awards were made on 21 October.

THE 1998 AWARD WINNERS

JJB Man of Steel
IESTYN HARRIS of Leeds Rhinos took the game's top individual award as the unanimous choice of a panel of officials and journalists as the personality who had made the most impact on the season. He received a trophy and a cheque for £5,000.

JJB Super League Players' Player of the Year
IESTYN HARRIS of Leeds Rhinos was voted Super League's top player by his fellow professionals and received a trophy and a cheque for £1,000.
Short-listed: Adrian Morley (Leeds R.) and Henry Paul (Wigan W.)

JJB Super League Young Player of the Year
LEE GILMOUR of Wigan Warriors was named the best young player of the year by a panel of judges. He played in all 30 of the club's Cup and League matches, including 17 as a substitute, and scored 10 tries. The 20-year-old had appeared only once the previous season, but made rapid progress in 1998 and after a few matches on the wing gained a regular place in the second row towards the end of season. He was a substitute for the Silk Cut Challenge Cup final, in the starting line-up for the Grand Final, played loose forward for Emerging England against Wales and crowned an outstanding first full season by making his Test debut for Great Britain against New Zealand. He received a trophy and a cheque for £1,000.
Short-listed: Paul Johnson (Wigan W.) and Chris Chester (Halifax B.S.)

JJB Super League Coach of the Year
JOHN PENDLEBURY of Halifax Blue Sox was adjudged the coach of the year in only his second season in charge of a senior team. He

became the first coach to win the award without his club having won a trophy during the season. But few opposed his nomination after he steered a Halifax side that had finished seventh in 1997 to third place. Pendlebury had quit for a few hours early in the season because of interference in team matters by some board members, but the players pleaded successfully with him to stay. He received a trophy and a cheque for £1,000.
Short-listed: John Monie (Wigan W.) and Graham Murray (Leeds R.)

CIS Super League
Referee of the Year
RUSSELL SMITH of Castleford was chosen as the top referee for the second successive season and for the third time altogether. The award was based on the official assessment of referees after each match and Smith received the highest marks. He had charge of the inaugural Grand Final and was the referee for all three Test matches Down Under between Australia and New Zealand. He received a trophy and a cheque for £1,000.
Short-listed: John Connolly (Wigan W.) and Stuart Cummings (Widnes)

JJB SUPER LEAGUE DREAM TEAM
Only three players have been selected for the Super League Dream team each year since its introduction in 1996. They are wingers Jason Robinson and Anthony Sullivan plus loose forward Andrew Farrell.
The 1998 team was selected by a panel of journalists, coaches and Super League officials, based on form throughout the season.

1. Kris Radlinski (Wigan Warriors)
2. Jason Robinson (Wigan Warriors)
3. Gary Connolly (Wigan Warriors)
4. Brad Godden (Leeds Rhinos)
5. Anthony Sullivan (St. Helens)
6. Iestyn Harris (Leeds Rhinos)
7. Gavin Clinch (Halifax Blue Sox)
8. Neil Cowie (Wigan Warriors)

9. Robbie McCormack (Wigan Warriors)
10. Dale Laughton (Sheffield Eagles)
11. Steele Retchless (London Broncos)
12. Adrian Morley (Leeds Rhinos)
13. Andrew Farrell (Wigan Warriors)

FASDA AWARDS
The First and Second Division Association arranged their own individual awards for the first time and made the presentations during the interval of the First Division Grand Final at the Alfred McAlpine Stadium, Huddersfield. Each category was chosen by a panel of journalists and officials.

First Division Player of the Year
STANLEY GENE of Hull Kingston Rovers received the award after another outstanding season in which he headed the First Division try chart with 28 and added six more in Cup-ties. The Papua New Guinea international half back missed only one of Rovers' 37 Cup and League matches.
Short-listed: Garen Casey (Wakefield T.) and Richard Chapman (Featherstone R.)

Second Division Player of the Year
PHIL JONES of Lancashire Lynx gained the award after a record-breaking season with the Second Division champions. He finished with two club season's records with 101 goals and 254 points, including 13 tries. The stand off also equalled two match records with 10 goals and 24 points against Workington Town.
Short-listed: Mike Edwards (Oldham) and Gary Barnett (Batley B.)

FASDA Coach of the Year
NEIL KELLY of Dewsbury Rams won the award, which covered both divisions, for lifting his side from First Division sixth in 1997 to third in 1998 with little money to spend on new players. It was the highest position Dewsbury had gained for 13 years.
Short-listed: David Harrison (Hull K.R.) and David Ward (Batley B.)

FASDA TEAMS OF THE YEAR

For the first time First and Second Division coaches were asked to submit their form side of 1998, without including players from their own club, enabling a panel of journalists and officials to produce the following composite teams.

First Division XIII
1. Martyn Holland (Wakefield Trinity)
2. Richard Baker (Hunslet Hawks)
3. Brendan Williams (Dewsbury Rams)
4. Garen Casey (Wakefield Trinity)
5. Karl Pratt (Featherstone Rovers)
6. Stanley Gene (Hull Kingston Rovers)
7. Ian Watson (Swinton Lions)
8. Tim Street (Leigh Centurions)
9. Richard Chapman (Featherstone Rovers)
10. Richard Hayes (Hunslet Hawks)
11. Andy Coley (Swinton Lions)
12. David Larder (Keighley Cougars)
13. Chris Charles (Hull Kingston Rovers)

Second Division
1. David Murray (Lancashire Lynx)
2. Chris Eckersley (Oldham)
3. Roger Simpson (Batley Bulldogs)
4. Shaun Austerfield (York)
5. Leigh Deakin (York)
6. Phil Jones (Lancashire Lynx)
7. Gary Barnett (Batley Bulldogs)
8. Barry Williams (Workington Town)
9. Darren Holt (Barrow Border Raiders)
10. Mike Edwards (Oldham)
11. Tony Miller (Doncaster Dragons)
12. Simon Smith (Lancashire Lynx)
13. Justin Eldershaw (Bramley)

WRITERS' PLAYER OF THE YEAR

IESTYN HARRIS of Leeds Rhinos picked up the first of his individual awards when the members of the Rugby League Writers' Association chose him as their top player.

Previous winners
1996 Apollo Perelini (St. Helens)
1997 Andrew Farrell (Wigan Warriors)

WRITERS' MERIT AWARD

ERIC ASHTON received the Rugby League Writers' Association Arthur Brooks Merit Award for services to the game. The former Wigan and Great Britain captain has been a distinguished figure in the game for more than 40 years as player, coach and official.

The merit award was introduced in 1982 and three years later became a memorial trophy in the name of Arthur Brooks, a former Rugby League journalist, most notably with the *Daily Mirror*.

Previous winners
1982 Geoff Fletcher (Huyton player and official), 1983 David Howes (RFL Press Officer), 1984 Tom Morton (Doncaster secretary), 1985 John Holmes (player), 1986 Roger Millward (Hull K.R. player and coach), 1987 Tom Bergin (RL Writers' Association life member), 1988 Trevor Foster (Bradford N. player and official), 1989 Gary Hetherington (Sheffield E. founder), 1990 Maurice Oldroyd (BARLA national administrator), 1991 John Joyner (player), 1992 David Oxley (RFL Chief Executive), 1993 Jeff Grayshon (player), 1994 Mal Meninga (player), 1995 Alex Murphy (player and coach), 1996 Garry Schofield (player), 1997 Lee Crooks (player).

LION OF THE YEAR

ROGER MILLWARD became the first winner of the Tom Mitchell Trophy as 'Lion of the Year' when he received it a few weeks after the death of the former Great Britain tour manager. The award will now become a feature of the Rugby League Lions Annual Luncheon and be presented to any past or present British Lion who, in the estimation of the Lions committee, has upheld the tourists' proud standard on and off the field.

Millward made three full tours Down Under in addition to World Cup trips and appeared in 29 Test matches for Great Britain.

HALL OF FAME

The official Rugby League Hall of Fame was introduced in 1988 to pay tribute to the game's select band of legendary players. Sponsored by Whitbread Trophy, a panel of League officials, journalists and historians restricted entry to the highest echelon of players, based on playing records and their rating as legends in the annals of the game. Only players who had played most of their career in Britain and had been retired for at least 10 years were considered.

Nine players made up the original Hall of Fame with Neil Fox being added in 1989 after he had been retired for 10 years. These are the elite ten:

BILLY BATTEN
1905-1927 Hunslet, Hull, Wakefield T., Castleford
BRIAN BEVAN
1945-1964 Warrington, Blackpool B.
BILLY BOSTON
1953-1970 Wigan, Blackpool B.
NEIL FOX
1956-1979 Wakefield T., Bradford N., Hull K.R. York, Bramley, Huddersfield
ALEX MURPHY
1956-1975 St. Helens, Leigh, Warrington
JONTY PARKIN
1913-1932 Wakefield T., Hull K.R.
GUS RISMAN
1929-1954 Salford, Workington T., Batley
ALBERT ROSENFELD
1909-1924 Huddersfield, Wakefield T., Bradford N.
JIM SULLIVAN
1921-1946 Wigan
HAROLD WAGSTAFF
1906-1925 Huddersfield

Brian Bevan: Magnificent Australian winger.

Billy Boston: Great Welsh winger.

MAN OF STEEL WINNERS

	Man of Steel	1st Division Player	2nd Division Player	Young Player	Coach	Referee
1977	David Ward (Leeds)	Malcolm Reilly (Castleford)	Ged Marsh (Blackpool B.)	David Ward (Leeds)	Eric Ashton (St. Helens)	Billy Thompson (Huddersfield)
1978	George Nicholls (St. Helens)	George Nicholls (St. Helens)	John Woods (Leigh)	John Woods (Leigh)	Frank Myler (Widnes)	Billy Thompson (Huddersfield)
1979	Doug Laughton (Widnes)	Mick Adams (Widnes)	Steve Norton (Hull)	Steve Evans (Featherstone R.)	Doug Laughton (Widnes)	Mick Naughton (Widnes)
1980	George Fairbairn (Wigan)	Mick Adams (Widnes)	Steve Quinn (Featherstone R.)	Roy Holdstock (Hull K.R.)	Peter Fox (Bradford N.)	Fred Lindop (Wakefield)
1981	Ken Kelly (Warrington)	Ken Kelly (Warrington)	John Crossley (York)	Des Drummond (Leigh)	Billy Benyon (Warrington)	John Holdsworth (Kippax)
1982	Mick Morgan (Carlisle)	Steve Norton (Hull)	Mick Morgan (Carlisle)	Des Drummond (Leigh)	Arthur Bunting (Hull)	Fred Lindop (Wakefield)
1983	Allan Agar (Featherstone R.)	Keith Mumby (Bradford N.)	Steve Nash (Salford)	Brian Noble (Bradford N.)	Arthur Bunting (Hull)	Robin Whitfield (Widnes)
1984	Joe Lydon (Widnes)	Joe Lydon (Widnes)	David Cairns (Barrow)	Joe Lydon (Widnes)	Tommy Dawes (Barrow)	Billy Thompson (Huddersfield)
1985	Ellery Hanley (Bradford N.)	Ellery Hanley (Bradford N.)	Graham Steadman (York)	Lee Crooks (Hull)	Roger Millward (Hull K.R.)	Ron Campbell (Widnes)
1986	Gavin Miller (Hull K.R.)	Gavin Miller (Hull K.R.)	Derek Pyke (Leigh)	Shaun Edwards (Wigan)	Chris Anderson (Halifax)	Fred Lindop (Wakefield)
1987	Ellery Hanley (Wigan)	Andy Gregory (Wigan)	John Cogger (Runcorn H.)	Shaun Edwards (Wigan)	Graham Lowe (Wigan)	John Holdsworth (Kippax)
1988	Martin Offiah (Widnes)	Steve Hampson (Wigan)	Peter Smith (Featherstone R.)	Shaun Edwards (Wigan)	Doug Laughton (Widnes)	Fred Lindop (Wakefield)
1989	Ellery Hanley (Wigan)	David Hulme (Widnes)	Daryl Powell (Sheffield E.)	Paul Newlove (Featherstone R.)	Graham Lowe (Wigan)	John Holdsworth (Kippax)
1990	Shaun Edwards (Wigan)	Andy Goodway (Wigan)	John Woods (Rochdale H.)	Bobbie Goulding (Wigan)	John Monie (Wigan)	Robin Whitfield (Widnes)

	Man of Steel	1st Division Player	2nd Division Player	3rd Division Player	Young Player	Coach	Referee
1991	Garry Schofield (Leeds)	Jonathan Davies (Widnes)	Tawera Nikau (Ryedale-York)	—	Denis Betts (Wigan)	John Monie (Wigan)	John Holdsworth (Kippax)
1992	Dean Bell (Wigan)	Graham Steadman (Castleford)	Iva Ropati (Oldham)	Wally Gibson (Huddersfield)	Gary Connolly (St. Helens)	John Monie (Wigan)	Robin Whitfield (Widnes)
1993	Andy Platt (Wigan)	Tea Ropati (St. Helens)	Paul Newlove (Featherstone R.)	Martin Wood (Keighley C.)	Jason Robinson (Wigan)	John Monie (Wigan)	John Connolly (Wigan)
1994	Jonathan Davies (Warrington)	Jonathan Davies (Warrington)	Martin Oglanby (Workington T.)	—	Andrew Farrell (Wigan)	John Joyner (Castleford)	John Connolly (Wigan)
1995	Denis Betts (Wigan)	Bobbie Goulding (St. Helens)	Nick Pinkney (Keighley C.)	—	Andrew Farrell (Wigan)	Graeme West (Wigan)	Russell Smith (Castleford)

	Man of Steel	Super League Player	1st Division Player	2nd Division Player	Young Player	Coach	Referee
1996	Andrew Farrell (Wigan)	Robbie Paul (Bradford B.)	Nathan McAvoy (Salford R.)	Stanley Gene (Hull K.R.)	Keiron Cunningham (St. Helens)	Shaun McRae (St. Helens)	Stuart Cummings (Widnes)
1997	James Lowes (Bradford B.)	James Lowes (Bradford B.)	Tevita Vaikona (Hull S.)	Richard Pachniuk (Rochdale H.)	Lee Briers (Warrington W.)	Matthew Elliott (Bradford B.)	Russell Smith (Castleford)

ATTENDANCES

CLUB ATTENDANCE REVIEW

The following is a review of clubs' home attendances for League matches from 1990-91.

The main figure is the club's average attendance for League matches that season. The figure in brackets indicates an upward or downward trend compared with the previous season.

Also indicated is the division the club competed in that season, i.e.,

1 – The old-style First Division/Centenary Championship/Super League

2. – The old-style Second Division, changing to First Division in 1995-96

3. – The old-style Third Division, changing to Second Division in 1995-96

Club	90-91	91-92	92-93	93-94	94-95	95-96	1996	1997	1998
Barrow B.R.	2 962 (−1035)	3 1003 (+41)	3 786 (−217)	2 1318 (+532)	2 957 (−361)	3 666 (−291)	3 630 (−36)	3 786 (+156)	3 1038 (+252)
Batley B.	2 1188 (−318)	3 1145 (−43)	3 925 (−220)	2 1227 (+302)	2 1509 (+282)	2 1305 (−204)	2 1358 (+53)	3 697 (−661)	3 632 (−65)
Blackpool G.	2 638 (−142)	3 309 (−329)	3 475 (+166)	—	—	—	—	—	—
Bradford B.	1 5274 (−310)	1 4725 (−549)	1 5082 (+357)	1 6513 (+1431)	1 5654 (−859)	1 4593 (−1061)	1 10346 (+5753)	1 15163 (+4817)	1 12,905 (−2258)
Bramley	2 805 (−177)	3 870 (+65)	2 980 (+110)	2 729 (−251)	2 758 (+29)	3 446 (−312)	3 456 (+10)	3 428 (−28)	3 576 (+148)
Carlisle B.R.	2 781 (+207)	2 800 (+19)	2 648 (−152)	2 603 (−45)	2 375 (−228)	3 495 (+120)	3 611 (+116)	3 424 (−187)	
Castleford T.	1 6019 (−409)	1 6465 (+446)	1 5658 (−807)	1 5555 (−103)	1 5090 (−465)	1 4072 (−1018)	1 5012 (+940)	1 5004 (−8)	1 6395 (+1391)
Dewsbury R.	2 955 (−272)	3 1140 (+185)	3 1108 (−32)	2 1366 (+258)	2 1859 (+493)	2 1324 (−535)	2 1477 (+153)	2 1470 (−7)	2 1155 (−315)
Doncaster D.	2 1458 (−507)	3 1158 (−300)	3 997 (−161)	2 1648 (+651)	1 3495 (+1847)	3 1026 (−2469)	3 966 (−60)	3 647 (−319)	3 507 (−140)
Featherstone R.	1 4722 (+453)	1 4001 (−721)	2 2670 (−1331)	1 4030 (+1360)	1 3683 (−347)	2 2097 (−1586)	2 1988 (−109)	2 2317 (+329)	2 1721 (−596)
Halifax B.S.	2 4458 (−1463)	1 7181 (+2723)	1 6452 (−729)	1 6608 (+156)	1 5600 (−1008)	1 4657 (−943)	1 5083 (+426)	1 5407 (+324)	1 5670 (+263)
Huddersfield G.	2 1306 (−328)	3 2271 (+965)	2 1985 (−286)	2 2227 (+242)	2 2904 (+677)	2 2427 (−477)	2 3344 (+917)	2 3723 (+379)	1 5142 (+1419)
Hull K.R.	1 4952 (+101)	1 4752 (−200)	1 3609 (−1143)	1 3403 (−206)	2 1900 (−1503)	3 1638 (−262)	3 1699 (+61)	2 2758 (+1059)	2 2306 (−452)
Hull S.	1 6699 (+481)	1 5892 (−807)	1 4860 (−1032)	1 4314 (−546)	1 4165 (−149)	2 2824 (−1341)	2 3008 (+184)	2 6268 (+3260)	1 5742 (−526)
Hunslet H.	2 767 (−279)	3 770 (+3)	3 724 (−46)	2 740 (+16)	2 852 (+112)	3 870 (+18)	3 1099 (+229)	3 1123 (+114)	2 1743 (+620)
Keighley C.	2 985 (+49)	3 1196 (+211)	3 2060 (+864)	2 3032 (+972)	2 3723 (+691)	2 3787 (+64)	2 4871 (+1084)	2 2662 (−2209)	2 2117 (−545)

(continued)

Club	90-91	91-92	92-93	93-94	94-95	95-96	1996	1997	1998
Lancashire L.	2 690 (−116)	3 394 (−296)	3 434 (+40)	—	—	3 501	3 416 (−85)	3 413 (−3)	3 743 (+330)
Leeds R.	1 11102 (−1149)	1 12164 (+1062)	1 11527 (−637)	1 9545 (−1982)	1 12516 (+2971)	1 11594 (−922)	1 8581 (−3013)	1 11005 (+2424)	1 12150 (+1145)
Leigh C.	2 1719 (−2849)	2 3014 (+1295)	1 3967 (+953)	1 3385 (−582)	2 1550 (−1855)	3 1195 (−355)	3 1142 (−53)	3 1188 (+46)	2 1140 (−48)
London B.	2 557 (−284)	2 724 (+167)	2 554 (−170)	2 734 (+180)	2 814 (+80)	1 2386 (+1572)	1 5699 (+3313)	1 5125 (−574)	1 3575 (−1550)
Nottingham C.	2 255 (−322)	3 270 (+15)	3 270	—	—	—	—	—	—
Oldham	1 5094 (+693)	2 3149 (−1945)	2 2809 (−340)	1 4062 (+1253)	1 3889 (−173)	1 3187 (−702)	1 3629 (+442)	1 3832 (+203)	3 1819 (−2013)
Paris St. Germain	—	—	—	—	—	—	1 8026 (−2538)	1 5488	
Prescot P.	2 632 (+179)	3 319 (−313)	3 378 (+59)	2 403 (+25)	2 550 (+147)	3 338 (−212)	3 431 (+93)	3 384 (−47)	—
Rochdale H.	1 2542 (+32)	2 1415 (−1127)	2 1308 (−107)	2 1063 (−245)	2 1089 (+26)	2 1298 (+209)	2 1271 (−27)	3 834 (−437)	2 875 (−41)
St. Helens	1 7391 (−1164)	1 8456 (+1065)	1 8908 (+452)	1 7264 (−1644)	1 7467 (+203)	1 7143 (−324)	1 10221 (+3078)	1 8823 (−1398)	1 7090 (−1733)
Salford R.	2 2314 (−1406)	1 3785 (+1471)	1 4098 (+313)	1 4106 (+8)	1 3600 (−506)	2 2610 (−990)	2 3495 (+885)	1 5206 (+1711)	1 4676 (−530)
Scarborough P.	—	3 777	—	—	—	—	—	—	—
Sheffield E.	1 4031 (−7)	2 2435 (−1596)	1 3069 (+634)	1 3050 (−19)	1 2661 (−389)	1 3106 (+445)	1 4613 (+1507)	1 3946 (−667)	1 4009 (+63)
South Wales	—	—	—	—	—	—	3 1328	—	—
Swinton L.	2 1737 (+59)	1 2702 (+965)	2 1051 (−1651)	2 788 (−263)	2 776 (−12)	3 757 (−19)	3 1506 (+749)	2 1543 (+37)	2 1229 (−314)
Wakefield T.	1 4848 (−580)	1 5022 (+174)	1 4505 (−517)	1 3822 (−683)	1 3438 (−384)	2 1824 (−1614)	2 2109 (+285)	2 1912 (−197)	2 1774 (−138)
Warrington W.	1 5915 (+503)	1 5204 (−711)	1 4550 (−754)	1 6188 (+1638)	1 5380 (−808)	1 4922 (−458)	1 5157 (+235)	1 5404 (+247)	1 4848 (−556)
Whitehaven W.	2 1035 (+74)	3 632 (−403)	3 1462 (+830)	2 1257 (−205)	2 1149 (−108)	2 1205 (+56)	2 1081 (−124)	2 1444 (+363)	2 1037 (−407)
Widnes V.	1 6793 (−1065)	1 6291 (−502)	1 5540 (−751)	1 4525 (−1015)	1 4086 (−439)	2 2908 (−1178)	2 2531 (−377)	2 2151 (−380)	2 2199 (+48)
Wigan W.	1 14493 (+520)	1 14040 (−453)	1 14553 (+513)	1 14561 (+8)	1 14195 (−366)	1 11947 (−2248)	1 10168 (−1779)	1 8865 (−1303)	1 10610 (+1745)
Workington T.	2 1426 (+735)	2 1884 (+458)	3 2040 (+156)	2 2603 (+563)	1 3776 (+1173)	1 3061 (−715)	1 2322 (−739)	1 1588 (−734)	3 812 (−776)
York	2 1857 (−638)	2 1181 (−676)	3 1701 (+520)	2 1311 (−390)	2 1120 (−191)	3 642 (−478)	3 668 (+26)	3 613 (−55)	3 792 (−179)

COMPETITION ATTENDANCE REVIEW

		90-91	91-92	92-93	93-94	94-95	95-96	1996	1997	1998
FIRST	Total	1,168,407	1,185,117	1,122,955	1,364,056	1,330,538	606,728	867,435	916,005	910,912*
GRADE	Av.	6,420	6,511	6,170	5,683	5,543	5,515	6,571	6,939	6,901

*Not including six 'On the Road' matches played at neutral venues with a total attendance of 31,387

		90-91	91-92	92-93	93-94	94-95	95-96	1996	1997	1998
SECOND	Total	371,398	204,304	168,069	315,841	328,377	236,132	265,315	278,388	259,442
GRADE	Av.	1,263	1,824	1,501	1,316	1,368	2,146	2,412	2,531	1,572
THIRD	Total	—	159,209	160,348	—	—	85,772	120,475	75,393	69,219
GRADE	Av.		875	1,027			780	913	685	865
LEAGUE	Total	1,539,805	1,548,630*	1,451,372*	1,679,897	1,658,915	928,632	1,253,225	1,269,786	1,239,573
TOTALS	Av.	3,235	3,253*	3,225*	3,499	3,456	2,814*	3,351*	3,607*	3,288
(1st & 2nd)										
***plus 3rd**										
CHALL-	Av.	6,748	6,899	7,771	5,907	5,821	—	6,891*	7,919*	6,321*
ENGE CUP *From 4th round										
REGAL	Av.	3,515	4,007	3,624	2,690	3,627	3,200	—	—	—
PREMIER	Av.	12,483	13,513	12,788	13,165	11,425	—	18,047	7,153	—
10,000+		43	49	38	41	51	20	24	49	41
(No. of)										

Including international matches

FIRST GRADE refers to the old First Division, the 1995–96 Centenary Championship and Super League from 1996
SECOND GRADE refers to the old Second Division and from 1995–96 the new First Division
THIRD GRADE refers to the old Third Division and from 1995–96 the new Second Division

RECORDS

Best First Grade season's average – 7,292 in 1988–89
Best First Grade club average – Bradford B. 15,163 in 1997

20,000-plus crowds . . . from 1988-89

22,968	Castleford v. Leeds	Yorks Cup final	Elland Rd, Leeds	16 Oct. 1988
20,709	Widnes v. Wigan	John Player final	Bolton W. FC	7 Jan. 1989
26,080	Leeds v. Widnes	RL Cup round 2	Leeds	26 Feb. 1989
26,529	Warrington v. Wigan	RL Cup semi-final	Manchester C. FC	25 Mar. 1989
21,076	Wigan v. St. Helens	Division One	Wigan	12 Apr. 1989
78,000	Wigan v. St. Helens	RL Cup final	Wembley	29 Apr. 1989
40,194	Hull v. Widnes	Premiership final	Manchester U. FC	14 May 1989
30,786	Widnes v. Canberra	World Club Challenge	Manchester U. FC	4 Oct. 1989
20,346	Britain v. New Zealand	Third Test	Wigan	11 Nov. 1989
27,075	Wigan v. St. Helens	Division One	Wigan	26 Dec. 1989
23,570	Leeds v. Wigan	Division One	Leeds	4 Mar. 1990
26,489	St. Helens v. Wigan	RL Cup semi-final	Manchester U. FC	10 Mar. 1990
24,462	Wigan v. Leeds	Division One	Wigan	10 Apr. 1990
77,729	Wigan v. Warrington	RL Cup final	Wembley	28 Apr. 1990
40,796	Bradford N. v. Widnes	Premiership final	Manchester U. FC	13 May 1990
24,814	Wigan v. Australia	Tour	Wigan	14 Oct. 1990
54,569	Britain v. Australia	First Test	Wembley	27 Oct. 1990
46,615	Britain v. Australia	Second Test	Manchester U. FC	10 Nov. 1990
32,500	Britain v. Australia	Third Test	Elland Rd, Leeds	24 Nov. 1990

(continued)

29,763	Wigan v. Widnes	Division One	Wigan	9 Apr. 1991
75,532	Wigan v. St. Helens	RL Cup final	Wembley	27 Apr. 1991
42,043	Hull v. Widnes	Premiership final	Manchester U. FC	12 May 1991
20,152	Wigan v. Penrith	World Club Challenge	Liverpool FC	2 Oct. 1991
26,307	Wigan v. St. Helens	Division One	Wigan	26 Dec. 1991
21,736	Wigan v. Warrington	RL Cup round 2	Wigan	16 Feb. 1992
20,821	Leeds v. Wigan	Division One	Leeds	15 Mar. 1992
77,286	Wigan v. Castleford	RL Cup final	Wembley	2 May 1992
33,157	St. Helens v. Wigan	Premiership final	Manchester U. FC	17 May 1992
20,534	St. Helens v. Wigan	Lancs Cup final	St. Helens	18 Oct. 1992
73,631	Britain v. Australia	World Cup final	Wembley	24 Oct. 1992
20,258	Leeds v. Castleford	Division One	Leeds	26 Dec. 1992
21,191	Wigan v. St. Helens	RL Cup round 2	Wigan	13 Feb. 1993
20,057	Leeds v. Wigan	Division One	Leeds	3 Mar. 1993
20,085	Bradford N. v. Wigan	RL Cup semi-final	Elland Rd, Leeds	27 Mar. 1993
29,839	Wigan v. St. Helens	Division One	Wigan	9 Apr. 1993
77,684	Wigan v. Widnes	RL Cup final	Wembley	1 May 1993
36,598	St. Helens v. Wigan	Premiership final	Manchester U. FC	16 May 1993
36,131	Britain v. New Zealand	First Test	Wembley	16 Oct. 1993
29,100	Wigan v. St. Helens	Division One	Wigan	26 Dec. 1993
22,615	Leeds v. Bradford N.	RL Cup quarter-final	Leeds	27 Feb. 1994
20,771	St. Helens v. Leeds	RL Cup semi-final	Wigan	26 Mar. 1994
78,348	Wigan v. Leeds	RL Cup final	Wembley	30 Apr. 1994
35,644	Castleford v. Wigan	Premiership final	Manchester U. FC	22 May 1994
20,057	Wigan v. Australia	Tour	Wigan	8 Oct. 1994
57,034	Britain v. Australia	First Test	Wembley	22 Oct. 1994
43,930	Britain v. Australia	Second Test	Manchester U. FC	5 Nov. 1994
39,468	Britain v. Australia	Third Test	Elland Rd, Leeds	20 Nov. 1994
20,053	Leeds v. Wigan	Division One	Leeds	11 Dec. 1994
23,278	Wigan v. St. Helens	Regal Trophy quarter-final	Wigan	8 Jan. 1995
21,485	Featherstone R. v. Leeds	RL Cup semi-final	Elland Rd, Leeds	1 Apr. 1995
26,314	Wigan v. St. Helens	Division One	Wigan	14 Apr. 1995
78,550	Wigan v. Leeds	RL Cup final	Wembley	29 Apr. 1995
30,160	Leeds v. Wigan	Premiership final	Manchester U. FC	21 May 1995
41,271	England v. Australia	World Cup	Wembley	7 Oct. 1995
26,263	England v. Fiji	World Cup	Wigan	11 Oct. 1995
30,042	England v. Wales	World Cup	Manchester U. FC	21 Oct. 1995
66,540	England v. Australia	World Cup final	Wembley	28 Oct. 1995
75,994	St. Helens v. Bradford B.	RL Cup final	Wembley	27 Apr. 1996
20,429	Wigan v. St. Helens	Super League	Wigan	21 Jun. 1996
35,013	Wigan v. St. Helens	Premiership final	Manchester U. FC	8 Sep. 1996
78,022	St. Helens v. Bradford B.	RL Cup final	Wembley	3 May 1997
33,389	Wigan W. v. St. Helens	Premiership final	Manchester U. FC	28 Sep. 1997
41,135	Britain v. Australia SL	First Test	Wembley	1 Nov. 1997
40,234	Britain v. Australia SL	Second Test	Manchester U. FC	8 Nov. 1997
39,337	Britain v. Australia SL	Third Test	Elland Rd, Leeds	16 Nov. 1997
60,669	Sheffield E. v. Wigan W.	RL Cup final	Wembley	2 May 1998
43,553	Wigan W. v. Leeds R.	SL Grand Final	Manchester U. FC	24 Oct. 1998
27,884	Great Britain v. New Zealand	Second Test	Bolton W. FC	7 Oct. 1998

1998 ATTENDANCE ANALYSIS

JJB SUPER LEAGUE

132 matches* 910,912*

Average 6,901

* *Not including six 'On the Road' matches played at neutral venues and attracting a total of 31,387 spectators.*

The third season of Super League and summer rugby saw a minimal drop in the total attendance from the previous year's record 916,005, averaging 6,939. And the 1998 figure was still well up on the inaugural Super League campaign of 1996 when the aggregate was 867,435, average 6,571.

Bradford Bulls were the best supported club for a third successive season, although their average home crowd of 12,905 was down on the previous year's 15,163, which remains the record for any club since the scrapping of the old one League system in 1973.

Of the 10 clubs who have appeared in Super League for the last two years, five showed an increase on 1997 and five suffered a drop in home crowds. Wigan Warriors gained the most new support, up from 8,865 to 10,610. Others to show an increase were Castleford Tigers, Halifax Blue Sox, Leeds Rhinos and Sheffield Eagles.

Bradford's average loss of 2,258 was the biggest fall in support. Surprisingly, Hull Sharks' first season in Super League resulted in a drop from the 6,628 average who watched them during their First Division championship-winning campaign to 5,742. But the home crowds of the other promoted club, Huddersfield Giants, shot up from 3,723 to 5,142 despite finishing at the bottom of Super League.

FIRST DIVISION

165 matches 259,442

Average 1,572

The average First Division attendance fell from 2,531 in 1997 to 1,572, but a meaningful comparison is difficult because of a different fixture format and an increase in the total number of matches from 110 to 165. All 11 clubs played 20 matches in 1997 and 30 a year later.

Hull Sharks' promotion also left the division without its easily best supported club. Hull averaged 6,268 in 1997, whereas Hull Kingston Rovers headed the 1998 crowd chart with an average of only 2,306.

Of the eight clubs who have remained in the First Division over the past two seasons only Widnes Vikings reported an increase, up slightly from 2,151 to 2,199. Even champions Wakefield Trinity's average home crowd dropped from 1,912 to 1,774.

SECOND DIVISION

80 matches 69,219

Average 865

The Second Division average increased from 685 to 865, but comparisons are again difficult to assess because of another major change in the fixture format. Eleven clubs each played 20 matches for a total of 110 in 1997, while eight clubs totalled only 80 matches in 1998, including games in the Red and White Rose championships.

Oldham had the best average in 1998 with 1,819 in their first season after being re-formed from the Super League club which folded at the end of 1997 when they had an average crowd of 3,832.

Barrow Border Raiders were the only other Second Division club to average four-figure home crowds with 1,038. Of the six clubs who were also in the Second Division in 1997 four showed an increase.

TOTAL LEAGUE CROWDS

377 matches* 1,239,573

Average 3,288

* *Not including six 'On the Road' matches played at neutral venues and attracting a total of 31,387 spectators.*

The overall average League match attendance across all three divisions was the lowest since the switch to summer rugby in 1996. A total of

374 matches in 1996 produced an average of 3,351 and in 1997 it was 3,607 from 352 matches.

SUPER LEAGUE PLAY-OFF

The inaugural Super League play-off, involving the top five clubs, produced six matches with an aggregate attendance of 93,727 giving an average of 15,621. The Grand Final between Wigan Warriors and Leeds Rhinos attracted a crowd of 43,553 to Old Trafford, surpassing the best for any Premiership Final which it replaced. In 1997 11 Premiership matches drew a total of 78,680 for an average of 7,153.

FIRST DIVISION PLAY-OFF

The inaugural First Division play-off, involving the top five clubs, produced six matches with an aggregate of 21,622 giving an average of 3,604.

SILK CUT CHALLENGE CUP

Starting from a 20-tie third round, when First and Second Division clubs were drawn at home to amateurs, 51 Cup-ties averaged 4,377 from an aggregate of 223,237. A year earlier the average was 5,268 from 268,650.

In the 31 ties after Super League clubs entered in round four the average was 6,321 from an aggregate of 195,943 compared with 7,919 and 245,489 in 1997 (not including replays).

FIVE-FIGURE CROWDS

There was a record total of 30 Super League attendances of 10,000 or more during the 1998 season. This is one more than the previous season and a big increase on the 19 five-figure crowds during the inaugural Super League season of 1996.

In the old Division One days the record was 33 in 1988-89 when 44 more matches were played.

Bradford Bulls again attracted 10,000 or more to each of their 11 Super League home matches in 1998, while Leeds Rhinos and Wigan Warriors had eight, St. Helens two and Huddersfield Giants one.

Including Cup and international matches there was a total of 41 five-figure attendances in 1998 compared with 49 in the previous season, which included eight in the World Club Championship.

The 10,000-plus crowds in 1998 were divided into the following categories:

Super League	30
Challenge Cup	4
Super League play-off	4
Test matches	3

The biggest attendance of the season was, as usual, at Wembley for the Silk Cut Challenge Cup final where 60,669 saw Sheffield Eagles beat Wigan Warriors. The other 20,000-plus crowds were 43,553 for the inaugural Super League Grand Final at Old Trafford, Manchester, between Wigan and Leeds Rhinos and 27,844 for the second Lincoln Test featuring Great Britain and New Zealand at Reebok Stadium, Bolton.

TREIZE TOURNOI

The inaugural Treize Tournoi attracted low attendances until the final at Toulouse pulled in a creditable 10,283 for the play-off between Villeneuve and Lancashire Lynx. Only approximate figures were given for most of the six other matches in France and they added up to 11,612. The six matches in England ranged from 247 to 1,506 for a total of 5,329.

1998 LEAGUE ATTENDANCE TABLES

(Home League matches only. Not including six 'On the Road' matches played at neutral venues and attracting a total of 31,387 spectators.)

SUPER LEAGUE

	Total	Average
1. Bradford Bulls	141,957	12,905
2. Leeds Rhinos	133,645	12,150
3. Wigan Warriors	116,706	10,610
4. St. Helens	77,994	7,090
5. Castleford Tigers	70,340	6,395
6. Hull Sharks	63,159	5,742
7. Halifax Blue Sox	62,368	5,670
8. Huddersfield Giants	56,564	5,142
9. Warrington Wolves	53,323	4,848
10. Salford Reds	51,432	4,676
11. Sheffield Eagles	44,098	4,009
12. London Broncos	39,326	3,575
Totals	**910,912**	**6,901**

FIRST DIVISION

	Total	Average
1. Hull Kingston Rovers	34,604	2,306
2. Widnes Vikings	32,988	2,199
3. Keighley Cougars	31,757	2,117
4. Wakefield Trinity	26,609	1,774
5. Hunslet Hawks	26,139	1,743
6. Featherstone Rovers	25,813	1,721
7. Swinton Lions	18,431	1,229
8. Dewsbury Rams	17,328	1,155
9. Leigh Centurions	17,097	1,140
10. Whitehaven Warriors	15,548	1,037
11. Rochdale Hornets	13,128	875
Totals	**259,442**	**1,572**

SECOND DIVISION

	Total	Average
1. Oldham	18,194	1,819
2. Barrow Border Raiders	10,381	1,038
3. Workington Town	8,125	812
4. York	7,924	792
5. Lancashire Lynx	7,434	743
6. Batley Bulldogs	6,324	632
7. Bramley	5,759	576
8. Doncaster Dragons	5,078	507
Totals	**69,219**	**865**

REFEREES

REFEREES' PERFORMANCE DIRECTOR

Fred Lindop: November 1988 - January 1993*
Greg McCallum: October 1994 - August 1997**
Geoff Berry: August 1997 - December 1998**
Greg McCallum: January 1999 -
*Title was then Controller of Referees
**Title was then Referees' Coaching Director

REFEREES' HONOURS 1998

Silk Cut Challenge Cup final:
Stuart Cummings

Super League Grand final:
Russell Smith

First Division Grand final:
Nick Oddy

Trans-Pennine Cup final:
Steve Nicholson

Treize Tournoi final
Graham Shaw

Great Britain v. New Zealand - 3 Tests:
Bill Harrigan (Aus)

Emerging England v. Wales:
John Connolly

Ireland v. France:
Claude Alba (France)

France v. Scotland:
Robert Connolly

Scotland v. Ireland:
John Connolly

Australia v. New Zealand - 3 Tests:
Russell Smith

CIS Referee of the Year:
Russell Smith

International panel 1998:
John Connolly
Stuart Cummings
Russell Smith

SENIOR REFEREES

● A two tier grading system was introduced at the start of 1995-96, Premier status referees taking charge of the Super League matches, Grade One the First and Second Division fixtures.

JOHN CONNOLLY (Wigan)
Date of birth: 30.9.59
Grade One: 1990-91

Divisional Premiership 1992-93, 1993-94, 1997
France v Great Britain 1993-94
Wales v New Zealand 1993-94
Wales v Australia 1994-95
France v Wales 1994-95
Emerging England v Wales 1998
Scotland v Ireland 1998
Cumbria v Australia 1994-95
Referee of the Year 1993, 1994

ROBERT CONNOLLY (Wigan)
Date of birth: 30.9.59
Silk Cut Plate final 1997
France v Scotland 1998
Grade One: 1990-91

STUART CUMMINGS (Widnes)
Date of birth: 17.11.60
Grade One: 1991-92
Challenge Cup 1996, 1997, 1998
Regal Trophy 1994-95
Premiership Trophy 1993-94, 1994-95, 1997
Divisional Premiership 1991-92, 1996
Lancashire Cup 1992-93
Charity Shield 1992-93
Australia SL v. New Zealand 1997
Scotland v Ireland 1996
Referee of the Year 1996

STEVE GANSON (St. Helens)
Date of birth: 4.1.70
Grade One: 1995-96

KARL KIRKPATRICK (Warrington)
Date of birth: 3.12.64
Grade One: 1994-95

Stuart Cummings: Wembley referee.

COLIN MORRIS (Huddersfield)
Date of birth: 11.3.57
Grade One: 1989-90
Premiership Trophy 1989-90
Papua New Guinea v France 1991
France v Papua New Guinea 1991-92
Wales v France 1991-92
Russia v France 1992
France v Great Britain Under-21s 1989-90
Charity Shield 1990-91
Cumbria v Papua New Guinea 1991-92
Cumbria v Australia 1992-93
War of the Roses 1991-92

STEVE PRESLEY (Castleford)
Date of birth: 4.4.57
Grade One: 1993-94
Great Britain Under-21s v Australia 1994-95

RUSSELL SMITH (Castleford)
Date of birth: 24.1.64
Grade One: 1991-92
Challenge Cup 1992-93, 1994-95
Super League Grand final 1998
Second Division Premiership Final 1994-95
Yorkshire Cup 1992-93
New Zealand v Australia (3) 1993, (3) 1998
New Zealand v Papua New Guinea (2) 1996
New Zealand v. Australia SL 1997
Wales v England 1994-95
France v Wales 1996
France v Great Britain Under-21s 1991-92
Referee of the Year: 1995, 1997, 1998

Grade One

DAVID ATKIN (Hull)
Date of birth: 19.12.64
Grade One: 1992-93

ALAN BATES (Workington)
Date of birth: 18.4.58
Grade One: 1993-94
France v Great Britain Under-21s 1994-95

ALAN BURKE (Oldham)
Date of birth: 21.1.57
Grade One: 1987-88
Lancashire Cup 1990-91

RAY CORNISH (Wigan)
Date of birth: 26.8.1961
Grade One: 1997

PETER GILMOUR (Workington)
Date of birth: 11.9.58
Grade One: 1990-91

RON LAUGHTON (Barnsley)
Date of birth: 13.7.1964
Grade One: 1997

PAUL LEE (Leigh)
Date of birth: 28.7.57
Grade One: 1994-95

STEVE LOWE (Leeds)
Date of birth: 8.12.57
Grade One: 1996

IAN McGREGOR (Huddersfield)
Date of birth: 27.12.53
Grade One: 1993-94

STEVE NICHOLSON (Whitehaven)
Date of birth: 5.4.61
Grade One: 1992-93
Trans-Pennine Cup final 1998

NICK ODDY (Halifax)
Date of birth: 16.4.62
Grade One: 1994-95
First Division Grand final 1998

GRAHAM SHAW (Wigan)
Date of birth: 11.9.70
Grade One: 1995-96
Treize Tournoi final 1998

PETER TABERNER (Wigan)
Date of birth: 24.6.60
Grade One: 1995-96

ALLIANCE

ALLIANCE CHAMPIONSHIP

	P.	W.	D.	L.	Dg.	FOR Gls.	Trs.	Pts.	Dg.	AGAINST Gls.	Trs.	Pts.	Pts.
Wigan W.	21	18	0	3	0	113	180	946	1	42	62	333	36
St. Helens	21	17	0	4	3	83	143	741	2	57	74	412	34
Salford R.	21	13	0	8	6	60	88	478	3	64	90	491	26
Halifax B.S.	21	10	1	10	0	67	97	522	2	64	92	498	21
Sheffield E.	21	10	0	11	0	79	113	610	2	71	105	564	20
Huddersfield G.	21	7	0	14	2	56	77	422	1	74	129	665	14
Widnes V.	21	4	1	16	1	37	60	315	5	88	130	701	9
Hunslet H.	21	4	0	17	5	47	66	363	1	82	142	733	8

ALLIANCE FIRST DIVISION

	P.	W.	D.	L.	Dg.	FOR Gls.	Trs.	Pts.	Dg.	AGAINST Gls.	Trs.	Pts.	Pts.
Hemel Hempstead	21	15	0	6	3	71	98	537	6	59	86	468	30
Keighley C.	21	12	0	9	4	73	111	594	1	68	77	445	24
Batley B.	21	12	0	9	4	84	97	560	4	56	79	432	24
Barrow B.R.	21	10	1	10	4	56	84	452	5	50	67	373	21
Whitehaven W.	21	10	0	11	4	57	86	462	2	69	94	516	20
Workington T.	21	9	2	10	5	45	68	367	1	54	82	437	20
Rochdale H.	21	8	0	13	6	51	77	416	7	71	109	585	16
Leigh C.	21	6	1	14	1	62	86	469	5	72	113	601	13

ALLIANCE CHALLENGE CUP FINAL
Batley B. 14 v. St. Helens 32
At Mount Pleasant, Batley, 26 September
Batley B: Craig Lingard; Carl Shuttleworth (1g), Ashley Fothergill (1t), Nick Simpson, Carl Riley (1t); Simon Jackson, Nigel Craven (1t); Mark Scott, Craig Stevens, Neil Hartley (Capt.), Leigh Grogan, Phil Hardwick, Richard Hewitt. **Playing subs:** Jeremy Dyson, Will Cartledge, Johnny Morgan, Steve Cowling
St. Helens: Jason Johnson; Joey Hayes (2t), Tony Stewart (1t), Alan Cross, Steve Hall; Scott Barrow (Capt.), Paul Wellens (4g); Andy Leathem, John Hamilton, Paul Mathison, Tim Jonkers (1t), Mark Edmondson, Chris Newall (1t). **Playing subs:** Nick Cammann (1t), Paul Haigh, Dale Holdstock, Mike Loughlin
Referee: Richard Silverwood (Dewsbury)

POT POURRI

DIARY OF LANDMARKS

1895 August 29 ... the beginning. The Northern Rugby Football Union formed at The George Hotel, Huddersfield, following the breakaway from the English RU by 21 clubs who wanted to pay players for taking time off work to play.

September 7 ... season opens with 22 clubs.

Joseph Platt appointed Rugby League Secretary.

1897 April 24 ... Batley win the first Northern Union — later Rugby League — Challenge Cup final.

Line-out abolished and replaced by punt from touch.

All goals to be worth two points.

1898 Professionalism allowed but players must be in full-time employment.

1899 Scrum if player cannot release the ball after a tackle.

1901 Punt from touch replaced by 10-yard scrum when ball is carried into touch.

1902 Two divisions introduced.

Punt from touch abolished completely. Touch-finding rule introduced with the ball having to bounce before entering touch.

1905 Two divisions scrapped.

Lancashire and Yorkshire County Cup competitions inaugurated.

1906 Thirteen-a-side introduced, from traditional 15.

Play-the-ball introduced.

1907 First tour — New Zealand to England. The tour party were RU "rebels".

First Top Four play-off for championship.

1908 Australia and New Zealand launch Rugby League.

First Australian tour of England.

1910 First British tour of Australia and New Zealand.

1915 Competitive rugby suspended for duration of First World War.

1919 Competitive rugby resumed in January.

1920 John Wilson appointed Rugby League Secretary.

1922 Title of Northern Rugby Football Union changed to Rugby Football League.

Goal from a mark abolished.

1927 First radio broadcast of Challenge Cup final — Oldham v. Swinton at Wigan.

1929 Wembley staged its first RL Challenge Cup final — Wigan v. Dewsbury.

1932 London exhibition match under floodlights at White City — Leeds v. Wigan.

1933 France staged its first Rugby League match — an exhibition between England and Australia in Paris.

London Highfield, formerly Wigan Highfield, became capital's first Rugby League team, also first to play regularly under floodlights.

1934 A French squad made a short tour of England before Rugby League was officially launched in France.

1935 European Championship introduced, contested by England, France and Wales.

1939 Second World War. Emergency war-time competitions introduced.

1945 War-time emergencies over.

1946 Bill Fallowfield appointed Rugby League Secretary.

First all-ticket match — Hull v. Hull K.R.

1948 King George VI becomes first reigning monarch to attend Rugby League match — Wigan v. Bradford Northern Cup final at Wembley.

First televised match — at Wembley — but shown only in London area.

Wembley's first all-ticket final.

International Board formed.

1949 Welsh League formed.

1950 Italian squad makes brief tour of England.

1951 First televised match in the North — Britain v. New Zealand at Swinton.

First floodlights installation by Northern club, Bradford Northern.

1952 First nationally televised Challenge Cup final — Workington Town v. Featherstone Rovers.

1954 First World Cup, staged in France.

1955 London stages series of televised floodlit matches for the Independent Television Association Trophy.

Welsh League disbanded.

1956 Sunday rugby for amateurs permitted by the Rugby Football League.

1962 Two divisions reintroduced, with Eastern and Western Divisions also formed.

1964 Substitutes allowed for injuries, but only up to half-time.

Two divisions and regional leagues scrapped. One league system with Top 16 play-off for championship.

1965 BBC-2 Floodlit Trophy competition begins

with regular Tuesday night series.
Substitutes allowed for any reason up to and including half-time.
English Schools Rugby League formed.

1966 Four-tackle rule introduced for Floodlit Trophy competition in October, then for all games from December.

1967 First Sunday fixtures played, two matches on December 17.

1969 Substitutes allowed at any time.
Universities and Colleges Rugby League Association formed.

1971 John Player Trophy competition launched.

1972 Six-tackle rule introduced.
Timekeepers with hooter system to signal end of match introduced.
Colts League formed.

1973 Two divisions reintroduced.
March 4 ... British Amateur Rugby League Association formed.

1974 Drop goal value halved to one point. Had been reduced earlier in international matches.
David Oxley appointed Rugby League Secretary.
David Howes appointed first full-time Public Relations Officer to the Rugby Football League.
National Coaching Scheme launched.

1975 Premiership Trophy competition launched.

1976 Differential penalty introduced for technical scrum offences.

1977 County Championship not held for first time since 1895, excluding war years.
Anglo-Australian transfer ban agreed.

1978 Papua New Guinea admitted as full members of International Board.

1981 Rugby League Professional Players' Association formed.
The Northern Rugby Football League retitled The Rugby League.

1982 County Championship scrapped.

1983 Sin bin introduced.
Try value increased to four points.
Handover after sixth tackle introduced, among several other new or amended laws following meeting of International Board.
Anglo-Australian transfer ban lifted.

1984 Alliance League introduced in reserve grade reorganisation.

1985 First Charity Shield match played in Isle of Man.

War of the Roses launched on Lancashire v. Yorkshire county of origin basis.
Relegation-promotion reduced to three down, three up.

1986 Relegation-promotion altered for one year only to four down, two up to provide a 14-strong First Division for the 1987-88 season.

1987 Premiership doubleheader at Manchester United's Old Trafford launched with introduction of a Second Division Final.

1988 Colts scrapped for new youth scheme.
Six-man League Board of Directors appointed.
Fred Lindop appointed first-ever Controller of Referees.

1990 Russia introduced Rugby League and sent 90-man squad on three-match tour to Britain.

1991 Russian eight-club league launched.
Three divisions introduced for 1991-92 season.
Academy Under-18 league formed.
Blood bin introduced.

1992 Maurice Lindsay appointed Rugby League Chief Executive on retirement of David Oxley.
Ten-metre play-the-ball rule introduced.

1993 Controller of Referees Fred Lindop included in League HQ redundancy programme.
Two divisions reintroduced with three bottom clubs demoted to non-League status.
National pro-am Conference League launched.
County Cups scrapped.

1994 Broadcaster Harry Gration appointed Rugby League Public Affairs Executive on resignation of David Howes.
Top Australian referee Greg McCallum appointed Rugby League Referees' Coaching Director.
League publish *Framing the Future* report

1995 Journalist Paul Harrison appointed Rugby League Media Manager on resignation of Harry Gration.
Disciplinary procedure of referees putting players on report introduced.
In-goal judges introduced.
Rupert Murdoch and News Corporation's £87m package launches Rugby League into revolutionary and controversial new era.
Centenary Championship and return to three

divisions for last season of winter rugby.

Crop of rule changes include: scoring teams to restart play, scrums to be 20 metres in from touch, ball must be played backwards at play-the-ball.

Four substitutes with six replacements introduced.

1996 Last Regal Trophy final.

Super League and summer rugby begins.

Squad jersey numbering introduced.

Video replays used for first time to assist referees with debatable try decisions.

Wigan and Bath RU meet in first cross-code club challenge matches.

League players start playing Rugby Union in winter.

Media manager Paul Harrison among League HQ redundancies.

RL (Europe) Ltd formed to market Super League.

1997 RFL-BARLA dispute ends with formation of Joint Policy Board.

Premierships last season.

1998 Salary Cap introduced.

Maurice Lindsay departs as RFL chief executive to become SLE managing director.

Neil Tunnicliffe appointed RFL chief executive.

Play-off and Grand Final to decide Super League and First Division Championships.

Maurice Lindsay: Appointed Super League (Europe) managing director in 1998.

DISMISSALS – AN EIGHT YEAR REVIEW

A season-by-season record of each club's total of first team dismissals.

(– Indicates club not in existence in that season.)

– club not in existence	1998	1997	1996	1995–96	1994–95	1993–94	1992–93	1991–92
Barrow B.R.	4	4	2	1	4	2	3	6
Batley B.	1	2	5	1	5	3	4	7
Blackpool G.	–	–	–	–	–	–	0	6
Bradford B.	5	2	3	1	2	2	0	4
Bramley	2	0	10	2	8	3	4	2
Carlisle B.R.	–	4	0	2	1	9	6	2
Castleford T.	0	1	3	0	3	1	3	3
Dewsbury R.	1	1	4	1	4	4	1	1
Doncaster D.	5	4	4	2	5	3	2	3
Featherstone R.	3	1	2	4	6	3	3	7
Halifax B.S.	3	1	3	3	1	1	1	2
Huddersfield G.	1	1	0	4	1	3	6	2
Hull K.R.	1	5	1	1	3	0	0	1
Hull S.	0	2	2	1	3	1	3	2
Hunslet H.	4	3	2	2	7	5	3	2
Keighley C.	3	2	0	0	3	3	2	4
Lancashire L.	0	2	1	1	–	–	0	5
Leeds R.	3	1	2	3	1	2	1	2
Leigh C.	6	0	4	0	3	3	1	3
London B.	1	2	3	0	2	1	5	2
Nottingham C.	–	–	–	–	–	–	2	2
Oldham	4	3	2	4	6	2	6	5
Paris S.G.	–	2	3	–	–	–	–	–
Prescot P.	–	1	1	5	5	3	7	7
Rochdale H.	2	3	2	1	5	1	2	4
St. Helens	1	4	2	6	4	3	1	6
Salford R.	2	2	1	3	1	1	0	0
Scarborough P.	–	–	–	–	–	–	–	1
Sheffield E.	1	0	1	1	2	1	4	7
South Wales	–	–	1	–	–	–	–	–
Swinton L.	2	3	2	0	6	2	3	4
Wakefield T.	6	0	3	1	1	3	1	3
Warrington W.	2	2	1	4	3	0	2	6
Whitehaven W.	1	4	1	1	7	4	1	5
Widnes V.	5	5	4	1	5	0	5	2
Wigan W.	0	0	0	1	3	1	2	2
Workington T.	3	2	3	0	2	2	4	6
York	5	3	1	2	4	4	2	1
Totals	**77**	**72**	**79**	**59**	**116**	**76**	**90**	**127**

DISCIPLINARY ANALYSIS 1998

The following is a club-by-club disciplinary record for 1998, showing the players sent off in first team matches and the findings of the League's Disciplinary Committee.

The committee's verdict is featured in the brackets after the player's name, each number indicating the match ban imposed. SOS stands for sending off sufficient punishment, MI for mistaken identity and NG for not guilty. A suspension reduced or increased on appeal is shown as follows, 6 to 4. Suspended players are also usually fined from £50 to £300.

Club	Total sent off	Dismissed player	Number of sin bins
Barrow B.R.	4	Stuart Rhodes (3), Stewart Quayle (1), Brett McDermott (NG), Shaun Wallis (2)	3
Batley B.	1	Gary Barnett (2)	4
Bradford B.	5	James Lowes (2 to 1), Sonny Nickle (NG), Jon Scales (SOS), Graeme Bradley (1 to SOS, NG)	12
Bramley	2	Eugene Currie (2), Anthony Gibbons (4)	6
Castleford T.	0	–	4
Dewsbury R.	1	Gary Rose (SOS)	10
Doncaster D.	5	Tony Miller (SOS), Lee Senior (SOS), Lance Busby (4,2), Andrew Rothwell (2)	11
Featherstone R.	3	Anthony Jackson (5), Carl Hall (2), Lee Maher (NG)	6
Halifax B.S.	3	Kelvin Skerrett (2), Karl Harrison (NG), Gary Mercer (Fined £300)	12
Huddersfield G.	1	Nick Fozzard (SOS)	10
Hull K.R.	1	Stanley Gene (SOS)	4
Hull S.	0	–	15
Hunslet H.	4	Craig Richards (2), Richard Goddard (1), Robert Wilson (NG), Christopher Ross (4)	11
Keighley C.	3	Robert Roberts (SOS,6), Mark Campbell (NG)	11
Lancashire L.	0	–	3
Leeds R.	3	Anthony Farrell (NG), Adrian Morley (1), Marc Glanville (SOS)	16
Leigh C.	6	Tim Street (SOS,2,SOS,3), Andrew Pucill (2), Shaun Geritas (4)	14
London B.	1	Peter Gill (SOS)	9
Oldham	4	Paul Round (NG,NG), Michael Edwards (NG), Peaufai Leuila (1)	8
Rochdale H.	2	Leo Casey (3), Kenneth Kerr (NG)	16
St. Helens	1	Paul Newlove (SOS)	15
Salford R.	2	Martin Crompton (2), David Bradbury (5)	10
Sheffield E.	1	Waisale Sovatabua (SOS)	4
Swinton L.	2	Paul Hulme (SOS), Wesley Rogers (1)	9
Wakefield T.	6	Andrew Fisher (NG), Sonny Whakarau (SOS), Carl Briggs (SOS), Francis Stephenson (SOS), Matthew Fuller (SOS,1)	9
Warrington W.	2	Jonathan Roper (SOS), Michael Eagar (SOS)	10
Whitehaven W.	1	Siose Muliumu (SOS)	10
Widnes V.	5	Ian Gildart (NG), Damian Munro (2), Dean Cross (1), Antonio Garcia (NG), Shane Wilson (2)	20
Wigan W.	0	–	7
Workington T.	3	Stephen Maguire (NG), Barry Williams (2), Peter Riley (1)	8
York	5	Craig Booth (2,NG,NG), Lea Tichener (NG), Stuart Flowers (1)	13

In addition, the following players were dealt with by the Disciplinary Committee after either being referred by the League's Board of Directors or placed on report by match referees:

Referrals

Bradford B.: Bernard Dwyer (1 & £150 fine to 0 & £250)

London B.: Peter Gill (Warning), Terry Matterson (Warning)

Oldham: Sean Cooper (90 days)

St. Helens: Christopher Smith (NG)

Sheffield E.: Keith Senior (4)

Warrington W.: Brendon Tuuta (1)

Workington T.: Gary Hetherington (4), Peter Riley (Warning)

York: Stuart Flowers (90 days)

Reported

Barrow B.R.: Ian Rawlinson (NG)

Bramley: Wayne Freeman (NG), Eugene Currie (4)

Dewsbury R.: Mark Haigh (Warning)

Doncaster D.: Gareth Pratt (2), Lance Busby (4), Lee Maher (4)

Featherstone R.: Shaun Irwin (2), Gary H. Price (2 & £75 fine to 1 & no fine, 1 to 0 & £75 fine)

Hull K.R.: Stanley Gene (NG)

Hull S.: Jason Temu (3)

Hunslet H.: David Plange (NG), Robert Wilson (No further action)

Keighley C.: Philip Stephenson (2), David Longo (1), Karl Smith (3), Robert Roberts (4)

Lancashire L.: Simon Smith (2)

Leeds R.: Tony Kemp (4 to 2)

Leigh C.: Nick Jenkins (NG)

London B.: Mark Carroll (2)

Rochdale H.: Paul Stevens (2), Jason Green (2)

St. Helens: Paul Davidson (1), Brett Goldspink (1)

Salford R.: Paul Forber (NG)

Warrington W.: Mark Forster (3 to 2), Adam Fogerty (Warning)

Whitehaven W.: Aaron Lester (Fined £100)

Widnes V.: Jamie Bloem (NG)

Wigan W.: Mick Cassidy (6)

Workington T.: Michael Bethwaite (1), Mark Keenan (3)

QUEEN'S HONOURS

Twelve Rugby League players have been awarded the MBE and four others the OBE by Her Majesty the Queen for their services to the game. Former Castleford player-coach Malcolm Reilly was awarded the OBE in June 1991, while Great Britain's full-time coach.

Player	Awarded MBE	GB Caps	Career	Clubs
Eric Ashton	June 1966	26	1955-69	Wigan
Geoff Gunney	June 1970	11	1951-73	Hunslet
Clive Sullivan	January 1974	17	1961-85	Hull, Hull K.R., Oldham, Doncaster
Chris Hesketh	January 1976	21+2	1963-79	Wigan, Salford
Roger Millward	January 1983	28+1	1963-80	Castleford, Hull K.R.
Neil Fox	June 1983	29	1956-79	Wakefield T., Bradford N., Hull K.R., York, Bramley, Huddersfield
David Watkins	January 1986	2+4	1967-82	Salford, Swinton, Cardiff C.
Ellery Hanley	January 1990	33+1	1978-95	Bradford N., Wigan, Leeds
Jeff Grayshon	June 1992	13	1970-95	Dewsbury, Bradford N., Leeds, Featherstone R., Batley
Jonathan Davies	January 1995	12+1	1989-95	Widnes, Warrington
Billy Boston	June 1996	31	1953-68	Wigan, Blackpool B.
Martin Offiah	January 1997	33	1988-	Widnes, Wigan, London B.
	Awarded OBE			
Malcolm Reilly	June 1991	9	1967-86	Castleford
Garry Schofield	June 1994	44+2	1983-	Hull, Leeds, Huddersfield G.
Shaun Edwards	January 1996	32+4	1983-	Wigan, London B., Bradford B.
Alex Murphy	January 1999	27	1956-75	St. Helens, Leigh, Warrington

Alex Murphy: Awarded OBE in New Year's Honours list.

THE RUGBY FOOTBALL LEAGUE

Address: Red Hall, Red Hall Lane, Leeds LS17 8NB; Tel: 0113-2329111; Fax: 0113-2323666

Patron: Her Majesty The Queen

Chairman: Sir Rodney Walker

President: Bill Garratt (Warrington Wolves)

Chief Executive: Neil Tunnicliffe

Board of Directors: Neil Tunnicliffe, Sir Rodney Walker (chairman), Non-executive finance director: Darryl Keys, Terry Sharman (Sheffield Eagles), Steve Wagner (Featherstone Rovers)

Advisory Panel (Including Disciplinary Committee): Bob Ashby, John Atkinson, Vic Bowen, His Hon. Judge Peter Charlesworth, Colin Clarke, Richard Evans, Derek Fox, Neil Fox, Peter Higginbottom, Ken Irving, Eric Lawrinson, Alan McInnes, David Poulter, Joe Seddon, Neil Shuttleworth, Jim Spencer, Prof. Sir John Wood, Phil Worthington, Malcolm Pike, Russell Bridge, Wilf George, Terry Flanagan.

Minimum Standards Committee: Steve Wagner (chairman), Neil Tunnicliffe, Dave Callaghan, Courtney Collins, John Lucas, (Gleeds Co.), David Wood (RFL); Robin Barron (English Sports Council, Yorkshire & Humberside Region), Jeff Perris (Sports Turf Research Inst.), Bob Fuller, Robin Hays, David Poulter, Paul Roberts, Max Woosey. Ex-officio: Harry Jepson.

All Parliamentary Group: Lord Lofthouse (Chairman); Lindsay Stott MP, Roger Stott, CBE, MP (Vice-Chairmen); Laurie Cunliffe MP (Treasurer); David Hinchliffe MP, James Clappison MP (Joint Secretaries)

The Rugby League Intergroup (European Parliament): Terry Wynn MEP (President); Freddy Blak MEP, Brian Simpson (Vice-Presidents); Tony Cunningham MEP (Secretary)

Deputy Chief executive, associate director of marketing and media: Dave Callaghan

Finance Executive: Peter Webster

Associate director of administration: Emma Rosewarne

Associate director of development: Tom O'Donovan

Operations Executive: Geoff Keith

Performance director: Joe Lydon

Referees' performance director: Greg McCallum

Referees' development officer: Geoff Berry

Public relations and media manager: John Huxley

SUPER LEAGUE (EUROPE) LTD

Address: Kings House, King Street, Leeds LS1 4UD; Tel: 0113–244 1114; Fax: 0113–244 1110

Managing director: Maurice Lindsay

Chairman: Chris Caisley (Bradford Bulls)

Board of Directors: Chris Caisley, Gary Hetherington (Leeds Rhinos), John Smith (Warrington Wolves), Nigel Wood (Halifax Blue Sox)

RFL Board Member: Terry Sharman (Sheffield Eagles)

Marketing director: Ian Robson

Media and broadcast manager: Andrew Whitelam

Marketing manager: Ian Riddoch

Operations manager: Sally Bolton

FIRST AND SECOND DIVISION ASSOCIATION

Address: Red Hall, Red Hall Lane, Leeds LS17 8NB; Tel: 0113-2329111; Fax: 0113-2323666

General Manager: Bob Scott (Huddersfield Giants) Tel: 01484-538774

Chairman: Bob McDermott (Dewsbury Rams)

RFL Board member: Steve Wagner (Featherstone Rovers)

● As at 1 January 1999

Laurie Daley: Australia's captain in first Test against New Zealand in 1998.

AUSTRALIAN RL

1998 Grand Final

League leaders Brisbane Broncos lived up to their ranking as 5-1 on pre-final favourites to recover from a 12-10 half-time deficit and race to an emphatic 38-12 victory over Canterbury Bulldogs in the newly-titled National RL* Grand Final at the Sydney Football Stadium. Following the merger of the Australian RL and Super League, the play-offs had been extended to the top ten of the enlarged 20-club table and Canterbury stormed through to the final from ninth place after twice coming from far behind to pull off remarkable victories in the earlier rounds.

Brisbane's Gorden Tallis took the Clive Churchill Medal as the man of the match with a typically aggressive second row performance that included a second half try. But it was essentially a great team effort that broke down the Bulldogs' early resistance. After a terrible start that led to Canterbury conceding a try following a handling error inside two minutes, they hit back to take the lead and look as if they might pull off a major shock.

An evenly contested first half began with Canterbury immediately put under pressure and when Willie Talua lost the ball near his own line Brisbane pounced for Michael De Vere to go over in the corner. Canterbury shrugged off the setback to battle back and within 22 minutes they were in front with Gateshead-bound Tony Grimaldi dummying and charging his way over. Daryl Halligan added the goal only for Canterbury to put themselves back under pressure with another error and Brisbane again took advantage for Kevin Campion to touch down shortly after going on as a substitute.

The thrill-a-minute first half had one final twist just before the interval when Talau made up for his early error to score Canterbury's second try and with Halligan kicking another goal the Bulldogs had their two-point half-time lead. But within two minutes of the restart Brisbane surged ahead with a try from Tonie Carroll and

maintained their increased tempo to run in four more tries without reply.

Travis Norton topped the tackle count with 30 for Canterbury, while Andrew Gee led Brisbane's defensive effort with 25.

* After just one season, News Corporation's Super League agreed to a merger with the Australian RL to form the National Rugby League Championship containing 20 clubs.

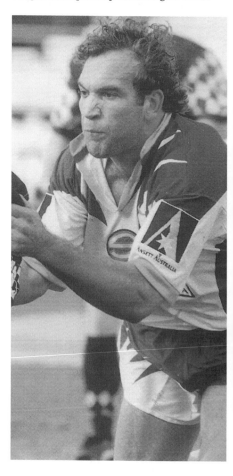

Gorden Tallis: Man of the Match in Grand Final.

NATIONAL RL GRAND FINAL

Sunday 27 September 1998   Sydney Football Stadium

BRISBANE BRONCOS 38   **CANTERBURY BULLDOGS 12**

Brisbane Broncos	Position	Canterbury Bulldogs
Darren Lockyer	Full back	Rod Silva
Michael De Vere	Wing	Gavin Lester
Steve Renouf	Centre	Shane Marteene
Darren Smith	Centre	Willie Talau
Wendell Sailor	Wing	Daryl Halligan
Kevin Walters	Stand off	Craig Polla-Mounter
Allan Langer, Captain	Scrum half	Corey Hughes
Shane Webcke	Prop	Darren Britt, Captain
Phillip Lee	Hooker	Jason Hetherington
Andrew Gee	Prop	Steve Price
Gorden Tallis	Second row	Tony Grimaldi
Brad Thorn	Second row	Robert Relf
Tonie Carroll	Loose forward	Travis Norton

Playing substitutes
Michael Hancock
John Plath
Kevin Campion
Petero Civoniceva

Playing substitutes
Steve Reardon
Troy Stone
Glen Hughes
David Thompson

T: De Vere, Campion, Carroll,
Sailor, Tallis, Lee, Smith
G: Lockyer (5)

T: Grimaldi, Talau
G: Halligan (2)

Coach: Wayne Bennett

Coach: Steve Folkes

Half-time: 10-12
Attendance: 40,857

Referee: Bill Harrigan
Clive Churchill Medal for Man of the
Match: Gorden Tallis (Brisbane)

Allan Langer: Brisbane Broncos captain.   *Wendell Sailor: Brisbane Broncos tryscorer.*

1998 NATIONAL RL TABLE

	P	W	D	L	F	A	Pts	Att.*
1. Brisbane Broncos	24	18	1	5	688	310	37	20,252
2. Newcastle Knights	24	18	1	5	562	381	37	20,023
3. Melbourne Storm	24	17	1	6	546	372	35	12,729
4. Parramatta Eels	24	17	1	6	468	349	35	11,709
5. North Sydney Bears	24	17	0	7	663	367	34	11,093
6. Sydney City Roosters	24	16	0	8	680	383	32	10,801
7. Canberra Raiders	24	15	0	9	564	429	30	10,086
8. St. George Dragons	24	13	1	10	486	490	27	10,394
9. Canterbury Bulldogs	24	13	0	11	489	411	26	8363
10. Manly Sea Eagles	24	13	0	11	503	473	26	10,512
11. Cronulla Sharks	24	12	1	11	438	387	25	11,370
12. Illawarra Steelers	24	11	1	12	476	539	23	9243
13. Balmain Tigers	24	9	1	14	381	463	19	10,576
14. Penrith Panthers	24	8	2	14	525	580	18	9257
15. Auckland Warriors	24	9	0	15	417	518	18	9230
16. N. Queensland Cowboys	24	9	0	15	361	556	18	17,083
17. Adelaide Rams	24	7	0	17	393	615	14	7818
18. South Sydney Rabbitohs	24	5	0	19	339	560	10	6085
19. Gold Coast Chargers	24	4	0	20	289	654	8	6599
20. Western Suburbs Magpies	24	4	0	20	371	802	8	7301

* *Average home crowd*

NATIONAL RL PLAY-OFF
Top ten clubs
Week One
Melbourne Storm 12 v. Sydney City 26
Parramatta 25 v. North Sydney 12
St. George 12 v. Canterbury 20
Canberra 17 v. Manly 4
Week Two
Newcastle 15 v. Sydney City 26
Brisbane Broncos 10 v. Parramatta 15
North Sydney 2 v. Canterbury 23
Melbourne Storm 24 v. Canberra 10
Week Three
Brisbane Broncos 30 v. Melbourne Storm 6*
Newcastle 16 v. Canterbury 28*
After extra time
Week Four
Brisbane Broncos 46 v. Sydney City 18**
Parramatta 20 v. Canterbury 32*
After extra time
Grand Final
Brisbane Broncos 38 v. Canterbury 12*
* *At Sydney Football Stadium*
** *At ANZ Stadium, Brisbane*

LEADING SCORERS
(Not including play-offs)
Tries
20 Darren Smith (Brisbane Broncos)
   Steve Menzies (Manly)
   Michael Buettner (North Sydney)
Goals
108 Ivan Cleary (Sydney City)
Points
268 Ivan Cleary (Sydney City)

BRITISH PLAYERS IN 1998 NRL
Harvey Howard (Western Sub.) 9+3 app.
Lee Jackson (Newcastle) 18+2 app. 2 tries

1998 STATE OF ORIGIN MATCHES (* Denotes captain)

NEW SOUTH WALES v QUEENSLAND

22 May
Sydney
Attendance: 36,070

New South Wales 23
Tim Brasher (South Sydney) 1t
Rod Wishart (Illawarra) 1t
Andrew Ettingshausen (Cronulla)
Terry Hill (Manly)
Adam MacDougall (Newcastle)
*Laurie Daley (Canberra) 1t
Andrew Johns (Newcastle) 1g, 1dg
Rodney Howe (Melbourne)
Geoff Toovey (Manly)
Paul Harragon (Newcastle)
Dean Pay (Parramatta)
Nik Kosef (Manly)
Brad Fittler (Sydney City) 1t
Subs: Matthew Johns (Newcastle)
    David Barnhill (Sydney City)
    Steve Menzies (Manly) 1t
Coach: Tom Raudonikis

Queensland 24
Darren Lockyer (Brisbane Broncos) 4g
Matt Sing (Sydney City)
Steve Renouf (Brisbane Broncos)
Darren Smith (Brisbane Broncos)
Wendell Sailor (Brisbane Broncos)
Kevin Walters (Brisbane Broncos) 1t
*Allan Langer (Brisbane Broncos) 1t
Shane Webcke (Brisbane Broncos)
Jason Hetherington (Canterbury)
Gary Larson (North Sydney)
Wayne Bartrim (St. George)
Jason Smith (Parramatta)
Peter Ryan (Brisbane Broncos)
Subs: Steve Price (Canterbury) 1t
    Martin Lang (Cronulla)
    Ben Ikin (North Sydney)
    Tonie Carroll (Brisbane Broncos) 1t
Coach: Wayne Bennett
Referee: Bill Harrigan

5 June
Brisbane
Attendance: 40,447

New South Wales 26
Tim Brasher (South Sydney) 1t
Rod Wishart (Illawarra)
Paul McGregor (Illawarra) 2t
Terry Hill (Manly)
Adam Mac Dougall (Newcastle) 1t
*Laurie Daley (Canberra)
Andrew Johns (Newcastle) 3g
Rodney Howe (Melbourne)
Geoff Toovey (Manly)
Paul Harragon (Newcastle)
Dean Pay (Parramatta)
David Barnhill (Sydney City)
Brad Fittler (Sydney City) 1t
Subs: Nik Kosef (Manly)
    Andrew Ettingshausen (Cronulla)
    Glenn Lazarus (Melbourne)
    Steve Menzies (Manly)
Coach: Tom Raudonikis

Queensland 10
Darren Lockyer (Brisbane Broncos) 1g
Matt Sing (Sydney City) 1t
Steve Renouf (Brisbane Broncos)
Darren Smith (Brisbane Broncos)
Wendell Sailor (Brisbane Broncos) 1t
Kevin Walters (Brisbane Broncos)
*Allan Langer (Brisbane Broncos)
Shane Webcke (Brisbane Broncos)
Jason Hetherington (Canterbury)
Gary Larson (North Sydney)
Gorden Tallis (Brisbane Broncos)
Brad Thorn (Brisbane Broncos)
Wayne Bartrim (St. George)
Subs: Steve Price (Canterbury)
    Martin Lang (Cronulla)
    Ben Ikin (North Sydney)
    Tonie Carroll (Brisbane Broncos)
Coach: Wayne Bennett
Referee: Bill Harrigan

19 June
Sydney
Attendance: 38,952

New South Wales 4
Tim Brasher (South Sydney)
Rod Wishart (Illawarra)
*Laurie Daley (Canberra)
Terry Hill (Manly)
Adam MacDougall (Newcastle)
Brad Fittler (Sydney City)
Andrew Johns (Newcstle)
Glenn Lazarus (Melbourne)
Matthew Johns (Newcastle)
Tony Butterfield (Newcastle)
David Furner (Canberra)
David Barnhill (Sydney City)
Jim Dymock (Parramatta)
Subs: Dean Pay (Parramatta)
    Robbie Kearns (Melbourne)
    Ken McGuinness (Wests) 1t
Steve Menzies (Manly)
Coach: Tom Raudonikis

Queensland 19
Darren Lockyer (Brisbane Broncos) 2g
Robbie O'Davis (Newcastle) 1g
Steve Renouf (Brisbane Broncos))
Ben Ikin (North Sydney) 1t
Wendell Sailor (Brisbane Broncos)
Kevin Walters (Brisbane Broncos) 1t
*Allan Langer (Brisbane Broncos) 1t
Shane Webcke (Brisbane Broncos)
Jamie Goddard (Gold Coast)
Gary Larson (North Sydney)
Gorden Tallis (Brisbane Broncos)
Jason Smith (Parramatta) 1dg
Darren Smith (Brisbane Broncos)
Subs: Steve Price (Canterbury)
    Matt Sing (Sydney City)
    Peter Ryan (Brisbane Broncos)
    Andrew Gee (Brisbane Broncos)
Coach Wayne Bennett
Referee: Bill Harrigan

ANZAC TEST
NEW ZEALAND 22 v. AUSTRALIA 16
Friday 24 April 1998, at North Harbour Stadium, Auckland
Attendance: 24,640
NEW ZEALAND: Matthew Ridge (Capt. 3g); Sean Hoppe (1t), Richard Blackmore, Ruben Wiki, Richard Barnett; Robbie Paul, Stacey Jones; John Lomax, Henry Paul, Quentin Pongia, Tony Iro, Jarrod McCracken, Logan Swann. **Playing subs:** Nigel Vagana, Terry Hermansson (1t), Kevin Iro (2t), Joe Vagana. **Coach:** Frank Endacott.
AUSTRALIA: Robbie O'Davis; Wendell Sailor, Terry Hill (2t), Steve Renouf (1t), Mat Rogers (2g); Laurie Daley (Capt.), Andrew Johns; Rodney Howe, Geoff Toovey, Paul Harragon, Steve Menzies, Brad Thorn, Brad Fittler. **Playing subs:** Darren Lockyer, Nik Kosef, Glenn Lazarus, Dean Pay. **Coach:** Bob Fulton.
Referee: Russell Smith (England)

AUSTRALIA 30 v. NEW ZEALAND 12
Friday 9 October 1998, at Suncorp Stadium, Brisbane
Attendance: 18,501
AUSTRALIA: Darren Lockyer (1t, 4g); Wendell Sailor, Steve Renouf, Darren Smith, Tim Brasher; Kevin Walters (1t), Allan Langer (Capt.); Shane Webcke, Andrew Johns (1g), Darren Britt, Gorden Tallis (2t), Robbie Kearns, Jason Smith. **Playing subs:** Ben Ikin, Brad Thorn (1t), Steve Price, Steve Menzies. **Coach:** Wayne Bennett.
NEW ZEALAND: Matthew Ridge (Capt. 1g); Richard Barnett, Ruben Wiki (1t), Kevin Iro, Sean Hoppe (1t); Robbie Paul, Stacey Jones; Joe Vagana, Syd Eru, Quentin Pongia, Stephen Kearney, Jarrod McCracken, Logan Swann. **Playing subs:** Gene Ngamu (1g), Tony Iro, Tony Puletua, Nathan Cayless. **Coach:** Frank Endacott.
Referee: Russell Smith (England)

NEW ZEALAND 16 v. AUSTRALIA 36
Friday 16 October 1998, at North Harbour Stadium, Auckland
Attendance: 24,470
NEW ZEALAND: Richard Barnett; Sean Hoppe, Kevin Iro, Ruben Wiki, Daryl Halligan (1t, 4g); Robbie Paul, Stacey Jones; Joe Vagana, Syd Eru, Quentin Pongia (Capt.), Jarrod McCracken, Stephen Kearney, Logan Swann. **Playing subs:** Gene Ngamu, Tony Iro, Tony Puletua (1t), Nathan Cayless. **Coach:** Frank Endacott.
AUSTRALIA: Darren Lockyer (1t, 3g); Tim Brasher, Steve Renouf (2t), Darren Smith (1t), Wendell Sailor; Andrew Johns (1g), Allan Langer (Capt.); Shane Webcke, Jason Hetherington (1t), Darren Britt, Gorden Tallis, Robbie Kearns, Jason Smith (1t). **Playing subs:** Ben Ikin, Brad Thorn (1t), Steve Price, Steve Menzies. **Coach:** Wayne Bennett.
Referee: Russell Smith (England)

Tony Iro: New Zealand Test forward.

PAPUA NEW GUINEA RL 50th ANNIVERSARY TOURNAMENT

(Each country given full international status except New Zealand Maoris)

Wednesday 7 October, At Lae
Papua New Guinea 46 (Tries: Raymond Karl, Adrian Lam, David Gomia, Leonard Tarum, Alfred Songoro, Marcus Bai, Stanley Gene, David Buko; Goals: John Wilshere 6, Adrian Lam)
Cook Islands 6 (Tries: Meti Noovao; Goals: Steve Berryman). Att: 8000

Wednesday 7 October, At Lae
New Zealand Maoris 23 (Tries: Tony Waikato 2, Jamie Stevens, Mike Luke; Goals: Paul Howell 3; dg: Chris Nahi)
Tonga 12 (Tries: Simone Nekesi 2, Sam Fukofuka). Att: (As above, double-header)

Sunday 11 October, At Wabag
Papua New Guinea 44 (Tries: Adrian Lam 2, David Buko 2, Raymond Karl, Alfred Songoro, Stanley Gene, Tom O'Reilly, Andrew Norman; Goals: John Wilshere 4)

Tonga 28 (Tries: Paul Koloi 2, Andrew Tangata-Toa 2, Andrew Lomu; Goals: Takai Taulanga 4). Att: 7000

Sunday 11 October, At Kokopo
Cook Islands 16 (Tries: Clive Arona, Meti Noovao, Ali Davys; Goals: Richard Piaura, Henry Turua)
New Zealand Maoris 8 (Tries: Paul Howell; Goals: Paul Howell 2). Att: 6000

Wednesday 14 October, At Kimbe
Papua New Guinea 46 (Tries: David Gomia 2, Tom O'Reilly, David Buko, Raymond Karl, Julias Krewanty, Richard Songoro, Adrian Lam; Goals: John Wilshere 7)
New Zealand Maoris 0 Att: 10,000

Wednesday 14 October, At Kokopo
Tonga 30 (Tries: Fred Typou 2, Paul Koloi 2, John Hopoate, Sam Fukofuka; Goals: Taikai Taulanga (3))
Cook Islands 22 (Tries: Denvour Johnston, Steve Berryman, Zane Clarke, Anthony Samuels; Goals: Berryman 2, Meti Noovao). Att: 6000

Final table

	P	W	D	L	F	A	Pts
Papua New Guinea	3	3	0	0	136	34	6
Tonga	3	1	0	2	70	89	2
Cook Islands	3	1	0	2	44	84	2
New Zealand Maoris	3	1	0	2	31	74	2

FINAL
Sunday 18 October, At Port Moresby
Papua New Guinea 54 (Tries: David Gomia 2, Stanley Gene 2, David Buko 2, Marcus Bai, Alfred Songoro, James Kops, David Westley; Goals: John Wilshere 6, Stanley Gene)
Tonga 12 (Tries: Saimone Nekesi 2, Richard Villasante). Att: 9000

THIRD PLACE PLAY-OFF
Sunday 18 October, At Port Moresby
New Zealand Maoris 28 (Tries: Shane Edwards, Phil Bergman, Frank Watene, Willie McLean; Goals: Paul Howell 6)
Cook Islands 6 (Try: Clive Arona; Goal: Steve Berryman)

SQUADS

Papua New Guinea: David Buko, John Wilshire, David Gomia, Alfred Songaro, Marcus Bai, Stanley Gene, Adrian Lam, Lucas Solbat, Leonard Tarum, David Westley, Raymond Karl, Tom O'Reilly, Peter Noki, Richard Mamando, Jim Wilson, James Kops, Andrew Norman, Julias Krewanty, Max Tiri, Ruben Ruing. **Coach:** Bob Bennett

Cook Islands: Tiri Toa, Ernest Paikura, Brian Atatoa, Anthony Samuels, Richard Paikura, Craig Bowen, Ali Davys, Jason Pekepo, Zane Clarke, Denvour Johnston, Patrick Kuru, Terrie Glassie, Alfred Manu, Steve Berryman, Sonny Shepherd, Meti Noovao, Clive Arona, Henry Turua, Alex Kermode, Adam Watene. **Coach:** Paul McGreal

New Zealand Maoris: Willie McLean, Charlie Kennedy, Jason Williams, Tony Waikato, Steve Matthews, Jamie Stevens, Phil Bergman, Jermmine Awahou, Paul Howell, Frank Watene, Ray Barchard, Michael Madsen, Kylie Leuluai, Shane Edwards, Dallas Mead, Chris Nahi, Chris McClausland, Nathan Picchi, Ari Shead, Mike Luke, Tawera Nikau. **Coach:** Cameron Bell

Tonga: Gregg Wolfgramm, Paul Koloi, John Hopoate, Fredrick Pongi, Saimone Nekesi, Joe Pomale, Willie Wolfgramm, Lamtau Ngata, Esau Mann, Alfons Massela, Solomon Haumono, Richard Villasante, Andrew Tangata-Toa, Vili Wolfgramm, Malupo Liutai, Samuela Fukofuka, Sione Tuliakiono, Andrew Lomu, Takai Taulanga, Peni 'Amato. **Coach:** Mike McClennan

OTHER INTERNATIONAL MATCHES

COOK ISLANDS 18 v. NEW ZEALAND MAORIS 10

Wednesday 24 June 1998, at Tereora National Stadium, Rarotonga
Attendance: 1500
Cook Islands: Tiri Toa; Daniel Tangapiri, Sonny Shepherd, Richard Piakura (Capt., 3g), Teauvira Williams; Darren Pitt (2t), Terry Piri; Ngere Tariu, David Tuteru, Scott Arlander, Lloyd Matapo, Patrick Kuru, Alex Kermode. **Substitutes:** Pare Rongokea, Tungane Tini (1t), Allan Tuara, Peckham Maoate. **Coach:** Jeffrey Murray.

New Zealand Maoris: Steve Matthews; Odell Manuel, Bryan Jellick, Boycie Nelson, Charlie Kennedy (1t); Paul Howell (Capt.), Hare Te Rangi; Paul Rauhihi, Tainui Raihe, Frank Watene (1t), Jason Kerapa, Jonathan Smith, Neville Ramsey. **Substitutes:** Corey Kingi, Fergie Edwards, Donovan Clark, Ray Barchard. **Coach:** Cameron Bell.
Referee: Taiesi Kirisome (Samoa)

COOK ISLANDS 14 v. NEW ZEALAND MAORIS 24

Sunday 28 June 1998, at Tereora National Stadium, Rarotonga
Attendance: 1700
Cook Islands: Tiri Toa; Tonga McBride, Lloyd Matapo, Richard Piakura (Capt., 1t, 1g), Johnny George (1t); Terry Piri (1t), Teina Pepe; Ngere Tariu, David Tuteru, Allan Tuara, Sonny Shepherd, Patrick Kuru, Alex Kermode. **Substitutes:** Pare Rongokea, Tungane Tini, Terii Aberahama, Peckham Maoate. **Coach:** Jeffrey Murray.

New Zealand Maoris: Steve Matthews; Bryan Jellick (1t), Boycie Nelson, Jason Walker, Charlie Kennedy; Corey Kingi, Hare Te Rangi; Paul Rauhihi, Paul Howell (Capt., 3t, 4g), Frank Watene, Ray Barchard, Jonathan Smith, Neville Ramsey. **Substitutes:** Fergie Edwards, Jason Kerapa, Odell Manuel, Donovan Clark. **Coach:** Cameron Bell.
Referee: Taiesi Kirisome (Samoa)

COOK ISLANDS 8 v. NEW ZEALAND MAORIS 24

Sunday 5 July 1998, at Tereora National Stadium, Rarotonga
Attendance: 2300
Cook Islands: Daniel Tangapiri (1t); Johnny George, Tiri Toa, Richard Piakura (Capt.),

Tonga McBride; Darren Piri, Terry Piri; Scott Arlander, David Tuteru, Ngere Tariu, Sonny Shepherd, Patrick Kuru, Alex Kermode. **Substitutes:** Teauvira Williams, Lloyd Matapo (1t), Pare Rongokea, Tungane Tini, Teina Pepe, Peckham Maoate. **Coach:** Jeffrey Murray.

New Zealand Maoris: Steve Matthews; Bryan Jellick, Boycie Nelson (1t), Jason Walker (1t), Charlie Kennedy; Corey Kingi (1t), Hare Te Rangi (1t); Paul Rauhihi, Paul Howell (Capt., 4g), Frank Watene, Ray Barchard, Jonathan Smith, Neville Ramsey. **Substitutes:** Fergie Edwards, Jason Kerapa, Odell Manuel, Donovan Clark, Tainui Raihe, Peter Lewis. **Coach:** Cameron Bell.

Referee: Taiesi Kirisome (Samoa)

TONGA 20 v. SAMOA 20
Saturday 7 June 1998, at Nuku'alofa
Attendance: 5000

Tonga: Samiuela Fotu; Sitiveni Osai, Siua 'Atoa, Maikeli Mohulamu (1t), Tonga Fili; Saineha Lautaimi, Samiuela Fukofuka (1t); 'Ofila Fifita, Peni 'Amato (Capt.), Sione Tuliakiono, Tu'l Ma'afu, Malupo Liutai (1t), Takai Taulanga (4g). **Substitutes:** Molisoni 'Otukolo, Makineti Langi, Lamatau Ngata, Vili Takapautolo.

Samoa: Faasao Viliopelu; David Fruean, Faamati Luamanuvae, Arona Sini (Capt.), Timoti Tuvale (1t); Richard Lauina, Alapati Leavasa; Kiliata Alai (2t), Eddie Couper, Faafouina Sua, Ivo Pesamino, Lafo Ah Ching (1t), Utulei Moananu (2g). **Substitutes:** Tanielu Sanerivi, Vitaliano Vaasili, Tuiavii Sua, Ropati Taunau.

TONGA 24 v. SAMOA 8
Tuesday 30 June 1998, at Nuku'alofa

Tonga: Samiuela Fotu; Makineti Langi, Lea Latunipulu, Maikeli Mohulamu (1t), Tonga Fili (2t); Molisoni 'Otukolo, Samiuela Fukofuka; Lamatau Ngata, Peni 'Amata (Capt.), Sione Tuliakiono, Tu'l Ma'afu, Malupo Liutai (1t), Takai Taulanga (4g).

Substitutes: Siua 'Atoa, Sila Pangai, Sefo Taufalele, Vili Takapautolo.

Samoa: Apolo Tua; David Fruean (1t), Faamati Luamanuvae, Arona Sini (Capt.), Faasao Viliopelu; Richard Lauina, Alapati Leavasa; Ropati Taunau, Falesiva Matafa, Tuiavii Sua (1t), Timoti Tuvale, Lafo Ah Ching, Utulei Moananu. **Substitutes:** Tanielu Sanerivi, Vitaliano Vaasili, Eddie Couper, Faafouina Sua.

TONGA 24 v. SAMOA 22
Saturday 4 July 1998, at Palalaua School Grounds, Siumu
Attendance: 2000

Tonga: Lea Latunipulu (1t); Makineti Langi (1t), Siua 'Atoa, Maikeli Mohulamu, Tonga Fili; Molisoni 'Otukolo, Samiuela Fukofuka, Lamatau Ngata, Peni 'Amato (Capt., 1t), Sione Tuliakiono, Vili Takapautolo, Malupo Liutai, Takai Taulanga (1t, 4g). **Substitutes:** Ofila Fifita, Sila Pangai, Sefo Taufalele, Viliami Soni.

Samoa: Apolo Tua; David Fruean (1t), Faamati Luamanuvae, Arona Sini (Capt.), Faasao Viliopelu; Richard Lauina, Alapati Leavasa; Ropati Taunau (1t), Falesiva Matafa (1t), Tuiavii Sua, Timoti Tuvale (1t), Lafo Ah Ching (1t, 1g), Utulei Moananu. **Substitutes:** Tanielu Sanerivi, Vitaliano Vaasili, Eddie Couper, Faafouina Sua.

TONGA (ARL) 14 v. FIJI 22
Wednesday 1 July 1998, at Teufaive Stadium
Attendance: 2500

Tonga: Vao Pako Pongi; Lolo Tu'ifua (1t), Sifa 'Aluesi (1g), Motuhi Tu'ipulotu, Vaha'l Totone; Tevita Kaufusi (1t), Paula Finau (1t); Lolo Mohi, Kapeli Kautai, Talakai Taani, Salesi Kaufusi, Kafa Losi, Sione Teaupa. **Substitutes:** Felti Pongi, Ngahe Tau, Vili Vaka, Soane Tupou Malohi.

Fiji: Orisi Kaloulasulasu; Timoci Saulekaleka Vatubuli, Matereti Naqau (3g), Joseph Lacacavibaua, Farasiko Tokarei; Penisoni

Namua, Alipate Naqaya (1t); Etuate Vakatawa, Jone Yabakindrau Koroi, Filimone Drua, Kaiava Salusalu (Capt.), Pita Nawaikula (1t), Toma Ratumaitadra. **Substitutes:** Basilio Kunavura (2t), Kalaveti Naisoro.

FIJI 14 v. PAPUA NEW GUINEA 16
Saturday 18 July 1998, at Churchill Park, Lautoka
Attendance: 1800
Fiji: Josefa Rasiga; Alipate Naqaya, Matereti Naqau (1t), Orisi Loco, Tomoci Vatabuli (1t); Farasiko Tokarei, Kalaveri Naisoro (Capt.); Etuate Rutidara Rutidara, Pita Nawaikula, Kaiava Salusalu, Filimoni Drua, Penisoni Namua, Alipate Tinivatta (1t). **Substitutes:** Paulaisi Tasere (1g), Jone Kuruduadua, Manasa Nawarkula, Tom Waqa. **Coach:** Paulasi Tabulutu.
Papua New Guinea: Ruben Ruing; James Kops, David Gomia (1t), Andrew Norman, Robert Volu; Robert Tela (2g), Dickson Sibya; Raymond Karl (1t), Leonard Tarum, Lucas Solbat, Chris Lome, Peter Noki (1t), Max Tiri (Capt.). **Substitutes:** Robert Sio, Brown Wilby, Francis Pegu, Tony Day. **Coach:** Bob Bennett.

PAPUA NEW GUINEA 34 v. FIJI 12
Wednesday 22 July 1998, at Minj RL Ground
Attendance: 5000
Papua New Guinea: Ruben Ruing; James Kops, David Gomia (1t), Andrew Norman, Robert Volu; Nissan Pakistan, Robert Tela (1g); Leonard Tarum (1t), Raymond Karl, Max Tiri (Capt.), Francis Pegu, Peter Noki (1t), Chris Lome (1t). **Substitutes:** Robert Sio, Brown Wilby (1t), Francis Pegu, Dickson Sibya (2t), Lucas Solbat (1t). **Coach:** Bob Bennett.
Fiji: Josefa Rasiga; Alipate Naqaya, Kalaveri Naisoro (Capt., 1t), Orisi Loco, Tomoci Vatabuli; Matareti Naqau (2g), Pita Nawaikula; Tom Waqa, Paulaisi Tasere, Etuate Rutidara, Filimoni Drua, Penisoni Namua, Alipate Tinivatta. **Substitutes:** Jone Kuruduadua (1t), Manasa Nawarkula, Etonia Nawasetawa, Maika Vunivere. **Coach:** Paulasi Tabulutu.
Referee: Taesi Kirisome (Samoa)

PAPUA NEW GUINEA 10 v. FIJI 14
Sunday 26 July 1998, at Lloyd Robson Oval, Port Moresby
Attendance: 1500
Papua New Guinea: Ruben Ruing; James Kops, David Gomia, Andrew Norman (1t), Robert Volu; Robert Tela (1g), Dickson Sibya; Raymond Karl, Leonard Tarum, Lucas Salbot, Max Tiri (Capt.), Tony Dai, Chris Lome. **Substitutes:** Robert Sio, Brown Wilby, Francis Pegu, Nissan Pakistan. **Coach:** Bob Bennett.
Fiji: Tomoci Vatabuli; Jone Kuruduadua, Alipate Tinivata, Orisi Loco, Alipate Naqaya; Matereti Naqau (3g), Kalaveri Naisoro (Capt., 1t); Etuate Rutidara, Pita Nawaikula (1t), Kaiava Salusalu, Basilio Kunavura, Tom Waqa, Manasa Nawakula. **Substitutes:** Etonia Nawasetawa, Maika Vunivere, Pauliasi Tasere, Penisoni Namua. **Coach:** Paulasi Tabulutu.
Referee: Taesi Kirisome (Samoa)

FIXTURES

SUPER LEAGUE 1999
● Dates and kick-off times are subject to change

JJB SUPER LEAGUE
Matches shown live on Sky TV are listed for the first half of the season (marked SKY). Matches for the second half of the season will continue to be televised on Fridays and Sundays, concentrating on those having a vital bearing on the challenge for a top five play-off place.

FRIDAY, 5 MARCH

SKY	Wigan Warriors	v.	Hull Sharks	7.30

SUNDAY, 7 MARCH

	Bradford Bulls	v.	Sheffield Eagles	3.00
	Castleford Tigers	v.	Wakefield Trinity	3.30
SKY	Gateshead Thunder	v.	Leeds Rhinos	6.35
	Halifax Blue Sox	v.	Warrington Wolves	3.00
	London Broncos	v.	Huddersfield Giants	3.30
	Salford Reds	v.	St. Helens	3.00

SUNDAY, 14 MARCH
Silk Cut Challenge Cup - Sixth Round

FRIDAY, 19 MARCH

SKY	Leeds Rhinos	v.	Wigan Warriors	7.30

SATURDAY, 20 MARCH

	Sheffield Eagles	v.	London Broncos	6.00

SUNDAY, 21 MARCH

	Huddersfield Giants	v.	Halifax Blue Sox	3.00
	Hull Sharks	v.	Bradford Bulls	3.15
SKY	St. Helens	v.	Gateshead Thunder	6.35
	Wakefield Trinity	v.	Salford Reds	3.30
	Warrington Wolves	v.	Castleford Tigers	3.00

SATURDAY, 27 MARCH
Silk Cut Challenge Cup - Semi-final (1)

SUNDAY, 28 MARCH
Silk Cut Challenge Cup - Semi-final (2)

THURSDAY, 1 APRIL

SKY	Bradford Bulls	v.	Leeds Rhinos	5.00

GOOD FRIDAY, 2 APRIL

	Castleford Tigers	v.	Halifax Blue Sox	7.30
	Gateshead Thunder	v.	Wakefield Trinity	3.00
	London Broncos	v.	Hull Sharks	3.30
	Salford Reds	v.	Warrington Wolves	3.00
	Sheffield Eagles	v.	Huddersfield Giants	
SKY	Wigan Warriors	v.	St. Helens	12.05

EASTER MONDAY, 5 APRIL

SKY	Hull Sharks	v.	Sheffield Eagles	12.30
	Leeds Rhinos	v.	London Broncos	3.00
	St. Helens	v.	Bradford Bulls	3.00
	Wakefield Trinity	v.	Wigan Warriors	3.30
	Warrington Wolves	v.	Gateshead Thunder	3.00

TUESDAY, 6 APRIL

SKY	Halifax Blue Sox	v.	Salford Reds	7.30

WEDNESDAY, 7 APRIL

	Huddersfield Giants	v.	Castleford Tigers	7.30

FRIDAY, 9 APRIL

SKY	London Broncos	v.	St. Helens	7.30

SUNDAY, 11 APRIL

	Bradford Bulls	v.	Wakefield Trinity	6.00
	Gateshead Thunder	v.	Halifax Blue Sox	3.00
	Huddersfield Giants	v.	Hull Sharks	3.00
	Salford Reds	v.	Castleford Tigers	3.00
SKY	Sheffield Eagles	v.	Leeds Rhinos	6.35
	Wigan Warriors	v.	Warrington Wolves	3.00

FRIDAY, 16 APRIL

SKY	Halifax Blue Sox	v.	Wigan Warriors	7.30
	Leeds Rhinos	v.	Hull Sharks	7.30

SUNDAY, 18 APRIL

SKY	Castleford Tigers	v.	Gateshead Thunder	6.35
	St. Helens	v.	Sheffield Eagles	3.00
	Salford Reds	v.	Huddersfield Giants	3.00
	Wakefield Trinity	v.	London Broncos	3.30
	Warrington Wolves	v.	Bradford Bulls	3.00

FRIDAY, 23 APRIL

SKY	Bradford Bulls	v.	Halifax Blue Sox	7.30

SATURDAY, 24 APRIL

	London Broncos	v.	Warrington Wolves	6.30

SUNDAY, 25 APRIL

	Gateshead Thunder	v.	Salford Reds	3.00
	Huddersfield Giants	v.	Leeds Rhinos	3.00
	Hull Sharks	v.	St. Helens	3.15
SKY	Sheffield Eagles	v.	Wakefield Trinity	6.35
	Wigan Warriors	v.	Castleford Tigers	3.00

SATURDAY, 1 MAY
Silk Cut Challenge Cup - Final

MONDAY, 3 MAY

	Castleford Tigers	v.	Bradford Bulls	
	Gateshead Thunder	v.	Huddersfield Giants	3.00
	Halifax Blue Sox	v.	London Broncos	7.30
	St. Helens	v.	Leeds Rhinos	3.00
	Salford Reds	v.	Wigan Warriors	3.00
	Wakefield Trinity	v.	Hull Sharks	3.30
	Warrington Wolves	v.	Sheffield Eagles	3.00

• The 3 May fixtures are subject to change once the Challenge Cup finalists are known. The SKY matches will be played on 3 May, kick off 12.00 and 5 May, kick off 7.30.

FRIDAY, 7 MAY

SKY	Huddersfield Giants	v.	St. Helens	7.30
	Leeds Rhinos	v.	Wakefield Trinity	7.30

SATURDAY, MAY 8

	Sheffield Eagles	v.	Halifax Blue Sox	6.00

SUNDAY, 9 MAY

	Bradford Bulls	v.	Salford Reds	7.30
	Hull Sharks	v.	Warrington Wolves	3.15
SKY	London Broncos	v.	Castleford Tigers	6.35
	Wigan Warriors	v.	Gateshead Thunder	3.00

WEDNESDAY, 12 MAY

	Bradford Bulls	v.	London Broncos	7.30
	Salford Reds	v.	Leeds Rhinos	7.30

FRIDAY, 14 MAY

SKY	Wakefield Trinity	v.	St. Helens	7.30

SUNDAY, 16 MAY

	Castleford Tigers	v.	Sheffield Eagles	3.30
	Gateshead Thunder	v.	Bradford Bulls	3.00
	Halifax Blue Sox	v.	Hull Sharks	3.00
	Salford Reds	v.	London Broncos	3.00
SKY	Warrington Wolves	v.	Leeds Rhinos	6.35
	Wigan Warriors	v.	Huddersfield Giants	3.00

WEDNESDAY, 19 MAY

	Gateshead Thunder	v.	Hull Sharks	

FRIDAY, 21 MAY

SKY	Leeds Rhinos	v.	Halifax Blue Sox	7.30

SATURDAY, 22 MAY

	Sheffield Eagles	v.	Salford Reds	3.00

SUNDAY, 23 MAY

SKY	Bradford Bulls	v.	Wigan Warriors	6.35
	Huddersfield Giants	v.	Wakefield Trinity	3.00
	Hull Sharks	v.	Castleford Tigers	3.15
	London Broncos	v.	Gateshead Thunder	3.30
	St. Helens	v.	Warrington Wolves	3.00

WEDNESDAY, 26 MAY

	Castleford Tigers	v.	St. Helens	7.30

FRIDAY, 28 MAY

SKY	London Broncos	v.	Wigan Warriors	7.30

SUNDAY, 30 MAY

	Bradford Bulls	v.	Huddersfield Giants	6.00
SKY	Castleford Tigers	v.	Leeds Rhinos	6.35
	Gateshead Thunder	v.	Sheffield Eagles	3.00
	Halifax Blue Sox	v.	St. Helens	3.00
	Salford Reds	v.	Hull Sharks	3.00
	Warrington Wolves	v.	Wakefield Trinity	3.00

WEDNESDAY, 2 JUNE

	Wigan Warriors	v.	Sheffield Eagles	7.45

FRIDAY, 4 JUNE

	Leeds Rhinos	v.	Gateshead Thunder	7.30
SKY	Warrington Wolves	v.	Halifax Blue Sox	7.30

SUNDAY, 6 JUNE

SKY	Huddersfield Giants	v.	London Broncos	6.35
	Hull Sharks	v.	Wigan Warriors	3.15
	St. Helens	v.	Salford Reds	3.00
	Wakefield Trinity	v.	Castleford Tigers	3.30

WEDNESDAY, 9 JUNE

	Halifax Blue Sox	v.	Wakefield Trinity	7.30
	Sheffield Eagles	v.	Bradford Bulls	7.30
	Warrington Wolves	v.	Huddersfield Giants	

SUNDAY, 13 JUNE

	Bradford Bulls	v.	Hull Sharks	6.00
	Castleford Tigers	v.	Warrington Wolves	3.30
	Gateshead Thunder	v.	St. Helens	3.00
	Halifax Blue Sox	v.	Huddersfield Giants	3.00
	London Broncos	v.	Sheffield Eagles	3.30
	Salford Reds	v.	Wakefield Trinity	3.00
	Wigan Warriors	v.	Leeds Rhinos	3.00

FRIDAY, 18 JUNE

	Halifax Blue Sox	v.	Castleford Tigers	7.30
	Leeds Rhinos	v.	Bradford Bulls	7.30

SUNDAY, 20 JUNE

	Huddersfield Giants	v.	Sheffield Eagles	3.00
	Hull Sharks	v.	London Broncos	3.15
	St. Helens	v.	Wigan Warriors	3.00
	Wakefield Trinity	v.	Gateshead Thunder	3.30
	Warrington Wolves	v.	Salford Reds	3.00

WEDNESDAY, 23 JUNE

	Hull Sharks	v.	Salford Reds	7.30
	Leeds Rhinos	v.	Castleford Tigers	7.30
	St. Helens	v.	Halifax Blue Sox	7.30

SATURDAY, 26 JUNE

	Sheffield Eagles	v.	Hull Sharks	3.00

SUNDAY, 27 JUNE

	Bradford Bulls	v.	St. Helens	6.00
	Castleford Tigers	v.	Huddersfield Giants	3.30
	Gateshead Thunder	v.	Warrington Wolves	3.00
	London Broncos	v.	Leeds Rhinos	3.30
	Salford Reds	v.	Halifax Blue Sox	3.00
	Wigan Warriors	v.	Wakefield Trinity	3.00

WEDNESDAY, 30 JUNE

	Sheffield Eagles	v.	Gateshead Thunder	7.30

FRIDAY, 2 JULY

	Leeds Rhinos	v.	Sheffield Eagles	7.30

SUNDAY, 4 JULY

	Castleford Tigers	v.	Salford Reds	3.30
	Halifax Blue Sox	v.	Gateshead Thunder	3.00
	Hull Sharks	v.	Huddersfield Giants	3.15
	St. Helens	v.	London Broncos	3.00
	Wakefield Trinity	v.	Bradford Bulls	3.30
	Warrington Wolves	v.	Wigan Warriors	3.00

WEDNESDAY, 7 JULY

	Huddersfield Giants	v.	Bradford Bulls	7.30
	Wakefield Trinity	v.	Warrington Wolves	
	Wigan Warriors	v.	London Broncos	7.45

SATURDAY, 10 JULY

	Sheffield Eagles	v.	St. Helens	3.00

SUNDAY, 11 JULY

	Bradford Bulls	v.	Warrington Wolves	6.00
	Gateshead Thunder	v.	Castleford Tigers	3.00
	Huddersfield Giants	v.	Salford Reds	3.00
	Hull Sharks	v.	Leeds Rhinos	3.15
	London Broncos	v.	Wakefield Trinity	3.30
	Wigan Warriors	v.	Halifax Blue Sox	3.00

FRIDAY, 16 JULY

Castleford Tigers	v.	Wigan Warriors	7.30
Leeds Rhinos	v.	Huddersfield Giants	7.30

SUNDAY, 18 JULY

Halifax Blue Sox	v.	Bradford Bulls	3.00
St. Helens	v.	Hull Sharks	3.00
Salford Reds	v.	Gateshead Thunder	3.00
Wakefield Trinity	v.	Sheffield Eagles	3.30
Warrington Wolves	v.	London Broncos	3.00

WEDNESDAY, 21 JULY

Sheffield Eagles	v.	Wigan Warriors	7.30
St. Helens	v.	Castleford Tigers	7.30

FRIDAY, 23 JULY

Leeds Rhinos	v.	St. Helens	7.30
London Broncos	v.	Halifax Blue Sox	7.30

SATURDAY, 24 JULY

Sheffield Eagles	v.	Warrington Wolves	3.00

SUNDAY, 25 JULY

Bradford Bulls	v.	Castleford Tigers	6.00
Huddersfield Giants	v.	Gateshead Thunder	3.00
Hull Sharks	v.	Wakefield Trinity	3.15
Wigan Warriors	v.	Salford Reds	3.00

WEDNESDAY, 28 JULY

London Broncos	v.	Bradford Bulls	7.45
Wakefield Trinity	v.	Halifax Blue Sox	3.00

SUNDAY, 1 AUGUST

Castleford Tigers	v.	London Broncos	3.30
Gateshead Thunder	v.	Wigan Warriors	3.00
Halifax Blue Sox	v.	Sheffield Eagles	3.00
St. Helens	v.	Huddersfield Giants	3.00
Salford Reds	v.	Bradford Bulls	3.00
Wakefield Trinity	v.	Leeds Rhinos	3.30
Warrington Wolves	v.	Hull Sharks	3.00

WEDNESDAY, 4 AUGUST

Hull Sharks	v.	Gateshead Thunder	7.30

FRIDAY, 6 AUGUST

Leeds Rhinos	v.	Warrington Wolves	7.30

SATURDAY, 7 AUGUST

London Broncos	v.	Salford Reds	6.30
Sheffield Eagles	v.	Castleford Tigers	3.00

SUNDAY, 8 AUGUST

Bradford Bulls	v.	Gateshead Thunder	6.00
Huddersfield Giants	v.	Wigan Warriors	3.00
Hull Sharks	v.	Halifax Blue Sox	3.15
St. Helens	v.	Wakefield Trinity	3.00

WEDNESDAY, 11 AUGUST

Huddersfield Giants	v.	Warrington Wolves	7.30

FRIDAY, 13 AUGUST

Halifax Blue Sox	v.	Leeds Rhinos	7.30

SUNDAY, 15 AUGUST

Castleford Tigers	v.	Hull Sharks	3.30
Gateshead Thunder	v.	London Broncos	3.00
Salford Reds	v.	Sheffield Eagles	3.00
Wakefield Trinity	v.	Huddersfield Giants	3.30

Warrington Wolves	v.	St. Helens	3.00
Wigan Warriors	v.	Bradford Bulls	3.00

WEDNESDAY, 18 AUGUST

Leeds Rhinos	v.	Salford Reds	7.30

FRIDAY, 20 AUGUST

Halifax Blue Sox	v.	Warrington Wolves	7.30

SATURDAY, 21 AUGUST

Castleford Tigers	v.	Wakefield Trinity	6.00

SUNDAY, 22 AUGUST

Bradford Bulls	v.	Sheffield Eagles	6.00
Gateshead Thunder	v.	Leeds Rhinos	3.00
London Broncos	v.	Huddersfield Giants	3.30
Salford Reds	v.	St. Helens	3.00
Wigan Warriors	v.	Hull Sharks	3.00

FRIDAY, 27 AUGUST

Leeds Rhinos	v.	Wigan Warriors	7.30

SATURDAY, 28 AUGUST

Sheffield Eagles	v.	London Broncos	6.00

SUNDAY, 29 AUGUST

Huddersfield Giants	v.	Halifax Blue Sox	3.00
Hull Sharks	v.	Bradford Bulls	3.15
St. Helens	v.	Gateshead Thunder	3.00
Wakefield Trinity	v.	Salford Reds	3.30
Warrington Wolves	v.	Castleford Tigers	3.00

SATURDAY, 4 SEPTEMBER

Sheffield Eagles	v.	Huddersfield Giants	6.00

SUNDAY, 5 SEPTEMBER

Bradford Bulls	v.	Leeds Rhinos	6.00
Castleford Tigers	v.	Halifax Blue Sox	3.30
Gateshead Thunder	v.	Wakefield Trinity	3.00
London Broncos	v.	Hull Sharks	3.30
Salford Reds	v.	Warrington Wolves	3.00
Wigan Warriors	v.	St. Helens	3.00

FRIDAY, 10 SEPTEMBER

Leeds Rhinos	v.	London Broncos	7.30
Halifax Blue Sox	v.	Salford Reds	7.30

SUNDAY, 12 SEPTEMBER

Huddersfield Giants	v.	Castleford Tigers	3.00
Hull Sharks	v.	Sheffield Eagles	3.15
St. Helens	v.	Bradford Bulls	3.00
Wakefield Trinity	v.	Wigan Warriors	3.30
Warrington Wolves	v.	Gateshead Thunder	3.00

FRI-SUN, 17-19 SEPTEMBER

Grand Final Play-offs

FRI-SUN, 24-26 SEPTEMBER

Grand Final Play-offs

SUNDAY, 3 OCTOBER

Grand Final Eliminator

SATURDAY, 9 OCTOBER

Grand Final

FIRST DIVISION

SUNDAY, 31 JANUARY
Silk Cut Challenge Cup - Third Round

SUNDAY, 7 FEBRUARY

Barrow Border R.	v.	Whitehaven Warriors	3.00
Batley Bulldogs	v.	Oldham	3.15
Featherstone Rovers	v.	Rochdale Hornets	3.30
Keighley Cougars	v.	Doncaster Dragons	3.00
Lancashire Lynx	v.	Bramley	3.00
Leigh Centurions	v.	York	3.00
Swinton Lions	v.	Hunslet Hawks	3.00
Widnes Vikings	v.	Dewsbury Rams	3.00
Workington Town	v.	Hull Kingston Rovers	3.00

SUNDAY, 14 FEBRUARY
Silk Cut Challenge Cup - Fourth Round

SUNDAY, 21 FEBRUARY

Bramley	v.	Keighley Cougars	3.00
Dewsbury Rams	v.	Leigh Centurions	3.00
Doncaster Dragons	v.	Swinton Lions	3.00
Hull Kingston Rovers	v.	Batley Bulldogs	3.00
Hunslet Hawks	v.	Workington Town	3.30
Oldham	v.	Featherstone Rovers	3.00
Rochdale Hornets	v.	Barrow Border R.	3.00

SUNDAY, 28 FEBRUARY
Silk Cut Challenge Cup - Fifth Round

SUNDAY, 7 MARCH

Barrow Border R.	v.	Featherstone Rovers	3.00
Batley Bulldogs	v.	Hunslet Hawks	3.15
Hull Kingston Rovers	v.	Oldham	3.00
Keighley Cougars	v.	York	3.00
Lancashire Lynx	v.	Dewsbury Rams	3.00
Leigh Centurions	v.	Whitehaven Warriors	3.00
Swinton Lions	v.	Bramley	3.00
Widnes Vikings	v.	Rochdale Hornets	3.00
Workington Town	v.	Doncaster Dragons	3.00

SUNDAY, 14 MARCH
Silk Cut Challenge Cup - Sixth Round

Dewsbury Rams	v.	Keighley Cougars	3.00
Doncaster Dragons	v.	Batley Bulldogs	3.00
Featherstone Rovers	v.	Widnes Vikings	3.30
Hunslet Hawks	v.	Hull Kingston Rovers	3.30
Oldham	v.	Barrow Border R.	3.00
Rochdale Hornets	v.	Leigh Centurions	3.00
Whitehaven Warriors	v.	Lancashire Lynx	3.30
Workington Town	v.	Bramley	3.00
York	v.	Swinton Lions	3.00

SUNDAY, 21 MARCH

Batley Bulldogs	v.	Bramley	3.15
Hull Kingston Rovers	v.	Doncaster Dragons	3.00
Hunslet Hawks	v.	Oldham	3.30
Keighley Cougars	v.	Whitehaven Warriors	3.00
Lancashire Lynx	v.	Rochdale Hornets	3.00
Leigh Centurions	v.	Featherstone Rovers	3.00
Swinton Lions	v.	Dewsbury Rams	3.00
Widnes Vikings	v.	Barrow Border R.	3.00
Workington Town	v.	York	3.00

SATURDAY, 27 MARCH
Silk Cut Challenge Cup - Semi-final (1)

SUNDAY, 28 MARCH
Silk Cut Challenge Cup - Semi-final (2)

Barrow Border R.	v.	Leigh Centurions	3.00
Bramley	v.	Hull Kingston Rovers	3.00
Dewsbury Rams	v.	Workington Town	3.00
Doncaster Dragons	v.	Hunslet Hawks	3.00
Featherstone Rovers	v.	Lancashire Lynx	3.30
Oldham	v.	Widnes Vikings	3.00
Rochdale Hornets	v.	Keighley Cougars	3.00
Whitehaven Warriors	v.	Swinton Lions	3.30
York	v.	Batley Bulldogs	3.00

FRIDAY, 2 APRIL

Batley Bulldogs	v.	Dewsbury Rams	7.30
Doncaster Dragons	v.	Oldham	7.30
Hull Kingston Rovers	v.	York	7.30
Hunslet Hawks	v.	Bramley	7.30
Keighley Cougars	v.	Featherstone Rovers	7.30
Lancashire Lynx	v.	Barrow Border R.	7.30
Leigh Centurions	v.	Widnes Vikings	7.30
Swinton Lions	v.	Rochdale Hornets	7.30
Workington Town	v.	Whitehaven Warriors	7.30

MONDAY, 5 APRIL

Barrow Border R.	v.	Keighley Cougars	7.30
Bramley	v.	Doncaster Dragons	7.30
Dewsbury Rams	v.	Hull Kingston Rovers	7.45
Featherstone Rovers	v.	Swinton Lions	7.30
Oldham	v.	Leigh Centurions	7.30
Rochdale Hornets	v.	Workington Town	7.30
Whitehaven Warriors	v.	Batley Bulldogs	7.30
Widnes Vikings	v.	Lancashire Lynx	7.30
York	v.	Hunslet Hawks	7.30

SUNDAY, 11 APRIL

Batley Bulldogs	v.	Rochdale Hornets	3.15
Bramley	v.	Oldham	3.00
Doncaster Dragons	v.	York	3.00
Hull Kingston Rovers	v.	Whitehaven Warriors	3.00
Hunslet Hawks	v.	Dewsbury Rams	3.30
Keighley Cougars	v.	Widnes Vikings	3.00
Lancashire Lynx	v.	Leigh Centurions	3.00
Swinton Lions	v.	Barrow Border R.	3.00
Workington Town	v.	Featherstone Rovers	3.00

SUNDAY, 18 APRIL

Barrow Border R.	v.	Workington Town	3.00
Dewsbury Rams	v.	Doncaster Dragons	3.00
Featherstone Rovers	v.	Batley Bulldogs	3.30
Lancashire Lynx	v.	Oldham	3.00
Leigh Centurions	v.	Keighley Cougars	3.00
Rochdale Hornets	v.	Hull Kingston Rovers	3.00
Whitehaven Warriors	v.	Hunslet Hawks	3.30
Widnes Vikings	v.	Swinton Lions	3.00
York	v.	Bramley	3.00

SUNDAY, 25 APRIL

Batley Bulldogs	v.	Barrow Border R.	3.15
Bramley	v.	Dewsbury Rams	3.00
Doncaster Dragons	v.	Whitehaven Warriors	3.00
Hull Kingston Rovers	v.	Featherstone Rovers	3.00

Hunslet Hawks	v.	Rochdale Hornets	3.30
Keighley Cougars	v.	Lancashire Lynx	3.00
Oldham	v.	York	3.00
Swinton Lions	v.	Leigh Centurions	3.00
Workington Town	v.	Widnes Vikings	3.00

SATURDAY, 1 MAY
Silk Cut Challenge Cup - Final

SUNDAY, 9 MAY

Barrow Border R.	v.	Hull Kingston Rovers	3.00
Dewsbury Rams	v.	York	3.00
Featherstone Rovers	v.	Hunslet Hawks	3.30
Keighley Cougars	v.	Oldham	3.00
Lancashire Lynx	v.	Swinton Lions	3.00
Leigh Centurions	v.	Workington Town	3.00
Rochdale Hornets	v.	Doncaster Dragons	3.00
Whitehaven Warriors	v.	Bramley	3.30
Widnes Vikings	v.	Batley Bulldogs	3.00

SUNDAY, 16 MAY

Batley Bulldogs	v.	Leigh Centurions	3.15
Bramley	v.	Rochdale Hornets	3.00
Doncaster Dragons	v.	Featherstone Rovers	3.00
Hull Kingston Rovers	v.	Widnes Vikings	3.00
Hunslet Hawks	v.	Barrow Border R.	3.30
Oldham	v.	Dewsbury Rams	3.00
Swinton Lions	v.	Keighley Cougars	3.00
Workington Town	v.	Lancashire Lynx	3.00
York	v.	Whitehaven Warriors	3.00

SUNDAY, 23 MAY

Barrow Border R.	v.	Doncaster Dragons	3.00
Featherstone Rovers	v.	Bramley	3.30
Keighley Cougars	v.	Workington Town	3.00
Lancashire Lynx	v.	Batley Bulldogs	3.00
Leigh Centurions	v.	Hull Kingston Rovers	3.00
Rochdale Hornets	v.	York	3.00
Swinton Lions	v.	Oldham	3.00
Whitehaven Warriors	v.	Dewsbury Rams	3.30
Widnes Vikings	v.	Hunslet Hawks	3.00

SUNDAY, MAY 30

Batley Bulldogs	v.	Keighley Cougars	3.15
Bramley	v.	Barrow Border R.	3.00
Dewsbury Rams	v.	Rochdale Hornets	3.00
Doncaster Dragons	v.	Widnes Vikings	3.00
Hull Kingston Rovers	v.	Lancashire Lynx	3.00
Hunslet Hawks	v.	Leigh Centurions	3.30
Oldham	v.	Whitehaven Warriors	3.00
Workington Town	v.	Swinton Lions	3.00
York	v.	Featherstone Rovers	3.00

SUNDAY, 6 JUNE

Barrow Border R.	v.	York	3.00
Featherstone Rovers	v.	Dewsbury Rams	3.30
Keighley Cougars	v.	Hull Kingston Rovers	3.00
Lancashire Lynx	v.	Hunslet Hawks	3.00
Leigh Centurions	v.	Doncaster Dragons	3.00
Rochdale Hornets	v.	Whitehaven Warriors	3.00
Swinton Lions	v.	Batley Bulldogs	3.00
Widnes Vikings	v.	Bramley	3.00
Workington Town	v.	Oldham	3.00

SUNDAY, 13 JUNE

Batley Bulldogs	v.	Workington Town	3.15
Bramley	v.	Leigh Centurions	3.00
Dewsbury Rams	v.	Barrow Border R.	3.00
Doncaster Dragons	v.	Lancashire Lynx	3.00
Hull Kingston Rovers	v.	Swinton Lions	3.00
Hunslet Hawks	v.	Keighley Cougars	3.30
Oldham	v.	Rochdale Hornets	3.00
Whitehaven Warriors	v.	Featherstone Rovers	3.30
York	v.	Widnes Vikings	3.00

SUNDAY, 20 JUNE

Bramley	v.	Lancashire Lynx	3.00
Dewsbury Rams	v.	Widnes Vikings	3.00
Doncaster Dragons	v.	Keighley Cougars	3.00
Hull Kingston Rovers	v.	Workington Town	3.00
Hunslet Hawks	v.	Swinton Lions	3.30
Oldham	v.	Batley Bulldogs	3.00
Rochdale Hornets	v.	Featherstone Rovers	3.00
Whitehaven Warriors	v.	Barrow Border R.	3.30
York	v.	Leigh Centurions	3.00

SUNDAY, 27 JUNE

Barrow Border R.	v.	Rochdale Hornets	3.00
Batley Bulldogs	v.	Hull Kingston Rovers	3.15
Featherstone Rovers	v.	Oldham	3.30
Keighley Cougars	v.	Bramley	3.00
Lancashire Lynx	v.	York	3.00
Leigh Centurions	v.	Dewsbury Rams	3.00
Swinton Lions	v.	Doncaster Dragons	3.00
Widnes Vikings	v.	Whitehaven Warriors	3.00
Workington Town	v.	Hunslet Hawks	3.00

SUNDAY, 4 JULY

Bramley	v.	Swinton Lions	3.00
Dewsbury Rams	v.	Lancashire Lynx	3.00
Doncaster Dragons	v.	Workington Town	3.00
Featherstone Rovers	v.	Barrow Border R.	3.30
Hunslet Hawks	v.	Batley Bulldogs	3.30
Oldham	v.	Hull Kingston Rovers	3.00
Rochdale Hornets	v.	Widnes Vikings	3.00
Whitehaven Warriors	v.	Leigh Centurions	3.30
York	v.	Keighley Cougars	3.00

SUNDAY, 11 JULY

Barrow Border R.	v.	Oldham	3.00
Batley Bulldogs	v.	Doncaster Dragons	3.15
Bramley	v.	Workington Town	3.00
Hull Kingston Rovers	v.	Hunslet Hawks	3.00
Keighley Cougars	v.	Dewsbury Rams	3.00
Lancashire Lynx	v.	Whitehaven Warriors	3.00
Leigh Centurions	v.	Rochdale Hornets	3.00
Swinton Lions	v.	York	3.00
Widnes Vikings	v.	Featherstone Rovers	3.00

SUNDAY, 18 JULY

Barrow Border R.	v.	Widnes Vikings	3.00
Bramley	v.	Batley Bulldogs	3.00
Dewsbury Rams	v.	Swinton Lions	3.00
Doncaster Dragons	v.	Hull Kingston Rovers	3.00
Featherstone Rovers	v.	Leigh Centurions	3.30
Oldham	v.	Hunslet Hawks	3.00
Rochdale Hornets	v.	Lancashire Lynx	3.00
Whitehaven Warriors	v.	Keighley Cougars	3.30
York	v.	Workington Town	3.00

SUNDAY, 25 JULY

Batley Bulldogs	v.	York	3.15
Hull Kingston Rovers	v.	Bramley	3.00
Hunslet Hawks	v.	Doncaster Dragons	3.30
Keighley Cougars	v.	Rochdale Hornets	3.00
Lancashire Lynx	v.	Featherstone Rovers	3.00
Leigh Centurions	v.	Barrow Border R.	3.00
Swinton Lions	v.	Whitehaven Warriors	3.00
Widnes Vikings	v.	Oldham	3.00
Workington Town	v.	Dewsbury Rams	3.00

SUNDAY, 1 AUGUST

Barrow Border R.	v.	Lancashire Lynx	3.00
Bramley	v.	Hunslet Hawks	3.00
Dewsbury Rams	v.	Batley Bulldogs	3.00
Featherstone Rovers	v.	Keighley Cougars	3.30
Oldham	v.	Doncaster Dragons	3.00
Rochdale Hornets	v.	Swinton Lions	3.00
Whitehaven Warriors	v.	Workington Town	3.30
Widnes Vikings	v.	Leigh Centurions	3.00
York	v.	Hull Kingston Rovers	3.00

SUNDAY, 8 AUGUST

Batley Bulldogs	v.	Whitehaven Warriors	3.15
Doncaster Dragons	v.	Bramley	3.00
Hull Kingston Rovers	v.	Dewsbury Rams	3.00
Hunslet Hawks	v.	York	3.30
Keighley Cougars	v.	Barrow Border R.	3.00
Lancashire Lynx	v.	Widnes Vikings	3.00
Leigh Centurions	v.	Oldham	3.00
Swinton Lions	v.	Featherstone Rovers	3.00
Workington Town	v.	Rochdale Hornets	3.00

SUNDAY, 15 AUGUST

Barrow Border R.	v.	Swinton Lions	3.00
Dewsbury Rams	v.	Hunslet Hawks	3.00
Featherstone Rovers	v.	Workington Town	3.30
Leigh Centurions	v.	Lancashire Lynx	3.00
Oldham	v.	Bramley	3.00
Rochdale Hornets	v.	Batley Bulldogs	3.00
Whitehaven Warriors	v.	Hull Kingston Rovers	3.30
Widnes Vikings	v.	Keighley Cougars	3.00
York	v.	Doncaster Dragons	3.00

SUNDAY, 22 AUGUST

Batley Bulldogs	v.	Featherstone Rovers	3.15
Bramley	v.	York	3.00
Doncaster Dragons	v.	Dewsbury Rams	3.00
Hull Kingston Rovers	v.	Rochdale Hornets	3.00
Hunslet Hawks	v.	Whitehaven Warriors	3.30
Keighley Cougars	v.	Leigh Centurions	3.00
Oldham	v.	Lancashire Lynx	3.00
Swinton Lions	v.	Widnes Vikings	3.00
Workington Town	v.	Barrow Border R.	3.00

SUNDAY, 29 AUGUST

Barrow Border R.	v.	Batley Bulldogs	3.00
Dewsbury Rams	v.	Bramley	3.00
Featherstone Rovers	v.	Hull Kingston Rovers	3.30
Lancashire Lynx	v.	Keighley Cougars	3.00
Leigh Centurions	v.	Swinton Lions	3.00
Rochdale Hornets	v.	Hunslet Hawks	3.00
Whitehaven Warriors	v.	Doncaster Dragons	3.30
Widnes Vikings	v.	Workington Town	3.00
York	v.	Oldham	3.00

FRI-SUN, 3-5 SEPTEMBER
Grand Final Play-offs

FRI-SUN, 10-12 SEPTEMBER
Grand Final Play-offs

FRI-SUN, 17-19 SEPTEMBER
Grand Final eliminator

SAT-SUN, 25-26 SEPTEMBER
Grand Final

TRI-NATIONS SERIES

SATURDAY, 16 OCTOBER

New Zealand	v.	Australia	At Auckland

FRIDAY, 22 OCTOBER

Australia	v.	Great Britain	At Brisbane

FRIDAY, 29 OCTOBER

New Zealand	v.	Great Britain	At Auckland

FRIDAY, 5 NOVEMBER

Final between top two teams	At Sydney